JEWISH NEW YORK

This work was made possible in part through the generosity of a number of individuals and foundations. Their thoughtful support will help ensure that it is affordable to schools, libraries, and other not-for-profit institutions.

The Lucius N. Littauer Foundation made a leadership gift before a word of this book had been written, a gift that set this project on its way. Hugo Barreca, The Marian B. and Jacob K. Javits Foundation, Mr. and Mrs. Peter Malkin, David P. Solomon, and an anonymous donor helped ensure that it never lost momentum. We are deeply grateful.

Jewish New York

The Remarkable Story of a City and a People

Deborah Dash Moore, Jeffrey S. Gurock,
Annie Polland, Howard B. Rock, *and*
Daniel Soyer

WITH A VISUAL ESSAY BY DIANA L. LINDEN

NEW YORK UNIVERSITY PRESS
New York

NEW YORK UNIVERSITY PRESS
New York
www.nyupress.org

References to Internet websites (URLs) were accurate at the time of writing. Neither the author nor New York University Press is responsible for URLs that may have expired or changed since the manuscript was prepared.

Library of Congress Cataloging-in-Publication Data
Names: Moore, Deborah Dash, author. | Gurock, Jeffrey S., 1949–   author. |
Polland, Annie, 1973–   author. | Rock, Howard B., 1944–   author. |
Soyer, Daniel, author. | Linden, Diana L., contributor.
Title: Jewish New York : the remarkable story of a city and a people / Deborah Dash Moore, Jeffrey S. Gurock, Annie Polland, Howard B. Rock, and Daniel Soyer ; with a visual essay by Diana L. Linden.
Description: New York : New York University Press, [2017] |
Includes bibliographical references and index.
Identifiers: LCCN 2017012920 | ISBN 9781479850389 (cl : alk. paper)
Subjects: LCSH: Jews—New York (State)—New York—History. | CYAC: New York (N.Y.)—History.
Classification: LCC F128.9.J5 M665 2017 | DDC 974.7/004924—dc23
LC record available at https://lccn.loc.gov/2017012920

New York University Press books are printed on acid-free paper, and their binding materials are chosen for strength and durability. We strive to use environmentally responsible suppliers and materials to the greatest extent possible in publishing our books.

Manufactured in the United States of America

10 9 8 7 6 5 4 3 2 1

Also available as an ebook

For Irene Golden Dash,
who made New York's Jewish history,
and for Elijah, Zoe, Rose, and Oren,
who are creating its future

Macy's Day Parade Watchers, 1954, by William Klein. "Pseudo-poster The American Dream: Italian cop, integrated Hispanic, Yiddish mama, African-American lady + beret . . . the Melting Pot." William Klein, *New York 1954–55* (Manchester, England: Dewi Lewis Publishing, 1995), 16. © William Klein. Courtesy of William Klein.

CONTENTS

MAP OF NEW YORK CITY, 1911

This 1911 Rand McNally street map of Manhattan and sections of three other boroughs highlights the new underground railroad system and demonstrates how the subways linked lower Manhattan to uptown and the Bronx. The western line would spur apartment construction on the Upper West Side (west of Central Park), while the line that swerved east heading north to the Bronx would stimulate extensive building in Harlem (north of Central Park) and the south Bronx. The uniform grid pattern of numbered streets, running east-west, and numbered avenues, running north-south, gradually would acquire attributes of neighborhoods. In 1911 Jews lived primarily on the Lower East Side (the bulge that protrudes toward Brooklyn) but rapid transit was already carrying them out of this immigrant neighborhood uptown to Harlem and the Bronx and across the bridges spanning the East River to Brooklyn. Courtesy of Stephen S. Clark Library, University of Michigan.

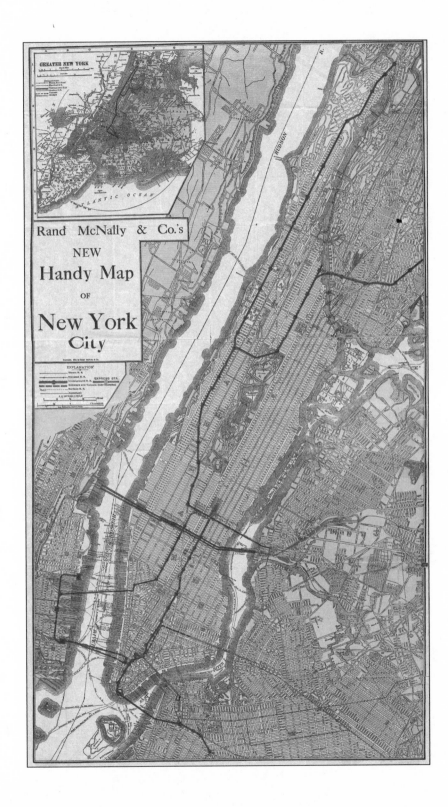

Aerial view of New York City focused on the southern tip of Manhattan island, with bulge of Lower East Side and three East River bridges visible; in the distance to the right is Queens. September 30, 1947. Courtesy of New York State Archives.

Introduction

How New York Became a Jewish City

"Of all the big cities," Sergeant Milton Lehman of the *Stars and Stripes* affirmed in 1945, "New York is still the promised land."[1] As a returning Jewish GI, Lehman compared New York with European cities. In the crucible of a devastating world war, many of those cities (perhaps with the exception of Paris, which was not bombed) looked miserable and definitely old, in stark contrast to New York. But even Jews who hadn't served overseas knew what made New York so desirable. First and foremost was security: Jews could live without fear in New York. Yes, they faced pervasive discrimination and occasional violence from tough and anti-Semitic young men, but in this city of almost eight million residents, many members of other ethnic and religious groups encountered prejudice. Jews contended with anti-Semitism in the twentieth century more than German Protestants or Irish Catholics dealt with bias, perhaps. But the Irish had endured vicious mockery and widespread antagonism in the nineteenth century, and Jews suffered less than African Americans, Latinos, and Asian New Yorkers. Furthermore, Jews could live freely as Jews. Close to two million New York Jews contributed to a pervasive sense of Jewishness in many parts of the city.[2] Their presence helped constitute much of what was distinctive about New York as an American city. In return, New York's size and diversity allowed Jews to understand that there were many ways to be Jewish. The city welcomed Jews in all their variety—rich and poor, religious and radical, bourgeois and bohemian. New York Jews saw the city as a place where they could flourish and express themselves. As a result, they came to identify with New York, absorbing its ethos even as they helped to shape its urban character. When World War II ended in Europe with victory over Nazi Germany, New York's promises glowed more brightly still.

New York's multiethnic diversity, shaped in vital dimensions by its large Jewish population, shimmered as a showplace of American democratic distinctiveness. In contrast to a continent that had become a vast slaughterhouse, where millions of European Jews had been ruthlessly murdered with industrial and military efficiency, America, and specifically New York, glistened as a place Jews could and did call home. Even as they tended to cluster together, Jews navigated shared spaces in New York and lived next door to diverse others: Germans, Italians, Irish, African Americans, Puerto Ricans, Chinese, even white Protestants. The city's famous skyline had defined urban cosmopolitanism in the years after World War I. Now its thriving ethnic neighborhoods—Jewish and Catholic, African American and Puerto Rican, Italian and Irish—came to represent modern urban American culture.

But as a poster city for immigration, with a majority population composed of immigrants and their children, New York also elicited negative perceptions. Many people in the United States derided New York as "un-American" because of its large Jewish and foreign population. Some even pictured it less as dominating the East Coast of the United States than as unmoored, located mid-Atlantic, halfway to Europe.³ A city of many languages, New York was, and continued to be, divided along multiple fissures of religion, race, ethnicity, class, and sexual orientation. Jews were part of this complex mix.

New York City represented more than immigrants. Its architecture and geography summoned icons of American culture, society, and economy. Wall Street had long symbolized finance capitalism. Times Square exemplified commercial performance culture, while Tammany Hall described not merely a building but a powerful Democratic political machine. Seventh Avenue named the garment center, Madison Avenue the heart of advertising, and Fifth Avenue elegant retail shopping. The Empire State Building, the city's and the nation's tallest in height for decades, stood as an emblem of twentieth-century urbanism and broadcast the global reach of U.S. power and influence. These associations evoked New York as the largest city in the United States, its financial, commercial, and cultural capital, as well as the city's political identity as a stronghold of the Democratic Party.

As the city flourished during and after the war, it maintained its political commitments to generous social welfare benefits to help its poorest residents. Jews advocated for and benefited from these policies; they supported efforts to establish a liberal urban legacy. In modeling a progressive and prosperous multiethnic twentieth-century American city, New York demonstrated what its Jews valued. "Its five boroughs were renowned for excellent public schools, pure and abundant water, spacious and well-kept parks, and matchless mass transit."[4] Versions of Jewish urbanism played not just on the political stage but also on the streets of the city's neighborhoods. Its expressions could be found as well in New York's centers of cultural production—in literature and publishing, theater, music, and visual arts.

By the middle of the twentieth century, no city offered Jews more than New York. It nourished both celebration and critique. New York gave Jews visibility as individuals and as a group. It provided employment and education, inspiration and freedom, fellowship and community. Jews reciprocated by falling in love with the city, its buildings' hard angles and perspectives, its grimy streets and harried pace. With tongue in cheek, the poet Milton Klonsky called it "Ghetto of Eden."[5] But by the 1960s and '70s, increasing numbers of Jews desired something different, a less pressured and more private mode of living. For many of the second and third generation who grew up on New York's sidewalks, immersed in its babel of languages and cultural syncretism, prosperity dimmed their affection for the working-class urban world of their youth. They aspired to American suburban pleasures of home ownership and privacy, grass and trees that did not have to be shared with others in public parks. This disaffection endured for a generation. But in the beginning of the twenty-first century, Jews, including suburban Jews, increasingly returned to the city. They sought its particular blend of cosmopolitan flair and intense Jewish milieus. There they joined the million New York Jews who had refused to decamp for greener pastures in the 1970s and 1980s. These diehard New Yorkers treasured their city in good times and bad. Throughout, New York City remained the wellspring of Jewish American culture, a resource of authentic Jewishness even for those who lived thousands of miles west of the Hudson River.

As a collaborative effort, this volume recasts the history of New York City by focusing on Jews who became New Yorkers. It puts the history of New York Jews in dialogue not only with Jewish history but also with Gotham's history and, by extension, American history.

By the beginning of the twentieth century, Jewish New York constituted the largest Jewish urban community in world history, and it retained that distinction for a century. Jews possessed a rich history of living in cities throughout Europe, North Africa and the Ottoman Empire, and as urbanization increased in the nineteenth century, Jewish immigrants to New York drew on that urban experience.[6] Yet despite significant continuities, New York also represented something unprecedented in its size and scale, density and diversity, newness and modernity. More Jews came to live in New York City than in England, France, Germany, Austria, Hungary, or Italy, inviting comparisons less with other cities than with Jewish histories of European nations. Of course, New York's Jewish history does not exactly tell a "national" story. Rather, it chronicles an urban history of one of New York's "ethnic" and religious groups: that is, its Jews. But in a way, their history might also be seen as having "national" dimensions, since in 1950, 40 percent of all American Jews lived in New York.[7] For decades in the mid-twentieth century, Jews occupied a singular position as the city's largest single ethnic group, over a quarter of its population. However, Catholics were the largest single religious group in the city. When coupled with neighborhood patterns of residence that segregated African Americans and separated Jews and Catholics in the city, these ways of thinking about group identity as either racial, religious, or ethnic helped to fashion New York's particular urban mix.

This book synthesizes varied perspectives of the historians who wrote three prize-winning volumes under the *City of Promises* umbrella. Despite different emphases, all agreed on the larger rubric of "city of promises" as the proper framework for research, paying homage to Moses Rischin's pathbreaking study of the Lower East Side, *The Promised City*. All put the process of urbanization and becoming city people in the forefront of their consciousness. City people learned to live cheek by jowl with others who were different. New York City people especially accustomed themselves to a high-density population, fast pace, noise, and dirt. Even today, outsiders associate these features with New York. But for Jews who settled in New York, the city offered more than overcrowded, hectic, filthy, miserable conditions. It also proffered promises.

New York provided life without a majority population—without one single ethnic or religious group dominating urban society. Jews were used to living as a minority in Europe and the Middle East. Now in New York, Jews could go about their business, much of it taking place within ethnic niches, as if they were the city's predominant group.[8] Jews had not always felt free to imagine the city as their special place. Indeed, not until mass immigration from Europe piled up their numbers, from the tens of thousands to the hundreds of thousands, had Jews laid claim to New York to influence its politics and culture. Its Jewish population soared from five hundred thousand at the turn of the twentieth century to 1.1 million before the start of World War I.[9]

When and in what sense did New York become a city of promises for Jews? It certainly was not in the colonial era. Yet during that period, seeds for future promises were planted, most importantly political, economic, and religious rights. While the city's few hundred Jews lived in the shadow of far more prosperous Jewish communities in London and Amsterdam, New York Jewish men enjoyed citizenship rights and responsibilities that their peers in London could only envy. These rights gradually led New York Jews to emerge from a closed synagogue society and to participate with enthusiasm in revolutionary currents sweeping the colonies. Jews in New York absorbed formative ideas regarding human rights; they tasted freedom and put their lives on the line for it during the American Revolution. They incorporated ideals of the American Enlightenment into their Jewish lives.

During the nineteenth century, these changes attracted increasing attention from European Jews. New York gradually acquired a reputation as a destination in itself. Arriving from Europe at Castle Garden at the foot of Manhattan, increasing numbers of Jewish immigrants decided to stay. Enticed by New York's bustling streets, with their opportunities for commerce and crafts, they put off riding west or south to peddle or settle. Sometimes, older brothers decided to stay, as did Jonas and Louis Strauss, who sent their younger brother, Levi, to the West Coast via steamship in 1853 to open a branch of their New York City dry-goods firm. Levi Strauss did better, perhaps, than they expected when he went into manufacturing copper-riveted denim work pants after the Civil War.[10] But such a move into garment manufacturing from selling dry goods and, especially, used clothing had already taken root in New York prior to the war. It formed the basis of an industry that became the city's largest. More than any other industry, garment manufacturing transformed New York into a city of promises.

What did the city promise? First, it promised a job. Close to half of all Jewish immigrants sewed clothing in hundreds of small-scale sweatshops that disguised an ever-burgeoning industry that soon became one of the nation's most important. Next, it promised a place to live. True, the overcrowded Lower East Side bulged with residents, even its modern tenements straining to accommodate a density of population that rivaled that of Bombay. Yet soon bridges to Brooklyn and rapid transit to Harlem and the Bronx promised improvements: fresh air, hot and cold running water, even a private toilet and bathroom. Third, it promised food. Jewish immigrants hadn't starved in Europe, but New York's abundance changed their diets and attitudes toward food and its simple pleasures. In New York, a center of the nation's baking industry, Jews could enjoy a fresh roll and coffee each morning for pennies. They savored meat regularly, often a rare treat in Europe. Fourth, it promised clothing. It didn't take long, especially laboring in the garment industry, for Jews to trade their old-world clothes for the latest ready-made styles. Thus properly attired, they looked and felt like modern men and women, able and willing to make their way.[11]

Such promises might be quotidian, but they opened Jews' eyes to other ones. Young Jewish immigrants embraced the city's promise of free education; they could attend public institutions starting in elementary school, ascending to secondary school, and culminating in college. However, a family economy privileged sons over daughters when decisions about post-elementary education had to be made. Nevertheless, while costs of forgoing income from teenaged children often required Jews to go to work and not attend school or to combine labor and learning, New York Jews increasingly enrolled in the city's free schools. Some immigrants, especially women, thought the city promised freedom to choose a spouse, though matchmakers also migrated across the ocean. Still others rejoiced in what they imagined was a promise of uncensored language: written and spoken, published and onstage, in Yiddish, Hebrew, German, Ladino, and English. Some conceived of the city's rough political democracy as holding a promise of solidarity among working men and women, an opportunity to promote radical social change, to overturn capitalism or at least to modify its worst excesses. A significant number demanded extension of civil and voting rights to women.

Then there were more ambiguous promises. Did New York offer Jews a chance to live without a formal legally constituted Jewish community? Did it suggest that Jews no longer needed to practice Jewish rituals or observe the Sabbath? Some Jewish immigrants thought they could leave behind old-world ways of thinking and acting; they secularized their Jewish lives, often starting the process in Europe even before they emigrated. Others developed ways of being Jewish, both secular and religious, in tune with New York's evolving cultures. Both groups identified their own visions of what it meant to be Jewish in America with New York itself.

This volume narrates the history of New York Jews with an eye to their distinctive story as well as a consciousness of how Jews embedded their particularity within the city's contentious past. New York has attracted extraordinary historical attention from its earliest existence as a small Dutch seaport to its current state as a world city, "capital of the American century."[12] New York Jews, by contrast, tend to figure most often in accounts of the heyday of immigration to the city, starting in the 1840s and extending until Congress cut it short in 1924. Historians of immigration continually have mined the rich and complex Jewish immigrant era. Far less often have historians of American Jews turned either to the colonial years that preceded it or to the rest of the twentieth century that followed. Each of those periods presents challenges. In the early period, Jews were such a small minority that it is hard to recognize their significance in establishing patterns of difference that gained acceptance by the majority and exerted a lasting impact. In the latter decades, Jews were so well integrated as a part of New York politics, economy, and culture that it was far easier for scholars to treat them simply as New Yorkers, without any identifying label. This volume argues that distinctive Jewish bonds did not dissolve even when Jews appeared to act largely as New Yorkers. Urban historians overlook critical sources of political, economic, and cultural productivity by ignoring those ethnic connections.

In order to present New York's Jewish history in its many aspects, this book moves thematically within a broad chronological framework.

The four parts of the book delimit overlapping eras in New York Jewish history. Part 1 covers the colonial period through the Civil War. Part 2 focuses on many features of the immigrant era, from 1865 to 1925, while part 3, from 1885 to 1975, develops themes that begin during immigration but extend through much of the twentieth century. The final section, part 4, from 1960 to 2015, brings the story into the twenty-first century, reaching back into mid-twentieth-century developments and carrying them forward. Chapters treat significant themes as they relate to both Jewish and American urban history.

Jews participated in building the Empire City by casting their lot with urbanism, even as they struggled to make New York a better place to live, work, and raise a family. Their aspirations changed New York and helped to transform it into a city of promises, some fulfilled, some pending, some beckoning new generations.

PART I

1654–1865

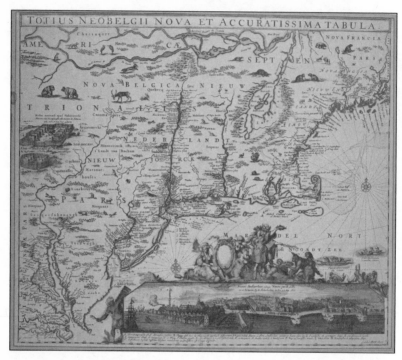

Restitutio View (detail), made by Hugo Allardt to honor the brief reconquest of New Amsterdam by the Dutch in 1673. The image shows a prosperous seaport with two docks, farms on the right, and a seafaring ship. Courtesy of the Miriam and Ira D. Wallach Division of Art, Prints and Photographs: Print Collection, New York Public Library.

1

Foundations

"This is Eden where the land floweth with Milk and Honey," proclaimed a Dutch poet upon seeing Manhattan Island in the seventeenth century. Three hundred years later, two million Jews would call this "land of milk and honey" home, making New York the world's largest and most prosperous Jewish city. In the process, Jews fashioned in New York their own Zion in America.[1]

The Jewish journey to this new world began in Spain and continued via Portugal, Holland, and Brazil before reaching Manhattan Island in 1654.

* * *

August 1492. Christopher Columbus gazed at the docks of the Spanish port. Thousands of Jewish refugees crowded under a sultry sun desperately trying to book passage. Facing a choice to either convert to Catholicism or flee Spain, these Sephardic, or Spanish, Jews held fast to their faith. Many others had already crossed the border to Portugal. But Portugal's reprieve lasted only five years. Then all Jews were forcibly converted to Catholicism. Some of them secretly retained elements of Judaism, passing a dim consciousness of their former Jewish identity to their children.[2]

Over many centuries, under Muslim and Christian rulers, Jews had lived and flourished in the Iberian Peninsula. Sephardic Jews occupied important positions in government; they counted in their ranks many creative Jewish poets and philosophers; their rabbis transformed Jewish mysticism into a complex system of kabbalah; they worked as artisans in Spanish cities; but most of all, they developed extensive trading networks throughout the Mediterranean. Built on bonds of family, trading partnerships survived the expulsion of Spanish Jews. Whether they settled in Italian city-states or the Ottoman Empire, in southern France or the Netherlands, Sephardic Jews stayed connected with converted family members who remained behind. As Columbus's journeys of discovery opened up new lands for European colonization, Sephardic Jews gradually forged a network linking port cities around the Atlantic Ocean.[3]

Sephardic Jews settled in Amsterdam as the Dutch Republic won its freedom from Spain in 1581, less than a century after the expulsion. A Protestant republic, Holland adopted principles of religious toleration and constitutional freedoms along with representative government. Its vibrant stock and commodities exchanges, innovative banking and credit facilities, strong army, heterogeneous population, and republican government offered Jews entrée into a new political and economic order. In Amsterdam, Sephardic Jewish merchants thrived in a milieu that appreciated Jewish capital, commercial acumen, and mercantile connections. The board of directors of the Dutch West India Company, established in 1621, included a significant minority of Amsterdam Jewish merchants. When the company established a foothold in Recife, Brazil, as many as a third of the city's Jewish population emigrated. Dutch Jews possessed manpower, capital, and connections with Portuguese merchants and the Brazilian trade.[4]

By contrast, the company's outpost on Manhattan island, ambitiously named New Amsterdam, offered pitifully few opportunities. Notwithstanding the poet's vision, early New Amsterdam bore more resemblance to Babel than Eden. Notoriously mismanaged, the colony attracted various nationalities, speaking eighteen different languages, and gained a reputation for drunkenness, promiscuity, and lawlessness. If Recife produced a profit for the company, New Amsterdam produced headaches.[5]

The company, attempting to salvage its North American outpost, appointed Peter Stuyvesant as director. A strict Dutch Calvinist, seasoned soldier (he had lost part of a leg in battle), and determined autocrat, Stuyvesant ruled New Amsterdam from 1647 until the British conquest in 1664. The peg-legged director brought order and growth, instituted a municipal government system, and refurbished the port. New immigrants arrived, houses rose in Dutch gabled style, and a merchant class assumed dominance. The seaport exported furs, tobacco, and foodstuffs.[6]

Just before the Jewish New Year of Rosh Hashanah in September 1654, the *St. Catrina* sailed into New Amsterdam's harbor and unloaded its cargo, including twenty-three Jewish refugees from Recife. Fleeing the Dutch surrender of Recife to the Portuguese, these refugees are often hailed as the first Jewish presence in what became New York, even if four other Jews preceded them. Their arrival has assumed legendary dimensions, as recounted by a Dutch Jewish poet. First captured by a Spanish ship and then recaptured by a French warship, the refugees looked to Providence for succor. "God caused a Savior to arise unto them, the captain of a French Ship," wrote the poet, "and he conducted them until they reached the end of the inhabited earth called New Holland." The poet's imagination successfully transformed a more complex and mundane reality into a providential arrival.[7]

In fact, messianic dreams coincided with pragmatic mercantile realities. Both motivated Sephardic Jewish merchants in Amsterdam to expand their Atlantic network and open new lands as havens for Jews. Their diasporic consciousness interpreted Jewish dispersion throughout the world as forerunner to the Messiah's arrival. In 1654, the Amsterdam merchant Jacob Barsimon left for New Amsterdam; the following year, his fellow Amsterdam Jew Menasseh Ben Israel traveled to London on a mission to secure the readmission of Jews to England.[8]

The 1654 fall of Recife to the Portuguese spurred the return of most Jews to Holland, except for the small group of twenty-three Jews. Four married men, six women (two widowed), and thirteen children intended to head to a Dutch colony in the Caribbean, one with a growing Jewish population. Forced by rough weather to land in Spanish Jamaica, they paid a heavy fee for passage to New Amsterdam, disembarking before Rosh Hashanah. They celebrated the holiday most likely with four other Jews who had preceded them on a ship from Europe: Barsimon, the attorney Solomon Pietersen, and Asser Levy, a butcher from Vilna, and his wife, Miriam Levy.[9]

Stranded in New Amsterdam, the twenty-three lacked sufficient funds to pay for their just-concluded passage. The captain sued for his money. Following the Dutch policy of religious toleration, the court first granted a delay in the proceedings for the two days of the Jewish New Year. Then the court agreed with the captain that he was owed money. But sale of the Jews' possessions failed to produce enough cash, although Christians helped them to raise funds. Desperate, the twenty-three appealed to Amsterdam Jews, who paid their debts.[10]

Stuyvesant, believing that "diversity and toleration would undermine social harmony" in New Amsterdam, petitioned the West India Company's directors for permission to deport the refugees. This "obstinate and immovable" people's settlement, he argued, would cause even more confusion by adding their practices to those of Catholics, Quakers, and Lutherans. He decried Jews' economic behavior, their selfishness, and their "customary usury and deceitful trading with the Christians," and he belittled their religion as poison. A "deceitful race," he pronounced, "such hateful enemies and blasphemers of the name of Christ." He warned that these Jews "owing to their present indigence . . . might become a charge in the coming winter." Thus, he concluded, it would be "useful for them in a friendly way to depart." Local magistrates and burgomasters affirmed Stuyvesant's request and pressed the recently arrived Jewish merchants to leave as well. With such a welcome, most left.[11]

What, then, is the significance of these first Jews? Although they left behind few other traces than their tale of woe, their celebration of the Jewish New Year, their refugee status, and their family composition speak to later self-understandings of American Jews. Like the poet, they, too, saw providential continuity and a potential haven for the displaced and persecuted as characteristic features of America, and especially of New York.[12]

Learning of Stuyvesant's letter to the West India Company asking to oust the recently arrived Jews, Jewish elders in Amsterdam wrote to both their city fathers and the company's board of directors. They explained that the "Jewish Nation" declared itself "well disposed" to set out for New Netherland, "on the same footing and condition extended to all," there to "enjoy freedom to exercise their religion as they were permitted in Brazil." If these conditions were met, as in Recife, many would settle in North America and "contribute considerably" to peopling the new colony. Jews sought "the same protection" as "other inhabitants," including "the same rights of housing, commerce, trade and liberty."[13]

Given the weight afforded economic reasoning in the Netherlands, substantial Jewish contributions to Recife, the influence and wealth of Amsterdam's Jews, and their presence in the West India Company, the company rejected Stuyvesant's proposal. If messianism contributed to Jewish efforts to win economic rights in port cities around the Atlantic and Mediterranean, mercantilism animated Amsterdam's merchants.

Noting Jewish sacrifice in Recife and the "large capital which they still have invested in the shares of the company," the directors declared that Jews could travel and trade to and in New Netherland and live and remain there, provided the poor among them would not become a burden to the company or to the community but would be supported by their own.[14]

Without the Amsterdam Jewish community, Jews in New Amsterdam would have had no opportunity to contend for their rights and Dutch citizenship. Nonetheless, those in New Amsterdam carried on the struggle. The company's directive allowed them to pursue their quest in a hostile climate. The next two years proved critical. Barsimon, Pietersen, and Levy led the mission to seek rights possessed by their Dutch brethren. These three Jewish merchants, who arrived before the twenty-three, possessed considerably greater stature than the Recife refugees did. Their political pursuit resembled similar efforts subsequently undertaken by Jews in other port cities, shaped, in part, by the spread of Enlightenment ideas.[15]

First these Jewish merchants sought religious privileges to build and worship in their own meeting place. Stuyvesant denied their request, explaining that giving Jews religious liberty, "we cannot refuse the Lutherans and the Papists."[16] Yet Jews persevered. They regularly refused to appear in court to answer a summons on a Saturday, their Sabbath, a position respected by the court. They obtained permission to "purchase a burying ground," which became the Chatham Street cemetery. They received a Torah scroll from Amsterdam. Jewish butchers were excused from slaughtering hogs, unkosher animals. Still, New Amsterdam proved unfriendly. Only Asser and Miriam Levy lasted the decade until the British arrived.[17]

Religious liberty did not suffice if one could not earn a living. New Amsterdam's Jews sought free access to the marketplace. Despite orders from the West India Company to give Jews full "civil and political" rights, Stuyvesant and the burgomasters resisted. Asser Levy and Jacob Barsimon requested permission to stand guard with other citizens rather than pay a tax for a substitute. They were denied due to "the disgust and aversion" of the citizens and because Jews were not citizens. When both men complained of the tax burden, the municipality instructed them to "go elsewhere." Levy persisted; eventually he won the right to do guard duty. Repeated appeals to the company's directors in Amsterdam also gained Jews rights to trade and purchase property, privileges long common to their Dutch counterparts.[18]

Yet full citizenship eluded Jews. Jewish merchants supported Asser Levy's petition for burgher rights of citizenship. Since Jews enjoyed these privileges in Amsterdam, New Amsterdam Jews were not requesting anything unprecedented. Finally, the city fathers caved. Jewish merchants prevailed, but not without repeated attempts and vital support from Amsterdam's Jewish community and directors of the West India Company.[19]

Jews built on the rights that had been hard won in New Amsterdam after the British arrived in 1664. They obtained permission to worship in public and to construct a synagogue. Without an established church in New York, unlike in some of the other British colonies in North America, Jews enjoyed religious liberty in the context of a multireligious, multilingual, and multiethnic society, exactly what Stuyvesant had feared. Not only Lutherans, Catholics, and Quakers but diverse Protestants, including Methodists, Baptists, and Presbyterians, all erected churches in the city. The 1740 naturalization act confirmed Jewish citizenship. New York, however, went further than other colonies. It fully emancipated Jews, granting Jewish men rights to vote and hold office on the basis of their economic standing. Enlightenment values of religious toleration influenced politics, as did mercantilist ideas. Jews traded freely throughout the colonies and the Atlantic world; they also pursued artisan opportunities unconstrained by guild restrictions.[20]

Port Cities

In August 1664, four English frigates sailed into New Amsterdam and demanded its surrender, though England and Holland were at peace. The British renamed the seaport New York. Despite subsequent wars, by 1700 New York was growing as an English colony. It joined a network of Atlantic, Mediterranean, and Caribbean port cities where Jews lived largely by trade and crafts. These port cities shared common characteristics and housed mixed populations of Sephardic and Ashkenazi Jews. The latter, like Asser Levy, came from German and eastern European lands.

Port cities held multinational, multireligious, and multilingual populations. Sephardic Jewish merchants who were engaged in international trade fit comfortably within this diverse milieu. They increasingly appeared to Christians to resemble other merchants, perceptions encouraged by Enlightenment ideas. Jews in port cities reflected a diversity of backgrounds, speaking many languages with different styles of religious worship. New York, with its small Jewish population, included both Sephardic and Ashkenazi Jews. Sephardic Jews often thought of themselves as Hebrews of the Portuguese nation, while Ashkenazi Jews considered themselves part of the Jewish nation. Although Ashkenazi traditions usually included Yiddish language and culture, Sephardic traditions reflected Ladino (Judeo-Spanish) language and culture. Other port cities, such as those in Italy, contained even more Jewish variety.[21]

Port cities served as formative nodes in emerging Jewish civic equality. They tendered considerable economic freedom, political security, and cultural opportunities. As a result, Jewish religious self-understandings underwent transformation in port cities as Jews adapted to changing political, social, and economic realities.[22]

Although New York Jews traded with port cities around the Atlantic, including larger Jewish communities in Surinam and Curaçao, London and Amsterdam mattered most. The 1656 readmission of Jews to London transformed it into an important trading partner for Sephardic Jewish merchants. New York Jews adopted their model of a "synagogue community," allocating to their only synagogue responsibility for all aspects of Jewish collective life. While Sephardic Jews established their religious practices in the city's first synagogue, they worshiped together with Ashkenazi Jews and shared leadership responsibilities.

New York's Jews began to gather for religious services in 1682. A house on Mill Street served as Congregation Shearith Jacob's first synagogue.[23] In 1730, the Jewish community, headed by prominent merchants, including Sephardi Luis Gomez and Ashkenazi Jacob Franks, raised funds to purchase a lot and construct a building, first home of the renamed Congregation Shearith Israel, also known as the Spanish and Portuguese synagogue. Contributions arrived from many Atlantic Jewish communities, reflecting connections binding port-city Jews. Numbering just 250 in the mid-eighteenth century, New York's Jewish community maintained a stronger sense of common identity than in either London or Amsterdam.[24]

The city's Jewish community exerted control over its members only by way of moral suasion and, if necessary, social ostracism. Living in a Christian society and constituting a mere 2 percent of the city's population, Jews made the synagogue their spiritual center of gravity and focus of their collective identity. Its rules and rituals articulated Jewish norms. These included a prohibition against riding on the Sabbath and adherence to Jewish dietary laws. Although it is impossible to know the extent of colonial Jewish observance, most Jews resided within walking distance of the synagogue. As the only synagogue in the thirteen colonies until 1763, New York's Shearith Israel drew Jews during the autumn High Holidays from as far as Halifax in Canada.

Shearith Israel's physical structures reflected New York Jews' commitment to provide for all Jews from cradle to grave, irrespective of socioeconomic status. These structures included the synagogue, a *mikveh* (ritual bath) using water from a spring, a two-story building to house a school and administrative offices, and a third building as a home for the congregation's *shamash* or caretaker, as well as a cemetery outside the city. The synagogue building copied London's and Amsterdam's Sephardic architectural style, with a balcony and separate entrance for women, an elevated platform for reading from the Torah scroll in the center, benches for seats, and room for those who were too poor to purchase seats to stand during worship.[25]

Jews who settled in colonial America, whether Sephardic or Ashkenazi, "aspired to become merchants participating in transatlantic commerce. Even if one began as a shopkeeper, he wanted to die as a merchant."[26] Such dreams animated New York Jews. They sought to enter the Atlantic trade as importers and exporters. Jews often placed their sons or sons-in-law in different seaports to expand and secure their business networks. Jewish merchants played an outsized role in the Atlantic trade, accounting for some 12 percent of port entries early in the eighteenth century. This prominence gradually diminished as New York grew in population while its Jewish population did not keep pace. Both Sephardic and Ashkenazi Jews engaged in such trade, and both contributed generously to New York's synagogue.[27]

Wills revealed New York Jews' extraordinary wealth. Joseph Bueno de Mesquita, a Sephardic merchant, left his wife £600, along with five slaves and the furniture of a prosperous home, including a leather couch, blue linen, and kitchen and dining room accessories. But more than that, Bueno also willed his descendants a Hebrew Bible and Torah with a silver bell. Just as the five slaves signified both his wealth and acceptance of colonial New York's social and economic mores, so did the Torah scroll, an expensive item, indicate the centrality of Judaism in his life.[28]

Real estate speculation, distilling rum, and supplying British military forces with foodstuffs complemented profits drawn from the Atlantic trade. On occasion, in recognition of money's power, political figures solicited wealthy Jewish merchants for help securing a lucrative position.[29] Nathan Simson, an English émigré who returned to Britain for the final years of his life with a fortune of £60,000, achieved such prominence that the New Yorker Francis Harison wrote him two letters asking him to intervene in Parliament for Harison to be given the position of comptroller of the Port of Boston. Harison's pleas indicated how powerful a wealthy

NEW YORK SLAVE MARKET ABOUT 1730 (1902.)

Slave market at the foot of Wall Street, 1700s. In 1711, a market in slaves was established on Wall Street, where slaves were sold or leased. Ultimately, black slaves composed over 15 percent of New York City's population. The city housed more slaves than any colony north of Maryland. Prosperous Jewish merchants accepted slavery as part of daily life. On average, they owned no more and no fewer slaves than their Christian peers did. Courtesy of the Miriam and Ira D. Wallach Division of Art, Prints and Photographs: Print Collection, New York Public Library.

Jewish merchant could be deemed by non-Jews. Yet because of Jews' extensive trade, legal disputes constantly troubled Jewish business careers. Colonial New York was a litigious society, and so were New York Jews. The merchant Moses Levy doggedly pursued Simson in chancery court for five years in 1722, contending that his brother, whose estate Simson represented, had thrown salt into a shipment of cocoa that his brother had then sold to him. Levy won his case.[30]

As Bueno's will reveals, slavery flourished in New York City during the colonial era. When the American Revolution occurred, more slaves lived in New York than in any colony north of Maryland. Men of both middling and genteel standing owned slaves. Slaves worked on the docks, as assistants to craftsmen, and, most commonly, as household servants. Wealthy slave owners leased slaves to tradesmen in need of temporary labor.[31]

Jews were no exception. Only a handful of Jewish merchants manumitted slaves. Some Jewish merchants and ship owners, often together with Christian partners, profited from New York's slave trade, though their consignments represented a small fraction of these enterprises. The slave trade enriched some leading Jewish families.[32]

Well-to-do Jewish merchants shared with Christians a common attitude toward slavery. They accepted it as part of daily life and the city's economy. On average, Jews owned no more and no fewer slaves than their non-Jewish peers did. At Passover seders, they did not relate the story of the Exodus from Egypt to African American slavery. Colonial Jews did not challenge a society in which slave owning was the norm.

Jewish women, like their Christian counterparts, generally lived lives dominated by domestic chores, marriage, childbirth, and child rearing. However, Jewish cultural practices also sanctioned women entering the marketplace. Some of these women worked in occupations available to females, such as teaching or the needle trades. Others opened retail stores or, on occasion, a kosher boardinghouse. Women most often entered the mercantile world only if they remained single or after the death of a spouse. Eighteenth-century society deemed it acceptable for a woman to adopt her husband's trade.[33]

As a port city, New York integrated Jews into its economic and political fabric, even as Jews maintained a measure of social distance. Christians viewed the synagogue community's intimacy as clannish, an attitude that reflected a long tradition of religious disdain for Jews. On occasion, Jews endured overt expressions of prejudice, often during moments when Jewish practices appeared in public, such as during a funeral procession to the cemetery. But usually Christian bias registered in subtle exclusions. For example, although as of 1740 Jewish male citizens, if freemen or property owners, possessed the vote and could run for office, the highest elective positions they held were constable, assessor, and collector of taxes. Wealthy Jewish merchants never won election to either the Assembly or Common Council. Had figures of their stature been Christian, they would have been on one or both of these bodies.[34]

Anti-Jewish attitudes did not, however, prevent Jews and Christians from cooperating in economic pursuits. Nearly every major Jewish merchant partnered with Christians. Artisans worked with Christian associates and journeymen as well as with a largely Christian clientele. To the extent that socializing extended economic ties, Jews and Christians also mixed. They joined the same Masonic lodges and served together in the militia. The elite members of the Jewish community in New York socialized with their Christian counterparts. And when disaster threatened, Christians accepted Jewish hospitality. During a smallpox epidemic, Mordechai Gomez housed the New York Assembly at his estate in Greenwich Village, even if the Assembly had grumpily resolved, unanimously, that Jews "ought not to be admitted to vote for Representatives in this Colony."[35]

The lure of acceptance challenged Jewish distinctiveness. Jews struggled not only for rights to live in New York, practice their religion, and seek their fortunes. They also strove to maintain a cohesive ethnic and religious society, to overcome forces of adaptation that inevitably pushed at so tiny a sector of the population, and to practice and preserve ancient rituals in a world that was ever more part of the Enlightenment. In this, they largely succeeded. Though their population did not grow as did the city's, with the help of immigration and an active synagogue, they sustained Jewish community, passing on key traditions to future generations.

Religious Community

Yom Kippur, the Day of Atonement, 1755. An oppressive heat blanketed the city on this mid-September day. After eating an early dinner,

New York's Jews hurried to Shearith Israel for the evening service initiating the solemn fast. At the synagogue, the men and women separated. The men entered the sanctuary, while the women took the separate door to the balcony, climbing its narrow steps carefully. Gitlah, the wife of Solomon Hays, chose a seat near an open window to enjoy a bit of air in the stifling synagogue, crowded to capacity with Jews visiting from distant colonies. She did not notice a thunderstorm brewing until a burst of rain poured through the window, drenching her fine clothes. Solomon, seeing her distress from his seat on the main floor, rushed outside and up to the women's gallery to close the window. As the atmosphere grew ever more unbearable, some women turned for help to the synagogue elders. Receiving permission, the women reopened the window. Frustrated, Gitlah closed it. This time, Lewis Moses Gomez, one of Shearith Israel's lay leaders, a man of great wealth and prestige, tramped upstairs himself to remove the entire window so it couldn't be shut. After services ended, Hays and Gomez confronted each other in the courtyard. Hays refused to recognize Gomez's authority as a synagogue elder. Soon words turned to fists, and Hays headed home with a bloody mouth, ejected from the synagogue.

Not one to acquiesce easily to congregational authority, Hays filed assault charges in a New York court. In response, Shearith Israel issued its first and only excommunication, read in public in February, May, and October of 1756, stating that members were to shun Hays: "because he has scandalized us amongst the Christians."[36] Jews often brought business complaints against each other to court, but taking a dispute over congregational matters to a colonial court was a highly unusual step, an airing of communal dirty laundry in public. The trial dragged on for nineteen days. The real issue, the prosecutor reasoned, didn't involve lack of respect for an elder of Shearith Israel but rather anger at Hays for having taken other actions, not named in the formal charges, that embarrassed the congregation. These included demonstrating that Moses Gomez's son Daniel was guilty of usury; exposing two Albany Jews as noncitizens, causing them to lose trading privileges; and revealing that the congregation had attempted to cause a Christian wife "to renounce her Savior, and become a proselyte to the Jewish religion." These incidents, the prosecutor claimed, led to an "inveterate hatred" toward

"Informer" Hays. The jury disagreed. It found the elders innocent and ordered Hays to pay the costs of the defense attorney.[37]

Hays sought revenge. He began writing a book detailing the synagogue's sins and vindicating his actions. But ostracism took its toll. Finally, Hays made "proper submission for the injuries done the Congregation," paid a hefty fine, gave bond for good behavior, and pledged to "deliver up a certain book in his possession wrote against [the congregation] Society." The elders then readmitted him as a member of the congregation.[38]

Although Shearith Israel put the matter aside, the incident revealed powerful tensions tugging at its religious community. Despite its best efforts to bring all Jews together under one roof and despite a colonial culture of deference to men of wealth and authority, the congregation struggled to achieve comity. Lay leaders held on jealously to their prerogatives. They desired to guide the Jewish community and were loathe to forfeit control. As a result, the congregation never sought a rabbi until the nineteenth century. The premise of Jewish religious community in New York rested on an active leadership of wealthy, married Jewish men.

Yet getting these prosperous, married merchants to agree to serve as *parnas*, the most important lay officer of the synagogue, proved difficult. Lewis Moses Gomez did it (as did several of his sons) but often reluctantly. The position consumed time, and its benefits were elusive. The *parnas* oversaw three paid officials; distributed funds to the poor (or secured their exit from the city); supervised the congregation's finances; and maintained order in the synagogue, including mediating disputes. A small governing board of distinguished Jewish citizens assisted the *parnas* and elected the next one. Shearith Israel counted as members only those who paid seat assessments; others stood at religious services, which could last several hours. Thus, synagogue culture emphasized class differences, making them visible to all.[39]

Shearith Israel employed three officials. Considered the congregation's spiritual leader, the hazan circumcised male newborns, prepared male youth for bar mitzvah, and, when a teacher was not employed, ran the school. He conducted services twice daily on weekdays and three times on the Sabbath. Though not ordained, he was fluent in Hebrew and could answer religious questions not demanding intensive Talmudic inquiry. The *shamash* assisted him, keeping the sanctuary clean and

Mill Street synagogue. The first synagogue built in the thirteen colonies, in 1730, Mill Street synagogue housed Congregation Shearith Israel and, together with a school, a ritual bath (*mikveh*), and a house for the caretaker, served as the center of a synagogue community in New York during the eighteenth century. Courtesy of Congregation Shearith Israel.

supplied with wood, water, and candles. The *bodeck/shochet* provided certified kosher meat for the community.[40]

Although Ashkenazim outnumbered Sephardim after 1720, the synagogue followed Sephardic traditions. It positioned the hazan in the center of the synagogue when leading prayers, facing the holy ark, which held the Torah scroll. Hebrew was pronounced in the Sephardic manner; morning blessings were said in synagogue rather than at home.[41]

Jewish religious traditions dictated life-cycle events. Circumcision, the foremost requirement, occurred eight days after the birth of a male child, provided a *mohel* (ritual circumciser) could be found in time. Male children became bar mitzvah at thirteen, which marked their religious coming of age. Celebration started immediately after the Sabbath service and ran for two days, during which time "anybody who was anybody" began to "blow their heads off." Saturday night was for dancing, and Sunday an open house. When children sought a marriage partner, first their parents and then the congregation had to agree. The two families prepared a carefully written contract, including sections ensuring the bride's financial security if widowed. Weddings occurred on Sundays in the bride's home, outside if weather permitted. For funerals, members of the congregation carried the coffin on their shoulders through the streets to the Jewish cemetery.[42]

The Sabbath anchored the week, a day of profound rest. From Friday evening to Saturday evening, Jewish law and custom permitted no work, no travel, no cooking, no writing, no transaction of business. "I never knew the benefit of the Sabbath before," observed Jacob Franks's wife, Abigail, "but now I am glad when it comes for his [Jacob's] sake that he may have a little relaxation from t[ha]t continual hurry he is in." Franks, a prosperous merchant, often chosen as *parnas* of Shearith Israel, refrained from commerce in honor of the Sabbath. It is impossible, however, to judge how widespread was such Sabbath practice. A Christian visitor to America in 1747 noted that New York's Jews "never cook any food for themselves on Saturday but that it is done on the day before."[43]

Kashrut, a critical area of ritual observance, distinguished Jews from Christians and involved supply and inspection of kosher meat. The congregation carefully supervised a ritual slaughterer (*shochet*). As members supplied kosher meat to coastal and Caribbean communities, the synagogue was determined to ensure its beef met Jewish legal requirements. Shearith Israel supervised kashrut on behalf of New York Jews, yet this communal responsibility did not necessarily dictate Jewish behavior either at home or when traveling among Christians. If Jacob Franks's wife, Abigail, is to be believed, some Jews worried about disregard for kashrut. Abigail, who did not cover her own dark hair according to expectations for a traditional married Jewish woman, nonetheless cautioned her son Naphtali not to eat anything but "bread & butter," even at her brother Asher's home in London or anywhere where "there is the least doubt of things not done after . . . strict Judaic method." Yet

Abigail also socialized with New York's Christian elite, as befit the wife of New York's most prominent Jewish citizen.[44]

Shearith Israel maintained a school, since New York lacked public education. Its first academy taught Hebrew, subsequently adding secular subjects. Wealthy Jewish New Yorkers sent their children to school, supplementing their education with private lessons. The school also accommodated less prosperous New York Jews, educating their children for free. Despite irregular sessions, school nonetheless increased Jewish and secular literacy, allowing the next generation to surpass their parents' education and fit more comfortably into colonial society.[45]

By contrast, Shearith Israel grudgingly assumed responsibility for assisting poor Jews, especially itinerants. One of its largest expenses, charity strained its resources, at times exceeding the hazan's salary. The congregation regularly resorted to sending the indigent to other communities after a couple of months of support, a fairly widespread and standard Jewish practice on both sides of the Atlantic.[46]

However, the elders' most difficult and time-consuming task involved maintaining peace in synagogue and community. Periodic congregational conflict threatened the very existence of the synagogue. Economic inequality and questions of status and authority generated the most disagreement. Recognizing how disrespect undermined community, the elders attempted to regulate respect by requiring those who were called to the Torah during Sabbath services to bless both *parnas* and congregation. Refusal incurred a fine. This regulation reflected efforts to discipline the more prosperous, since the honor of being called to the Torah involved a financial contribution to the congregation.[47]

If conflict roiled congregational and communal life, early wills expressed piety and devotion to the synagogue. Although most colonial Jews apparently "never doubted that there was life after death," few articulated a belief in resurrection in their wills. Business reversals reminded Jews of life's fundamental instability and how much lay in God's hands.[48]

Two translations of prayers manifested Jews' adaptation to colonial society as well as their adherence to traditional practices. The first English translation of Jewish liturgy in America, a special 1760 service of thanksgiving for the British victory in the French and Indian War, indicated how Jews had come to identify as British subjects. Indeed, until the Revolution, the congregation regularly recited a prayer in Spanish for the British king. A subsequent translation of both Sabbath and High Holiday services justified conducting services in Hebrew in "veneration" of the "sacred" language. However, as Hebrew was "imperfectly understood by many, by some, not at all," a translation was needed. The service itself followed traditional practice and would have been immediately familiar to any Jews visiting New York.[49]

Two noteworthy Christians, Peter Kalm, a Swedish botanist, and Alexander Hamilton, a Scottish physician, visited Shearith Israel and recorded their impressions. Kalm emphasized the modernity of the service, noting that both men and women "dressed in the English fashion" and that during prayer, men wore their hats and "spread a white cloth [tallit] over their heads," with the wealthier sporting a "much richer cloth than the poorer ones." He noticed that men had Hebrew books for prayer and song and that the hazan read prayers while elevated in the center of the room. Hamilton peppered his observations with his opinions. He described "an assembly of about fifty of the seed of Abraham chanting and singing their doleful hymns." He too noticed how the men wore their hats in the synagogue, unlike Christians, and how the men "had a veil of some white stuff which they sometimes threw over their heads in their devotion," a reference to a tallit. Try as he might, he could not get the "lugubrious songs" out of his head for a day. But he also paid attention to the women, some of whom he thought were very pretty. He commented how "they stood up in a gallery like a hen coop" and watched as they sang or paused and "talked about business." Kalm described an educated, modern religious congregation, Hamilton an exotic scene. Much lay in the eye of the beholder. Modern in the street, New York's Jews followed venerable traditions in their sanctuary.[50]

Yet Enlightenment ideas reached New York Jews. Abigail Franks's letters reveal a good dose of skepticism. Abigail possessed a strong personality. A highly educated, well-read woman, she expressed impatience with Judaism, especially the Judaism practiced in New York. She confessed, "I can't help condemning the many superstitions we are clogged with & heartily wish a Calvin or Luther would rise amongst Us." She yearned for reforms because she did not think religion consisted of "idle ceremonies." Even while advising her son to observe strictly the dietary laws and noting the Sabbath's beneficial impact on her husband, she condemned many Jewish customs as outdated superstitions. Abigail

Franks also had little use for the traditional concept of resurrection. But Abigail possessed a pious side. Learning of the death of her son's infant child, she counseled that it was "the will of that Divine Power to which all must submit and say with Aaron it's the Lord's doing and we must be silent." Her reference to Aaron's loss of his two sons uncovers how

Abigail Franks, c. 1735. This portrait of the wife of Jacob Franks, a wealthy merchant in colonial New York, hints at her self-confidence. A well-read woman, she was a deeply committed Jew. She wears an elegant, low-cut velvet dress but no jewelry; nor does she cover her long, dark hair. Courtesy of the American Jewish Historical Society.

much she had internalized scripture's religious message. When it came to times of crisis, traditional Judaic piety prevailed. Probably Abigail was not alone in these sentiments.[51]

Social and Cultural Practices

A resident standing outside the newly constructed Mill Street synagogue on a Saturday morning could not have missed the arrival of the family of Lewis Moses Gomez, one of the city's wealthiest Jewish merchants. His large family of six sons marched in procession, led by the elder Gomez. His personal slaves followed them, carrying the family's prayer books and prayer shawls, since Jews were forbidden to carry on the Sabbath. In a ceremony symbolic of the deferential nature of colonial American society, upon reaching the synagogue, the slaves entered, placed the books and shawls on the proper benches, and left as the family took their seats.[52]

Slave ownership exemplified only one facet of adaptation confronting all New York Jews. Jews also struggled to sustain their small community as the seaport grew from approximately 10,600 total population in the 1730s. This expansion turned its three hundred Jews into a small and shrinking minority of New York's population. Jewish families usually had an average of five children, though not all lived to adulthood. Immigration augmented these numbers, but Jews came at a slower pace than others did. New York Jews faced the question of whether their children would marry other Jews and sustain Jewish communal life.

Women married around the age of twenty, men at twenty-seven; marriages lasted close to thirty years. But many young Jewish men and women remained single. In New York, 45 percent of men and 41 percent of women did not marry. Possibly the paucity of mates who were considered appropriate by parents, the transience of men seeking fortunes in the West Indies, and the shame of marrying outside the religion kept so many young Jews single. The intermarriage rate hovered between 10 and 15 percent. With rare exceptions, Shearith Israel did not sanction conversion as a solution to intermarriage. Opposition stemmed from lack of a rabbi to perform a conversion ceremony and fear of angering Christians. These patterns enhanced the importance of Jewish immigrants to ensure a population adequate to maintain a community, however small.[53]

Most married Jewish women devoted their time to running a household and raising their children. If they maintained a kosher kitchen, they assumed responsibilities for cooking and baking. Servants could not work in the kitchen without immediate supervision by the woman of the house; otherwise, the dwelling would be *trefa* (nonkosher). A member of Shearith Israel reminisced that the "women of the congregation were real actors in [the] kitchen business." If a woman suspected a violation of the rules of kashrut, including separate dishes for meat and dairy products, she was obliged to report it to the synagogue. The burdens of maintaining a kosher kitchen gave special, even mystical meaning to life, but it also meant added work.[54]

Jewish women apparently attended synagogue regularly, though attendance was considered optional except on Purim and the High Holidays. Few could see clearly from their seats in the balcony behind a latticed "breast work as high as their chins," which echoed contemporary architectural visions of Solomon's Temple. None participated in the service's rituals, although women contributed to the synagogue's aesthetics. For the High Holidays, they donated "White decorations" for the Torah scrolls and a "Curtain" for the ark, which the congregation celebrated with a special blessing. Many women could follow the worship service due to Jewish education and a stress on literacy.[55]

Women also possessed traditions of private Jewish prayer. Female devotional petitions (*tkhines*) addressed personal issues, including those specifically relating to women, such as pregnancy and childbirth. Personal piety opened avenues for religious solace, allowing women to express their spiritual striving within a Jewish framework.[56]

Married women had access to the mikveh and its embodied sacred and physical cleanliness. Laws for menstruating women required them to bathe each month in the *mikveh* after they finished their menstrual cycle in order to resume sexual relations. Sephardic Jews endowed the mikveh with even greater significance. They understood its structure, drawing upon underground springs of water, as predicting messianic dreams of redemption. In addition, the colonial mikveh reflected elements of spa culture, popular Protestant notions of the benefits of water cures. The mikveh thus offered married Jewish women a higher status, elevating them socially as well as religiously, their monthly baths helping to hasten the Messiah.[57]

Snuff box, by Myer Myers, 1760–1770. This gold snuff box displays a scene of a man bringing agricultural tribute to a king, who sits on a throne with three armed soldiers by his side. The talented Jewish silversmith Myer Myers enthusiastically adopted popular rococo style that required exceptional skill in engraving. He produced work for wealthy merchants as well as religious objects for synagogue use. Courtesy of the Metropolitan Museum of Art.

When affluent colonial Jews died, their possessions were often inventoried, providing insight into the material culture of prosperous New York Jewish life. Wardrobes and tables, plates and pots, candlesticks and kiddush cups, and even *etrog* holders for the holiday of Sukkot open a window into the world of New York Jews. In addition, more valuable objects, including portraits and silver, expressed Jewish aspirations and integration into New York culture. Jews lived within intersecting cultural milieus that simultaneously integrated them into the city's life and distinguished them from other New Yorkers.

The Jewish silversmith Myer Myers, one of the city's most success-ful, produced elegant silver finials for Torah scrolls for his congrega-tion, Shearith Israel, along with objects for daily use by wealthy New Yorkers, such as silver tankards and graceful pear-shaped coffee pots. The former, adorned with ornate gold crowns, featured miniature bells dangling from each of its three curved balls that would chime as the Torah was carried from the ark to be read. The latter reflected the new popularity of coffee and tea, socially prestigious drinks, facilitated by booming Atlantic trade networks. Myers stayed abreast of European trends. His style progressed from the rococo, with curvilinear elegance in the natural beauty of shells and flowers, to neoclassicism, centering on restraint, balance, and proportion of geometric forms. Considered a merchant-artisan, Myers entered a partnership with a Christian and also gave out work to other craftsmen. His rococo style shared common elements with popular British silverware, even as his success spoke to Jewish contributions to colonial culture.[58]

Food and drink united Sephardic Jews, much as did their Jewish language, Ladino. Forged over centuries in Spain, Sephardic "cuisine became the culinary equivalent of Ladino." Food bound Jews to each other, not just because of kosher requisites but also because of specific tastes and flavors that encouraged Jews to feel part of an extended fam-ily. Throughout the Jewish Atlantic world, Sephardic Jews possessed a "penchant for pungent foods alongside foods that are rich, complex, sweet, and colorful."[59] Exchanging food as gifts reinforced kinship ties, while saying grace after meals brought to consciousness spiritual dimen-sions of eating. New York Jews necessarily engaged in food production in order to fulfill the demands of kashrut. In addition, observance of kosher laws distinguished Jews from Christians, creating simultaneously insiders and outsiders. Yet even as Jews integrated new foods into their diets, they retained a distinctive palate that marked a home as Jewish.

That home, if among the wealthy elite, often boasted a portrait of its owner and his wife and, occasionally, his children. Jacob Franks com-missioned such paintings from one of the established portrait artists of the colonies. His picture features a prosperous personage, wearing an elegant maroon velvet coat and a stylish wig. His left hand points toward a large ship sailing on the ocean, indicating the source of his wealth as a merchant. By contrast, the portrait of his wife, Abigail, portrays her as elegant and proper, wearing a low-cut blue dress but without jewelry. Her dark hair, parted in the middle of her head, curls gracefully over one shoulder. These portraits of a prominent New York Ashkenazi Jewish family, one devoted to Judaism and among the leadership of Shearith Israel, eloquently demonstrate the attractions and rewards of the city's colonial culture.[60]

Pioneering Jews repeatedly strove to establish religious, cultural, and social foundations that would promote a sense of security and identification with other New Yorkers. Over the course of a little more than a century from the mid-1660s to the mid-1770s, Jews transformed their relationship to the city, its citizens, and its leadership.

Colonial New York Jews established key foundations for future Jewish life in the city. Political and economic freedoms, religious community, social fellowship, and integration into the cultural mores of colonial New York characterized Jewish society. Jews differed from their fellow citizens, but their differences remained muted. Mostly Jews appeared to add elements of diversity to a robust and bustling seaport, testifying to its openness and acceptance of non-Christians. Jews of colonial New York identified with British American culture, an affiliation that led many to cast their lots with their fellow Americans in the ensuing Revolution.

Revolution and Change

On the fourth of July in 1788, Philadelphia held a grand parade to celebrate Pennsylvania's ratification of the new Constitution of the United States of America. In scorching summer heat, Philadelphia's Jews lined up to walk alongside their fellow countrymen. Gershom Seixas, New York's first native-born hazan, marched at the front, linking arms with clergy of different Christian denominations. Observers watched as the handsome and beardless Jewish clergyman, with his large nose, curly black hair, and a penetrating gaze, strode steadily, apparently at ease in his position of prominence. Seeing him among the Christian clergy, they could not resist reflecting on the symbolism he represented. Seixas's presence announced forcefully the new nation's religious tolerance, evident in its willingness to include non-Christians in such a public, patriotic event. The United States, the parade apparently proclaimed, welcomed

Jews as part of its civic and religious democracy. When the marchers finally reached their destination, they enjoyed a feast that featured a separate kosher table for Jews. Philadelphia's parade recognized both Jewish similarity and difference, allowing Jews to participate as Americans and as Jews.[61]

How did Gershom Seixas, renowned as the hazan of Shearith Israel, come to be marching at the head of a parade in Philadelphia celebrating the Constitution? The answer reflects the transformation wrought by the American Revolution on New York's Jews.

Shearith Israel's hazan, only thirty-one years old in 1776, perceived American colonists as defenders of liberty. Seixas had been at his post for eight years. That Seixas, who was born and educated in New York, assumed the responsibilities of hazan announced the successful maturation of the city's Jewish community. Seixas testified to its ability to transmit Jewish knowledge and commitment to the next generation. Like his fellow New Yorkers, Seixas mourned the deaths of eight minutemen on the bridge at Lexington, carefully followed proceedings of the Continental Congress in Philadelphia, cheered the courage displayed at Bunker Hill, and welcomed the appointment of George Washington as commander in chief. But when the British arrived on Staten Island in the summer of 1776 with the largest flotilla yet seen in North America, carrying a force of thirty thousand British soldiers and Hessian mercenaries, he knew, as did even conservative New Yorkers, that he had to make a decision.[62]

With invasion imminent, Seixas beseeched God to change the hearts of King George and his advisers. He rejoiced as the Declaration of Independence, signed on July 4, 1776, was read with great ceremony to Washington's Continental army. Like many New England ministers, he divined sacred meaning in revolutionary events. But he preferred to close the synagogue "rather than let it be a Tory congregation." Although his final sermon lamented that this might be the last service at Shearith Israel, he did not hesitate to carry most of the synagogue's Torahs and valuables in a locked box out of danger rather than leave them where they might fall into the hands of despised Tories.[63]

Seixas's congregants, too, had to choose either to join the American patriot cause or to remain loyal to George III. The first option likely meant leaving the city; the second choice allowed Jews to stay. It was not an easy decision. Some argued that to flee New York would mean the end of Shearith Israel, the oldest synagogue in the thirteen colonies. Others demurred. Most congregants chose exile, a familiar Jewish condition.

Jews shared with their fellow New Yorkers a growing alienation from the British. The freedom, respect, and economic opportunity that Jews enjoyed in New York allied many with rebel leaders of the colony, their partners and compatriots. Jews lived in a colony, now a state, that offered them full rights of citizenship, including the vote, whereas the English government still treated its Jewish citizens as "second class." Indeed, "New York in 1777 became the first state in the western world to confer total citizenship upon the Jews." At the state's founding convention, held during a moment of wartime peril, John Jay, later chief justice of the United States Supreme Court, told fellow New Yorkers that they were born "equally free with the Jews," a people notable for their resistance to tyranny. Jay portrayed Jews as an exemplary people for a new nation. It is no wonder so many New York Jews took up the revolutionary cause.[64]

Between Washington's retreat and Evacuation Day in November 1783, the British established their military headquarters in New York City. Loyalists seeking refuge under British military protection replaced New Yorkers who fled. The city's population swelled, taxing its resources. African Americans pursuing freedom crowded its outskirts. The military commandeered most public buildings and churches. The city remained under martial law throughout its occupation, although British military officers enjoyed theater productions and parties.[65]

Roughly 30 Jews stayed loyal to the crown; 16 joined 942 New Yorkers who signed an "Address of Loyalty," affirming Great Britain's supremacy over the colonies. Preservation of Shearith Israel preoccupied these remaining Jews. The elders left Torah scrolls for their use. The British army contemplated converting the synagogue into a hospital, but several Jews persuaded military authorities to spare it. The British valued Jewish support and severely punished two soldiers who vandalized the synagogue, burning Torah scrolls. But the small number of Jews weakened the synagogue community and made it difficult to secure a quorum (minyan) of ten men for Sabbath services.[66]

The real story of New York Jews during the American Revolution occurred in Philadelphia, where most of them found refuge. Prior to the war, Philadelphia had a small Jewish population of perhaps twenty-five families. However, as the capital of the new republic, the city attracted many Jewish refugees. For New Yorkers, it became their home away from home. They both established themselves in trade and remade the city to resemble their former life. New York's Jews spurred Philadelphians to erect the first synagogue in the city, leaving behind rental quarters. A New Yorker headed the committee to build a synagogue for Mikveh Israel, a red-brick building similar to Shearith Israel; former New York elders wrote the congregation's bylaws. Mikveh Israel then hired Gershom Seixas as hazan.

Most New York Jews followed their hazan to Philadelphia and joined the patriot cause. Some volunteered for militia service. Others used their experience in privateering gained in the French and Indian War to disrupt British shipping. Still others assisted in finance, securing needed loans to keep the Continental army provisioned. Seixas offered spiritual support.[67]

Gotham's Jews possessed political equality and wanted these same rights in Pennsylvania. The commonwealth's new constitution contained a "test oath" requiring affirmation of the "divine inspiration" of both Old and New Testaments. Jews could not take such an oath. Seixas and others wrote those who were charged with reviewing Pennsylvania's constitution, explaining that the Test Act was a "stigma" on both Jews and the commonwealth. The Test Act contradicted the commonwealth's constitution, which stated that "no man who acknowledges the being of a God" could be deprived of his civil rights. As revolutionaries, Jews had proven that they were "as fond of liberty as other religious societies can be." Seixas argued passionately that if the Test Act were eliminated, Jews would thrive in Pennsylvania, adding to its prosperity. If not, they would go elsewhere.[68]

In 1787, Jews tried again to eliminate Pennsylvania's test oath, this time by writing to the Constitutional Convention meeting then in Philadelphia. While the convention's federal mandate did not include state laws, delegates did unanimously approve a clause providing "that no religious test shall ever be required as a qualification to any office of public trust under the United States." These efforts to eliminate test oaths became part of a legacy of political equality that New York's Jewish leaders bequeathed to Jews of the new republic and enshrined in the federal Constitution. (In 1790, Pennsylvania finally dropped the offend-ing clause.)[69]

As the new nation's most prominent Jewish clergyman, Seixas, who had returned to New York, now went back to Philadelphia for the pa-rade, glorying in freedom's accomplishments. After the British depar-ture, he had accepted Shearith Israel's offer to resume his duties as hazan in New York with a salary that placed him among the city's upper middle class. He then pressed in his inaugural sermon for "stricter attention" to rules of "decency & decorum." Services should command "respect" instead of "contempt," he urged. An ardent revolutionary, Seixas desired a dignified republican order.[70]

Although Shearith Israel's lay leaders subsequently came to share Seixas's emphasis on decorum and respect, they initially saw messianic tidings in the Revolution's success. First, they penned a Hebrew prayer praising the Revolution's achievements and its blessings of peace, fore-shadowing a future redemption. Then, as soon as the New York Legisla-ture passed an act allowing for incorporation of religious societies, the congregation quickly crafted articles of incorporation and established a governing Board of Trustees. But then it hesitated, choosing not to promulgate its first constitution until after ratification of the federal Constitution in 1789. Two years later, the trustees took over all fiscal and religious supervision of the congregation.[71]

With an incorporated religious society and Board of Trustees, the "synagogue community" yielded to an American corporate model. In colonial times, Jews lived within a Christian world but largely social-ized among themselves. After the Revolution, Jews became part of the commonwealth, their synagogue a chartered institution of the state. They embarked on building a new type of urban American Judaism in New York.

The Five Points, 1828. This engraving from *Valentine's Manual* (1861) depicts a profusion of classes, men and women, mixing in the streets. Although densely crowded and the poorest section of New York, the Five Points offered immigrants opportunities to establish a foothold in the city.

2

Shaking Off Constraints

A series of dramatic changes swept through New York City beginning in 1791 that changed the character of Jewish communal life, ultimately destroying the synagogue community of colonial times. Following the American Revolution came upheavals associated with Jeffersonian democracy that broadened the electorate and disrupted long-established patterns of deference. Economic innovation accompanied these political and religious experiments, fostering rapid expansion of the city's population through immigration. This urban transformation made New York the nation's largest metropolis. Its pluralism and diversity promoted significant alterations in the fabric of Jewish life that transformed Judaism into a distinctively urban religion. Concomitantly an industrial and commercial revolution facilitated new modes of work, housing, culture, religion, and politics. As civil conflict loomed, New York Jews bore few resemblances to the small, tightly knit and contentious community that had faced the revolt against British colonialism in 1776. Instead, democratic modes of Jewish communal life established patterns for a pluralistic urban American Judaism.

New York's Jews joined the rest of the growing seaport community in one of the greatest contests in American political history: the battle over the legacy of the American Revolution. With the new nation deeply divided over the meaning of 1776, passionate political debates erupted. The Hamiltonians, subsequently the Federalist Party, sought a strong central government. They passed legislation creating a potent national bank, encouraged growth of manufacturing, including factory production, and staunchly supported Britain while fiercely opposing the French Revolution. Federalist ideology championed deference rather than egalitarianism, contending that people with less wealth ought to allow men with standing to guide the helm of nation, state, and city. Jeffersonians responded by forming the nation's first political party, ancestor of today's Democratic Party. Supporters of an agriculturally based society with a weak central and stronger state governments, they disliked financial speculation and regarded banks with fear and suspicion. They preferred that factories remain in England. Many initially opposed the Constitution. They supported the French Revolution and saw Britain as a foe of American independence. Advocates of political egalitarianism, they argued that a shoemaker could make as wise a choice regarding government policies as a learned attorney.[1]

Jews entered this political fray. In the tumultuous 1790s, while Jews aligned with both parties, most joined the Jeffersonians. However, the Hamiltonian version of republicanism that stressed deference and tradition found a home in Shearith Israel even as the egalitarian Jeffersonian strain was winning at the polls. As the city fathers attempted to establish order within a republican framework by laying out the rectangular street grid that was to define Manhattan Island, so, too, prominent Jewish leaders of Shearith Israel tried to inaugurate an ordered republican structure. They sought through constitution writing to remake their synagogue in the image of American republicanism.[2]

This first constitution tried to navigate opposing tendencies in New York political culture and to wed synagogue traditions with republican ideals. Its preamble echoed the initial lines of the Bill of Rights. But even as its bylaws opened membership to Jewish males who were at least twenty-one years old, they rejected indentured or hired servants and those who were intermarried. A further clause forbade any Jew who violated "religious laws by eating trefa, breaking the Sabbath, or any other sacred day" from being called to the Torah or running for congregational office. Yet this new compact allowed all members to vote for members of the board, gave three members the right to call a synagogue meeting, and directed arbitration to end divisive internal controversies.[3]

Shearith Israel remained the only synagogue in New York throughout the first thirty-five years of the early republic, but it no longer served as the cornerstone of Jewish life. Efforts to create a republican congregation failed to keep pace with the city's growing Jewish population. Membership could not compete with other choices for fellowship, such as the Masonic Order or the Mechanics Society. However, on the High Holidays, nonmembers purchased seats and filled the synagogue. For many Jews, the synagogue assumed relevance for only part of their lives: primarily life-cycle ceremonies and the High Holidays. Thus began practices that became increasingly common throughout the United States.[4]

Shearith Israel struggled as a result. It endured repeated financial crises. Its Mill Street building gradually deteriorated. But it adamantly resisted all proposed reforms, rejecting a request for a choir, the right not to wear a prayer shawl, and any innovations in worship. This increasing rigidity rested on a new constitution that contained neither a bill of rights nor a statement proclaiming the right to enact compacts. It named only a single governing body, the Board of Trustees, with the *parnas* as president. The constitution stressed order and decorum, sustained by substantial fines. The Board of Trustees exercised tight control over hazan, *shochet*, and *shamash*, disbursed charity, and supervised the school. Though the hazan was a respected religious leader, the board governed. The trustees expected obedience.[5]

Jeffersonian influences battered Shearith Israel. The right to challenge authority, a key Jeffersonian tenet, sparked controversies. Intrigues among synagogue leadership and bitterly contested elections revealed how members shunned deference to oust traditional leadership. Generational tension and friction between Ashkenazi and Sephardi members contributed to these conflicts. Most significantly, Jeffersonianism spurred a revolt of Ashkenazi members that produced a second synagogue. Jefferson had affirmed that a people under a government that denied them "the inalienable rights of life, liberty and the pursuit of happiness" possessed the right "to alter or abolish it, and to institute new government." This spirit fostered the birth of B'nai Jeshurun in 1824.[6]

From the colonial period until the beginning of the nineteenth century, most Jews, like most New Yorkers, lived and worked in the area south of City Hall. But gradually more prominent Jews moved farther north, west of Broadway, to "quiet, tree-shaded blocks." From there, New York's wealthier families could still walk to their businesses and places of worship. Poorer Jews from England and central Europe also settled to the north, albeit east of Broadway. But while Protestants could choose among an array of churches, many reflecting class, denominational, and ethnic differences, all Jewish New Yorkers, regardless of wealth, headed to Shearith Israel, the city's only synagogue, on Mill Street since the eighteenth century. Contemporary observers blamed the breakup of Shearith Israel on the growing geographic spread of the Jewish population. The city's geography began to shape Jewish life, even as Jewish life shaped the geography of New York. But other forces were also at work.[7]

An Ashkenazi faction organized, seeking to implement a form of equality among Jewish men as well as greater religious observance than was the norm at Shearith Israel. While they pledged loyalty to Shearith Israel, they emphasized strict performance of Jewish law and attendance at services. More surprising, they established rotation in office, with an executive committee of five elected members to govern for three-month terms followed by a new committee. Believing in transparency, they opened committee meetings to the public and adopted a majority rule for accepting new members. The group promised to distribute honors democratically rather than in accordance with wealth. They intended to foster Ashkenazi identity and to increase religious observance by establishing egalitarian governance and democratic procedures in Jewish ritual practice.[8]

When Shearith Israel's Board of Trustees refused to sanction a separate faction within the synagogue, the dissidents seceded. Explaining their decision to establish a new congregation, they wrote to the board a list of their grievances. First, being "educated in the German and Polish minhog," they found it "difficult" to practice Sephardic ritual. Second, despite the still-small Jewish population in New York and sparse synagogue attendance, a growing Jewish community made it impossible for Shearith Israel to handle all Jewish congregants, "particularly on Holidays." Third, the distance "of the shool" from their homes made it hard to attend services. The secessionists did not "capriciously withdraw" from this "ancient and respectable congregation." Rather, echoing the Declaration of Independence, they declared it "nature's necessity." In closing, they invoked a shared identity "as Brethren of one great family." As part of a Jewish community larger than any one synagogue, the new congregation, B'nai Jeshurun, trusted that their endeavor would "be recognized."[9]

Shearith Israel's board considered the letter, postponed action, and never responded. However, it soon recognized the new congregation. Shearith Israel loaned B'nai Jeshurun four Torah scrolls for the dedication of its synagogue in a remodeled First Coloured Presbyterian Church in the very heart of New York's immigrant working-class neighborhood. Each congregation offered prayers for the welfare of both sets

of trustees. Prominent members of Shearith Israel had signed the secessionists' letter.[10] It was time to let their fellow Jews go. The growing city
could encompass more congregations.

This division of B'nai Jeshurun and Shearith Israel marked a turning point in New York Jewish communal life. Shearith Israel was New
York's first synagogue, but B'nai Jeshurun was the first of many new
synagogues. Bolstered by increasing numbers of immigrants, congregations split and split again as egalitarian republicanism and rampant
congregationalism blossomed in the city. B'nai Jeshurun represented a
younger generation with fewer men of wealth and prestige, but it rapidly
became one of the city's largest synagogues, inaugurating new patterns
of growth and expansion.[11]

Prior to the Civil War, 150,000 Jews arrived in the United States as
part of the central European migration, which included eastern European Jews from Russia and Poland who came by way of the German
states. While many traveled on to midwestern cities like Chicago, Cleve-
land, Cincinnati, and St. Louis, thousands remained in New York. As
central Europe transitioned from a society of estates, in which Jews
served as middlemen between peasants and nobles, to an industrial society, many Jews faced dismal economic prospects. The slightly better
off moved to larger cities in search of work; the poor migrated to the
United States. Immigration not only took Jews from small towns to the
metropolis but also transported them from a premodern society to a
rapidly modernizing urban center. Letters home and newspaper articles
heralded economic opportunities, accelerating migration and creating
a chain guiding Jews. Jewish immigrants thus joined a great migration
streaming out of various regions of central Europe.[12]

Immigration changed New York's Jews. By the mid-1840s, a quarter
of the American Jewish population lived in the city. By 1859, New York's
Jewish population numbered near forty thousand (5 percent of the city's
general population), half of them central European Jews. They came
from lands intermittently hostile to Jews, restricting access to professions, trades, real estate, and even marriage. Whether they left Prussia,
Bavaria, or Bohemia, young immigrant Jews shared common characteristics: lack of formal education, little money, no spouse, and hardly any
knowledge of English.[13]

B'nai B'rith certificate, 1876. Jewish immigrant men in New York City established the Independent Order of B'nai B'rith, the Jewish fraternal society, in 1843. Initially designed to succor German-speaking immigrants, it grew rapidly, and many lodges switched to English before the Civil War. This certificate portrays the order's charitable activities as well as its motto of "benevolence, brotherly love, and harmony." Courtesy of the Prints and Photographs Division, Library of Congress.

Alternative Identities

October 1843. The Jewish cycle of High Holidays, culminating with celebration of the harvest festival of Sukkot, had just ended, and the regulars had gathered at Sinsheimer's Café in the German Kleindeutschland (Little Germany) neighborhood of Manhattan for beer, conversation, and fellowship. While they were looking forward to the New Year that had just begun, their frustrations with, as they put it, "the deplorable condition of Jews, in this, our adopted country," rankled. The congregations weren't doing anything; they were too busy fighting over issues of ritual and liturgy. The new literary club that Henry Jones had joined hoping it would mediate between the congregations had succumbed and joined the fray. A born organizer, Jones, a serious, dark-haired, and bespectacled young man with a prominent nose and cleft chin framed by a fringe of beard, desperately wanted to foster a spirit of cooperation among New York Jews. He and several of the regulars had joined the Masons or Odd Fellows lodge, but a recent incident excluding Jews from a lodge irritated them. They needed something different.[14]

Seeking to rise above New York Jews' internecine wrangling, the Sinsheimer regulars decided to create an alternative to both religious congregations and secular lodges: a secular Jewish fraternal society. They named their invention B'nai B'rith (Sons of the Covenant). This fraternity combined traditions of Judaism and Freemasonry and replaced the synagogue with the lodge room. Incorporating special handshakes and passwords, B'nai B'rith spoke to central European Jewish immigrants, offering a form of sociability that men once had enjoyed in synagogue. As the fraternal organization spread to many American cities, Jews found fellowship in its lodges and security in its insurance policies. B'nai B'rith members also strove to support "science and art," to help "the poor and needy," to come "to the rescue of victims of persecution," and to bridge gaps between immigrant standing and citizenship. In short, they laid out for themselves basic demands of Jewish communal responsibility couched in universal language. Within less than a decade, New York enrolled seven hundred members, with more lodges opening each year. Before the century ended, New York Jews had exported their innovative form of Jewish secular fraternity across the ocean to Europe and the

Middle East. Other Jewish fraternal orders followed, at times rivaling B'nai B'rith in numbers.[15]

As B'nai B'rith grew, it devoted itself to helping immigrants integrate into American society. Here, indeed, was a modern form of Jewish brotherhood, true "sons of the covenant," whose fellowship knew no national boundaries, unconstrained by struggles over religious ritual. Responding to a Baltimore lodge's request to admit non-Jews, the New York chapters replied that the order is "adapted . . . solely for Israelites." Members organized the Maimonides Library "to provide instruction for the masses." The library held eight hundred books available for loan for a dollar-a-year membership fee. B'nai B'rith lodges acted as adult literary societies guided by German liberal intellectual ideas. Lodges sponsored cultural evenings. On the eve of the Civil War, as immigrants prospered, lodges switched from German to English and dropped many secret rituals.[16]

Freedom from constraints of the "synagogue community" unleashed enormous creativity among New York Jews. They initiated new forms of Jewish communal organization that responded to opportunities and demands of urban living and remade Jewish life in the city. As the Jewish population diversified through immigration from central and eastern Europe, a more pronounced upper class and a growing working class emerged, products of urban growth. This combination spurred establishment of independent charitable organizations, including the city's first Jewish hospital, as well as a wide array of social welfare, cultural, and communal groups.[17] Though Jews composed less than 5 percent of New York's population in the pre–Civil War decades, they supported almost as many organizations as non-Jewish ethnic and religious groups did. Organizational diversity—and competition—came to characterize New York's Jews.

Synagogues multiplied but struggled to keep pace with Jewish institutional innovation. New immigrants from towns throughout central and eastern Europe sought familiarity in worship among their fellows as well as greater stringency in observance of Jewish law. Leaving towns that often restricted their freedom to marry and start a family, individual Jewish men found American democracy and freedom intoxicating. They aspired to leadership positions within congregations and willingly experimented by creating new organizations. No single institution could contain these variations. Neither could one congregation accommodate all would-be leaders, who, over a thirty-year period, established twenty-seven congregations. When Jews did go to synagogue, they went to pray and to socialize.[18]

Isaac Mayer Wise, the leader of Reform Judaism in America, reminisced that in 1846, when he first disembarked as a young man in New York, most poor Jews were ignorant of Jewish learning, while the better off "kept aloof from Hebrew society" and "despaired of the future." Yet neither abandoned Judaism. Their "psychological and emotional needs" kept them "within the fold." Immigrant Jews needed each other in a foreign land. Common ties of ethnicity, language, and culture endured, while deeply ingrained traditions, practices, and commonalities encouraged many native-born Jews to remain loyal to family and faith. But if the synagogue, despite its strong presence in New York, would not or could not fully satisfy desires for connections, where would these yearnings find an outlet?[19]

New York Jews spent most of their time outside synagogues—in tenements, on the streets, in workshops, and in the marketplace. They interacted with non-Jewish New Yorkers on a daily basis, forming relationships that influenced synagogue life and encouraged new patterns of Jewish association. Synagogue-goers adapted what they learned from New York politics, business, and society to introduce such new trends within the synagogue as elected officers. Synagogue leaders also decided to hire Jewish ministers able to represent the congregation in ecumenical gatherings and to deliver English-language sermons. The arrival of these first rabbis in the 1840s challenged previous patterns of lay leadership.

But daily life in New York also inspired formation of alternative forms of Jewish community—newspapers, social clubs, libraries, hospitals, lectures, and charities. Thus, the story of New York synagogues and their various divisions, while telling, is not *the* story of Jewish New York. Rather, the story of the urban origins of American Jewish life flourished in the markets, tailor shops, saloons, and butcher stores where Jews formed an ethnic economy and forged neighborhood networks. These more informal connections shaped new forms of associational life.

Jewish creativity also found outlets in the arts. The Italian Opera Company under Max Maretzek briefly exceeded even dancing in popularity. Born in Moravia, Maretzek came to New York after time in London as a conductor. He formed his own company, supported by fellow

Jews who relished his productions of European operas. Other Jews tried their hand at theater, building playhouses and offering single-price tickets in a democratic move. On occasion, the local Jewish press boasted of Jewish contributions to the city's culture. Yet such praise could be double-edged, with Jews accused of controlling New York's cultural offerings and lowering their quality.[20]

As audience members, New York Jews evidenced diverse tastes in theater. They could be found in the dress circle of the City Theater and at Barnum's Museum, where they watched plays that were "more intensely effective representations of real life" than elsewhere in the city. They also patronized the German National Theater as well as Fellow's Minstrels, an entertainment parodying blacks, with whites wearing blackface and imitating black dialects. Participation in the arts offered the middling and newly affluent Jewish community opportunities to mix with Christians on equal terms, promising social acceptance in a broader urban public community.[21]

The literary society, an alternative fraternal outlet, attracted ambitious young Jewish men. Literary societies exemplified attempts to encourage fraternization by German-speaking Jewish immigrants, joined by non-German newcomers and native-born Jews seeking greater refinement. They aimed to integrate better into American society and discuss critical contemporary issues. Typical debates, for example, concerned whether "a woman ought to move in the same sphere as men" or whether fashion benefited humanity. Political issues, such as comparisons between Russian serfdom and American slavery, also animated discussion. Jewish, secular, optimistic, and ambitious, literary societies enrolled low numbers since most New York Jews focused on getting an economic foothold in the new country. Yet their ambitious intellectual agendas reflected energies and enthusiasms nurtured in the growing metropolis.[22]

As Jews achieved economic security, they embraced ever more lavish festive occasions. They attended dinners sponsored by literary and benevolent societies, enjoying music and dancing. In 1861, Meyer S. Isaacs, the twenty-one-year-old son of the editor of the *Jewish Messenger*, founded the Purim Association to raise funds for worthy causes. Its annual Purim Ball quickly became the social event of the year, celebrated with elaborate gaiety, despite the ongoing Civil War. Demand for invitations was intense; nobody of means wanted to be left off the list.

More and more tickets were printed, as upward of three thousand fashionable Jews attended. Perhaps most sumptuous, the 1863 ball featured the Seventh Regiment band, with sixty-five musicians playing varied dance numbers. Remarkable elaborate costumes rarely referenced either Queen Esther or Mordecai, the holiday's heroes. Adopting Christians' New Year's Day tradition, Jews opened their homes on Purim for visits. The Purim Ball marked the end of "ball season," a season that encompassed synagogue and benevolent-society affairs and exclusive social gatherings, as well as public lectures and concerts.[23]

German influence on New York Jewish organizational practices spurred a secularization that extended to Sabbath observance. An exasperated editorialist complained that the average Jewish New Yorker desired to keep the Sabbath but felt that America's "climate" created "something in the air that opposes his intention." This pattern persisted. Fifty years later, a staunch crusader for Sabbath observance claimed that immigrants seeking freedom and economic opportunities "seemed to think there was something in the American atmosphere which made the religious loyalty of their native lands, and especially the olden observance of the Sabbath, impossible."[24]

Indeed, something in New York's "climate" did make regular Sabbath observance difficult, if not impossible. Sabbath practices differentiated not only Jew from Christian but also Catholic from Protestant and, significantly, German from Anglo. New Yorkers debated the Sabbath, how it should be observed, and whether it should be observed at all. German Christian immigrants contributed to this debate over appropriate behavior on the American Sunday. Even those who attended church regularly considered "secular activities" part of their Sunday routine, but these elicited criticism from native-born white Protestants. While some wished to reserve Sunday for rest and churchgoing, other definitions of Sunday behavior included attendance at a library, voluntary association, or lecture hall. Many immigrants championed a "Continental Sabbath," which encompassed leisure and amusement. Theaters, dance halls, and saloons beckoned city dwellers but irked those who favored a government-protected Sunday as a day of church attendance and quiet contemplation. German immigrants organized to protect their right to spend their day off work as they pleased, appealing to American separation of church and state and individual liberties to fight Sunday blue laws.[25]

Jews, too, joined these debates. Sermons and publications noted that Jews shirked their religious responsibilities. Jewish communal leaders denounced Sabbath desecration but also argued over Christian worship patterns. Some claimed that Jews' ability to open their stores on Sunday actually illustrated "American freedom, a striking instance of

Landing immigrants at Castle Garden, New York City. Engraving from *Harper's Monthly Magazine*, June 1884. New York became a city of immigrants prior to the Civil War, with most arriving at Castle Garden at the southern tip of Manhattan. Immigrants transformed New York into the nation's largest metropolis. Around 150,000 Jews, many of them from central Europe, figured among the immigrants coming to America in these years, and thousands remained in the city.

independence and equality." Others rejected that argument. On a practical and personal level, New York Jews grappled with whether to work on Saturday, simultaneously the Jewish day of rest and an important commercial day. Jewish networks of peddling and business failed to insulate Jewish peddlers and businesspeople from the pull of the city's commercial demands and the lure of its economic opportunities.[26]

The growing presence of secular Jews in an increasingly immigrant city complicated what it meant to be Jewish. No longer was Jewishness defined by religious practice and congregational membership. Yet both Christians and Jews assumed that these nonobservant New Yorkers remained Jews. Their irreligious behavior challenged the boundaries of the city's burgeoning and diversifying Jewish community and transformed characteristics of Jewish identity. On the one hand, in the formation of B'nai B'rith, the founding of Jews' Hospital, and the inception of ninety-three different societies ranging from small burial societies to the Hebrew and German benevolent societies, Jews determined to bond with each other, often by nationality. On the other hand, Jewish families welcomed the public school, the institution that offered the quickest mode of acceptance for immigrant children into the greater community. Similarly, in Jews' immersion in the arts, as in business, they chose to join Christian New Yorkers without distinction, to sit side by side at the Astor Opera House, the Academy of Music, and the Broadway theaters. Jewish identity and Jewish integration remained challenging and elusive as Jewish life increasingly became more complex, diverse, and urbanized, no longer centered on the synagogue. Instead, Jewishness acquired secular urban dimensions rooted in common experiences of immigration, occupational choices, and residence.

Immigrant Urbanism

The American Revolution had unleashed New Yorkers' entrepreneurial expectations and generated remarkable urban growth. No city could match New York's merchants, artisans, or manufacturers. Jews freely ventured into all arenas of the marketplace. Whether it was Asher Myers crafting bells for City Hall, Harmon Hendricks constructing a copper-rolling mill, or Sampson Simson launching clipper ships, Jews exploited the new opportunities. But even as an open market widened horizons of economic enterprise for aspiring artisans, merchants, and manufacturers, it increased economic stratification: by 1800, 20 percent owned 80 percent of the city's wealth, while the bottom half owned less than 5 percent. This inequality grew even greater over the century.[27] These changes were mirrored among New York Jews.

Soon after the Revolution, New York became the nation's financial center. Four Jewish businessmen joined together with twenty other New Yorkers to found the New York Stock Exchange in 1793. The city's merchants cornered the cotton trade, became expert at speculation and insurance, and launched ambitious economic adventures. With the opening of the Erie Canal, New York began its journey to become a world-class metropolis. The entry point for immigrants, the city's port also served as the entrée for a majority of the nation's imports as well as a site for transatlantic shipping of many exports from the West.[28]

Housing the New York Stock Exchange and the Gold Exchange, New York flourished as the American center of market speculation. Its banks provided investment capital for the West and South. The California gold rush brought the city both capital in newly minted gold and an outlet for its manufactories supplying western speculators. New York maintained close ties to the South: its bankers accepted slave property as collateral; its brokers hawked southern railroad and state bonds; its wholesalers sold southerners household goods; its traders and shipowners monopolized the sale of cotton.[29]

New York became the axis of the nation's communication network. Telegraphy permitted almost instantaneous news of business and current events. A new invention, the rotary press, allowed an 80 percent drop in the price of a newspaper. Dailies and weeklies bloomed, enticing both elite and working classes with news, politics, sports, court trials, theater, investigative exposés, and gossip about the rich and famous. The weeklies included two English-language newspapers aimed at Jews: the independent *Asmonean*, edited by the English immigrant Robert Lyon, and the Orthodox *Jewish Messenger*, edited by Samuel Isaacs, the rabbi of Congregation Shaaray Tefilah.[30]

Before mass immigration from central Europe began in the 1840s, New York's Jewish population most commonly fell within the middle or lower middle classes. Relatively few Jews entered the professions. However, as early as the 1790s, the first American-born Jewish physician graduated medical school at Columbia College. He pioneered in what became a common Jewish profession in New York. Most Jews worked as merchants, auctioneers, and brokers; smaller numbers labored in crafts. The expansion of printing in the city enticed Jewish artisans to enter the field. Yet even with a booming economy, poverty, disability, mental illness, and crime also existed among the city's Jews, albeit in unknown proportions. New York's wealthy Jews did not keep pace with this changing city; they no longer possessed the economic standing of earlier years. But Jews continued to own slaves as commonly as their non-Jewish peers did, until slavery was abolished in New York State in 1827.[31]

A major engine of social and economic transformation came with thousands of immigrants who crowded into New York in the thirty years before the Civil War. Pushed out by a potato famine in 1845 that spread from Ireland to the southern and western German states, the failure of the German Revolution of 1848, and widespread unemployment in Britain, an average of 157,000 emigrants arrived annually at Castle Garden at the tip of Manhattan. Approximately one of every five or six remained in the city, where they were joined by thousands of native-born Americans who left their farms or workshops to try their luck in the metropolis. By 1855, immigrants, mostly from Ireland and Germany, made up over half the city's population. Two of every three adults in Manhattan were born abroad. New York's urban revolution transformed it into an immigrant city, an identity that endured for over a century.[32]

Most newcomers considered life in New York better than in Europe, with more meat and nicer furniture, but they remained one bad recession away from the pawnshop. Many Germans lived in tenements in Kleindeutschland in lower Manhattan. A mere twenty-five feet wide and only seventy feet deep, of three to five stories, a tenement housed twenty-four two-bedroom apartments, each with only a single window for families and their boarders. Usually over 150 tenants crowded into a single tenement.[33]

In the era's robust economy, at least a quarter of immigrant Jews attained middle-class standing by the 1850s, joining native-born Jews as merchants, wholesalers, retailers, skilled craftspeople, and professionals. Some did even better. During the Panic of 1857, a harrowing recession caused by the overextension of banks and a fall in the price of wheat, the *Asmonean*, hoping to persuade wealthy Jews to help those without work, published the names of fifty leading Jewish firms, averaging 278 employees each. Most were in textiles, a few in importing and dry goods. Many of the men heading these companies had connections in the South and West, including Joseph Seligman, whose family firm made a fortune supplying the California gold rush, and Levi Strauss, who achieved legendary success outfitting miners in California, while his purchasing office and manufacturing operations remained with his older brothers in New York. This wealth, immigrant and nonimmigrant, provided resources to build Jews' Hospital and the Hebrew Orphan Asylum, to patronize the arts, and eventually to construct elaborate synagogues.[34]

Urbanization transformed the world of Jewish women as well as men. Unmarried women—whether widows or daughters—often worked as peddlers, washerwomen, domestics, and tailors. In the Five Points immigrant neighborhood just north of City Hall, almost half of employed women worked in the needle trades and a quarter as domestic servants. Some seamstresses labored in workshops; many sewed in their apartments. Irrespective of other employment and marital status, most women kept house. The majority of households had between three and six children. Whether through wage work or housework, shared occupations and responsibilities of the Five Points Jews created informal but vital neighborhood networks.[35]

Except for several women who achieved notoriety as feminists, few New York Jewish women participated in the women's rights movement. However, many heard of the Seneca Falls convention of 1848 and its manifesto demanding equality. The *Asmonean* even printed a parody of the proclamation that it was time for the women to "break off the chains which Fashion has thrown among them." Judging from newspaper columns, most Jewish men rejected women's equality, echoing nineteenth-century middle-class norms that women belonged neither in the marketplace nor in the public square but rather in the home, at the center of domestic life. Men did support secular education for girls as well as boys, but if pages of advertisements for pianos are any evidence, religious training and participation remained peripheral to women's lives. By contrast, attendance at concerts, dramas, and operas suggested that middle-class Jewish women embraced the arts and rarely frequented the synagogue gallery.[36]

New York's urban expansion produced distinctive residential neighborhoods that reflected variations in class, occupations, and points of

origin. Residential stratification changed the character of daily interactions. Within each neighborhood, different modes of life took root,
increasing social distance between Jews. While the more established
Shearith Israel leaders living west of Broadway and just north of City
Hall might have used oil lamps, coal stoves, and iceboxes, those east of
Broadway inhabited dilapidated and hastily subdivided wooden homes
and depended on candles, oil lamps, and found wood. Much of the
native-born Jewish population moved to the Lower West Side, north of
Canal Street (Shearith Israel built a new synagogue on Crosby Street in
1834 in recognition of this residential clustering), while immigrant Jews
settled among Catholic and Lutheran German immigrants. The bulk of
their synagogues clustered in a section of Kleindeutschland on the East
Side. Thus, class divisions separated Jewish congregations even as they
stratified Protestant churches.[37]

Jewish immigrants usually spent their first years in Five Points, the
city's immigrant neighborhood, where familial and communal ties mitigated difficult living conditions. Five Points, so called due to the five-
cornered intersection of five streets, acquired a reputation as a place of
crime, prostitution, and disorder. But it primarily served as a home and
workplace for a struggling and burgeoning working-class population.
By the mid-nineteenth century, Irish immigrants and their children—
the largest immigrant group in New York City—constituted 75 percent
of Five Points' population. German-speaking immigrants composed
the second-largest group (approximately 20 percent), and of these, approximately half were Jewish. Most of the Jews living in Five Points came
from Posen, Polish territory then governed by Prussia.[38]

The city had created the Five Points neighborhood by filling in and
building over the Collect Pond. Never properly drained, the pond regularly flooded the two-and-a-half-story wooden structures constructed
on it. Yet Five Points' stables, workshops, and factories provided a convenient combination of work and residence, making it a prime destination for tens of thousands of immigrants who sought affordable rent
and housing close to work. As a result, the dilapidated wooden homes
contained far more inhabitants than one might expect. The first floors
often housed stores, and backyards had additional sheds and worksta-
tions. Soon, a great demand for homes and work in this neighborhood
led property owners to tear down the old wooden structures in order to

build brick tenements. But the tenements' crowdedness, dark interior spaces, and cellars made for miserable housing.[39]

Like other ethnic groups, immigrant Jews settled in specific blocks and even certain tenement buildings. But blocks with a high proportion of an immigrant group retained a heterogeneous population. In other words, just because a block was known as "Jewish" did not mean that all the shops or all the residences were necessarily Jewish.[40]

Newcomers often relied on ethnic ties to gain a foothold. Employers, conversely, looked to members of their own ethnic groups as workers on whom they could rely and with whom they could easily communicate. Neighborhoods like Five Points offered not only jobs but also Jewish community networks. These helped newcomers directly even as more established Jews used them to create an American Jewish identity that involved caring for coreligionists in need. Informal neighborhood networks developed fundamental elements of more formalized charitable organizations as the numbers of Jews grew. In an ethnic economy, people depended on those whom they knew, usually from a shared hometown and family, to get started. This help benefited the giver, too. Such work propelled individuals forward, even as it knit together a tight ethnic economy.[41]

Thus, while Jews might bicker in their synagogues, they forged ties with one another in the streets. They helped one another find jobs, expand business networks, and form community in shops and on street corners. Over time, this community even survived its members' dispersal. As Jews moved uptown with socioeconomic success, they still returned to Five Points to visit the old synagogue, patronize Jewish book dealers, and buy Passover groceries and matzo. They relied on Five Points for jobs for their children, Jewish connections and sustenance, and social ties for themselves.[42]

New York in the three decades before the Civil War emerged as the nation's most vigorous municipality. It grew to a metropolis numbering 814,000 in 1860. At the hub of the nation's growing rail system, Gotham became America's leading manufacturing center. The city housed the heart of the nation's garment trade, major iron works, and a multitude of assorted industries such as the Singer Sewing Machine Company. New York's merchants established the country's first department stores.[43]

These opportunities for labor attracted immigrants, but they clustered in specific industries and occupations, initially reflecting skills and experience they had brought with them. Subsequently, ethnic connections facilitated finding work and expanded economic niches. Irish immigrants arrived extremely poor, with only agricultural experience, and most entered laboring jobs. By the mid-nineteenth century, they composed the majority of New York's longshoremen, shipyard and warehouse workers, quarrymen, and construction workers. Germans possessed more money and experience in trades and crafts such as carpentry, tailoring, shoemaking, tanning, pottery, bricklaying, and weaving. They found work in many trades and also introduced new ones, such as piano manufacture, to the city.[44]

Immigrant Jews similarly found their niche, most importantly in peddling and selling used clothing. Given a "hastily fixed up basket," a new immigrant was "hurried into the country." Jews applied their old-country experience to their new situation, supplying demand in city and countryside. Perhaps half of immigrant Jews took up peddling when they arrived. Peddling involved Jews who settled in small towns in the South and new cities in the Midwest. Many peddlers assiduously worked to ascend the socioeconomic ladder that led from peddler to dry-goods merchant. The myth of ascent appealed to many immigrants, but some preferred the security of the ethnic neighborhood. Others worked as tailors or shoemakers, also using skills they had previously learned. These Jews joined their fellow German immigrants laboring in similar trades.[45]

Peddlers expanded their businesses by developing ties with Jews elsewhere in the country, much as Jewish merchants had developed networks around the Atlantic in the previous century. By 1860, the majority of the sixteen thousand peddlers in the United States were Jewish, which enabled New York Jewish merchants to take advantage of regional and even national markets. Thus, Jewish peddlers facilitated the growth of New York suppliers. Subsidiary wholesale and manufacturing centers, like Cincinnati, emerged, led by transplants from the shops and warehouses of New York.[46]

Jewish peddlers often specialized in the sale of secondhand clothing. In these years, only men at the bottom of the socioeconomic ladder—sailors, miners, or slaves—wore ready-made clothing. Most Americans stitched clothes at home, had clothes sewn by a custom tailor, or bought reconditioned used garments. While few Jews worked as custom tailors, many Jews were secondhand clothing merchants, who took in, cleaned, and renovated old clothing, preparing it for both retail and wholesale markets. Often "an object of ridicule and contempt," the secondhand clothing trade facilitated Jews' contribution to an emerging garment industry, despite the fact that they played no role in such technological advances as the invention of the sewing machine. Jewish secondhand traders actually "renovated" the traffic, incorporating innovative commercial ideas as well as experimenting with production of new clothes on the side. At first, New York Jews dabbled in the production of cheap clothing—"slops." A dry-goods merchant with cloth in stock risked little by hiring workers to produce inexpensive ready-made clothes, a process of gradual transformation from merchant into small manufacturer.[47]

Opportunity and mobility existed for a minority. Contemporary observers credited Jewish peddlers with introducing the installment plan (selling on "time"), direct selling, and lower prices, made possible by a willingness to maintain a smaller profit margin. Connections with Jews in London encouraged a transatlantic traffic in used clothes and facilitated a transition for some from peddler to merchant standing within a decade. Workers in the nascent garment industry joined successful peddlers and native-born Jews in manufacturing and selling clothes, wholesale or retail.[48]

Jews in New York acquired a reputation especially for their shops downtown in the Chatham Square neighborhood. "Clothing stores line the southern sidewalk without interruption, and the coat-tails and pantaloons flop about the face of the pedestrian," wrote an observer. "In front of each, from sunrise to sundown, stands the natty, blackbearded and fiercely moustached proprietor," the account continued. "Stooping as you enter the low, dark doorway, you find yourself in the midst of a primitive formation of rags, carefully classified into vests, coats and pantaloons." These Jewish shopkeepers embarrassed Rabbi Isaac Mayer Wise, who was always well dressed with vest, jacket, tie, and crisp white collared shirt. He deemed the area a "disgrace." However, these modest Chatham shops formed the nucleus of a rapidly expanding international trade and a growing ready-made clothing industry. On the eve of the Civil War, the value of the clothing market in New York reached $17 million.[49]

The Civil War demanded production of uniforms, and Jewish merchants eagerly filled orders. This effort helped to propel Jews from the margins to the center of clothing manufacture. Both those already involved in the clothing business and those lacking any experience whatsoever jumped at the contracts to set up shop. Without time to measure each soldier, suppliers developed a system of standardized sizes. This facilitated rapid production of uniforms but also mass production for a civilian market.[50]

As the Civil War helped transform an undesirable secondhand-clothing trade into a garment industry, so some Jewish owners of Chatham dry-goods shops made a comparable transition to proprietors of small firms. This transformation materialized in cast-iron loft buildings arising on Broadway, that long street that ran from the base of Manhattan diagonally up to its northern tip. Walking up Broadway from Canal Street to Union Square, an observer noted how the occupants of some four hundred buildings were almost all "Hebrews," counting "over 1000 wholesale firms out of a total of 1200." More than Broadway bore witness to Jewish commercial mobility since Jewish firms similarly predominated "in the streets contiguous to Broadway."[51] But even as these impressive buildings had risen, with the names of Jewish merchants above their doors, thousands of Jewish immigrants were pouring into miserable tenements to the east. When the owners of the Broadway warehouses had lived on those streets, they had been a part of Kleindeutschland. Now their employees found themselves on the renamed Jewish East Side.

Religious Quarrels

In the years leading up to the Civil War, specifically Jewish religious quarrels divided New York Jews. Their struggles with each other over questions of tradition reflected not merely efforts to fashion a mode of religious life compatible with metropolitan demands but also desires to articulate a vision to guide the future of Judaism in the United States. The movement to reform Jewish religion in both its rituals and core doctrines agitated Jews in New York and throughout the United States. Ultimately, as it produced numerous variations, it transformed all forms of Jewish religious practice into minority expressions. While the battle for the hearts and minds of American Jews began in Charleston, South Carolina, in the 1820s, it reached new dimensions in New York. The city's affluence encouraged congregations for the first time to recruit rabbinic leaders, who carried in their baggage some of Europe's contentious debates over religion. Their vigorous arguments, amplified by New York's position as the nation's leading media center, mobilized masses of supporters that produced key institutions influencing the rise of not only Reform but also modern Orthodox and Conservative Judaism. Moments of cooperation accompanied the ebb and flow of disputes determining a distinctively urban form of Judaism in the city, its lineaments shared by the entire spectrum of Jewish religious practice.[52]

Rooted in central Europe, Reform Judaism spread with Enlightenment ideas in response to a protracted emancipation process granting Jews civil and political rights. Seeking Christian approval for full citizenship and desiring to have Judaism reflect the spirit of the age in order to be intellectually and spiritually satisfying, European reformers adjusted Judaism to modern behavioral norms and philosophy. They hoped this process would also inspire and retain new generations of Jews. Reformers tinkered with Sabbath services, shortening them, adopting stricter rules of decorum, and adding instrumental music. Rabbis introduced reading the Torah on a three-year rather than annual cycle and abolished the second day of festivals. Yet even such modest changes as German-language sermons, mixed choirs of men and women, and organ music encountered resistance. Whether opposition came from Jewish or governmental authority, it hampered the "free development" of Reform.[53]

No such restrictions constrained Reform in the United States. Reform Judaism prospered in the United States, where religious freedom and capitalist enterprise encouraged dramatic changes and where opportunities for full expression prevailed. As Jews struggled to fulfill the obligations of traditional Jewish practice, they simultaneously established Orthodox congregations and ignored demands of personal observance. Many immigrants, intent on getting businesses off the ground or enjoying newfound social opportunities, neglected both synagogue attendance and regular daily prayers. Statistics suggest that half of all American Jews chose not to affiliate with any congregation by 1850. No centralized authority guided congregations as they attempted to alter traditions to modernize worship. Self-governing, congregations made their own rules and elected their own ministry. This freedom produced variations, as each congregation found its own way to reconcile Judaism with American culture.[54]

While many Jews gave up on congregational life or chose a secular alternative to the synagogue in B'nai B'rith, a handful decided to try to remake the synagogue. The founders of Temple Emanu-El, much like the men of B'nai B'rith, also worried that existing synagogues repelled youth. But unlike B'nai B'rith, they explicitly desired a new religious community. In choosing the name Emanu-El—"God is with us"— they expressed their intention to stay within the bounds of Judaism. While they hoped that reform would enable them "to occupy a position of greater respect" among their fellow citizens, they also yearned to "worship with greater devotion." Eager to keep Judaism relevant to others like themselves, they embraced reform in order to "save Judaism" from a perceived straitjacket of outdated forms imposed by fanatical traditionalists.[55]

New York's first Reform congregation slowly altered worship to blend devotion to the divine and fidelity to the new age, initially mostly through decorum that matched its aesthetic aspirations. Keeping the traditional prayer book, the congregation added vocal music, German-language hymns, and a German-language sermon. Yet the congregation also initially upheld many critical elements of traditional Jewish life, practices they would later reject: Jewish dietary laws (kashrut), separation of men and women during prayer, and prayer shawl and head covering for men. Overall, Emanu-El's approach attracted new members, enabling it to expand. Moving into a former church spurred additional reforms. Emanu-El decided to read the Torah on a three-year cycle, introduced an organ, and minimized requirements for boys studying to become bar mitzvah. In short, it strove to modernize in order to strengthen, not diminish, Judaism.[56]

Each of these changes alienated some congregants and elicited ire from traditionalists in the press, but Emanu-El flourished. It drew ever more worshipers and grew bolder in its reform initiatives. It introduced a new prayer book that eliminated a host of theological beliefs (the concept of a chosen people, the coming of a personal Messiah and resurrection of the dead, restoration to Zion, and resumption of sacrifices) and ritual practices (observance of the second day of festivals). Soon

Temple Emanu-El, the city's only Reform congregation, grew rapidly from a
small discussion group. In 1854, it purchased a large Baptist church on
Twelfth Street. Transforming the church into a synagogue, Temple
Emanu-El ended the traditional Jewish practice of separate seating of men
and women. Temple Emanu-El became one of the city's most influential
synagogues, supported by many wealthy Jewish immigrants. Reproduced
from *Synagogue Architecture in the United States: History and Interpretation*
by Rachel Wischnitzer by permission of the University of Nebraska Press.
Copyright 1955 by the Jewish Publication Society of America.

other Reform congregations adopted the prayer book, a sign of Emanu-El's influence. Emanu-El also abandoned prayer shawls and no longer required hats. Then, in an aggressive move, it required all men to go bareheaded.[57]

Most boldly, the congregation introduced family seating. Emanu-El was the first Jewish congregation in New York and only the second in the United States to allow men and women to sit together during services as they did in mainstream Christian denominations. While a radical innovation from the perspective of Judaism, Emanu-El's family seating seemed to its members merely the next step in its efforts to meet American social standards. To seat men and women together distinguished Emanu-El even from Reform practice in Germany. Other New York congregations that had adopted some of Emanu-El's reforms at first shied away from family seating, as did reforming congregations in other American cities. (New York's second-oldest synagogue, B'nai Jeshurun, adopted family seating in 1875 only after a fight that led to a civil court case.)[58]

Debates over mixed seating reflected reconsiderations of women's position in Judaism. Emanu-El replaced the bar mitzvah service, which made "no impression on the boy," with a confirmation ceremony that received "sons and daughters into the same covenant." Gender egalitarianism expressed, in part, a desire to emulate the spiritual milieu of Protestant churches, where women's presence mandated conventions of dignified bourgeois behavior. Nineteenth-century American Christianity underwent a period of "feminization" as women became mainstays of church congregations, the most reliable attendees at Sunday services, the most conscientious members of committees, and the most pious congregants. Jewish women's fate was entwined with the Jewish community's quest for respectability in the Christian world. But this was only one consideration. Reform ideology extended beyond emulation of Protestant society to reinforce the movement for women's political, social, and economic equality. Rabbi Isaac Mayer Wise termed a traditional morning prayer in which a man thanked God that he was not created a woman "an insolence."[59]

Such concerns for women's rights did not extend to synagogue governance. A tradition of male lay control held sway at Emanu-El as in other Jewish congregations. The temple's trustees included some of the city's most prosperous central European immigrants. Its ritual committee regularly overruled its rabbi, who could conduct no marriage ceremony without the board's permission. Concerned with decorum, the board paid attention not only to what Jews said during worship and how they prayed, but also to how they dressed. It expected elegant clothes on the part of men and women attending services. The board regularly invited prominent reform figures to lecture and recruited talented, highly educated leaders. Under this spirited management, Emanu-El grew rapidly both in numbers and in wealth.[60]

With Temple Emanu-El as the Reform movement's base, reformers challenged traditionalists in debates that reverberated in the streets, pulpits, and Jewish press. Reformers grounded their creed in a wedding of science and Judaism, arguing that Judaism must stand the test of modern investigation. This included thought and ritual. Reformers argued that Judaism evolved over the centuries. Talmud mirrored a distant past containing wisdom but also ceremonies and commandments that were lifeless in the modern era. Many rabbinic customs (*minhagim*) derived from cultures of nations with whom Jews lived in the Diaspora. Science demonstrated that the Bible was divine in its creation but Talmud was not. Reformers harshly condemned many Jewish rituals. For example, they ridiculed the requirement that a man cease shaving for thirty days after the death of a mother or father and disparaged the eleven months of mourning.[61] They attacked kashrut, a bastion of traditionalism; a kosher table should not be the "diploma of a good Jew."[62]

These spirited attacks did not go unanswered. By midcentury, New York emerged as a center of both Reform and Orthodox Judaism due to the presence of leading intellectuals in both camps. Reform Jews had a voice in the influential *Asmonean* and Orthodox Jews in the *Jewish Messenger*. New York housed the nation's foremost Reform synagogue, Emanu-El, supported by the city's wealthiest Jews, as well as Shearith Israel, its oldest Orthodox synagogue.

Growth in both population and affluence facilitated recruitment of men educated in Jewish learning and secular studies. Their arrival in Gotham transformed the city into American Judaism's intellectual center. The most prominent Orthodox leaders were Samuel Myer Isaacs of Shaaray Tefilah and Morris Raphall of B'nai Jeshurun. Isaacs, a tall and somewhat dour personage with mutton-chop whiskers, cut a very different figure from the short and stout Raphall. Both, however, had spent time in England before coming to New York City, thus helping to knit an English-speaking diaspora connecting the United States with Great Britain. Both gave sermons on a regular basis. Raphall eagerly spoke wherever he could, traveling throughout the country. Isaacs used his *Messenger* newspaper to spread his ideas and attack reform.[63]

Despite rabbis' superior knowledge of Jewish religion and history, they deferred to boards of trustees, which remained by law the congregational governing bodies and zealously guarded their prerogatives. Each considered its rabbi an employee, along with the *shochet* and *shamash*. The boards did not want any employee speaking about controversial subjects, jeopardizing its standing in the community.[64]

New York congregations occupied all points on a spectrum from traditional orthodox practice through to radical reform. On average, a new congregation appeared each year for various reasons. Most new congregations organized around immigrants' place of origin. But other issues prompted splits: a willingness to accept proselytes, contested elections to the Board of Trustees, demands for religious observance outside synagogue, hiring of a *shochet*, even antagonism to new immigrants. These schisms demonstrated the influence of New York's religious pluralism and openness to religious entrepreneurship, which transformed disputes over ethnicity, personality, and ideology into new congregations.[65]

Yet in moments of crisis, New York Jews temporarily put aside their religious differences. The largest outcry arose over the Mortara case in 1858, in which a Jewish child was torn from his home in Italy under Catholic law because a family servant had secretly had him baptized at age six. Synagogues led and hosted protest gatherings. At a mass meeting, the assembled adopted a resolution condemning the "kidnapping."[66]

This mobilization instigated an effort to establish an American Jewish union. The Orthodox *Jewish Messenger* pleaded for a national board of Jewish congregations to enable Jews to have a greater influence in national affairs. Almost two dozen congregational representatives from cities ranging from New Orleans to St. Louis met in New York and established the Board of Delegates of American Israelites with headquarters in New York. It pledged no interference in either party politics or internal congregational affairs. But this did not prevent Reform congregations from boycotting along with Shearith Israel, which never felt comfortable with Ashkenazi congregations.[67]

Leopold Newman, in uniform. A Columbia-educated attorney and poet, Newman joined New York's Thirty-First Regiment and fought at the battles of Bull Run and Antietam. Rising to lieutenant colonel, he was hit by grapeshot in the leg and taken to Washington, DC, where he died while surgeons amputated his leg. President Lincoln visited him at bedside and promoted him to brigadier general. Courtesy of the New York State Military Museum.

Changes wrought by successive revolutions in industry and commerce, politics and society, religion and culture transformed New York City into a major metropolis, filled with immigrants as well as an extraordinarily wealthy elite. New York Jews participated in these transformations that dramatically recast their religious and communal worlds. As the Civil War approached, they stood poised to confront decades of contention pitting competing groups of Jews against each other. Yet these civil conflicts served as both prelude to and context for significant struggles to forge forms of community among New York Jews.

Debating Slavery

Abraham Lincoln had just been elected president of the United States. South Carolina and other southern states were seceding from the union, although Lincoln had not yet been sworn into office. The future did not look promising that Sabbath in January 1861 as Rabbi Morris Raphall ascended the bima (elevated platform) of B'nai Jeshurun and surveyed his congregants. His congregation, the first one to break away from Shearith Israel, had prospered, moving uptown to a new and more spacious building on Greene Street, north of Houston. Rabbi Raphall, too, had flourished in the city. His English-language sermons had vaulted him to an enviable position as New York's most prominent Jewish spiritual leader, the first rabbi invited to open a session of Congress in 1860. Now, with the union in peril, the bearded and bespectacled Raphall stepped forward to tackle the tough question of slavery and the Bible. Though no "friend to slavery in the abstract" and still less "to the practical working of slavery," he claimed that his personal feelings were irrelevant. Invoking the biblical story of Noah and his son Ham, the Orthodox rabbi concluded that, aside from family ties, slavery was the oldest form of social relationship. For viewing his father's nakedness, Ham and his descendants, the black race, were cursed to become slaves.

The Bible, Raphall explained, differentiated between enslaved Hebrews, who as slaves for limited periods were to be treated as any other Hebrew, and non-Hebrew slaves and their progeny, who were to remain in bondage during the lives of their master, his children and his children's children. Non-Hebrew slaves provided the relevant model for southern slavery. Hebraic law permitted masters to chastise these slaves short of murder or disfigurement and required that a slave who fled from Dan to Beersheba be returned, as must the slave absconding from South Carolina to New York.[68] While Raphall cautioned southerners that slaves must be protected from lustful advances, hunger, and overwork, he emphatically concluded that the Bible sanctioned slave property.[69]

Raphall's sermon created a sensation. Three New York newspapers published the text in full. Southern sympathizers distributed it throughout the country.[70] Raphall was not the first New York Jew to enter the debate on slavery, however. Several influential newspaper editors preceded him.

The question of slavery dominated politics in the antebellum era, reaching a fever pitch in the 1850s and drawing Jews into its debates. Most prominent Jewish leaders in New York opposed abolition and, to varying degrees, supported slavery. While they spoke for themselves, the absence of strong voices in favor of abolition differentiated Jewish leaders from New York Christian spokespeople. In 1856, a straw poll of "twenty-five of the prominent clergy" in New York revealed that twenty-three of them backed the Republican antislavery candidate for president.[71] Jewish rabbis' reluctance to support antislavery candidates for president suggested that many Jews acquiesced in slavery and did not desire to abolish it. These attitudes among Jewish and Christian clergy initially emerged in the 1840s.

Considered by many Christians to be the "most important Jew in America," Mordecai M. Noah, a playwright, former U.S. consul at Tunis, sheriff and surveyor of New York, Democratic Party leader, and newspaper editor, proudly declared, "I was always a friend of the south." Through his paper, he encouraged New Yorkers, particularly merchants, to develop close ties with southerners. He considered slavery a common good. Blacks, he claimed, were "anatomically and mentally inferior a race to the whites, and incapable, therefore, of ever reaching the same point of civilization, or have their energies roused to as high a degree of enterprise and productive industry." They could be content only in servile positions. Emancipation would jeopardize the country's safety. Noah wished to make publication of antislavery literature a punishable offense. Abolitionists were dangerous. They strained relations between merchants and southern traders. At war with America, they jeopardized the Union.[72]

Robert Lyon, the editor of the *Asmonean*, also edited the *New York Mercantile Journal*, a paper reputed to carry "great influence over the minds of many commercial men." His newspapers reached both local and national audiences. A Jewish religious progressive, Lyon opened the pages of the *Asmonean* to advocates of reforming Judaism. A staunch Democrat, he endorsed prosouthern Democrats for president and governor in 1856. Given Lyon's detailed knowledge of the Jewish commercial world and his consultation of "the wishes and desires of the majority of [the paper's] supporters," his political leanings likely reflected those of the city's Jewish business community. Lyon despised abolitionists as much as Noah did and urged Americans "to crush out for once and forever the attempt to plunder our Southern citizens of their property."[73]

The *Asmonean* supported enforcement of the controversial Fugitive Slave Act, which required police to turn over an alleged fugitive solely on the affidavit of a master, denying the fugitive the right to speak in court. The act was "the law of the land." While Jews might purchase a slave's release, they could not endanger "national and even international peace by gaining his freedom through violence," he wrote. Jews owed their renewed sense of self-confidence and comfortable position to America; they must "stand by the constitution, now and forever."[74]

These outspoken leaders expressed views held by many Jewish New Yorkers. An abolitionist report perspicaciously noted, "Jews of the United States have never taken any steps whatever with regard to the Slavery question," although Jews were often "the objects of so much mean prejudice and unrighteous oppression." Most Jews avoided the subject of slavery, nervous that Jewish political engagement might spark anti-Semitism. Jews observed how the Irish suffered after their more forceful entry into local politics. When Raphall delivered his controversial proslavery sermon, B'nai Jeshurun's board did not reprimand him over his position on slavery but rather objected to "the impropriety of intermeddling with politics." In 1860, Abraham Lincoln commanded only 35 percent of the city's vote. German-immigrant wards where most Jews lived voted two to one against him.[75]

Abram J. Dittenhoefer, who grew up in South Carolina, was an exception among New York Jews. He not only championed abolition but also worked on Lincoln's campaign. Dittenhoefer attended Lincoln's Cooper Union address in 1860, and despite the raspy quality of Lincoln's voice, thought "his earnestness invited and easily held the attention of his audience." The address launched Lincoln's successful run for the Republican nomination. Dittenhoefer later called it "epoch-making." Few New York Jews shared these sentiments. In fact, Dittenhoefer's father counseled his son, when he was a young law student, to become a Democrat as a public career because a Republican "would be impossible in the City of New York." He later reminisced, "One can hardly appreciate to-day what it meant to me, a young man beginning his career in New York, to ally myself with the Republican Party. By doing so," he explained, "not only did I cast aside all apparent hope of public preferment, but I also subjected myself to obloquy from and ostracism by acquaintances, my clients, and even members of my own family."[76] Dittenhoefer made an unusual decision. Most New York Jews aimed to fit into society. Unpopular positions did not win friends.

Only rarely did New York Jews identify southern slavery with the Israelite sojourn in Egypt; Dittenhoefer did. He pointedly observed that an Israelite, "whose ancestors were enslaved in Egypt, ought not to uphold slavery in free America, and could not do so without bringing disgrace upon himself."[77] Each year, numerous Passover articles in the Jewish press refused to equate the two. Ancestral Israelites and black slaves existed in two different worlds. Racism undoubtedly pervaded Jewish society as it did much of American culture.

By 1860, many of New York's Jews—merchants, wholesalers, retailers, and even garment workers—considered the southern trade their lifeblood. Southern planters and merchants owed New York firms $200 million in 1860; war would wipe out that enormous debt. Unsurprisingly, New York capitalists desperately sought compromise, sending delegations to Washington, DC, in hopes of preventing secession. Jews and others faced loss of trade and the panic of bankruptcy if the Union dissolved. For many, this proved reason enough to oppose the Republican platform. In addition, the Union's collapse imperiled political security. The Constitution of New York State and the U.S. Constitution provided protections for Jews that existed in few other places in the world.[78]

The Civil War triggered a spike in anti-Semitic sentiment. It had grown as the city's Jewish population increased, neighborhoods became recognizable as Jewish, and Jewish merchants gained financial standing. Visibility worsened impressions of Jews. Newspapers and magazines

Street barricades in New York, 1857. When the Republican state legislature, led by temperance reformers, attempted to implement prohibition of alcoholic beverages, riots resulted. Irish and German immigrants fought militias in the streets. This violence foreshadowed other conflicts between Republicans and Democrats in the city. Courtesy of the New-York Historical Society.

commonly pictured them as parvenus rapaciously climbing the economic ladder as they flaunted material success and opulence. Unlike other forms of anti-immigrant sentiment that singled out the poor for attack, anti-Semites targeted those who achieved financial stability. Even reputable papers that were favorably inclined toward Jews reported stories confirming a Jewish propensity for dishonest commerce and targeting Jews working in the stock market. By 1860, the terms "Jew" and "Jew one down" as verbs, meaning to haggle on a price and bargain in a miserly way, had entered the American lexicon, nowhere more so than in New York. Religiously motivated attacks on Jews as infidels and "malicious, bigoted hypocrites" accompanied a revival of evangelicalism. Educated men harbored anti-Jewish feelings. A Walt Whitman prose sketch described "dirty looking German Jews," while a Herman Melville short story about Manhattan depicted "a Jew with hospitable speeches, cozening some fainting stranger into ambuscade, there to burk him."[79]

But these attacks paled in comparison with General Order No. 11, "the most sweeping anti-Jewish regulation in all of American history," which rattled the Jewish community of New York. On December 17, 1862,

General Ulysses S. Grant, terming Jews "a class violating every regulation of trade established by the Treasury Department," commanded
their immediate expulsion from his military department, an area that
included northern Mississippi and parts of Kentucky and Tennessee.
Once a Jewish emissary informed Lincoln of the act, he immediately re-
voked the order. But that didn't satisfy New York Jews. When a "committee of Jews" in the city "took it upon themselves" to applaud Lincoln for
"annulling the odious order," the "bulk" of the city's Jews rebuked them,
according to the *New York Times*. Grant, they averred, should have been
summarily dismissed.[80]

By comparison, other anti-Semitic slurs seemed almost routine.
These slanders claimed that Jews were cowardly and crooked, lacked
patriotism, favored the draft, and remained far from the battlefield while
they profited from shoddy war production. Some charged that Jews ma-
nipulated the gold exchange. Others accused Jews of being copperheads
(southern supporters), claiming that the banker August Belmont, "the
Jew banker of New York," was leading a conspiracy of Jewish bankers
in a plot to support the Confederacy. Belmont represented the Jewish
banking house of Rothschild in the city and was an ardent Democrat,
serving as chair of the Democratic National Committee in the late 1850s.
He had converted to Episcopalianism, but that did not prevent people
from identifying him as a Jew. The anguish of a long, bloody war heightened anti-Semitism in the city.[81]

These simmering ethnic, religious, and racial conflicts burst out into
the open in the summer of 1863. Enraged over a lottery draft, Irish and
German workers rioted as resentment soared against blacks, blamed
as the cause of the war, and against the wealthy, who could buy out of
the draft. For three days, gangs stalked New York's streets. Barricades
blocked avenues and alleys. Crowds attacked German garment stores,
including those owned by Jews, and houses in wealthy neighborhoods.
Mobs lynched blacks in the streets and set fire to the Colored Orphan
Asylum. The official count listed 2,000 wounded and 118 dead, though
many more may have perished. The riot, "considered one of the worst
civil insurrections in American history," ended when the secretary of
war ordered soldiers fresh from the battle of Gettysburg to the city.
The Jewish General William S. Mayer, an immigrant from Austria, received a personal note of thanks from President Lincoln for his service
during the uprising. Mayer had raised a regiment from New York as

a colonel, although he was too recent an immigrant to have acquired citizenship.[82]

In 1864, Lincoln carried only 33 percent of the city's vote, doing no better than in 1860 despite recent Union victories presaging an end of war. But some Jewish attitudes toward the war had shifted, as most industrialists and merchants turned to the Union side. After a difficult initial year, the city's men of commerce had prospered. The Hendrickses' copper manufactory, founded by Harmon Hendricks, one of the city's wealthiest Jews, operated at full capacity during the conflict; garment manufacturers, like Joseph Seligman, supplied the army's seemingly endless needs. Republicans and industrialists forged a common economic bond. But the working classes suffered. Wages stagnated as inflation eroded living standards. The working-class vote produced a sizable Democratic majority. Still, while Germans favored the Union more than the Irish did, not a single German ward in Kleindeutschland gave a majority of its votes for Lincoln. German Jews tended to identify with Christian Germans, so their vote probably did not differ from that of their fellow immigrants.[83]

Lincoln's assassination and Union victory gradually changed Jewish attitudes. New York Jews turned out to mourn the murdered president as his body traveled by train across the country, through the city, and back to Springfield, Illinois. B'nai B'rith marched in the funeral procession, and even B'nai Jeshurun participated in the memorial ceremony. The arrival of hundreds of thousands of Jewish immigrants in the years after the Civil War transformed Jewish attitudes toward Lincoln. These newcomers brought an implicit sympathy for "honest Abe" on the basis of European depictions of him. In later decades, rabbis regularly honored Lincoln as the great emancipator, integrating him into a Jewish pantheon of heroes, recalling his rise from humble beginnings, and quoting his biblically phrased speeches. New York Jewish support for slavery and the South faded from memory, as new immigrants arrived with no experience and little knowledge of the Civil War.[84]

These immigrants entered a very different city from the southern-sympathizing one of the pre–Civil War era. Although they built on foundations established by Jews who had preceded them, they also innovated. As their numbers soared to over a million, New York Jews gradually transformed the city itself, remaking its politics, reinterpreting its culture, and enhancing its economic power.

PART II

1865–1925

City of Ambition, by Alfred Stieglitz, 1910. Born in Hoboken and raised in New York, the German Jewish photographer Alfred Stieglitz sought to transform photography from a commercial practice into an art. Picturing New York from the ferry approaching lower Manhattan, he captured the city's explosive energy in a photograph of lyrical, urban modernism. Courtesy of Yale University Beinecke Rare Book and Manuscript Library.

3

One City, Two Jewish Worlds

"I am not pretty, my father is not rich, and I am not going to marry, but before I die, all New York will know my name!" So reputedly affirmed Julia Richman to a friend when she was eleven or twelve. When she died, her prophecy proved true: she had not married, and all of New York knew her name as the first woman and first Jew appointed district superintendent of public schools. Her district included the Jewish Lower East Side. On her way to that renown, she became the city's first Jewish public school principal and the first female principal in Manhattan. Her vision of the proper path to Americanization for immigrant children left its mark on New York City.[1]

Strong willed and ambitious, Richman grew up partly in New York's teeming Kleindeutschland neighborhood and partly on Central Park West as the daughter of middle-class Jewish immigrants from Prague. She battled her parents to let her attend the newly organized Female Normal College (later Hunter College). After graduating at the age of seventeen, she began a forty-year career in education with a position as a public schoolteacher. At the same time, she started teaching Sabbath School at Congregation Ahawath Chesed. That work connected her with other central European Jews increasingly concerned about Jewish immigrants from eastern Europe. Richman soon helped to organize charitable associations, including the Young Women's Hebrew Association (YWHA). Her involvement simultaneously in public and Jewish education, in uptown religious and charitable endeavors focused on downtown problems, made her a key figure in the transformation of the city and New York Jews at the turn of the century.

Like many New York Jews of central European background, Richman championed Americanization, understood as raising "a race of worthy citizens." Educated as the daughter of immigrants in public schools, she valorized them. "Between the alien of today and the citizen of to-morrow stands the school," she wrote, "and upon the influence exerted by the school depends the kind of citizen the immigrant child will become." Many Lower East Side parents undoubtedly agreed, since almost all sent their children to public school, reserving Jewish education for supplementary, after-school study if they provided any Jewish education at all. But Richman enraged immigrants in clashes over Christmas observances and speaking Yiddish in school—a sin that she reportedly punished by washing out a child's mouth with soap. Despite several campaigns to remove her from her post by immigrant parents unafraid to challenge the school system, she retained the friendship and support of prosperous Jewish leaders, who sat on the Board of Education.[2]

Richman's vision extended beyond the public schools to the neighborhoods surrounding them. She advocated for the establishment of kindergartens; cheap, nutritious lunches; supervised playgrounds; and health examinations. She also possessed a gendered understanding of education, championing "domestic science" for girls and "manual training" for boys.[3] Her activism and influence, stemming from both her position as district superintendent of the Lower East Side and her extensive connections with wealthy Jews, exemplified one model of "uptown" and "downtown" interaction among New York Jews.

Downtown and Uptown

The two monikers of "downtown" and "uptown" derived from New York's geography. They came to characterize two groups of Jews separated not only by physical space but also by class, occupation, education, language, and Americanization. Uptown Jews, like Julia Richman, often were born and educated in the city, the children of immigrants or the second generation. Most were socioeconomically secure, all spoke English, many were middle or even upper class. Indeed, had not thousands of Jewish immigrants arrived in the city in the 1870s and 1880s, distinctions between uptown and downtown might never have emerged. Yet these new immigrants, although they followed patterns laid down by earlier Jews, dramatically transformed New York Jews.

Eastern European Jewish immigrants, uprooted by economic change in their home countries, arrived in New York seeking opportunities. Throughout eastern Europe—Russia, Austria-Hungary, Romania—industrialization dislocated struggling merchants and artisans, while

restrictions on Jewish educational, residential, and occupational options further provoked young Jews to pursue a better life in America.
Rapid Jewish population growth compounded economic stress, spurring
migration to large cities throughout Europe and the United States. Between 1880 and 1924, two and a half million eastern European Jews came
to the United States. Close to 85 percent of them landed in New York
City, and approximately 75 percent of those settled initially on the Lower
East Side. By 1890, the downtown neighborhood "bristled with Jews."
These Jewish immigrants far outnumbered the previous ones. They also
came at a time of unprecedented immigration to the United States, when
twenty-three million immigrants arrived. Unlike many of their fellow
migrants, Jews intended to stay. Strikingly, 33 percent of the total immigrant population returned to their old homes, while only 5 percent of
Jews made that decision.[4]

Jews also settled in New York City in larger numbers than other immigrant groups did. The Jewish East Side served as a gateway to America. In addition to meeting Irish, German, and Italian immigrants, many
Jewish immigrants encountered Jews from different regions or towns.
While an observer might consider the Lower East Side to be one homo-
geneous neighborhood, simply a "Jewish ghetto," a closer look revealed
multiple subethnic enclaves. Hungarian Jews clustered together, as did
Galician Jews; Romanian and Levantine Jews shared streets, while Russian Jews lived everywhere, but especially south of Grand Street. Jews'
disparate backgrounds shaped their interactions with New York beginning with the Lower East Side. Immigrants sought out former neighbors
(landslayt) to share distinctive foodways and religious customs, adapting old-world networks to their new urban geography. Of these various
streams of Jews, Levantine Jews, those arriving from Turkey, Greece,
and Syria, appeared most distinct. Although small in number, Levantine Jews included hundreds of Jews from Greece, who settled in both
Harlem and the Lower East Side; Arabic-speaking Jews from Aleppo,
Syria, who opened shops on Grand, Allen, and Orchard Streets; and
more well-educated, Ladino-speaking Jews from Constantinople and
Salonica, who settled in a section between Houston and Canal Streets
and Chrystie and Essex Streets.[5]

Languages reinforced differences between these two groups of Jews,
one from eastern Europe and the other from the Ottoman Empire. The

latter identified with Ladino or Judeo-Spanish, which flourished around the turn of the century as a language of journalism and popular literature. By contrast, most eastern Europeans, irrespective of their country of origin, shared a lingua franca in Yiddish, a language that emerged in German lands and expanded throughout eastern Europe. An extensive secular literature developed in Yiddish, especially in the nineteenth century. Yiddish synthesized German with Hebrew and Aramaic.[6]

Irrespective of the streets Jewish immigrants settled or the languages they spoke, all found homes in tenements. For the many immigrants who arrived as children and for those children born to immigrant parents in America, the tenement experience defined their identity more than an increasingly remote Romanian, Hungarian, Russian, or Ottoman town did. Tenements staged immigrants' first encounters with American daily life. By 1900, over 90 percent of Jews lived in them. Tenements even blanketed many Jewish areas outside the Lower East Side, including Harlem and Brooklyn's Brownsville.[7]

Tenements became synonymous with overcrowded and unsanitary conditions, but the first ones were built to solve overcrowding. Irish and German immigrants had started to subdivide one-family homes, stringing up sheets to serve as "walls." Tall tenements, with five or six floors of apartments, offered each family its own space and kitchen and appeared to dispel the crowdedness of subdivided two-story homes. The same lot that uncomfortably held three families now accommodated well-partitioned space for twenty families and two stores. But extensive construction of tenements severely restricted light and air. Tenement buildings filled 90 percent of the lot, leaving no room for side windows, and each new tenement further strengthened the barrier between tenement dwellers and sun and sky. While front rooms of front apartments looked onto the street, and front rooms of rear apartments overlooked a rear yard, all interior rooms lacked exterior windows.[8]

Of course, tenements did not grow by themselves. Landlords, many of them immigrants who had accumulated some savings, bought narrow lots as investments and stepping-stones to prosperity. Hoping to reap as much profit as possible, they created as many rental units as feasible. Incoming immigrants provided incentive to build, while the city did little to regulate construction. With each passing year, the housing stock deteriorated, as increasing numbers of immigrants crowded into available apartments. Moved to respond, the city passed a law in 1879 mandating the "dumbbell tenement," so named because the buildings' shape resembled a dumbbell, narrow in the middle and wider at each end. When two such tenements adjoined, their narrow waists formed a shaft designed to admit light and air to interior rooms. Yet these small air shafts failed to provide ventilation and often served as garbage receptacles. This law created the most infamous housing stock in the nation's history.[9]

A typical tenement hallway was dark, because wooden doors at both back and front blocked out the sun without interior gas lighting. In some tenements, landlords cut windows into apartment walls next to hallways so that the unlit hallways could leech light from the apartments. Most immigrants lived in 325-square-foot apartments without indoor plumbing. Water needed for laundry, cleaning, and cooking had to be fetched from a faucet in the rear yard, which also housed laundry lines and privies. Bare-boned tenement kitchens had room for a coal and, later, gas stove and a sink (but no running water). No refrigeration and very little storage necessitated daily shopping. Privacy didn't exist. Despite the darkness of tenement halls, a tour through them produced sensory overload: the aroma of a neighbor's cooking, screeching of toddlers, odors of chamber pots, brisk footsteps of a contractor bringing in the next bundle of clothes to be stitched, a Yiddish conversation among housewives, echoes of children's street games from street or roof, and the never-ending hum of sewing machines.[10]

The 1901 Tenement Housing Law, the first comprehensive and retroactive law, radically restructured these preexisting tenements as well as molded future ones. Landlords had to improve lighting in public hallways and individual apartments and provide one toilet per two families. This often required adding skylights, installing gas lighting fixtures, and stealing space from bedrooms to create room for toilets and air shafts. But many of these changes came too late for the first generations of immigrants, who had moved to other neighborhoods. Those who remained now had running water, indoor toilets, and a bit more light and air along with overcrowding and poverty.[11]

Even crowded tenement apartments sometimes reflected immigrants' hopes for respectability and material comfort. The right kinds of furniture set in rooms differentiated by function marked a family as having middle-class aspirations, if not income. Immigrant householders preferred "colored wallpaper, brightly patterned linoleum, and yards of lace and fabric trimmings." Above all, they favored heavy, plush upholstered furniture. Neighborhood merchants catered to these tastes, advertising in the Yiddish press and offering the option of buying on the installment plan.[12]

Ambitious Jewish families also desired a piano. A "piano in the parlor" signaled a rise to "the height of social respectability," made possible by installment plans and the Steinway Company's affordable and less-space-consuming upright model. The piano served a number of purposes, all related to enhancing social status. "I got busy, busy, busy," recalled the Yiddish theater composer and conductor Joseph Rumshinsky. "From ten in the morning until three in the afternoon I taught young women, recently married, who wanted to show their husbands they play the piano. From three until seven I taught schoolchildren. And from then until ten or eleven in the evening I taught shop girls and office girls who wanted to get married." This rage for a piano opened Jewish homes to popular culture in the form of sheet music of Yiddish songs and English ones from "Tin Pan Alley."[13]

Neighborhood social connections facilitated Jewish adaptation to New York. After finding work, immigrants immediately set about transforming themselves from a greenhorn into an American through a purchase of new clothes. Having completed this significant transition, this new American Jew then proceeded to a photographer's studio to have a picture taken to send to European relatives. Jews presumed that American goods were superior to those of Europe, quite apart from their higher social status. "Everything had to be American," recalled one memoirist. "Clothes from home were defective, even if they were of good quality and well sewn. Going to the stores with the greenhorn was a joyful procedure, like a Jew back home picking out an *esrog*" for the Sukkot holiday. Jews were not the only immigrants to reinvent themselves through dress, but since so many Jews worked in the garment industry, attuned to American fashion, they often demonstrated greater stylishness.[14]

New clothes symbolized New York's open and apparently egalitarian class structure. With mass production of clothing, middle- and even working-class people could wear apparel previously within reach only of the upper class. Each level of store copied the one above it. Since working-class Jewish women wearing "imitations" of Fifth Avenue style often had sewn the originals, their copies could be exact. Moreover, Jewish immigrants measured their transformation against the norms of Europe, where lower-class women wore shawls and only ladies wore hats. Here, any woman could don a hat and become a "lady," while her male counterpart became a "gentleman." New York promised a kind of conversion, a self-reinvention whether by means of a new suit of clothes or a piano in the parlor.[15]

A different kind of self-invention animated the wealthy bankers, entrepreneurs, industrialists, and professionals who frequented the midtown Harmonie Club's sumptuous rooms. One of the oldest, most exclusive, and best appointed social clubs in the city, with a strictly limited membership, it catered exclusively to Jews. It did not, however, advertise its Jewish character, in part because the men sought to mold a cohesive class with its own mores, manners, and attitudes. Established by central European Jews in 1852 as an immigrant cultural society, it evolved after the Civil War in response to growing social anti-Semitism. It became a kind of exclusive club, similar to those that increasingly excluded Jews and were favored by white Protestant elites. As a new group of wealthy New Yorkers prospered after the war, creating chasms between rich and poor never previously seen in the city, these largely Protestant millionaires disdained Jews, refusing to admit them to their social clubs or their children to expensive private schools. Even Joseph Seligman suffered rebuff, most notably being turned away by a Saratoga hotel where he and his family had regularly spent summers. In response, wealthy Jews started their own city and country clubs, summer resorts and vacation spots.[16]

Most Harmonie Club members claimed central European descent. Though English became the club's dominant language by 1905, older members still conversed in German. Members indulged in reading in the library, smoking in a lounge, playing cards, bowling, or exercising in the gymnasium. A few patronized the bar. Sometimes their wives and sisters joined them for dinner in the elegant dining room or for a dance in the palatial ballroom.

But change overtook this uptown institution. Balls and "large entertainments" fell out of fashion. Members' own big and opulent residences accommodated most major family social events. A new clubhouse uptown, a tall Renaissance palace designed by Stanford White, eliminated the ballroom and catered mainly to men. It guaranteed that Harmonie remained a leader among the dozen Jewish social clubs in the city.[17]

Downtown's social scene differed dramatically. Rather than private clubs, immigrants used the city's public spaces, like street corners and parks, to socialize. Women as well as men participated in heady conversations about politics and art, working conditions and literature. When they had a little extra money, Jewish immigrants patronized humble commercial establishments like Goodman and Levine's basement café. Clusters of Jewish men and women, modestly dressed with a certain bohemian flair, descended its steps and opened the door to an array of strong smells: "roast herring and cooked fish, sour borsht, fried pancakes, bad coffee, scalded milk." Despite calloused hands of building-trades workers or factory operatives, some patrons knew that they were really literary women and men, members of a revolutionary new generation of Yiddish poets. Braving "barely endurable" food, a haze of cigarette smoke, the owners' hostile stares when they did not spend enough money, kitchen heat in the summer, and icy draughts in the winter, these young writers came night after night to discuss literature and gossip.[18]

Far from exclusive, Goodman and Levine's was one of nearly three hundred Jewish cafés on the Lower East Side. Eastern European Jewish immigrant working-class cafés actually served more tea than coffee, along with food, and even more talk. Unlike saloons, traditionally American workingmen's "clubs," these cafés offered little alcohol. Instead they attracted an aspiring intellectual and artistic clientele that established their reputation as vibrant centers of debate on politics, art, and society. Most significantly, the cafés appealed to women as well as men, unlike either workingmen's or upper-class clubs. Lower East Side cafés specialized. Radicals congregated at the Monopole, while theater people met at the Café Royale, which eventually became the preeminent café of the Yiddish-speaking intelligentsia.[19]

Strikingly different in terms of class, language, customs, and ethos, the uptown club and downtown café epitomized only part of a vast range of Jewish cultural expressions in New York. Indeed, as New York became simultaneously the nation's cultural capital and its Jewish capital, Jews increasingly produced and consumed all sorts of music, literature, drama, and visual art. As artists, producers, consumers, and critics, Jews also contributed to the city's urban, but not explicitly Jewish, culture. Their presence registered especially in commercialized culture—popular music and theater, movies, the mass-circulation press—typically seen as "American" and in modernist movements considered avant-garde. Fluid boundaries characterized Jewish and general culture, commercial and modernist.

New York City assaulted the eyes of its residents with a plethora of signs pasted on billboards and store windows, crowded streets filled with pedestrians, vehicles of all sorts from horse-drawn wagons to streetcars to rapid-transit trains roaring overhead. This visual cacophony regularly drew stares from New Yorkers and visitors, who recognized in the city's towering buildings and constant bustle the components of a modern metropolis. Contrasts heightened in these years between the relative serenity of uptown and the chaos of downtown. Public spaces in the city, its parks and streets, attracted artists and photographers. The latter particularly gravitated downtown, seeking to bring their vision of "the other half" to elegant parlors uptown through magic-lantern shows. Jacob Riis, a pioneering Christian reformer who hailed from Denmark, used his bulky camera to invade the narrow nooks and alleys of the Lower East Side and to illuminate its dark tenements with his magnesium flash. Riis captured poor Jews through his lens, along with Italians and other immigrants. He helped to make the neighborhood a site of photographic experimentation.[20]

Alfred Stieglitz, by contrast, disdained such slumming on behalf of housing reform and strove instead to elevate photography into an art form. Born in Hoboken and raised in New York, the son of prosperous German Jewish immigrants, Stieglitz fell in love with photography, "his passion." His midtown gallery at 291 Fifth Avenue and his magazine, *Camera Work*, catered to uptown Jews and other New Yorkers interested in European modernist art as well as photography. Even before the 1913 Armory Show that shattered New Yorkers' assumptions about art, Stieglitz featured some of Europe's best modern painters along with American artists. He "stood at the center of a movement which sought to produce a new American art and culture, a movement openly critical of the aggressive commercialism, hypocritical moralism and empty conventionality of the reigning culture."[21] His own photographs of New York, including a classic image taken from a Brooklyn ferry approaching Manhattan, called *The City of Ambition*, conveyed the power of lower Manhattan, its tall skyscrapers rising dramatically against a cloudy sky. Ultimately Stieglitz's reputation rested on a strikingly different image, *The Steerage*, taken on a ship heading to Europe. Its clean lines and straight technique, juxtaposing men and women outdoors on the crowded steerage deck with a gangplank and smokestack, captured and aestheticized the human drama of migration.[22]

New York City public schools proved to be another place that shaped a generation of English-speaking Jewish consumers of the city's cultural offerings. Public education introduced Jews to British high literary culture, which led a number of them not only to name their children after famous British writers—Sidney, Irving, Milton—but also to plunge into the business of book publishing in New York. Jews began their "passionate love affair" with the public schools as early as the 1860s, taking advantage of the free school system while continually chipping away at its curriculum's Christian elements. Secularization of the public schools proceeded in fits and starts, not completed until well into the twentieth century. But while overtly Christian aspects gradually diminished, the schools' vaguely Protestant culture persisted because it dovetailed so closely with educators' conception of true Americanism. With the influx of immigrant children, public schools redoubled their efforts at Americanization, stressing English, hygiene, etiquette, citizenship, and vocational training. Teachers, few of whom were Jewish, denigrated Yiddish, the children's home language.[23]

Jewish children growing up in the tenements gained a reputation for intellectual precociousness, even aggressiveness, an image happily burnished in retrospect by American Jews. The socialist Yiddish daily *Forverts*, downtown's most influential newspaper, even found it necessary to warn Jewish parents not to push their children too hard to excel in school and extracurricular studies. But this myth exaggerates a Jewish love of learning. For every Jewish youth debating Marxist doctrine or devouring books in the local public library, more were wandering the streets, fighting with rival gangs, playing baseball in city sandlots, and swimming in the East River. Most young Jews left school before graduating in order to earn a living. Nevertheless, they did learn English.[24]

Arriving as New York developed into a preeminent Jewish city, immigrants and their children took advantage of the city's relative openness

Macy's Herald Square, New York City, 1907. Owned by the brothers Nathan and Isidor Straus, Macy's opened its stunning new department store, a nine-story castle of commerce on Thirty-Fourth Street in 1902. One of the world's largest department stores, the building cost $4.8 million to construct and heralded the rapid rise of Jews in retailing. Courtesy of Prints and Photographs Division, Library of Congress.

to remake themselves, their New York, and by extension, American culture as a whole. Following the establishment of a city of five boroughs in 1898, Jews, immigrant and native-born alike, increasingly came to see themselves as New Yorkers. Part of becoming New Yorkers involved learning the language of class struggle.

Capitalists and Workers

By the turn of the century, increasing numbers of New York Jews of central European background had built their modest businesses in commerce and manufacturing into substantial enterprises. Department stores ranked high among those enterprises, changing how many middle-class New Yorkers shopped. Amid considerable competition, R. H. Macy's made a bid to become the store associated with the city when it opened its a nine-story castle of commerce on Thirty-Fourth Street on a site that had once housed B'nai Jeshurun's synagogue. Fanfare and hoopla accompanied the 1902 inaugural event. Two red-marble pillars flanked the Broadway entrance. Overhead, an arch showcased a bronze clock and statues of Greek maidens. Though bronze letters spelled out the name of the store's founder, R. H. Macy, Isidor and Nathan Straus, the current owners, engineered the move and the stunning $4.8 million construction. Their father had come to the United States in 1852 and started a general store in Talbotton, Georgia. After the Civil War, Isidor brought the family to New York City to open a wholesale crockery business. In 1874, they acquired the concession for Macy's china and glass department.[25]

By the time the Strauses acquired Macy's in 1896, it had long surpassed other New York department stores. The Strauses built on that success, continuing to innovate as well as moving uptown and constructing one of the world's largest department stores. Macy's enticed New York women to pursue happiness through consumption, as they handled the finest linens, tried on the most fashionable dresses, and purchased English teas. An army of workers created meticulously arranged departments and splendid display windows, encouraging a popular New York practice of window-shopping. The frequent touting of best prices promoted purchases. The move to Thirty-Fourth Street escalated the store's glamour. Increased space meant more goods to peruse (additional departments) and unsurpassed grandeur. Macy's close attention to holidays, including its orchestration and expansion of the Christmas holiday season, extended practices initiated by Stewart's, Wanamaker's, and other department stores owned by Christian businessmen. Macy's continued success enabled the Straus brothers (a third brother, Oscar, did not join Isidor and Nathan in the business but went into law and politics instead) to pursue Jewish philanthropy and public affairs.[26]

While some Chatham Street shopkeepers and their descendants transformed their old-clothes trade into the ready-made garment industry, others headed into dry goods and charted their advance through retail. Department stores represented the next rung in commerce, one pioneered by such Christian New Yorkers as A. T. Stewart prior to the Civil War. Stewart opened his marble palace of commerce on Broadway and Chambers, collecting a number of departments under one roof. In so doing, he transformed shopping. Instead of traipsing from one retail firm to another, walking into and out of shop after shop, middle-class women found all their needs under one roof. Consumption became an elegant, convenient experience at A. T. Stewart's, where New Yorkers could dine and socialize as well.[27]

Ten years after Macy's grand opening on Thirty-Fourth Street, Sender Jarmulowsky presented the Lower East Side with its first high-class office skyscraper, proudly emblazoned with his name and housing his eponymous bank. Full-page advertisements announced its opening, proclaiming a *yontef*, or holiday. The ads promised special promotions throughout the month of May. Jarmulowsky's bank changed the Lower East Side's cityscape. No longer would its banks operate from typical neighborhood three-story commercial structures or nondescript tenement storefronts. When earlier enterprising bankers had festooned their buildings with terra-cotta beehives or wrought-iron initials, they had merely scratched the surface, dressing up ordinary structures but leaving the streetscape largely untouched. Exiting the noise and chaos of Canal Street, immigrants entering Jarmulowsky's bank gazed up at a grand clock surrounded by rosettes and allegorical figures representing industry and commerce. But the two-story marble banking room, which rivaled those of established uptown banks, probably excited tenement dwellers even more.[28]

Jarmulowsky's building drew on a Jewish model for inspiration, the 1906 J. & W. Seligman & Co. headquarters in the Wall Street financial district. Both banks had rounded corners, announcing their structures' significance at street level, while circular towers at the roofline proclaimed their majesty far and wide. Jarmulowsky's modeling his bank after that of the "American Rothschilds" signaled his esteem for these successful central European Jewish bankers as well as his distance from the workers whose deposits had enriched him. Jarmulowsky's eye-catching rooftop, a domed circular pavilion wreathed by eagles, also elicited comparisons to the nearby Municipal Building, a city landmark. The bank's popular neo-Renaissance-style building linked the Lower East Side to the rest of the city.[29]

In 1873, Jarmulowsky, a Russian-born Talmudic scholar turned Hamburg banker, had decided to try his luck in New York City. Five years later, he rented an office on the southwest corner of Canal and Orchard, helping to expand the boundaries of the Lower East Side. There he catered as a fledgling banker to many of the 240,000 eastern European Jews who arrived in the 1880s, 391,000 who came in the 1890s, and 1,387,455 who landed between 1901 and 1914. In the early years, bankers like Jarmulowsky served primarily as "ship ticket agents and money forwarders," helping immigrants send funds, and eventually tickets, to relatives in Europe. A banker had to inspire trust. Jarmulowsky advertised that his ship-ticket services were "Solid! Secure! Real!"[30] He cultivated an enviable reputation as an honest businessman, assuming a paternal persona to the entire community.[31]

Jarmulowsky cut a distinguished and pious figure on the streets of the neighborhood, with his covered head, full (albeit trimmed) beard, arched eyebrows that framed pale, wide-set eyes, and a determined mouth. Though he and other successful eastern European businessmen and philanthropists no longer lived downtown, their businesses thrived on the burgeoning East Side. They returned each morning to serve and profit from their ethnic constituency. In many cases, they invested money that they had earned through business, whether dry goods, cigars, or the garment industry, in real estate, first on the Lower East Side, then uptown in Harlem, and in Brownsville, Brooklyn, and in the Bronx, wherever Jews were moving.[32]

Jarmulowsky's bank symbolized both eastern European immigrant Jews' thrift and their entrée into New York capitalism. When the fall busy season hit its stride, Jarmulowsky urged garment workers to "save what you can for the future." As a convenience to workers, his bank kept its doors open until nine p.m., so no one need "stop his work and lose time during the day."[33]

Regardless of background or occupation, immigrants worked day and night to maintain themselves and their families. In return for six days of running, doing, and working, they received a week's wages or netted a sales profit. After they had paid rent, shopped for food, and purchased stock for the cart or placed a deposit on the next contract, some of this money found its way into a bank. In this way, local banks reflected immigrants' ambitions and disappointments. Whether socialist, anarchist, Orthodox, or atheist, all immigrants worked, and most of them struggled to save money.

Passbooks from Jarmulowsky's bank gave many immigrant families keys to New York's "golden door," the powerful concluding words of

Jewish poet Emma Lazarus's sonnet "The New Colossus," affixed to the Statue of Liberty. Immigrant banks indicated the importance of neighborhood and ethnic economic niches, which helped newcomers adapt to the city and become actors in its industrial capitalism, especially in the garment trades, street commerce, and real estate. Yet as important as these neighborhood networks were, banks also revealed the significance of the immigrant Jewish family, the basic economic unit that strategized to eke out a living in the tenement districts and negotiated adjustment of Jewish traditions to New York life.

Jarmulowsky, arguably the most famous of the East Side bankers, had plenty of company. A 1903 survey of East Side banks counted hundreds of bankers there. Some boasted deep roots in the neighborhood; others were "bankers by the grace of having come over a steamer or two ahead of the other fellow." Bankers thrived in immigrant neighborhoods because they met critical needs of their communities, uniting friends and family, dispensing news, and most importantly, selling ship tickets. These bankers fueled the transatlantic migration of hundreds of thousands of Jewish immigrants, in part through prepaid tickets sold on installment. An immigrant banker like Max Kobre at his peak in 1914 held accounts of twenty-three thousand depositors, who had placed $3,700,000 in his Lower East Side and Brownsville banks, far surpassing the fifteen thousand depositors with $1,667,000 in deposits in Jarmulowsky's bank. Immigrant bankers like Kobre were "the transnational broker who made migration possible; his bank was the 'clearing house' where [immigrants] exchanged news from the entire region."[34]

In New York, ethnicity divided the banking business. Bankers accommodated their fellow ethnics, since the city's "more established financial institutions . . . tended to eschew immigrant neighborhoods."[35] Immigrants who had succeeded as grocers, saloon keepers, and merchants often started banking as a side business. In addition to ship tickets, they offered installment plans that made large purchases possible, watched over their patrons' savings, adjusted their hours to fit their clientele, and provided business loans and credit. In turn, bankers invested in real estate, spurring development of the Lower East Side and neighborhoods in Harlem and the Bronx. Some bankers would take funds entrusted to them to more established banking houses to collect interest, while some would "borrow" these funds for their own business needs. Overall, these Jewish immigrant banks became "reservoirs for local investment capital," enabling small entrepreneurs to access capital and also directly invest funds in real estate. Gradually, the growth of immigrant businesses attracted the city's larger banking houses. Still, most immigrants patronized immigrant bankers.[36]

Yet even as immigrant bankers prospered by investing the hard-earned savings of workers, they did not always return the trust they had won. Spectacular bank failures periodically revealed the precariousness of such well-known banks as Jarmulowsky's and Kobre's, their inability to resist unsecured expansion, temptations of investments in New York real estate, and on occasion, mismanagement. Because these banks were located in New York City, home of Wall Street finance, their failures sent ripples beyond the ethnic world of immigrant Jews and prompted political figures to contemplate regulation. While such laws helped in the future, they did not return lost deposits to devastated customers.

Immigrant depositors storm Adolf Mandel's Rivington Street Bank, February 1912. After hearing rumors that the bank had run dry, Jewish immigrants raced to retrieve their funds. One of the most famous of the Lower East Side bankers, Adolf Mandel started his business in 1883 and maintained an excellent reputation. Jewish bankers catered to Jewish immigrants, helping them to purchase ship tickets to reunite with family members left behind. Courtesy of Prints and Photographs Division, Library of Congress.

Many immigrants eventually turned to labor unions and their own co-operatives to entrust their funds, seeking alternative forms of capitalist organization.[37]

But before immigrants could save their money, they needed to work. Most relied on family and neighborhood connections to find jobs. While Jews generally arrived with more urban skills than other immigrant groups did, they still needed to adjust to New York's industrial conditions. A survey of 333 Lower East Side wage earners in 1909 found that two thirds of arriving immigrants secured jobs in occupations different from those they had held in Europe. Thus, social connections in New York proved critical; these could be rekindled in immigrant neighborhoods and tenements.[38]

Jews who came before the Civil War set many of the patterns followed by later immigrants, especially visible in the rise of a garment industry that expanded to include women's clothing and became a pillar of New York's economy and its Jews. The city's assets spurred growth of the needle trades, enabling clothing manufacturing to increase 600 percent between 1860 and 1880. New York already had numerous garment firms, which benefited from New England textile mills as well as European textiles and fashion ideas. New immigrants provided cheap labor and fed a growing retail market in the city itself. The simultaneous increase of catalogues, advertising, and department stores expanded markets across the nation. Finally, New York's role as the nation's financial capital offered access to money for new and old firms eager to expand. While the city's lack of open space hindered other industries, the adaptability and flexibility of clothing manufacture allowed for decentralization. Manufacturers purchased, designed, and cut fabric but relied on contractors who managed the assembly and production of finished clothes in tenement apartments throughout the city but especially in lower Manhattan.[39]

New York Jews used their experience in the garment industry and wholesale and retail trade to direct this expansion, with the help of cheap labor that came in the form of eastern European Jewish immigrants after the Civil War. As they arrived in New York and settled in the same neighborhoods that had once nurtured the central European Jewish secondhand market, they soon learned of the garment industry's importance and employed neighborhood networks to find jobs.

By 1890, one-half of all eastern European Jewish immigrants in New York worked in the clothing industry; ten years later, they composed the majority of both workers and employers. Jews viewed the garment industry as a means to an end, much as previous Jewish immigrants had thought of peddling. Many remained in garment manufacture only as long as necessary. Economists found that the longer an immigrant lived in the United States, the less likely he or she was to work in the clothing industry.[40]

Most Jewish newcomers to the city secured their first employment in the needle trades, a change from the popularity of peddling in the decades prior to the Civil War. Yet both peddling in the 1850s and the needle trades in the 1890s exerted similar appeal: the tasks could be learned quickly, and language did not prove a barrier. As suppliers provided credit for peddlers starting out, so did contractors employ "learners" for no pay. In the early twentieth century, the garment industry employed 53 percent of Russian Jewish men and 77 percent of Russian Jewish women workers. Because garment-industry mechanization and its breakdown of tasks could be easily mastered, many Jewish immigrants became "Columbus tailors," discovering the needle in America.[41]

Weaving through the pushcarts, boys carried bundles of fabric already cut to pattern to tenement contractor shops throughout the East Side neighborhood, where workers assembled them into garments. The contracting system relieved manufacturers of responsibility for managing a workforce. Manufacturers employed skilled workers to design garments and cut fabric. A contractor hired sewing-machine operators, pressers, basters, and finishers and organized assembly of the garments, which were then returned to the manufacturer. This flexible system expanded during the busy season and contracted during slack season, leaving both workers and contractors bereft of work and pay but insulating manufacturers from any wasted expenditures for overhead and wages. The contracting system put relentless downward pressure on wages and conditions. It also allowed workers to become "bosses" by opening their own shops with little capital. All they needed was a sewing machine, a pressing table, and a stove for the irons. Sewing machines could be purchased on installment, and one could use a tenement apartment for space. Immigrants also required a strong competitive will and an ability to face failure. A third of all contractors went out of business each year.[42]

Necktie Workshop in a Division Street Tenement, by Jacob Riis, c. 1899. A pioneering urban reformer, Jacob Riis, a Christian immigrant from Denmark, photographed the sweatshops of the Lower East Side. Jewish manufacturers and contractors, often called "the moths of Division Street," sweated labor from their Jewish workers, men and women, pictured here. Courtesy of the Museum of the City of New York.

Tenement sweatshops became infamous for their crowded and unsanitary conditions. Laborers worked up to fourteen hours a day during the busy seasons, and the stove, needed to heat the irons, operated even throughout torrid summers. Sewing-machine operators sat by the windows for light, but in winter, the light weakened by late afternoon, straining their eyesight. The term "sweatshop" referred not to the heat but rather to the manner in which manufacturers "sweated" profit from contractors, who in turn "sweated" profit from laborers. Given the system's close margins and the fact that a contractor received a fixed, often low price per garment from a manufacturer, a contractor's only chance of gaining a profit came from "sweating" as much work out of his or her workers for as little wages as possible. Despite opportunities for mobility, the garment industry regularly produced setbacks: "today's workers might become tomorrow's bosses and today's bosses could easily fall back into the ranks of the proletariat."[43]

Growing availability of electric sewing machines, coupled with increasing regulation of tenement factories, encouraged manufacturers to relocate to more spacious uptown lofts with electricity. Between 1901 and 1911, eight hundred new loft buildings rose along Broadway and on Manhattan's West Side, providing ample space for garment shops. Compared to tenement sweatshops, these factories boasted high ceilings and sun-washed spaces. They especially appealed to young women—often teenagers—who entered the industry and preferred these factories to cramped tenement sweatshops. But although physical conditions improved, exploitation endured. Women especially suffered from male bosses who sought sexual favors.[44]

With "restless ambition," Jewish immigrants who had adapted to New York began to take advantage of its economic opportunities. Some improved their status by remaining in the garment industry as contractors or even becoming manufacturers. In fact, by the end of the nineteenth century, most manufacturers as well as workers hailed from eastern Europe. Others deserted "the clothing industry to go into such occupations as small shopkeepers, insurance agents and clerks." Most immigrants exited the working class by opening their own small businesses.[45]

According to one Lower East Side survey, 24 percent of Jewish immigrants worked as "merchants," a deceptive category divided equally between pushcart peddlers and proprietors of their own stores. If a newly arrived immigrant did not enter the garment shop, he or she often began as a pushcart peddler. It cost only ten cents to rent a cart, and initial inventory could be acquired on credit. A peddler did not need to know English. Jewish immigrants established stationary pushcart markets on the Lower East Side, despite municipal ordinances designed to keep peddlers moving. By 1900, the city counted twenty-five thousand pushcart peddlers, many of them Jewish immigrants. While Italian and Greek peddlers specialized in fruits and vegetables, Jews dominated sales of nonfood items such as eyeglasses, shoes, fabrics, clothing, toys, books, and hardware. Their prices attracted shoppers from beyond the East Side. Peddlers earned fifteen to eighteen dollars a week, compared to half that amount earned by garment workers. Many saved enough to open their own stores within five or six years.[46]

Most peddlers harbored ambitions to become shopkeepers and used both savings and loans to achieve their goal. Self-employed, storekeepers curried respect. They were their own bosses. Nevertheless, shopkeepers often worked themselves—and their families—as hard as contractors drove their workers. Family members played essential roles in store management. Husbands and wives, as well as daughters and sons, kept shop. "Who's minding the store?" for good reason often greeted a couple seen together at some occasion.[47]

Irrespective of an immigrant's job, he acquired additional expenditures when reunited with his family. Simply put, the dollar went further in Russia than it did in New York. Supporting a wife and children in the tenements strained resources. Often, Jewish families came as part of a chain migration, with husbands and fathers leaving first, securing a job and a place to live, and then sending funds to bring over the rest of the family. "Jewish immigrants are burdened with a far greater number of dependents than any other immigrant people," explained one observer. Because of the high proportion of women and children, 45 percent of Jews arriving in the United States listed "no occupation." Even though they usually traveled alone, Jewish immigrants reconstituted families once they arrived, increasing pressure to find jobs immediately. Each male Jewish wage earner supported 1.8 people, as compared to a non-Jewish immigrant, who supported 1.3 people. Between 1899 and 1914, women constituted 30 percent of all other immigrant groups to the United States, while Jewish women accounted for 44 percent and children under the age of fourteen made up 25 percent of Jewish immigrants.[48]

Jewish immigrants negotiated this strain, in part, by taking in boarders and relying on their children's wages. Forty-three percent of Jewish homes housed boarders. This mutually beneficial situation enabled a boarder to pay several dollars a week for room and board and not be bothered with housecleaning or food preparation, while a family earned extra income. Often half a dozen boarders would sleep in a room. Wives cleaned and cooked. "The main meal in the evening always consisted of the same courses, namely a piece of herring or chopped liver, pea or barley soup, cooked meat, and cooked plums, always accompanied by a pickle and a glass of beer."[49]

The labor of tenement wives generated income from boarders. Women handled the cash transactions and work involved. Keeping boarders reflected women's role as chief manager of household funds and allowed them to pay rent and put food on the table. This work demanded physical strength and keen strategizing, not to mention constant social networking as boarders came and went. Women shopped daily and lugged water for cleaning, cooking, and laundry up and down stairs. Boarders, almost by definition, were transitory and would have to be replaced; rent was not.[50]

Family members formed an economic unit, with mothers working at home or in family businesses and fathers and eldest children, both male and female, earning wages. More than any other immigrant group, Russian Jews depended on their children's income. Whereas foreign-born families in general derived 21 percent of their household income from children's work, Russian Jewish children brought in 31 percent of the household income. Only younger children attended school. Contributing to the family economy affected children's long-term life prospects. Before World War I, Jewish immigrant children achieved only an eighth-grade education, if that. The age at which students left school correlated directly with the age that minors could obtain working papers. When twelve-year-olds could get working papers, the sharpest decline in school enrollment in Lower East Side schools happened at that age. When the age for working papers rose to fourteen, the steepest drop occurred at that grade level. Of course, if a boy were big and mature looking, he could often manage to get papers even younger than the legal age.[51]

This family economy that drove youths to labor as soon as they had working papers also fueled revolts against exploitive working conditions. Teenage boys and girls regularly walked off the job in protest. Strikes erupted periodically on the Lower East Side, on occasion sustained by socialism. Some older Jewish immigrant workers imbibed socialist ideas in Europe; others discovered socialism preached on the streets of New York or at rallies and strike meetings. Socialism's promise of an alternative system of labor and living energized Jewish workers, channeled their anger, and carried them into bitter efforts to unionize, especially in the garment industry. In 1888, three unions, together with socialist intellectuals, formed the United Hebrew Trades (UHT) in an effort, modeled on the United German Trades, to coordinate and further unionization. Though initially consisting of only a handful (a mere eighty members), two years later the UHT had recruited twenty-five unions with an estimated membership of thirteen thousand. Gradually, Jewish workers acquired visibility, if not clout, with nine thousand marching in the 1890 May Day parade, while fifteen thousand turned out for September's Labor Day parade.[52]

Leaders of the UHT spoke tirelessly at strikes and rallies, eventually attracting all types of Yiddish-speaking unions. When Orthodox religious-school teachers and kosher butchers organized, they both joined the UHT, despite its socialist commitment. Gradually, the UHT grew and expanded. A number of "elements combined to make the Jewish labor movement such a potent force in New York City." These included "the rise of an enormous Jewish working class concentrated in an economically strategic industry, the frequency of class conflict, the early support from German socialists, the unchallenged leadership of radical intellectuals, the collapse of old elites, and a comparatively free environment for cultural and political activity before World War I."[53]

These battles possessed political dimensions as well as reflecting generational struggles. Over the course of several decades, they permeated the culture and shaped the convictions of New York Jews. They laid the basis for growing dedication to progressive socialist values alongside democratic ones. By the early decades of the twentieth century, as the tempo and pace of labor struggles intensified, conflicts between workers and capitalists propelled New York Jews onto a larger urban stage beyond family, neighborhood, and community. Ultimately, Jews forged new forms of democratic community, using not only political resources but also religious and cultural reserves transplanted from Europe and transformed in New York.

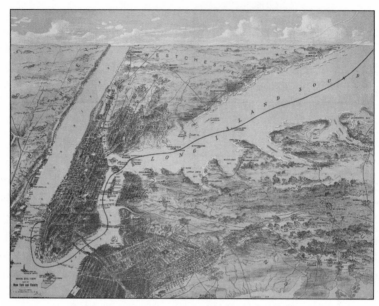

Bird's-eye map of New York City, 1909. This view of the city of five boroughs shows the heavily populated areas of Manhattan and Brooklyn and the relatively unpopulated sections of the Bronx and Queens. The city's Jewish population grew by 1910 to reach a million, out of almost five million New Yorkers. Jews settled in Brooklyn and the Bronx in increasing numbers. By the turn of the century, New York was the largest Jewish city in the world. Courtesy of the Miriam and Ira D. Wallach Division of Art, Prints and Photographs: Print Collection, New York Public Library.

4

Forging Community

New York Jews shared a palpable sense of living in a city that was changing before their eyes, on its path to becoming a major metropolis.
Certainly Jews grasped the immensity of their challenges after the 1898
consolidation that created Greater New York, a city of five boroughs.
The Brooklyn Bridge spanned the East River and connected two large
cities (Brooklyn ranked as the fourth-largest city in the United States
in 1890), but Jews struggled to develop an overarching vision of democratic community that would provide a means of unifying yet respecting
diversity. Given divisions of class, language, religion, ethnicity, and
geography, how might New York Jews bridge their own differences? Two
comparable yet separate Jewish communities had developed in Manhattan and Brooklyn, each with its own array of organizations and leaders
who jealously guarded their prerogatives. Although many Brooklynites
worked in Manhattan, they claimed allegiance to their own local neighborhoods, such as Williamsburg, Brownsville, and Borough Park. Yet
gradually New York Jews developed a collective vocabulary in which
to couch their differences. This means of communication emerged out
of understandings of their commonalities as Jews, especially bonds of
peoplehood that transcended past European histories and present local
attachments, specific religious commitments and secular political ideologies. Ultimately, their compromises and innovations reverberated well
beyond the island city's borders.

The Rise of Denominationalism

December 14, 1870. Almost five hundred New Yorkers—Christians
and Jews alike—mounted a makeshift platform on Lexington Avenue
and Fifty-Fifth Street. The sun shone brightly as ticket holders filed in
to take their seats for a cornerstone-laying ceremony. "Adorned with
flags," the platform covered a construction site for what would become

Congregation Ahawath Chesed's new synagogue. Despite very little for the eye to behold—yet—the day's speeches evoked pride in the heights achieved by an erstwhile tiny immigrant Kleindeutschland congregation and roused attendees to anticipate the future structure that would soon tower over its brownstone neighbors.[1]

Ahawath Chesed's Reform leaders used the occasion to invite prominent Reform rabbis, Christian neighbors, city politicians, and local religious and communal figures to celebrate a tolerant, cosmopolitan city and nation. Together they acknowledged a shared American identity elastic enough to contain individual and group differences. Isaac Mayer Wise, the country's leading Reform rabbi, headquartered in Cincinnati, delivered the keynote speech. He praised the new "temple" about to be built.[2]

Those who were gathered ostensibly came to witness the laying of a physical cornerstone for a grand Moorish synagogue. But the event's symbolic significance expressed Jews' intangible but very real sense of security and confidence in their city and country. In this way, Wise's use of the word "temple" could refer both to a chain of Jewish synagogues across time and place and also specifically to those forward-thinking and tolerant houses of worship in New York and America for "all the families of man," Christian or Jewish.

New York hosted more Moorish-style synagogues than did any other city in the world. The city's openness, tolerance, and cosmopolitanism enabled its Jewish congregations to alter their rituals and customs to conform to American cultural standards, even as they maintained their distinctiveness. Observers recognized that these synagogues were "monuments of Christianity as well as of Judaism." They testified "not only of constant Jewish zeal and munificence, but also of increased Christian humanity and tolerance." These buildings on New York's cityscape reminded passersby of an American spirit that reveled in the march of both Gothic churches and Moorish synagogues down its prominent avenues. In New York, where Jews faced no constraints on synagogue building styles, Judaism could be understood as a component in the creation of a pluralistic city. If Jews used Moorish style to proclaim a sense of distinctiveness, it did not threaten their social position. Rather, Moorish synagogues helped to shape New York's cityscape.[3]

Central Synagogue, 1872, photograph by C. K. Bill. Ahawath Chesed's Moorish structure towered over its brownstone neighbors when it opened in 1872. The building was later renamed Central Synagogue, and its towers, keyhole windows, and arches distinguished it from contemporary religious and commercial buildings in New York City. Courtesy of Central Synagogue Archives.

Moorish style in New York spoke less to religious preferences and more to Jews' freedom and comfort. Congregations contended with each other along a wide spectrum of religious identification, from Reform to Conservative to Orthodox, but with few exceptions, they all sought to forge a workable New York Judaism. Moorish style transcended Jewish religious differences. It marked a wider Jewish engagement with modernity and with surrounding religious and secular cultures. The Reform movement took the lead, but many Orthodox synagogues, though hewing to Jewish law and tradition, similarly wished to adapt their Judaism to America.[4]

After the Civil War, affluence fueled growth and corresponding religious disunion. Postwar prosperity positioned leading Jewish, Catholic, and Protestant congregants to funnel their success into the design and construction of magnificent houses of worship. Between 1860 and 1870, synagogue construction, chiefly in New York City, increased New York State's synagogue property value by over 200 percent, to close to $2 million, and doubled its seating capacity to 21,400. Moves from repurposed Christian churches to purpose-built synagogues cost money. One estimate suggested that the Jewish sanctuaries on average cost $12,000 more than most Protestant churches did. These synagogues announced the Jewish community's rise in wealth and social standing, marking it as a worthy peer of proper Christian society. Yet synagogues still fell miserably short of accommodating the city's Jews, had they all desired to attend Sabbath services. Congregations imagined their synagogues as monuments to religious amity, but in truth, they appealed to only a minority of New York Jews. Congregations faced a crisis regarding their ability to remain relevant to Jews in the modern world, even to those who wished to retain their religious identity.[5]

New York City's open atmosphere not only lent entirely novel meanings to Moorish style but also encouraged development of new spiritual expressions for those American Jews who congregated within these buildings or even just walked by them. Their diversity and commonalities expressed a panoply of ways to be Jewish in New York. Freedom from state-sponsored religious authority allowed each congregation to develop on its own, creating competition. Each congregation defined itself not only though its endorsement of reform or defense of tradition but also in comparison with its neighbors.

But one problem plagued all congregations. Maintaining the traditional Jewish Sabbath proved difficult for all because it conflicted with the standard American workweek. Both Reform and Orthodox wrestled with the problems of Sabbath observance and synagogue attendance. Some Reform congregations experimented by offering Sunday sermons in addition to Saturday services. But even Temple Emanu-El's rabbi, Samuel Adler, firmly opposed a proposal to shift the sermon from Saturday to Sunday. Congregants may not have attended Saturday services, but they often wanted their temples to hold them.[6]

Threats to the Jewish Sabbath, which had secured Jewish life for centuries, came from several directions. Finding jobs that allowed for Saturday rest became increasingly difficult after the garment industry's shift to uptown factories and away from downtown neighborhood shops. One solution, to open one's own business, allowed one to set one's own hours. But storekeepers still contended with unpredictable enforcement of Sunday blue laws that prohibited, or at least severely circumscribed, Sunday business.[7]

Sabbath observance came with a cost. Wage-earning Sabbath observers worked in Orthodox newspapers and businesses that sold religious goods, such as sacramental wine stores or matzo factories. Sabbath observers in the building industry could find work with Harry Fischel, who not only offered his laborers Saturdays off but also paid them for a half day. Many memoirs, however, attest to meager pay from more marginal jobs. On occasion, nonobservant children toiled on the Sabbath to subsidize a father's desire to desist from such labor. Some immigrant Jews rationalized their Sabbath employment by arguing that one could break the Sabbath to save a life, thus excusing Sabbath desecration by those who worked to support their families. Most rabbis rejected this interpretation, but they also offered no tangible means to resist a six-day workweek that included Saturday.[8]

Another kind of threat issued from within the Jewish community. Although Sabbath observance was both a labor and religious problem, few labor leaders who adhered to radical secularist ideologies cared about it. Some anarchist organizers actively railed against religion, even organizing Yom Kippur balls, raucous celebrations heaping scorn on traditional piety. As a socialist fraternal organization, the Workmen's Circle forbade religious officials from holding office and regularly scheduled lectures against religion. But gradually the organization softened its stance, in part because it embraced tolerance as an American principle and in part out of a practical recognition that most immigrants fell somewhere along the middle of a spectrum that stretched from free thought to traditional Judaism. Many Workmen's Circle members appreciated both secular ideas and religious customs.[9]

Despite all these difficulties, the Sabbath left its mark on Jewish neighborhoods and homes. Beginning on Thursday nights and accelerating on Friday morning, Jews poured onto the streets for heated rounds of shopping and bargaining. Even the tenements dressed for the Sabbath: "On Friday afternoons the facades of many of the tenements were almost obscured by pillows and blankets being freshened, in conjunction with other pre-Sabbath sprucing measures." Settlement-house and social workers reported that a flurry of street activity on Thursday and Friday transformed Jewish homes. Families' efforts to create a distinct and meaningful Sabbath atmosphere testified to their continued respect for the day of rest. Children often patronized the public library on Fridays to borrow books for Saturday. (Other children preferred to go to the movies instead.)[10]

Yet just as central European immigrants to New York often neglected strict Sabbath observance in favor of economic integration, so too did eastern European Jews, despite the fact that many labored for Jewish garment manufacturers. New York's Jews grappled with the city's blue laws and Saturday work. The clash of calendars forced Jewish immigrants who wanted to preserve their Orthodoxy to hunt for jobs that allowed them to rest on the Sabbath. If one did have to work on the Sabbath, how could one remain an observant Jew? Uptown, Ahawath Chesed and Emanu-El had responded in part by emphasizing Friday-night services and promoting a Reform agenda that minimized Jewish law. Downtown, aside from proclaiming that members could not "publicly desecrate" the Sabbath, a leading Orthodox congregation, the Eldridge Street Synagogue, offered no official answer for Jews who worked on the Sabbath.[11]

Indeed, only a minority of New York Jews observed the Sabbath or affiliated with a synagogue. Observers estimated that perhaps 20 or 30 percent prayed weekly and that somewhere between 5 to 40 percent belonged to a congregation. But many more, perhaps as many as three-quarters, attended synagogue annually on the High Holidays. In a pragmatic move, the Eldridge Street Synagogue provided a venue for eastern European Jews who did not attend daily or even weekly to participate in services according to holiday or life-cycle schedules. A substantial portion of its income came from sale of High Holiday tickets, many of them to nonmembers, Sabbath desecrators, who nevertheless desired to worship in an established synagogue during the Jewish New Year. Similarly, it made special fee-based accommodations for nonmembers who needed a place for a son's bar mitzvah.[12]

With so much accommodation characterizing New York's religious Jews, a committed young man, Felix Adler, decided to take a bold step. The son of Rabbi Samuel Adler of Reform Temple Emanu-El, Felix rejected his father's compromises. In 1876, he split from Reform Judaism. He rejected not only a Saturday Sabbath but much of Judaism's distinctiveness. "Judaism is dying," he pronounced as he gathered like-minded individuals, many of them young native-born Jewish New Yorkers, to form the Society for Ethical Culture. Brilliant, regal looking, and with a doctorate in philosophy from Heidelberg, Felix Adler embraced an optimistic universalism characteristic of Reform thinkers. "The intellectual and ethical challenges of the day" demanded a strong, humanitarian, and truly universal effort, the ambitious twenty-five-year-old proclaimed. Ethical Culturists met on Sundays to absorb the ideas of all world religions and to consider progressive action in their own city. In particular, they sought to model new forms of education for workers' children, establishing a school that would teach the tenets of Ethical Culture. The society attracted only a small percentage of New York Jews (many of whom also retained their membership in Reform congregations). But Adler's defection, and his religious challenge, provoked Reform rabbis.[13]

Vigorous debate issued from pulpits about the proper direction for American Judaism. New York congregations paid attention to each other's choices, as did national Jewish papers and religious leaders. These arguments reverberated beyond the city's limits.[14]

Debates over specific reforms shaped trajectories of individual congregations within a broadening spectrum of religious identification. Ahawath Chesed embraced mixed seating and a mixed choir in its elegant Moorish temple on Lexington Avenue, but it never took the lead in radical reform. In 1884, the congregation hired a new rabbi, Alexander Kohut, a graduate of the Breslau Theological Seminary who had already completed several volumes of a Talmudic dictionary. Ahawath Chesed's choice of Kohut demonstrated a tentative stance toward Reform, unlike Temple Emanu-El, and a continued respect for tradition.[15]

Within weeks of Kohut's New York arrival in 1885, this handsome, broad-shouldered man with a full beard commenced a series of lectures on the Talmudic text *Ethics of the Fathers*, using it to challenge Reform ideology and practice. Without Jewish law, he argued, Judaism was a "deformity—a skeleton without flesh and sinew, without spirit and heart. It is suicide, and suicide is not reform." Kohut hoped to advance "the old and the new in happy and blended union," along more "conservative lines" that recognized the importance of Jewish law. Rabbi Kaufman Kohler, the leader of Temple Beth El, just eight blocks north on Lexington Avenue, took the bait. Kohler, a devoted bearded Reform rabbi with a penetrating gaze and over a decade of experience in the American rabbinate, responded in kind. He delivered five discourses defending Reform. The two men's exchanges attracted press attention. Known as the "Kohut-Kohler affair" and translated into English, they sparked debates in newspapers and within synagogues.[16]

Rebekah Bettelheim, the daughter of a San Francisco rabbi and soon-to-be fiancée of Alexander Kohut, recorded her apprehension upon attending an open meeting at Temple Emanu-El in which prominent rabbis, including Kohut and Kohler, had gathered to discuss "the conflict between science and religion." She had been following debates among rabbis in the press and feared experiencing acrimony in action. However, the proceedings pleasantly surprised her. Kohut's address garnered admiration, if not assent. "I remember with what gratification I saw Dr. Kohler rush forward and congratulate his antagonist." Bettelheim also noted the pleasures of open meetings and vigorous argument. New York's geography—with diverse temples within blocks of each other—surely heightened this dynamic, as crowds overflowed each rabbi's synagogue. The sheer concentration of leading congregations and rabbis distinguished New York from other American cities.[17]

These religious debates catalyzed two important events, both of which asserted New York's centrality in American Judaism. First, Kohler summoned like-minded Reform rabbis to Pittsburgh for a convention. While Reform leaders had previously attempted to unite rabbis around an ideological justification for Reform, they had never succeeded. This time they did. The resulting Pittsburgh Platform, an eight-point articulation of American Reform Judaism, wielded tremendous power through the 1930s. The platform rejected the Talmud's hold on modern Jews, eliminating laws such as regulations on diet and dress that did not meet the standards of "modern civilization." As importantly, the platform championed an enlightened and universalistic spirit that encouraged Jews to espouse Judaism's ethical teachings. The Pittsburgh Platform viewed Judaism as a "progressive religion ever striving to be in accord with the postulates of reason." Thus, debate spurred Kohler and his colleagues to hammer out a milestone in the American Reform movement.[18]

In turn, the Pittsburgh Platform's rejection of the Talmud and the binding force of Jewish law pushed Kohut to join with other like-minded rabbis to establish a rabbinical seminary. At the Jewish Theological Seminary (JTS), students would learn to deliver English sermons and immerse themselves in Western thought but continue to study Talmud and traditional texts. Kohut had preached this balance to his congregation and hoped that such a synthesis could ensure proper leadership for American Jewry. Initially, lack of funds limited JTS's influence. But by the turn of the twentieth century, a tremendous demand by eastern European immigrants for new leadership that balanced tradition with American culture prompted the wealthy philanthropist Jacob Schiff and the lawyer Louis Marshall to support the institution's renewal. Under Solomon Schechter's leadership, JTS expanded its reach, training not just rabbis but also teachers through its Teachers Institute. By the second decade of the twentieth century, JTS began slowly to shift away from Orthodoxy to create Conservative Judaism, a third branch of American Judaism. As Rebekah Kohut concluded, "Thus one of the great seats of learning, the training-place of many of the most distinguished leaders of today, the home of the greatest Jewish library in the world, owes its existence to the fevered controversy of the 1880s."[19]

Comparable contests occurred downtown among immigrants from eastern Europe. Arriving in multitudes, they settled in the very same streets that had made up Kleindeutschland, now called the Lower East Side. Five-story tenements filled up with Yiddish-speaking immigrants, and some of the garment shops owned by Ahawath Chesed's members employed eastern European Jewish workers. Just as German-speaking immigrants had gathered to lead Orthodox services, these newcomers adapted storefronts and tenement rooms into houses of prayer.

Eastern European Jewish men in New York City tended to form small congregations and, lacking funds, rented halls for their worship services. They took turns leading services or, if more established, hired cantors and preachers to chant the prayers and deliver occasional Yiddish sermons. While uptown congregations built synagogues, eastern European Jews took over their old former churches. A church that had once been the home of Temple Emanu-El now housed the eastern European Orthodox Congregation Mishkan Israel Suvalk. But most downtown congregations blended modestly into the Lower East Side streetscape.[20]

Then Beth Hamedrash took a bold step: the congregation decided to build its own new synagogue on Eldridge Street, to remain Orthodox, and to stay on the Lower East Side. Members aimed to disprove assumptions that as Jews Americanized, they would modify their liturgy, change their religious beliefs, and abandon traditional Jewish observances. These committed Orthodox Jews, as prosperous congregants, also implicitly challenged the prevailing practice that saw Jews shift their religious identification as they moved up in socioeconomic class position.

The trustees of the renamed Kahal Adath Jeshurun watched construction of their new synagogue as bills piled up. A significant disparity loomed between the congregation's 150 members and the new sanctuary's capacity of 735. Just as lay leaders of uptown temples had to calculate how they would finance and maintain their new structures, using the sale of seats as basis for support, so too did leaders of Kahal Adath Jeshurun. Thus, the congregation crafted and circulated seat contracts. In a competitive milieu of 130 downtown congregations, where immigrants often selected congregations on the basis of hometown ties, the leaders of Kahal Adath Jeshurun needed to "market" their congregation in novel ways.

The Moorish structure arising on Eldridge Street might have called to mind uptown temples. For those who had such impressions, the seat contract offered swift and unequivocal reassurance: "As it is the intention of all persons connected with said congregation to preserve, maintain and adhere to the strict Orthodox faith," it stated, "it is hereby agreed, that, if at any time an organ should be used in connection with

Eldridge Street Synagogue, photograph by Kate Milford. Opening on September 4, 1887, the Moorish synagogue of Kahal Adath Jeshurun on Eldridge Street proclaimed the accomplishments of eastern European Jewish immigrants downtown. Like the magnificent synagogue buildings uptown, Eldridge Street Synagogue paid tribute to the optimism and security of New York Jews. Courtesy of the Museum at Eldridge Street.

the service, if males and females are allowed to sit together during divine services; or if a mixed choir (males and females) is allowed to sing during divine services," a seat owner could recover not just the money invested but double the amount.[21] The women's balcony guaranteed more than a physical separation of the sexes; it marked a rigid conceptual dividing line between Reform and Orthodox Judaism. Ahawath Chesed's mixed choir and mixed seating—elements that marked it as Reform—would not be countenanced downtown.

Hopes of opening in time for the High Holiday season were fulfilled. Throngs, including some uptown Jews curious to see what this new structure portended, attended a dedication ceremony. Nothing in the neighborhood's architecture announced its Jewish presence as strikingly as the Eldridge Street Synagogue. Though it lacked a corner location, its three-lot perch in the center of the street still impressed, especially in contrast to the surrounding tenements. From afar, six-pointed Stars of David atop finials stood out. Uptown visitors praised the building, even calling it among the finest synagogues in the city. While the brownstone of Lexington's synagogue connected it with neighboring brownstone townhouses, the cream-colored brick of Eldridge Street Synagogue linked it with adjacent red-brick tenements. Once inside the sanctuary, an Ahawath Chesed member might have been reminded of his own synagogue's stained-glass windows and delicate pillars but would have been discomfited by a bima (platform) set in the midst of the sanctuary instead of in the front.[22]

Eldridge Street Synagogue and its wealth rebuked uptown Jewish ways of reconciling Jewish and American identities. Unlike traditional prayer groups in tenements, Orthodox worship in an architecturally prominent building raised eyebrows. The ability to build such a synagogue implied that a significant segment of the congregation had Americanized sufficiently to raise funds and navigate courts. They used their American business sense to proclaim their Orthodoxy. The speeches that resounded throughout the handsome interior finishes of cherry and ash signaled an adamancy with which this congregation defined itself in contrast to Reform Judaism. Reform, in this view, threatened to lead to apostasy.[23]

Retention of Orthodox liturgy did not stop Eldridge Street from hiring a renowned cantor to lead the prayer service and to help avoid what some Jews considered a cacophony of worshipers reciting prayers at their own pace. In addition, the congregation created a system by which trustees stationed throughout the sanctuary could signal the *shames* if crowds became too noisy. In response, the *shames* would thump the reading table with his fist, "and a sort of small thunder reverberated through the synagogue."[24]

Like uptown temples, Eldridge Street depended on its lay leaders. It constantly battled neighboring congregations for the Orthodox public's allegiance. The most pressing challenges occurred within a decade of its opening, as its most successful members, the men who built the synagogue, began to migrate out of the Lower East Side to Harlem and the Bronx. They wanted to take the congregation with them. Rather than move the synagogue uptown as previous generations of Jews did, lay leaders of the Eldridge Street Synagogue constantly sought new ways to attract members. When necessary, they secured mergers with other congregations to maintain its downtown presence.[25]

Just as Ahawath Chesed became a place where Bavarian, Bohemian, and Prussian immigrants formed an American Reform Judaism, so too did the Eldridge Street Synagogue become a place where Jews from throughout eastern Europe, along with some who were American born, undertook a similar project to create an American Orthodox Judaism. As Ahawath Chesed relied on German to bind newcomers from throughout central Europe, so did Eldridge Street employ Yiddish to unify diverse eastern European Jews.[26]

Eldridge Street Synagogue did not have its own rabbi, so it joined forces with fourteen downtown congregations to form the Association of Orthodox Hebrew Congregations. These congregations wanted to address chaos in the regulation of kosher meat and adjudication of Jewish law. They knew they needed an eastern European luminary to rally support from immigrants. Thus, in 1888, they hired Rabbi Jacob Joseph from Vilna. However, although they could import the rabbi and offer him a handsome salary, they could transplant neither eastern European Orthodox communal structures nor respect for rabbinic authority. New York City Jews remained a voluntary religious community. Rabbi Joseph failed to gain widespread support despite a warm welcome. Matters deteriorated further when the association decided to tackle the issue of kashrut. To help pay for Joseph's salary, the association placed a tax on kosher meat. Downtown consumers ridiculed the tax as a bitter reminder of the hated tsarist meat tax. Rival rabbis, seeing an opening, elected themselves chief rabbis. Hopes for a citywide Orthodox Jewish authority vanished.[27]

Largely ignored in life, Rabbi Joseph in death assumed prominence as a symbol of Orthodox Judaism in America. Tens of thousands of mourners turned out on a hot July day in 1902 for his funeral procession, which wound its way from his house on Henry Street, along Grand Street, toward the ferry to Brooklyn and the cemetery. This public mourning demonstrated the power and maturity of downtown Jews in New York. However, the funeral has been remembered mainly for a melee that broke out between some of the mourners, workers at the R. H. Hoe factory on Grand Street, and the police. Yet local newspapers praised the funeral's dignity. Moreover, a mayoral commission exonerated the mourners of any blame in the disturbance and disciplined the police captain.[28]

On Eldridge Street, Moorish finials and stenciled gilded stars shielded a congregation of Jews crafting an American form of Orthodoxy. Congregational leaders understood the broader challenges confronting Jews beyond the stained-glass windows. Though the chief rabbi experiment had failed, the congregation tried again to organize Orthodox Jewry by leading an initiative for an Orthodox Union in 1898. The Orthodox Union united both uptown Orthodox rabbis and downtown leaders. It lobbied to defend the interests of Orthodox Jews, especially around Sabbath observance. While it opposed Reform, the union shared a common desire to guide "immigrants to balance their allegiance to Judaism with the drive to Americanize."[29]

Not all downtown Orthodox Jews agreed. Resisters, organized in the Agudath Ha-Rabbannim (Union of Orthodox Rabbis of the United States and Canada), viewed any compromise with American culture as a threat to a traditional Judaism as practiced mainly in eastern Europe. They lamented the introduction of English-language sermons and opposed modernization of the curriculum in Yeshiva Etz Chaim, an Orthodox yeshiva (elementary school) established on the Lower East Side, and the Yeshiva Rabbi Isaac Elchanan, emerging as the primary training school for Orthodox rabbis. The Agudath Ha-Rabbannim ordained the early rabbis trained at the Elchanan Yeshiva but scorned those studying at JTS as deficient in Talmudic learning. Although members of Agudath Ha-Rabbannim had chosen to immigrate to the United States, they were well aware that among their fellow rabbis in Europe, America enjoyed a reputation as "a treyf land where even the stones are impure." It was not an easy place for pious Jews.[30]

New York's capitalist economy and democratic society not only challenged male rabbis seeking to reassert religious authority but also freed women to organize and speak up on their own behalf. Given the chaos and competition that ruled in the kosher meat business, housewives decided to take matters into their own hands. In 1902, furious over a jump in the price of kosher meat from twelve to eighteen cents a pound, Jewish women sprung into action. Thousands of women "streamed through the streets of the Lower East Side, breaking into butcher shops, flinging meat into the streets and declaring a boycott." Termed "rioters" in the English press and "strikers" in the Yiddish press, they attacked customers of those kosher butchers who remained open, seizing and destroying purchased meat.[31]

A mere four days after the strike started, it spread beyond the Lower East Side to Harlem, Brooklyn, and the Bronx. The women were ready to organize beyond mass meetings. "We will not be silent; we will overturn the world," they yelled. Hundreds of women participated in meetings; dozens volunteered to boycott stores. Their presence on the streets in front of kosher butcher shops and their aggressiveness in preventing other women from entering and purchasing meat, not to mention their willingness to smash store windows, led to scuffles with the police and arrests. Brought before a judge who asked, "Did you throw meat in the street?" one of the ringleaders replied, "Certainly. I should have looked it in the teeth?" With the lines clearly drawn, initially by the women boycotters, who secured broad neighborhood support from Orthodox and socialist men alike, and with wide swaths of neighborhood women steadfastly participating, the wholesale butchers capitulated.[32]

"Despite their superficial similarity to earlier food riots, the kosher meat riots of 1902 give evidence of a modern and sophisticated political mentality emerging in a rapidly changing community. With this issue of the high price of food, immigrant housewives found a vehicle for political organization. They articulated a rudimentary grasp of their power as consumers and domestic managers." Categorizing Jewish immigrants according to ideologies did not do justice to the mutability of immigrant identities, religion, or politics. "Boundary lines were fluid and socialist rhetoric tripped easily from the tongues of women who still cared about kosher meat, could cite Biblical passages in Hebrew, and felt at ease in the synagogue." Indeed, the women went into synagogues to interrupt the reading of the Torah because a matter of justice was at stake. "When one irate opponent roared that [a woman] speaking thus from the bima was an effrontery [*chutzpa*] and desecration of God's name [*chillul ha'Shem*]," the outspoken housewife "responded that the Torah would pardon her."[33]

Thus, New York Jews adumbrated a full spectrum of religious observances and ideologies to accompany them, including opening doors for women's activist participation in shaping religious life. One side of that spectrum ranged from an Ethical Culture movement that stepped outside Judaism and extended through permutations of Reform and on to modes of Conservative practice. The other side included pious, rejectionist rabbis and their congregations through diverse forms of immigrant congregations based on hometown connections all the way to versions of modern Orthodox Judaism. On rare occasions, these male religious groups cooperated with each other. More often, they competed for members, leadership, and authority. Their debates proved productive

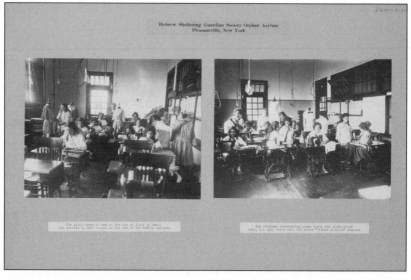

Hebrew Sheltering Guardian Society Orphan Asylum, Pleasantville, New York, c. 1900. Fearful of proselytizing by Protestant and Catholic child-welfare orphanages, New York Jews organized to care for Jewish children at risk. This photograph depicts girls learning what were considered useful skills, namely, sewing, to prepare them to support themselves. Courtesy of Harvard Art Museum / Fogg Museum, Transfer from the Carpenter Center for the Visual Arts, Social Museum Collection, 3.2002.150. Imaging Department © President and Fellows of Harvard College.

of institutional innovation, such as rabbinical seminaries and unions of rabbis. But while religious bonds linked some Jews with each other, these ties nurtured sectarianism and, eventually, denominationalism. They failed to provide a blueprint for communal cohesion. Religious affiliation would remain a choice of a dedicated minority of New York Jews.

Charity versus Self-Help

As New York City became an industrial metropolis with sharp contrasts of wealth and poverty, Jews struggled with which new forms of charity to adopt, who would get to lead modern Jewish philanthropies, and even if American traditions of self-help should be preferred. The city's capitalist entrepreneurial spirit inspired many Jews to experiment with philanthropic forms, mixing traditions of Jewish collective responsibility with American Christian modes of the "gospel of wealth." Simultaneously, recipients of charity registered their anger at the disdain that accompanied aid and did their best to reject noblesse oblige through formation of mutual benefit societies that provided social welfare insurance. The process of competition and cooperation changed Jewish understandings of both charity and self-help, as new opportunities opened for both women and men.

Between 1870 and 1915, the city's population expanded dramatically from one and a half million (including areas incorporated into Greater New York in 1898) to five million. The needs of a growing population prompted citizens of all backgrounds to step into the breach, especially religious groups. Most philanthropic enterprises organized along confessional lines in both the city and the United States, as they did in Europe. Protestant agencies even delivered publicly funded services. Missionary activity often accompanied charitable work, forcing the Catholic and Jewish poor to endure a dose of preaching with their aid. This outreach challenged Jews to save vulnerable members of their community from Protestant missionaries. As immigration swelled the potential clientele, both Catholics and Jews expanded and institutionalized their charitable efforts, resulting in a "mammoth enterprise of social service" that sought to care for "the sick, the elderly, orphans, the unemployed, prison inmates, the hungry, and the destitute." Severe economic downturns like the Panic of 1873 further spurred creation of private charities to tend to the poor.[34]

Urban charitable trends influenced Jewish forms of giving. In a rapidly changing city, well-to-do Jews fashioned distinctive charitable and social work roles that offered women possibilities of involvement in public affairs. Jews also sought to provide opportunities for Jewish doctors who confronted anti-Semitic prejudice when they tried to gain hospital privileges.[35]

The rise of substantial numbers of Jews into the ranks of the middle and upper classes enabled this surge in charitable activity. An 1890 census focusing on 18,031 American Jewish families who had been in the country for at least five years found that they generally had achieved middle-class standing. Throughout the nation, Jews had worked their way up from peddler to small business owner, wholesaler, and professional. Nearly two-thirds of the families surveyed employed at least one servant.[36]

Many New York Jews had attained middle-class status, but in comparison with a national sample of American Jews, the city had a heavier concentration of both wealthy and poor. Just as the majority of the city's sixty thousand Jews reached the middle class by 1880, hundreds of thousands of newcomers arrived to reinforce the city's Jewish working class. Simultaneously, New York's vitality as the nation's economic center produced a moneyed elite. By the last quarter of the nineteenth century, the nation's wealthiest and most illustrious Jews lived in New York City, including famed financiers like Joseph Seligman and Jacob Schiff.[37]

Jewish leaders not only enlarged the agendas of congregations and other associations to include increased charity for immigrants but also created entirely new forms of communal support to connect brownstone Jews with tenement Jews, to bring uptown to downtown. Charity work emphasized a sense of social responsibility toward newcomers by those who were more established. But translating charitable impulses into formal networks and institutions took years and sparked heated debates. Immigrants often preferred their own fraternal orders or mutual benefit societies built on town of origin (*landsmanshaftn*) as alternative models of communal organization stressing self-help. These competing modes and visions of community eventually bridged uptown and downtown, although charitable networks and institutions served as the communal core and structure.

Caring for the significant population of working-class Jews shaped the community's agenda as it integrated *tsedakeh* (usually translated as charity) into an urban world. Previously synagogues and their associated societies had directed the community's charitable impulses. Beyond the synagogues, benevolent and philanthropic associations as well as individuals sponsored a Jewish hospital, orphanages, and other institutions in the city. But after the Civil War, a need for strong, centralized action, as well as models set by both the Jewish community in London and Christian missionaries in New York, prompted Jewish communal leaders to campaign for a United Hebrew Charities to supplant a myriad of smaller charitable organizations.[38]

Samuel Isaacs came to this realization in 1865. He had tried unsuccessfully to revive an 1858 Passover union that he had established in response to the financial panic of 1857. Gradually he recognized that the problem was more fundamental than the poor in need of matzo. The Passover season exposed the fact that an organized community was required "all year round." So Isaacs took matters into his own hands by appealing directly to his *Messenger* readers for support. "We cannot send the poor away empty handed," he implored, "and we certainly cannot from our limited means relieve all applicants." The *Messenger* informed interested readers that the paper "shall be happy to take charge of any donations that they may please forward to [its] office."[39]

In the absence of a united congregational front or even a federation of benevolent or mutual benefit societies, the newspaper knit the community together. The *Messenger* acknowledged the plight of the "unsynagogued" and spearheaded efforts to help them. With the rise of American newspaper culture and without a strong rabbinate, editors assumed a leadership role. Their editorials could criticize the community; unlike pulpit sermons, they did not fear offending well-heeled congregants. While Isaacs issued the call for funds, and many male readers donated, women actually distributed the Passover aid.

As the Panic of 1857 had fueled the formation of the Association for Free Distribution of Matsot to the Poor in 1858, the Panic of 1873 hastened the foundation of the United Hebrew Charities the following year. During the Panic of 1873, approximately 25 percent of New Yorkers lost their jobs; those who held on to employment found their wages decreased by one-third. Jews suffered along with other New Yorkers. Boom-and-bust cycles jeopardized immigrants' economic fortunes.[40]

Yet while it took an economic crisis to propel the Jewish community to reform its charitable societies, the plan and method had been patiently devised and stridently publicized for years. The *Messenger* had been promoting a "radical reform" of existing charitable societies. Typically, the Jewish press had used the term "radical reform" to refer to heated debates over ritual, belief, and practice between emerging Orthodox and Reform movements in Judaism. Isaacs, however, shifted focus away from arguments over religion to a broader challenge posed by poverty. In the *Messenger*'s call for professionalization of charities, it relentlessly criticized those merchants who carelessly gave money to professional beggars. Despite good intentions, failure to pay attention to how money was used allowed professional Jewish beggars to prosper, while deserving Jewish families suffered. Systematized charity would find employment for a head of household rather than simply doling out funds. Yet leaders of the Hebrew Benevolent and Orphan Society, one of the city's most prominent Jewish charitable organizations, resisted Isaacs, revealing just how formidable and radical was any plan for union.[41]

Isaacs contended that personal charitable impulses, no matter how praiseworthy, needed to be adapted to modern times. "It has always been our boast that, while the Israelites support the public charities, they take care of their own poor. What we lack is not the will or the spirit to give, but the knowledge how to give wisely."[42] What might have worked in the old neighborhoods could not meet broader communal needs. Even under American conditions of voluntarism, the *Messenger* showed that other religious and ethnic groups had devised united charities. "The secret of success has been union," Isaacs reiterated.[43]

A unified community response in New York recognized that elemental social and economic conditions produced widespread penury. As long as there was immigration, there would always be a poor, working-class segment of Jews. Moreover, though the city offered opportunity and mobility, capitalism created instability. To care for the poor in the most up-to-date manner, the *Messenger* held up the example of the London Jewish charity, which hired professionals to supervise requests for aid and determine scientifically which should be approved and for how much.[44]

As part of an effort to systematize service delivery, the *Messenger* divided the city into districts and sent uptown women to take charge of Jewish communities within an assigned district. Because many of the needy, especially those deemed "deserving" by their benefactors, were ashamed to ask for assistance, aid groups directed representatives to scout various neighborhoods in search of the "deserving" poor. Division into districts also reflected a need to replace informal neighborhood connections with a formal structure.[45]

Finally, in October 1874, five core institutions formed the United Hebrew Charities (UHC).[46] In subsequent years, the UHC helped thousands of families pay their rent and purchase food. Those families lived "crowded in tenements, deprived of sufficient air, exposed to disease and crushed in spirit." UHC also tackled "ways to reduce desertion among Jewish husbands." Economic vicissitudes, increasingly congested neighborhoods and tenement dwellings, and family strife abetted by dislocations of migration plagued many Jewish New Yorkers. The UHC desired to restore families to "self-support." So it purchased sets of tools, pushcarts, and in some cases, stock for small stores. While an initial payment might have helped women whose husbands deserted them pay rent and purchase food, it didn't answer long-term needs. Becoming a tailor did, since it allowed women to work at home, near their children. By 1875, thirty-five thousand women in New York worked as dressmakers or milliners. The UHC encouraged this trend by providing sewing machines.[47]

New York Jews followed Protestant philanthropies in instituting a modernized "scientific" approach to charity, which increased Jewish women's prominence. Jewish women delivered goods to tenement districts, staffed downtown offices, served as partners in the newly established United Hebrew Charities, and held major leadership positions in congregational sisterhoods that provided many direct services to the poor. These uptown women devised new models of Jewish womanhood. In their adoption of "scientific" methods of social work and expanded notions of women's proper sphere, sisterhoods drew much from their Protestant neighbors, even as they retained, privileged, and created their own distinctive Jewish female identity.[48]

As both a middle-class New Yorker and Jewish woman, Rebekah Bettelheim Kohut, together with other sisterhood women, participated in broader urban trends that charted the incipient professionalization of social work. Previously, women's congregational charitable work had consisted of sewing circles and raising money, activities that kept most members in their own neighborhood parlors. The growing women's club movement propelled Jewish women outside their homes to work directly with the poor. They set priorities, managed budgets, and cast their net far beyond the confines of home, synagogue, or neighborhood. Inspired by Christian women's organizations, synagogue sisterhoods emphasized their Jewish identity. Their work benefited coreligionists, and they viewed this labor as religious.[49]

When Rebekah Kohut traveled a short two miles to the pushcart-packed streets of the Lower East Side, she left a world in which Judaism towered above the streetscapes in Moorish synagogues and middle-class Jews casually gathered with Christian neighbors on brownstone stoops. She entered a world where immigrants worked for fourteen hours a day hunched over sewing machines in tenement apartments, worshiped in spaces carved out of tenement halls, and socialized outdoors on dirty sidewalks. This alternative Jewish milieu transported sisterhood women. Kohut confessed to a "fascination" in walking along downtown streets "and losing one's self in the throngs of newcomers to America." Not content, as other uptown visitors, merely to sample the "Oriental bazaar" of the market, sisterhood women plunged further into the neighborhood's heart. They established an office downtown and monitored their district, which ambitiously covered the entire Lower East Side.[50]

The work of these women differed qualitatively from past types of Jewish women's charity with regard to both mission and organizational networks. "We do not wait until the poor comes to our house but by means of our society we go out to meet the poor," relayed their annual report.[51] In forming and leading the second sisterhood in the United States in 1889, Rebekah Kohut and her congregation used a shared religion, a heightened sense of women's role in the world, free time secured by middle-class status, and tenets of social work to build a more direct connection to downtown's Jews. In six years, Kohut's sisterhood recruited a membership of 350. They ran a kindergarten, a sewing circle for girls, and a religious school at their headquarters; they dispersed throughout the neighborhood to "alleviate the misery and relieve the wants of 200 destitute families." In 1890, they joined forces with the United Hebrew Charities, and six years later, ten sisterhoods formally organized an umbrella organization, the Federation of Sisterhoods of Personal Service. As a measure of respect, the UHC accorded to each its formal district of responsibility.[52]

Sisterhood women regularly discussed their work and its larger significance relative to class and religion. They emphasized that they labored in part to surmount class differences and develop mutuality. Uptown sisterhoods aimed "to overcome the estrangement of one class" of Jews from another and "to bring together the well-to-do and the poor," in a relationship "not of patron and dependent, but of friend and friend." Eastern European Jews merited real relationships. Moral, educational, and religious activities ultimately seemed more valuable than did more easily measurable material goals and outcomes.[53]

Initially the United Hebrew Charities received strong support from the Jewish community: its subscriptions more than covered expenditures. But by the 1880s, UHC faced financial difficulties. It could not cope with the sheer numbers of eastern European Jews. Yet even then, the UHC still served one out of ten Jewish immigrants.[54]

The UHC's building "gave the Jews a headquarters." This three-story structure, with large, arched windows and ornamental cornice that "suggested a Florentine Renaissance palace," stood at the corner of East Twenty-First Street, in neutral territory—several blocks north of downtown's Lower East Side, where many clients lived, and well south of uptown's fashionable neighborhoods, where its patrons resided. A number of important Jewish social welfare agencies lined its corridors. It hosted major events, including the founding meetings of the American Jewish Committee in 1906 and the New York Kehillah in 1909, and projected an image of professionalism and solidity to Jews and non-Jews alike.[55]

But new immigrants saw charity's limitations and organized on their own behalf. Many joined older organizations established by earlier immigrants. Jewish fraternal orders attracted a new cohort of members, eager for their insurance benefits. In the early twentieth century, these orders peaked with half a million members nationwide.[56]

The number of independent mutual benefit societies also exploded, catering to immigrants and their needs for fellowship, insurance, health benefits, and religious bonds. In 1918, the *Jewish Communal Register* located 1,016 in New York, certainly an undercount. Most were *landsmanshaftn*, consisting of immigrants from a particular hometown in eastern Europe. *Landsmanshaftn* often reflected an array of political, social, religious, and gender divisions in the community. As a result, one small European town could give birth to multiple societies in New York bearing its name. The town of Rakov, Belarus, for example, had four *landsmanshaftn* in New York: the first one, a religious congregation, organized in 1890; the second one, founded by young men, appeared in 1904; and the third became Branch 428 of the Workmen's Circle, a sò-cialist fraternal order. Finally, in 1931, women established their own club. This dynamic multiplied among immigrants from larger cities, such as Warsaw or Minsk, which could have dozens of societies in their name.[57]

Landsmanshaftn and other societies schooled members in American culture on terms defined by immigrants, not by their uptown coreligion-ists or public schools or politicians. Their meetings alone constituted civics lessons in which members learned the meanings of citizenship in a free republic. No matter their ideological orientation, they all pos-sessed the same basic structure, derived from American sources. Immi-grants gleaned these rules from either experience in older organizations or a variety of instructional manuals published in Yiddish.[58]

One member recalled the profound transformations that could take place within a society. As a newcomer, he had been depressed about his lack of success in adjusting to New York and had considered returning to Europe. But then, he said, "something else happened, something ex-traordinary, that affected me very strongly and completely knocked out of my head the idea of going back." What happened? "During the months that I was hanging around like that, my *landslayt* brought me into a society. And there I was, sitting at a meeting when one of the members—a man with a very good appearance—was speaking about a question very intel-ligently, nicely, and logically in good . . . Yiddish." Intrigued, the young newcomer inquired who he was. "When I was told his name my mind was changed completely—my thoughts about going back disappeared." Here is the memoirist's explanation:

> What had happened? Here I must tell a little of the past of the man, the
> speaker at the meeting, who had made such an impression on me. He was
> a childhood *landsman* of mine, from the same street and from the same
> synagogue. As children we kept far away from each other. He was very
> poor, of a bad, even ugly appearance—dirty and ragged. He did not study

in either a *heder* or a modern school. It is likely that he could not even read the prayers, though he used to hold the prayer book open. I quickly left him behind and forgot about him until this encounter at the meeting.

So my whole way of thinking took a turn. A poor boy there! A fine, intelligent householder here, with a nice family and fine children! Dirty there! How clean and neat he is here! Of ugly appearance there! How nice and respectable he is here!"

Mulling over this transformation "from there to here," he resolved "no longer to think of going back": "Here in America, in the free land with all opportunities for everyone equally, here is my home. I shook off the last bit of dust from the old country."[59] This memoirist was not alone. Hundreds of thousands of immigrants "shook off the last bit of dust from the old country," prepared to take advantage of New York's social and economic opportunities surrounded by others from the same old country town.

Soon *landsmanshaftn* combined into federations based on country or region of origin. These Russian, Polish, Galician, and two competing Romanian federations amplified the voice of the societies in the larger Jewish community. As constituents of federations, societies built practical institutions such as hospitals and contributed to efforts to forge larger Jewish communal structures. The federations elevated a new class of leaders to represent the immigrant masses, "a type of truly democratic servant of the people, a type which possesses American energy and Jewish loyalty." These physicians, lawyers, and politicians had immigrated as children or teenagers and possessed English fluency. They interacted and competed with the wealthy "uptown" elite.[60]

Eastern European Jews did not neglect charity and created their own philanthropic institutions, sometimes directly responding to perceived deficiencies in established agencies. In Mount Sinai Hospital, for example, attitudes toward its immigrant patients often seemed indistinguishable from those of the Protestant missionaries, whom it was originally designed to displace. Mount Sinai refused to provide kosher food, and its Americanized Jewish staff and lay leaders evidenced especial contempt for practices of Orthodox eastern Europeans who composed an increasing proportion of their clientele. Reports of hospital staff shaving the beards of pious patients further roiled Orthodox circles.[61]

Furious, a group of forty Orthodox Jewish men gathered in a tailor shop in 1890 to discuss the possibility of opening a hospital for impoverished immigrants crowding into the Lower East Side. Despite limited resources, founders of the Beth Israel Association of New York moved with remarkable speed. They opened Beth Israel Hospital in leased quarters in the heart of the Lower East Side the following year. Not only did the new hospital make a point of serving kosher food, but its doctors and nurses also conversed with their patients in Yiddish. Demand quickly outpaced the space available in the twenty-bed hospital, and Beth Israel expanded rapidly.

By 1917, Beth Israel boasted a hospital, free dispensary, school for nurses, and work treating recently arrived immigrants threatened with deportation because of trachoma. With the hospital about to move into a new building just outside of the Lower East Side on East Sixteenth Street, its leadership represented a new "downtown" elite. While a German-born investment banker presided over Mount Sinai, a cloak and suit manufacturer who had arrived in New York from Poland at the age of ten took the helm of Beth Israel.[62]

Beth Israel's success inspired imitation. Building a Jewish hospital served a burgeoning Jewish population, provided opportunities for Jewish doctors to work, and elevated ambitious Jewish philanthropists to communal leadership positions. Brooklyn's Jewish elite opened the Jewish Hospital of Brooklyn to much fanfare, while Lebanon and Montefiore Hospitals provided medical care in the Bronx. Several *landsmanshaft* federations also ran their own small hospitals.[63]

Eastern European Jewish immigrants similarly disliked the UHC and determined to establish their own charitable organization, the Hebrew Immigrant Sheltering and Aid Society, known as HIAS. HIAS originated in two separate organizations: the Hebrew Sheltering House Association, founded in 1889 under the leadership of the Orthodox Yiddish newspaperman Kasriel Sarasohn, to provide shelter for homeless immigrants; and the Hebrew Immigrant Aid Society (also called HIAS). The latter grew out of a crisis when a *landsmanshaft* committee sent to Ellis Island to investigate the pauper's burial of a *landsman* decided to form a permanent agency to assist needy newcomers. Then it discovered that the UHC representative at the immigration station was unable to speak Yiddish. HIAS struck a chord in the immigrant community and raised enough money to place its own Yiddish-speaking worker at Ellis Island. In 1909, the two organizations merged.[64]

By 1917, HIAS headquarters in a four-story building on East Broadway inscribed the word "Welcome" in English above the door. The agency maintained its Ellis Island bureau, as well as branches in other port cities. It helped immigrants "to land"; provided information; guided newcomers to locate relatives, jobs, and lost luggage; assisted with the process of naturalization; offered free legal advice; looked after transportation for immigrants traveling beyond New York; sheltered thousands in its hostel; distributed clothes to the needy; and staffed a Social Service Bureau and an Agricultural Bureau. HIAS distinguished itself by its energy and determination to assert immigrants' rights. It vigorously appealed deportation orders, investigated conditions on arriving ships, and lobbied for pro-immigrant legislation. Over time, HIAS helped hundreds of thousands of newcomers.[65]

New York City expanded enormously after the Civil War, but its Jewish community grew even more quickly, becoming increasingly complex and differentiated by class, country of origin, religious inclination, politics, and language. Face-to-face informal neighborhood networks endured but proved inadequate to meet communal needs. So New York's Jews elaborated a system of formal institutions to take care of the poor, the sick, the orphaned, and the widowed. They reached beyond boundaries of individual congregations and mutual benefit societies, creating broader communal structures that transcended internal differences and gave women a central role in these emerging core communal institutions. Jews followed patterns common in the city as a whole, in which most social welfare agencies adhered to denominational lines. Continued immigration ceaselessly produced poverty, but New York enabled Jews to acquire the means to succor those who struggled. Gradually philanthropy defined an organized Jewish community, competing with, and ultimately winning out over, other models such as those set by fraternal orders.

As New York City became a city of five boroughs and began building the transportation networks to link these disparate worlds together, New York Jews similarly forged connections through charity and gender, knitting together new types of Jewish communities that occasionally surmounted divides of class, neighborhood, language, country of

Rose Schneiderman, c. 1905. Immigrant Jew, cap maker, union activist, socialist, and feminist, Rose Schneiderman forged cross-class and cross-ethnic alliances through her leadership of the Women's Trade Union League in support of both suffrage and labor unions. In her work for New York State's Factory Investigating Commission, she helped to spur the passage of dozens of laws governing workplace safety and health. This photo captures Schneiderman at work sewing. Courtesy of Kheel Center, Cornell University.

origin, and religious beliefs. New York Jews sometimes sought unity, but most often their organizations divided them into multiple Jewries—left wing and right wing; uptown and downtown; rich and poor; immigrant and native born; and speaking English, German, Yiddish, and Ladino. Religion, too, fractured Jews into secular and Reform camps as well as varieties of traditionalists. New York gave Jews freedom to organize their communal life as they saw fit and allowed them to define Jewishness on their own terms. New York Jews responded by creating a panoply of organizations catering to any number of desires and needs. Jewish collective community would need to arise from unimaginable diversity.

Public Culture

New York Jews forged a vibrant center of Jewish culture in several languages. Indeed, New York Jewish cultural politics began with language. Each language spoken by Jews—English, Yiddish, German, Russian, Hebrew, Ladino—carried cultural, class, and ideological freight. Did English signify assimilation and abandonment of Jewish identity? Did German gesture to a European Enlightenment heritage of philosophy, music, and spirituality? Did Russian point to a potent transnational blend of intellectualism and radicalism? And what of those identifiably "Jewish" languages of Yiddish, Hebrew, and Ladino? Hebrew possessed status as a holy tongue, the language of sacred scriptures and often of prayer. But Hebraists desired to revive Hebrew as modern language integral to the Zionist project of restoring the Jewish nation to its ancient homeland and establishing a Jewish commonwealth there. Yiddishists often demurred. They sought to elevate Yiddish, the lingua franca of millions of Jews not just in New York but also throughout Europe and wherever Jews had immigrated around the globe. Anyone who wanted to reach the masses, which included socialist intellectuals as well as novelists, playwrights, and poets, turned to Yiddish. As for Ladino, it seemed to be the only way to knit together clusters of multilingual Jews from the Ottoman Empire. Gradually, each language came to be associated with ideologies: democratic, Zionist, progressive, radical.[66]

New York Jews mainly spoke English at the beginning of the nineteenth century, but central European immigration placed German almost on a par with English as the community's public language. Rabbis extolled German's virtues from the pulpit, and organizations kept their minutes in it. Jews joined German singing societies, attended German theater, and read German newspapers. But a substantial proportion of central European Jewish immigrants were only thinly "Germanized." Nearly half came not from states later unified as Germany but from Bohemia and Moravia, Hungary and Alsace, areas where many Jews still spoke Yiddish. These immigrants continued to speak Yiddish at home and on the street, though they used standard German in more formal settings. However, English made steady inroads, as demonstrated by the Harmonie Club's linguistic evolution.[67]

Before New York Jews could be thoroughly re-Anglicized, millions of immigrants arrived from eastern Europe's Yiddish-speaking heartland, making Yiddish an important language of public and private discourse. Almost immediately, it began to absorb English influences. Many loanwords came from the sphere of work and business: *shap* (shop), *payde* (from "payday," meaning "wages"), *opreyter* (operator, of a sewing machine), *nekst* (next, meaning "turn"), and, along with *okay*, one of the most popular words, *sharup* (shut up). Hybrid words included *alraytnik* (someone who has worked his way up) and *nogoodnik*. English correspondingly influenced Yiddish syntax, as did German, especially in the press and organizations, where Jews borrowed terminology from their German counterparts. Newcomers complained that they could barely understand the Yiddish spoken and printed in America, but they soon learned it.[68]

Yet even as English was seeping into Yiddish, Yiddish was repaying the loans, influencing American English, especially in New York. The American writer Henry James feared immigrants' propensity to "play, to their heart's content, with the English language." Yiddish imperiled the purity of English, he thought, threatening to transform it and corrupt American culture. Initially Yiddish influenced American English indirectly via loanwords in German, partly through underworld speech: *ganef* (thief), *kosher* (okay, reliable), *meshugeh* (crazy). H. L. Mencken, who championed American English, reported that many New Yorkers, Jewish and non-Jewish, understood dozens of Yiddishisms. Mencken lists "schmoosing" (*sic*) as garment workers' slang for "idling around and talking shop." Entertainers spread Yiddishisms outside the city. (See the Marx brothers: "Hurray for Captain Spalding, the African explorer. Did someone call me *shnorer*?")[69]

When the American Jewish poet Emma Lazarus, who was of old-stock Sephardic origin, penned "The New Colossus" to support a campaign to raise funds for a base for the Statue of Liberty, she referenced masses of Yiddish-speaking immigrants along with others arriving at New York's Castle Garden. As she welcomed them through the "golden door," she embraced possibilities for cultural change. Although she could not anticipate what these newcomers might bring, she saw "tempest-tost" immigrants as central to American society. Eventually, Lazarus's own poetry acquired public dimensions, contributing to an understanding of fundamental American values as a nation of immigrants. Situated at an intersection expressive of both American and Jewish culture, Lazarus came to be seen as a New York poet, shaped in part by the powerful effect of immigration on her imagination.[70]

New York Jews learned much from their urban contemporaries in poetry, drama, fiction, and journalism. Gotham's Yiddish literary scene intersected both the German- and English-language cultural arenas, with mutual benefit to all New Yorkers. The Lower East Side's physical proximity to Greenwich Village encouraged Jewish café devotees to interact regularly with bohemians.

Greenwich Village attracted native-born, English-speaking New York Jews committed to modernism and political radicalism. They mingled there with non-Jewish figures in literature and the arts. In Village cafés, writers, artists, patrons, and intelligent consumers met to eat cheap food and discuss literature and social problems. These new bohemians, some of them with impeccable pedigrees and Ivy League educations, migrated to New York, where, they felt, "something considerable may happen." As the greatest immigrant city in the country, New York enticed them with its potential. In contrast to most of New York society, bohemians accepted Jews and nourished Jewish cultural creativity. Some of these Jews, such as Walter Lippmann, Waldo Frank, and James Oppenheim, were American born and hailed from affluent backgrounds. Others, such as Ariel Durant and Konrad and Naomi Bercovici, came from immigrant families.[71]

This milieu spawned a number of little magazines, such as *The Masses* and *The Seven Arts*. Frank and Oppenheim helped found the latter. It also fostered influential journals of opinion, such as the *New Republic*, which Lippmann helped to establish. These magazines allied Jewish intellectuals with Gentile thinkers who shared similar political and cultural commitments that wedded progressivism and modernism. Bohemians sometimes took a direct interest in immigrant Jewish community and culture, visiting the Lower East Side, Yiddish theater, and Jewish cafés. Several Jewish immigrants facilitated exchanges between Yiddish and English culture, especially the socialist editor of the Yiddish daily *Forverts*, Abraham Cahan (1860–1951), and the Romanian-born and Paris-educated Konrad Bercovici (1881–1961).

More than Bercovici, Cahan represented the highly politicized connections between immigrant and native intelligentsias. Born in 1860, Cahan grew up in Vilna, the intellectual capital of Jewish Lithuania. He received a traditional education and then attended the Vilna Jewish Teachers' Seminary, a Russian-language school that trained its students to become officially recognized Jewish communal functionaries. Although he never attended university, Cahan fell in with a crowd of Russian-speaking revolutionary intellectuals, was forced into hiding, and, in 1882, fled Russia. That same year, he gave the first Yiddish socialist speech in America. A serious personage, with spectacles, a bushy mustache, and thick, dark, wavy hair, Cahan quickly learned English well enough to teach it to newcomers. He became an accomplished English-language writer.[72]

Cahan mediated between two cultural worlds, often guiding American intellectuals who wanted to get to know the immigrant quarter. Cahan first met the dean of American letters, William Dean Howells, in 1892, when Howells sought him out as an informant on working conditions and the labor movement on the Lower East Side. The two hit it off, partly because of their shared admiration for Russian realist writers. Later, Cahan shepherded Hutchins Hapgood through the Yiddish cafés when Hapgood was researching his book *Spirit of the Ghetto*. Hapgood's sympathetic collective portrait introduced English readers to the immigrant Jewish neighborhood and popularized its characterization as a "ghetto."[73]

If the social democrat Cahan nurtured bonds between immigrant radicals and progressive Gentile intellectuals, the radical anarchist Emma Goldman distanced herself from the Jewish immigrant milieu. Fiery and charismatic, the editor of *Mother Earth* was temperamentally the opposite of her dour *Forverts* counterpart. Born in Kovno, Lithuania, in 1869, Goldman moved with her family to St. Petersburg, Russia, at the age of twelve. There she became a factory worker and gained a revolutionary education through reading Russian literature. In constant conflict with her father, disgusted by the oppressive tsarist system, and facing an arranged marriage, Goldman fled Russia to join a sister in Rochester, New York. Dissatisfied, she escaped again, this time to New York City. The execution of the Chicago Haymarket martyrs, convicted of exploding a bomb during an 1886 labor rally that killed several policemen, cemented her commitment to anarchism. Gradually she gained a reputation as both a "mesmerizing" speaker and "the most dangerous woman in America," an image enhanced by the confession of President William McKinley's assassin that he had been inspired by her writings.[74]

Goldman possessed a knack for self-promotion. Her lectures, as much spectacle as edification, entertained audiences; she even appeared at Oscar Hammerstein's theater, between a dog act and a dance routine. Her physical appearance belied her great energy: "Spectacled and severe, [she] dressed in a simple shirtwaist, tie, and skirt, her hair pulled back in a bun," looking like a "severe but warm-hearted school teacher." Her anarchism owed much to an American tradition of individualism. She placed more stock in a spirit of personal rebellion against constraint than in collective class action. She attacked such conventional institutions as marriage as particularly oppressive to women, advocating free love and birth control. But she viewed suffrage as a trap to enmesh women by the state.[75]

Fluent in Russian, German, and Yiddish, in addition to English, Goldman believed that "real social changes could be accomplished only by the natives" and so set out to spread "propaganda in English among the American people." In fact, she expressed contempt for her Jewish comrades, whom she accused of "sell[ing] their Anarchism in real estate, or in playing dominoes in restaurants." Anglo-Americans, by contrast, "live Anarchism."[76]

Some Jewish immigrants pursued different passions. A thirteen-year-old cigarette maker with a mop of dark curly hair and dreamy eyes named Boris Thomashevsky teamed up with a Jewish saloon keeper to import a troupe from London. Together they mounted the first professional Yiddish theater production in New York. The performance flopped, but within a decade, Yiddish drama flourished in city theaters. Rival troupes, led by such stars as Thomashevsky and his wife, Bessie, competed vigorously for a growing audience.[77]

Popular productions of low artistic quality, known as trash (*shund*), characterized early Yiddish theater. Writers churned out biblical spectaculars, domestic melodramas, and overwrought commentaries on current events. Often they simply plagiarized plays, transposed the setting to a Jewish venue, and gave characters Yiddish names. Crowds came for performers and spectacles, not scripts, which actors seldom followed closely anyway. Boisterous audiences provided their own entertainment, a common feature of nineteenth-century popular theaters catering to working-class patrons. Yiddish music halls also thrived; for a bargain price, families could enjoy "songs, dances, sketches, and jokes, usually spiced with double entendres and suggestive gestures."[78]

Gradually, a more sophisticated Yiddish theater emerged. When the playwright Jacob Gordin attended his first New York Yiddish play shortly after immigrating, he was astounded and dismayed: "Everything I saw and heard was far from real Jewish life. All was vulgar, immoderate, false and coarse. 'Oy, oy!' I thought to myself, and I went home and sat down to write my first play." Gordin elaborated, "I wrote my first play the way a pious man, a scribe, copies out a Torah scroll." A Russified radical intellectual with a full beard and an aristocratic mien, Gordin advocated a "realistic," socially conscious Yiddish drama. His didactic plays proffered a modern moralistic take on burning social and cultural issues. Gordin aroused controversy. His fans idolized him, while critics often excoriated him. When he died in 1909, his body lay in an open casket onstage surrounded by flowers (both practices defying Jewish funeral traditions) as thousands came to mourn and acclaim him. One was tempted, wrote a journalist, to cry, "Bravo, Gordin, bravo," almost expecting the playwright to arise for a bow at his final performance.[79]

Other serious playwrights followed, writing naturalistic plays and adding complexity to Yiddish theater productions. Many explored vital issues in immigrant life. A new generation of actors and directors promoted more sophisticated theater. In 1918, Maurice Schwartz founded the Yiddish Art Theatre. His expressive face—dark eyebrows with deep-set eyes and long nose—served him well in multiple acting roles. But he also desired to produce literary, modernist plays for the people. With his wife as his business partner, Schwartz's first production at the Yiddish Art Theater featured Celia Adler, daughter of the great Yiddish actor Jacob Adler and one of several siblings (Stella, Luther) who achieved renown onstage in English and Yiddish. But despite critical praise, serious Yiddish plays struggled to find an audience outside small circles of Yiddish-speaking intellectuals. *Shund* retained its popularity.[80]

Fluidity in language and popular appeal encouraged some Yiddish actors to try the English stage. Bertha Kalich, dubbed the "Yiddish Bernhardt," succeeded. Strikingly beautiful and regal in her bearing, Kalich began her career in Europe in Polish, Yiddish, Romanian, and German theaters. Fearing an assassination plot by jealous rivals, she came to New York and starred in Yiddish theater. Then she appeared on the English stage and garnered wide approbation. But when her emotional style lost favor, she returned to Yiddish theater, using her experience on the American stage to boost her cachet.[81]

As in theater and literature, New York emerged as the nation's center of journalism. Giants of publishing, both Jewish and Christian, battled for a rapidly growing readership. Jews participated in New York's mainstream English-language press as editors, journalists, and owners. Indeed, Jews shaped two opposite ends of the newspaper spectrum: the rise of "yellow journalism" through Joseph Pulitzer's *World* and the emergence of stuffy but reliable journalism in Adolph Ochs's *Times*. Both men sustained complicated relationships to Jewishness. Ochs shied away from Jewish political issues, although he remained a devoted Reform Jew. Pulitzer converted to Catholicism yet often suffered from anti-Semitism by critics of his journalism innovations. Both entered New York's newspaper business as young men. Pulitzer was only thirty-six years old, an immigrant from Hungary with a background in German-language journalism in St. Louis when he purchased the flagging *New York World* in 1883. Ochs was thirty-eight, a native-born Jew raised in Knoxville, Tennessee, with experience as a printer's helper, business manager, and owner of a Chattanooga paper, when he took over an ailing *New York Times*, with a circulation of just nine thousand and on the edge of bankruptcy.[82]

Pulitzer revolutionized American journalism. His newspaper introduced banner headlines, pictures, color cartoons, and a sports page. Pulitzer wanted punchy language, ran more human-interest stories, and focused his newspaper's attention on details of violence, scandals, and executions. Writing sympathetically about the working class and immigrants and supporting progressive politics, the paper's journalists played to ethnic tastes and prejudices. By appealing to the first- and second-generation Irish, Germans, and Jews who made up a majority of New York's population, Pulitzer raised his newspaper's daily circulation from 15,000 to 450,000 by 1895.[83]

Realizing the futility of competing either with Pulitzer's *World* or William Randolph Hearst's *New York Journal*, Ochs decided to rebuild the *Times* as a "high-standard newspaper, clean, dignified and trustworthy" for "thoughtful, pure-minded people." The following year, he introduced the *Times*' now famous motto: "All the news that's fit to print." Conservative and stodgy, the *Times* kept a studied distance from the urban crucible in working-class immigrant neighborhoods. Instead Ochs established the paper as the standard for honest, objective reporting, the vaunted "newspaper of record."[84]

Jewish critics complained that Ochs failed to take strong and open stands on Jewish issues. The one exception came during the Leo Frank case. Convicted of murdering a teenage female employee of his Atlanta pencil factory, Frank was sentenced to death, a sentence commuted to life imprisonment by the governor. Anti-Jewish rhetoric filled the local press as mobs gathered outside the courthouse. Perhaps because Ochs hoped to show that the South was not anti-Semitic given his own southern background, he took a personal interest in the case, going so far as to try to persuade southern newspapers to reprint *Times* editorials. Frank's lynching in Georgia in 1915 and callous responses from southern journalists shook Ochs profoundly. He reacted by further distancing the *Times* from Jewish causes, although he did prepare a guide for journalists on the proper use of the word "Jew" to assist B'nai B'rith's Anti-Defamation League, itself formed in part in response to Frank's arrest.[85]

Press freedoms in New York, coupled with expanding numbers of Jews, produced innovative Yiddish papers that were often exported back to Europe. The first giant of Yiddish journalism, Kasriel Zevi Sarasohn, got his start in 1874 as a thirty-nine-year-old printer, in America just three years. Eleven years later, his *Yidishes tageblat* (Jewish daily news) absorbed the weekly he had founded to become the first commercially successful Yiddish daily. A portrait of him as an older man reveals a determined gaze and set jaw, with a clipped beard and large, round yarmulke. He imbibed the spirit of Enlightenment in Europe but remained traditionally observant. His newspapers, Orthodox in religious orientation and politically conservative, pioneered the use of yellow journalism in the Yiddish press, a winning combination mixing piety and sensationalism.[86]

Immigrant Jewish radicals also gained journalistic experience in New York with their own newspapers. In 1897, a group of socialists decided to form a new newspaper, the *Forverts* (Forward), to appeal to the masses. Its first editor, the veteran Yiddish socialist propagandist Abraham Cahan, left after a few months, frustrated at his comrades' inability to transcend old sectarian habits. He then spent almost five years as an English-language reporter for one of the country's premier muckraking newspapers, absorbing American popular journalistic methods and progressive politics. When he returned to the *Forverts*, he purposefully applied those methods and politics. Cahan possessed a keen sense of his readers' tastes and interests. His detractors among the left-wing Yiddish intelligentsia, including many of his writers, grumbled that he neglected serious issues, pandering instead to his uneducated readers with sensational stories on tenement fires and celebrity love triangles.[87]

Under Cahan's autocratic editorial control, the *Forverts* soared in readership, becoming both the world's premier Yiddish daily and America's leading socialist daily. It gained this position with a shrewd mix of political earnestness and sensationalistic reporting. The *Jewish Daily Forward*, as it was known in English, printed Cahan's high-minded realist drama and literary criticism alongside installments of trashy novellas. News analysis by some of Europe's leading socialist thinkers appeared next to local human-interest stories. Cahan's most famous innovation—an advice column called the *bintl brief* (bundle of letters)—featured queries from readers seeking solutions to their problems. Many reflected particular cultural crosscurrents stirring the Jewish immigrant working class. In the 1920s, the paper published a regular rotogravure section featuring photographs of Jewish life and general subjects. By 1911, the paper claimed a circulation of 123,000 (compared to the *Tageblat*'s 69,000). The following year, it erected a ten-story tower on East Broadway, pursuing the footsteps of other newspaper giants like the *New York Times*, which built on Longacre Square at Forty-Second Street. While the *Times* gave its name to Times Square, municipal authorities named Rutgers Square in honor of the Jewish philanthropist Nathan Straus, who died on the *Titanic*.[88]

The Yiddish press counted some 150 publications in the forty-five years after 1872, when the first one had appeared in New York. In 1917, its five daily newspapers boasted a combined circulation in New York of over three hundred thousand. The most significant dailies besides the *Forward* and *Tageblat* were the *Morgen zhurnal* (Morning journal), which had supplanted the *Tageblat* as the city's leading Orthodox newspaper; the *Varhayt* (Truth), a paper inclined to support the Democratic Party; and the *Tog* (Day), which adopted a liberal, Zionist editorial stance. These dueling papers championed competing ideologies as well as taking positions on political issues. In addition to dailies, weekly, monthly, annual, and occasional publications ranged from the anarchist *Fraye arbeter shtime* (Free voice of labor) to the *Vegvayzer in der amerikaner biznes velt* (Guide to the American business world).[89]

The Yiddish press published the early "Sweatshop Poets," who got their nickname not only because most of them labored in the shops but also because workers' travails often animated their poetry. These poets penned melancholy laments over the plight of sweated workers, stirring calls to revolutionary action, and an occasional anthem of Jewish nationalism. They intended their poems to be declaimed or sung. Set to music, many became standards at socialist meetings in the United States and Europe.

Morris Rosenfeld (1862–1923) became the first Sweatshop Poet to reach an English audience. "A man of flamboyant temperament inclined to lapses into depression," Rosenfeld received a traditional Jewish education. He immigrated to New York from Russian Poland, becoming a presser in the garment industry, one of the least skilled jobs. A charismatic orator with deep-set eyes and a fine tenor voice, he declaimed his verse at socialist and union meetings. His poems, regularly published in the press, expressed his identification with his audience of poor workers:

> The groan of slaves, when they are tired,
> awake my songs;
> it's only then that I'm inspired:
> I reckon up their wrongs.

Rosenfeld struggled until the Bialystok-born Harvard professor Leo Wiener "discovered" him and published a volume of translations, *Songs from the Ghetto* (1898). The book's success led to additional translations of Rosenfeld's work into other languages. For a time, Rosenfeld earned a living speaking and reading at colleges and settlement houses, while also writing for the Yiddish press. But a series of reverses along with the death of his son embittered him, and changing literary styles deepened his isolation. When he died in 1923, the mainstream of Yiddish literature had passed him by.[90]

In fact, some of the regulars at Goodman and Levine's led a revolution in Yiddish poetry around 1907–1908. Known as *di yunge*, the young ones, they grouped around a journal, *Di yugnt* (Youth). Most earned a livelihood as manual workers. Some engaged in radical politics. But they sought to separate their art from politics, disparaging the older sweatshop poets as nothing more than "the rhyme department of the Jewish labor movement." Instead of lamentations over the proletariat's fate, they desired poetry for poetry's sake. "Poetry was for us young ones the entire content of our lives," recalled one of their leading lights, Mani Leyb (1883–1953). "Poetry illuminated our gray days of hard physical labor at the sewing machine, the scaffolding, or the hatter's block." They found inspiration in Jewish folksong and modernist European poetry.[91]

"Tall, thin, somewhat slouching and handsome," Mani Leyb (Brahinsky) was perhaps the "most attractive member of the group," not only for his prominent chin and high cheekbones but also for his dreamy "poetic personality." His autobiographical poem "I Am . . ." expresses a sentiment almost exactly opposite that of Rosenfeld. While Rosenfeld denied any aesthetic intention apart from expressing the suffering of his class, Mani Leyb, a shoemaker by trade, proclaimed that his poet's heart set him apart from his fellow shoemakers:

> In Brownsville, Yehupets, beyond them, even,
> My name shall ever be known, oh Muse.
> And I'm not a cobbler who writes, thank heaven,
> But a poet who makes shoes.[92]

These poets created a new kind of literary art in Yiddish, one dependent on an elite audience that embraced modernism. A sophisticated milieu nurtured this new generation of Yiddish writers, a subculture of immigrant Jews. The Lower East Side remained its hub, but as with the population as a whole, its members increasingly lived elsewhere. The Bronx possessed an especially lively cultural scene and fostered "an atmosphere of creativity."[93]

Joseph Opatovski, a young immigrant engineering student who was born into a Hasidic family, lived in the Bronx and achieved fame as the novelist Yoysef Opatoshu (1886–1954). Opatoshu joined the staff of the *Tog* and regularly wrote short stories as well as novels. He took Jewish New York as his subject, publishing such novels as *Hibru* (Hebrew), a devastating look at Jewish education in the city, and *Arum Grand Strit* (Around Grand Street) about the Lower East Side. He also tackled interethnic and interreligious tensions in a series of short stories, *Rase* (Race).[94]

As a distinguished Yiddish prose writer, Opatoshu had few peers in New York. Sholem Aleichem, renowned as a founder of modern Yiddish literature, arriving at the end of 1914, encouraged Opatoshu. However, Sholem Aleichem, like Rabbi Jacob Joseph, suffered from neglect in America, only to be mourned with a massive funeral procession in May 1916 that drew between 150,000 and 250,000 people. Jews lined the streets as Sholem Aleichem's casket made its way from the Bronx through Harlem and down to the Lower East Side before crossing over to a Brooklyn cemetery. Opatoshu's other peer, Sholem Asch (1880–1957), wrote very different types of novels. Asch came to New York in 1914, stayed for decade, and later returned.[95]

Both Opatoshu and Asch treated eastern European and American themes, including the city itself, but their experiences with translation into English brought them different audiences. Asch's epic novel *East River* explores themes of intermarriage of a Jewish man and a Catholic woman, religious commitment, and familial devotion. *East River* "makes room for a wide-ranging cast and a series of discourses on social phenomena, including the connection between dance crazes and women's rights." It contrasts with Asch's powerful short novel *Uncle Moses*, which depicts the exploitation of Jewish workers by their *landsman* and a doomed marriage of a hapless daughter of a poverty-stricken worker to his boss. Both novels, however, reached audiences in English through translation. *Uncle Moses* also became a Yiddish film. Its wedding scene captures the simultaneous anguish and joy of this arranged marriage held in a crowded tenement apartment. Opatoshu similarly turned to the complexities of New York's Jewish world and tensions around Americanization. But unlike Asch, who hewed to realism, as early as 1914, Opatoshu adopted modernist techniques of multiple voices, for example, in his short story "Fun Nyu Yorker Geto." Opatoshu vividly explored social turmoil and psychological distress in several New York novels. Yet relatively few of Opatoshu's novels were translated, and as a result, he did not acquire an English audience. In the cultural politics of Jewish literature, translation played a key role in bringing Yiddish writers to English readers and thereby shaping what they understood as Jewish writing.[96]

The world of Jewish immigrant letters extended beyond Yiddish to other languages. Eastern European migration brought sufficient numbers of committed Hebraists to sustain publications and cultural organizations. The latter sponsored lectures that drew hundreds of people, including students, teachers, workers, merchants, professionals, and even peddlers. "For people like me, who were slaves all week in factories," one memoirist recalled, Sunday meetings of Hebraists "were truly refreshing."[97]

As with Yiddish, a younger cohort emerged. They started a sophisticated weekly literary journal and established a national organization to promote Hebrew. American Hebraists saw the United States as an important potential center of Hebrew renaissance. They aimed to further Hebrew's revival for modern cultural expression. Hebraists never attracted large numbers, but they influenced American Jewish culture. In part through the establishment of Hebrew teachers colleges, they came to dominate supplementary Jewish education, which became the most popular form of Jewish education for the children and grandchildren of immigrants.[98]

Surrounded by well over a million Ashkenazi Jews, New York's estimated twenty thousand recent Sephardic immigrants lived as a minority within a minority. They too established their own press in Ladino—traditionalist (the weekly *La Amerika*), socialist (*La boz del pueblo*), and even satirical (*El kirbatch Amerikano*). Despite the limited circulation of the Ladino press, it guided new immigrants, offered advice columns, connected diverse groups of Sephardic Jews, and reported on communal activities.[99]

Jewish journalists also contributed to immigrant publications in non-Jewish languages. Jews wrote much of New York's Russian-language papers before World War I. In fact, for a time, Jewish radicals largely produced the Russian press for Jewish readers. Many pioneers of Russian journalism went on to write for and edit Yiddish publications as well as later Russian-language newspapers.[100]

Yet even as Jews wrote in many languages, they did not neglect English. Cahan had company. Other Jewish journalists made names for themselves. Columnists like Walter Lippmann acquired devoted followings. Emma Goldman's anarchist journal *Mother Earth* championed women's equality, birth control, union organization, and sexual freedom. "I want freedom, the right to self-expression, everybody's right to beautiful, radiant things," she wrote.[101]

The public culture of Jewish New York sustained a rich diversity of creative expression in multiple languages. Multilingual immigrants savored poetry and prose, theater and journalism, in many settings, just as writers and dramatists, editors and actors, moved between languages and venues. While Jews competed for audiences and influence, they also freely borrowed from each other and from the city's cultural scene, sharing a common New York language. Jews helped to introduce modernism in literature and culture and pushed the city toward social democracy, which was seen as intertwined with modernism.

Capital City

New York's rapid rise to prominence as the nation's capital city for everything except federal politics exerted a gravitational pull on ambitious American Jews across the nation. Their presence in the mix that was becoming New York Jewry proved crucial to the establishment of collective dimensions of Jewish life. Possessed with a grasp of both the breadth of the United States and the possibilities of New York's position within it, they imagined the city as the new capital of American Jews and the place where the lineaments of a distinctive American Jewish politics and community could emerge. They joined forces with talented and wealthy immigrants willing to finance their ambitious proposals. In turn, migration of native-born Jews to the city contributed to its rising significance as a Jewish center. Not only immigrants like Jacob Schiff arrived from Germany eager to prosper and lead but also such men as the lawyer Louis Marshall from Syracuse and the Reform rabbi Judah

Magnes from Oakland. A cadre of exceptional women joined them, such as Henrietta Szold from Baltimore, Sadie American from Chicago, and Lillian Wald from Rochester, all of whom fashioned powerful new Jewish organizations.

These men and women moved to New York, drawn in part by its promises as mass immigration reshaped the future of world Jewry, presaging a shift in prominence from Europe to the United States. The chaos and energy of immigrant life simultaneously pointed to the need for organization and the importance of New York in this era of Jewish history. It was becoming the largest Jewish city in history. Leadership of New York Jews was open and augured a prominent position among American Jews. Farsighted Jewish men and women aspired to such a leadership that would emerge from a union of the masses with the classes. They aimed both to co-opt immigrants and to create consensus. As they confronted questions of anti-Semitism at home and abroad, they stepped onto the world stage and secured New York's importance as Jews' capital city.

Although some native-born Jews worried that their association with uncouth newcomers might undermine an already shaky social status, they firmly rejected calls for immigration restriction. In addition, New York Jews strove to awaken sympathy for Russian Jewry among government officials, contending that persecution forced Jews to immigrate. In the early 1890s, as immigration accelerated, communal leaders mobilized. They convinced the president to name a special commission to survey sources of the mass migration from Europe to the United States, engineered replacement of the American envoy to Russia with one more sympathetic to Jews, and paid for a *New York Times* correspondent to go to Russia and report back on the dire Jewish situation.[102]

Simultaneously, social welfare agencies confronted problems of poverty and adjustment in the wake of immigration in the spirit of Progressive social reform that was animating so many well-to-do Americans. The United Hebrew Charities (UHC) moved away from its previous emphasis on aid and attacked behaviors and dysfunctional family structures that were deemed causes of poverty. The UHC came to see husbands' desertion of their families as a central problem, reflecting widespread American assumptions that married men should be supporting their families. Desertion's ripple effects, according to the UHC, included prostitution and increased institutionalization of children.[103]

By 1911, widespread desertion warranted its own agency: the National Desertion Bureau. In its first six years, the bureau handled nearly ten thousand cases, hunting down husbands and either effecting reconciliations (some apparently forced), securing family support from husbands, or remanding them to police authorities for prosecution under a law that criminalized nonsupport (17 percent of cases). "Man left family in Brooklyn without warning; had been away for almost a year and made no contribution toward their support," began a typical case account. "Through publication of the man's picture in our 'Gallery of Missing Husbands' he was located in Selma, Ala. He had established a business in that city and was induced through our correspondence with a rabbi there, to send for his family." The large number of desertions moved the Yiddish daily *Forward* to collaborate with the National Desertion Bureau and establish an innovative regular feature: the "Gallery of Missing Husbands," with photographs of men being sought by their abandoned wives. The report concluded with pride: "The reconciliation was complete as our applicant later advised us." The bureau even helped families deserted in Russia, once they arrived in New York, to find a missing husband.[104]

More innovative social welfare institutions gradually eclipsed the UHC, including the "settlement house," a concept imported from Britain. The settlement house differed from traditional charities in that its workers, usually idealistic young college graduates, the majority women, actually lived in houses in the midst of immigrant slums they hoped to improve. Motivated by the "social gospel" to apply Christian ideals to problems posed by urbanization, immigration, and industrialization, settlement workers brought English, citizenship classes, and welfare services to the urban poor. They often worked for progressive reform, espousing a moderate socialism.[105]

Lillian Wald, founder of Nurses' Settlement in 1895, achieved renown as New York's most famous settlement worker. Born to German Jewish immigrant parents in Ohio in 1867, Wald came of age in Rochester, New York. There she grew up on the fringes of an acculturated German Jewish milieu. Her family raised her in a universalistic spirit that drew more from liberal Christianity than from Jewish traditions. With her dark eyes and hair and full lips, Wald shied away from Jewish identification, self-conscious about her "Oriental" appearance. She ardently believed in the "fundamental oneness of humanity."[106]

Yet Wald did not hesitate to use her Jewish social connections to convince the financier Jacob Schiff to underwrite her Nurses' Settlement, purchasing its house at 265 Henry Street. Soon known as the Henry Street Settlement, it offered services common to settlements: classes in English, citizenship, arts and crafts, and home economics as well as a venue for youth clubs, lectures, and amateur theater. Wald started New York's Visiting Nurse Service as another program before it became an independent agency. She fought to improve the neighborhood through parks and playgrounds, public health measures, and better housing and working conditions. She tendered the Henry Street Settlement's parlor to help launch the National Association for the Advancement of Colored People (NAACP). A pacifist, she actively opposed American entry into World War I and defended civil liberties. In short, New York's Jewish milieu gave her both opportunities and reasons to become a pioneering social activist, contributing to the city's importance as a center of progressive reform.[107]

A few blocks away from Wald's resolutely secular Henry Street Settlement, Jewish philanthropists founded the Educational Alliance as an explicitly Jewish institution. The Educational Alliance blended Jewish education with Americanization, in the process antagonizing immigrants who held very different views about how to become American Jews. It used civics and English courses and exuberant celebrations of national holidays for Americanization. But it also promoted a modern Jewish identity through Hebrew lessons, Sabbath services, and Jewish holiday observances. Seeking to combine Jewish and American practices, the Alliance wanted to create a new American Judaism. However, its ideas of appropriate Jewish religious observances often irritated immigrant Jews. For example, when Hebrew schoolteachers complained that boys wore their caps inside the classroom following traditional Jewish practice, the Alliance distributed yarmulkes as a substitute. As a board member reported, "It gives the classroom the appearance of uniformity and is a marked improvement over the former boorishness and un-American custom of wearing hats in the class room." Uniform yarmulkes solved the dilemma of how to reconcile the traditional Jewish

practice of covering one's head when studying Hebrew and sacred texts
with American norms of going bareheaded indoors. Yet this "solution"
also exacerbated intergenerational conflict, with children observing different religious behaviors than their pious parents did.[108]

When the Educational Alliance moved into a magnificent new building that collected multiple programs under one roof, it implicitly adapted
uptown's department-store model. Its expansive five-story, "yellow

EDUCATIONAL ALLIANCE, EAST BROADWAY, NEW YORK.
(From a photograph.)

Educational Alliance building. This mammoth, five-story, yellow-brick building on
East Broadway dominated the cityscape of tenements that surrounded it. In 1889, three
prominent Jewish institutions—the Hebrew Free School Association, the Young Men's
Hebrew Association (YMHA), and the Clara Aguilar Free Library—merged; in 1893,
they became the Educational Alliance, which blended Jewish education with Americanization. Like department stores, the Educational Alliance included a wide array of
offerings on its floors. Courtesy of the Miriam and Ira D. Wallach Division of Art,
Prints and Photographs: Print Collection, New York Public Library.

pressed brick" corner building stood out as an island of order, light, and American Jewish culture in a congested, dim, and chaotic neighborhood. The lower level held an auditorium for concerts and lectures. The main floor housed offices, an industrial school, and kindergarten classrooms. On the second floor, additional classrooms served students who gathered after school for art and music classes, drama groups, Hebrew studies, and clubs of all kinds. The third floor included a chess and conversation room as well as the Aguilar Free Library and reading room holding twelve thousand books. Those who climbed the stairway up to the fifth floor found a gymnasium "on the most approved plan" and "a series of baths, walled in with marble, and lockers with open wire panel construction." For a breath of fresh air, local residents gathered on its roof garden.[109]

The Educational Alliance, contending with outspoken immigrants furious at its practices, slowly altered its programs. Initial methods of religious instruction reflected the founders' uptown Reform sensibilities, but immigrants preferred services closer to Orthodox practice. Following local public schools, the Alliance banned Yiddish on its premises but then relented. Its programs struggled to connect immigrant parents and children. Leaders on the socialist left and the Orthodox right criticized its mixed motives of social concern and social control, evident especially in its rigid rules for gendered recreation. Gradually, however, as the Alliance changed, it won grudging respect. By World War I, the socialist *Forward*, suspicious of uptown interventions and indifferent to religion, responded favorably to its work. The masses spoke with their feet, and those feet actually wore out the marble stairs within thirty years.[110]

Across the river in Brooklyn, the Hebrew Educational Society (HES) occupied a comparable position in Brownsville and reflected similar concerns. Brooklyn's Jewish elite anxiously read editorials criticizing uncouth Brownsville immigrants. But they also nervously eyed their bigger and richer Manhattan counterpart, motivated to show "that the Brooklyn Hebrew is not behind his New York brother." The HES building housed "children's and youth clubs, English and citizenship classes, religious instruction and worship, a gymnasium, a variety of manual training and vocational courses, a kindergarten, recreation rooms, a seasonal children's farm garden, a summer roof garden, a milk station and baby clinic, a library, a branch of the penny provident bank, a music school, a citizenship bureau, community theaters in English and

Yiddish, a study room, dances, and holiday celebrations." As many as 360,000 people used the building each year.[111]

These organizations reflected Jewish iterations of the spirit of Progressivism sweeping through American cities. Although they contended with specific Jewish issues relating to immigration, religion, and politics, they shared many common features with other programs of social reform. Their innovations, as in the National Desertion Bureau or Visiting Nurse Service, represented imaginative responses to problems of poverty and social dislocation that helped make New York a model for the nation. While some organizations catered specifically to Jewish immigrants and their children, others adopted universal approaches even as they also remained largely within a Jewish milieu. Both types of urban organizations served as laboratories and inspirations for new modes of Jewish institutional activity that looked beyond the city's borders.

The widespread spirit of organization among Jews received an ironic boost when New York City police commissioner Theodore A. Bingham published an article in 1908 on "foreign criminals in New York." Using statistical evidence to support his accusations, Bingham blamed immigrant Jews for much of the city's crime, way beyond their proportion of the total population. "They are burglars, firebugs, pickpockets, and highway robbers—when they have the courage; but though all crime is their province, pocket-picking is the one to which they take most naturally." New York Jews reacted angrily; the Yiddish press and many organizations and leaders demanded Bingham's resignation. But questions lingered, even after Louis Marshall quietly brokered an agreement that had Bingham retract his statements in return for Lower East Side Jews ending their campaign against him.[112]

Many Jews suspected that Bingham had told an unfortunate truth. Indeed, significant Jewish criminal activity among immigrants on New York's Lower East Side had drawn official inquiry before. Two investigations had uncovered Jewish involvement in political corruption, prostitution, and extortion. By the time Bingham made his accusations, Jews controlled much, though apparently not a majority, of the prostitution in the city. The article provoked the attention of Jewish men to what had been an outspoken concern of the National Council of Jewish Women, namely, extensive Jewish involvement in the international "white slave" traffic. The question of Jewish criminality added fuel to a movement among Jews toward greater centralized organization.[113]

Rabbi Judah Magnes called on New York Jews to form a "permanent and representative organization that may speak on their behalf, that may defend their rights and liberties and that may also cope with the problems of criminality." A month later, a committee of downtown notables, headed by Magnes, convened a conference to discuss creating just such an organization. That meeting led to the official founding convention of the Kehillah (Jewish community) of New York City, an attempt to merge traditional corporate Jewish communal organization with an American ethos of democracy and Progressive-era faith in technical expertise. The founding convention at the UHC building demonstrated that the Kehillah movement had a mass base. Three hundred delegates attended representing 213 synagogues, charitable associations, mutual benefit societies, lodges, educational institutions, Zionist groups, *landsmanshaft* federations, and other organizations. Magnes also convinced the leading lights of the recently established American Jewish Committee (AJC), including Schiff and Marshall, to participate.[114]

Judah Magnes (1877–1948) held together this fragile coalition of downtown and uptown, Zionists and antinationalists, Orthodox and Reform, radical and conservative. Born in San Francisco in 1877, he grew up in Oakland, California, excelling in journalism, sports, and oratory. Ordained as a Reform rabbi by Hebrew Union College, he arrived in New York and by 1908 was rabbi of Temple Emanu-El, the congregation catering to the city's Jewish upper class. His marriage to Marshall's sister-in-law and his membership in the AJC cemented his personal and political ties to the elite. Yet Magnes hardly typified its social milieu. Indeed, he cultivated a varied range of connections with immigrant Jews. Rabbi of the flagship Reform temple, he occasionally prayed at a small Orthodox congregation in a tenement basement. An outspoken Zionist, he inclined to radicalism and pacifism and enjoyed the company of Yiddish intellectuals. A brilliant preacher, Magnes was uniquely positioned to lead this Kehillah experiment.[115]

Magnes compared the Kehillah to a municipal government. One arm represented the democratic polity. Affiliated organizations sent delegates to the annual convention, which expressed Jewish public opinion and set policy. The founding convention resolved, uneasily, two contentious

Judah Magnes. Born in Oakland, California, Magnes migrated to New York City after being ordained a Reform rabbi at Hebrew Union College in Cincinnati. Drawn to the city's dynamism and possibilities, he worked as rabbi of Temple Emanu-El and as leader of the New York Kehillah to surmount differences between uptown and downtown, Zionist and antinationalist, Orthodox and Reform, radical and conservative. Courtesy of Prints and Photographs Division, Library of Congress.

issues. First, delegates passed a clause in the constitution that barred noncitizens from serving as convention delegates after Magnes argued that it was necessary if the Kehillah was to avoid the image of an *"imperium in imperio."* Second, the convention accepted a compromise in the relationship of the Kehillah to the American Jewish Committee. The AJC disliked the idea of a democratic community but agreed to transform the Kehillah's executive committee into a local district of the AJC. This gave the AJC veto power over Kehillah involvement in matters beyond New York City's boundaries. The AJC need not have worried. Its members consistently fared well in elections to the executive committee, often much better than self-proclaimed tribunes of the Lower East Side.

The Kehillah's professional bureaus constituted the second arm of Magnes's Jewish municipal government. Here it faced serious clashes between uptown and downtown as it tried to get Orthodox to cooperate with Reform. It first opened an Education Bureau; subsequently it established bureaus of social morals, industry, and philanthropic research. In addition, the Kehillah founded a School for Jewish Communal Work and even organized a Board of Orthodox Rabbis. Run by salaried staff, these bureaus attempted to coordinate, modernize, and professionalize Jewish activities. The Bureau of Jewish Education created model schools and issued curricula and teaching materials; the Bureau on Social Morals worked with police and maintained a staff of agents to gather intelligence on prostitution, gambling, and other vice in Jewish neighborhoods; the Bureau of Industry sought to mediate labor disputes between workers and manufacturers. The Board of Orthodox Rabbis attempted to set standards for certification of kosher meat.[116]

Samson Benderly, an educational reformer who headed the Kehillah's Bureau of Jewish Education, estimated that less than a quarter of Jewish children who attended public school received any sort of Jewish instruction at any given time. Though this meant that, over the course of their school careers, 68 percent of boys and 21 percent of girls acquired at least some Jewish education, Benderly argued that what they got was dismally below public-school standards. At best, wrote an associate, *heder* teachers were "earnest, mediaeval men, zealously trying to impart unwished for knowledge to the unwilling youngsters of the new world." At worst, they were ignorant peddlers and shop workers who passed themselves off as teachers to equally ignorant parents. Benderly believed the problem stemmed from lack of systematic coordination and professionalism. So the bureau raised pedagogical standards and called for more professional training and institutional coordination. But resistance to Benderly's efforts from traditionalist rabbis led him to focus on girls, whose education was less constrained by European practices.[117]

Despite the Kehillah's significant accomplishments, it floundered when the United States entered World War I. Many of its problems stemmed from its attempt to form an all-encompassing corporate democratic Jewish body in an open, voluntarist, and pluralistic society. Even at its height, the Kehillah never won over more than a tenth of the thousands of individual Jewish societies and congregations. Among those who *did* affiliate, it struggled to impose order. The Orthodox Agudath Ha-Rabbannim failed to understand why it should follow the dictates of Reform Jews; the AJC resisted democratically-arrived-at decisions of the conventions; the large labor and socialist sector refused to commit to an exercise in class collaboration. The war further damaged the Kehillah. Having taken an outspokenly antiwar position, Magnes could no longer supply the glue to keep the enterprise together. It dissolved officially in 1922.[118]

If the Kehillah represented a vision of a democratic Jewish polity based on mass suffrage, the Federation movement that succeeded it structured membership in an official Jewish community on an ability to provide charitable support to others. Dozens of Jewish philanthropic institutions, many of them with professional staffs, served a population of one and a half million and often competed for attention and dollars. Big donors, headed by the German-born Felix Warburg of the investment bank Kuhn, Loeb & Company, initiated a new round of centralization, this time in the form of a Federation for the Support of Jewish Philanthropic Societies. Federation intended to provide joint fund-raising for its constituent agencies, which retained their autonomy. The goal aimed to reduce duplication in fund-raising and improve efficiency in service delivery by reducing pressure on organizations to raise their own money.[119]

New York, in fact, came late to the Federation model, which had been pioneered elsewhere. Even Brooklyn had a jump on Manhattan, having organized its own Federation of Jewish Charities in 1909. But the Manhattan and Bronx Federation dwarfed them all, raising over $2 million for eighty-four agencies by January 1917. It quickly assumed a prominence and authority rooted in its leadership, its ability to solicit a staggering amount of money, and its effective co-optation of organizations.[120]

Federation attempted to mobilize a broad cross-section of New York Jews—a minimum contribution was ten dollars—and the initial campaign attracted ninety-five hundred subscribers, upped to seventy thousand in January 1918. Gradually Federation established itself as a means through which middle- and upper-class Jews "paid their dues" for membership in the New York Jewish community. Rather than creating a board of delegates from constituent agencies, Federation adopted a military model, with Warburg at the top of a bureaucracy of solicitors. As general, he commanded colonels, who held leading positions in various trades in which Jews had established ethnic niches. By 1921, this model of fund-raising around trade groups, structured hierarchically in a Business Men's Council, established a form of philanthropic leadership for New York Jews that eschewed any claim to political representation. Federation's leadership concentrated in the hands of the wealthiest Jews, initially of central European origin. In fact, Federation often held its meetings at Warburg's Fifth Avenue mansion, until it moved them to the nearby Harmonie Club. Federation thus encouraged a "deferential community based on wealth," far from any democratic vision of connecting downtown with uptown and forging a unified organization to lead New York and, by extension, American Jews.[121]

Emma Goldman speaking at Union Square, 1916. Fiery and charismatic, Emma
Goldman vaulted into public politics through her speeches and anarchist journal,
Mother Earth. Unlike Rose Schneiderman, she placed more stock in a spirit of personal
rebellion against constraint than in collective class action. A feminist, she advocated
free love and birth control rather than suffrage. Courtesy of the Lower East Side
Tenement Museum.

5

The Power of Politics

Politics offered an alternative to efforts to forge a New York Jewish community. In both its formal and informal dimensions, democratic politics attracted Jews eager to engage with American society and culture. Some sought change; others hungered for influence. Some propagated compelling alternatives; others desired a livelihood. Some moved from the local arena to a national stage; others gazed overseas to Europe, seeking audiences and approbation from abroad. Politics existed on the local level of clubhouses and street-corner rallies as well as on a national level of discourse and debates over ideas and ideologies. Some Jews wielded a pen or brush to condemn or magnify America; others turned to ballot boxes to push New Yorkers onto different paths. Irrespective of Jews' motivations and aims, their methods and approaches, New York's political and public cultures gave them a taste of power, both its limitations and its diverse possibilities.

Transnational Jewish Politics

In April 1903, the Yiddish press splashed a dreadful story on its front pages: a vicious pogrom in Kishinev, Bessarabia, slaughtered over forty Jews. The horrible news galvanized Jewish immigrants. The *Forward* called for a "monster demonstration," collected funds for relief, and gathered signatures on a protest petition. Although some Jewish socialists objected to what they saw as a wave of nationalist hysteria, others defended concern for their fellow Jews.[1]

The Jewish elite soon responded as well. Jacob Schiff took the lead and organized a "Bankers' Committee" that procured over $1 million, completely dwarfing British Jewry's £4,000. The effort established the world preeminence of New York and American Jews. Meanwhile, B'nai B'rith initiated diplomatic efforts, presenting a protest petition to a sympathetic but reluctant President Theodore Roosevelt to convey to the Russian government, which refused to accept it.[2]

Kishinev foreshadowed a wave of bloody pogroms that prompted downtown and uptown to work together. At a 1905 meeting held at Temple Emanu-El, the flagship Reform synagogue, "there were the 'native born,' the German element, Nationalists, Zionists, Reformers, Orthodox, Social Revolutionaries—in short . . . a united Jewry." The resultant American Committee for the Relief of Russian Jews quickly solicited $1 million, half of which came from New York City. At the same time, a group of "Socialist Revolutionaries" issued a call for a Jewish Defense Association (JDA) to fund the purchase of arms for Jewish self-defense units. JDA recruited not only socialists but also Zionists. The Zionist rabbi of Temple Emanu-El, Judah Magnes, headed the effort. A charismatic speaker with a gap-toothed smile, Magnes imagined that the JDA might evolve into a permanent organization to bridge divides among New York Jews.[3]

Magnes wasn't the only one dreaming of organization. New York Jewish men aspiring to lead American Jews recognized a need for a permanent national organization to defend Jewish rights. Given their desire to control its direction, they turned to Louis Marshall, who invited a small group of "leading Jews" from across the country to a closed-door meeting at the UHC building. Most were successful businessmen, lawyers, and rabbis of central European or American birth. Most adhered to Reform Judaism and rejected nationalist views that Jews constituted a people apart from religious belief and practice. Several of them, including Schiff and Marshall, had acted as Jewish intercessors with the U.S. government on an unofficial basis. Only a handful represented the growing immigrant community or Zionist or radical political perspectives. Nonetheless, their move to create a New York–based organization challenged the leading midwestern Jewish establishment: the headquarters of Reform Judaism in Cincinnati and offices of B'nai B'rith in Chicago.[4]

After much debate, those who were assembled rejected proposals for a democratically elected representative body—a Jewish "congress"—and settled on a small, self-selecting group of sixty. Although the resultant American Jewish Committee (AJC) included members from all regions of the country, and its first president was a Philadelphian, New Yorkers formed its executive committee's inner circle. They represented a rather insular group, united by background, occupation, wealth, and family ties. The location of the AJC's small office and staff in the UHC building bolstered their dominance, as did the New Yorkers' tremendous individual wealth and personal influence. Yet their two most important leaders had not grown up in New York but rather migrated to it.[5]

Jacob Schiff (1847–1920) and Louis Marshall (1856–1929) dominated the AJC. Born in 1847 into a prosperous family in Frankfurt-am-Main, Schiff immigrated to the United States just after the Civil War. After a brief sojourn back in Germany, he returned to the U.S., where he joined the investment bank Kuhn, Loeb & Company, married Loeb's daughter, and ascended to head the firm. "Medium in build and fastidiously groomed," he sported a goatee, a walking stick, and a quick temper. As a leading financier, Schiff, one of the wealthiest men in America, gave generously of his fortune to Jewish and non-Jewish causes. In fact, it sometimes seemed that scarcely a Jewish cause existed that did not receive funding from Schiff. Although a Reform Jew himself, he contributed liberally and ecumenically to any undertaking that he felt furthered Jewish learning or defended Jewish rights. To fight Russian anti-Semitism, he had helped finance the Japanese war effort during the Russo-Japanese War, a contribution lauded by the Japanese government. His extensive connections with Jews and Jewish organizations abroad allowed Schiff to fill the role of "elder statesman."[6]

Marshall, a close ally of Schiff, became the AJC's second president in 1912. A talented corporate lawyer, Marshall was born in 1856 in Syracuse, New York, to recently arrived German immigrants. A "short, stocky man of stern appearance," Marshall was always "confident in his opinions" and impatient with those who disagreed. His dour public persona certainly did not recommend him for mass leadership, and he harbored a suspicion of too much democracy in Jewish life. But his tireless efforts on behalf of Jewish rights and interests elicited respect beyond the narrow confines of his social milieu. At one point, he even learned Yiddish and underwrote a Yiddish newspaper to reach the immigrant community. By the 1920s, his influence was so pervasive that critics complained that American Jewry lived under "Marshall Law."[7]

The AJC ambitiously aimed to defend "the civil and religious rights of Jews in any part of the world," to "secure for the Jews equality of economic, social and educational opportunities," and to provide "relief from calamities." It preferred to work quietly, behind the scenes, through intercession with people in power and through force of moral argument based on carefully gathered and presented evidence. Accordingly, the AJC established a bureau of statistics and undertook to issue the *American Jewish Year Book*. The AJC opposed questions regarding race on the U.S. Census, limitation of naturalization rights to non-Asians, and local laws banning kosher slaughtering. It defended Russian Jewish revolutionary exiles faced with extradition, the rights of Balkan Jews, and Mendel Beilis, accused of ritual murder in Russia. In 1913, it helped push through the New York State Legislature a civil rights bill banning discrimination in "public resorts."[8]

The AJC launched a campaign to address Russian discrimination against Jewish travelers bearing American passports, despite provisions of an 1832 commercial treaty between the U.S. and Russia. The AJC called on President Roosevelt to abrogate the treaty. This abrogation campaign gained support from a wide swath of American Jewry, including B'nai B'rith and the Reform movement. In 1913, the United States finally terminated the treaty.

From the inception of the AJC in 1906, it fought to keep the borders of the United States open to Jews and all other immigrants. It lobbied Congress and presidents, testified before committees, produced pro-immigrant studies, and interceded with immigration officials in procedural and administrative matters. Cooperating with other organizations, the AJC for years managed to prevent enactment of a literacy test for entry into the country and to fend off an explicit exclusion of "Asiatics" from citizenship.[9]

The National Council of Jewish Women (NCJW) shared a common sensibility with male-dominated New York Jewish organizations. It saw family stability as a cornerstone of healthy communal life and undertook practical work with new immigrants. Headquartered in Chicago, the NCJW grew out of a dynamic meeting of Jewish women under the auspices of the World Parliament of Religions at the Chicago world's fair in 1893. It expanded rapidly, recruiting prosperous Americanized women, many of them Reform Jews. It soon claimed a national membership of ten thousand.[10]

But as the numbers of immigrants escalated, the NCJW moved away from its early emphasis on religious self-education to focus on social service. It blended a Reform Jewish commitment to "universal ethics" with a gendered sense that women possessed a special talent for ameliorating social problems. When the New York State Legislature revealed the extent of Jewish involvement in prostitution, NCJW members resolved to protect immigrant women from the dangers of international prostitution, or the "white slave trade." They threw themselves into work on Ellis Island and also agitated, albeit unsuccessfully, for Jewish men to make the issue a priority.[11]

This emphasis on immigration pushed the NCJW's New York section to the forefront of the organization's work and drew an ambitious Sadie American (1862–1944) to New York. With her dark eyes, large nose, and prominent chin, she often served as the NCJW's public face, first as corresponding secretary and then as paid executive secretary. Daughter of a successful German immigrant merchant, American brought her experience at both Chicago's Maxwell Street Settlement and Temple Sinai's religious school to New York. She spearheaded the NCJW's activities on behalf of immigrant women, establishing an aid station at Ellis Island staffed by Yiddish-speaking social workers. They interviewed every Jewish female immigrant between the ages of twelve and thirty, counseling them on prospects for settlement and warning them emphatically about dangers posed by pimps and traffickers. NCJW tried to provide a "complete chain of protection" to vulnerable single immigrant women, starting with its Ellis Island station and extending into help for women to settle into their homes.[12]

But American attracted controversy with her "brusque manner and autocratic style," combined with increasing resentment over New York's immigration work. Her observance of a Sunday Jewish Sabbath hurt her, as did her reputation for extravagance. Finally, in 1914, allegations of financial mismanagement forced her out of her national position and eventually her New York section presidency. She left NCJW and never returned.[13]

By contrast, the separate Brooklyn section avoided controversy. Its activities followed national and New York priorities: immigration work, mostly at HES in Brownsville; assistance to Jewish women incarcerated or on probation; education in housekeeping; and aid to the blind. It maintained a Home for Jewish Girls in Jamaica, Queens, for girls at risk of delinquency. Rose Brenner, elected section president in 1912 at the age of twenty-eight, provided dynamic leadership, increasing membership fivefold during her tenure. A Brooklyn native, daughter of a local judge, and member of the Reform Congregation Beth Elohim, Brenner rose to head the NCJW in the 1920s.[14]

With so many organizations in New York, the AJC's position as representative of American Jewry did not go unchallenged. It claimed to speak for American Jewry as a whole, but it was not a representative body. Its members jealously guarded their status as the country's "leading Jews." Hostile to Zionist aspirations, AJC expressed the opinions of those who regarded themselves Jews by religion, not nationality or ethnicity.

A transnational Jewish movement, Zionism emerged out of desires to respond to enormous changes occurring in the Jewish world. Zionists dreamed of a Jewish national revival. It claimed a mass base among immigrants and a small but intellectually impressive following among educated Americans. It championed Jewish cultural renewal and democratization of Jewish life. Early on, the Sephardic poet Emma Lazarus proclaimed herself "one of the most devoted adherents to the new dogma." But at the grassroots, Zionist clubs formed mainly in immigrant neighborhoods of New York and Brooklyn. These groups coalesced into the Federation of American Zionists (FAZ). Although most of its leaders were eastern European intellectuals such as Kasriel Sarasohn, publisher of the conservative *Yidishes tageblat*, the FAZ attracted some American-educated Jews, including its first chairman, the Columbia University Semitics professor Richard Gottheil, and Reform rabbis Judah Magnes and Stephen S. Wise. FAZ initially followed Theodore Herzl's political Zionism, but it soon embraced cultural concerns, developing allied organizations such as a fraternal order and youth group.[15]

Zionism included many alternative branches, all of which found adherents in New York. The Mizrachi movement organized those who sought to combine modern Jewish nationalism with traditional Judaism. Opposing them, Poale Zion (Workers of Zion) united Zionism with socialism. It proposed to liberate the Jewish working class through a socialist Jewish state in Palestine. A tiny party, it expanded its reach through its respected journal, *Yidisher kemfer* (Jewish militant) and its allied fraternal order.[16]

Zionism spoke to women as well as men. In February 1912, seven women decided that it was time "stop talking and start doing something" for the Zionist cause. They had been studying Zionism as members of

JDC food packages in New York, c. 1921. World War I prompted New York Jews to organize a massive effort of relief that led to the creation of the Joint Distribution Committee (JDC or Joint). After the war, New York Jews continued to contribute funds to help those who were suffering in Russia. The photo depicts graphically what a ten-dollar contribution conceivably could buy as part of a food remittance package for the relief of Russian war sufferers. Courtesy of the Joint Distribution Committee.

a study circle. Sensing that the "time was ripe for a large organization of women Zionists," they founded Hadassah—the Women's Zionist Organization of America. Their ambitious call to organize eventually produced both America's largest Jewish organization and its most successful women's volunteer association. Although the women of Hadassah did not "stop talking," they transformed medical care in Palestine on the basis of their dual ideology of "collective motherhood" and practical action. As a deeply committed Zionist organization, Hadassah ignored male criticism that its pragmatic idealism lacked sufficient ideological rigor even as it continued to educate its members and the public in Zionist philosophy and Jewish history and culture.[17]

Henrietta Szold (1860–1945) guided Hadassah in its formative years. By the time she helped found Hadassah, the dynamic and determined

Szold was an accomplished Jewish communal activist and probably the most influential female member of the Jewish establishment. Born in Baltimore in 1860, she received an American high school education and a thorough Jewish education from her rabbi father, whom she served as amanuensis, translator, and editor. An early lover of Zion, she became the only woman member of the FAZ Executive Committee. "I became a convert to Zionism the very moment I realized that it supplied my bruised, torn, and bloody nation, my distracted nation, with an ideal," she recalled, "an ideal that can be embraced by all, no matter what their attitude may be to other Jewish questions." Szold came to New York in her forties to study at the Jewish Theological Seminary. Her long face with deep-set eyes framed by short hair parted in the middle gave her a serious demeanor. Had she been able, she would have become a rabbi; instead she promised not to make that request in return for an opportunity to learn. She joined an FAZ study circle.[18]

The promise of Jewish spiritual regeneration attracted Szold to Zionism, but a trip to Palestine with her mother turned her in a more material direction. Disgusted with the disease and poverty that she saw, Szold returned home and formulated a plan modeled after American settlement houses. She sought to aid Jewish communities in Palestine by providing the best American medical practices. With funding from Nathan Straus, the non-Zionist philanthropist and co-owner of Macy's department store, Hadassah sponsored the first American nurses in Palestine just prior to World War I and opened a clinic in Jerusalem. Committed to serving all—Jews, Christians, Arabs, and Muslims—without regard to race or religion, according to Progressive American ideals, Hadassah gradually constructed a modern Jewish medical infrastructure in Palestine.[19]

Zionism also attracted American-born Jews distant from Jewish life in the United States, such as the prominent Boston attorney Louis D. Brandeis. Then World War I catapulted Brandeis to leadership, and FAZ enrolled tens of thousands of new recruits. By 1917, hundreds of Zionist societies, branches, lodges, and even synagogues flourished in New York City, especially in neighborhoods of eastern European immigrants and their children. College students at City College, Columbia, Hunter, the Jewish Theological Seminary, New York University, and the Yeshiva Rabbi Isaac Elchanan rallied to the Inter-collegiate Zionist Association.

Two Hadassah sections covered "New York" and Brooklyn. Of the 119 Young Judea clubs in the city, 28 existed in Brownsville, where Zionist youth could be seen collecting money along its main shopping street, Pitkin Avenue, for the Jewish National Fund.[20]

While Zionists advocated Jewish national revival in the Land of Israel, and the AJC called for integration of a Jewish religious community into the United States, Jewish socialists harbored a range of attitudes toward the twin questions of the nature of Jewish identity and the shape of the Jewish future. Some socialists struck a resolutely cosmopolitan stance, insisting that they looked forward to a world without national divisions. They hesitated to join efforts that they felt raised national, ethnic, or religious solidarity above that of class.

But increasingly, socialists adopted a more positive stance toward Jewish national identity, encouraged by Chaim Zhitlovsky (1865–1943), the most important intellectual proponent of a synthesis of political radicalism and Jewish nationalism. Born in 1865, Zhitlovsky grew up in a Hasidic family in Vitebsk, Belarus, and did not immigrate to New York until his forties. Radicalized in his youth, he remained an adherent of a non-Marxist form of socialism. After experiencing a reawakening of his Jewish identity, he developed a theory of diasporic Jewish nationhood expressed through the Yiddish language. A "handsome man with sparkling blue eyes and thick blond hair and beard," Zhitlovsky possessed a "sonorous voice," with which he spoke elegantly in Yiddish, Russian, and German. He captivated audiences as a brilliant speaker and formidable debater. Although he could be rigid and dogmatic in his espousal of a modern, secular Jewish culture in Yiddish, Zhitlovsky influenced a range of radical Jewish movements, convincing their adherents to see no conflict between Jewish peoplehood and socialist internationalism.[21]

Supporters of this national-radical synthesis grew in number in New York due to immigration of politicized Jewish intellectuals, along with Jewish socialists and nationalists, after the failure of the 1905 Russian Revolution. Entering the immigrant labor movement, they made it more overtly Jewish. In the Workmen's Circle socialist fraternal organization, they pushed for cultural projects—publications, classes, lectures, a theater, and eventually, a network of children's schools—that would propagate a modern Yiddish culture, "purely secular" and "thoroughly Jewish." Hesitant to join cross-class alliances, these Jewish socialists nonetheless

Meyer London campaigning, 1914. In 1914, the Lower East Side sent the socialist labor lawyer Meyer London to the House of Representatives. His oratorical skills and ability to connect with ordinary people helped propel Jewish immigrant socialism to Washington, DC, one expression of the rise of a Jewish style in New York politics. Courtesy of Prints and Photographs Division, Library of Congress.

spoke out vociferously on "Jewish issues" at home and abroad. They contended that a distinct Jewish people within an American "nation of nations" could flourish in the United States. Their experience in New York, with its enormous immigrant population, sustained their inherently transnational vision.[22]

New York Politics

Election Day 1914. Even before the polls closed, people began to stream from all corners of the Lower East Side toward the Forward Building that towered over East Broadway. By nightfall, crowds filled Rutgers Square and flowed into the surrounding side streets. People in the throng jostled for a better view of a screen hanging on the façade of the ten-story Forward Building, where election results would be projected. They were hoping for a socialist victory in the heavily Jewish Twelfth Congressional District, a seat long held by a Jew, Democrat Henry M. Goldfogle.

The Socialist Party candidate, a popular labor lawyer named Meyer London, had run unsuccessfully twice before. This time, it seemed he might win. But for hours, there was no news. Only partial returns trickled in, and rumors spread that the Democratic machine was up to its old tricks, falsifying returns to swing the election. At eleven o'clock, the Republican Yiddish daily the *Tageblat* came out with an "extra" announcing Goldfogle's victory. Still the crowd lingered, waiting for word from the socialist *Forward*.

Finally, at two o'clock in the morning, the official results appeared. Goldfogle conceded. London had won. The crowd erupted. People danced, sang, embraced, and kissed. At four o'clock, London arrived, borne aloft on supporters' shoulders. A spontaneous procession snaked through the Lower East Side, the marchers waving brooms to signify a political housecleaning.[23]

The Forward Building, in competition with Jarmulowsky's bank, assertively proclaimed the rise of a socialist sun in the Jewish community. Indeed, etchings of suns ran in bands along the top of the building. Overlooking Rutgers Square and Seward Park, the building advertised the newspaper and its cause. Emblazoned in large Yiddish and English letters on top of the façade, the *Forward*'s name joined the Socialist Party's arm-and-torch emblem. Its builders envisioned it as the main address for the Jewish labor and socialist movements. The building fulfilled those expectations. It housed the *Forward*'s editorial and business offices and printing plant as well as meeting rooms and a thousand-seat auditorium. The Jewish labor fraternal order, the Workmen's Circle, located its headquarters there, as did the United Hebrew Trades and the Jewish Socialist Federation. Union locals and radical *landsmanshaftn* used the meeting rooms.[24]

Not quite two miles to the north, near Union Square, stood Tammany Hall, headquarters of the Democratic Party's dominant faction in Manhattan. The Society of Saint Tammany, a fraternal group, formed the political machine's inner circle. Called "the wigwam," the three-story red-brick and marble edifice similarly contained meeting rooms and a large auditorium. A roof pediment sported a larger-than-life statue of an American Indian chief—St. Tammany, the order's legendary patron. While Tammany's chieftains operated in upstairs offices, they leased downstairs to Tony Pastor's New Fourteenth Street Theater, a variety house. Tammany Hall, too, embodied the political power of an important ethnic group. Irish politicians dominated its leadership and base.[25]

The mood at Tammany Hall reflected the Democrats' poor showing in 1914. London's victory exposed the Democratic machine's weakness on its own front stoop. The machine had worked hard to recruit newer immigrant groups pouring into lower Manhattan, long a Tammany bastion. Jewish socialists represented an ethnic as well as political challenge, injecting a whole new style into New York politics.

The Forward Building and Tammany Hall symbolized opposing pulls on Jewish political allegiances. Until London's victory, New York's politics had stymied Jews, even as their increasing numbers held out the possibility of influencing elections. Jews could join Tammany Hall but soon ran into an "emerald ceiling" that prevented non-Irish from gaining power. They could enroll in the Socialist Party. But socialists could not break out of their Jewish electoral ghetto and so proved of limited use for exerting influence. The Republican Party might be more open to newcomers than Tammany was, but as a minority party in the city, it offered few prospects. Other options also appealed: reformers of various stripes and all sorts of radicals. New York promised Jews that they would be able to participate in the city's political life. Jews grabbed the promise: as voters, activists, and candidates. But only with the emergence of large and dense Jewish districts did a distinctive Jewish position in New York politics develop.[26]

Gradually what was characteristic of Jewish politics became a hallmark of New York City's political culture, namely, its practical use of government to counter a capitalist market in favor of social justice, whether on the municipal, state, or national level. Even before the rise of the New Deal, Jewish political activists worked diligently to channel progressive politics toward more-far-reaching social and economic change. Ultimately, in alliance with such progressive politicians as Governor Al Smith, President Franklin D. Roosevelt, and Mayor Fiorello La Guardia, New York's Jewish social reformers and socialists entered the mainstream to build New York's unusual social democratic polity.[27]

Socialist power resulted from a long process, beginning in the nineteenth century, of recruiting potential Jewish voters, immigrants from eastern Europe. These early Jewish socialists learned from German radicals in New York. With their help, most Jewish radicals found their way to Marxism and a predominantly German Socialist Labor Party.[28]

In 1886, Jewish workers, caught up in the mood of labor unrest that swept the city and nation, went on strike. On May Day, the Jewish Workers' Association led some three thousand Jewish workers as they marched to Union Square together with tens of thousands of German, Irish, and native-born American workers to demand an eight-hour day. The Jewish Workers' Association also galvanized support among immigrants for strikes of non-Jewish streetcar workers, waiters, and musicians.

The Jewish Workers' Association threw itself into the struggle that fall for the mayoral campaign of Henry George, who was running on a platform calling for higher pay; shorter hours; better working conditions; public ownership of railroads, telegraphs, and streetcars; no more police harassment of labor assemblies; and an end to collusion between politicians and business against workers' interests. Above all, George stressed his signature issue, a single confiscatory tax on real estate, which, he believed, would finance a range of public welfare measures and end the monopoly on land that led to overcrowded housing conditions for the poor.[29]

Despite the enthusiasm of George's followers, he lost the election to a Democrat, though he finished ahead of the Republican Theodore Roosevelt. George carried German and Irish working-class neighborhoods. He probably won a plurality of the small Jewish vote. The radical press hailed the results as a tangible demonstration of working-class mobilization. But soon the class-based coalition that had backed the campaign fell apart, and the movement dissipated.[30]

Gradually Jewish socialists attracted a following as they overcame their resistance to using Yiddish. Some immigrant Jews found in socialism an answer to questions that plagued them: their downward social mobility in both old country and new, the long hours they worked in factories, the miserable conditions in tenements, and their marginalization as an ethnic minority.[31]

Socialists slowly constructed an organizational infrastructure to touch the lives of tens of thousands of immigrants. Taking advantage of New York's opportunities to organize, ten workers met in an Essex Street tenement to establish a class-conscious Jewish mutual benefit society. Called the Arbeter Ring, or Workmen's Circle, it aimed not only to help its members by providing medical care and burial expenses but also explicitly to emphasize education and solidarity with the working class in its "struggle against oppression and exploitation." In 1900, several branches reorganized as a national fraternal order. By 1917, the Workmen's Circle had 240 branches in New York City alone, enrolling twenty-five thousand members.[32]

Even more than the Workmen's Circle, the *Forward* guided the rise of the socialist movement. The paper strove to be lively and engaging, written in language accessible to average working-class immigrant readers with interests broader than orthodox socialist doctrine or internecine party squabbles. Still, the *Forward* preached socialism. It covered major events from a radical perspective. It reported on labor struggles, Jewish and non-Jewish, as a passionate partisan, often raising money to aid striking workers. Organized as an association, the *Forward* contributed some of its profits to strike funds and socialist campaign coffers. In election season, it urged its readers to vote the Socialist Party ticket.[33]

The Socialist Party became the main socialist political body after the turn of the century. Its big tent accommodated progressive reformers and ardent revolutionaries, Christian socialists and Marxist freethinkers, Oklahoma farmers and urban industrial workers. Joining the Socialist Party linked immigrant New York Jews to midwestern labor leaders like Eugene Victor Debs, the party's perennial presidential candidate, and political operatives like Victor Berger, head of a successful Socialist Party political machine in Milwaukee. In New York, the party counted members of all ethnicities, but Jewish neighborhoods emerged as its main bastions.[34]

Socialist-led unions, especially in the garment industry, provided the final pillar of socialist strength. Between 1909 and 1914, the International Ladies' Garment Workers' Union (ILGWU) and other unions waged a series of giant, mostly successful strikes, mobilizing tens of thousands of members. This "Great Revolt" shook the garment industry and Jewish immigrant community. In 1909, the United Hebrew Trades enrolled just 5,000 workers in 41 unions. Five years later, its 111 affiliates claimed 250,000 members.[35]

The opening battle came with the "Uprising of the 20,000," a strike of shirtwaist makers, two-thirds of them young Jewish women and most of the rest Italian. That summer and fall, strikes had erupted. The ILGWU's

Local 25 pressed for a general strike in the industry, but the parent union resisted, afraid that it lacked resources to wage such a broad struggle. Finally, at a mass meeting at Cooper Union, a twenty-three-year-old member of Local 25's executive committee interrupted the leaders' speeches to appeal for a strike. "Curly-haired, dark-eyed, flirtatious," Clara Lemlich had arrived from Ukraine six years earlier. She had already established a reputation as a passionate socialist street speaker in Yiddish and English and a militant striker willing to brave physical danger. Lemlich's brief speech, recounted in many variations, became legendary in the Jewish labor movement: "I am a working girl, one of those striking against intolerable conditions. I am tired of listening to speakers who talk in generalities. What we are here for is to decide whether or not to strike. I offer a resolution that a general strike be declared—now." The next day, the first fifteen thousand workers went out on strike.[36]

The strike achieved a qualified success. The largest companies held out longer than small firms did, resorting to violence and brutal arrests to intimidate strikers. But violence helped to win over public opinion for the young women, especially when a notable contingent of middle- and upper-class allies from the Women's Trade Union League (WTUL) joined their protests. The strike ended without an industry-wide contract or union recognition in the big shops, but workers secured gains in pay and working conditions. Most importantly, membership of Local 25, about five hundred before the strike, now stood at twenty thousand.[37]

Five months later, seventy-five thousand cloak-maker members of the ILGWU, most of them Jewish men, walked off their jobs. The cloak makers succeeded in gaining union recognition. With the intervention of uptown Jewish lawyers and business leaders such as Louis D. Brandeis, Louis Marshall, and Jacob Schiff, union lawyers led by Meyer London forged an agreement with the employers' association. The "Protocol of Peace" established the garment industry's first permanent mechanism for settling grievances. Soon 90 percent of New York's cloak makers joined the union.[38]

Socialists boasted that they had the most articulate and intelligent leaders of all the political factions within the community.[39] Morris Hillquit (1869–1933) fit that mold. Born in Riga, Latvia, in 1869, Hillquit (né Hilkowitz) was a native German speaker but received a Russian-language gymnasium education. He immigrated in 1886 and went to work sewing shirts. Soon he left to work full-time in the labor and socialist movement. After mastering Yiddish and writing for the Yiddish radical press, Hillquit turned to English-language writing and speaking, popularizing socialist ideas. He graduated from New York University Law School and began to practice law. Hillquit, square-jawed with a trim mustache and broad brow, earned a good living as a corporate lawyer, though he also took pro bono civil liberties cases and served as counsel to various unions.[40]

As Hillquit immersed himself in the socialist movement on a national level, he distanced himself from its New York Jewish sector. He periodically returned to assist the garment unions in their struggles, and to run for office. In one of those contests, he succumbed in a three-way race for Congress in Harlem against an Orthodox Jew and a Zionist. Liked and respected, Hillquit never attracted a mass following, due in part to his retiring public personality and ambiguous stance on immigration restriction, the result of efforts to find common ground with the pro-restriction mainstream labor movement but unpopular among immigrant Jews.[41]

Meyer London's career resembled Hillquit's with one important difference: London continued to feel at home in the Jewish immigrant community and remained intimately connected with its life and institutions. Born in 1871, London grew up in Ukraine. He received both a traditional Jewish and modern Russian education. London arrived in New York in 1891, going to work in his father's radical print shop. Clean shaven and bespectacled, with a large nose and high forehead, London learned English and soon entered New York University Law School. Quickly Americanized, he was one of the first Jewish socialists in New York to join up with the midwestern socialist group headed by Debs. But unlike Hillquit, London continued to live on the Lower East Side, where his saintly nature became legendary. As attorney for tenants, workers, and unions, he often refused payment for his services.

With London's generosity, empathy for the powerless and oppressed, and devotion to the labor movement, he exemplified a great "socialist man." He spoke to audiences "from the heart to the heart" about the world's injustice. He also considered himself a member of the immigrant *Jewish* community. Unlike Hillquit, London consistently opposed immigration restriction. When World War I broke out, London headed the labor movement's effort to raise funds for Jewish war victims. Upon his election to Congress in 1914, he told a celebratory audience, "I hope that my presence will represent an entirely different type of Jew from the kind that Congress is accustomed to see." Conscious of his visibility as a Jewish immigrant socialist, London accepted his pioneering role in formulating a new form of American Jewish politics simultaneously committed to social justice and sensitive to ethnic concerns.[42]

Then came that infamous Saturday in March 1911, just over a year after the "Uprising of the 20,000," which brought thousands of shirt-waist workers into the streets to fight for better wages, decent working conditions, and union recognition. Sometime after noon, a fire burst out on the three top floors of a modern loft building occupied by the Tri-angle Shirtwaist Company. Triangle did not run a sweatshop. Rather, it employed hundreds of workers in a large (twenty-seven thousand square feet) factory in the Asch building. A block east of Washington Square, it boasted twelve-foot ceilings and elevators. Spacious, light, and airy, it was considered fireproof. Unfortunately, the factory's contents—the fab-ric and the workers—were not fireproof. A carelessly discarded cigarette close to quitting time ignited tons of cotton scraps and cloth bundles scattered around Triangle's three floors. Panic ensued as workers tried to escape through locked doors or doors that opened inward, down in-adequate fire escapes that buckled under their weight and the heat, or on packed elevators that stopped running when the heat became too intense for their operators. Many victims fell eight, nine, or ten stories to their deaths, shredding fire-department nets. Onlookers, including policemen who just thirteen months earlier had battled some of these same workers during their great strike, watched with horror the falling bodies from the streets below. Triangle had been one of the large firms that had resisted the union and its demands for safety precautions.[43]

Within about half an hour, 146 workers, most of them young women, immigrant Jews and Italians, died. Devastating to the communities that suffered most of the losses, the fire shook the entire city and set it on a course of social reform under an unlikely leadership of a coalition of Tammany Hall stalwarts and earnest reformers. The fire also stoked a Socialist Party upsurge in the Jewish community. The next day, the *For-ward* banner headline, "The Morgue Is Full with Our Sacrifices," pro-claimed, "Yesterday was one of the most horrific days in the history of the Jewish quarter." Equally distraught, a *Morgen zhurnal* headline captured the calamity: "Grieving and Wailing in All the Streets." For days, the press filled with graphic accounts and images of the disaster. The Triangle fire influenced the direction of politics in New York for the next several decades and demonstrated the central role that Jews had come to play in the city's economic, social, and political life.[44]

A flurry of activity—protest meetings, memorial gatherings, relief drives—culminated in a symbolic funeral for the last unidentified victims and a mass meeting at the Metropolitan Opera House. Class tensions flared. Fearful that a mass funeral would get out of hand, Jewish philanthropists, along with the mayor, tried to stop it. But a committee of Local 25, the WTUL, the Socialist Party, the United Hebrew Trades, and other unions, chaired by the shirtwaist maker and author Teresa Malkiel, proceeded with a procession to the Workmen's Circle cemetery. On a dreary and wet day, thirty thousand people solemnly accompanied the carriages to the pier.[45]

At the Metropolitan Opera House meeting, workers filled the galleries, while wealthy philanthropists and reformers sat in the orchestra. Rabbi Stephen S. Wise of the Free Synagogue pointedly reminded the crowd that the tragedy had not been an act of God. Rather, it resulted from "the greed of man." However, Rose Schneiderman best captured labor's defiant mood. At four foot nine, the redheaded Schneiderman, a former cap maker, a union activist, and a socialist, served as vice president and chief organizer of the WTUL's New York chapter. Schneiderman forged a career through cross-class alliances with middle-class friends of the labor movement. But that day she challenged them. She spoke bitterly to the assembled notables:

> The old inquisition had its rack and its thumbscrews and its instruments of torture with iron teeth. We know what these things are today: The iron teeth are our necessities, the thumbscrews are the high-powered and swift machinery close to which we must work, and the rack is here in the firetrap structures that will destroy us the minute they catch fire. . . .
>
> This is not the first time girls have been burned alive in this city. Every week I must learn of the untimely death of one of my sister workers. Every year thousands of us are maimed. The life of men and women is so cheap and property is so sacred!

Looking at her well-dressed audience, she bluntly told them, "I can't talk fellowship to you who are gathered here. Too much blood has been spilled. . . . It is up to the working people to save themselves."[46]

Schneiderman was not the only one to draw radical class-conscious conclusions from the fire. At a cloak makers' rally, a worker in the crowd shouted, "Why shouldn't the working class elect its own candidates?" when a conservative labor leader called for election of "honest men." At another meeting, a socialist editor declared, "We have the votes," and asked, "Why should we not have the power?"[47]

Mainstream politicians also chose to act. Tammany assemblyman Al Smith, who represented part of the Lower East Side in Albany, went to the morgue to talk with his constituents affected by the fire. When a group of reformers approached him about setting up an investigative committee, he suggested it be made a committee of the legislature with political teeth. And when the Factory Investigating Commission (FIC) was established, Smith joined state senator Robert F. Wagner as co-chair. In the course of the commission's four-year life, it heard hundreds of witnesses and compiled thousands of pages of testimony. Its members traveled around the state, visiting factories and other workplaces, viewing for themselves the conditions under which New York's workers toiled.

The FIC was a milestone. First, it proposed and saw passed dozens of new laws governing workplace safety and health issues, as well as wages and hours. Second, it brought elements of Tammany Hall into league with the sort of high-minded social reformers who would never have collaborated just a short time earlier. In part, this resulted from a conscious effort by Tammany to shore up its shaky support among Jews and the working class. But it also reflected a personal awakening by Smith and Wagner, both of whom went on, Smith as governor and Wagner as a U.S. senator, to develop key features of the welfare state on both state and national levels.

Third, the FIC demonstrated how central Jews had become to the political life of the city and state. Of its members, the publisher and fire buff Simon Brentano and AFL chief Samuel Gompers were Jewish, despite little connection to Jewish culture or community. But its staff included Jews closely identified with either Jewish philanthropic circles or immigrant labor. The investigatory staff chief, George Price, an immigrant physician, had authored pamphlets and articles in Russian and Yiddish on Jewish immigrant life in America. Three Jewish women, Rose Schneiderman, Clara Lemlich, and the labor activist Pauline Newman, all worked for the FIC, with Newman especially important in guiding Wagner and Smith through the state's industrial netherworlds.[48]

Notwithstanding the FIC, a socialist surge began in 1914 with Meyer London's election to Congress and continued for more than half a decade. The maturation of the Jewish labor movement contributed to London's victory, but so did his personality and willingness to view himself as a representative of an ethnic as well as a class community. London eagerly appealed to a constituency beyond the proletariat by portraying himself as the most viable alternative to Tammany. As one shopkeeper who intended to vote for London explained, "The politicians sap the blood of us businessmen," but London would "liberate us from graft." Leftists in the Socialist Party criticized his campaign's personal and "racial" appeals and muttered about a supposed unofficial "split for London" strategy. But Jewish voters responded, giving London 49.5 percent of the vote to Goldfogle's 41.1 percent.[49]

The following year, Brownsville, Brooklyn, a heavily Jewish immigrant neighborhood, sent the socialist Abraham Shiplacoff to the state Assembly, the first of a number of socialists to represent Jewish districts in the state legislature and the city's Board of Aldermen. For the next several years, socialists seriously contested every local election, sometimes as the largest party, in working-class Jewish areas of Manhattan, Brooklyn, and the Bronx. In Brownsville, socialists assumed a formidable presence in the neighborhood and helped to build the Labor Lyceum to provide programs in Yiddish and English. A neighborhood home of the Workmen's Circle and garment unions, the Lyceum offered concerts, lectures, debates, socials, dances, and holiday celebrations. At election time, it served as Socialist Party campaign headquarters.[50]

The socialist high point came in 1917 when Morris Hillquit mounted a vigorous "peace and milk" campaign for mayor in a four-way race. By that time, the "fighting" reform mayor, John Purroy Mitchel, had worn out his welcome among large swaths of the electorate. The United States' entry into World War I also became a major bone of contention. Attempting to seize the mantle of patriotism, Mitchel called himself a "100 percent American mayor" and attacked his Democratic opponents as allies of the Hohenzollerns and Habsburgs. Unfortunately for Mitchel, large

sections of the Irish, German, and Jewish populations in New York harbored antiwar sentiments.[51]

The Democrats that year put up a machine mediocrity, John "Red
Mike" Hylan, a Brooklyn judge. On domestic issues, Hylan took a popu-
list stance, vowing to hold down subway fares and calling for municipal
ownership of public utilities. He tried to straddle the war issue, proclaiming support for the war effort but decrying Mitchel's militarism.[52]

Hillquit criticized Mitchel's "cold business administration" and
pushed a socialist program of social transformation. But the war issue
really generated enthusiasm around his campaign. With Hillquit voic-
ing his party's unambiguous opposition to the war, his campaign acquired such momentum that Tammany took fright. It sent in "wrecking
crews" to break up socialist street meetings and solicited warnings by
Jewish Democratic stalwarts that a large Hillquit vote would stir up anti-
Semitism. With the election being a referendum on the war, the Socialist
Party expanded its support in German and Irish districts, but Hillquit
received a majority of votes only in Jewish neighborhoods. In the end,
Hylan beat Mitchel decisively. Hillquit finished a strong third. That year,
socialists sent a delegation of ten to the state Assembly and seven to the
Board of Aldermen. The Jewish socialist Jacob Panken won election to
the municipal court for a ten-year term.[53]

Although the war helped propel New York socialists to their highest
level of support in 1917, it also sowed seeds of dissension within their
ranks and contributed to their subsequent rapid electoral decline. London spoke out against the war, but he took what he saw as a responsible
position as a member of Congress. This meant that he voted against
the declaration of war and conscription but supported the sale of Liberty Bonds once the United States had entered the fray. The party's left
wing—soon to split to form the Communist Party—excoriated him for
his compromises, while prowar groups attacked him as a traitor. London
also forfeited support from Labor Zionists when he refused to endorse
the British government's Balfour Declaration favoring a Jewish homeland in Palestine. He lost his seat in 1918.[54]

London returned to Congress after the 1920 elections, which also sent
five socialists to the state Assembly in what turned out to be the Socialist
Party's last hurrah. In addition to internal dissension over the Bolshevik
Revolution and new Soviet government in Russia, socialists confronted

a focused attack from their political opponents who gerrymandered districts to dilute socialists' voting strength. The Board of Aldermen categorically refused to seat the two socialists elected in 1919 until weeks before the 1920 election. In a case that became a cause célèbre, the state legislature ejected the five socialists elected to the Assembly in 1920. Finally, Democrats and Republicans united to run fusion candidates against the socialists. In the face of gerrymandered districts, fused opposition, state repression, internal dissension, and a dose of old-fashioned Tammany intimidation, socialists lost their toehold in the electoral system. By 1923, only Judge Jacob Panken remained as a socialist elected official; his ten-year term ended in 1927.[55]

In the midst of this political ferment, Jewish male voters provided critical support for the 1917 referendum that gave women suffrage in New York State. The Jewish labor movement and Socialist Party contributed to this victory, as did a decade of suffragist activity aimed directly at capturing immigrant Jewish votes. The upsurge of Jewish and Socialist votes stimulated by Hillquit's campaign helped push the referendum over the top only two years after it had failed. Although Tammany Hall also favored votes for women, its core constituency—Irish Catholic men—remained the least positively inclined toward female suffrage.[56]

Jewish supporters of suffrage emphasized its link to labor. "The manufacturer has the vote; the bosses have votes, the foremen have votes, the inspectors have votes. The working girl has no vote," Lemlich stressed. Jewish women worked alongside Jewish men in the garment industry; as coworkers, their presence pointed to shared concerns for better conditions in the shops and at home. As Lemlich put it, "The bosses can say to the officials: 'Our votes put you in office. . . . Never mind what they say[,] . . . they can't do anything.' That is true," Lemlich admitted. "For until the men in the Legislature at Albany represent her as well as the bosses and foremen, she will not get justice; she will not get fair conditions. That is why the working-woman now says that she must have the vote," she explained. Suffrage organizations successfully lobbied the Yiddish press, all of which, from left to right, supported suffrage by 1917. The ILGWU and the United Hebrew Trades endorsed suffrage. Suffragists recruited uptown Jews as well. The central body of Reform rabbis endorsed votes for women, as did an outstanding progressive figure, Rabbi Stephen S. Wise.[57]

New York Jewish support for suffrage pointed not only to possibilities to exercise power in the city but also to types of issues that united Jews across class, religious, and political differences. Jews articulated a wide range of ideologies stretching from a nascent communism all the way through to a liberal republicanism that changed New York. For much of the twentieth century, Jews in all their diversity helped to make the city's reputation as the vibrant cultural capital of the country and the site of a relatively well-developed social democracy.

World War I and Its Aftermath

New York reverberated with conflicts occurring overseas. Its large immigrant population and their children, comprising a majority of New Yorkers, lived attuned to events happening in their countries of origin. Fighting in Europe between nations echoed on the city's streets as neighbors battled each other, upholding often opposing political viewpoints. Thus, wartime sparked internal debate and innovation at the same time as it united Jews to help their overseas brethren. New York Jews drew on their several decades of experience in building organizations and developing modes of cooperation for charitable purposes in their efforts to respond to the unfolding tragedies of wartime.

World War I devastated the dense Jewish communities of central and eastern Europe, where a majority of world Jewry lived. Armies fought their way back and forth through Jewish cities and towns. Jewish civilian populations suffered from the general ravages of war and from attacks specifically directed against them as Jews. Jewish men fought against each other as combatants on both sides. The war uprooted hundreds of thousands and turned them into refugees in Russia and Austria. Material losses were staggering. Moreover, hostilities severed previous channels of aid from Berlin, London, or Paris to poverty-stricken populations in eastern Europe and Palestine and disrupted communal structures, whether traditional or modern.

American Jews almost alone remained unscathed by the war. Safe and relatively prosperous, they realized they had a special responsibility to aid their fellows in war-torn areas of Europe and the Middle East. The Yiddish daily *Tageblat* expressed an opinion heard often as newspapers detailed the misery caused by the war: "It is important for American

Jews to keep in mind that we are the only large Jewish community which is not caught up in the horrible tumult. We are the only part of the Jewish people which is living in peace and tranquility, so we should help, when we are able, the Jews on the other side of the ocean."[58] Bonds between recent eastern European immigrants and their hometowns endured. Reports of devastation coming from those towns hit close to home.

Landsmanshaftn responded quickly. In the months following the outbreak of the war in August 1914, disparate societies overcame their ideological and other differences to form united relief committees for their towns. Radical Workmen's Circle branches, Orthodox congregations, and everyone in between put aside their differences to solicit thousands of dollars through mass appeals, theater parties, and balls. They held meetings where members heard firsthand accounts from recently arrived townspeople. *Landsmanshaft* federations channeled money to the old country and information to the new. But getting money across the front lines to its intended recipients proved difficult, since many had fled and dispersed. By the end of hostilities, *landsmanshaft* relief committees had accumulated considerable sums.[59]

The war-relief crisis stimulated calls for more centralized organization. Three national relief committees obtained funds from distinct constituencies: The Central Relief Committee for the Relief of Jews Suffering through the War (CRC) approached the Orthodox segment of the community; the American Jewish Relief Committee (AJRC) worked mainly with wealthy Jews associated with the AJC; and labor and socialist activists formed the Jewish People's Relief Committee of America (PRC). In an effort to rationalize the delivery of aid, however, all three united in the American Jewish Joint Distribution Committee (JDC or Joint) to give relief with the "greatest directness and least duplication." The JDC ultimately survived the immediate crisis to become one of the most important international American Jewish organizations, providing material assistance to less fortunate Jews around the world.[60]

The war also prompted renewed calls for a centralized national organization that would speak for American Jewry on political matters at home and, especially, abroad. Proponents of an American Jewish Congress favored a more democratic, activist, and militant approach than did the American Jewish Committee. The idea of a congress garnered most support among those who were inclined toward Zionism or other

Jewish Relief Campaign. During and after World War I, the American Jewish community, represented here by a female allegorical figure bearing a tray of food, raised tens of
millions of dollars for the Jews of war-torn Europe, pictured pitifully in the foreground
as ragged mothers and children. Note the New York skyline with the Statue of Liberty in
the background. Courtesy of Prints and Photographs Division, Library of Congress.

national conceptions of Jewish peoplehood, thereby generating more enthusiasm from eastern European Jews than from well-established central Europeans. Nevertheless, such "uptown" Zionists as Rabbis Judah Magnes and Stephen S. Wise, as well as the newly converted Zionist leader, Louis D. Brandeis of Boston, outspokenly championed the congress idea.[61]

The Zionist movement expanded greatly due both to the prestigious leadership of Brandeis, who stressed the compatibility of Jewish nationalism and American patriotism, and to American Jews' reaction to war's devastation. Membership in the Federation of American Zionists (from 1918, the Zionist Organization of America) soared from 7,000 in 1914 to 150,000 in 1918. New York became temporary headquarters for the world Zionist movement when the Provisional Executive Committee for Zionist Affairs (PEC) relocated at the start of the war. Leading Zionists such as David Ben-Gurion and Yitshak Ben-Tzvi arrived in New York, having been expelled from Palestine by the Ottomans as nationals of a hostile power. They added prestige to the movement. PEC procured funds for the Jewish community in Palestine and for refugees who had been expelled, negotiated with the British for recognition of Palestine as a Jewish national home, and agitated for an American Jewish Congress.[62]

As Brandeis gradually withdrew from active leadership after his appointment to the Supreme Court, Wise took the reins of the movement. Born in Budapest to a rabbinic family, Wise came to the United States at the age of six. A graduate of City College, with a doctorate from Columbia University, he received private ordination and embarked on a career as a Reform rabbi. Wise rejected an offer of the pulpit at New York's prestigious Temple Emanu-El because its trustees would not guarantee him enough independence to preach as he pleased. Instead, he founded the Free Synagogue, "based on freedom of pulpit, free pews to all without fixed dues, outspoken criticism of social ills, the application of religion to their solution, and an extensive program of social welfare." With an aquiline nose, jutting chin, and flowing mane, Wise became known for his soaring oratory and dramatic flair. An ardent liberal in politics and a passionate Zionist, he was, like Magnes, an uptown Reform rabbi who attempted to connect to immigrant Jews downtown.[63]

For three years, Jews debated the congress idea. A dizzying array of players held meetings, attended rallies, and attempted negotiations.

Finally, they reached compromises: the congress would seek to protect Jewish civil rights. "Group rights" were out, but the "rights of peoples," including the "Jewish people," were in. Three-quarters of the delegates were to be elected in open balloting and the rest appointed by organizations.

Elections occurred over two days in June 1917. In New York City, upward of 130,000 Jews voted at almost fifty polling stations located in public and Hebrew schools, synagogues, clubrooms, and YMHAs and YWHAs. Nationally, over 300,000 people participated at polling stations across the country. Women enjoyed equal suffrage, a right they won in November elections in New York State but not throughout the United States. However, fewer people voted than organizers had predicted, possibly because of a last-minute socialist boycott. Labor Zionists won representation among the elected delegates, but no mainstream socialists. Nevertheless, these elections constituted an unprecedented demonstration of communal democracy.[64]

When the American Jewish Congress finally met in Philadelphia in December 1918, a month after the war had ended, it named a delegation to represent American Jewry at the Versailles peace talks. There, experienced diplomats of the American Jewish Committee, especially Louis Marshall, carried out effective behind-the-scenes work. American Jews toiled to write minority rights into agreements leading to the independence of Poland and other new central and eastern European states emerging from the ruins of the Russian and Austro-Hungarian empires. Unfortunately, these liberal provisions for minority rights were more often violated than honored, handing American Jews plenty to do in defense of Jewish rights abroad. In response, the American Jewish Congress subsequently reconstituted itself as a membership organization, with Wise at its head. Indeed, the war unleashed previously unimagined hatred and violence against Jews in Europe and spurred anti-Semitism in the United States that resounded on New York streets. New York Jews, no matter their politics, of necessity took note of the changed conditions.[65]

* * *

Before Rabbi David de Sola Pool began his Passover sermon, he paused to look at his congregants in Shearith Israel, the nation's oldest synagogue, now located on Central Park West. "The opening chapters of

Louis Marshall. Born in Syracuse, New York, Marshall came to New York City to practice law and rose to an eminent position of leadership of the American Jewish Committee as its second president. After World War I, he spoke out forcefully against immigration restriction, nativism, and anti-Semitism in the United States. His tireless efforts on behalf of Jewish rights and interests elicited respect beyond the narrow confines of his social milieu. Courtesy of Wikipedia Commons.

Exodus give us the earliest examples of anti-alien legislation on record," he proclaimed, drawing a parallel between Pharaoh's oppressive policies and new immigration quotas gaining momentum in Congress. "While the measures which Pharaoh took were barbarous," he warned, "the spirit of the Egypt of his day is not dead." Other Jewish sermons in 1924 spoke even more directly: "The immigration restriction bills are a denial and reversal of long-cherished American ideals and traditions, an affront to the memory of the founders of the Republic, a dagger thrust into the hearts of thousands of human beings who yearn for an opportunity to lead the normal decent life which their own lands deny them and a staggering blow to humanitarians everywhere."[66]

As anti-immigrant sentiment peaked in the form of severely restrictive immigration laws, New York Jewish congressmen, rabbis, intellectuals, and communal leaders joined other New Yorkers to champion a pluralist vision of an American nation made richer by their own and other immigrants' experiences. Though they failed, and Congress enacted anti-immigrant quotas, their fight speaks of their deep faith in the promise of inclusion and tolerance, best fulfilled in New York City. Despite quotas and nativist sentiment, New York Jews continued to craft American identities rooted in the city's pluralist cosmopolitanism.

Immigration restriction marked the triumph of a nativist movement energized by World War I. While social anti-Semitism had flourished in the city for decades, its effects most often hurt prosperous central European Jews who were denied access to private schools and clubs. Now an atmosphere of supercharged wartime patriotism spurred attacks on German Americans as well as radicals like Morris Hillquit and Meyer London, who opposed American entry into the war, and "hyphenated Americans," who were seen to have loyalties outside the borders of the United States. Passage of the Espionage Act in 1917 and Sedition Act the following year chilled free speech in the city. The U.S. Postal Service threatened to withdraw second-class mailing privileges from the Yiddish *Forward*, forcing the paper to translate all articles about the war to be censored. The war unleashed anti-Bolshevik sentiment, leading to a Red Scare. The U.S. attorney general authorized raids to round up radicals and ship them out of the country. Emma Goldman, long an outspoken foe of militarism, was deported. After the war, many Americans feared that immigrants would spread the revolutionary contagion sweeping

Europe, especially communism. The Ku Klux Klan revived, this time targeting Jews and Catholics, along with African Americans. It epitomized the reactionary, anti-modern, anti-urban, racist, and xenophobic mood of much of the country.[67]

Anti-Semitism gained new legitimacy in certain local circles. Madison Grant, a patrician New Yorker and founder of the New York Zoological Society, expressed some of the racial anxieties of the times. In Brooklyn, a group of citizens published the *Anti-Bolshevik*, which described itself as "A Monthly Magazine Devoted to the Defense of American Institutions against the Jewish Bolshevist Doctrine of Morris Hillquit and Leon Trotsky," two Jewish New Yorkers, as Trotsky had lived briefly in the Bronx. The most admired industrialist of the era, Henry Ford, further emphasized the political dangers posed by a secret, international Jewish cabal. Beginning in 1920, Ford's *Dearborn Independent* began a ninety-two-week campaign against "Jewish influence" in American culture. Distributed in the hundreds of thousands through his car dealerships throughout the country, the newspaper even reprinted an adaptation of the tsarist forgery, *The Protocols of the Elders of Zion*.[68]

The main Jewish defense agency, the American Jewish Committee, vociferously denied any Jewish link to communism but hesitated over how to respond to Ford. Although anti-Semitic conspiracy theorists named the AJC's chairman, Louis Marshall, as the chief Jewish conspirator in the United States, the organization ultimately maintained its standard low-key, reasoned approach. Appealing to "enlightened" public opinion, it commissioned and distributed several books and pamphlets rebutting the *Protocols* and highlighting Jewish contributions to American culture and Western civilization. It lobbied former and sitting presidents to speak out, with some success. However, against Marshall's advice, the Jewish journalist Herman Bernstein sued Ford for libel after the *Independent* named him as its source for the *Protocols*. Bernstein's suit went nowhere. But one by the Californian attorney Aaron Sapiro, accused by Ford of dominating American agriculture on behalf of the Jewish conspiracy, forced the industrialist to retreat. Although the matter was settled out of court, in 1927, Ford issued an apologetic statement that had been written for him by Marshall.[69]

But much legislative damage had been done. Congress had been slowly adding categories to the kinds of people barred from entering the country. By World War I, laws banned convicts, prostitutes, "idiots," "lunatics," contract laborers, polygamists, anarchists, Chinese laborers, and people deemed likely to need public support. In 1917, Congress added illiterates to the list and created an "Asiatic barred zone" that effectively excluded almost all Asians. The Immigration Act of 1921 set an overall numerical limit of 350,000 immigrants each year. Afraid that the nation would be polluted by an influx of "abnormally twisted," "unassimilable" Jews, Congress aimed to shape immigration qualitatively. Passed overwhelmingly despite objections by Meyer London and other immigrant and Jewish representatives, the law established annual quotas for each country equaling 3 percent of the number of individuals from that country present in the United States in 1910.[70]

But when the 1921 law failed to stem immigration to the extent desired, Congress reexamined the issue in 1924. New legislation cut national quotas to 2 percent of people from a given country in the United States as of 1890. This law blatantly excluded most southern and eastern Europeans and barred Asians. Representatives of immigrant districts put up a last-ditch defense. New York's delegation included four Jewish members: Democrats Samuel Dickstein, Emanuel Celler, and Sol Bloom and Republican Nathan Perlman. Dickstein and Perlman were foreign-born, while Bloom was the son and Celler the grandson of immigrants. Much of the debate centered on the effects that the bill's anti-Asian provisions would have on U.S.-Japanese relations, but New York City's Jewish congressmen joined with most of their New York colleagues, as well as Catholic and Jewish representatives from other states, to defend immigrants and criticize nativist bigotry. Celler gave his first important speech in the House on the subject; he would not rest until he managed to liberalize immigration laws forty years later. Notably, twenty out of twenty-two of New York State's Democratic House members issued a public statement opposing the bill. But they failed to convince their fellow legislators. The bill passed overwhelmingly.[71]

This nativist triumph after World War I overshadowed persistent alternative visions articulated by many New York Jews. Some held onto their faith in the power of the melting pot to Americanize immigrants and their children. Others, such as Horace Kallen (1882–1974), a distinguished philosopher, proposed "cultural pluralism," in which diverse groups would retain their ethnic distinctiveness even as they contributed to create a new American society. A rabbi's son who came to the United States as a child, Kallen spent most of his long life in New York at the New School for Social Research, where he was a founding member. In his influential essay "Democracy versus the Melting Pot," he argued passionately for "cultural pluralism" as a defining feature of American life. Critiquing strident advocates of Americanization, he contended that you could change your name (and many Jews did), you could change your spouse (not a popular choice until after World War II), but you couldn't change your grandparents (suggesting an ongoing racial essentialism). The Columbia University anthropology professor Franz Boas (1858–1942), an immigrant to the United States from Germany, attacked the basis of racial exclusion by contending that environment exerted more influence than birth in determining individual and group characteristics. Of Jewish origin, though uninvolved in New York Jewish life, Boas thus attacked racialist ideas underpinning the new restrictive laws.[72]

This legislation dramatically affected immigration in general and Jewish immigration in particular. Numbers of new arrivals plummeted from 357,803 in 1923–1924 to 164,667 in 1924–1925; altogether 223,000 Jews came to the United States from 1920 to 1924, but only 36,000 came from 1925 to 1929 after enactment of the 1924 law.[73] Without a massive influx of immigrants, New York Jewry began a slow transition from a Yiddish-speaking immigrant community to a native-born and English-speaking one.

The community's demographic transformation occurred gradually. Not only did a trickle of legal immigrants continue to arrive, but so did smaller numbers of illegal immigrants. A largely Jewish network of smugglers that until this time had focused its energies on helping migrants sneak *out* of Russia now turned its attention to enabling its clients to *enter* the United States, often through either Cuba or Canada. New York remained a magnet for Jewish immigrants, as much because of family ties as because of economic opportunity.[74]

The failure of Jews to influence U.S. policy on immigration had profound repercussions on New York Jews, many of which did not register until the decades after the Second World War. Meanwhile, in the interwar years, local politics assumed more significance as Jews labored to set down roots in the city and make themselves at home. Neighborhood ties subsequently strengthened Jewish political activism and channeled it in new directions.

PART III

1885–1975

View from the Roof of the St. George Hotel, by Samuel H. Gottscho. Looking across the river from Brooklyn at Manhattan's midtown skyline, punctuated by the Empire State Building, the Brooklyn-born Jewish photographer Samuel Gottscho captured the sense of how "the city" appeared to many Jewish residents of New York's outer boroughs. No one did more than Gottscho to fix the image of New York as a city of towering heights and glorious panoramas. Although the Squibb Pharmaceutical factories dominate the foreground, one's eye gravitates to Manhattan soaring in the background. Courtesy of the Museum of the City of New York.

6

Jewish Geography

Even while the Lower East Side dominated popular imagination as the center of New York Jewish life, it actually provided a way station for millions of immigrants who passed through the area en route to another urban neighborhood, one that promised better housing, more air and light, and easy access to work. In the movement of eastern European Jews out of the Lower East Side, they occasionally followed in the footsteps of central European Jews who had preceded them. But as the city grew to include Brooklyn and Queens alongside Manhattan and the Bronx, as bridges traversed the East River, and as rapid-transit facilities tied together once-distant districts, Jewish immigrants and their children often made their own way, establishing new neighborhoods throughout the city.

Jews not only participated in this geographical expansion of the city; numbers of them helped to construct the physical city itself. Although most Jews were satisfied with renting their apartments, some entered the booming world of real estate development and construction, fashioning whole neighborhoods in the process. Others turned to building factories and lofts that anchored the garment and printing industries in mid-Manhattan. As successful speculative builders and landlords, these Jews amassed an ability to influence politics and exerted a different kind of power unrelated to voting strength. The distinctive feel of a New York street, especially in its residential neighborhoods lined with apartment buildings, owed much to Jewish builders and their vision of modern urban living.[1]

A process of internal migration through the city—of people and firms—never ceased, although housing shortages, two world wars, and the Great Depression slowed it down. New York was a city of renters, and Jews moved often as they married, had children, earned a stable living, or suffered financial reverses. Yet because the links of chain migration drew Jews to some areas and not to others, neighborhoods

Simpson Street, Bronx, 1920. This photograph shows a typical streetscape that characterized many new working-class Jewish neighborhoods in the Bronx. Along such streets in Hunts Point, modern tenements of five and six stories exuded an aura of secure well-being where Jewish life flourished. The stores on East 163rd Street, a major thoroughfare with streetcars, sold clothing and hats, while on the second floor, a dentist established an office. Courtesy of the Museum of the City of New York.

gradually acquired personas. Jews who lived or grew up in them came to identify themselves not with New York as much as with their own particular place in the city.

A City of Neighborhoods

Neighborhoods nurtured shared experiences of Jewish diversity, albeit divided by class. As Jewish real estate speculators, builders, landlords, and workers filled in open spaces with tenements and tore down individual houses to construct apartment blocs, Jews dispersed in sections throughout Manhattan, Brooklyn, and the Bronx. An ethnically segregated construction industry spurred growth that structured daily New York Jewish life.

Watching Lower East Side Jewish immigrants in the 1890s pursuing potential profits from real estate, Abraham Cahan observed how "a fever of real estate speculation" raged. "Lots, completed buildings and half-completed buildings were bought and sold," he recalled with a measure of distaste. "Anyone who had a couple hundred dollars dove into real estate."[2] The tenement real estate market's hierarchy, with layers of investors and workers, paralleled that of the garment industry. With so many middlemen seeking returns, tenants suffered just like sweatshop workers. While both investments offered opportunity for modest capitalists, they posed tremendous risks. More established, uptown Jews bought large parcels of land along planned subway routes, divided them, and sold these lots to smaller investors, who in turn sold them to builders, often downtown Russian Jews who secured loans from immigrant bankers. Builders quickly erected tenements, which they often sold to purchasers, who then sought lessees to collect rent and manage the property. The lessee earned a profit by raising rents and spending little on repairs.[3]

Construction along subway routes created both working-class and middle-class neighborhoods accessible to Lower East Siders. Harlem, located just north and east of Central Park, initially attracted central European Jews. But by the turn of the century, rapid building drew eastern European Jewish immigrants as well as second-generation Jews. In East Harlem, "new law" tenements offered Jewish tenants slightly more modern conveniences and space than they could easily obtain on the Lower East Side. In bourgeois Central Harlem, buildings advertised apartments with all the "latest improvements," including bathrooms with porcelain tubs, electric lights and buzzer systems, hot and cold running water, dumbwaiters, and especially, light and air. Middle-class Jews eagerly snapped them up.[4]

Working-class Jewish immigrants moved to Harlem in part because they were pushed from the Lower East Side. In 1892, 75 percent of the city's Jews lived on the Lower East Side. But expansion of elevated railroads and construction of a subway system in 1904 and the opening of the East River bridges—Brooklyn in 1883, Williamsburg in 1903, and Manhattan in 1909—destroyed thousands of tenements for access ramps, displacing hundreds of thousands of residents. Seeking new homes, Jews moved not only to Harlem but also across the river to Williamsburg and Brownsville in Brooklyn. By 1903, the Jewish Lower East

Side housed only 50 percent of the city's Jews, a figure that declined to 25 percent by 1916.[5]

Despite steady out-migration throughout the 1920s that left behind only one hundred thousand Jews in the Lower East Side, the neighborhood still anchored Jewish life in the city. In the interwar years, 39 percent of the Lower East Side's residents were Jewish, but Jews owned 75 percent of the businesses. Ironically, the area's commercial vitality actually increased as those who had moved away returned to shop and dine. Communal affection and responsibility bound New York Jews to the Lower East Side. Organizations flourished in the neighborhood; Yiddish theater and newspapers were located there.[6]

Another immigrant quarter emerged in Brownsville, Brooklyn, where open spaces and garment factories attracted Jews. First they lived in modest wood-frame, two-family houses, but soon new multifamily tenements erected by Jewish builders and real estate speculators eclipsed these wooden homes. Construction transformed swampy wasteland into "rows miles long of four and five story modern pressed brick tenement houses." By 1920, 80 percent of the roughly one hundred thousand residents of Brownsville were Jewish, and the neighborhood resembled the Lower East Side in its density, poverty, and Jewishness.[7]

Christians and Jews clashed, especially along Brownsville's shifting borders. "Since [Jews'] advent to this portion of the town not a day has passed without a fight of some kind," the *Brooklyn Eagle* claimed. "In fact, many an unfortunate Christian who has had occasion to pass through the streets of Brownsville at night has been roughly handled." Tough Brownsville Jews also joined forces with Christians. The neighborhood notoriously nurtured Murder, Inc., an ethnically mixed gang that flourished in the interwar decades, especially during Prohibition.[8]

Informal interactions of Brownsville residents shaped its Jewish character. The outdoor marketplace on Belmont Avenue came alive on Thursdays and Fridays as housewives and their husbands shopped for the Sabbath. Stalls lined the sidewalks selling fish, live fowl, vegetables, salt herring, rye bread, and dry goods. Pitkin Avenue, Brownsville's mile-long main shopping street, held food and clothing stores, as well as Jewish-owned banks, theaters hosting movies and Yiddish plays, kosher delis, and Chinese restaurants. Newsstands sold Yiddish as well as English newspapers.[9]

Jewish immigrants and their children also settled in the Bronx. Early arrivals hunted for signs of Jewishness, which soon appeared "in the windows of the butcher stores, on the shelves of the bakery stores." Jews brought urban development as well: "As the gentiles left, the grass on the hills, the bushes, plants, and flowers gradually disappeared. More stores and tenement houses grew up in their place." Yet the Bronx, with more parkland than any other borough, provided all its residents communal backyards filled with trees and lawns, rivers and gardens.[10]

Much of a district's Jewish character came from the people walking its streets, attending to their daily business of buying and selling. Styles of commerce and goods aimed at Jewish customers identified a street as Jewish. Pushcart markets, a Jewish innovation in the city, arose in such neighborhoods as Harlem, Brownsville, and Mott Haven in the Bronx. Establishments satisfying Jewish culinary tastes and kosher requisites gave neighborhoods a distinctive quality.[11]

Besides kosher meat and live chickens, certain foods stood out as Jewish favorites. Soda water's popularity, which when unflavored became seltzer, the "workers' champagne," gave rise to more than one hundred Jewish-owned soda-water companies, 90 percent of such firms in the city. Jews also ate more fish than other ethnic groups did. This proclivity, along with kosher demands to separate milk and meat, helped transform fish stores and herring stands into "appetizing stores" selling prepared fish, salads, and dairy products. Delicatessens, which Jews inherited from German immigrants, sold sausages and other cooked meats—salami, pastrami, corned beef, tongue, and bologna. Delis became such an iconic New York Jewish institution that their presence often identified a Jewish neighborhood more clearly even than that of a synagogue.[12]

Full-fledged "sit-down" restaurants sometimes evolved out of delicatessens, "coffee and cake parlors," and Romanian wine cellars. A handful of large, elegant kosher restaurants appeared in both Jewish sections and midtown Manhattan, where they served a clientele of garment-industry manufacturers and upwardly mobile families. In addition to meat restaurants, "dairy restaurants" offered vegetarian dishes. Even when restaurants were not actually kosher, their division between meat and milk symbolized Jewish culture. Later, in the interwar decades, another ethnic preference appeared in Jewish neighborhoods: Chinese restaurants, especially popular among immigrants' children. In time, Jewish taste for Chinese food became a kind of in-joke among Jews and an easy reference for stand-up comics.[13]

Jews also put public spaces to different uses than did other New Yorkers. Jews avidly patronized local public libraries, giving the Seward Park branch a reputation as the city's busiest. Similarly, the Brownsville branch library "immediately filled to capacity" with the largest annual circulation in Brooklyn. To relieve overcrowding, a separate children's branch opened, housed in its own imposing building. In the Bronx too, libraries flourished as Jews entered the neighborhood; tastes in reading matter changed, tending toward European literature and books on social problems. Jews congregated in local parks to discuss politics or enjoy holiday promenades.[14]

New York had always been a walker's city. Strollers loved passing friends on neighborhood avenues. Window-shopping, a favored pastime, generated crowds during holiday seasons. Customers journeyed by foot in and out of stores across wide expanses of commercial districts in search of bargains. Residents and visitors enjoyed perambulating as they took in the sights and sounds of the metropolis's entertainments, even if a bus, trolley, or subway had brought them close to their destinations. But in 1919, a disgruntled New Yorker told state officials that "her shoes had been worn out" beating the pavement in a totally unsuccessful quest. She had marched all around town in search of decent housing for her family and was "unable to find better quarters." Her husband, children, and so many others were stuck together, "crowded in dark, ill-smelling apartments."[15]

New York teetered on the brink of failing to fulfill a most basic promise to its citizenry: to provide decent and safe places to live. Housing authorities reported that "over twenty thousand of the worst dwellings in the city that were not in use in 1916 were back on the market" because there were "practically no unoccupied apartments that are fit for human habitation." Even apartments in the better class of buildings were "unobtainable" as "rents . . . were rising and families were 'doubling up.'" War industries had attracted hundreds of thousands of workers, many of them African Americans from the South, and governmental restrictions during the European hostilities on all but essential construction had severely constricted housing starts. Both new settlers and immigrants who arrived just before quotas became the law in the early 1920s competed with longtime residents for limited space. From 1915 to 1920, the population within the five boroughs rose by six hundred thousand.[16]

In 1921, the Board of Estimate passed a tax-exemption ordinance that galvanized new construction. The law, extended several times, basically freed "all new buildings planned for dwelling purposes" from ten years of real estate taxes. This far-reaching solution to New York's most pressing dilemma profoundly affected how its Jews lived, worked, and in many cases prospered during the next two decades.[17]

This mandate energized local builders and real estate operators. Many new buildings differed little from prewar construction of four- and five-story "walk-ups" even if promoted as "up-to-date." But in the Bronx in 1922, the first "million dollar apartment house" signaled a new era of housing for the middle class. This nine-story building on the Grand Concourse boasted "modern, fire proof apartments arranged so that each living unit occup[ied] an entire wing of the structure, equipped with high speed elevators, intercommunication system [and] a steam laundry in the building." Such construction set a pattern for future developments. The previously underpopulated borough of Queens sprouted new neighborhoods. In Manhattan, Riverside Drive, Central Park West, and Park Avenue arose as elegant communities of large apartment buildings.[18]

Prospective tenants appreciated these houses' location within "subway suburbs." A quick and cheap commute on the subway to Manhattan offices, factories, or stores appealed to New York Jews. It allowed a merchant, a manufacturer, or even a worker to relocate the family to a wholesome, albeit urban, setting. Migration out of the Lower East Side did not necessarily signal movement into the middle class. Rather, it indicated greater stability in income, an ability to spend a bit more on housing, and the impact of unionization, as well as social and occupational mobility. Sometimes, children convinced parents to seek these better neighborhoods. But a cheap commute from home to job was critical. So "long as dwellings are within the 5 cent zone, such as new rapid transit routes afford," a real estate journal observed, "tenants are willing to go to the boroughs."[19]

Whole new communities coalesced within walking distance of rapid-transit lines. The South Bronx had elevated railroad links to downtown very early. However, a number of new subway lines after 1917 made much-larger regions accessible. Trains running over and under the East River brought Brooklyn and Queens neighborhoods closer to Manhattan. The Independent subway line (IND), built during the Depression, provided fifteen-minute service to Manhattan and transformed additional neighborhoods.[20]

As backers, beneficiaries, and builders of an expanding and refashioned New York, Jews continued their long-standing patterns of economic, industrial, and social behavior.[21] Becoming a builder involved knowing how to assemble workers and financing: from the architect to design and file the plans, to bosses who knew how to navigate an ethnically divided construction industry, to bankers who provided loans for each stage of construction. Jews moved from manufacturing buttons to building apartments with little difficulty. Where Jews built and worked, fellow Jews settled. This ethnic connection drove both construction and residential choices. Indeed, "the bonds of ethnicity supported ethnically separate construction industries catering to an ethnically distinct housing market."[22]

Rapid housing construction opened employment opportunities for Jewish skilled laborers. To gain a foothold in those industries, painters, plasterers, paperhangers, and decorators worked as scabs, agreeing to wages considerably less than those of other tradespeople. These maneuvers earned Jews the enmity of Irish-dominated construction trades unions, which usually denied membership to Jewish workers. So Jews formed their own "alteration unions," working on remodeling buildings.[23]

Once a building was ready to rent, entrepreneurs who owned and managed apartment houses got their message out to fellow Jews— through either word of mouth or local advertising. Then a chain migration commenced from older neighborhoods. For Jews who had risen out of factory work to owning a small business, an apartment on one of the major tree-lined avenues in the Bronx or in Brooklyn signaled success in America. Economic and social calculi called for them to invest heavily in their shop or industry while setting aside enough money to rent an appropriate home. Buying a house did not appeal to many; it promised neither status nor security and fulfilled no personal dream unavailable in a spacious apartment.[24]

Most New York Jews associated with their own kind, but some ventured into emerging Christian preserves and encountered rebuff. Such exclusions did not approach the discrimination that African Americans faced, but they were nonetheless insulting and influenced Jewish residential patterns. Edward McDougall, principal of the Queensboro Corporation, conceived of "a completely planned and largely self-contained community" in Jackson Heights, Queens, for Christians only. He built "the nation's first garden apartment suburb . . . for upper-middle-class New Yorkers." Like New York Jewish builders, the Protestant McDougall capitalized on the extension of rapid-transit links. By 1919, he planned for his customers to buy, rather than rent, their own apartments. Quickly, some six hundred families purchased homes. But he accepted neither Jews nor Catholics nor, for that matter, dog owners.[25]

McDougall advertised his intentions on city buses with real estate code words: "Restricted Garden Residential Section." Nonetheless, some determined Jews tried to buy an apartment. The routine went as follows: "A man went there and applied for an apartment and would be then taken by the agent on the way to be shown the apartment. . . . He would give his name and if it was a Jewish name he was immediately notified that there was no use looking any further that they would take no Jews." These details entered public record when McDougall sued a contractor for failure to fulfill a mortgage obligation. The contractor claimed that Queensboro had acted "arbitrarily or capriciously in the selection or rejection . . . of tenants," which had limited his pool of applicants. The judge sided with McDougall and affirmed his right to exclude "persons of Jewish name, origin or parentage who were otherwise desirable . . . and financially solvent." That decision kept Jews out of Jackson Heights until the 1950s.[26]

Residential discrimination against Jews also occurred in the Forest Hills Gardens section of Queens. Envisioned as a "planned residential community" by reformers for "persons of modest means," its preferred clientele excluded Jews and Catholics. Some Jews broke into the restricted Gardens, but more often Jews lived on its outskirts. Benjamin Braunstein designed elegant apartments on the periphery of Forest Hills to "resemble the . . . Gardens architectural pattern." With classy names like Devon Hall, buildings sported "Doric front columns, arched windows and colonial revival pediments" and rented to Jews.[27]

On the threshold of congressional immigration restriction in 1924, Jewish households helped to define New York as a Jewish city. Jewish New Yorkers, mostly immigrants and their children, constituted close to 28 percent of the city's population. How people dressed and talked, how they furnished their apartments, what they ate and did with their leisure time—all contributed to a sense of Jewishness conditioned by both class and distance from immigration. The Jewish home, less crowded than it had been on the Lower East Side, was the ultimate Jewish space. Decisions made at home by parents and their children influenced the street, since local businesses gratified collective proclivities of nearby residents, and tastes intersected with resources to afford types of housing that produced distinctive neighborhood styles of life.[28]

Interwar-era New York Jews found their niches in a wide variety of urban milieus. These Jewish neighborhoods included grimy tenement districts, blocks of well-appointed elevator apartment buildings, and leafy streets of single- and two-family homes. Some housed poor Yiddish-speaking immigrants and their children, others relatively secure working-class families, still others a striving native-born English-speaking middle class. Then there appeared a few areas for those who had already reached the top. Divided by class, Jewish sections also acquired varied religious, political, and cultural attributes.[29]

The Upper West Side, whose cavernous streets were lined with elegant apartment buildings, epitomized the opposite of the Lower East Side. The city's wealthiest Jewish neighborhood, often called "a gilded ghetto," the area housed prosperous manufacturers, professionals, and other businesspeople, with a median family income almost seven times that of the older area. Some upwardly mobile Jews found apartments in new buildings and remained downtown, where the city's poorest Jews resided. Most preferred newer sections with recently constructed apartment buildings, complete with elevators. If they struck it rich, they moved to the Upper West Side.[30]

Jews moved from crowded working-class areas, but they also rapidly abandoned Central Harlem, once home for a rising Jewish bourgeoisie. Tens of thousands of prosperous Jews left as African Americans moved in, although prior to World War I, Jews lived next door to African Americans. Jewish residents of Harlem had no memories of Jewish

2781–2785 Broadway, October 25, 1946, by Irwin Underhill. Underhill's photograph portrays the mix of buildings at the northwest corner of 107th Street and Broadway, part of the heavily Jewish neighborhood of the Upper West Side. A tall elevator apartment building shares the block with modest five-story modern tenements. Many Jewish garment manufacturers and businesspeople lived in the neighborhood as well as Jewish professionals and intellectuals. Courtesy of the Museum of the City of New York.

attitudes toward slavery in the city, but many gradually came to share a pervasive American bias that considered African Americans undesirable neighbors. However, Jewish landlords rented to African Americans. A federal housing study concluded that while the children of immigrants possessed the "possibility of escape, with improvement of economic status to more desirable sections of the city," among African Americans, "definite racial attitudes favorable to segregation interpose difficulties," restricting access to better residential areas. Jews could settle in Washington Heights, which abutted northwestern Harlem, for example, but a Neighborhood Protective Association pressured landlords, many of them Jews, to sign racially restrictive agreements.[31]

Jewish workers benefited from another important piece of state legislation: a 1926 law granted tax breaks to builders who limited dividends to 6 percent, established moderate rents, and opened their doors to tenants with low incomes. The Amalgamated Clothing Workers Union, among the largest predominantly Jewish labor groups, with a rank and file of some 175,000, secured mortgages from its own Amalgamated Bank, from the Yiddish socialist newspaper the Forward Association, and once the building was completed, from the Metropolitan Life Insurance Company. With these funds, the Amalgamated constructed a cooperative near Van Cortlandt Park in the West Bronx. These six cooperative apartment buildings, grouped around shared gardens, reflected the success of the Jewish socialist labor movement. The apartment complex bore witness to the union's recognition that it needed to address the cost of living for its members not just through wages but also through consumption. The Amalgamated cooperative represented upward and outward mobility through working-class collectivism.[32]

In the Amalgamated co-op, a family could occupy an apartment in a six-floor walk-up for a modest $500 investment per room—$150 down payment with monthly installments spread out over the next ten years—and an $11-per-month carrying charge. By contrast, just to rent a three- to five-room apartment on the Grand Concourse cost between $55 and $85 a month. Luckier co-op residents enjoyed "a view of Van Cortlandt Park, the waters of the city reservoir, and the palisades of the Hudson," as well as access to "tennis courts, ice skating and other outdoor recreation" available in the park. Subsequent construction added the convenience of elevators and expanded the co-op to some seven hundred families. Everyone enjoyed "landscaped gardens" around the buildings, and many participated in cooperative cultural and purchasing projects. A single meter registered electric usage in all of the co-op's apartments, and the co-op paid for electricity just as it did for heat. Residents also took advantage of rapid-transit facilities for "a quick and easy commute to jobs in Manhattan's garment district."[33]

Other ideologically committed Jewish laborers, like Jewish communist garment workers, joined co-ops facing Bronx Park, a few miles east from the Amalgamated. This radical project acquired financing through loans extended by its party's Yiddish newspaper, the *Morgen freiheit* (Morning freedom). The co-op offered deals to its residents comparable to the Amalgamated's. Concomitantly, Yiddishists established their Sholem Aleichem Houses, another Bronx cooperative. Similarly committed socialist Zionists created the Farband Houses. In each project, developers did more than provide housing. They built libraries, auditoriums, day-care nurseries, classrooms, and gymnasia, all aimed at creating and nurturing an ideological community of neighbors.[34]

Because migration within New York sorted people according to ethnicity, religion, politics, and class, Sephardic Jewish families who left the Lower East Side also regrouped. Many Syrian Jews, for example, headed for Brooklyn, specifically the Bensonhurst neighborhood, which also attracted second-generation Italian New Yorkers.[35]

On the eve of the Great Depression, Brooklyn and the Bronx surpassed Manhattan as centers of Jewish residence. Whether rich or poor, struggling or just surviving, New York Jews of the interwar decades lived largely in distinctive, identifiable neighborhoods. A decade of extensive intracity migration "produced the seeming paradox of concentrated dispersal" as "the process of migration intensified Jewish residential segregation," with two-thirds of New York Jews living in their own ethnic areas.[36]

Almost half the city's Jews lived in Brooklyn. Brooklyn neighborhoods ran the gamut, yet class did not always correlate with religion, culture, or politics. Some neighborhoods of working-class immigrants and their children became bastions of pious Orthodoxy, and others harbored a strong radical contingent. Similarly, middle-class areas could be strongly modern Orthodox or identified with Conservative Judaism and Zionist politics. Jews moved from one area to another, usually based on class aspirations or for good public schools for their children. Occasionally some sought specific religious options.[37]

In the Bronx, where Jews made up nearly half the borough's population, upwardly mobile families moved from east to west. In the largely working-class but heterogeneous East Bronx, Yiddish-speaking manual workers and their families inhabited gritty industrial and tenement districts. The critic Irving Howe recalled that Fox Street symbolized for his parents the depths to which one might fall during the Great Depression. "At least we're not on Fox Street," his father would say philosophically during a crisis. Better-off workers occupied blocks around Crotona Park, living in moderately priced modern apartment buildings. The Workmen's Circle and garment unions gave the East Bronx a reputation for radicalism, secured by cooperative housing projects. To the west lay the Grand Concourse, the Bronx's "Fifth Avenue," though its white-collar residents were more middle class than wealthy, with average incomes lower than those of Brooklyn's better neighborhoods. As bourgeois and American as the Concourse seemed, moreover, it was 75 percent Jewish, one of the most solidly Jewish neighborhoods outside of Brownsville. Jewish families often traversed these neighborhoods as they climbed the socioeconomic ladder.[38]

The Great Depression put a crimp on Jewish mobility, except downward mobility. One by one, the experiments in cooperative housing, except for the Amalgamated, succumbed; unable to pay their debts, they were acquired by capitalists. Their demise amplified the voices of those who were most dedicated to class justice. Jewish communists especially redoubled efforts to prevent evictions and force landlords to roll back rents. The aptly named "Great Rent Strike War of 1932" mobilized thousands. Protestors fought pitched battles with police to prevent neighborhood people from being put out into the gutters. Communist leadership attracted the support of fellow Jews who harbored no partisan loyalties but empathized with those who suffered loss of their homes. In Brownsville, Jews fought evictions by distracting the police and moving families' furniture back into their apartments. At times, fighting evictions mobilized an entire neighborhood.[39]

New York neighborhoods gave Jews a sense of being at home within a multiethnic city that sometimes seemed remote, unwelcoming, and inaccessible. "We were of the city, but somehow not in it," the literary critic Alfred Kazin wrote of his own second generation. "I saw New York as a foreign city," he confessed. " 'New York' was what we put last on our address, but first in thinking of the others around us. *They* were New York, the Gentiles, America." Others echoed this sentiment, whether they came from Brownsville, like Kazin, or from the East Bronx. A sense of alienation from the city ran as an undercurrent within Jewish consciousness, inflecting their position as a minority, albeit a significant one, of New York's population. Wide swaths of the city—most of Queens and Staten Island and substantial pockets of Manhattan, Brooklyn, and even the Bronx—remained the property of others, not just, or even primarily, established Anglo-American Protestants, but various Catholic ethnic groups, which by this time together constituted a religious majority.[40]

Yet many Jews growing up in New York in the 1930s and 1940s enjoyed a sense of security in their neighborhoods that came from the
streets, schools, and extended families living nearby. "As a kid, I thought
everyone was Jewish," recalled Adolph Schayes, who grew up on Davidson Avenue, off Fordham Road in the Bronx. He had good reason to feel
that way. Although Jews shared the Fordham neighborhood with the
Irish, everywhere Schayes turned he saw Jews and Jewishness around
him. As a child, he accompanied his mother shopping at Kasowitz's
fruit store, Israel's meat market, and Efron's bakery. His peer group of
Jews, with "a token Irish," formed a club, the Trylons, named for the 1939
world's fair centerpiece. They walked their streets wearing their dark-
blue jackets, with the club's name lettered in orange on the back, and
hung out together. They found their competitive edge in sports. Schayes
grew up to be six foot eight and played basketball, eventually going on to
a professional career. But as a child, he lived in a Jewish world, including
the public schools he attended. So many Catholic kids went to parochial
schools that Jews made up the majority of students in public school and
many of the teachers. Schayes's experience typified that of many children of Jewish immigrants in New York.[41]

Despite a stable population just under eight million, New York continued to change. New construction added depth to Jewish neighborhoods. After World War II, the Amalgamated co-op in Van Cortlandt
added two large-scale, high-rise buildings assisted by government aid
and union activism. Cooperatives received a boost in 1955 when the New
York State Legislature passed the Mitchell-Lama law, providing for tax
abatement on middle-income cooperatives and authorizing power of
eminent domain in return for limitations on profits and income of cooperators. Jewish builders and residents employed these regulations to
maintain New York's reputation as "the unrivaled co-op housing capital
of the nation."[42]

Postwar Developments

In the postwar years, real estate operators and construction companies
helped build a new cityscape, modulating the interwar urban ideal.
Queens Boulevard joined "the great boulevards of Brooklyn [and] the

Bronx" as "essentially 'Jewish' avenues, built by Jewish developers for a Jewish clientele." Newspapers described "suburban apartments which provide open-air balconies or terraces . . . and garage spaces for tenants' automobiles," not only on Long Island but also within the city limits. The speed of new construction amazed New Yorkers. One Jewish builder bragged that he set a "postwar record" in completing a six-story elevator apartment house in only four months. Financed in part by the sale of a Bronx apartment building, he and his associates constructed the Rhoda House (probably named for his wife) in Forest Hills. They outfitted each of the forty-two apartments with fancy "household appliances, such as refrigerators and modern kitchen ranges."[43]

Other Jewish developers of housing in Queens pitched their postwar enterprise to appeal to Jews contemplating suburbanization. Claiming affordable elegance only a brief subway ride "to the office, the Fifth Avenue shops, the theatre," they described their "three luxurious 21 story skyscrapers" as "an entire suburb within a suburb," minus the hassle of commuting. They capitalized on the prime flaw of suburban life: the daily trek of breadwinners to jobs in the city. They advertised, "78% of the land given over to landscaped private grounds, malls, fountains!"— amenities that reflected a popular urban architectural concept of the tower in the park. All apartments possessed "unobstructed views, . . . covered balcony terraces, . . . Westinghouse air conditioning," and "uniformed doormen." Residents "marked their upward passage by moving from elevator buildings to so-called 'luxury apartments.'" Each advertised item—balconies, views, air-conditioning, garages, private gardens, and uniformed doormen—signaled status within reach of middle-class Jews, much as elevators, windows in every room, modern plumbing, gas stoves, and light and air had previously promised American living for aspiring immigrants and their children.[44]

Jewish builders operated at both ends of the socioeconomic spectrum. The LeFrak family built extensive projects in Queens for "the masses not the classes." Like other Jewish builders whose sons entered the family firm, LeFrak drew on a heritage dating to the early years of the century, when immigrant father Aaron and his son, Harry, focused on housing for working-class Jews, first on the Lower East Side and then in Brooklyn. Their most ambitious early efforts involved construction of small houses and walk-up apartment buildings in Brooklyn. After the war, the family, now headed by Harry and his son, Samuel, shifted to Queens, starting off with a 136-family project named the Colorado. With the rise of LeFrak City, a mammoth complex of five thousand apartments that took a decade to build, the family acquired a reputation of "giving the people what they wanted, at a price that they could afford to pay." Modest monthly rents of "$40 a room or $120 for a one-bedroom apartment" provided tenants with "total facilities for total living," which included tennis and swimming. These middle- and upper-class sports required expensive equipment, unlike basketball and baseball, which were most popular among working-class New York Jewish boys. In the 1960s, the heyday of this construction, LeFrak "built an apartment every eighteen minutes."[45]

Textures of Jewish life endured in the Bronx as many Jews saw no reason to leave their no-longer-new neighborhoods. Memoirists reflected on continuities in lifestyle and street culture. Ruth Glazer, who in 1949 was doing research and editorial work for the Amalgamated Clothing Workers Union, thought there was "more life, vigor and excitement in one single Bronx apartment house at six o'clock in the evening than in a thousand elm-lined Main Streets on a Fourth of July." She described the West Bronx as a "community whose residents seem occupied full time in discovering the wonderful things produced in the world that can be had for even the moderate amount of money at their disposal." Like those who rhapsodized in the 1920s about all that was right in their neighborhood, Glazer wondered "what streets anywhere can match them in their sheer number of food stores, ice-cream parlors, delicatessens, restaurants, specialty shops for women and children." In these venues, neighbors enjoyed sociability. Even in the butcher shops "a leisurely, almost club-like atmosphere" flourished among women, especially on Thursday mornings when Sabbath shopping began. "Then the butcher holds court, announcing his opinions on the world, commenting on departing customers." Just like in the past, "the role of the Concourse in Bronx life, like its geographical location is central." While "its once aristocratic buildings have become shabby and it no longer has its former prestige," still "it is a name to conjure with." Ultimately, for Glazer, "the present generation" embellished "Bronx style."[46]

The writer Vivian Gornick evoked similar street scenes within the West Bronx. Everywhere she turned, there "was Jewishness in all its rich variety. Down the street were Orthodox Jews, up the street were Zion-ists, in the middle of the street were shtetl, get-rich-quick Jews, European humanist Jews." Irrespective of their level of commitment, "Jewishness was the leveler." Coming from a radical, secular background, Gornick recalled that "observance" involved watching other Jews on the avenue on Jewish holy days. "The whole world shut down, everyone was dressed immaculately and a sense of awe thickened the very air we breathed. The organic quality of the atmosphere told us who we were, gave us bound-ary and idiomatic reference, shaped the face of the culture in which each one of us assumed a vital, albeit primitive, sense of identity."[47]

Even as many Jews, especially those who had served in the military and benefited from the GI Bill, left the city for the suburbs, New York Jews maintained a style of life inherited from their parents ensconced in their neighborhoods. The arrival of refugees and survivors of the Holo-caust changed the character of some neighborhoods, such as Washing-ton Heights and Williamsburg, without disrupting established patterns. Although interethnic tensions, especially with the Irish, diminished, definable turfs within and among neighborhoods endured. Youth gang warfare neither targeted Jews as victims nor engaged them as antago-nists. Around half of New York Jews lived in neighborhoods where they made up at least 40 percent of the population. Thus, they experienced the city in the postwar decades as even more Jewish than it was, since Jews constituted less than 30 percent of the city's total population.[48]

New York Jews' possession of a neighborhood meant that the sounds, smells, and sights of their own ethnic bonds abounded and radiated from the streets. On their own turf, New York Jews answered unself-consciously to no other voices or commands. They spoke their own lan-guage, usually unaccented English flavored with Yiddish idioms, told their own insider jokes, relished their favorite foods, observed their own calendar, and socialized with friends who understood their idiomatic New York culture.

Residential segregation characterized New York City. Jews knew that African Americans also lived in the city, but they rarely encoun-tered them. For example, as of 1957 on the Grand Concourse, African Americans constituted only 3.5 percent of its population. A comparable story could be told in Brooklyn. In some sections, almost no African Americans lived—a couple hundred in Borough Park, a few thousand

Co-op City, 1973, by Gary Miller. Co-op City, a massive housing project in the North Bronx, under construction in this photo, represented the culmination of New York's investment in cooperative housing for working- and middle-class residents. Pioneered by Jewish immigrants and produced most successfully by the Amalgamated Clothing Workers Union in the interwar decades, cooperatives were adopted as a tool of urban renewal after World War II. Co-op City drew thousands of Jews from other Bronx neighborhoods, especially the Grand Concourse, hastening their decline. Courtesy of Prints and Photographs Division, Library of Congress.

in Flatbush. These areas, respectively, housed 63,000 and 123,000 Jews. By contrast, in poverty-stricken Bedford-Stuyvesant, two-thirds of its 253,000 residents were black, but only 11 percent were Jews. Even when African Americans made up a quarter of the population, as they did in Crown Heights, Jewish children growing up didn't notice them. The historian Mark Naison recalled, "there were only a sprinkling of black families in the fifteen blocks between Eastern Parkway and Kings County Hospital," his key neighborhood landmarks, and "most of them seemed solidly working class." He frankly allowed that most blacks in Crown Heights were seen only by day as domestics, "girls" who "arrived in a group on the Kingston Avenue bus from Bedford-Stuyvesant and left by the same route in the evening." To the extent that there were subsurface "racial issues in my neighborhood," he added, they "did not have much impact on my early childhood." Jewish children growing up in New York City in the 1950s lived in a multiethnic city and attended public schools, but most of them remembered instead secure childhoods in largely white Jewish neighborhoods.[49]

New York Jews were comfortable where they were and among whom they lived, and they took the cheap and quick, if often crowded, subways together to work, as their parents did before them. Urban residential areas "linked to the central business district by the extraordinarily rapid transit facilities" were "the real 'bedroom communities' . . . even more so than the classic suburban county of Westchester." As late as 1948, a single ride cost but five cents; only after 1966 did the fare rise above fifteen cents. Bronx garment workers—cutters, pressers, or finishers—could leave their homes at 7:30 a.m. and be certain to punch the clock in the Garment Center by 8:00. They returned home to shop and socialize among Jews.[50]

Public transit facilitated enjoyment of the city's culture, an alternative to suburbanization and its private pleasures. An inexpensive night out on a warm summer's evening might include an open-air concert on the hard stone seats of CCNY's Lewisohn Stadium, where the New York Philharmonic performed outdoors. Alternatively, local movie theaters offered double features in air-conditioned comfort. Or Jews might "gather in groups on weekday evenings to watch their favorite shows." Aware of suburban options, many New York Jews eschewed them. Their children laughed at *Mad* magazine's send-up of suburbanization by Jewish writers and illustrators who had grown up in the Bronx. Listeners to one of Brooklyn-born Carole King's early records might have noticed that "Pleasant Valley Sunday" critiqued suburban life in what she called "status-seeker land." Yet King, the daughter of a New York schoolteacher and a firefighter, also enjoyed spending summers in a bungalow colony in Connecticut that was founded by the Ner Tormid Society, the Jewish firefighters' fraternal organization.[51]

Growing older, members of an American-raised generation felt impatient with their neighborhoods. Eager to claim Manhattan's cosmopolitan opportunities, they discovered that these had been shaped in many ways by the cumulative impact of immigrant Jews. As Jews became "walkers in the city," they grasped how generations of Jewish immigrants had bequeathed to New Yorkers patterns of association, labor, culture, politics, and religion. Moorish synagogues in midtown spoke to the way Jewish synagogues helped cultivate New York's tolerance and pluralism; Macy's and other department stores advertised specials for Jewish holidays, reminding consumers of Jewish engagement with commerce; garment factories in the West Thirties attested to the centrality of this city industry; rallies in Union Square pointed to the strength of radical and labor movements.

Despite Jewish New Yorkers' feeling that their neighborhoods stood somehow apart from the city as a whole, New York had already become in some senses a "Jewish city." At over a quarter of the population, Jews profoundly influenced the city's culture, politics, and economy. Of course, the city shaped them as well. This was perhaps especially true of the second and third generations, those who were born or raised in New York, who were becoming the dominant segment of the community.

Chalk Games, by Arthur Leipzig, 1950. Inspired by a Breughel painting of children playing, the Brooklyn-born Jewish photographer Arthur Leipzig set out to photograph children's games throughout the city. Street games defined growing up in the city for Jewish children, as much a part of their formative experience as living in small apartments. His image of chalk games played by boys on a city street illustrates aspects of an urban working-class childhood characteristic of the lives of children of Jewish immigrants in New York: gendered, unsupervised play on streets designed to accommodate traffic. © Arthur Leipzig. Courtesy of Howard Greenberg Gallery.

7

Raising Two Generations

September 1960. For two days, on Thursday and Friday, the New York City public schools closed their doors to honor the Jewish New Year. This unprecedented recognition of Jewish religious identity marked one kind of arrival of New York Jews. For years, demographers trying to estimate the Jewish population of the city had used "the Yom Kippur method," which counted the number of absences in public schools on that day, compared them to a "standard" day, and then extrapolated an approximate total population count from the presumed absent Jewish students. Of course, not only Jews took off on Yom Kippur. Especially in schools with largely Jewish student bodies, Christian students often yielded to temptation to enjoy a break from their lessons since not much was done in mostly empty classrooms. But by 1960, although Jewish children made up only a third of the public school students, Jewish teachers constituted 45 percent of the teaching staff, and Jews were a majority among school principals. A mix of pragmatism and politics suggested that closing the public schools would relieve widespread absences at the same time as it gestured to a significant Jewish presence in the city. Thus, the High Holidays joined Christmas in the New York City public school calendar along with combined Easter and Passover vacations.[1]

Jews' massive numbers and concentrated distribution throughout the city allowed them "to embrace a vision of the city as a whole," without losing sight of themselves as a distinct group.[2] Raising children in New York, Jewish parents—both immigrant and second generation—sought to find ways to participate in American life even as they maintained a sense of Jewishness. Unlike other large cities, New York offered a free education extending from elementary school through college. Thus, many New York Jews aspired to acquire a college education, even if only a small percentage fulfilled this dream. Jews also observed the city's religious and ethnic diversity, borrowing ideas and practices from their Catholic neighbors to fashion new ways to be Jewish. While Jews faced ongoing discrimination in opportunities for work, they possessed the possibility of establishing ethnic niches in the city that sustained them during economic crises, like the Great Depression, and provided socioeconomic mobility during periods of prosperity. Out of this mix of promise and prejudice emerged several generations of New York Jews.

Religious Innovations

Rhythms of Jewish living traditionally revolved around weekly Sabbath observance and an annual cycle of holidays punctuated by life-cycle events. Jewish modes of observance informed daily living, especially in food consumption but also in regular morning, afternoon, and evening prayers. Men and women participated differently in these religious patterns, since only men were expected to lay tefillin each day as part of their prayer ritual and to attend worship services on Sabbaths and holidays. Women fulfilled their religious obligations domestically, lighting Sabbath candles and making sure, through their shopping and cooking, that their homes were kosher, fit for their families. Parents shared responsibilities for raising children, teaching them how to read Hebrew and how to pray, along with knowledge of Jewish culture, ethics, and history. But even here gender differences dictated how boys and girls learned to be Jewish.[3]

New York City—its economic demands, Americanization pressures, and political attitudes—assaulted male normative practices, especially those of public prayer, while allowing for preservation by Jewish immigrants and their children of a new mix of folk, domestic, and elite forms of Judaism. This blend emphasized annual holiday and life-cycle events, especially bar mitzvah and marriage. Simultaneously, capitalist markets, congregational freedoms, and organizational initiatives encouraged innovative forms of urban Judaism. Eventually religious pluralism came to characterize experiences of Jewish lived religion in the city. As with other aspects of New York Jewish culture, religious experiments that took root in the city found adherents among Jews across the United States.

Faithfulness to dietary laws, or kashrut, signaled observance of Jewish traditions. Eastern European Jews created a large market for kosher goods, and many companies, whether owned by Jews or non-Jews, sold kosher products. Food manufacturers targeted Jewish consumers with advertisements explicitly touting their products as kosher. Some companies established by immigrant Jews, such as Gellis, Horowitz-Margareten, Rokeach, and Hebrew National, catered mainly to a kosher market. They added rabbinic seals of approval to their packages testifying to their ritual purity. Even before World War I, national brands such as Quaker Oats, Babbitt's Cleanser, Borden's Condensed Milk, Uneeda Biscuits, Proctor & Gamble Crisco shortening, and many items from General Foods and Heinz 57 Varieties carried rabbinic seals as well.[4]

Yet as it became easier to keep kosher, a contradictory trend developed: fewer Jews chose to maintain kosher homes, though they might adopt stricter standards at holiday times. Consumption of kosher meat in New York City fell even before immigration restriction. Simultaneously, many Jews transferred their previous concerns for ritual purity to sanitary standards in processed foods. Advertisers soon recognized the implicit equation. As early as 1912, Borden's adopted the slogan "Pure Means Kosher—Kosher Means Pure." As New York Jews abandoned kashrut, they embraced a modern preference for recognizable brands of packaged goods with reliably predictable quality. Many Jews, however, favored distinctive items, chosen in response to advertising that set their diets apart from non-Jewish New Yorkers. This innovation took kashrut observance away from rabbinic authority and placed it in the hands of individual consumers, who decided what to purchase. "Kosher style," an alternative to kosher, signaled Jewish partiality for certain flavors, such as pastrami and pickles, and disdain for others, such as cheeseburgers that mixed meat and dairy.[5]

Food also played a key role as New York Jews elaborated life-cycle events. They especially endowed bar mitzvahs as occasions for celebrations that gradually shifted the focus away from the synagogue toward the catering hall. Relatively modest parties in honor of a thirteen-year-old boy achieving adulthood within the context of Jewish religious practice expanded into expensive events, with formal invitations, music, dancing, and large catered meals. Recognizing a need to provide some ritual for these Saturday-evening parties, Brooklyn Jewish caterers invented a candle-lighting ceremony that improvised on American birthday celebrations. At the high point of the evening, a cake topped with thirteen candles arrived and the bar mitzvah boy called on thirteen adults, usually family members whom he wished to honor, to light a candle. The new ritual caught on and spread beyond the city.[6]

Bar mitzvahs pulled teenagers and their families into synagogues during one year, but after that year passed, many New York Jews reverted to a practice common already in the nineteenth century of attending services only on the High Holidays. A pre–World War II survey showed that religious social activities—not to mention services—ranked dead last among some fifty leisure-time activities for Jewish teens, males and females, and those in their early twenties. Many enjoyed simply "walking or hanging around." The neighborhood mattered more than the synagogue.[7]

Mordecai M. Kaplan, among the most innovative rabbis in New York City, proposed a major change in Jewish religious life when he called up his oldest daughter—he had four of them—to read from the Torah one Sabbath in 1922 when Judith was thirteen. Moved by the recent passage of the Nineteenth Amendment, which gave women the right to vote, Kaplan reasoned that girls as well as boys should be initiated into Jewish adulthood through a parallel ritual of bat mitzvah demonstrating their mastery of Hebrew prayers and Torah reading. Judith's father considered this invention part of his challenge to Judaism's status quo on many theological and ritual fronts, leading eventually to the rise of Reconstructionist Judaism. But it also reflected, as Judith Kaplan Eisenstein recalled decades later, "a conscious feminism in our household." The Kaplans were far ahead of their time; bat mitzvah did not become commonplace until after World War II. Although this novelty appalled Kaplan's Orthodox mother, who warned him that his rabbi father was turning over in his grave, Kaplan persisted in his insistence that Jewish women were equal to Jewish men and that both deserved to participate in public Jewish religious ritual.[8]

New York Jews also innovated at the end of life. Traditionally, Jews allocated responsibility for burying the dead to a voluntary association, *hevre kadisha* (holy association), which ritually washed and dressed the body (*tahara*), prepared the simple pine coffin (when coffins were required for burial), and escorted the body to the cemetery. Men cared for men, and women cared for women. Jews established cemeteries at the city's edges since Judaism required the dead to be buried beyond residential areas. Often the purchase of land for a cemetery preceded the organization of a congregation in a city. The dead needed a place to rest among Jews; the living could live among non-Jews.

But as New York grew, distances between where Jews lived—and died—increased until Jews had to hire transportation to take their dead for burial. Communal practices that had taken care of interment struggled to keep up with a burgeoning Jewish population. More and more people died in hospitals, necessitating two trips: first to take the corpse home and then to the cemetery. The undertaker, a "species of middleman made necessary by the complexities of the modern city," gradually superseded the traditional burial society.[9]

At this point, enterprising Jewish delivery drivers and undertakers realized that they could expand their business if they offered additional services. Jews rejected embalming, which swept the United States as a result of the Civil War. Nor did they care for cremation. But crowded tenement apartments made purifying a corpse difficult, even with the requirement of immediate burial, usually within twenty-four hours. In addition, modern bureaucracy requiring registration of deaths spurred specialization. So the delivery drivers and undertakers teamed up to assume these tasks. They handled the city-mandated details, removed the corpse to a funeral "parlor" that mimicked the room where a family would have placed the dead at home, prepared and clothed the body according to Jewish ritual, and transported it to the cemetery. Soon they tendered additional funeral "services," including a religious functionary to read psalms and give a eulogy. "By 1910, if not earlier, it was possible to bypass synagogue, hevre kadisha and lodge and go directly to a funeral director who would provide all of the necessary services, arrange for the purchase of a burial plot and secure the ministrations of a rabbi and cantor for the funeral."[10]

So popular did these commercialized and privatized funeral practices become that generations of New York Jews accepted them as traditional. Jewish undertakers evolved into funeral directors and established a number of large family chains of funeral homes, similar to those of Christians. Handling Jewish deaths in New York became a big business.[11]

In new neighborhoods settled by Jews after World War I, Sabbath and kashrut observance devolved largely into matters of personal concern,

Mother and Child, by Rebecca Lepkoff, c. 1950. Growing up on the Lower East Side, Rebecca Lepkoff started taking photographs in the 1940s. Her classes at the heavily Jewish New York Photo League encouraged her to develop a point of view. She trained her camera on her own neighborhood world, picturing those quotidian moments that captured relationships among people struggling to make a living. For much of the first half of the twentieth century, most Jewish women left paid employment after children were born. © Rebecca Lepkoff. Courtesy of Howard Greenberg Gallery.

while religious issues among Jews focused on synagogues, previously the domain of men. Even as eastern European and Sephardic Jews caught up to central European Jews who had made the Bronx and Brooklyn their homes when these boroughs were still remote, outlying districts, cultural divides persisted. Many of the former hesitated to join Reform congregations, preferring to start their own. Religious pluralism soon characterized many New York Jewish neighborhoods, where Orthodox and Conservative synagogues stood across the street from Reform temples.

Religious leaders of all Jewish movements bemoaned the empty seats in their sanctuaries on the Sabbath; however, Rabbi Kaplan proffered the most creative solution to Jewish disengagement with congregations. His "synagogue center" idea popularized a strategy that those who came to play might in time be convinced to stay to pray. Kaplan left his first experimental synagogue center, the Jewish Center in Manhattan, to establish the Society for the Advancement of Judaism and a new religious movement. Articulated in his magnum opus, *Judaism as a Civilization: Toward a Reconstruction of American-Jewish Life* (1934), Reconstructionism promulgated the concept of Judaism as an evolving civilization. Kaplan urged synagogues to become centers of neighborhood life, for families and not just for men, to exemplify Judaism's multiple dimensions, especially its cultural expressions. Synagogue centers could embody diverse modes of Jewish worship—in fact, the Jewish Center retained its commitment to modern Orthodoxy—along with gyms and pools in their shuls.[12]

According to Kaplan's formula, in the synagogue center, "all the members of the family would feel at home during the seven days of the week." An ideal synagogue-center building boasted not only a swimming pool and gym, together with spaces for worship both large and small, but also classrooms for religious education, a kosher kitchen and restaurant for elegant dining, a social hall for celebration of bar mitzvahs and weddings, a room for theatrical productions and public lectures, a library, and rooms for conversation and discussion. Such an elaborate, multifaceted building cost money, and many synagogue centers charged hefty dues for membership. Kaplan aimed to build social connections, using the center to make Jews more fully Jewish in all aspects of their lives. Israel Levinthal, a Kaplan disciple and rabbi at the Brooklyn Jewish

Brooklyn Jewish Center, Wurts Brothers, 1924. In new neighborhoods throughout Brooklyn and the Bronx, Jews erected synagogue centers. These impressive buildings combined religious worship with education and recreation. Often called "the shul, with a pool and a school," a synagogue center catered to the entire family rather than just to male worshipers, as had characterized many immigrant congregations. It also appealed specifically to local neighborhood residents, rather than to European hometown associations. Courtesy of the Museum of the City of New York.

Center, believed there was "magic" in this methodology. He thought the "magic" would appear when a "young man, entering the gymnasium class, would notice the announcement on the bulletin board that on the next evening a meeting would be held in the interest of Jewish refugees or for relief." With the young man's "interest aroused," he would then come to a weekday Forum lecture. "The chairman would announce that on the coming Friday eve, the rabbi would speak on this or that subject. . . . He would come to the services. If the services appealed to him, he would come again."[13]

Although a string of interwar synagogue centers in New York adopted this approach, they failed to inculcate regular attendance at religious services in many members. Those who placed worship at the heart of Judaism questioned whether athletes or artists would ever find their way from the synagogue's gym, classrooms, or auditorium to its sanctuary. During the Great Depression, many people with time on their hands turned to synagogue centers as secular Jewish retreats. Singers such as Sophie Tucker or Belle Baker performing at a congregational benefit packed the house and contributed toward filling strapped coffers. But such events that "blurred the boundaries between the world of Broadway and the world of the synagogue" did little to increase regular worship participation. In the Bronx, four thousand Jews may have attended High Holiday services at one synagogue center, not to mention those who, as always, congregated outside, but during the year, half-empty sanctuaries predominated.[14]

After World War II, synagogue centers acquired a new appeal as a means of inculcating Jewish identity in children. Neighborhood religious culture of Jewish Queens, described as a "midway point" between "the Big City and suburbia," did not initially radiate Jewishness. For many families from Brooklyn and the Bronx, their move to Queens "involved a new adventure in Jewishness, expressing itself in formal affiliation, for the first time in their lives, with a Jewish community institution." These Jews lived in a tolerant environment, where they watched a strengthening of social ties between their children and Christian friends that filled them with anxiety. Some parents trusted a Jewish center to entertain their children. They hoped that rather than congregating with a mixed crowd "at the neighborhood movies or ice-cream parlor, hanging out on the corner or even in the basement playrooms of one another's homes," Jewish boys and girls would gravitate to a center.[15]

The Forest Hills Jewish Center started when Jews, a small minority, kept a low social profile, but it enjoyed a heyday after World War II, when the neighborhood became distinctively Jewish. Rabbi Ben Zion Bokser expanded the center to include a commodious sanctuary, an auditorium for social activities, and a youth center. Some thirty social clubs and basketball, swimming, and boxing leagues attracted almost seven hundred children to its Hebrew school, with many bar and bat mitzvahs every week. The synagogue center thus adopted activities once associated with settlement houses and YMHAs. Only now parents, rather than Jewish philanthropists, paid for these.[16]

Orthodox Jews increasingly addressed identity issues less through their synagogues, which remained the domain of men, than through an emphasis on modern parochial schools. These differed from the yeshivas of the interwar period. Adopting the neutral term "day school," this movement moved beyond its core constituency of parents committed to traditional religious observance with the opening of the Ramaz School in Manhattan in 1937. Concerted efforts recruited children from families that were less committed to Orthodox Judaism. Ramaz convinced them of the value of parochial education.[17]

Such an effort appeared in Queens as well. Samuel Spar recruited six youngsters from observant families, starting with his son, to a fledgling school that offered a modern religious Zionist orientation. When it acquired its own building, it had seven grade levels. Initially, it relied on enrollment of children of Orthodox refugees from Hitlerism or survivors of the Holocaust who had settled in Queens. Soon pupils from "non-Orthodox" homes throughout the borough joined them.[18]

But religious heterogeneity stimulated tensions within the Yeshiva of Central Queens. The school day opened with recitation of morning prayers from the siddur (the Orthodox prayer book), grace accompanied meals, and boys wore yarmulkes and tzitzit (the fringed undergarment worn by Orthodox Jews). However, Conservative families objected strenuously when the school administration "introduced segregation of the sexes . . . not only in the class room, but also in the dining room and playground." Gender segregation in school, as in synagogue, proved to be a critical line dividing Orthodox from other modern forms of Judaism. Ultimately, those who "desire[d] a more liberal approach to Jewish education" determined that they had to have a school of their own. So they established the Solomon Schechter Day School of Queens. Subsequently Conservative day schools all over the country turned to this New York Jewish educational initiative as a model.[19]

Many Holocaust survivors gravitated to New York and made up a large proportion of roughly 130,000 German and Austrian Jews in the city. Anti-Semitism of a different sort propelled thousands of Sephardic Jews to America and especially to New York in the postwar decades. Driven by Arab anger over the rise and military successes of the State of Israel, popular animosities and governmental policies forced Jews from

Syria, Lebanon, Iraq, and Egypt to flee. Special congressional legislation passed in 1957 to help "victims of persecution," designed to assist Hungarian refugees from communism, also eased the way for Egyptian Jews to enter the United States.[20]

These Jewish newcomers, like so many immigrants before them, searched for familiar faces, essentially those men and women who shared their ethnic, social, and religious sensibilities. Orthodox Jews from eastern Europe gravitated to Brooklyn neighborhoods. The co-ops of the Bronx welcomed those who espoused socialist traditions. German-speaking Jews reconnected with refugee establishments in Washington Heights, while others settled on the West Side of Manhattan and in Queens. Sephardim moved into Brooklyn enclaves in Bensonhurst. Most noticeable of these newcomers, varying sects of Hasidic Jews established themselves in Williamsburg, Brooklyn, where they intensified the neighborhood's Orthodox Judaism.[21]

These pious Jews, following their rabbis' commands, not only "established their own new religious and communal centers" but also "changed the appearance of the neighborhood by" maintaining European habits and customs. Disdaining secular amusements, they converted local movie theaters into yeshivas. The streets filled daily with "men with long beards, kaftans, and all varieties, types and sizes of black hats, and women with wigs or kerchiefs and dark stockings." To the uninitiated, all of these Hasidim looked pretty much alike. But while Satmarer from Hungary were the largest new group in Williamsburg, the neighborhood housed more than a dozen sects from different parts of eastern Europe, each eager to preserve its own distinctive behaviors. Propinquity heightened another European tradition: disputes and rivalries among different Hasidic groups, each loyal to its own religious leaders' ideologies and practices. The leaven for controversy rose out of the city's ecology. Members of Hasidic courts, whether from Klausenberg or Belz or Munkacz or Vizhnitz, "that had once sprawled from Bratislava to Odessa," now nestled cheek by jowl and of necessity shared the sidewalks.[22]

By changing the neighborhood's character, survivors and refugees hastened the relocation of many erstwhile Jewish residents of Williamsburg to other parts of the city and suburbia. While they might have looked back with some disdain at an enclave referred to derogatorily as "refugeetown," their exodus opened up the area to even more Hasidim, who filled newly vacant apartments. A different Williamsburg resulted. After Hasidim from Williamsburg settled en masse in Borough Park in the 1960s, less pious American Jews relocated again.[23]

Crown Heights also become a Hasidic hub, home to the Lubavitchers, whose influence on Jewish life extended well beyond their neighborhood. Here, too, a transfer of Jewish populations occurred. While Lubavitchers followed their leader to the neighborhood, they still shared the streets with middle-class American Jews and other ethnic groups. As the Lubavitcher presence expanded, Crown Heights attracted Jewish visitors. Both the faithful and curious came to hear and see the popular rebbe Menachem Mendel Schneerson. His weekly Sabbath public lectures inspired his followers. Thousands crammed into the headquarters at 770 Eastern Parkway to listen. Eventually the world became his neighborhood as he broadcast his discourses, first on radio and then on television and video.[24]

Hasidim returned a visible Jewish religious presence to New York City. As the Lower East Side had advertised its religious Jewishness through signs for kosher butchers, matzo factories, and religious bookstores, Brooklyn's Hasidic neighborhoods refocused Jewishness on men and women walking the streets in their distinctive garb. These neighborhoods, even more than the Lower East Side, shut down on the Sabbath as well as Jewish holidays. They also reinvigorated public displays of Yiddish. Although they appeared to be in the city but not of the city, Hasidic Jews played an increasingly significant role in New York politics. Their growing numbers helped to distinguish New York Jews from Jews in other American cities. Their most significant innovation came from the Lubavitcher rebbe. Motivated by John F. Kennedy's call for a Peace Corps, Schneerson adapted the president's notion of service—in this case, to all Jews but especially unaffiliated ones—to recruit an army of emissaries spreading the possibility of doing a single mitzvah (commandment) on the streets of New York. From New York, these emissaries fanned out into the rest of the world, seeking to transform and redeem Jews, to bring them back to Jewish religious practice. For Lubavitch Hasidim, Brooklyn, not New York (and certainly not Israel), became the center of the Jewish world.[25]

Girl Learning to Skate, by N. Jay Jaffee, c. 1950. After serving in World War II, N. Jay Jaffee returned to his hometown of New York and started to photograph the city. He often pictured familiar working-class Brooklyn Jewish neighborhoods like Brownsville and East New York. Roller-skating was both a popular pastime for boys and girls and a fast means of getting around the neighborhood. Skates were strapped to shoes, and their clamps were tightened with a key; sidewalks provided ideal surfaces for speed. © N. Jay Jaffee. All rights reserved. Used by permission of The N. Jay Jaffee Trust, www.njayjaffee.com.

Higher Education

As more second-generation New York Jews graduated high school, many of them aspired to attend the city's colleges and universities, particularly its free, municipal-run institutions. A combination of prejudice and penuriousness brought most to local schools of higher education. There they made enduring friendships as they imbibed the intellectual excitement and political ferment that pervaded undergraduate life.

Informal and formal quota systems severely limited the numbers of Jews who attended the nation's elite private universities, especially from New York. Even if students changed their name on their application and fibbed in answering other personal information questions, a Brooklyn address, their parents' names and places of birth, a photograph that revealed to prejudiced admissions officers "semitic features," and a public school transcript announced that they were Jewish. Discrimination reduced the percentage of Jewish students at Columbia, New York City's only Ivy League school, from 40 percent in the early 1920s to 22 percent ten years later.[26]

Less prominent schools accepted Jewish students. Land-grant universities opened their doors. But it took both an adventurous, self-confident, and perhaps most importantly, sufficiently affluent young man or woman to seek these distant frontiers of learning. When New York Jews did arrive on these campuses and walk up to Jewish fraternities or sororities in search of friends, they discovered that Jews from other parts of the country rarely welcomed them. Other American Jews considered New Yorkers "undesirable." They were "loud, unrestrained, poor (or 'new rich'), lower-class, un-American . . . and either too traditionally religious or politically radical" to fit in.[27]

New York University, less prestigious than Columbia, tendered a mixed reception to Jews. Actually, NYU represented "the most striking dualism, a house divided against itself, to be found in the academic world." The school possessed a bucolic Bronx campus, founded before the borough became so Jewish, "as a men's country college, with the good old American collegiate spirit." However, the so-called old guard at NYU considered their "quiet, retired hill-top" world changed and undermined when "aliens," many of them Jews, began to attend. Anxious to restore the school's presumed racial-religious balance, school officials instituted "personal and psychological" tests to weed out Jews. They succeeded.[28]

The "other" NYU, particularly its undergraduate Colleges of Commerce and Education and its Washington Square College in Greenwich Village, where the school began back in the 1830s, extended a more hospitable welcome to Jewish men and women. In the 1920s, James Buell Munn, dean of the liberal arts college, Washington Square, spoke warmly of a mission to provide children of immigrants of both genders with "natural cultural opportunities" within his school. He wanted it to be a "laboratory" for inculcating American values while students strived to fashion productive careers. New York Jews responded by enrolling downtown in all three available branches. Whether or not Jewish undergraduates related to Munn's assimilatory message, they understood that they were welcome downtown. Munn facilitated a process of molding "an ethnically-diverse, cosmopolitan, largely urban intelligentsia" not only with his vision but also with money he inherited. Jews quickly constituted a majority of students at Washington Square College, many of them commuting each day back home.[29]

But most college-bound male Jews applied to New York's own competitive municipal colleges, especially City College of New York (CCNY), "the Cheder [Jewish school] on the Hill," in upper Manhattan. City College was their "Proletarian Harvard," where in the 1930s, close to 90 percent of the student body was Jewish. Those who got in understood what it meant to be beneficiaries of their school's century-old tradition of free tuition. The future *New York Times* editor A. M. Rosenthal recalled of his time as a high school senior, "I had absolutely no conversations with any of my classmates or with my parents about what college I would enter or try to enter." For Rosenthal, "there was only one choice. You either got into City College or you looked for a job in the Post Office." At no other college in America did the total daily cost of attendance reach "about 30 cents, . . . 10 cents for the round trip subway ride and about 20 cents for food."[30]

CCNY remained open and free largely due to the efforts of a galvanized student body. In 1932, during the Great Depression, students protested the city's attempt to "save $1,500,000 at the expense of the City College students." In an impassioned plea, they argued that the "establishment of fees would seriously cripple" the school's "enviable reputation" for "intellectual vigor," transforming a college renowned for its students' "mental ability" and bringing it "a step nearer to some of our country club establishments."[31]

The best CCNY students more than rewarded their alma mater for its uninterrupted largesse. A year after the tuition threat passed, three young men from poor Jewish families, who subsequently won Nobel Prizes in the sciences, enrolled. They were among seven CCNY men who were so honored for scientific research during the generation that spanned the Depression and the early postwar years. But perhaps Jonas Salk best epitomized how New York City, through its distinctive educational promise to its residents, benefited the nation and the world.[32]

The dark-haired research physician with thick eyebrows who ended the scourge of polio for millions entered CCNY at age sixteen. Salk started college aspiring to be an attorney. But poor grades and pressure from his mother moved him to the premed program, where he excelled. He focused intently on "class work, preparation and exams. . . . He joined no clubs, held no offices, won no honors, played no sports," and unlike most CCNY fellows, "made no life long friends." But upon graduation in 1933 at age nineteen, he had prepared for medical school.[33]

Salk, brilliant and lucky, gained admission to NYU's School of Medicine, where "tuition was comparatively low; better still, it did not discriminate against Jews." He then secured a coveted internship at Mount Sinai Hospital. But anti-Semitism almost denied him more advanced research opportunities. After Rockefeller University turned him down, a non-Jewish former mentor secured him a position at the University of Michigan. In order for Thomas Francis to get his disciple the opportunity, he had to refute the notion that Jews did not get along with people. From 1942 to 1947, Salk worked under Francis. Then he left for the University of Pittsburgh to direct its new viral-research program. Eight years later, he won international acclaim as "the man who saved children."[34]

The serious tenor that students like Salk brought to CCNY resembled that of most classmates intent on graduating, desiring to secure decent employment during the difficult Depression years. Living at home and commuting to school, they rushed back to part-time jobs. Without dormitories, CCNY fostered a different collegiate reality.[35]

Jewish women at Hunter College similarly found college life transitory. As at CCNY before World War II, Jews made up 80–90 percent of the student body. These undergraduates spent "more than half as much time in their underground campus—the subways"—as they did in classes, lectures, and laboratories. During such journeys, female students at Hunter and at Brooklyn College, which opened as a coed institution in 1930, perfected "the art of studying while straphanging." Yet undergraduates knew that they were a privileged minority. In many families, young women sacrificed their chances at higher education to give their brothers the opportunity to work only part-time while attending college. Jewish women contented themselves with jobs as bookkeepers, in sales, or as secretaries. Jewish male high school graduates were twice as likely as females to continue their education. Jewish men attended graduate and professional schools at a ten-to-one ratio to Jewish women.[36]

Liberal learning at CCNY offered unrivaled opportunities for a political education. Gathered in alcoves of the school's cafeteria, doctrinaire advocates of socialism and communism competed to convince others of the rightness of their cause. CCNY's indoor Jewish street possessed many kiosks, each manned by ideologists who engaged in legendary debates with Jewish spokesmen for different brands of radicalism, positioned provocatively in the next alcove. Alcove 1 contained a mix of "right-wing Socialists . . . to splinters from the Trotskyist left wing" to an even more "bewildering" array of "Austro-Marxists, orthodox Communists, Socialist centrists," not to mention "all kinds of sympathizers, fellow travelers, and indeterminist." When these peripatetic debaters were not battling among themselves, starting out with a civil call—"let's discuss the situation"—they engaged in intellectual combat with the people in Alcove 2, the home of the pro-Stalinist Young Communist League, headed by Julius Rosenberg.[37]

These advocates shaped campus culture. They attracted students to the alcoves to listen to arguments. "When that happened," one veteran of these battles has recalled, "a crowd gathered around the contestants, the way kids do, waiting for a fight to explode. But there were no fist fights, even when the provocations seemed unbearable." However, once the noise and excitement died down, listeners who did not share the depth of the alcove spokesmen's concerns drifted away to their worldly

Antiwar rally at the City College of New York, c. 1938. New York's free municipal colleges, especially City College for men and Hunter College for women, attracted large numbers of Jewish students, who set a tone of political activism and academic striving. For many New York Jews, City College was their "Proletarian Harvard," where close to 90 percent of the student body was Jewish in the 1930s. Courtesy of Archives, City College of New York, CUNY.

pursuits, classes, or part-time jobs. On the one hand, Irving Kristol, a youthful radical at CCNY who became an articulate neoconservative thinker, noted, "because of the kinds of kids that went there," from working-class Jewish backgrounds, possessed of some degree of radicalism in their families' traditions, "the entire student body was to one degree or another political." On the other hand, "most were passive politically, [and] the active types numbered in the hundreds." This endemic passivity frustrated radicals seeking to take their fights out of the alcoves and into the streets beyond CCNY.[38]

Women radicals at Hunter College similarly endured disappointment with their rank and file's unwillingness to commit to their causes. The most dedicated members of the college's Young Communist League endeavored to do it all. They traveled long distances from home, held part-time jobs, distributed party literature, solicited names on petitions, sold the *Daily Worker* on Manhattan street corners, and attended interminable political meetings on campus even as they made sure not to miss classes. Notwithstanding their activism, they, too, sought to earn credits for a teaching degree. Most other Hunter students, including many who agreed with activists' feelings about changing society, neither could nor would juggle home, job, social, and educational demands. Some feared that if word got out that they were troublemakers, they might lose their part-time jobs. Aspiring teachers understood that if the city Board of Education's Board of Examiners designated them as a "potential threat to the school system," they would be denied a coveted teaching license. Challenged and conflicted, most Hunter students lingered on the sidelines.[39]

The socialist Hal Draper, who first spoke out at Brooklyn College and remained with radical movements long enough to link up with New Left operatives in the 1960s, looked back at his and his comrades' efforts to create ideological strongholds in New York City colleges in the 1930s and estimated that only 1 percent joined the student groups. But their impact extended to "concentric rings of influence embracing different portions of the student body" around them. Some supported particular campaigns when issues touched home. Radical organizations found their widest and staunchest support at CCNY, Hunter, and Brooklyn in 1932, when they championed the students' ultimate gut issue: the crusade to maintain free tuition. Draper also argued that even those who never attended meetings and focused on their books and jobs "could not help absorbing the climate of ideas which pervaded the political life of the campus as a part of the larger society."[40]

Some students actively opposed leftists on campus.[41] The most aggressive opponents enrolled in the Reserve Officers Training Corps (ROTC). Like all organizations at the school, ROTC consisted predominantly of Jews.[42] These students opted to take two basic courses in military science as part of their college curriculum and upon graduation earn a commission in the United States Army. The corps also had its extracurricular component, including a band, a monthly, the *Lavender Cadet* (a reference to CCNY school colors), and a rifle team. It regularly conducted review parades through campus. Some students signed up because grading was apparently higher in military-science courses than in hygiene, while others joined on the eve of World War II in anticipation of U.S. involvement. But numbers enlisted because they agreed with the administration's social and political values. In the 1930s, CCNY, the renowned radical campus, had "the largest voluntary unit in the nation."[43]

After World War II, the percentage of Jewish students at CCNY gradually declined as opportunities for a college education in New York expanded to include additional four-year colleges as well as two-year community colleges and a graduate school. Many Jewish students understood a college education as a means of socioeconomic mobility. Getting into CCNY required a high grade point average that excluded most high school graduates. In 1970, in response to African American protests and political pressure, the City University of New York decided to guarantee all high school graduates an opportunity to enroll in college. This "open admissions" policy enormously increased the numbers of students on CCNY's campus, straining its resources. But by this time, many middle-class Jews chose to attend schools away from home. They matriculated either in the moderately priced, growing state university system or in private institutions that had once discriminated against Jews. NYU was still the city's second-largest Jewish school, with its sixteen thousand students uptown and downtown (40 percent of the student body). Columbia enrolled some sixty-five hundred Jews, 25 percent of its student body.[44]

New York's widening web of higher education—all of the boroughs acquired four-year free colleges as part of an expanded City University of New York—provided Jews with a ladder of opportunity unavailable elsewhere. Increasingly, New York Jews assumed that they could obtain a college education if they had the grades and worked hard enough. As attending college became routine for women as well as men in the post–World War II era, Jews shifted their occupational patterns and sought employment in those middle-class positions that required knowledge skills. Their rising educational status and investment in securing cultural capital prepared the children and grandchildren of immigrants for a changing city economy.

Occupational Niches

Immigrant Jews arrived in a city with a diversified and expanding economy encompassing manufacturing, commerce, transportation, construction, and finance. They quickly entered that world mostly as workers, finding employment through family and friends in industries dependent on the relative success of Jewish entrepreneurship. These patterns produced economic niches, with Jews working at all levels of an industry. Jews dominated the garment industry, one of the city's top sources of wealth and jobs, but they also concentrated in construction, printing, metal and machinery, baking and kosher meat, cigars and cigarettes. New York's industries, like its commerce, often consisted of relatively small units clustered throughout the city but most prominently in Manhattan and Brooklyn. Such economic structures encouraged entrepreneurship, spreading opportunities to rise into the middle class and distributing New York Jews along a broad socioeconomic spectrum. Indeed, most immigrants, after fifteen years of living in the city, earned as much as native-born workers did. Capitalism tempted Jews to try to change their position from worker to boss, and mobility characterized immigrant occupations. While many failed, those who succeeded recognized the fluidity of their class position, especially since the Great Depression dramatically reduced the livelihoods of all New Yorkers. New York Jews moved up and down the economic ladder, but gradually, immigrants, their children, and their grandchildren, the second and third generation, steadily enjoyed increased prosperity and security.

"Economic insularity, the availability of internal mobility ladders, the advantageous location of Jews in an industry that was rapidly growing for which they brought relevant skills, and the unusual overlap of segregated workplaces and homes" produced a "great paradox." This long "initial stage of segmented economic incubation" turned out to give Jews an exceptional platform for achievement. Jews faced discrimination in a host of occupations, most of them in large industries such as utilities, insurance, or telephone companies. *Fortune* magazine assured its readers in the midst of the Depression that Jews "very definitely" did not run banking. Nor did they work in large insurance companies, and they played a limited role in the stock exchange. Except as taxi drivers, most New York Jews did not work in transportation. Not until Mayor Fiorello La Guardia opened up civil service positions to merit-based examinations could they aspire to work in the city's many bureaucracies. La Guardia's merit-based appointment system benefited Jews in their battles for city jobs against the Irish, who often lacked academic credentials. Many New York Jews sought the security that a civil service job offered. But with Depression cutbacks, neither a high school diploma nor a college degree guaranteed employment. These exclusions forced Jews to rely on each other for employment and to employ themselves in their own small retail and commercial establishments. As Jews organized unions not just in the clothing industry but also of retail clerks, teachers, social workers, and pharmacists, they often confronted other Jews with demands for decent pay and working conditions. Jews thus continued a tradition of radicalization and support for socialism and communism into the 1930s.[45]

Second-generation Jews replicated many patterns of behavior of their immigrant parents. Although many of the second generation attained much higher education levels and even attended college, they reconcentrated in new economic niches. So many Jews entered such fields as law, medicine, accounting, and public school teaching that cultural stereotypes appeared. "My daughter, the teacher" took her place next to "my son, the doctor" in the proud litany of a stereotyped Jewish mother. Yet as with industrial and commercial employment, Jewish lawyers worked in Jewish law firms, not the leading "white shoe" corporate firms; Jewish hospitals admitted Jewish doctors, though many remained general practitioners. Even professional degrees did not promise prosperity. Those who broke through difficult barriers to become physicians and dentists did not get lucrative positions. Often professional practitioners relied on an informal network, as Jews turned to other Jews as clients, patients, and customers.[46]

But the enormous expansion of a public hospital system in New York City along with extension of mandated public education to four years of high school greatly enhanced Jewish occupational opportunities. For decades, Jews made up substantial percentages of new teachers entering the city's public school system; its enlargement created avenues of internal mobility for men and women to become principals. This career, popular among Jewish women and men, also connected Jews with other Jews in the city despite competition. Many of the brightest Jewish college graduates turned to secondary school teaching. However, growth of the City University of New York promised the most intellectually accomplished a chance to teach at the university level if they successfully pursued advanced study. Anti-Semitic policies that had excluded Jews from university employment retreated after the Second World War under the impact of the GI Bill and intensive Jewish efforts to challenge discrimination through legislation.[47]

This dynamic interplay of opportunity and promise, combined with exclusion and concentration, spurred Jewish economic innovation. Embracing canonical traditions associated with English and American literatures, New York Jews dove into the business of culture. They entered not just mass entertainment industries such as radio and television but also high-cultural industries like publishing, as well as those located midway between the popular and elite, such as theater and journalism. Leading second-generation Jews of central European background shifted from money making to culture making, sensing opportunities to earn a livelihood in these expanding fields. While eastern European Jewish immigrants enjoyed reading some of the great European writers in Yiddish translations, their children, educated in public schools that taught Shakespeare and George Eliot, absorbed English literature even as some of them recognized its specifically Christian bias. So inspired, a number desired to become cultural authorities themselves.

"Precisely because they were discouraged from pursuing careers in English departments, blackballed from genteel publishing firms, and excluded from meetings of the most prestigious publishers and advertisers," New York Jews "had to create alternative mechanisms of cultural expression and dissemination." Thus, they entered high-culture industries as "a subversive force" and changed the nature of the literary field. Beginning with Alfred Knopf, who left Doubleday to found his own

Blanche and Alfred Knopf. Although the publishing house bore Alfred Knopf's name, Blanche Knopf played a key role in its success. The center of publishing as well as printing shifted to New York City in the twentieth century as Jewish editors, writers, and publishers introduced new types of books (such as paperbacks), innovative modes of marketing (such as Book of the Month Club), and translations of European authors. Courtesy of the Prints and Photographs Division, Library of Congress.

firm with his wife, Blanche, Jews upended the city's publishing industry. A number apprenticed with Knopf and then went on to start their own firms: Horace Liveright of Boni and Liveright, Richard Simon and Max Schuster of Simon and Schuster, George Oppenheimer of Viking Press. Ultimately Bennett Cerf of Random House swallowed up Modern Library and Knopf itself.[48]

These Jewish publishers transformed the industry and successfully competed with Boston firms, making New York City the center of trade-book publishing in the United States. They provided sustenance for New York Jewish writers, bohemians, and radicals to earn a paycheck and especially gave professional Jewish women a place to work. They not only published translations of European writers, risked publishing writers who challenged obscenity laws, and brought new authors to a burgeoning American middle class, but they also created new markets and ways to reach them through innovative advertising, inexpensive paperback books, and fresh marketing and distribution techniques (e.g., selling books in train stations). In short, they revolutionized the industry and "the very texture of American culture itself." And in patterns familiar to New York Jews, many of these editors, writers, publishers, and other white-collar workers in the industry chose to live near each other, either uptown on the West Side of Manhattan or downtown in Greenwich Village.[49]

Jewish entrepreneurs cultivated a willingness among their fellow New York Jews to pay for culture. One leading sociologist emphasized that "large symphony orchestras, the theatres, trade-book publishing, the avant-garde magazines, the market for drawings and paintings, all have as their principal audience and consumer, the Jewish middle-class." Middle-class Jews running small businesses generated enough money to sustain a vibrant culture scene in the city because they possessed disposable income that they were ready to spend on books, art, theater, and music, rather than on suburban houses, fancy cars, boats, and expensive sports. Thus, "the entrepreneurial wealth of small-unit firms" fueled diverse cultural activities in the city, both popular and elite.[50]

As most Jewish workers left the garment industry when ready to enjoy Social Security benefits and union pensions, smaller numbers continued as manufacturers and designers. The latter group introduced Jewish fashion ideas to American culture. Not since Levi Strauss developed blue jeans or Ida Cohen Rosenthal, Enid Bisset, and William Rosenthal created the Maidenform bra had Jews helped to shape clothing design for so many Americans. The "enterprising garment industry" carried a Jewish stamp even if fewer Jews actually produced clothing on Seventh Avenue, the new location where garment factories had migrated. Jews continued to sell clothing, through diverse venues ranging from Fifth Avenue and Brooklyn department stores to Fifty-Seventh Street specialty shops to cut-rate operations on Manhattan's Union Square and Fordham Road in the Bronx. The clothing industry remained relatively easy to enter as an entrepreneur. Surviving required similar techniques of cost cutting employed by Jewish manufacturers in the years of mass immigration, even if unionization had helped to reduce sweatshop conditions.[51]

Both Ralph Lauren and Calvin Klein, who attended the same Bronx elementary school, dreamed of becoming wealthy through the garment industry. Lauren (né Lifshitz), while still a high school student, already tried to dress like a fashion designer. He haunted Paul Stuart and Brooks Brothers, among the most upscale haberdashery stores in the city, sampling suits, jackets, ties, and other accessories. Finding the styles wanting, he began to sketch his own clothing lines. At age twenty, he dropped out of CCNY to pursue his ambition, catching on initially as a salesman at Brooks Brothers. Though it took several years before Lauren earned his first million, he was heading up and away from his Bronx origins.[52]

Unlike Lauren, Klein wanted to design women's clothing like his role model, his maternal grandmother, a seamstress. Predictably, his unconventional occupational desires did not play well among neighborhood boys. A handsome man with thick, spikey hair, a wide mouth, and broad brow, Klein possessed effeminate mannerisms, though his homosexuality was fully closeted, a common life-style choice for gay men in those years. Klein left his local neighborhood behind when he enrolled in the High School of Industrial Arts in Manhattan and subsequently matriculated at the Fashion Institute of Technology. His courses helped him develop a more sophisticated appreciation of styles, fabrics, and colors.

Upon graduation, Klein hooked up with one of the top "cloak and suit houses." Dissatisfied, he moved on to a more prestigious firm, where he met a pattern maker, Abe Morenstein. They joined forces. But neither had sufficient capital to fulfill their dreams. So Klein returned to the Bronx and turned to a Jewish boyhood friend, a supermarket owner who had given him part-time work. With Barry Schwartz's money, Morenstein and Klein established an unofficial partnership. In return for the financial backing, Schwartz requested a large piece of the enterprise. In 1967, Calvin Klein incorporated Calvin Klein Ltd. with Schwartz as a 50 percent "silent partner." Klein cut Morenstein out, a move not unprecedented in the highly competitive world of Seventh Avenue. Less than a year later, Schwartz became far more than a disengaged investor. When his Sundial Supermarket in Harlem was ransacked in riots following the murder of Dr. Martin Luther King Jr., Schwartz shifted his energies to the Jewish clothing industry. Ten years later, both men were drawing salaries in excess of $4 million.[53]

The stellar success of Klein and Lauren spoke not only to their talent in designing clothing and mastering the arts of promotion and production central to the industry but also to the enduring, if decreasing, power of ethnic niches to propel New York Jews to take advantage of the city's changing economy. Most second- and third-generation Jews did not follow their fathers into family businesses, whether those firms manufactured music or machines, but struck out in new areas opened up by declining anti-Semitic exclusion and a changing urban economy. New York reached its peak as the nation's premier manufacturing center during the 1940s, while retaining its prominence as the country's financial center and a major commercial city. After the war, this diversified economy shifted. Manufacturing left for southern towns and eventually moved overseas, in part driven out by bankers and developers who coveted factories' land for more "valuable" uses, in part enticed by cheap labor, and in part made obsolete by new technologies (e.g., in printing). As Jews saw some of their ethnic niches disappear, they responded by creating new ones and by gradually integrating into white middle- and upper-class positions in a city increasingly divided by the conjunction of race and class.[54]

Cathedrals of Broadway, by Florine Stettheimer, 1929. Born in Rochester, New York, to German Jewish parents, Florine Stettheimer moved to New York City to study at the Art Students League. She used her wealth to support herself as well as other artists. Her paintings often can be read as an homage to her adopted city. Here Mayor Jimmy Walker throws out the first pitch in a newsreel, while around him shimmer the names of famous Broadway theaters, many, like the Roxy, built by Jewish builders. Courtesy of the Metropolitan Museum of Art.

Making New York Jews

February 1924. Well-dressed music patrons, including "a gaggle of musical luminaries," made their way up Forty-Second Street to Aeolian Hall, eager to hear an afternoon concert billed as "An Experiment in Modern Music."[1] Paul Whiteman had assembled for his orchestral band a sampling of jazz music, commissioning George Gershwin to write a piece. Known for his popular songs, especially "Swanee," that appealed to the masses, not the classes, Gershwin had put off the commission until the newspaper announced the date. Then he dashed off a duo-piano version in two weeks and handed it to Ferde Grofé to orchestrate. Gershwin decided "to kill" the "misperception" that jazz music had to "cling to dance rhythms." He told his first biographer that he initially heard the piece "as a sort of musical kaleidoscope of America, of our vast melting pot, of our unduplicated national pep, of our metropolitan madness." Appropriately, Gershwin wanted to call the piece "American Rhapsody," a reflection of his belief in "the democratic potential of music" and his ambition to write "original, rootedly American music that various audiences would appreciate." But his brother nixed the title. "Rhapsody in Blue" grabbed its audience as soon as its long clarinet glissando opening ended and the handsome twenty-six-year-old Gershwin began to improvise at the piano.[2]

"Rhapsody in Blue" achieved "instantaneous popular success. Victor made a recording that sold a million copies," earning Gershwin a quarter of a million dollars in its first decade. As MacDonald Moore has observed about the piece, "a collaborative effort, it boosted the reputations of all concerned: Gershwin, Whiteman, and Grofé." Gershwin was born in Brownsville but grew up on the Lower East Side and Harlem—his father moved the family twenty-eight times between 1900 and 1917. He fell in love with music and pursued it, studying piano, orchestration, harmony, and theory. Then he found work as a song plugger, promoting sheet music for a successful Tin Pan Alley publisher, until he broke onto the Broadway stage, all the while privately writing classical music. Critics mulled over Gershwin's melding of jazz and classical music even as they wondered whether his Tin Pan Alley and Broadway melodies were jazz.[3]

These extramusical debates about New York Jewish cultural production raised the significance of what Gershwin and other Jewish New Yorkers were doing. "Using the criterion of the aesthetic of identity, critics deemed music composed by Jews reflective of Jewish values and roles. Proponents of modernism, the stereotypical 'New York Jew' became identified with a racial tradition midway between Yankees and Negroes." Perhaps "most troublesome" for some champions of elite classical music, "Jews tried to participate in the sacred ceremonies of national autogenesis through culture. It seemed that Jewish composers intended to obliterate the root distinction between high culture and merely anthropological culture. Classical and vernacular, traditional and avant-garde, white and black, hedonism and mechanism: all appeared to enter the Jewish melting pot."[4]

By the time Gershwin stepped onto the stage at Aeolian Hall and sat down at the piano, concepts of "New York Jews" circulated freely among locals and outsiders alike. A second generation born and bred in the city produced an efflorescence of cultural styles that mixed categories often thought distinct, especially by those white Protestants who considered themselves guardians of American culture. New York City left its imprint on Jewish immigrants and their children. New York Jews returned the favor, eagerly seeking to imagine a place for themselves in the city as the vanguard of American culture. They took basic ethnic attributes of language, religion, and family and "transformed these into a generic Jewish urban 'character.'"[5] This synergy often led supporters and detractors alike to merge the identities of New York and its Jews.

Literary and Visual Cultures

Jews participated in forming a cultural community as distinctly New York styles of speaking, writing, seeing, and listening took shape over the course of the twentieth century. This urban cultural milieu celebrated and critiqued the city's multiplicity and diversity, its many voices and styles. Jews added their own perceptions, often taking the city itself as a subject for prose, poetry, music, and art. Gotham became, in Benjamin

Pollak's characterization, "the most capacious and contentious site of the Jewish literary encounter with American modernity." Eventually Jewish writing crafted an "intertextual cityscape" that "imbued specific neighborhoods and spaces with heightened meaning." The rise of New York as the nation's intellectual and cultural center amplified the voices and opinions of Jewish critics. Their ongoing engagement with an intertextual urban literature periodically prompted productive revisiting of previously published works by Jewish writers. These "second lives" often launched New York Jewish literatures into influential careers beyond their original circulation.[6]

Abraham Cahan inaugurated this urban tradition with *Yekl: A Tale of the New York Ghetto* (1896). Cahan's realist fiction captured sexual tensions between a Jewish immigrant who has eagerly Americanized and his traditional wife, who arrives several years later. Published in both English and Yiddish versions, the novella did not reach as wide an audience as Cahan's English magnum opus, *The Rise of David Levinsky* (1917). *Levinsky* told an epic story of Jewish immigration through the eyes of one immigrant who acquires wealth as a garment manufacturer only to lose his soul. However, Yekl enjoyed a reprise performance in a movie version, *Hester Street* (1975), that brought a distinctly feminist interpretation to its tale of unrequited love, divorce, and remarriage. Cahan relished mediating as an English-language writer interpreting "the ghetto" to literate native audiences and as a Yiddish editor interpreting America to immigrants.[7]

Anzia Yezierska (1885–1970) similarly made a mark on American culture through writing drawn from her New York experiences. Like Cahan, she wrote fiction about immigrant life. Since, like him, she often wrote in the first person about characters who superficially resembled the author, her work is often taken to be autobiographical. But while she clearly drew on her own involvement in the tenements and shops, she just as clearly differed from her characters. Yezierska graduated from college and spoke educated, unaccented English, while her heroines usually speak in Yiddish cadences. In fact, having arrived in the United States as a child, she really pioneered as a second-generation writer, expressing a sense of alienation from both her old-world parents and her new-world culture.[8]

Yezierska shrouded her early life in a mist largely of her own creation. She frequently fought with her father, and a father character typically appears in her stories as a misogynistic petty tyrant. Yezierska attended public schools and earned a degree in home economics from Teachers College of Columbia University. She taught in public school but disliked both the profession and her subject. Charismatic, vivacious, and beautiful, with "thick red hair, prominent blue eyes, and a creamy complexion," she briefly aspired to a stage career. In 1915, she published her first story, "Free Vacation House," which describes the disappointment and humiliation a poor Jewish immigrant woman faces with condescension from charitable do-gooders. Yezierska was already a published author when she met the philosopher John Dewey, "the love of her life," though the relationship apparently remained platonic. Her relationship with Dewey ended after about a year. However, the figure of an Anglo-American Protestant intellectual mentor/lover appeared in a number of her subsequent stories. But racial and cultural differences stymie any liaison between the Jewish female protagonist and the professor.[9]

Yezierska's stories often depict the heroine's tortured ambivalence, longing to escape a suffocating Jewish culture yet feeling alienated from mainstream America. Her story "Fat of the Land" (1919), about the loneliness of an immigrant woman supported by her successful American children, won a prize for best short story of the year. Her subsequent anthology, *Hungry Hearts* (1920), garnered generally positive reviews but little commercial success. Still, Samuel Goldwyn not only bought the movie rights but also brought Yezierska to Hollywood to help write the screenplay. Repelled by the crass commercialism and mercenary attitudes of writers in Hollywood, she soon returned to New York. After some continued success in the 1920s, her fame faded, until historians of American women rediscovered her in the 1970s as part of a new women's history.[10]

Like Yezierska's fiction, Henry Roth's complex and brilliant novel of the Lower East Side, *Call It Sleep* (1934), owed its prominence to republication. In 1964, a younger generation of literary critics, including Irving Howe, rediscovered and championed it. Hailed as a masterpiece, the novel sold a million copies in paperback and stayed for weeks on the best-seller list. Initially published during the Depression, it recounted a bittersweet coming-of-age story of a Jewish immigrant boy. Roth's imaginative use of language moved the immigrant New York novel out of social realism into the realm of multilingual modernism. In *Call It Sleep*, when characters speak Yiddish, their language is presented in elegant English; by contrast, the English language of the street appears coarse, ungrammatical, and accented. Playing with language, Roth made English unfamiliar to readers even as he familiarized them with Yiddish and Hebrew, in part through his "translation" into resonant English. Roth (1906–1995) came to New York as a child, lived with his parents on the Lower East Side before moving with his family to Harlem, attended City College, joined the Communist Party, and found a sponsor and lover whose support allowed him to write the novel. But then Roth moved to Maine and fell silent until he published *Shifting Landscape* (1987), a collection of essays, followed by his monumental *Mercy of a Rude Stream* in four volumes.[11]

Among many New York Jewish writers who extended the reach of New York language, Grace Paley (1922–2007) stood out for her "ability to reconcile the sounds of Yiddish, Russian, Polish, and English, along with the signs of Jewish and Christian culture." Born in the Bronx into a comfortable middle-class, left-wing immigrant family, Paley grew up surrounded by the city's multilingual speech. She attended public high school and college but did not find her own voice until the 1950s. Then she recognized that it needed to be both loud and clear in order to be heard. In her short story "The Loudest Voice" (1959), Shirley Abramowitz, a daughter of Jewish immigrants who fearlessly speaks her mind, describes her neighborhood: "There is a certain place where dumbwaiters boom, doors slam, dishes crash; every window is a mother's mouth bidding the street shut up, go skate somewhere else, come home." But Shirley's voice was the loudest. That gift leads to the choice of Shirley to narrate her public school's Christmas play and occasions dispute between her parents on the appropriateness of a Jew telling this central Christian story. As in many Paley stories, the conflicts hang in the air, unresolved, even as the parents' debates over assimilation and Jewish identity reflect central concerns of New York Jews.[12]

The blend of politics and culture that is visible in Paley's stories—"In Palestine the Arabs would be eating you alive," the father counters the mother's concerns; "Europe you had pogroms. Argentina is full of Indians. Here you got Christmas"—took root in a host of magazines that merged Jewish issues with those of American culture more broadly. This process began with the *Menorah Journal*, the product of a Jewish collegiate movement that wrestled with the heavily Protestant dimensions of elite American culture. The *Menorah Journal* opened its pages to artists and writers, critics and public intellectuals. Lionel Trilling, who made a career at Columbia University as a pioneering tenured Jewish faculty member in the English Department, published early pieces there alongside innovative rabbis like Mordecai M. Kaplan and historians like Salo Baron, the first professor of Jewish history at Columbia University. Its managing editor from 1925 to 1931, Elliot Cohen (1899–1959), who later became the first editor of *Commentary* magazine, aspired to foster a Jewish renaissance built on secular and ethnic understandings of Jewishness. As Cohen later explained in *Commentary*, "People continually ask whether a cultural product is 'Jewish' or 'American,' seeming to assume that these two traditions be mutually exclusive." But in this important area of life, "you can be in two places at once." In short, Cohen rejected both a hyphenated identity and a binary division between Jewish and American.[13]

Cohen did not exclude art. Indeed, only magazines devoted to art regularly published more illustrations. While traditional images of ritual objects appeared, the *Menorah Journal* favored the work of living Jewish artists, especially modernist ones, both European and American. Transnational in its vision, its reproductions introduced readers to an exceptionally wide array of visual styles, from cubist to constructivist to futurist to abstract. However, while it embraced a capacious definition of Jewish artists, Jewish subject matter achieved pride of place. "Artists who did not depict recognizably Jewish subjects had to be positioned in such a way as to recoup their Jewishness," usually accomplished through sequencing of images. "This also worked to secure the Jewish identity of the artist."[14]

Jewish engagement with the visual arts emerged closely tied to literary spheres. A generation of Jewish painters and sculptors helped to revolutionize American art. Most were either immigrants from eastern Europe or children of immigrants. Their experiences as newcomers and their relationship with the diverse, turbulent city informed their art, leading them away from academic tradition toward modernism in style and subject matter. They encountered an openness in New York's art scene despite "contemporary American debates over art that saw modernist painting and sculpture as 'Ellis Island Art,' that is, a foreign import and therefore un-American." Nonetheless, Jewish painters enjoyed

I Glorify New York, a Symphony in Lines, by Abraham Walkowitz, 1913. Born in Siberia, Abraham Walkowitz immigrated as a young child to New York and fell in love with the city. Although he went to Paris to study, he returned as a confirmed American modernist. He exhibited in the path-breaking Armory Show of 1913 and gravitated to the circle of modernist photographers and artists around Alfred Stieglitz and his gallery. His drawings and prints often take the city as their subject. © Abraham Walkowitz. Courtesy of Beth Urdang Gallery.

support from established artists, critics, gallery owners, and teachers—both Jewish and not Jewish—who shared their aesthetic sensibilities and interest in urban themes.[15]

New York Jewish artists, like Abraham Walkowitz and Max Weber, went to Paris but then returned. Walkowitz came back as what one art historian called the "first American modernist." Weber, a friend of *di yunge*, fell under the influence of Cézanne, Matisse, and Picasso in Paris. Walkowitz and others showed their work in both the famous 1913 Armory Show and the subsequent *Forum Exhibition of Modern American Painting*, which highlighted American artists who had been slighted at the Armory Show. That one-third of the organizing committee and nearly a quarter of the artists featured in the *Forum* show were Jews demonstrated their growing importance in the New York art scene. Apart from Alfred Stieglitz's own work as a pioneering photographer, he played a critical role introducing European modernist currents to American audiences. He exhibited Rodin drawings and Matisse paintings at his gallery but also backed young American modernists as well as the pioneering work of such Jewish photographers as Paul Strand. Strand's photograph of Wall Street, with its slanting shadows of miniature workers walking past an immense granite wall, conveyed an almost abstract modernist image along with a powerful critique of the city's financial capital.[16]

Florine Stettheimer (1871–1944) similarly nurtured modernist artists in her salon even as she also painted. She used her wealth from her German Jewish parents to support her own art and that of others. Born in 1871 in Rochester, New York, the fourth of five children, she began her education in Germany, returning in 1892 to study at the Art Students League in New York. Her paintings from 1917 until her death in 1944, the years that she lived with her mother and two sisters in the city, form an "unprecedented pictorial category that is part portraiture, part history painting, and part genre painting." Many works can be read as biographical since they depict her and her family. Stettheimer also collaborated with the poet Gertrude Stein and the composer Virgil Thomson by producing sets and costumes for their modernist opera, *Four Saints in Three Acts.*[17]

An eclectic combination of settlement houses, radical activists, and non-Jewish art teachers nurtured immigrant Jewish artists. Beginning in 1892, the Educational Alliance began to organize annual exhibitions, using pieces loaned from private collections, as part of its mission to

Americanize immigrants and improve their "standards of taste." Well over one hundred thousand visitors came to see one 1895 exhibit. This outpouring revealed a thirst for fine art among immigrant Jews comparable to their children's embrace of high literary culture available in public libraries. In 1895, the Alliance started art classes as well. Subsequently, when the artist and critic Henry McBride taught at the school, he added life drawing, industrial design, and painting to the curriculum. But the Alliance soon suspended art classes because increasing numbers of immigrants taxed its resources.[18]

The anarchist Ferrer Center (also called the Modern School), founded in 1911, stood at the "nexus between radical politics and the artistic avant-garde," as well as between Greenwich Village and the Lower East Side. Most of its teachers and leaders, including the prominent Ashcan school painters Robert Henri and George Bellows, were not Jewish, but most of the students were Jews. Under Bellows and Henri's anti-academic tutelage, instruction included such techniques as "rapid sketching and the short pose," intended to encourage freedom and discourage academic rigidity. The artist Moses Soyer, a teenager when he attended Henri's class, recalled that Henri, a brilliant teacher, permanently altered his own approach—and those of his brothers Raphael and Isaac, whom he told about his experience.[19]

When the Educational Alliance restarted its art school, its new director, Abbo Ostrowsky (1889–1975), a Jewish immigrant from Russia who had studied at the National Academy of Design, inclined toward radical politics, not avant-garde art. Louis Lozowick (1892–1973), who taught there, thought the school fostered a "definite social orientation." He observed that a student "is made to feel his identity with the community of which he is a product by drawing inspiration from its life, reflecting the peculiarities of its environment and embodying in permanent form its cultural heritage." Although conceived as a "community art center," the art school assumed a more professional character under Ostrowsky.[20]

Comparable bonds among second-generation Jews shaped the emergence of the New York school of abstract expressionists. Painters such as Barnett Newman (1905–1970) and Mark Rothko (1903–1970) turned to abstraction and what became known as "color field" paintings after World War II. Both had previously experimented with myth but came to see an art of "pure idea" as best able to speak to humanity's tragic condition, amply on display during the Holocaust. They pared away narrative, figuration, and detail in favor of lyrical and often shimmering colors. "I paint out of high passion," Newman affirmed, claiming that his deceptively simple paintings—a field of color divided by a line or two, what he called a "zip"—emerged out of a "difficult and complex process." Unlike Rothko, who immigrated as a child to Portland, Oregon, and came to New York after two years at Yale, Newman grew up in New York, attended City College, and worked at his father's clothing firm until his wife insisted that he give it up for painting full time.[21]

Rothko studied with Max Weber and joined a circle of painters around Milton Avery that included Newman and Adolph Gottlieb. As with many Jewish writers, Rothko took the city, its streets and subways, as subjects that possessed political valences. However, only after his turn to abstraction brought financial success did he forgo his job teaching art to children at the Center Academy, a Jewish progressive parochial school under the auspices of the Brooklyn Jewish Center. His teaching ultimately influenced his painting, bringing him to recognize that one starts with color, not drawing, as basic to a modern understanding of art. The career trajectories of both Newman and Rothko reveal alternative forms of economic support proffered by New York Jewish institutions that allowed Jewish artists to develop.[22]

As photography gained recognition in the midst of the Great Depression for its visual power to document contemporary life, two young New York Jews—Sid Grossman (1913–1955) and Sol Libsohn (1914–2001)—joined together to create the New York Photo League, a mixture of school, exhibit venue, and club with a left-leaning social agenda favoring documentary photography. The Photo League "believed that photographers had an obligation to illuminate and record the world they lived in." Photo League members encouraged "art with social purpose, photography that could improve living conditions and better civil liberties." At the Photo League, classes, community, exhibits, education in the history of photography, and shared ways of thinking about photography—including what to photograph (people), how to photograph (straight photography), where to photograph (outdoors with natural light)—all converged. The Photo League integrated women into its classes and documentary projects, implicitly welcoming their perspectives, though it had no language to discuss gender. Most members were young, some still in their teens. Photography engaged Photo League members, but so did a stew of progressive and leftist politics.[23]

New York Jewish backgrounds that seldom needed articulation also linked members of the Photo League. Many grew up as children of immigrant parents. Morris Engel (1918–2005) joined the Photo League in its early years when he was a teenager. He described its quarters as "a refuge, a home": "It filled a gap in my emotional life. I entered and pleasure came." Photo League members shared styles of talking, habits of looking, and categories of perception. A city that felt half Jewish colored their common fund of experiences. Through their intense, ongoing discussions about photography as a group activity, Photo League members came to work within linked discourses of aesthetics and social action. The non-Jewish photojournalist W. Eugene Smith marveled, "they carried on some of the best debates about photography I ever heard." Taking their Jewish identity for granted and, therefore, a feature easily ignored, these photographers discovered that their shared assumptions as New Yorkers facilitated creative conflict. They were freed to argue about what made for good photographs without having to deal with an establishment that disdained Jews.[24]

In many ways, the Photo League typified a form of Jewish cultural organization that was characteristic of second-generation New York Jews. Unlike the Educational Alliance, which was supported as a specifically Jewish organization by wealthy philanthropists, the Photo League relied on its membership to survive. Unlike the Ferrer Center, where mostly non-Jewish painters taught mostly Jewish students, the Photo League's teachers and students included only a minority of non-Jews. In short, the Photo League was not explicitly Jewish, either religious or sectarian, but its membership and teachers shared common cultural backgrounds as New York Jews. Despite its relatively brief life, the Photo League's imagery influenced what subsequently came to be known as the New York school of photography: gritty, experimental, focused on people on the city's streets, sharing a commitment to photography as documentary, postmodern. A significant number of its students subsequently went on to introduce college courses in photography, extending the impact of New York Jewish photographers.[25]

If photography straddled art and commerce, moving pictures entered New York's popular culture as commercial entertainment. Beginning with nickelodeons in 1905, movies took off in various formats. Hundreds of thousands of people flocked to them each day, with Jews and other immigrants the prime audience for this new, cheap, and thrilling form of amusement. "When you go through the streets of our neighborhood you will be amazed by the mass of moving picture houses," the *Forward* reported. "Four or more 'shows' can be found on one street." An informal atmosphere resembling that of the Yiddish theater took hold in movie houses.[26]

Jewish entrepreneurs quickly stepped into this new market. Adolph Zukor (1873–1976), a thirty-year-old immigrant and successful furrier, opened an arcade on Fourteenth Street with kinetoscopes (very short peep-show films) with a partner. He later operated conventional nickelodeons as well. Marcus Loew (1870–1927), a native New Yorker who had grown up in an immigrant family in the heart of Kleindeutschland, started with nickelodeons. Then he branched out into vaudeville and Brooklyn, and soon Loew owned forty theaters throughout the city. William Fox (1879–1952), born in Hungary and brought to New York as an infant, had already enjoyed success in the garment industry when he began to renovate dilapidated theaters in Brooklyn.

Zukor, Fox, Loew, and others changed the way movies were made and exhibited, pioneering production of feature films and showing them in ever larger and more luxurious surroundings. As Zukor later put it, the "nickelodeon had to go, theaters replaced shooting galleries, temples replaced theaters, and cathedrals replaced temples." As early as 1908, Fox's thousand-seat Dewey Theater on Fourteenth Street offered programs of vaudeville and movies for as little as a nickel or a dime, all under the watchful eyes of red-uniformed ushers. At the same time, Loew also showed a combination of vaudeville and movies. Then he methodically expanded his chain beyond New York, until it spread throughout the United States and Canada. Loew's large, luxurious, and conveniently located theaters attracted respectable middle-class families. In New York, they dotted the entire city, reaching into outer-borough neighborhoods, where their patrons increasingly lived.[27]

Zukor and the German Jewish immigrant Carl Laemmle concluded that audiences would be more than willing to sit through longer movies, especially to see their favorite stars. After importing European feature films, Zukor formed Famous Players Film Company, with the established Jewish American theatrical impresarios Daniel and Charles Frohman and David Belasco producing their own films. In 1913, they released the tremendously successful *The Prisoner of Zenda*. Success inspired mergers.

Famous Players became Famous Players-Lasky Corporation, which in turn took over the distribution company Paramount Picture Corporation. Enlisting the help of the Jewish Wall Street firm Kuhn, Loeb and Company to raise the capital to open a string of first-run movie palaces across the country, the company combined production, marketing, and distribution.[28]

While New York nurtured the early movie industry and executive offices lingered in the city, movie production rapidly shifted to Hollywood. Still, New York itself proved a powerful presence in American movies, fully a third of which in the 1920s and '30s featured the city as their setting. Hollywood became a sort of colony of Jewish New York, broadcasting New York Jewish style throughout the nation. Jews supplied much of the creative talent to Hollywood, and later radio and television, reaching national and international audiences.[29]

Immigration restriction gradually reduced audiences for Jewish immigrant culture. The community's German-speaking element had faded almost entirely, hastened by anti-German sentiment in World War I. The Yiddish sector slowly shrank, although it retained heft and originality throughout the interwar years and World War II. The modernists of the *in zikh* (introspectivist) group superseded *di yunge* as the vanguard of Yiddish poetry. Newcomers, including the brothers Israel Joshua and Isaac Bashevis Singer and the poet Kadya Molodovsky, arrived during the Depression. Their presence bolstered Yiddish prose and poetry. Molodovsky (1894–1974) learned Yiddish from her paternal grandmother and Hebrew from her father, who also hired Russian-language tutors for his brilliant daughter. A classic Jewish beauty, with dark eyes and hair, a long nose, and wide lips, she received an unusual education for a shtetl childhood. After the Bolshevik Revolution, she married and moved to Warsaw, where she worked as a teacher and published several volumes of poetry, along with children's poems. Settling in New York unleashed a flurry of new writing, including a fictional diary, *Fun Lublin biz Nyu-York* (From Lublin to New York), as well as a play. In her novel-cum-journal, Molodovsky played with the process of learning English. Writing in variations of Yiddish that identified class position and level of Americanization, and then integrating English words and sentences, she charted a changing female consciousness. Molodovsky also edited a Yiddish literary journal, *Svive* (Surroundings), the only woman to do so.[30]

Similarly, Israel Joshua Singer (1893–1944) found New York to be a fruitful intellectual milieu that saw the publication of three major novels, including *Di brider Ashkenazi* (*The Brothers Ashkenazi*) as well as the dramatization of his second, most successful novel, *Yoshe kalb* (*The Sinner*). Singer found translators for his novels, unlike Molodovsky, and reached an English-speaking audience as a result. His younger brother, Isaac Bashevis Singer (1902–1999), flourished in New York; he continued to write in Yiddish and to see his work translated into English.[31]

Yiddish audiences ceased to grow in this interwar period despite ongoing cultural creativity. Art theater maintained high standards, attracting critical admiration from beyond the Yiddish-speaking world. Although the Yiddish press continued to count its readers in the hundreds of thousands, it, too, crested. Even before restrictive legislation limited immigration, readers opted for English-language newspapers. A shrinking public gradually marginalized New York Yiddish culture. The future of Jewish culture lay in English, albeit with a Yiddish substratum.[32]

Indeed, by the interwar period, the association of Jews with New York culture was so pervasive that for many Americans, the two were nearly synonymous. By the mid-1920s, "New York had become the geographical code word for the mass media, for Jewishness, for jazz and the avant-garde, for the assorted urban ills of contemporary American civilization." Many Americans "were fascinated by New York," writes MacDonald Moore, "as they were fascinated by Jews. They didn't care to think where one left off and the other began." Jewish influence existed on a number of levels: Yinglish slang fused with earlier Irish and German elements in New York speech; Jewish energy contributed to the speed with which events seemed to move in New York compared to the rest of the country; Jews in the New York garment industry set clothing styles for other Americans; Jewish inroads in book publishing introduced new forms of middle-brow literature and, in several important court cases, challenged social conventions of obscenity. Whether cultivated by the Jewish labor movement or the public schools, Jews formed much of the market for both popular and "high" culture. In the 1930s, Jews made up more than half the subscribers to the New York Philharmonic; in the 1960s, they constituted half of Broadway's audiences.[33]

Performing American Jewishness

When musical theater became Broadway's lifeblood, Tin Pan Alley, the popular music writing and publishing business, relocated to an expanding theater district. Songwriters regularly interpolated ragtime tunes into Broadway hits. Irving Berlin (1888–1989)—operating out of the Strand Building on Forty-Fifth Street, where he opened his publishing firm in 1919—knew that one or two first-rate songs could make a show. Residuals from publication of his sheet music provided him with steady income long beyond the run of any theater production. In 1931, music publishers, both large and small, filled the upper floors of the Brill Building on Forty-Ninth Street and Broadway, so named because Morris Brill had his clothing store on the ground floor. Ambitious songwriters knocked on one door after another, eager to sell their wares.[34]

Some of Tin Pan Alley's stars expanded its reach beyond New York. For generations, Jewish popular-music composers and publishers had provided songs for the nation. At the turn of the century, Harry Von Tilzer, having left his native Detroit to join a circus as a teenager, had become arguably "the most prolific song writer in the annals of Tin Pan Alley." His ballad "Wait Til the Sun Shines, Nellie" inspired relief workers to sing a parody, "Wait Til the Sun Shines, Frisco," hoping to cheer up San Francisco residents after the 1906 earthquake. Then Harry's brother, Albert, wrote the anthem of the national pastime, "Take Me Out to the Ball Game," though he had never attended a baseball game. During the depth of the Depression, Hollywood lured New York talent. Renowned composers and lyricists trekked across the country to join a burgeoning movie scene. There, sitting by a pool, Berlin wrote his Jewish fantasy, dreaming of "A White Christmas." It swept the nation, even though it carried no reference to the birth of Jesus, the reason for the holiday.[35]

Jewish fans of popular-song writers, sitting at a soda fountain and tapping out their favorite tunes, using silverware as their instruments and plates as their tin pans, rhapsodized about what successes these fellow Jews had made of themselves. Walking through Crotona Park, a young man and his date imagined they were Fred Astaire and Ginger Rodgers, "dancing cheek to cheek," a song that they knew Berlin wrote for the 1935 hit movie *Top Hat*. Most did not know that he penned perhaps his most famous song, "God Bless America," at Camp Upton, New

York, during World War I when he served in the U.S. Army. But New York Jews swelled with pride when Kate Smith belted out Berlin's alternative national anthem at both major political conventions in 1940. In its mix of prayer and pride, it exemplified Jewish affection for America, "land that I love."[36]

A new generation of Jewish songwriters, composers, and performers arose in New York. Jerome Kern and Oscar Hammerstein II, grandson of the impresario, collaborated on *Showboat*, based on a story by the Jewish writer Edna Ferber, which revolutionized the Broadway musical in 1927 by integrating music and plot. A decade later, the Gershwin brothers, George and Ira, brought *Porgy and Bess* to the stage. This tale of love and betrayal set in Charleston, South Carolina, yoked Jewish and African American themes and music, complicating Jewish artists' relationship to African American culture and moving decisively away from blackface to a more respectful stance.[37]

Other Jewish composers of classical music, like Aaron Copland (1900–1990), aggressively embraced American and Christian melodies, leaving behind their more modernist, urban compositions. Copland grew up in Brownsville, Brooklyn, a neighborhood he characterized as "drab." Like Gershwin, he sought out music teachers, finally securing an opportunity to study with Nadia Boulanger in Paris. When he returned, Copland achieved success in getting his modernist compositions performed. But he rejected modernism for more accessible music. His *Appalachian Spring* score for Martha Graham's modern dance of the same title exemplified this trend, using a Shaker hymn as its theme. Copland had proposed to Graham a dance based on immigration, but the non-Jewish dancer rejected it.[38]

As a Jewish presence grew in American classical music, literature, dance, and the visual arts, it allowed individual Jewish artists increasing freedom to explore. Indeed, critics debated whether there was anything identifiably Judaic about contributions by individual Jews. Yet they recognized how New York Jews sustained possibilities for Jewish creativity through their patronage, enthusiasm, and openness to experimentation.

Leonard Bernstein (1918–1990) exemplified these opportunities as a composer of classical music and Broadway hits as well as conductor of the New York Philharmonic. His conducting style, personal dynamism, athleticism, handsome and expressive face, and thick mane of hair captivated audiences. His opening triumph—when he stepped in to conduct the New York Philharmonic for an ailing Bruno Walter—hit the front page of several newspapers. Years later, with inordinate enthusiasm, his brother, Burton, claimed that Bernstein's elevation to music director of the Philharmonic was "a watershed moment in American history," given a strong bias against American-trained conductors that predominated in the classical music world.[39]

Bernstein's New York Philharmonic concerts played to national audiences, taking advantage of broadcasting's prominence in the city. A long-standing New York Philharmonic radio-network hook-up transmitted his inaugural concert and many subsequent performances. Bernstein also turned to the new medium of television to reach audiences. At a time when critics characterized television as a "vast wasteland," he contributed to the best it had to offer. He used the ninety-minute award-winning *Omnibus* series not only to present concerts but also to instruct viewers in appreciation of classical music. As music director, Bernstein initiated fifty-three Young People's Concerts, live from Carnegie Hall. Adults brought their children close to the television set and closer to high culture. Together they watched Bernstein explain to enraptured New York children "what is a concerto" or "humor in music" or "the sound of an orchestra." Eventually the series reached twenty-nine countries, a major New York contribution to the world of performing arts. In turn, New York made Bernstein "a household name even to people who only dreamed of visiting the city, who never set foot in a concert hall, or went to a production on the Great White Way."[40]

Bernstein also pursued a career as a composer on Broadway. He collaborated on a musical with the writers and lyricists Betty Comden and Adolph Green and the choreographer Jerome Robbins, all children of Jewish immigrants establishing careers in the performing arts. *On the Town* celebrated the city's excitement, vitality, and opportunities through the adventures of three sailors who careen through the city during their twenty-four-hour shore leave. The play opened on December 28, 1944, when Americans were focused on the Allies' desperate and successful fight against the Germans in the Battle of the Bulge. It ends on a serious note as the young men return to war duty. Still, audiences remembered that New York was "a helluva town."[41] A Hollywood version subsequently seduced a national audience.

On the Town's upbeat vision of New York City contrasted sharply with the 1948 documentary-style crime drama *Naked City*. Using images from a best-selling book of street photographs of the same name, taken by Weegee (the immigrant Jewish photographer Arthur Fellig), *Naked City* emphasized, in striking black-and-white scenes shot in New York, the city's dangerous, poor, and working-class character, along with its corrupt elegance. Thus, two very different Jewish interpretations of New York reached Americans, though few at the time recognized how their contrasting perspectives reflected what might be understood as a Jewish debate about the city and its possibilities.[42]

Bernstein, too, understood the corroding effect of prejudice and juvenile delinquency on New York's promises. In 1957, he collaborated again with Robbins and two other New York Jews, the playwright Arthur Laurents and a newcomer, the lyricist Stephen Sondheim, in producing *West Side Story*. Through a retelling of Shakespeare's *Romeo and Juliet* in contemporary New York ethnic terms, the four men addressed the blight of youth gang warfare in the city. Initially imagined as "East Side Story," it had focused on conflict between a Catholic and Jewish family on the Lower East Side, with anti-Semitism directed at a Jewish gang by the Italian American Jets. But Laurents noted that as early as the 1920s, a long-running Broadway show, *Abie's Irish Rose*, had dealt with family tensions over a Catholic-Jewish intermarriage. This was an old story; the men needed something new. Reading newspaper reports about marauding youth gangs in Los Angeles's barrios, Bernstein nailed the contemporary problem as racial, with Italians and Jews perceived as white. Religious differences no longer provoked ethnic conflict. He called for "an out and out plea for racial tolerance." Thus, the protagonists ironically became two Catholics, a Puerto Rican young woman and her ultimately doomed, Italian boyfriend, victims of senseless hatred. *West Side Story* ran on Broadway for over seven hundred performances. Critics treated it as a documentary rather than as an interpretation of Shakespeare. A movie version appeared, filmed on location in a tough working-class West Side neighborhood just before its tenements were razed to build Lincoln Center.[43]

Jews made their presence felt throughout the city's cultural worlds. One observer asserted, "the city could still be intrigued by the flavor of the East Side when recaptured by playwrights, novelists, and musicians." He considered it ironic that while "immigrant parents and Jewish garment workers have almost vanished from real life, sentimental portraits of their idiosyncrasies and relations with American-born children and grandchildren have become more common." What he dubbed "matzo-ball soap operas" achieved Broadway success in the postwar decades, appealing to "American-born Jewish audiences and large numbers of non-Jews too."[44]

Certainly Paddy Chayevsky's *The Tenth Man*, a hit on Broadway, reso-nated with Jewish audiences. In this updated version of the "dybbuk" story, a staple of Yiddish theater, a demon invades the soul of a young woman who lives in Mineola, Long Island. Cast as the protagonist, Jacob Ben Ami, long a star of the Yiddish Art Theatre, directly linked Second Avenue and Broadway. The play pivots around a search for a tenth man to fulfill the quorum for prayer in order to exorcise the demon. That mystical religious quest allowed Chayevsky to contrast sympathetically the values of old-timers—characters drawn from men he had known in his Bronx neighborhood—with the vacuous and materialistic attitudes of younger members of the synagogue and their "go-getter" rabbi. "This conflict between older, devout Jews and a younger generation in whom faith has grown dim," as one critic described the play's ultimate theme, portrayed suburban versus urban Jewish ways of looking at life.[45]

No one charted New York Jewish journeys as astutely as Gertrude Berg (1899–1966), who created the character of Molly Goldberg. Berg not only played Molly but also researched and wrote the scripts, often traveling down to the Lower East Side to listen to its street speech and get ideas for the show. A successful businesswoman, Berg grew up in New York and spent summers at her parents' resort hotel in the Catskills, where she met her husband. There she first experimented with present-ing shows. Her radio series, *The Rise of the Goldbergs*, began in 1929 and portrayed the saga of a second-generation Jewish family making their way in New York City, adjusting to the promises and challenges of America. The show went on to become one of the longest running radio series in history.[46]

From the family's East Tremont apartment in the Bronx, the Gold-bergs acquainted listeners with some basic rituals and customs of Ju-daism through discussions of upcoming major Jewish holidays. The television version premiered in 1949, representing the program's third incarnation. Several times, television cameras placed the Goldbergs in a synagogue on Yom Kippur, treating viewers "to an elaborate liturgical service." TV audiences immediately grasped the informal community life still part of the Jewish Bronx at 1038 East Tremont Avenue. Every

Molly Goldberg on set. Gertrude Berg created the irrepressible character of Molly Goldberg, a Bronx Jewish mother and housewife who dispensed wisdom and humor in fractured and Yiddish-accented English. Starting in 1929, *The Rise of the Goldbergs* became one of the longest running radio serials in history. Molly Goldberg moved to television after World War II. She was most Americans' image of a Jewish New Yorker. The Goldberg family acquainted listeners with some basic rituals of Judaism through discussions of major Jewish holidays. Berg's business acumen and her use of gendered expectations drove much of the show's humor. Courtesy of Getty Images.

episode opened with Molly, an irrepressible but scatterbrained house-wife, rolling up her kitchen window and calling out, "Yoo-hoo, Mrs. Bloom!" to greet her neighborhood friend. The plump, fair-skinned, and round-faced Molly also leaned out her window to sell products of her show's sponsors. Berg produced intimacy with her audience, encouraging them to conflate her with Molly. In 1951, Philip Loeb, who played Molly's husband, Jake, was blacklisted. Although Berg defended him, she eventually yielded to the network's demand that he be fired.[47]

Toward the end of the show's run, the Goldbergs moved to suburbia, at the behest of apprehensive network executives who wanted the series to be more reflective of the emerging American scene. The newly arrived family in an aptly named Haverville addressed, in their own comedic way, some of the dilemmas of their decision to leave the city, most critically whether "it's still possible to have good neighbors and be a cohesive family." This question particularly concerned Jews, who worried what their Protestant and Catholic neighbors would think of them. Berg answered that Jewish food—a stand-in for abundant love—would win them over. Ever the successful businesswoman, Berg collaborated on the *Molly Goldberg Jewish Cookbook*, which presented eastern European Jewish recipes as accessible to all Americans through humorous stories accompanying each recipe. After all, if Molly's Irish neighbor loved matzo brei, the distinctive Jewish egg and matzo pancake eaten on Passover, so could any American. Berg's business acumen and her use of gendered expectations drove much of the show's humor. Behind her "image of a simple housewife and mother stood one of the few women," writes Jeffrey Shandler, "who maintained creative control over her work in American broadcasting for decades."[48]

In music, art, literature, theater, and other cultural arenas, Jews worked alongside non-Jews. Together they established New York as an international center of the arts—so much so that scholars came to speak of a "New York school," applying the phrase to abstract-expressionist art, documentary photography, public intellectuals, and even poets. Active in these fields, New York Jews infused American culture with a range of expressions influenced by their own experiences as immigrants or children of immigrants in the nation's largest, most cosmopolitan, most multiethnic and multireligious city. Living and working in the cultural capital of the United States, New York Jews brought their creative sensibilities to bear on American culture.

Anti-Nazis hold a demonstration, March 15, 1937. Thousands of opponents packed
Madison Square Garden in a demonstration of support for a boycott of Nazi Germany.
Facing an increasingly dire situation in Germany, the socialist Jewish Labor Committee and Zionist American Jewish Congress joined forces to keep up economic pressure
on the Third Reich. With the help of sympathetic longshoremen and labor leaders,
they cooperated in prosecuting a boycott of German products and services at the port
of New York. Those who attended the rally hoped to influence Franklin Delano
Roosevelt, who had just been elected to a second term as president. Courtesy *New York
World Telegram & Sun* Newspaper Collection, Library of Congress.

9

Wars on the Home Front

After the American Revolution, New York was never a war zone until September 11, 2001. Still, reverberations from overseas wars reached the city and fomented conflict. Ideological and theological beliefs inflected Jewish attitudes toward European political struggles. Even when compromise seemed to be required due to looming catastrophe abroad, often one or another group dissented and refused to go along with a majority perspective. Critical times nudged Jews to bury some of their intramural differences to cooperate, but crisis simultaneously exacerbated internal arguments when so much was at stake.

New York Jews lived at the center of American Jewish national and international politics, connecting them to key decisions, involving them in bitter debates, and allowing them to influence public affairs. As the crucial Holocaust decade from 1938 to 1948 unfolded, American Jews' responses to the genocide of European Jews and establishment of the State of Israel took shape in the city. The Cold War against the Soviet Union, an ally of the United States during the Second World War, followed in the wake of that war, provoking attacks on Jewish political radicals, especially communists and those fellow travelers who had supported a Popular Front against fascism. Jewish political activity suffered significant travails that narrowed the range of New Deal Democrats, socialists, progressives, and radicals that had characterized New York Jews. By the mid-1950s, Jewish organizations had revamped their programs to focus on civil rights and Cold War internationalism, cleansed their memberships of Jews suspected of "subversion," and aligned in support of Israel. A decade later, many New York Jews regrouped around a new cause consonant with the Cold War: the rescue of Soviet Jews.[1]

World War II

March 1937. Thousands of people made their way to Madison Square Garden, filling its seats to rally against Hitler and Nazi Germany. These men and women had disrupted their regular routines to come to the Garden in the hopes that their presence might exert some political pressure on Franklin Delano Roosevelt, who had just been elected to a second term as president. The situation for Jews in Germany continued to deteriorate with little progress made in finding homes for desperate refugees. Recognizing a common cause in opposing Nazism, the socialist Jewish Labor Committee and Zionist American Jewish Congress had joined forces to brand "Hitlerism" as "the gravest menace to peace, civilization and democracy." To keep economic pressure on the Third Reich, they cooperated in a boycott of German products and services at the port of New York. With the help of sympathetic longshoremen and labor leaders, the boycott, initiated in 1933, also involved Jewish women who pledged not to purchase German-made goods.[2]

Then, in the aftermath of the 1938 November pogrom in Germany, more than twenty thousand people jammed another mass meeting at Madison Square Garden. This rally of working-class Jewish and non-Jewish organizations aimed to "protest Nazi outrages." Side streets filled with thousands more who listened through loudspeakers. At the podium, Zionist, socialist, and communist representatives stood shoulder to shoulder calling for an end to persecutions. New York Jews' ideological diversity—encompassing a handful of Republicans, large numbers of liberal New Deal Democrats, and voluble supporters of various iterations of socialism and Zionism as well as progressivism and communism—influenced their political posture. But in 1938, all of them opposed Nazism. This moment of unity did not endure.[3]

Hundreds of Jewish political, social, and religious groups, across the broadest of spectrums, maintained offices in the metropolis. Although the seat of the United States government was 250 miles away, seemingly all major deputations to influence leaders in Washington, DC, originated in New York. Jewish organizations spread within midtown across Forty-Second Street, east to west. Two major defense organizations, the American Jewish Congress and the American Jewish Committee, with often opposing approaches to Jews' monumental problems, stood at opposite sides of this famous New York street. The American Jewish Congress, a Zionist mass-membership organization with headquarters on the West Side off Eighth Avenue, led by Rabbi Stephen S. Wise, advocated public demonstrations to draw attention to Jewish suffering. The American Jewish Committee, a bastion of elite leadership located on the East Side on Lexington Avenue, prized quiet diplomacy. However, both walked together in harmony when they received an opportunity to speak to government. Jews who set foot among the powerful, they agreed, had to do so with respect and dignity.[4]

The offices of the Joint Distribution Committee and the American section of the Jewish Agency for Palestine also faced each other across the street between Park and Madison Avenues. The JDC acquired renown for sending supplies to Jews in eastern Europe before, during, and after the war, but its focus on European Jews disturbed Zionists who favored directing aid to Palestine. The Jewish Agency, the pre-state Jewish government in Palestine, shared space with its most dynamic publicity arm, the American Zionist Emergency Council, and its primary fund-raising group, the United Palestine Appeal. In 1939, however, the United Palestine Appeal and the fund-raising arm of the Joint Distribution Committee joined forces, despite their differences, to establish the United Jewish Appeal (UJA). The increasingly dire situation in Europe and Palestine warranted cooperation.[5]

Future leaders of American Judaism's religious movements studied in Manhattan. Rabbis and religious teachers learned at the Orthodox yeshiva Rabbi Isaac Elchanan Theological Seminary and its undergraduate school, Yeshiva College, in Washington Heights. Sixty blocks south, the men and women of the Jewish Theological Seminary prepared either to become Conservative rabbis or, in the women's cases, to graduate as Hebrew teachers. Even further south stood the Jewish Institute of Religion, a liberal rabbinical school for men, led by Rabbi Stephen S. Wise.

Volunteer workers and advocates for Zionist organizations, with different strategies for how Palestinian Jews should fight for their freedom and varying visions of what sort of state Jews might create, passed one another daily on the way to their offices in the Chelsea section of Manhattan. At lunchtime, Madison Square Park served as an informal spot for unscheduled debates between supporters of the David Ben-Gurion–led Histadrut, the "umbrella framework of the Labor Zionist movement in Palestine," and the confrontational New Zionist Organization (Revisionist), headed by Ze'ev Jabotinsky. In the critical postwar years, Histadrut supporters pleaded that the British could be convinced through diplomacy and cooperation to leave Palestine. Their interlocutors, Revisionist Zionists, sought to drive out the English through violence and intimidation. This debate continued wartime disputes between Wise's American Jewish Congress, allied with Ben-Gurion, and Jabotinsky's Revisionists over how to convince the United States government to rescue Jews. They disagreed over whether Roosevelt had Jewish concerns at heart. Wise believed in and trusted FDR; the Revisionists did not. If the American Jewish Congress spoke to the powerful with respect, the Revisionists—who rarely could get audiences with government— harangued and condemned, especially in the press.[6]

In another part of the park, Mizrachi members sermonized about the glories of a future Jewish state rising in the Land of Israel, "in the spirit of the Law of Israel." These Religious Zionists munched on sandwiches from home or purchased at Lugee's Kosher Restaurant nearby.[7] Yet despite a shared commitment to Zionism, they differed profoundly from Labor Zionists, who rejected religion. Instead these socialists, headquartered further south near Union Square, advocated for the power of labor to transform Jews and the land itself. Identified with the kibbutz movement and other forms of collectivism, they published a lively English-language journal, *Jewish Frontier*, along with the *Yidisher kemfer* (Jewish militant), to spread their message.[8]

Two other groups stood even further apart ideologically, sharing little aside from a common Jewish background: communist members of the Jewish People's Committee and the Agudath Israel, representative of Orthodox rabbinical refugees and their followers. Yet despite communists' antinationalist ideology, during the Popular Front era, they put international revolution on the back burner. They became American and Jewish patriots eager to make common cause with Zionists and others against fascism and Nazism. The Agudath rejected the ideal of restoring Jews to their ancient homeland. Attuned to the unfolding tragedy, they dedicated themselves to saving remnants, especially pious Jewish men, rabbis and their disciples, from the Nazis' hands. In this emphasis, they resembled the social democratic Jewish Labor Committee, which worked hard to rescue socialists, both Jewish and non-Jewish, from fascist persecution.[9]

As the nation's media center, New York both disseminated information and molded public opinion. Its newspapers published terrifying news about the Holocaust as well as reports about the Jewish commonwealth in Palestine. Efforts to reach Americans began with gaining space in New York's newspapers, weekly and monthly magazines, and radio outlets. Nine English-language dailies competed for readers in America's information capital, from the popular tabloid the *Daily News*, with close to two million readers, to the staid *New York Times*. Borough-based organs had their own loyal subscribers. David Sarnoff's National Broadcasting Company (NBC) operated out of Manhattan, as did its competitor, William Paley's Columbia Broadcasting System (CBS). These two Jewish media magnates promoted both sponsored and sustaining programs as they sought to win listeners throughout the country. CBS hired Edward R. Murrow in 1935 to provide real-time news coverage, while NBC expanded the reach of AM radio. Scores of periodicals, from the newsweeklies *Time* and *Newsweek* to the photo magazines *Life* and *Look*, published out of the metropolis.[10]

Jewish media followed suit. The city housed the Jewish Telegraphic Agency; it fed reports to the four Yiddish dailies and a myriad of journals and Anglo-Jewish periodicals. Operatives of the Jewish Labor Committee (JLC), which before and during the war was one of the most aggressive Jewish organizations dedicated to fighting fascism and Nazism and preventing "the spread of Fascist propaganda in America," did not have to go far to hear the most important reports. Its offices rented space downtown in the Forward Building.[11]

Manhattan also provided a prime venue for public Jewish protest. Rallies at Madison Square Garden, with its approximately twenty thousand seats within the main arena and room for thousands more under its famous rotunda on the street, regularly attracted press attention. In December 1940, the Jewish Labor Committee and the American Jewish Congress sponsored another mass meeting to protest Nazi conquest of eastern and western Europe. This time, they turned to Christian leaders, since communists hewed to a pacifist position, opposing U.S. involvement in World War II in line with the 1939 nonaggression pact between Germany and the Soviet Union. This rally attacked both "Nazi terrorism and Soviet aggression." Two years later, as word of the systematic murder of European Jewry in the death camps filtered into the city, the Jewish Labor Committee, American Jewish Congress, and B'nai B'rith gathered even more solemnly to decry these murderous onslaughts. They listened to a message from President Roosevelt promising that "the American people would hold the perpetrators of these crimes accountable on the day of reckoning."[12]

Dueling Jewish political organizations competed to use the power of Madison Square Garden to amplify their message. A week after the American Jewish Congress packed the Garden for a "Stop Hitler Now" rally, which beseeched FDR to rescue Jews, the Emergency Committee to Save the Jewish People of Europe took over the arena to stage a dramatic pageant titled "We Will Never Die." For the Revisionist Zionist leader Peter Bergson and his followers, this event, which filled the Garden, represented the culmination of a yearlong media torrent designed to energize its supporters to embarrass the U.S. government into making saving European Jews a priority. Previously, the Emergency Committee had taken out full-page newspaper ads that proclaimed, "At 50$ a Piece Guaranteed Human Beings," pleading with the Allies to ransom Jews. Now, through a cantata that the Hollywood screenwriter Ben Hecht wrote and the Broadway impresarios Moss Hart and Billy Rose directed and produced, child actors dressed as shadowy, shrouded figures, representing the doomed Jews of Europe, called out, "remember us," to a hushed gathering. After recitation of the kaddish, memorializing the dead, attendees filed out silently as if they were leaving a cemetery.[13]

But any group could rent the Garden. It hosted rallies of a very different sort designed to send opposing messages to the U.S. government and people. Most disturbing, from a Jewish point of view, was the German-American Bund's 1939 "'Americanism' rally and Washington's Birthday celebration." Through visual pageantry of uniformed marchers carrying flags with swastikas and the Stars and Stripes together to the podium, these American Nazis projected themselves as patriotic defenders of the United States. A crowd of twenty-two thousand heard the Bund leader recite a list of Jews whom he said controlled America, its media, and its president, all part of a Jewish conspiracy, "the driving force of Communism" in the U.S.[14]

May 1942. At a low point in the war, with no Allied victories in sight, Jews gathered at the Biltmore Hotel in midtown Manhattan. Six hundred delegates from every American and world Zionist organization, including Chaim Weizmann, president of the World Zionist Organization, and

David Ben-Gurion, attended this Extraordinary Zionist Conference. They demanded that "the gates of Palestine be opened." Three years had passed since the 1939 British White Paper severely limited Jewish immigration to Palestine. In anticipation of a far-from-certain Allied victory, the meeting proclaimed "that Palestine be established as a Jewish Commonwealth integrated in the structure of the new democratic world."[15]

A year later, as Allied armies made gains in North Africa, hundreds of delegates from virtually every Jewish organization in the United States descended on New York's Waldorf Astoria Hotel to attend the American Jewish Conference. By an overwhelming vote of 478 to 4, an almost unified American Jewish community agreed to prod its governmental officials and members of the international community to support a Jewish commonwealth in Palestine.[16]

Thus, New York Jews actively sought to rouse coreligionists and fellow citizens everywhere in the nation to Jewish suffering and advocated both rescue and a Jewish commonwealth. Almost two million strong, they stood closest to the center of home-front action. They could fill the Garden, and perhaps do more, to prove that American Jews cared about the fate of European Jewry and the destiny of Jewish Palestine.

Occasionally religious Jews took extraordinary measures to emphasize to those thousands of unaffiliated Jews just how grave the situation was during the Holocaust. In January 1941, even before Germany invaded the Soviet Union and started to murder Jews en masse, two Brooklyn Orthodox rabbis, emissaries of Agudath Israel's Rescue Committee, drove around wealthier sections of Brooklyn on a Saturday to solicit badly needed funds. Their seeming violation of Sabbath strictures against driving was understood correctly as far from a transgression. They were acting appropriately, within the spirit and letter of Jewish law, to save lives in a critical emergency. The sight of these pious Jews in their cars on the holy Sabbath dramatized their doomed brethren's desperate situation.[17]

In the autumn of 1942, a group of students at the Jewish Theological Seminary, shocked by public confirmation of the death camps and determined to do more than just attend Garden rallies, organized an Inter-Seminary Conference of Christian and Jewish Students. Meeting at the JTS, these future leaders of many faith communities called on the United States to throw open the nation's doors to Jewish refugees who had managed to elude the Nazis and to create temporary internment camps within the United States. The students' call for greater activism, published in Mordecai M. Kaplan's *The Reconstructionist*, spurred support by the Synagogue Council of America, a national organization of rabbis and lay leaders of all Jewish religious movements. The council summoned some three thousand synagogues and Jewish schools nationwide to use the weeks between the holidays of Passover and Shavuot, days historically associated with Jewish tragedy, to observe special memorial days and partial fast periods, to raise additional funds for relief organizations, and to curtail "occasions of amusement" during this time of contemporary tragedy. Subsequently, JTS students appealed for a rabbinical march on Washington, DC. In 1943, five hundred Orthodox rabbis cried out on the steps of the Capitol.[18]

That year, on Washington's birthday, the New York Jewish Education Committee conducted a "Children's Solemn Assembly of Sorrow and Protest." Some thirty-five hundred children, their teachers, and leaders from community Talmud Torahs, congregational schools, and Religious Zionist day schools and youth movements descended on the New York City Center in Manhattan. Through melodramatic scenes displaying grief and anger, the gathering attempted not only to deepen the students' and their parents' awareness of the dimensions of the Holocaust but also to enlist the sympathies of all New Yorkers. The city radio station WNYC broadcast the show to its listeners; the next day, newspaper readers saw the participants' anguished faces. Other cities replicated this New York protest model.[19]

Rabbi Joseph Lookstein of Yorkville's Kehilath Jeshurun, who presided at this impressive youth gathering, determined to sensitize his congregants to the fate of European Jewry. In April 1943, as Jews in the Warsaw Ghetto began their courageous revolt against their Nazi oppressors, Lookstein distributed black ribbons to his congregants to wear for seven weeks of mourning. He pleaded at the traditional memorial service concluding Passover for increased contributions to the recently established United Jewish Appeal. Finally he directed congregants to recite special prayers at "the close of the main meal in every home."[20]

Nonetheless, activists failed to enlist consistent widespread support. Even the trumpeted Garden events occupied less than a score of nights in seven years (1938–1945). Multiple stumbling blocks prevented activist Jews from galvanizing continuous community engagement. War news of death and destruction dominated newspapers and airwaves. The unbelievable details and extent of atrocities made the unfolding genocide difficult to grasp. Fears for loved ones in military service overseas took precedence over Jewish suffering abroad. Yet a kind of callousness also seemed to exist. How else can we explain, in light of what the Germans were actually doing, publication of a spoof in Yeshiva College's student newspaper to celebrate Purim, a feast day that commemorates Jewish escape from certain death in ancient Persia? The headline read, "Adolf Hitler Was Once Teacher Here." A year later, all too many students still ignored the unfolding Holocaust, protected from military service by draft deferments for divinity students.[21]

At the Jewish Theological Seminary, its president, Rabbi Louis Finkelstein, "neither responded to direct appeals to participate in protest actions . . . nor involved the Seminary in any public activity about the Holocaust." Seeking to explain his inaction, a historian has suggested that Finkelstein "did not have a clear sense that European Jewry would not be able to reconstitute itself" and "misunderstood the reasons for the Nazi assault on the Jews, blaming it on Nazi animosity for the monotheistic idea." Yet Finkelstein, his students, and their rank-and-file counterparts at Yeshiva College could be counted among those New York Jews who were most committed to their people's destiny.[22]

While the *New York Times* published basically "a story every other day" on the destruction of European Jewry, it never "presented the story of the persecution and extermination of the Jews in a way that highlighted its importance." The paper resisted making "what was happening to the Jews . . . the lead story even when American troops liberated the Buchenwald and Dachau concentration camps." Accounts of the "discrimination, the deportation and ultimately the destruction" of European Jews appeared on the front page only twenty-four times and never repeatedly. Editors only "intermittently editorialized about the extermination" and rarely highlighted it in the "Week in Review" or magazine sections. With Holocaust articles tucked away "on inside pages amid thirty or so other stories," all but the most acutely aware readers "would not necessarily focus on the stories because they were not presented in a way that told them they should."[23]

By contrast, from the very start of the war in September 1939, the Jewish Telegraphic Agency fed verified reports and eyewitness testimony that was consistently picked up by Yiddish dailies and not long thereafter by the English-language Jewish press. Still, even with these terrifying reports in hand, a gap remained between hearing and reading, believing and acting.[24]

Meanwhile, theological and political disagreements among New York–based Jewish organizations and leaders who clearly understood the dimensions of the Nazis' murders stymied unified community-wide efforts. While thousands of schoolchildren assembled at Manhattan City Center, those who attended Brooklyn yeshivas did not. Their schools' leaders refused to cooperate in an event that included non-Orthodox and nonreligious Jewish schools. Organizers of the gathering harbored their own political prejudices. They did not invite Revisionist Zionists because of their confrontational style. Rabbis also refused to join together in a Jewish interdenominational prayer meeting in May 1943. Rejection of Reform and Conservative rabbis took precedence over joint prayer for European Jews.[25]

By contrast, New York Jews knew for sure their obligations as loyal citizens. The United States demanded that they actively participate in the war effort, a commitment they enthusiastically assumed. As patriots, immediately after the bombing of Pearl Harbor, young Jewish men in the thousands signed up for military service. After the Women's Army Auxiliary Corps (WAAC) was organized, some Jewish women joined it. Occasionally, volunteering spawned tensions between dedicated sons and their parents, who not only feared for their safety, as all American mothers and fathers did, but also had to overcome a repugnance to army service grounded in myths of tsarist conscription. But this new generation of New York Jewish men understood that the U.S. military was an entirely different army, fighting a war that mattered immensely to Jews. While most non-Jewish soldiers enlisted eager to defeat the Japanese for their attack on Pearl Harbor, Jews in the barracks wanted to take on Hitler. On the most visceral level, they saw themselves fighting for their people and against Nazism and doing so as American Jewish men. They also recognized that their presence in the armed forces answered canards that American Jews avoided military service.[26]

For some Jewish men who took up arms, exigencies of the day trumped politics. One CCNY graduate, who as a left-leaning student in late 1930s had taken the Oxford Oath, reneged on that pledge never to fight in a war in order to battle a greater enemy: Nazism. Though he had a high draft lottery number and an essential home-front job, he forsook his potential exemption and was called up. Other, more doctrinaire former students, particularly some anti-Stalinist Trotskyists, who in the prewar years dominated their CCNY alcoves, bristled at these transformations. Irving Howe considered the war "the literal last convulsions of capitalist interminable warfare," he wrote; "both sides fight for the retention of their reactionary status quo." Howe penned these and other words against FDR, Churchill, Hitler, and Stalin for *Labor Action* while serving as a private first class, stationed in Alaska.[27]

Once in the army, Jewish soldiers received support from their families and communities, as did most GIs. New York Jewish delis urged Jewish parents, "send a salami to your boy in the army." Such packages gave their boys a taste of home. Army rations did not include kosher food; pork was a popular source of daily protein. Even many Jews who did not particularly keep kosher disdained eating ham.[28]

New York Jews on the home front participated enthusiastically in neighborhood war drives. They bought war bonds, gave blood, rolled bandages, collected scrap metals, organized block observances memorializing those who had fallen, and attended first-aid and civilian-defense activities. Local Jewish organizations used patriotic naming opportunities to raise funds for the United States and demonstrate their engagement in the war effort. Five days after Treasury Secretary Henry W. Morgenthau called on all New Yorkers to "start digging down into their pockets" to raise billions for the war-bond drive, a chapter of the American Jewish Congress in the Bronx contributed its first $5,000 toward financing "a bomber bearing the name 'The American Jewish Congress.'" In the Syrian Jewish community of Bensonhurst, members of its Magen David congregation demonstrated their loyalty by raising $300,000 for a two-engine B-25 Mitchell bomber named "Spirit of Magen David."[29]

Jews also challenged fellow Jews to avoid exploitation of wartime shortages. During Passover of 1943, peak season for kosher-meat sales, 150 Bronx kosher poultry retailers joined a "selling strike" designed "to force wholesalers into lower price levels." They closed their stores for three days to demand prices be pegged in accord with Office of Price Administration (OPA) regulations, which monitored rationing of consumer goods during the war.[30]

Brooklyn's insular Syrian Jewish community demonstrated unwavering patriotism in support of its young men in uniform. The war empowered a group of women to stay connected to their soldiers, relieving homesickness. They created a newsletter, *The Victory Bulletin*, which shared events at home with roughly one thousand Syrian Jews in uniform both stateside and overseas. Many of these young women discovered the transforming effect of their activism, perhaps "equal in impact to that of the boys who went off to fight a global war." These activists broke out of long-standing passive female roles and assumed leadership positions to a degree previously unseen within this traditional Jewish community.[31]

A consciousness of becoming American permeated diverse communities of Jewish New Yorkers during the war. *Victory Bulletin* editorials reminded readers of their ongoing obligations as patriotic Americans to show unquestioning support for the war effort. Through all the twists and turns in the priorities and conduct of the war, *The Victory Bulletin* expressed only total support for FDR. When it came to controversial war policies, like when and where to open a "second front"—an allied invasion in western Europe to complement the Soviet Union's titanic struggle with Germany from the east—*The Victory Bulletin* instructed its readers to write to Roosevelt and tell him, "I am behind you in your efforts." The one article that explicitly discussed the verified reports about the murder of Jews under Hitler criticized neither FDR nor his subordinates. But it did pillory the Red Cross for its failure to "utilize their financial resources and power to their utmost." It also called on the Allied nations "to threaten a terrible vengeance should such a crime"—the murder of an estimated four million additional Jews—"be perpetrated." The editors did not call for extraordinary measures to rescue doomed Jews.[32]

The Syrian community's unwavering support for the president paralleled the sentiments of most New York Jews. Although Peter Bergson's group of Palestinian Jewish activists and American supporters relentlessly criticized FDR, they remained an outspoken minority. When the president died, New York Jews mourned. Many had only known one president: Roosevelt. Rabbi Wise eulogized him as "a beloved and immortal figure," who "felt the misery of the Jewish people in Europe" with "compassion."[33]

New York Jews had joined Roosevelt's bandwagon in the late 1920s, helping to elect him governor. Gradually they entered the Democratic

political column and became loyal members of an emerging urban coalition of ethnic minorities that backed candidates who favored social
welfare legislation. Many understood their politics as congruent with
normative, American ways of acting, even as they continued to favor
policies championed by neighborhood socialists. Support for FDR
spiked after passage of New Deal legislation designed to help working
men and women. Roosevelt appointed unprecedented numbers of Jews
to high administrative offices. Jews commended his courage, especially
since their presence in government provided grist to anti-Semites who
charged that "Jew Deal" operatives controlled Washington.[34]

Eventually even committed socialists lined up with FDR. Abraham
Cahan's appeal to his comrades to "give up their theories and back Roosevelt's specific polices" resonated in the streets and at the ballot boxes.
Beginning in 1936, those who refused to vote the Tammany party ticket
could support FDR on the new American Labor Party (ALP) line. New
York garment-union leaders established this so-called Jewish third
party to strengthen their political clout and garner moderate left-wing
backing for FDR at the same time as they drew Jewish votes away from
the socialists. In 1936, the ALP contributed nearly a quarter of a million votes for Roosevelt—a substantial component of the 90 percent of
New York Jewish votes for FDR—and for the Jewish Democrat Herbert
Lehman, who was running for governor. By the 1944 election, the ALP
captured within one heavily Jewish Bronx neighborhood some 40 percent of the vote. Many socialists and communists eventually joined the
ALP, with only a handful, along with a staunch minority of Republicans, standing apart from this Jewish political alliance with the White
House.[35]

Yet their wartime anxieties as Americans and Jews did not erase
desires to live as normally as possible under the circumstances. Trying concerns—worries about family, fear over what was really happening to Jews in Europe, struggles to cope with consumer deprivations,
demonstrations of their loyalty to the United States and eagerness to
trust Roosevelt—coexisted with mundane daily realities. In extraordinary times, New York Jews also lived ordinary lives, displaying a mixed
set of priorities that balanced wartime apprehensions with local needs.
Ambiguities of communal life—conflicting priorities of commitment to
Jewish rescue and realties of an American war together with a desire to

maintain institutional equilibrium—surfaced among many Jewish religious organizations.[36]

A rabbi like Lookstein might plead for his congregants to remember Jewish suffering abroad, but such exhortations did not cast a mournful pall on synagogue life. At Kehilath Jeshurun, for example, its "Annual Smoker" for men went off as scheduled in January 1944, despite Lookstein's pleas. The next night, couples attended "a sellout" theater party on Broadway. Such events, not to mention the congregation's annual dinner, followed guidelines that the synagogue's president had articulated back in 1941. As the congregation made plans to celebrate its seventieth anniversary, its president asserted, "our common prayer should be that neither personal sorrow nor universal hardship may mar our proposed celebration and that it may be observed amidst a world enjoying the blessings of peace."[37]

Given a decidedly mixed record of Jewish congregational activity during wartime, most New York Jews who did not affiliate with a synagogue similarly behaved in normal ways. During World War II, Sylvia and Jack Goldberg harbored no strong Jewish organizational ties. Perhaps their story of how they coped, more than the saga of activists and those who had conflicting communal priorities, exemplified a quintessential New York Jewish home-front narrative. Living in the Bronx, their local religious involvement consisted of Jack's accompanying his wife's stepfather on the High Holidays to one of the older Orthodox synagogues in the neighborhood. In thinking about those days more than half a century later, Sylvia insisted that they "had absolutely no idea" about the Holocaust. "The press did not write about it, and we read the papers every day." Nor were they aware in retrospect of the public protests by Wise or Bergson. Their issue was not even the war effort, although they surely were patriotic. Rather, they wanted Sylvia to live a normal life raising their infant child, while Jack, drafted in 1943, served in England and then in France and Germany with the Third Army. He did not see his daughter until he was discharged in 1945.[38]

Sylvia lived rent-free with her mother and participated in an informal support circle of eight Jewish couples from the neighborhood. In addition to keeping daily tabs on each other while three of the husbands were in the service, they met monthly, as they had done before the war, at each other's homes. Their friendship had blossomed in the 1930s on the handball courts of the Castle Hill Pool, a blue-collar Jewish swim and sports club. Occasionally, they went to the Catskills for a weekend of rest and recreation. It helped them to cope with their daily cares and floating anxieties about their loved ones at war. They obtained a group discount by calling themselves "The Sylvia Goldberg Association," since Sylvia made the reservations. Comfortable in this upstate, bucolic Jewish space, as they ate to their hearts' content from an extensive menu of Jewish delicacies, they temporarily put their cares behind them and did not worry about the fate of their loved ones in uniform. Yet they remained conscious of how they had found personal normalcy during extenuating times. One woman took home a hotel dinner menu as a souvenir and commented with a mix of amazement and irony, "Would you believe this is war time?"[39]

Cold War

It seemed that no sooner had the Japanese surrendered and the millions of soldiers shipped back stateside than a new wartime footing emerged. The Cold War that took hold following World War II between the United States and the Soviet Union encouraged New York Jews to align themselves against the Soviet Union and adopt an anticommunist position. But for a brief moment in 1947, as the United Nations voted to partition Palestine into Jewish and Arab states, both the Soviet Union and the United States landed on the same page. Their support for the new State of Israel, established in May 1948, allowed Zionists and communists, socialists and capitalists, to coalesce into a single outpouring of enthusiasm for the beleaguered Jewish state. Such unanimity was short-lived. The 1948 presidential campaign fractured that unity, as New York Jews split their votes between the Democratic Party nominee, President Harry Truman, and the Progressive Party's standard-bearer, former vice president Henry Wallace, with a handful of Republicans voting for New York Governor Thomas Dewey. Yet by the 1950s, despite the Cold War, New York Jews increasingly integrated support for Israel and consumption of Israeli culture into their lives. Subsequently the Cold War facilitated a decision to embrace a decades-long campaign to speak out on behalf of Soviet Jews and to rescue them from an anti-Semitic government. A generation of New York Jews growing up in the postwar decades determined to enlist in a new Jewish cause that would rectify the scales of history. Some claimed to learn from what they understood as their parents' failures to save European Jews, while others challenged decisions made by members of what came to be called "the greatest generation."

The Holocaust cast a long shadow over New York Jewish politics. It shook up committed socialists, like Irving Howe, who had seen no difference during the war between Churchill and Hitler, Stalin and FDR. Nazism's branding of Jews as a race galvanized men and women to oppose discrimination in New York on the grounds of race, religion, and national origin. Jewish defense organizations revamped their programs. But the rise of a new anticommunist movement, identified with Senator Joseph McCarthy of Wisconsin, complicated New York Jewish politics. In 1948, many New York Jews, especially in the Bronx, had voted for Henry Wallace and his Progressive Party. With McCarthyism sweeping the country, New York Jews wrestled with their own, more intimate question of where they stood on communism and the Soviet Union. Watching "the trial of the century" unfold in Manhattan, they furiously debated the political issues swirling around the defendants, Ethel and Julius Rosenberg, arrested in 1951 for conspiracy to commit espionage.[40]

Although the charge was conspiracy, most observers thought of this Jewish couple, convicted based on the testimony of other Jews, as atomic spies. The drama of their trial, played out before a Jewish judge, with dueling Jewish prosecutors and defense attorneys, seemed to implicate all New York Jews. The trial pitted Julius and Ethel Rosenberg, both born and bred on the Lower East Side, children of struggling Jewish immigrants, against an ambitious, young assistant prosecuting attorney who grew up on the Grand Concourse before moving to Park Avenue. They stood before another Jew, a "boy judge" who aimed for respectability. The trial's drama presented a stark choice for Jews: "between those who had made it and those who still struggled on the edge of poverty, between the values of Park Avenue and those of the Lower East Side, between a religious Jewish identity and a secular radical one, between those clothed in the power of the state and those who wore only their own ideology." When the jury agreed that Julius had served as a spy for the Soviet Union, recruiting Ethel's younger brother, David Greenglass, and had been helped by Ethel, who appears to have been framed by the

FBI with her brother's assistance, the judge sentenced them to death. He accused them of "devoting themselves to the Russian ideology of denial of God, denial of the sanctity of the individual and aggression against free men everywhere instead of serving the cause of liberty and freedom."[41]

In the two years of appeals preceding the Rosenbergs' execution, neither side wavered. The Rosenbergs asked for justice, not mercy. The judge replied, "I consider your crime worse than murder." Subsequent appeals were rejected. The outbreak of the Korean War further inflamed passions, as did McCarthyism, which endangered so many left-wing Jews with loss of their livelihoods through blacklists and loyalty oaths, investigating committees, and prosecutions. The Rosenberg case threatened to implicate a significant segment of New York Jews and their synthesis of political radicalism with Jewish ethnicity.[42]

The Rosenbergs' execution occurred on a Friday evening in June 1953, as hundreds of New Yorkers gathered in Union Square in a silent vigil. The Jewish communist novelist Howard Fast took the microphone to announce that there was no more hope for reprieve. When Fast proclaimed that Julius Rosenberg was dead, "tears and sobs seized the crowd." A teenager later recalled, "We had stood there, silently, from late afternoon until that moment thinking that against all odds our presence might somehow persuade President Eisenhower to grant executive clemency." It was not to be. Yet in other parts of the city, where Jews mingled with their Italian American neighbors on Brooklyn streets, cheers greeted news of the couples' deaths, broadcast live from Sing Sing prison. An enormous burden on New York Jews had been lifted.[43]

The Rosenbergs' execution, coupled with difficulties defending a position that was neither communist nor liberal in an environment dominated by McCarthyism, contributed to the decision of a number of left-leaning Jewish intellectuals, including graduates of CCNY's alcoves like Irving Howe, German refugee scholars like Lewis Coser, and Ivy League–educated writers like Norman Mailer, to launch a new magazine, *Dissent*. Although the American Jewish Committee had underwritten the new Jewish intellectual magazine *Commentary* after World War II, its perspectives tended to support U.S. Cold War policy. *Dissent* and *Commentary* shared many writers, part of a circle of New York intellectuals, many of whom lived on the Upper West Side, increasingly an ethnically and socioeconomically diverse neighborhood. Both magazines attracted a mix of Jewish and non-Jewish men and a few women (especially once the feminist movement arrived) who sought to shape American political life. However, *Dissent*, lacking any Jewish organizational support, regularly critiqued United States politics from a democratic socialist position. It challenged the bureaucratization of American life, addressed rampant socioeconomic inequalities, and mounted substantial cultural criticism against bland, middle-brow culture, while publishing avant-garde writers. Its cultural criticism at times overlapped with *The Village Voice*, a weekly alternative paper that regularly published many New York Jewish columnists.[44]

A number of these men, "New York Intellectuals," had considered themselves in their college days to be "citizens of the world," cosmopolitans who set themselves apart from parochial sympathies and patriotic American realities. In the postwar years, their consciences raised by communist aggression, by Soviet anti-Semitism, and most profoundly by the horrors of the Holocaust that reminded them of their Jewish backgrounds, they refashioned themselves as self-conscious Jews. Living together on the "Upper West Side kibbutz," as they jokingly referred to the neighborhood, a number of them, including Daniel Bell, Nathan Glazer, and Irving Kristol, met regularly with their wives to study Talmud and Maimonides's *Mishneh Torah*. They wrote for a cluster of new journals that appeared after the war, including *Dissent* and *Commentary*, as well as two influential quarterlies, *Judaism* and *Midstream* (a Zionist publication). A few of these intellectuals, notably Kristol, transformed into Cold Warriors and, using *Commentary* and other magazines to its political right, influenced the rise of American neoconservatism.[45]

Aside from sharing a neighborhood and a passionate commitment to politics and intellectual debate, many New York Jewish intellectuals admired the new Jewish state. Their fierce arguments prior to May 1948 on whether a state should be established faded in the face of Israel's war against Arab nations. Israel's socialist leadership, its kibbutz experiment, its extraordinary effort to gather in displaced European Jews who had survived the war and to absorb Jews from Arab lands who fled persecution all elicited approbation. However, popular efforts to glorify Israel, such as Leon Uris's best-selling novel *Exodus*, provoked disdain for its "pro-Israel sentimentality."[46]

Enthusiasm for Israel extended beyond intellectuals to increasingly wide circles of New York Jews, who gave generously to the United Jewish Appeal's annual campaigns for financial support. In 1948, the campaign raised unprecedented sums that produced private worries among New York Jewish Federation leaders about such formidable competition for funds. Gradually, New York Jews integrated consciousness of Israel into their urban culture. Synagogues added the Israeli flag to the American one, flanking the ark or bima (platform); Jewish events often began with singing the Israeli national anthem. An organization like the 92nd Street YMHA encouraged Israeli dancing as it shifted away from Americanization activities. Its regular weekly sessions, which combined teaching new dances with old favorites, drew participants from around the city. Once a year, beginning in 1952, troupes from diverse venues converged on Hunter College for the annual Israeli folk-dance festival. It subsequently grew so big that it shifted to larger quarters at Carnegie Hall.[47]

By the 1960s, New York City enabled sustained advocacy for Jews trapped in the Soviet Union. More than ever, New York assumed visibility as an international media capital, even as it continued as the country's Jewish capital city. It also harbored the United Nations, only blocks from midtown Jewish organizational headquarters. The fight for Soviet Jewry ultimately ended in victory, with close to a quarter million settling in New York. Many of those who chose the United States over Israel in the 1970s and 1980s were not Zionists. Their choice to seek America's promises rankled Israeli officials who had been the first to fight for their right to emigrate, albeit often behind the scenes. Subsequently, the dissolution of the Soviet Union sent well over a million Jews and family members to Israel because the U.S. no longer considered them refugees.[48]

Although the struggle to rescue Soviet Jews occurred in the city, conflicts over tactics often reverberated with debates over how best to address Jewish crises. Recriminations over what Jewish "establishment" as opposed to "grassroots" leaders did, or did not do, during the Holocaust fueled these arguments. Such designations as "establishment" and "grassroots" were redolent with meaning and passion. Divergent views of the world from headquarters versus neighborhoods loomed large, even if everyone shouted, "Never Again."[49]

The Soviet Jewry movement also recruited a younger generation. Jacob Birnbaum (1926–2014) arrived in New York armed with a vision

Student Struggle for Soviet Jewry, Freedom Day Rally at the Soviet UN mission, May 1, 1988, by Abraham Kantor. New York City housed the United Nations and also served as America's media center. This combination amplified the voices of New York Jews when they rallied to rescue Soviet Jews. The movement regularly recruited young Jews. In the 1970s, many were veterans of 1960s protest movements (such as the civil rights movement and antiwar movement). Courtesy of Judith Cantor, Student Struggle for Soviet Jewry Records, Yeshiva University Archives, New York.

of how to attack the Soviets and free Soviet Jews. This cause became his life's work. Born in Hamburg, Germany, to a distinguished family of Yiddishists, he escaped to Britain on a Kindertransport. After the war, he moved to France to help survivors. When he came to New York City at age thirty-eight, he imagined a mass movement, a "tidal wave of public opinion," that would take the message of freedom to the streets, making the enemy decidedly uncomfortable through unfavorable publicity. Bearded and balding, wearing a black yarmulke, he planned to recruit his shock troops among Jewish students in the city. Living a few blocks from Yeshiva College, he found young Orthodox men and women ready to fulfill the religious obligation of "freeing captives." Birnbaum also reached Jewish students at Columbia University, where he founded the Student Struggle for Soviet Jewry (SSSJ). On May Day 1964, the group organized its first protest rally and picketed the Soviet UN mission. SSSJ appeared repeatedly at the United Nations. Its protest themes melded Jewish historical and religious imagery with contemporary political objectives, as demonstrations enacted Jewish identification. A Passover "Night of Watching" linked Soviet Jews with the Israelite Exodus from Egypt.[50]

Birnbaum's tactics resonated with Jewish college students, veterans of contemporary American protest movements. A full half of SSSJ members had been involved in anti–Vietnam War movements, while more than a quarter had fought for civil rights. Jewish engagement with civil rights involved both efforts to dismantle discrimination in college admissions, employment, and housing in New York and participation in efforts to integrate schools, public transportation, restaurants, and hotels in southern states. Protests against the Vietnam War took Jewish students out into the city's streets, where they occasionally encountered counterprotests from supporters of the president and America's involvement in Vietnam.[51]

Meir Kahane (1932–1990) and his Jewish Defense League (JDL) similarly despised the establishment. But Kahane also deemed nonviolent confrontations to be weak-kneed and "dangerous" because they provided "a false sense of activism." While in JDL's ongoing battles with New York's black militants, members only threatened to use any means available to them, when it came to harassing Russians living in the city, they fought both within and without the law. JDL derived from the Holocaust the "lesson" that Jews stood alone and that those who were content just to "hold rallies and mimeograph sheets of paper" would "doom" Soviet Jewry. Seeing themselves as struggling against the world and shamefully wrongheaded Jewish leaders, JDL members rejected respectability. They pledged "to do what must be done" so that the U.S. would have no alternative but to demand justice for Jews.[52]

With the crisis of Soviet Jews increasingly in the headlines, a new National Conference on Soviet Jewry (NCSJ) obtained Jewish communal funding along with its cooperating organization, the Greater New York Conference on Soviet Jewry (GNYCSJ). These organizations quickly "assumed the posture of the Student Struggle emphasizing mass demonstrations." The JDL also influenced their militancy. These new organizations feared leaving the field of protest to the lawless Kahane. But this turn did not augur a unified front among nonviolent advocates.[53]

Still, Solidarity Sunday, an annual event started in 1971, exemplified a community engaged in nonviolent protest. It attracted up to one hundred thousand marchers down Manhattan's Fifth Avenue to the UN. Beyond proving the people power of New York Jews with numbers that activists had dreamed of for generations, Solidarity Sunday also intensified the Jewish identities of many who participated. Those who stood in the streets, wearing bracelets bearing the names of oppressed Soviet Jews and carrying signs that called for their release and emigration, experienced the day as a secularized holy moment.[54]

JDL redoubled its militancy. It attacked Soviet newspaper and tourist outlets in New York and disrupted performances of Russian cultural troupes. It took to firing shots into the Soviet UN mission. Most egregiously, it bombed the offices of Sol Hurok Productions in Manhattan, killing a Jewish employee and injuring fourteen others. Hurok, a Jewish impresario, had gotten his start in Brownsville's Labor Lyceum and worked to help Soviet artists appear in the United States, using cultural exchange to overcome Cold War antagonisms. Seemingly, Kahane answered to no one except the police and the FBI, which monitored his activities. But actually, Lubavitcher Hasidic leaders along with Manhattan-based Jewish establishment opponents harshly called him to task. The former feared that his protests would undermine their own clandestine efforts to smuggle Jewish religious articles into Russia and to spirit Jews out of the Soviet Union. These Orthodox diplomats shared common tactics with Manhattan Jewish leaders.[55]

Jewish efforts on behalf of Soviet Jews fit comfortably within U.S. Cold War culture. In 1972, Senator Henry Jackson proposed a bill to tie release of Soviet Jews to Moscow's desire to be accorded "most favored nation" status. The Jackson-Vanik amendment stipulated that the Soviets would be denied specific trade and credit benefits unless they agreed to release annually large numbers of Jews—the target number became sixty thousand—and to end harassment of both politically outspoken dissenters and Jews who wanted to leave the Soviet Union. All groups of New York Jews involved in advocacy for Soviet Jews supported the legislation. However, when it became law in 1975, these organizations again diverged, some favoring protest and others opposed.[56]

Activists on behalf of Soviet Jewry achieved impressive victories within their organizers' lifetimes. They also provoked antagonisms and exacerbated divisions separating New York Jews. But just as the movement drew on the city's unique geography, its neighborhoods that clustered Jews according to class, religion, and politics, so did New York Jews' experiences resound beyond the city's boundaries. Despite inroads of suburbanization and diminution of New York City's Jewish population, its over a million Jews in the 1970s and 1980s still sustained sufficient diversity to fuel activist dreams, create communities of solidarity, and transform promises into realities.

PART IV

1960–2015

Mothers and Children, HIAS, by Sonia Handelman Meyer. Sonia Handelman (Meyer) gravitated to the New York Photo League to learn photography and then pictured Jewish life in New York. After World War II, she photographed survivors of the Holocaust as they struggled to build new lives. HIAS, formed initially to assist Jewish immigrants in the 1890s, offered these newest Jewish refugees help adjusting to life in the city. The arrival of survivors and refugees changed the character of some Jewish neighborhoods. © Sonia Handelman Meyer.

10

Old Turf, New Turf

August 1965. Emmanuel Celler, longtime congressman from New York City representing a Brooklyn district, finally reached a goal that had eluded him for over forty years. Immigration legislation passed Congress dismantling the infamous quota system established when Celler had begun his political career. The "bouncy and brash" Celler had tried repeatedly and unsuccessfully to change the law, although he did succeed in passing legislation admitting two hundred thousand displaced persons after World War II outside of the quotas.[1] Born and educated in Brooklyn, Celler, tall, blue-eyed, "bandy-legged and slope shouldered," consistently championed liberal Democratic politics. He drafted civil rights legislation and shepherded the landmark 1964 Civil Rights Act through the House. "I feel like I've climbed Mount Everest," he sighed after it passed. Once asked about his accomplishments as a congressman, he replied, "To be a successful Congressman, one must have the friendliness of a child, the enthusiasm of a teen-ager, the assurance of a college boy, the diplomacy of a wayward husband, the curiosity of a cat and the good humor of an idiot."[2]

Although Celler and others, including President Lyndon Johnson, who signed the bill at the foot of the Statue of Liberty, assured Americans that this new immigration legislation would not change the country's culture, they were wrong. By increasing the numbers of immigrants who could enter the United States each year and opening immigration from Asia and Africa (even as it placed restrictions on Latin America), the Hart-Celler bill dramatically shuffled the population of the United States and especially New York City. In the postwar period, only African Americans and Puerto Ricans had settled in the city in significant numbers. After the new law took effect, immigrants from the Dominican Republic and China, Haiti and India, Mexico and Jamaica, along with substantial numbers of Soviet Jews and Israelis and smaller numbers of Jews from Iran, Syria, and South Africa migrated to New York. By

2010, children speaking ninety-two languages attended the city's public schools. Once again, New York became an immigrant city, with "arguably the most diverse population of any major city in the world." Over a third of its population, or some three million residents, were born abroad. Immigrants mitigated the city's population decline due to the rapid exodus of New Yorkers during the 1970s, including tens of thousands of Jews; stabilized the city's population in the following decade; and increased it by the year 2000, when New York finally became a city of over eight million.[3]

Celler's legislation transformed the city, returning it to its historic character as an immigrant metropolis without a majority population, with immigrants and their children making up more than half of its residents. While Jewish immigrants figured in the mix, especially a large number of Jews from the Soviet Union, most Jewish New Yorkers fell into the census category of "white." In contemporary ethnic calculus, Jews constituted a significant percentage of white New Yorkers, a little less than a third. But since the number of whites was shrinking in the city, declining from a majority of 76 percent in 1970 to a minority of 44 percent in 2000, Jews' overall percentage of the population declined. However, Jews did not follow trends of other whites. The number of Jews declined less than the number of whites did in the 1990s and the number of Jews increased to over a million in the first decade of the twenty-first century while whites continued to decline. Both high birthrates among Hasidim and increased longevity contributed to Jewish population increases.[4]

Most New York Jews were college educated; many possessed advanced degrees. Having overcome occupational discrimination that lingered into the 1960s, Jews held jobs in real estate, finance, publishing, education, law, and medicine in this postindustrial city. They still congregated in neighborhoods, but Queens attracted more Jews than the Bronx did. They still worked in commerce, usually as managers of large stores rather than as owners of small ones. They still debated how to observe Jewish rituals and holidays. Most still refused to join a congregation, yet many retained a consciousness of being Jewish.[5]

Often Jewish differences grew out of family bonds; for some, their sense of Jewishness flowed from work or neighborhood or culture or politics. A visible minority rigorously observed the strictures of Judaism, and their presence gave other Jews a kind of yardstick by which to judge themselves. Despite their greatly reduced numbers, the city still honored Jewish holy days by adjusting its mundane rhythms. In fact, accommodations made for Jews, such as closing the public schools for the Jewish High Holidays, served as precedents for other non-Christian groups in the city, specifically Muslims and Chinese, who lobbied for similar recognition. In short, Jews exchanged old turf for new turf, but the battles behind those exchanges produced a Jewish New York that differed in significant ways from its working- and middle-class, progressive roots.

Housing, Racism, and Public Schools

Postwar champions of urban renewal urged wholesale destruction of tenement neighborhoods. Seeking to make the city attractive to white middle-income families, city officials used urban redevelopment to increase residential segregation. They displaced tens of thousands without giving any thought to where these New Yorkers might go. The abandonment and destruction of housing in expanding poor neighborhoods exemplified the "New York approach." Urban redevelopment, "the most important public policy undertaken by New York City after World War II, . . . transformed the city." These projects dislodged over one hundred thousand low-income people, 40 percent of them African American and Hispanic, in order to safeguard middle-class professionals who worked in the city's skyscrapers, medical centers, and universities. While these middle-class enclaves "bore the hopes" of liberals to secure a viable city, most of these urban activists refused to recognize "the moral paradox of a liberal policy that left social wounds." In fact, redevelopment produced a city "more divided by income and race." Many Manhattan Jewish liberals supported urban renewal, and Jewish unions took advantage of federal funds to build cooperatives in the 1950s. But Bronx Jews mobilized to fight it when it struck their neighborhood.[6]

Most New York City Jews in the 1950s lived securely among friends and family in their own enclaves of long standing, but residents of a one-mile strip of Bronx territory felt tremors of crisis. A massive city project that was destined to change the face of the entire metropolis threatened to obliterate their neighborhood. Robert Moses, who at one point reigned simultaneously as head of some dozen city and state offices, saw this land as an essential link in his master-builder road plan to modernize New York. He aimed to construct the Cross Bronx Expressway connecting the city with New Jersey, Long Island, and New England. With the support of the mayor and city officials, he informed 1,530 families housed in some 159 buildings that they had ninety days to move out of their condemned buildings. Unlike Jewish immigrants who had acquiesced to the destruction of thousands of tenements on the Lower East Side to build ramps for bridges spanning the East River, Moses's edict ignited a half-decade battle. During these skirmishes between Moses and neighborhood activists, Moses resorted to cutting off heat and hot water in some protestors' buildings. In the end, he won.[7]

Removing these five thousand residents, most of them Jewish, marked the beginning of the end of the neighborhood. As construction of "Heartbreak Highway" ensued, starting with noisy, dirty, and toxic excavation work, some ten thousand additional residents moved out. Those with more money, mostly the younger generation, looked for housing in the suburbs or the suburban-like Bronx community of Riverdale. Soon religious organizations followed.[8]

As Jews vacated East Tremont's apartments, many of the city's poorest, mostly African Americans, moved into the increasingly dilapidated buildings. Families on welfare found shelter in the neighborhood, sent by social welfare agencies. Fears and realities of muggings, robberies, break-ins, and violence reverberated through the neighborhood, accelerating a chain migration out of the area. As each additional cluster of Jews left a building, word spread next door and then around the corner. Co-ops and other middle- and lower-middle-class developments absorbed those who could flee. But the poor and elderly remained trapped in what were later described as "ravaged hulks"; people were "barricaded in their freezing apartments." Jewish communal discussions ignored these Jewish poor until the 1970s, when crusading journalists focused attention on their problems. East Tremont produced a compelling formula for decades of urban crisis. Such changes disrupting the fabric of Jewish neighborhoods drove Jews to move.[9]

Moses, exercising power as head of the New York City Housing Authority, similarly disturbed the working-class Jewish community of Brownsville. He determined that the "community would be a dumping ground for those displaced." To win local support, he used the promise of large-scale public housing. Brownsville's Jewish residents welcomed these proposals, believing in the city's responsibility to construct affordable housing for the working class. But the Brownsville buildings proved to be cheap, shoddily built, with small, narrow apartments that lacked modern amenities. Still, when the first developments opened in 1948, Jews eagerly sought apartments, which were better than decaying tenements. They occupied the majority of the thirteen hundred units; African Americans lived in the others. However, restrictions on income forced the most successful to leave. In their stead, came a different class of African Americans, many of them newcomers from the South. As racial balances started to tip, city practices exacerbated change by giving preference to African Americans who had been displaced by urban renewal, including many euphemistically called "problem families." Juvenile delinquency and gang violence gradually entered Brownsville's housing projects. Crime and fear traumatized more than just the immediate victims. One family's departure inspired others.[10]

Prejudice and discrimination deterred working-class African Americans from obtaining housing. Federal Housing Administration programs that provided white former GIs with mortgages to live in a suburbia that was off-limits to blacks denied African Americans opportunities to purchase homes. Practices known as "red-lining" blocked loans by banks in Brownsville and other poor city neighborhoods since these loans would not be secured by federal mortgage insurance. Such discriminatory practices rendered impossible either new private investment or capital improvements for store owners and landlords. These federal and city policies guaranteed Brownsville's decline from a working-class area into an urban slum.[11]

This compound of poverty, violence, fear, flight, and racism, exacerbated by unscrupulous real estate operators who capitalized on these tensions, ended Jewish life not only in Brownsville but also in adjoining areas. As Jews had speculated on tenement properties when immigrants poured into the city, some now engaged in "flipping" houses, using racial change as a means to make money. Most Jews left Brownsville, except for the elderly and destitute. Such spiraling dynamics transformed a neighborhood in just five short years from 66 percent white and heavily Jewish in 1957 to 75 percent African American and Latino. Although these neighborhood transformations surely strained relations between Jews and blacks, an absence of expressed, intense racial animosities tapped down their volatility. While Jews who remained in these areas in the early 1960s "felt increasingly uncomfortable in a sea of black and Latino faces, . . . there were no race riots or significant confrontations."[12]

Perhaps the hardest feelings emanated from the streets of Crown Heights, a formerly middle-class neighborhood adjoining Brownsville where Jews often lived in private homes. African Americans migrated in large numbers from Brownsville. Block-busting devastated Crown Heights. The process involved real estate agents selling a house on a block to an African American family and then sowing fear among neighbors that their property values would decrease as a result, thus leading to panicked sales. Street crime escalated. But even as Crown Heights was changing, Rebbe Menachem Schneerson told his followers that the Lubavitcher Hasidim would not leave an enclave that they had labored to build. They would not abandon its network of schools, shuls, shops, and other communal institutions.[13]

Following his rebbe's decision yet anxious to protect fellow Hasidim, Rabbi Samuel Schrage organized Jewish street patrols, dubbed the Maccabees. To many African Americans in Crown Heights, the Maccabees' activities smacked of vigilantism that indiscriminately targeted blacks. Conversely, some Jews saw criminals as anti-Semites. A city investigation attempted to set that record straight. It determined that muggers, burglars, and other criminals were essentially opportunists—black and white. This analysis also mandated that street patrols include both Jews and blacks. Schrage eventually changed his group's name to Crown Heights Community Patrols, helping to calm angry community voices.[14]

Yet the Lubavitchers' effective manipulation of the city's political system chafed their neighbors, who by the 1970s included Jamaican and Guyanese immigrants. By that time, Lubavitchers were the fastest growing segment of the neighborhood. Local Lubavitch organizations purchased apartment buildings for their members, including recent converts, and used government loan and subsidy programs to partially cover rental costs. To help their own poor, Hasidim effectively gained control of a local community planning board and directed public funds their way, to the exclusion of others in need. Seeking to expand their presence in Crown Heights, Hasidim literally knocked on African Americans' doors asking whether their houses were on the market. By 1978, the angriest black voices spoke of "Jewish expansionist aggression." Jews worried about rising crime and blamed first their neighbors and then the police for insufficient protection. But African Americans still thought that Jews engaged in racial-profiled vigilantism. They also resented special treatment accorded the Lubavitcher rebbe by the police.[15]

Unlike in Crown Heights, Brownsville, and East Tremont, most African Americans and Jews, living in an increasingly segregated city, did not confront or even engage one another. They rarely lived next door to each other, and their children attended largely segregated schools. Only in places of commercial amusements, like Coney Island, did Jews share the beaches and boardwalks with African Americans. The historian Eli Lederhendler, who grew up in the Bronx, recalled living "in a kind of conditioned ignorance where black-white relations in our city were concerned." Despite "an active desire to put things right," that is, with regard to "principled politically sanctioned segregation between people of different backgrounds," the question of "just why basic services like public schools should have been inadequate" for African Americans or "why de facto residential segregation by color was a way of life in New York" eluded him. He did not recognize that his "own mixed Jewish-Catholic, middle- and lower-middle-class neighborhood constituted a pocket of relative privilege." Many New York Jews failed to see racism underlying de facto segregation in the city. Unless parents brought segregation to consciousness, most New York Jews did not realize that their home turf was racially segregated.[16]

These childhood experiences, coupled with a familial belief in "social justice," allowed many New York Jews to applaud the efforts of Martin Luther King Jr. to integrate the South, to take pride in the civil rights activism of Rabbi Abraham Joshua Heschel, and to mourn the trio of black and Jewish martyrs, Goodman, Schwerner, and Chaney, murdered in Mississippi during the 1964 freedom summer. Many subsequently came to see themselves as "part of that last generation of New York Jews who believed in the existence of a special relationship and a commonality of fates" linking them with African Americans, despite radically different "social and economic positions both in the city and nationwide." However, these commitments "were never tested."[17]

When race riots broke out in Harlem and in Bedford-Stuyvesant in Brooklyn in the summer of 1964, sparked by the murder of a teenage African American by a policeman, thousands of angered residents "raced through the center" of the neighborhood, "shouting at policemen and white people, pulling fire alarms, breaking windows and looting stores." White store owners tallied up their losses. Rioters seemingly targeted "only businesses owned by white persons." *New York Times* editorialists minced no words when they opined that "the deepest reason for the rioting" was "the horrible ghetto condition, . . . stinking tenements, the lack of good schools, the inadequate recreational facilities, the shortage of job opportunities." High on the list of malefactors were rapacious landlords and storekeepers, "greedy white folks" and "prejudiced employers." Routinely characterized as part of the "white power structure," these exploiters were not labeled Jews, as opposed to whites, neither in rioters' rhetoric nor in commentators' criticisms, even if Jewish names abounded on lists of local shopkeepers whose places were looted. "No observer at any of these first series of riots recalled hearing anti-Jewish slogans," wrote a sociologist several years later. Such silence contrasted pointedly with strident voices heard during violence in other cities. Similarly, a local Brooklyn Jewish paper did not claim anti-Semitism.[18]

In some ways, these responses recalled earlier interpretations of Jewish-black confrontation, such as a 1960 NAACP campaign against Harlem liquor stores—most, they said, owned by Jews—that were "closed to Negro salesmen." Local residents expected more out of Jews than from the general white population. A spokesman for the NAACP "expressed amazement" that, given "the closeness that has existed between Jews and the Negro community," Jewish store owners did not immediately accede to their requests.[19]

The turning point in black-Jewish relations in New York occurred in 1968 when the two groups confronted each other in a political battle over power in the public schools. Here questions of leadership and influence were at stake. Jews had entered the city's public school system in large numbers, establishing an ethnic niche as teachers. By the postwar years, many had risen to administrative positions as principals. Strong traditions of support for unions led most to join the United Federation of Teachers (UFT), especially after postwar anticommunist crusades forced many radical Jewish teachers and their communist New York City Teachers Union out of the schools. African Americans, repeatedly stymied in their efforts to use public education to engineer opportunities for social mobility due to the abysmal quality of New York's segregated schools, sought control over their local schools in order to transform them. The prime combatants pitted a heavily Jewish union against black parents, even if neither group precipitated the dispute. The confrontations elicited vituperative anti-Semitic and racist sentiments from both sides.[20]

Confrontation between the members of the United Federation of Teachers and the Ocean Hill–Brownsville Community, 1968, by Sam Reiss. African Americans, repeatedly stymied in their efforts to use public education to engineer opportunities for social mobility due to the abysmal quality of New York's segregated schools, sought control over their local schools in order to transform them. The prime combatants pitted a heavily Jewish union against black parents, even if neither group precipitated the dispute. Sam Reiss Photographs Collection. Courtesy of Tamiment Library, New York University.

In 1967, the president of the Ford Foundation turned his attention to ameliorating racial inequality, championing a plan for community control and self-empowerment in New York City public schools. Initially, union leaders supported decentralization plans to revitalize depressed, underfunded, and overcrowded schools. Some even walked arm in arm with local parents to Board of Education headquarters to advocate for more funding. For the UFT head, Albert Shanker, these early protests reflected his past pedigree of support for civil rights. He had marched in Selma. However, when the plan was implemented in the Ocean Hill–Brownsville experimental school district, it immediately provoked conflict between teachers and parents.[21]

This struggle pitted black nationalists eager to exercise political power against Jewish unionists determined to protect their positions as teachers. As rhetoric escalated, so did actions by Jewish teachers and African American parents and leaders. In the aftermath of the murder of Martin Luther King Jr., anger and hopelessness about possibilities for dismantling a racist society spread among African Americans in the city. The head of the African-American Teachers' Association spoke bitterly of "death for the minds and souls of our black children" due to "the systematic coming of age of the Jews who dominate and control the educational bureaucracy of the New York public school system." The new administrator of the experimental district moved to fill administrative vacancies with those who shared these sentiments. The UFT quickly protested that he did so without following promotion guidelines. However, his unilateral move of summarily dismissing nineteen teachers and administrators in May 1968 galvanized union opposition. All but one was Jewish, many closely aligned with the UFT.[22]

The UFT initially turned to the courts, which granted relief because of lack of "due process," only to have Mayor John Lindsay refuse to implement the decision. With Shanker now at odds with both City Hall and his African American opponents in Brooklyn, he called his rank and file out on the first of three strikes that effectively closed down the entire city school system for close to three months. Charges and countercharges of anti-Semitism and racism fouled the city's air. An unsigned letter that found its way into the mailboxes of UFT teachers in one of the Brooklyn district's schools exacerbated matters. It read in part, "It is Impossible for The Middle East Murderers of Colored People to Possibly Bring To This Important Task" the qualities that are necessary to teach "African American History and Culture . . . to our Black Children." Shanker quickly distributed half a million copies of this letter. Anti-Semitism also infected the airwaves in a WBAI radio broadcast of a poem "dedicated" to Shanker, written by a fifteen-year-old schoolgirl. She rhymed, "Hey, Jew Boy with that yarmulke on your head / You pale-faced Jew boy—I wish you were dead."[23]

National and international developments intensified these tensions, especially the impact of Israel's 1967 war. That anonymous letter writer's referencing "Middle East murderers" reflected a growing African American identification with the Third World and its denigration of Israel as a colonialist state. African Americans translated this ideology into local politics and projected Jews as oppressors in the city. By contrast, the Israeli victory inspired many New York Jews to stand tall against all enemies, foreign and domestic. They "concluded that they could and must fight like hell for themselves," specifically in the schoolteachers' case for their jobs and, more generally, against anti-Semitism. Shanker's supporters saw him as a "tough Jew," a battler for his people in New York civic life.[24]

If these conflicts underscored the reality that while Jews and African Americans lived in the same city, they lived largely in different economic, social, and political worlds, these tensions also revealed serious fault lines within the Jewish community. In circles close to Shanker were Jews who hardly perceived him as a hero. Though their presence was barely noted, UFT opponents of long-standing, erstwhile members of the radical Teachers Union identified with black aspirations. Many of the Teachers Union's rank and file lost their jobs during the McCarthy Red Scare of the early 1950s for their alleged, or real, communist affiliations. Some refused to sign loyalty oaths that were demanded of teachers. Others continued to teach in the public school system even after their labor organization disbanded.[25]

More significantly, young Jewish teachers—40 percent of the replacement cohort brought into the Ocean Hill–Brownsville district in 1968—publicly denied that anti-Semitism pervaded the schools. A twenty-three-year-old recent graduate of Long Island University who secured one of those jobs characterized his group as "younger and better educated" than UFT stalwarts, with more experience working against the system and committed "to social change." He criticized the UFT for its "skillful use" of anti-Semitism "to intensify the fears of the liberal Jewish community."[26]

Older strikers disliked this youthful rhetoric. As they reviewed their own lives and careers, they contended that they were drawn back to a neighborhood that was once "theirs" to teach a new group of underprivileged students. They had empathized with their charges because they, too, had been poor children of immigrant newcomers to New York, growing up in Brownsville. In the spirit of egalitarianism of these formerly Jewish streets, they had cooperated with responsible local black parents to improve students' lives. And now arrogant young colleagues chastised them while black anti-Semites pilloried them as racists.[27]

Ira Glasser, the executive director of the New York branch of the American Civil Liberties Union, a group with many Jewish supporters, strongly seconded the younger teachers' sentiments. Challenging the UFT's motives and methods, he spoke as a liberal Jew and pointedly "blamed Shanker for whipping up the anti-Semitism issue" in order to undermine the entire decentralization effort. As far as black anti-Semitism was concerned, he alleged that the UFT's evidences were "half truths, innuendoes and outright lies." Another outspoken Jewish supporter of civil liberties, *Village Voice* journalist Nat Hentoff, not only "opposed the union stance and its supporters" but also addressed the alleged volatility of reading an anti-Semitic poem on the radio. Hentoff upheld the station's right to permit its shows' hosts and guests to speak their minds. While the rhetoric was unfortunate, he expected that the ensuing discussion would make clear that Jews were not the blacks' real enemy.[28]

Meanwhile, operating out of a totally different Jewish space, Rabbi Meir Kahane imagined his people under existential attack. Turning his position as managing editor of the Brooklyn weekly *Jewish Press* into a pulpit, Kahane repeatedly argued that the anti-Semitism emanating from the teachers' strike was but the latest manifestation of black antipathies suffered by his Jews of Brooklyn. He used this opportunity to mount one of his favorite soapboxes to ridicule the "establishment Jew" as "a rich Jew who lives in Scarsdale," removed from the realities of city life and without any feeling for the "grass-roots." Kahane viewed the city as "polarized beyond hope" with "anger, hate, frustration." He and his paramilitary activists used every means to answer anti-Semitism both within and without Brooklyn. They picketed WBAI's offices, calling on the Federal Communications Commission to revoke its license. They even extended their fight in Manhattan to the steps of Temple Emanu-El, protesting the liberal and wealthy Reform Jewish congregation's invitation to a member of the Black Panther Party to present his claims for reparations from whites for the exploitation of blacks.[29]

Kahane's Jewish Defense League (JDL) also pilloried Leonard Bernstein and his wife, Felicia, when they hosted a fund-raising gathering in their Park Avenue duplex in support of the (Black) "Panther 21," on trial for conspiring to blow up the Bronx Botanical Gardens. For Kahane, Bernstein epitomized the elite "radical chic" New York Jews at the center of "liberal and intellectual circles [who] lionize the Black Panthers."

While asserting that JDL defended "the right of blacks to form defense groups," Bernstein and his friends, in Kahane's view, went "beyond this to a group which hates other people."[30]

Kahane's rhetoric, and especially his methods, did not capture the hearts and minds of most New York Jews. But his articulation of Brooklyn-versus-Scarsdale or Bronx-versus-Manhattan dichotomies reflected real disagreements among Jews over turf as well as competition for leadership. The splits also measured the comfort level of Jewish groups and enclaves within the metropolis. While Jews seemingly agreed that black anti-Semitism was increasing, levels of anxiety varied. Depending on where they lived, often a measure of their socioeconomic position, Jews held fundamentally different views of the role of the municipal government in addressing their concerns. One sociologist argued that the Ocean Hill–Brownsville controversy transformed "outer borough Jews" from "optimistic universalism" to "nervous parochialism," while most Manhattan Jews maintained their liberal equilibrium.[31]

A public-opinion poll conducted half a year after the strike picked up an even more complicated range of attitudes across the city. Manhattan and Brooklyn Jews fundamentally differed. For example, less than one-half of the Jews in Manhattan perceived a rise of "anti-Jewish feeling in the city," while almost two-thirds of those in Brooklyn felt an increase in such tensions. Brooklynites also "tended to deny that discrimination against blacks takes place," often subscribing to racist stereotypes, while Manhattanites disagreed. Twice as many Manhattan Jews as Brooklyn ones thought that African Americans' demands were "justified." While a quarter of Manhattan Jews thought their neighborhoods were "going down," one-third still enthused about where they lived. By contrast, almost no Brooklyn Jews felt good about their area. On one fundamental question—the perception that "white teachers discriminated against black youngsters"—reflecting the crisis between the UFT and the Ocean Hill–Brownsville community, more than a quarter of Manhattan Jews agreed. Almost no Brooklyn Jews concurred.[32]

In general, Jews polled in Queens mirrored perspectives of those in Manhattan. They, too, rated their neighborhoods favorably. Fewer Queens Jews estimated a "rise in anti-Jewish feeling" citywide than coreligionists elsewhere did. "Manhattan and Queens Jews were most agreed that anti-black discrimination does exist," and a majority of Queens Jews felt that blacks' demands were "justified."[33]

Jews in the Bronx presented a very different picture. On the one hand, they appeared to be the most apprehensive about the future of their residential areas, probably reflecting "a recent influx of blacks and Puerto Ricans." But on the other hand, when it came to attitudes toward these newcomers, Bronx Jews held fast to their progressive values. Of all New York Jews, Bronx Jews did not see anti-Jewish feeling rising in the city, and a majority perceived that blacks suffered from discrimination and were "justified in [their] demands."[34]

The mix of attitudes of Bronx Jews reflected demographic changes taking place. In older sections, like the Grand Concourse, Jews pointedly observed, "affluent Jews who live in expensive apartments in Manhattan do not have to worry about the likelihood of a large-scale black influx." But they could have said the same thing about the "under-thirty-five," upwardly mobile, "well educated" Jewish crowd moving to the growing Riverdale section of the Bronx. This new generation of Bronx Jews identified with the social values of those in Manhattan and scored high on every quotient of tolerance. Meanwhile, in largely segregated apartment developments, no racial turmoil existed. In cooperative housing projects built by the unions, Jews espoused ideologies that supported integration and opposed racism, even if relatively few African Americans lived in their apartment buildings.[35]

In short, New York Jews held varied views on African Americans. With well over a million Jews living in the city, Jews could afford the luxury of dissension. Their lack of unanimity translated into diverse politics, struggles over turf, and competition for leadership.

This diversity of Jewish opinions on where the city was heading and their place within the changing urban mix registered when Mayor John Lindsay ran for reelection in 1969. Previously New York Jews had split between those who voted for one of their own—Controller Abraham Beame, a Democrat, would have been the first Jew to occupy Gracie Mansion—and those who voted for the young Republican Lindsay, also the standard-bearer of the Liberal Party. The major issues then focused on "fiscal responsibility," "political extremism," and "police misconduct." Only the third smacked of race. Lindsay supported establishing a civilian police review board, while his opponents demurred. But that issue did not turn the election. Actually, more African Americans voted for Beame than for Lindsay.

For Jews, the choice narrowed to ethnic heritage versus reform politics and hope for a new start for New York. Lindsay campaigned vigorously for Jewish support, his nylon yarmulke perched high on his head. Beame's appeals to group pride fell flat among many Jewish voters, as the Protestant outsider picked up traction among portions of the controller's natural constituents. When the votes were tallied, Jewish districts in Manhattan and Queens leaned toward Lindsay, while some Brooklyn neighborhoods supported Beame. Beame held his own in "Jewish middle-income, non-professional neighborhoods." This election was not a referendum on the place of Jews in the city.[36]

But four years later, Jews could not ignore the city's exploding racial tensions when they went to the polls. Now the incumbent faced the Democratic challenger, Controller Mario Procaccino, and the Republican and Conservative candidate, John Marchi. Lindsay retained only his Liberal Party line. His Honor had not sided with Shanker in 1968. Lindsay's proposal to enforce alternate-side-of-the-street regulations on the High Holidays angered Jews who would not move their cars on Rosh Hashanah or Yom Kippur. Many Jewish residents of Queens felt that the administration failed to provide proper city services, especially in snowstorms. But Lindsay retained the allegiance of "Manhattan" Jews and those who saw him as a progressive, with a compassionate and optimistic vision of the city's promise for all groups. Procaccino lampooned these Jewish voters and their Christian counterparts as "limousine liberals," a caricature of those insulated by wealth from traumas of crime, neighborhood change, and racial extremism. That image of privilege played well among Jews who were alienated by the mayor.[37]

New York Jews split their votes along class lines. Affluent Jews in Manhattan and those "who lived in Brooklyn and Queens and still worked as schoolteachers, wholesalers, accountants, and dentists" made different choices in an election in which "for the first time in New York City's history . . . racial conflict became determinative for the city's politics." Ultimately, "an unusual combination of support from higher income New Yorkers and low-income Negroes and Puerto Ricans" put Lindsay back into office. Better-off Jews, content with their lot in the city, lined up with blacks and Latinos, dissatisfied with the city's promises, while middle-class Jews voted with other white ethnic groups that were unhappy with New York's direction.[38]

Just a few months later, these profound differences resurfaced as the crux of an intense internal Jewish debate over the future of Forest Hills, Queens. The controversy arose in reaction to a plan to build low-cost housing to end racial segregation. Opponents imagined poor African Americans bringing crime and racial turmoil that had undermined other Jewish enclaves. Many protestors considered themselves urban "refugees," asserting, "many of us come from formerly Jewish communities in the Bronx and Brooklyn where an influx of low-income people meant that our children could not play safely in the streets and grown men were afraid to go out after dark." They perceived themselves as victims of an insensitive Lindsay administration that had taken their Jewish liberalism for granted. Had not most Jews of Forest Hills stood with the mayor in the recent election? In fact, he had garnered six thousand more votes than Beame had in that district. Those who now increasingly felt at odds with their city's policies and its lack of concern about their needs noted that the mayor had backed off from comparable initiatives in adjoining, predominantly Italian enclaves because politicos understood that Italians would resist African Americans moving next door.[39]

But Rabbi Ben Zion Bokser, the spiritual leader of the neighborhood's largest congregation, stood apart from his community's fearful and biased sentiments and absorbed much criticism for his liberal stance. In sermons and essays in his synagogue's bulletin, he consistently supported Lindsay's plan and forthrightly addressed its racial subtext. Sanguine about what changes would mean for the improvement of Jews' lives in Forest Hills, he allowed, "The initial impact [of] more contact with Negroes in our places of business, in our schools, in our home neighborhoods will produce many incidents of tension, but in the fullness of time this will be a source of blessing to all of us." Integration, he continued, "will give each of us unanticipated opportunities to widen our understanding of life." Bokser's plea for the power of multiculturalism, before the term existed as a rallying cry among liberals, spoke powerfully to a new Jewish vision of pluralism that could be nurtured in New York.[40]

On the other side, the JDL prepared to fight forced racial integration. Kahane recognized how crisis at the doorsteps of Forest Hills' Jews changed their political perspectives and turned them toward militancy. He mused, "It's easy for the Jew in Forest Hills to be liberal in Mississippi, [but] when a low-income housing project comes to Forest Hills, suddenly all these Jews that used to get up in the Forest Hills Jewish

Center [Rabbi Bokser's congregation] and say that JDL uses violence and they're bad, come over to me and say, 'Listen, if that housing project goes up, can you blow it up?' "[41]

Though not advocating violence, Rabbi Harry Halpern of Brooklyn's Flatbush Jewish Center confided his fears to Bokser. "People have a right to be alarmed by the influx of such a large number of low income residents. I know that in schools where there has been considerable bussing there are numerous threats against children who will not yield their money to those who wield knives." From a racially changing Upper West Side Manhattan neighborhood came another rabbinical warning: "If you do not want Queens Boulevard to be transformed to Upper Broadway, where Jewish women cannot walk down the street unmolested, you will reverse your opposition on this Forest Hills project." Mediation efforts of the Queens lawyer and future governor Mario Cuomo, together with intercession from the federal government, eventually transformed the project into a cooperative, which stilled angry voices. Erected on the border of neighboring Corona, an area with many African American musicians, civil rights leaders, and athletes, it housed largely white, elderly Jews until the 1990s.[42]

Many of these simmering tensions between Jews and African Americans in an integrated neighborhood boiled over two decades later on a hot day in August 1991. Menachem Mendel Schneerson, the Lubavitcher rebbe, was returning to his office on Eastern Parkway from a visit to his wife's grave. The rebbe did not travel alone. He received a police escort, ironically due to concerns over violence arising from intra-Hasidic struggles between the Lubavitchers and their Satmar enemies from Williamsburg. The rebbe's motorcade also included a station wagon that held members of his staff. As the wagon crossed the intersection of Utica Avenue and President Street, a car heading north on Utica struck it. The wagon careened onto the sidewalk, where Gavin Cato, a seven-year-old boy from Guyana, was learning with his cousin how to ride a bike. Both children were crushed and gravely wounded. Emergency vehicles rushed to the site of the accident, as did police. An Orthodox Jewish volunteer ambulance service arrived first, followed by New York's Emergency Medical Services. The latter treated the critically injured children on the spot, while the former, on instructions from police, took the driver and occupants of the wagon to the hospital. But Gavin Cato died before reaching the hospital.[43]

Incited by local demagogues to avenge Cato's "murder," black youths rampaged through the night destroying property and attacking Jews and police. The mob caught twenty-nine-year-old Yankel Rosenbaum, identified as an Orthodox Jew by his beard, dark clothing, and visible *tzitzit* (the ritual fringed undergarment). Beaten and stabbed, Rosenbaum subsequently died of his wounds. But his death did not end the riots, which lasted for three days.

Some Jews called the violence a pogrom, suggesting that it unfolded due to the government's, specifically Mayor David Dinkins's, behavior. New York's first African American mayor, unpopular among Orthodox Jews, was pilloried for his slow response to the violence. But African Americans characterized the events as a race riot, linking it to other past outbursts in the city. These alternative interpretations magnified political differences in the city between Jews, especially those in Brooklyn, and African Americans.[44]

These confrontations over housing and schools served as dress rehearsals for more extensive struggles over New York's promises to its people. Jews of Manhattan, Brooklyn, Queens, the Bronx, and Staten Island drew different lessons from these tumultuous years. Some determined that living in a multiethnic and multiracial city without any buffer from insular neighborhood enclaves no longer was worth the personal price of insecurity. Kahane himself decamped to Israel, where he started a political party that transferred to local Palestinian Arabs some of his racial animosity toward New York's African Americans. Others renewed their commitments to a changing city, unwilling to abandon the love affair that had carried Jews for generations. Many remained ambivalent. They walked away from these disputes increasingly of several minds over how comfortable they were, unsure of whether promises or nightmares would be theirs in their city.

Changing Neighborhoods

When Molly Goldberg wanted America to feel the vibrancy of New York Jewish neighborhood life, she projected 1038 East Tremont Avenue as the quintessential windows-open, door-unlocked, Bronx apartment-house community. Helen Lazarcheck, who really lived in that area in the 1950s, felt that warm embrace. "Everyone seemed to help one another. If there was trouble everyone would do something for you if they could.

They were always coming in and sharing what they had." Despite this friendliness, the Jews of East Tremont did not agree on political issues. "The Yiddishist and Hebraist each had his following with a supporting system of cultural clubs, bookstores, debating societies," as did radicals, both socialists and communists. Even the rabbis of the area's seven synagogues competed for religious allegiances. Jews debated contrasting worldviews on weekends or on Jewish holidays at crowded park benches in Crotona Park or on Southern Boulevard. But a palpable feeling of belonging united the neighborhood. Patterns of street life reassured everyone. Continuity characterized this place where neighbors had grown up and were raising their children and where they expected to grow old among friends.[45]

Yet this continuity belied significant changes. During the 1950s and 1960s, Jews began to leave New York, seeking suburban pleasures, economic opportunities, or a sun-dappled retirement in fast-growing cities like Miami and Los Angeles. By 1970, New York's Jewish population had dropped to 1.4 million, a 43 percent decrease over two decades. But when the city's fortunes plummeted, Jewish migration from New York accelerated, offset only by tens of thousands of poor immigrants from the Soviet Union, as well as thousands from Israel and Syria. The dramatic decline that occurred in the 1970s and 1980s brought the total Jewish population below a million by the new century.[46]

A significant worldwide recession began in 1973. Many major commercial banks, concerned with their own liquidity, demanded that the municipality pay back loans, which they had for years encouraged New York to assume. These lending institutions also pushed strongly for diminutions in city services, freezes and reductions in city jobs, and rolling back long-standing municipal labor benefits. Attempting to respond, the city instituted a wide range of budget cuts that produced hard feelings citywide. Several firehouses were closed. Police and teachers were laid off. In 1976, the City University ended its 129-year tradition of no tuition. Coming on the heels of open admissions that expanded educational opportunities for African Americans and Latinos, the new fees appeared to be yet another example of racism, especially since they coincided with the first majority-nonwhite class of students enrolled. Despite these cuts, the city found little sympathy from either bankers or politicians in Washington, DC, where there was a sense that the metropolis was being repaid for its longtime irresponsibility and arrogance.[47]

The collapse of manufacturing in the city brought massive unemployment to recent migrants and African Americans. Those who had never shared equally in the city's economic promises found fewer opportunities than ever within the depressed pool of entry-level industrial occupations. Many tenants were unable to pay their rents unless supported by the Welfare Department. People doubled up in apartments as others had done during the Depression. Streets teemed with youth. Some turned to peddling drugs as addiction and crime rates increased. Landlords took advantage of a vacancy-decontrol law to extract whatever money they could from their poor tenants. The law allowed owners to hike rents in rent-controlled apartments every time there was a turnover in what were increasingly becoming transient populations. In each instance when a welfare family was moved in and out, fees and charges could go up without any improvements on the property. Yet if a landlord desired to upgrade his holdings, "red-lining" by banks prevented the requisite extension of loans and mortgages.[48]

After a certain point, landlords escaped this spiral of deterioration by abandoning their buildings to avoid real estate taxes. On the way out, the most unscrupulous torched their investments to collect insurance. Nefarious "finishers" found lucrative opportunities to help complete the job. Before the suspicious fires, these criminals stripped a building of salvageable parts, even as the destitute still lived there. The epidemic affected neighborhoods all over the city from the Lower East Side to the Bronx to Brooklyn's Brownsville.[49]

Frustrated, an aide to the Bronx borough president complained that while the media was keenly aware of housing problems elsewhere in the city, "we sure would like to dramatize the abandonments" in the Bronx. "But we can't get the newsmen to come up to blocks like Charlotte Street." Seven years later, he got his wish when President Jimmy Carter visited, followed by a gaggle of news media. New York provided the classic city-in-decline scenario: rent-control conundrums, white working-class exodus, job loss, rising unemployment, drugs, crime, and housing abandonment. Then, in the hot summer of 1977, physical decimation intensified beyond all limits. During a region-wide electrical-grid blackout, marauding gangs of youths, angrily characterized by the press as "vultures," looted much of these areas' remaining businesses.[50]

These years severely tested New York Jews' faith in the metropolis. The issue centered on whether they still felt secure. Differences in perspectives appeared in the sharpest relief between relatively optimistic "Manhattan" and deeply pessimistic "Brooklyn" Jews, and their counterparts in other boroughs. Tens of thousands answered the basic existential question of whether they belonged in New York with an unqualified no. They joined and actually constituted a significant component of the middle-class exodus of those years. The numbers show a net loss of one hundred thousand Jews from the five boroughs. For the first time, New York Jews were as "equally suburbanized" as the general population was. The Bronx suffered the steepest decline and contributed half of the number leaving. Congregations folded. Jews with preteen and teenage children worried about the quality of public education as schools enrolled African American and Latino children. Public schools shifted from white to black and Latino.[51]

Bronx Jews who wanted to stay in the city moved in large numbers to Co-op City. They had been enticed away from their stable and affordable communities, most notably from the Grand Concourse, by this gigantic, 15,400-unit apartment complex in a northeastern corner of the Bronx. It promised a bucolic and modestly priced residential environment "for friendly people living together," in the spirit of previous union cooperative initiatives. Supported by tax abatement, these apartments included free electricity and air-conditioning. Previously Jews had sprawled on fire escapes or sat on park benches long into the hot summer nights. This planned community for working-class people and their children boasted shopping centers, schools, parks, and abundant parking, in effect offering residents suburban amenities within the metropolis. Bronx Jews were attracted by these offers and often frightened by African Americans and Latinos moving into their neighborhoods. Between twenty-five and forty thousand of them (estimated as 50–80 percent of the initial residents) left for Co-op City.[52]

Moving made abundant sense to "the salesmen and civil servants, the accountants and bakers," many approaching retirement age, who perceived their new homes as "the only way station between the decaying neighborhoods they escaped and the affluent suburbs they can not afford." They hoped to re-create at least part of the friendly street culture of the old neighborhood. Indeed, when the complex opened, "long after night fall elderly men and women [would] stroll along the expansive greens or chat on benches." On Jewish holidays, residents promenaded in a style reminiscent of old. There were "no iron gates on the stores," no graffiti, and very little crime. A thirty-five-man "security force armed with night sticks" enforced an eleven o'clock weekday and a midnight Saturday curfew that annoyed youngsters but kept them in line. It appeared to be a Jewish working-class haven.[53]

But poor planning plagued Co-op City. Carrying costs, which included mortgage payments and rising fuel prices, became an increasingly onerous burden on residents who had qualified for apartments precisely because of their limited incomes. Initially, 40 percent of occupants were over sixty-five years of age, many living on union pensions and Social Security. Despite their age, these "cooperators" had not lost their combative spirit, honed for decades as unionists. In 1975, with a 25 percent rent increase threatened, residents took to their own streets and withheld monthly payments, setting off a thirteen-month rent strike. They demanded that the government increase its subsidies. Driving around the complex, block captains, elected by a steering committee, boomed out announcements as bed sheets supporting the effort hung from windows. Strike leaders collected some $15 million in rent checks, which they kept secretly. But the co-op board resigned. Without a program for ongoing rent stability, the cost of living in Co-op City remained a burden for many residents. Israel Schwartz, who moved in soon after it opened, looked back on his experiences after ten years and asserted, "It's a dud, a complete dud. We were taken in, suckered right from the start. We were promised the Garden of Eden, but they inveigled us to get us in and then started to pile the charges on."[54]

In many ways, Co-op City represented simultaneously the apogee and downfall of state-supported cooperative apartment buildings in New York. A tradition that began with unions and radical Jewish immigrants in the interwar decades blossomed into an extensive construction program that built large-scale cooperative houses, often in conjunction with urban renewal, not only in the Bronx but also in Manhattan, Brooklyn, and Queens. Despite financial problems that plagued most of the early co-ops, postwar construction of union-sponsored and state-supported projects provided comfortable housing for thousands of the city's middle and working classes, including large numbers of Jews in the postwar decades. Many Jews embraced the principle of cooperation as a dignified and humane alternative to an exploitative landlord-tenant relationship or private home ownership. Co-ops pioneered a vision of affordable urban

community where neighbors shared responsibility for living
Their financial collapse cast a pall on future programs.

Religious Pluralism

New York Jews lived in a city divided by fissures of class and
sexuality, which spurred many to recognize its increasing
diversity. The baby-boomer Jewish generation no longer sense
whole world was Jewish or desired that it be that way. Not on
they lived but also where they worked shifted as Jews moved ou
parents' ethnic niches in manufacturing and retail, civil serv
public school teaching, into the professions, finance, higher edu
medicine, and real estate. When surveyed, close to half indicat
their three closest friends were not Jewish. They did, however, m
one long-standing tradition that had been widely observed for
century in New York City: they shunned synagogues that were ea
welcome them. In 1981, more than 40 percent of these young me
women never attended religious services, and another quarter app
only on the High Holidays.[55]

Creative religious leaders sought to engage these Jews by emplo
modern publicity methods. Lincoln Square Synagogue of the Up
West Side initiated its "Turn Friday Night into Shabbos" program v
a plan redolent of Madison Avenue. Its pitch to those who frequen
local singles bars was, "How about sharing red wine for Kiddush inste
of white wine for cocktails?" Or "How about a $10.00 ticket for a Sha
bos meal instead of a $40.00 ticket for the Theater?" The synagog
promised not a formal service but instead a "real Shabbos meal, . . . lo
of singing, maybe some dancing" of the Jewish and not disco variet
Those who came within its orbit discovered rabbis willing to work pa
tiently to convince them to "usher in the Sabbath in the same way their
ancestors have ushered it in for centuries."[56]

In the 1980s, a discernible surge in affiliation with synagogues in
Manhattan neighborhoods reflected a process of gentrification. Affluent young Jews were returning to the city, even deciding to raise a family
in an apartment—more often one they purchased as a condominium,
rather than rented—bucking the trend toward suburbanization. As
young children appeared on neighborhood streets, their parents turned

toward synagogues. Having decided to raise a family in the city, they looked to build affective communities, which included other Jews. Synagogues like B'nai Jeshurun, a Conservative congregation on the Upper West Side, which had teetered on the verge of closing, revived under a socially engaged activist rabbi, Marshall Meyer. Another Upper West Side synagogue, Ansche Chesed, opened its doors to a variety of alternative Jewish prayer groups, a mix of lay-led, egalitarian, and participatory fellowships (havurot) and prayer groups (minyanim). These clusters of like-minded Jews who wanted to live in New York, many of them highly educated, took root in Manhattan as baby boomers scorned its established synagogues as too formal and, often, as sexist. As these alternative Jewish prayer groups attracted more members, they needed space larger than a city apartment for prayer and study. Ansche Chesed's offer represented a creative response by its own aging congregation, which did not want to change its forms of Conservative religious worship. The presence of young Jews meeting in classrooms and assembly halls helped save the multistory, urban synagogue.[57]

These decisions to affiliate extended to homosexual and lesbian Jews who desired to affirm Jewish identity and spirituality but were alienated from synagogues that did not countenance their sexuality. In the wake of the 1969 Stonewall Riot, they created their own alternative religious community. Beth Simchat Torah brought together for religious devotion and camaraderie a largely professional and artistic class of Jews who had helped to gentrify the West Village area. For some gay Jews in 1973, a gay synagogue reflected an attitudinal shift from rebellion against convention to a desire for belonging. "We wanted a shul," explained a founding member; "anything else, if it interferes with the service we say 'No!' Those who leave . . . say that we are too traditional, which means we are not a social center." The congregation did make an important stand for gay rights, beginning with its participation in a gay rights parade. But Jewish spirituality took pride of place.[58]

Even as Congregation Beth Simchat Torah faced devastation wrought by the AIDS epidemic, it grew from a few hundred members to over one thousand and inspired comparable gay religious efforts across the country and internationally. Its rabbi, Sharon Kleinbaum, arrived in the midst of the AIDS crisis. She sought to bring healing to a congregation struggling with death. Ordained at the Reconstructionist Rabbinical College and an articulate feminist, she explained, "I did not become a rabbi to sell Judaism." Rather, she affirmed, "I became a rabbi because I believe in the power of religious community to overcome the culture in which we find ourselves, the culture of despair." Raised in an activist family, the petite, dark-eyed rabbi's knowledge spanned all varieties of Jewish religious experience. She embraced social justice movements and led protests for human rights—for women, blacks, gays and lesbians, immigrants, and Palestinians.[59]

The excitement of the city scene and new neighborhood dynamic of sharing space with others while deciding how and when to identify as Jews did not touch those Jews who were elderly, poor, widowed, or divorced. The Bronx (except Riverdale) remained the borough of Jewish seniors.[60] Yet occasionally an eclectic congregation, like the Intervale Jewish Center, survived against all odds. Located in the South Bronx, which lost more than three hundred thousand residents in the 1970s, roughly 40 percent of its population, the congregation soldiered on due to an unusual man, a baker who assumed the responsibilities of a "rabbi" for his diverse flock. Founded in 1917, the congregation at its peak drew as many as five hundred to services. But by the 1980s, "death lurked in the background," observed the anthropologist Jack Kugelmass, "showing its face now and then but always dispelled through blind determination." This small, impoverished, and abandoned Jewish community exemplified a spirit of resilience and creativity in the face of urban violence and decline.[61]

In Brooklyn, the Lubavitcher rebbe initiated a remarkable program of outreach to Jews. Young Hasidim loyal to the Rebbe manned "Mitzvah Mobiles," step vans outfitted with free information about Judaism and designed to introduce Jews to basic religious practices and precepts. They fanned out on Manhattan's streets and accosted likely passersby to inquire, "Are you Jewish?" When the answer was affirmative, they offered an opportunity to step inside the van to lay tefillin. A man did not need to know how to do this basic daily mitzvah since a Hasid would guide him in placing the small black box on his forehead and wrapping the straps on his arm. The outreach of Lubavitch, often called by the acronym Chabad, rapidly spread beyond New York to other cities in the United States and then gradually throughout the world. Soon 770 Eastern Parkway in Brooklyn served as headquarters for a vast network of emissaries, seeking to entice, persuade, and welcome Jews to observe a mitzvah that potentially would not only change their lives but also hasten the coming of the Messiah.[62]

Purim, c. 1980s, by Bill Aron. Orthodox Jews shunned such holidays as Halloween but enjoyed their own costumed festival during Purim. Bill Aron's photograph of a young boy dressed in beard, glasses, and hat comments not only on the holiday but also on three generations of Jews. The grandfather, with a small goatee, fedora, and necktie, represents modern Orthodox Judaism, increasingly rejected by traditionalizing sons. His son, also pictured here, wears a full beard, no tie, and a *shtrayml*, the fur-rimmed hat of Hasidic Jews. Borough Park, Brooklyn, the site of the photo, transitioned after World War II into an exclusively Orthodox Jewish neighborhood. © Bill Aron. Courtesy of Bill Aron.

Schneerson was not the only one concerned about all of those unaf-filiated Jews. Esther Jungreis, a Hungarian rabbi's wife (*rebbetzin*) who survived the Holocaust, established an outreach organization in Man-hattan called Hineni (Here am I) that was designed to compete with cults for the attention of young, single Jews. A dynamic and powerful speaker, the blond and elegantly dressed Jungreis attracted a substantial following in New York and then around the world through her many speeches, classes, extensive writings, and television programs. "Her lec-tures invoked stirring images of traditional Jewish life and the Holo-caust, and culminated in dramatic pleas to assimilated Jews to explore their heritage." Her message particularly inspired those Jews returning to Judaism, complemented by her vaunted matchmaking prowess.[63]

New York City remained fertile soil for Jewish religious experimenta-tion. Its size and diversity stimulated innovative forms of religious au-thority, ranging from hip versions of modern Orthodoxy to politically engaged gay congregations to media-savvy modes of Hasidism. These New York products exerted influence throughout the Jewish world.

Feminism

When Congresswoman Bella Abzug (1920–1998) ran for mayor in 1977, she understood the frustrations that her generation of New York Jews felt toward their native city's faltering promises. To a great extent, she shared their values and experiences. A product of the South Bronx dur-ing its Jewish interwar heyday, she had joined the radical Zionist youth group Hashomer Hatzair. A child of the working class, Abzug lived at home while attending Hunter College. She spent Saturdays at her father's Live and Let Live Meat Market in Manhattan's meatpacking district. The "abandonment" and "debris around those places" that she once called home saddened and angered her. She cared about the city's future. But there was far more to Bella Abzug that set her apart from those who focused narrowly on specific crises. She aspired to be not just some-one who would improve city conditions. Rather, she desired to cap her career as a transformative figure, a catalyst for a more egalitarian society within and without the metropolis. She sought to be the first female mayor of New York City. Once again, out of New York Jewry arose an activist bearing hopes for transcendent change. Her supporters in this campaign recognized that quintessential quality and embraced "her image as a fighter." One local politico understood Abzug as the uncommon leader who "stirs up the people who want to kick the backsides of the powerful."[64]

By the time Abzug ran for mayor at age fifty-seven, she had distinguished herself as an aggressive advocate. Short and energetic, she learned early in her career that no one paid attention to a diminutive woman. So she decided to wear hats, which drew attention and became her trademark. Abzug had earned high marks as a lawyer in labor and civil rights cases in the 1940s, as a defender of Senator Joseph McCarthy's targets in the 1950s, and as a founder of Women's Strike for Peace in the 1960s. An unabashed liberal, she won election to Congress in 1970 representing a downtown Manhattan district. Once in the House, she pressed for legislation that women needed most: securing reproductive rights, banning gender discrimination, and helping women gain childcare. Abzug served three terms and barely lost the New York State Democratic primary for Senate in 1976 before entering that crowded mayoral contest a year later.[65]

Abzug failed in that citywide election, losing to Ed Koch, the city's second Jewish mayor. Still, she remained an iconic figure who personified feminism. Her life story bridged generations in the struggle for the liberation of women. This movement possessed deep New York roots and a profound Jewish texture. Abzug followed in the footsteps of exceptional, radical New York Jewish women, like the communist Clara Lemlich Shavelson, who had fought for women's rights.[66]

New York also welcomed migrants like Betty Friedan (1921–2006), who spent formative years after college in the city as a radical labor journalist. However, she wrote her groundbreaking book *The Feminine Mystique* from her suburban home. Friedan claimed solidarity with other housewives struggling with the "problem that has no name." She asserted that, like other middle-class, educated, suburban women, she had been forced into a "comfortable concentration camp" of a bored, unfulfilling life of affluent routine. Once she articulated dilemmas with which so many identified in her best-selling book, she and her family returned to Manhattan's Upper West Side, the neighborhood she had previously abandoned. Then Friedan helped to found the National Organization of Women (NOW), serving as its first president. She subsequently became a major spokeswoman in the National Women's Political Caucus (NWPC). There she worked with Bella Abzug and the black congresswoman Shirley Chisholm, who represented Bedford-Stuyvesant as the first African American woman to serve in Congress.[67]

Competition as well as cooperation characterized the woman's movement. Gloria Steinem (b. 1934), who grew up outside of New York, joined her sister activists in the city in promoting women's liberation. Like Friedan, Steinem attended Smith College and aimed to be a writer and journalist, but unlike Friedan, she did not marry. Steinem moved to New York to pursue her career, only to find doors closed to serious employment opportunities. Furious at women's marginalization, she worked as a Playboy Club bunny and then wrote a damning piece exposing the sexist exploitation of these underpaid waitresses. With her founding of *Ms.* magazine, Steinem acquired a feminist pulpit to galvanize women across the nation.[68]

This triumvirate of activists differed over directions the movement should take and who should lead it. Friedan often attacked Abzug for "invading her turf" and took on Steinem for allegedly "ripping off the movement for personal profit." Abzug, in turn, publicly questioned Friedan's claim to the "motherhood" of feminism. Still, for all of their jealousies and misunderstandings, another form of marginality united them: anti-Semitism. Lumped together as "leaders of the Jewish conspiracy to destroy the Christian family," they suffered indiscriminate attacks. Steinem, born to a Jewish father and Christian mother and baptized as a Congregationalist at age ten, responded to this animus by averring, "never in my life have I identified myself as a Christian, but wherever there is anti-Semitism, I identify as a Jew."[69]

Steinem, Abzug, and Friedan also confronted prejudices from women within their own movement. At the first United Nations International Women's Decade Conference, they witnessed Israel pilloried as a racist state and their, and their country's, support for the Jewish state roundly denounced. The three endured similar calumnies five years later in Copenhagen, where delegates angrily contended that "Gloria Steinem, Betty Friedan and Bella Abzug all being Jewish gives the women's movement a bad name." Friedan retreated to a church away from the official gathering to express her views and reflected ruefully on how far their enemies had strayed from a promised sisterhood designed to ameliorate real problems of women worldwide.[70]

Another group of Jewish feminists in the city, born after World War II, "could not define themselves solely through their feminist ideology and affiliations." With Jewishness fundamental to their identities, they determined to free themselves from constraints that tradition had imposed on women's participation in religious rituals and leadership. Their solutions transformed the way Jewish women and men ordered their religious and communal lives in the United States and around the world.[71]

Most of these activist women found each other and coalesced into an influential community on Manhattan's Upper West Side, the same neighborhood that housed Jewish intellectuals and academics as well as young Jewish professionals. Many belonged to the New York Havurah, an experimental Jewish religious community. Some were pursuing graduate study at nearby Columbia University and the Jewish Theological Seminary (JTS). The flagship school of the Conservative movement, JTS admitted women to its graduate and teacher-training programs but not to its rabbinical school. Jewish feminist activists considered this situation discriminatory and worked to change it.[72]

Havurahs attracted committed women and men in their early twenties who chafed at what they perceived as the shallowness of synagogue life. In their quest to change the Jewish world, they sought kindred spirits eager to experiment with ritual, song, and liturgy, to imbibe an authentic communal experience at Sabbath and holiday meals, and most important, to engage Jewish texts by applying modern methods and sensibilities to received teachings. Feminists who were "dissatisfied with the strong bias in Jewish religious learning" also established a study group "to subject the Jewish tradition to serious scrutiny as women." As they learned more about themselves and Jewish women's history, they expected to convince the men around them to recognize how integral women were to Judaism. This would be a crucial first step toward consciousness-raising throughout the wider Jewish community. But these women of the New York Havurah discovered to their dismay that while their male counterparts determined to find new ways of living and acting Jewishly, they did not consider amelioration of female concerns as primary, or even worthy, objectives. The women realized that they had to work for change on their own.[73]

The women decided to focus on JTS. Many had been groomed to be future intellectual and communal leaders. They had been star pupils in Conservative religious schools, regular attendees at services, participants in Conservative youth groups and leadership-training fellowships, and campers and counselors at Camp Ramah, the movement's renowned summer educational program. In all regards, they were educated like their brothers, even so far as to enroll in JTS's coeducational undergraduate program. But gender equality ended when it came to full participation as adults in religious observances or congregational leadership.

Paula Hyman (1946–2011) explicitly articulated "the conflict between the way [women] are educated [Jewishly] and the kind of role [they] are allowed in the Jewish community." A student of modern Jewish history, she came to Columbia after completing a degree at Boston Hebrew Teachers College while taking her undergraduate degree at Radcliffe. In classic Havurah style, Hyman turned to the sources for religious validation of her discomfit with the status quo. She observed, "when tradition was incompatible with your sense of self, and some of your basic ethics, then you have to go back and examine the tradition."[74]

In 1972, Hyman, whose blond hair and blue eyes accompanied a brilliant intellect, joined others in drafting a manifesto: "Jewish Women's Call for Change." It demanded that women be counted in a minyan, given full equality under Jewish law, and allowed decision-making power in synagogues and general communal activities, and that "women be permitted and encouraged to attend rabbinical and cantorial schools, and to perform rabbinical and cantorial functions in synagogues." Hyman subsequently wrote on behalf of the New Jewish Sisterhood urging acceptance of the provisions of the "Call for Change." Rebuffed, the Sisterhood concretized into an advocacy group, Ezrat Nashim. The name meant literally "aid to women," but it also denoted the subordinate women's section of a traditional synagogue, away from liturgical action and powerful domains occupied by men. Self-empowered, they decided to confront Conservative rabbis directly and drove up to the Catskills to distribute their "Call for Change" at the rabbinical convention. Refused a place on the program, they held "countersessions" within earshot of the delegates.[75]

The Ezrat Nashim women, in asserting themselves, readily acknowledged that just as Abzug followed Shavelson, they too walked in the footsteps of exceptional Jewish women who strove to reorient traditions. They retold the story of Henrietta Szold through feminist eyes, turning her into an iconic figure. Szold, "by the standards of her time, . . . was blessed with an intellectual and professional freedom, which only a handful of women enjoyed in her era." But "by the standards of the current Women's Liberation movement, she was exploited and harassed throughout the best working years of her long life." She "harbored two ambitions—one for a brilliant career, the other for a brilliant marriage." These dreams, her biographer quickly noted, "many 'liberated' women today will tell you are incapable of peaceful coexistence in a 'male-dominated' world." Most poignantly, she asserted her right and obligation to say kaddish, the memorial prayer, for her own mother rather than have a man recite it in her stead. Scrutinizing rabbinic law, she observed, "elimination of women from such duties was never intended by our law and custom." Szold inspired a new generation of feminists.[76]

The women of Ezrat Nashim recognized as well that some of their members had benefited personally from previous accommodations of

Members of the Commission on the Ordination of Women Rabbis, Jewish Theological Seminary. The members listen to Chancellor Gerson Cohen (back to camera) at one of the early meetings. From left to right: Francine Klagsbrun, Fishel A. Pearlmutter, Haim Z. Dimitrovsky, Norman Redlich, Gordon Tucker, Rivka Harris, Wilfred Shuchat, Elijah J. Schochet, Victor Goodhill, Marian Siner Gordon and Seymour Siegel. Hidden from the camera were the two other members, Milton Himmelfarb and Harry Plotkin. From the Jewish Theological Seminary Chancellor's Report 1977–1979. Courtesy of the Ratner Center for the Study of Conservative Judaism.

Judaism to feminism, such as the new tradition of bat mitzvah, which became commonplace after World War II. They also appreciated Reform Judaism's steps to empower women. Unbound theologically by strictures of religious legal precedent, Reform Judaism had always been capable, according to its own Jewish system, of ordaining women as rabbis. But unyielding social mores within Reform leadership and its congregational ranks had stymied all initiatives. In 1972, however, the Hebrew Union College–Jewish Institute of Religion ordained Sally Priesand as its first woman rabbi. She came as an assistant rabbi to the Stephen S. Wise Free Synagogue in New York on the Upper West Side, strengthening its reputation as a site of religious innovation.[77]

Seeking to expand the reach of Jewish feminism, five hundred delegates arrived in New York City for the first National Jewish Women's Conference. They emphasized the need to create meaningful life-cycle observances for females. They redoubled efforts to identify and honor women's role in Jewish history. They succeeded within their own lifetimes. In the United States, not just in New York, mothers and fathers welcomed publicly the birth of daughters; new life-cycle rituals celebrated all stages in women's lives. Formalized bat mitzvah events even became part of Orthodox practice in communities that disdained feminism. Ezrat Nashim's extensive political advocacy led to admission of the first female candidates to JTS's rabbinical school in 1984. A year later, women danced in the streets when Amy Eilberg, who had studied intensively for several years at JTS hoping for a change in policy, was ordained as the first Conservative rabbi.[78]

These young feminists fortified the Jewishness of leading political activists like Bella Abzug. Certainly, the congresswoman's presence and address at the National Jewish Women's Conference spoke loudly of the integration of the women's rights movement and the struggle for equality within Judaism. Her new level of Jewish involvement constituted a return to greater religious and ethnic identity and a chance to salve some old wounds. She had grown up in a kosher home where Sabbath traditions were respected even as her father, of necessity, labored on Saturday. She received a quality Hebrew education. As a young woman, after studying in a local Hebrew high school and at JTS's coeducational teachers' program, she worked part-time in a Bronx Jewish center. From her neighborhood's secular Zionist Hashomer Hatzair youth group, she gained the "moral fervor, social idealism and pioneering militancy" that guided her public life. But she chafed at religious gender inequalities. She did not like being segregated in the women's balcony and took offense, as had Szold, when she was told that she was forbidden to say kaddish for her father.[79]

As Jewish feminists developed new rituals, like their own Passover seder with Moses's sister, the prophetess Miriam, as a central historical figure, both Friedan and Steinem gravitated toward a sense of religious sisterhood. Friedan admitted that such affirmations were a far cry from the "agnostic, atheistic, scientific, humanist" sensibilities that had guided her family life. For Steinem, congregating with Jewishly committed women gave her a more positive identity. Steinem's cofounder and editor at *Ms.* magazine, Letty Cottin Pogrebin, agreed. Pogrebin hailed from a traditional Jewish background. She briefly attended the Yeshiva of Central Queens. But like so many other women, a negative kaddish experience, that denial of such a basic filiopietistic right to public prayer upon the death of a parent, fueled her teenage rebellion against Judaism. Anti-Semitism in Copenhagen partially pulled her back. However, new Jewish feminist rituals and associations, such as monthly meetings with other women on the occasion of the new moon, or Rosh Hodesh, gave her a greater personal stake in helping to redefine Judaism.[80]

Standing with Abzug as a featured speaker at that first women's conference, Blu Greenberg (b. 1936), a mother of five and the wife of a leading modern Orthodox rabbi, was hardly alienated from Judaism. Yet she readily admitted that Ezrat Nashim initiatives impressed her. Leaders of the conference welcomed her since they aspired to create a movement that spoke to all Jewish women, religious and secular. Greenberg learned from that experience the necessity of a cohort of the like-minded to engender the requisite "support, the testing of ideas, the cross-fertilization." Concomitant with Greenberg's personal journey toward feminism, a cohort like the one that she prayed for began to emerge, albeit independent of her, among younger Orthodox women on the Upper West Side of Manhattan.[81]

On the festive fall holiday of Simchat Torah, which celebrates the completion of reading the Torah scroll over the course of a year and then starting over again, Rabbi Steven Riskin of Lincoln Square Synagogue authorized the first Orthodox all women's *tefillah* (prayer) service. Women were permitted to dance with the Torah scrolls and then read, as the men did in the main sanctuary, the concluding portions of the five books of Moses and the opening chapter of Genesis. This new practice complemented the synagogue's unusual, clear, plastic *mehitzah* that physically separated men and women but allowed the latter to see all of the ritual, including reading from the Torah. Then the congregation experienced another "watershed moment" when Riskin officiated at the synagogue's first bat mitzvah. A precocious female pupil in his Hebrew school petitioned for the right to mark her coming of age just like the boys by reading the prophetic portion during Sabbath morning services. "Playing it by ear," trying "to figure out what to do for a bat mitzvah" in an Orthodox congregation, Riskin "could not give her everything she wanted." But he and his cantor devised a ceremony that permitted her to read portions of the book of Ruth at a Friday night service. Many years later, Riskin proudly remembered that event as constituting part of his education when Elena Kagan was nominated by President Barack Obama to the United States Supreme Court.[82]

Decades later, leaders of New York's women's prayer groups made common cause with Blu Greenberg, ultimately establishing the Jewish Orthodox Feminist Alliance (JOFA). Started "around a member's kitchen table," this advocacy group took Orthodox women's concerns out of its constituents' homes and local neighborhoods in the hope of transforming the wider Jewish world. Their efforts contributed to Rabbi Avi Weiss's decision to designate Sara Hurwitz as the "Maharat" (a spiritual, legal, and Torah leader) of his Hebrew Institute of Riverdale in 2009. Then he titled her "Rabba," another neologism that sounded much like "rabbi." While many of Weiss's colleagues castigated his move, forcing him temporarily to withdraw the term, others wished he had just called Hurwitz "rabbi." But former Ezrat Nashim members appreciated the impact of their activism. A vision of women's equality hatched at New York City study sessions and later around urban kitchen tables had transformed significant segments of the Jewish world.[83]

Writing on the Wall, by Shimon Attie. "I remember when we lived in a tenement on the top floor in very bad condition. It was like a dream . . ." Part of a series, "Between Dreams and History," created by the Jewish photographer Shimon Attie, this image of the Lower East Side combines interviews with senior residents of the neighborhood projected with lasers on tenements and other buildings (in this case, part of a synagogue). A site-specific project, it shows how this iconic immigrant Jewish neighborhood entered into history. © Shimon Attie. Courtesy of Shimon Attie.

11

A Changing City

October 1977. With the eyes of millions of viewers coast-to-coast on the screen watching the second game of the World Series, commentator Howard Cosell looked up beyond the diamond to the view outside Yankee Stadium. "Ladies and gentlemen," he announced in his acerbic fashion, "the Bronx is burning!" A popular Jewish sports commentator, Cosell prided himself on "telling it like it is." So although he misidentified the source of the conflagration—he said it was an apartment building, but it was an abandoned school—Cosell pointed out to the nation that his native city was ablaze, a blighted, steeply declining metropolis under siege. Cosell did not pause to note the symbolism of the action on the field. The game pitted the Los Angeles Dodgers—that once-adored neighborhood-hugging franchise that had abandoned Brooklyn and contributed to a decline in the borough's self-esteem—against the Yankees, long emblematic of the city's power and dominance but presently rife with internal strife and controversy. For Abraham D. Beame, the city's first Jewish mayor, New York City needed such negative publicity like a hole in the head. But Cosell's pronouncement etched itself into national consciousness. Everyone now saw New York as a city of broken promises.[1]

Cosell's stinging jab came just a few days after President Jimmy Carter had made his surprise visit to the South Bronx. Newspapers and television reported that "he viewed some of the country's worst urban blight." Carter delivered a powerful media blow to Beame's city. Arriving by way of the southernmost part of the Grand Concourse, described as "a decaying remnant of a once fashionable boulevard," he walked on Charlotte Street, near Crotona Park, "through two blocks of rubble that looked like the result of wartime bombing." Less than two years earlier, a *Daily News* headline had screamed, "Ford to City: Drop Dead." While President Gerald Ford took offense at this tabloid's characterization of his response to New York's appeal to the federal government to prevent

Embattled Mayor Abraham Beame with the famous *New York Daily News* front page: "Ford to City: Drop Dead," November 3, 1976. The *Daily News* headline captured the sentiment of Washington toward New York's fiscal crisis. Identified as a Jewish and Democratic city by leading Republican politicians, New York garnered little sympathy for its financial woes. Many New York Jews decamped during this decade of crisis, although others contributed funds and expertise to help rescue New York from potential municipal bankruptcy. Photograph by Bill Stahl Jr. / *NY Daily News*. Reprinted with permission.

municipal bankruptcy, Ford asserted strongly that the "people in New York have been the victims of mismanagement."[2] Twenty-five years later, when two planes crashed into the twin towers of the World Trade Center, sending both of them up in flames and leading to the deaths of thousands of people, President George W. Bush recognized that an attack on New York City was an attack on the United States of America.

In the intervening decades between Ford and Bush, New York's fortunes plummeted and then rebounded as the city came to occupy a singular position as America's global metropolis, "capital of the American century." Although Jews left New York in large numbers during the 1970s, the remaining 1.1 million understood how tightly connected was Jewish American life—Jewish culture, religion, politics, and economy—with the nation's largest city. "New York stands apart from the other great capitals" of the world "in that its population diverges sharply from the nation of which it is the largest and chief city." This is because "New York is a Jewish city." Jews may be a tiny fraction of the American population, but they make up a significant percentage of New York's population. Furthermore, Jewish "political orientations, occupational pursuits, and cultural tastes [distinguish] American Jews from their fellow Americans." As a result, through New York, Jews have exerted an influence on the nation, especially in these areas, as they moved from ethnic niches on the fringes of the economy and city to its center.[3]

Three Jewish Mayors and the Politics of Crisis

Behind Cosell's and Ford's injurious rhetoric lay a confluence of social, economic, and political crises that had brought the city to the brink. Long active in New York City politics and contributing significantly to its progressive democratic traditions, Jews did not win the mayoralty until the election of Abraham Beame (1906–2001). But when Beame took office, while the explosive, racial name-calling had abated, he faced an explicit challenge to the city's storied commitment to help the poor and working class.[4] Ironically, Jewish mayors, starting with Beame and followed by Ed Koch (1924–2013), dismantled much of the progressive political heritage that Jewish immigrants and their children had labored mightily to erect. Instead, they oversaw the emergence of a neoliberal, postindustrial city attuned to upper-class concerns. Under Beame's watch, New York's years as an industrial center ended. The city's revenue base declined, and it succumbed to an orchestrated assault by bankers and corporate executives on its generous social democratic practices. A group of investment bankers stepped in to regulate city finances, securing money from both state and nation in return for significant changes in the city's budget. The willingness of the city's civil service unions and their Jewish leaders to invest their substantial pension funds in city bonds staved off default and bankruptcy.[5]

Metropolitan fortunes rose under Koch's first administration. This new Jewish incumbent and his constituents rode the crest of an improving national economy. Koch amplified the city's renewed cachet and popularity among the wealthy. When he appeared before congressional committees seeking financial assistance, he pointed to his aggressive posture in dealing with municipal unions in contract negotiations. As the quintessential unmarried Manhattanite, tall and bald, he personified the advertising slogan "I Love New York." Frequenting upscale restaurants, nightclubs, and athletic events, Koch constantly asked, "How am I doing?" Without waiting for a reply, he let anyone within earshot know that he and New York were doing just fine.[6]

Koch's ebullience eventually rubbed off on his fellow New Yorkers. He enjoyed popularity, benefiting from both the positive tone he had previously set for city life and the reality that his administration returned city services to pre-fiscal-crisis levels. Wealthy New Yorkers were conspicuous in their consumption. Lost from view but noticeable to those who walked the city was the suffering of a growing underclass of homeless people, many of them African American. Their fate little concerned the mayor. Race relations—the calmest critics spoke of economic disparities among groups; others shouted racism—became an issue in the 1985 campaign. African Americans sparred with Koch over the rise of Rev. Jesse Jackson as a national political candidate. They reacted excitedly to Jackson's aspiration to capture the Democratic nomination for president and responded to his message that they whose ancestors "once picked cotton could now pick a President." Koch heard Jackson differently, taking umbrage at his earlier characterization of New York as "Hymietown." The mayor interpreted this remark as proof that Jackson disliked Jews. Never one to mince words, Koch positioned himself as an unintimidated Jewish advocate. Koch returned for the third time to the mayor's office. He did not win a fourth election.[7]

During Koch's final four years in office, a confluence of problems made him politically vulnerable. A series of citywide corruption scandals undermined his standing. A stock-market crash ended a period of unbridled optimism about the city's progress. Despite Koch's tough rhetoric, events and rising crime aggravated racial tensions. Two Jewish candidates challenged Koch, arguing that his tenure had lasted long enough. They preached good government practices and pledged to clean up City Hall. But the African American Manhattan borough president David Dinkins mounted the strongest opposition. Primary results revealed that Koch won just five Democratic Brooklyn and Queens areas with largely Jewish and Catholic populations. Dinkins did well enough among voters in other predominantly white areas to carry him into the general election with his African American and Latino base.[8]

To white New Yorkers, Dinkins projected reconciliation and moderation. He spoke warmly of New York as a "gorgeous mosaic" of peoples. He emphasized to Jewish voters his condemnation of the Nation of Islam leader, Louis Farrakhan. Moreover, Dinkins pointed out his long and enthusiastic support for Israel and concern for freedom for Soviet Jews. However, Koch's supporters feared that under Dinkins, African Americans would be favored over whites. These fears versus the promise that New York under Dinkins would be a gentler and more inclusive city divided Jewish voters. Dinkins made far more than just the expected courtesy calls on local rabbis to allay community suspicions. But the Republican candidate, Rudolph Giuliani, swept heavily Hasidic neighborhoods of Brooklyn, as well as Jewish sections of Forest Hills.[9]

Dinkins won the election. His winning coalition included approximately 40 percent of the Jewish vote, primarily in liberal Jewish neighborhoods. In the Bronx, Dinkins ran extraordinarily well in minority communities. But he also did well in the untroubled Riverdale section and in the racially harmonious Co-op City–Pelham Parkway region. Dinkins succeeded with an often-elusive electoral coalition of African Americans and Latinos, reminiscent of the groups that secured John Lindsay's reelection some twenty years earlier. In retrospect, Dinkins's victory revealed that "despite deep racial cleavages within New York City," this town differed "from other older industrial cities," due in part to its large and variegated Jewish population. An effective black politician, who articulated a "bi-racial rhetoric," received a fair hearing.[10]

Dinkins also may have tapped into distinctive values that made these Jewish voters receptive. More than any other city in the United States, New York housed nonprofit foundations, many attuned to "social and urban issues." In fact, one-third of the largest foundations in the United States had offices in Manhattan. Many of their staff members shared a positive "orientation towards social justice and urban issues rather than merely economic issues." At the same time, rapid growth of nonprofit organizations strengthened city leaders' embrace of neoliberalism and helped to pave the way for the privatization of public responsibilities. Like Brooklyn Jews who generalized from their experiences working as civil servants with the city's poor and needy, these Jewish employees of nonprofit foundations drew on their urban knowledge in voting.[11]

However, the black-Jewish violence that erupted in Crown Heights, Brooklyn, damaged Dinkins's promise to fashion a gorgeous urban mosaic. Instead it opened the door to Rudolph Giuliani's politics of white backlash. When Dinkins ran for a second term, he lost to Giuliani, who garnered a significant percentage of Jewish votes.[12]

As mayor, Giuliani did not disappoint his Jewish core constituency. He visited Israel during the first Intifada to show his solidarity with victims of bombings. He also publicly snubbed Yasser Arafat. Giuliani announced that the Palestinian leader was unwanted at a Lincoln Center concert that the city hosted for United Nations delegates. Even as a debate roiled within and without Israel over whether, and how, to negotiate with Arafat, New York's mayor declared, "Israel may have to make peace with the man. But I don't have to extend any courtesies to him." Giuliani was uplifted, said his office, by the "more than 1,000 phone calls of support" that he received.[13]

Giuliani's act, however, did not play well among many New York Jews. They resented his meddling in international diplomacy and potentially undermining a complicated peace process then under way. Jews split again: Manhattan versus Brooklyn. Tensions boiled over publicly when the National Jewish Community Relations Advisory Council invited Arafat to address 150 of its leaders from around the country in Manhattan the same week as the mayor's snub. While one delegate calmly explained, "every time Arafat repeats his support of the peace process and appears conciliatory, it creates a new reality, one that he has to deal with back home," two protestors shouted, "Arafat is a murderer," leaving "the audience embarrassed at this breach of etiquette."[14]

Giuliani's undiplomatic outspokenness energized his supporters and troubled his opponents, but by the end of his first term, both groups of Jews grudgingly acknowledged that his administration had improved the quality of their lives. In his early years in City Hall, Giuliani rode the boom on Wall Street, which painlessly increased municipal revenues, helping him funnel monies into essential services. But his signature accomplishment, the continuing drop in crime, reassured law-abiding citizens. A *New York* magazine cover story, "The End of Crime as We Know It," said it all.[15]

Changing Jewish political attitudes registered clearly when Giuliani ran for reelection. The race pitted a Jewish, liberal civil libertarian from Manhattan on the Democratic ticket against a pugnacious Italian American Republican, running with Liberal Party endorsement. Manhattan borough president Ruth Messinger (b. 1940) had no standing with the Brooklyn Orthodox Jewish crowd, which actively slighted her as a woman and a liberal. Tall and thin with a wide smile, Messinger had compiled a broad record of activism in support of liberal causes alongside a steadfast devotion to Conservative Judaism. A daughter of the city, she had grown up in New York in the postwar decades and remained committed to making its urban promises available to newcomers. "I am a New Yorker, born and bred," she announced. "I walk fast, talk fast, think fast and, most importantly, stand up fast when the best interests of my city are being sold down the river." Messinger characterized Giuliani as "strident, mean spirited," and promised "to bridge ethnic and racial divisions" that he had exacerbated. She positioned herself more in Bella Abzug's tradition, which no longer spoke to well-heeled Jewish professionals. They had conveniently forgotten the largely invisible working class in this increasingly immigrant city. Nor did they pay attention to the growth of a substantial informal shadow economy of domestic workers, home health aides, and others who could not find regular employment.[16]

The mayor carried whites by a four-to-one margin and outpolled Messinger among women by nineteen points. He lost only in poor areas of the Bronx and among African Americans. Most strikingly, he won 75 percent of the Jewish vote. One Messinger supporter mused regretfully, "this is a time, certainly, when people have become more concerned about their private lives" than with larger societal issues. New York Jewish concern for struggling workers and immigrants, which had shaped the city's progressive politics for over a century, evaporated into a blend of economic and religious self-interest. The city's Jewish population had changed by the 1990s; economic inequality had burgeoned in New York, with most poor Jews either elderly immigrants or devoutly religious. However, Messinger turned her loss into a gain for American Jews. Leaving city politics, she accepted a position as the president and executive director of the American Jewish World Service (AJWS), a small organization that aimed to help secure human rights throughout the developing world. Messinger transformed AJWS into an imaginative powerhouse, at times serving as the conscience of American Jews, as during her efforts to stop the genocide in Darfur, Sudan.[17]

The terrorist attack on the World Trade Center on Tuesday, September 11, primary day in New York City, dramatically thrust New York's mayor into the limelight. Around the country, men and women hailed Giuliani as "America's mayor." He cultivated an image of a steadfast figure who kept New York together under the most extreme circumstances. The tragedy contributed to his standing; it helped his successor on the Republican ticket, Michael Bloomberg (b. 1942), win office. Bloomberg became the third Jew to occupy City Hall.[18]

The 2001 election pitted two Jews running for mayor and divided the Jewish vote. City Advocate Mark Green, on the Democratic ticket, possessed the active support of "numerous communal leaders . . . and leading rabbis" and had spent much of his career cultivating that ethnic vote. Yet Michael Bloomberg, a wealthy businessman entering politics for the first time and running on his own money, won an equal share of Jewish support. Disarray within Democratic political ranks contrasted with Bloomberg's non-confrontational style, which spoke of the challenges faced by all city dwellers.[19]

The Massachusetts-born media tycoon enjoyed exceptional financial success on Wall Street. As mayor, Bloomberg moved into echelons of power and privilege and said and did all the right things about Jewish issues. But he bore no resemblance to previous Jewish mayors, neither Beame nor Koch. Of average height and modest demeanor, he displayed his wealth in custom-tailored suits and a habit of disappearing over weekends on his private jet to get away from the city's pressures. He conscientiously downplayed his religious background and had no neighborhood roots or any affinity for New York's Jewish street culture that linked him to the group's past in the metropolis. He did not build his electoral appeal on a defined Jewish base. While still a candidate, he told an inquiring, provocative Jewish journalist, "Am I glad to be born a Jew? I never even thought about it in that context. You are what you are."[20]

Bloomberg spoke softly about his goals of improving public education and the hospital system, banning illegal guns, and balancing the rights of minority communities with sympathy for the police, whose law enforcement strategies targeted blacks and Latinos. If he possessed his own autocratic streak and sometimes could not resist instructing citizens on how to live their private lives, the generally circumspect mayor tended to avoid posturing. Yet he also contributed substantially to the growth of economic inequality in the city, assuming that what was good for billionaires would benefit all New Yorkers. The construction of skinny, enormously tall residential towers in midtown whose apartments cost many millions of dollars symbolized the enormous gulf between their wealthy owners and most city residents, who struggled to find affordable housing.[21]

Michael Bloomberg did not strike up a deep love affair with those New York Jews who cherished religious and cultural distinctiveness or who espoused a progressive political agenda. The latter bristled at the enormous rise in stop-and-frisk policing, which targeted African Americans and Hispanics, even as the city's crime rate continued to decline. Bloomberg's third term, which he won in 2009 after convincing the City Council to lift its restrictions on term limits, garnered support from whites and older New Yorkers in Manhattan and Queens, many of them Jews, although nearly three-quarters of New Yorkers said he should not have been allowed to run for a third term.[22] By the time the 2013 election rolled around, Democrat Bill DeBlasio swept first the primaries and then the mayoralty election with political promises closer to those cherished by New York Jews in the past.

Support from New York's newest progressive third party, the Working Families Party (WFP), helped anchor DeBlasio's campaign. The Working Families Party started in 1998, growing out of disgust with the Liberal Party's endorsement of Giuliani. As with the ALP and the Liberal Party in its earlier incarnation, labor unions headed by Jewish leaders (in this case, the Service Employees International Union) and grassroots groups funded and controlled the WFP board. Unlike either the ALP or

Liberal Party, WFP has sought to build a national constituency, taking New York's politics to other cities and states. Bloomberg, too, desired to take his neoliberal politics to the nation. But his posture represented a far cry from the transformative vision of Jewish immigrants, their children, and their grandchildren, who imagined the city as forging a pluralist path in the urban wilderness that potentially would guide all Americans. WFP's success has transformed New York. "America's largest city has gone from being run by a billionaire mayor and a party-machine council to being steered by a progressive mayor and progressive-driven council."[23] WFP has reminded the city of its working-class heritage.

A New Mix

The revival of Jewish immigration, albeit not on a scale equal to the early years of the twentieth century, fostered a new mix of Jewish creativity in

Musicians in Williamsburg, Brooklyn, by William Meyers, July 2, 2005. William Meyers decided to photograph New York's outer boroughs, capturing their distinctive housing styles and people. This image of musicians in a Williamsburg venue conveys the spirit of the klezmer revival that flourished in New York during the 1970s and 1980s. At the same time, it documents the rise of a new arts scene in Williamsburg, a neighborhood previously identified with Hasidic Jews and Puerto Ricans. © William Meyers. Courtesy of William Meyers.

New York City in the latter decades of the century. This burst of intellectual, literary, musical, and visual culture, along with scholarship, was drawn equally from New York natives, Jews from the suburbs who gravitated to neighborhoods their parents or grandparents had fled, newcomers who arrived as children, and those who came as immigrants. It complemented the rise of young, wealthy, ambitious Jewish men and women eager to profit from novel forms of financial markets, gentrification of neighborhoods, and technological innovations. Simultaneously, the city produced ever greater disparities of income as it reduced social welfare programs that had helped to lift earlier generations of Jewish immigrants out of poverty. By 2010, a portrait of New York Jews revealed enormous diversity in ethnicity, race, religious identification, and sexual orientation. It also highlighted sharply drawn distinctions between the upper 15 percent of the population who were wealthy and almost a third of Jews who struggled to make ends meet.[24]

As in earlier periods of New York history, over the course of the twentieth century, Jews developed and popularized forms of commercial entertainment, at times endowing them with a seriousness of purpose that expanded their purview. Although television production followed movies, moving across the continent to Hollywood from its early live-studio stages in the city, music recording industries, theater, and trade-book publishing—including such relatively new fields as graphic novels and children's books—remained in the city. Many occupied significant physical spaces in New York, districts that acquired their own characteristics. Some of these areas also assumed a Jewish ethnic New York flavor in the restaurants and clubs where deals were made, authors feted, and musics savored.

The flavors of the city changed, however, and Jews embraced Japanese sushi with as much fervor as earlier generations had feasted on Chinese food. In fact, as the restaurant business increasingly fluctuated with fads and styles, much like the clothing industry, it tempted Jews to try their hand at inventing different dining experiences. Previously Jews had experimented with the delicatessen, expanding its reach so that local delis came to characterize New York neighborhoods. Some were kosher, others were kosher style, and still others served pork, even as many avoided offering dairy products. New Jewish restaurant businesses bore scant resemblance to delicatessens; rather, they mixed all sorts of cuisines in eclectic combinations.[25]

Opportunities that were previously closed to Jews opened in such fields as advertising, engineering, academia, finance, and an array of medical disciplines. As medical care expanded, cadres of medical professionals settled in the city alongside increasing numbers of academics who sought employment in the city's numerous universities, colleges, and technical schools. Even as early as 1980, over a third of Jewish men living in Manhattan held graduate degrees, with another two-fifths possessing a four-year college degree. Women were not far behind. This "educational advantage translated into an income advantage." The Jewish median income of $34,000 exceeded the national median of $20,000. Other Jews, especially Brooklyn Jews who did not have advanced secular education, entered different economic niches. The growing presence of Hasidim stimulated growth in such fields as diamonds, transforming New York into the American center of an international industry and Manhattan's Forty-Seventh Street into the heart of the diamond district. Continuities endured as well. Orthodox, Sabbath-observant Jews still found self-employment a valuable option. Some of them, especially Syrian Jews, a tight-knit, Brooklyn-based, prosperous community, expanded retail operations in new areas like music recordings and electronic equipment alongside older economic niches, such as inexpensive clothing stores. Gradually a number moved into retail real estate, focusing on Manhattan.[26]

As New York Jews entered Wall Street finance, a field largely closed to Jews until after World War II, they introduced fresh approaches to banking and the market that upset established practices. Some of these Jews ended up going to jail for their innovations, which not only skirted the law but actually broke it. Others managed to succeed in leveraged buyouts, junk bonds, and corporate raids that shook up Wall Street and helped to produce a number of bubbles that subsequently burst, with serious consequences for many Americans. The most dramatic crash occurred in 2008 when, in echoes of the spectacular bank failures of Max Kobre and Jarmulowsky, the once-vaunted Jewish firm of Lehman Brothers collapsed. Its demise threatened the entire banking system, until the federal government stepped in to shore up banks that were deemed "too big to fail." In the 1930s, anti-Semites had falsely accused Jews of running Wall Street when they could not get a foot in the door. By 2008, Jews worked in many Wall Street firms together with other, non-Jewish New Yorkers, prospering with them and suffering when the Great Recession occurred.[27]

Those Jews who chose to stay in the city during the tumultuous decade of the 1970s often lived in different neighborhoods than in the past. A wave of cooperative and condominium conversions swept the city, transforming rent-controlled apartments on the Upper East and West Sides and in Washington Heights. Jews who decided to purchase rather than rent signaled their commitment to New York even as its future appeared clouded. Indeed, immigrants and their children remained the majority population among New York Jews. As gentrification gathered momentum, Jews moved to areas in Brooklyn, like Park Slope and Brooklyn Heights, that had previously housed few Jews. Chelsea, long a working-class district in Manhattan, evolved into a section attractive to gay and lesbian New Yorkers, who wanted a more subdued, middle-class style of living than what was available in the West Village. Their presence helped propel the neighborhood's gentrification, displacing working-class Catholics. Over the course of several decades, New York real estate markets boomed repeatedly, pushing out artists who had settled in the factory loft district in SoHo, forcing musicians to leave the Lincoln Center area for Washington Heights, fostering a revival in downtown Brooklyn's warehouse district, bringing young single men and women to Williamsburg's Orthodox enclave, and even carrying whites back to Harlem and Bedford-Stuyvesant.[28]

Young Jewish professionals participated actively in neighborhood gentrification during the Wall Street boom of the 1990s. Sounding like Jews of earlier eras, those who helped restore "the Brooklyn brownstone belt" bragged that it took only fifteen minutes to reach their managerial or executive jobs in Manhattan investment banks, law firms, or software companies. Those who were making even more money settled in luxury lofts within an expanding district that had begun its redevelopment a generation earlier. These new residents renewed the city tradition of walking to work. By 2010, upper-class Jews lived on both East and West Sides of Manhattan as well as in Chelsea. In Harlem, gentrification fulfilled a prediction that "affluent whites" would "inevitably" migrate there due to its stock of transformable low-cost housing and its "location just a few miles from midtown." Jews participated in these new patterns of settlement, drawn in part by Jewish speculation in real estate and engagement in both new construction and renovation. By the end of the first decade of the twenty-first century, census returns showed "Greater Harlem" no longer to be majority black for the first time since the 1920s.[29]

Middle- and upper-class New York Jews savored stability. Those who had decided to remain in the city ensured that textures of community life continued. Affluent Jewish enclaves dotted four of the five boroughs. In Manhattan, the Upper West Side retained its idiosyncratic character as an intellectual Jewish neighborhood, where "two populations distinct in their levels of Jewish affiliation and practice" lived side by side. One group joined synagogues, visited Israel, and enrolled children in Jewish day schools, while the other group rejected affiliation and often intermarried, if choosing to marry at all. But both types of Jews valued urban life, relished ethnic and religious diversity, subscribed to liberal politics, and cherished education.[30]

If Molly Goldberg had epitomized an earlier New York ethnic Jewish ethos of striving, leavened with humor, Woody Allen portrayed a new urban generation's Jewish neurotic aspirations with wit. Many young New York Jewish professionals saw their own pathologies and behaviors mocked in Allen's movies. He resolutely resisted Hollywood and stayed in the city, the "reigning auteur" of "urban angst during the eighties." Like many people born in Brooklyn, the Bronx, and Queens, Allen pictured Manhattan as New York City. The "Manhattan" he satirized was "inhabited mainly by Jews and WASPS." Allen rarely noticed African Americans, Hispanics, Chinese, or even Italians and Irish. His city dwellers were affluent, possessing "a sense of style and good taste." One analyst of locations that Allen used to tell the story of *Hannah and Her Sisters* (1986) identified no fewer than thirty venues, ranging from a downtown loft on Grand Street to the Carlyle Hotel uptown on Madison Avenue to restaurants in SoHo to the jogging track and Sheep Meadow in Central Park—places that Allen, like his characters, frequented.[31]

But many of these Jewish characters appeared unhappy with their lives of material achievement. In such movies as *Annie Hall* (1977) and *Crimes and Misdemeanors* (1989), Allen demonstrated how attuned he was to their, and his own, feelings of acute anxiety over "the competitiveness of their jobs, . . . guilt over their greed and meaningless acquisitiveness." As Allen portrayed them, these "self-seekers" ended up in troubled relationships with families in neighborhoods they had abandoned. One critic lauded Allen as "the urban poet of our anxious age—skeptical, guiltily bourgeois, longing to answer the impossible questions." Another observer credited him with possessing a keen sense for "some large philosophical dualities" that undermined the lives of men and women who had broken from their pasts but were uncertain about their futures.[32]

By contrast, Brooklyn's old neighborhoods expanded their strict Orthodox environments while families coped with poverty. Some fifteen thousand Jews headed to the quasi-suburban locale of Staten Island. It attracted a culturally diverse crowd that included better-off Orthodox Jews from Brooklyn, prosperous Russian immigrants, and native-born Jews with little interest in Jewish causes. Despite suburbia's ongoing appeal, by the 1990s, rates of out-migration slowed. In 2002, the total number of Jews in New York dropped, for the first time in more than a century, to just under one million. However, "unlike other East Coast and Midwestern Jewish communities whose suburbanization has resulted in a restructuring of the center of Jewish life," the city remained the unofficial Jewish capital of the area and country. Suburban Jews retained urban connections for both business and cultural activities. In addition, the New York Federation of Philanthropies expanded its fundraising reach to include the city's New York State suburbs, or what it called the "metropolitan" area.[33]

By 2010, New York City's Jewish population rose again to over a million, with increases registering in Brooklyn, the Bronx, and Queens. Russian Jewish immigrants arrived in significant numbers after the collapse of the Soviet Union. Many secular immigrants from Russia and Ukraine settled in Brooklyn's Brighton Beach, transforming the area into "Little Odessa." Traditionally religious Bukharan Jews opted for Forest Hills, Queens, earning it the nickname "Queenistan." "They've done in 20 years what it took other Jews at least 40 years," one observer marveled, reflecting on freshly built mansions, evidence of Bukharan Jews' prosperity. These eclectic homes all shared "a flair for the flamboyant." While both enclaves spoke a common Russian language, they differed in their attitudes toward religion and their prosperity, with Bukharan Jews both more pious and more prosperous.[34]

Immigrants endowed New York culture with distinctive accents, perhaps most often heard through a burst of literary activity. As memoirs acquired popularity, New York Jewish voices introduced readers to far-reaching experiences. André Aciman and Lucette Lagnado, both born in Egypt, wrote compelling memoirs of their families, especially their fathers, and the difficulties of moving from one multicultured world, where they had money and status, into another one, where they lacked wealth and all reasonable reference points. Aciman ended up with an academic appointment even as he continued to write, while Lagnado plied the trade of a journalist, also continuing to publish books that drew on her family's experiences. The memoir format inspired other immigrant Jewish journalists to write their New York stories. Joseph Berger, the son of Polish survivors of World War II who settled in the city after the war, wrote not only of his experiences but also of his parents and, by extension, of so many survivors and their children who made new lives in New York after the war. Similarly, Gary Shteyngardt chronicled in humorous fashion his travails as a Russian Jewish boy growing up in Queens, emblematic of so many other Russian immigrant children.[35]

These newcomers entered the city with little knowledge of its past history and few connections to its present culture. By contrast, Jews from the suburbs gravitated to New York often to study at its universities or to forge a career. Diverse aspects of the city drew them, and some stayed long enough to shape its culture. In certain fields, like theater and visual art, New York remained the place by which success was judged.

Two outstanding playwrights, Wendy Wasserstein (1950–2006) and Tony Kushner (b. 1956), introduced Jewish characters to the stage that were a far cry from the nostalgic shtetl Jews of *Fiddler on the Roof*. The latter production, with its theme of struggle between tradition and modernity, particularism and universalism, endured not only as a Broadway hit show but also as an extraordinarily popular musical throughout the globe in both professional and amateur productions. Wasserstein and Kushner brought distinctly different Jewish sensibilities to the stage. Wasserstein, who grew up first in Brooklyn and then on the Upper East Side, took women as the subjects for her plays. Her Broadway comedy hit *The Sisters Rosenzweig* not only explored what it meant to be Jewish through three very different women who come to terms with their Jewishness but also "celebrated the possibilities of a middle-aged woman." Wasserstein, a plump, short woman with wide-set eyes, a ready smile, and a mass of curly hair, claimed that her "notion of theater derived from her Jewish identity." She explained, "I think in many ways my idea of show business comes from temple; not that I really practice, but that sense of community, melancholy, and spirituality is there."[36]

Tony Kushner migrated back to New York, his birthplace, from New Orleans, where he grew up, to attend Columbia University. Like Wasserstein, Kushner placed Jewish characters onstage, most notably in his seven-hour Pulitzer Prize–winning play, *Angels in America: A Gay Fantasia on National Themes*. Although one of its leading characters, Louis, is a gay Jew, two other Jewish figures—Roy Cohn, whose legal career hunting communists got its start as an assistant prosecutor in the Rosenberg trial, and the ghost of Ethel Rosenberg, who blames Cohn for her death—play important roles that dramatize the political dimensions of the AIDS crisis. Kushner's consciousness of history informs his play, as is true for Wasserstein's Pulitzer Prize–winning play about feminism, *The Heidi Chronicles*.[37]

At the turn of the twenty-first century, history and memory, heritage and inheritance, figured far more prominently among New York Jews. Increasingly aware that the city had become "the old home" or point of origin for many American Jews, supplementing if not supplanting Europe, New Yorkers took it upon themselves to recover and represent their past. Four established organizations that collected documents, maintained archives and libraries, held exhibits, published scholarship, and supported research agreed to relocate to a new Center for Jewish History, joined by the American Sephardi Federation. Pooling some of their resources, they hoped to spur interest in modern Jewish history and make the center a site for students and scholars, visitors to the city as well as residents. This ambitious endeavor spoke to aspirations among New York Jews to reinforce the city's importance as a repository of American Jewish historical memory.[38]

Sites of Memory

The Holocaust cast a shadow over Jews in New York, not just because of the presence of the largest number of survivors in any American city. With so many New York Jews only a generation removed from immigration, they felt the losses of the Holocaust and deaths of family members with particular immediacy. Yet not until the 1980s did Jews manage to organize to commemorate those terrible years with a physical monument, despite early efforts to erect a statue right after the war ended. Then a mix of politics and real estate, memory culture and history, converged to allow for the establishment of the Museum of Jewish Heritage—A Living Memorial to the Holocaust, built on landfill in lower Manhattan, part of an expensive project called Battery Park City.[39]

The pull of history and memory registered in other parts of the city, not just on recent landfill. As New Yorkers realized after the razing of the elegant Pennsylvania Station in 1963 that not every old building should be torn down for a new one and that not all "creative destruction" in Manhattan was desirable, Jews also began to reconsider their particular urban heritage. Even as Lower East Side streets lost much of their mundane Jewish character, Jews redoubled efforts to concretize the history of this once-extraordinary Jewish place. Starting in the 1980s, organizations like the Museum at Eldridge Street, the Lower East Side Tenement Museum, and the Lower East Side Conservancy worked to entice visitors downtown through exhibits, walking tours, and cultural programs exploring how Jews and other immigrants made their way in New York. By the new millennium, these organizations had earned city, state, and national funding to raise historical awareness of the Lower East Side's significance as an immigrant entrepôt.[40]

This historical consciousness accompanied a transformation of the Lower East Side as artists and young Jewish capitalists returned to the site of their grandparents' beginnings. A chic sensibility replaced the neighborhood's legendary ethnic quality. Entrepreneurs in pursuit of "their version of the American dream," and with a ready customer base, established "boutiques featuring their own designer labels or a bar with great vodka martinis, or a vintage furniture store." Now observers spoke of the "intersection of new and old, of people of disparate cultures and points of view" on Orchard Street. However, Jews living elsewhere in the city no longer felt a tug to repair to Delancey Street for its sights and sounds and to savor ethnic delicacies as in the past. A few stalwarts survived. Many still lined up at Katz's Delicatessen. The counterman stood behind a sign reminding customers that this store once sent salamis to boys in the army. Others frequented Russ & Daughters, which published a mix of recipes and memoir about the "house that herring built" in 2013. But famed Jewish manufacturers, including Streit's matzo factory, left the neighborhood, unwilling to resist the astronomical prices offered for their now valuable real estate.[41]

When the Lower East Side ceased to be a center of Jewish population and activity during the Great Depression, it became, instead, "a primary site of Jewish memory and a physical space for the invention of Jewish identity in America." American Jews forged a collective consciousness for themselves through the Lower East Side, developing a narrative of arrival, suffering, adaptation, and eventual triumph. The neighborhood emerged as "a living reminder of an idealized immigrant world as well as a mirror of the past that reflected the extent of Jewish progress." Nostalgia allowed Jews to articulate a common account of their urban origins. The "neighborhood represented poverty but also the possibility for upward mobility; it testified to the existence of a vibrant, ethnic culture but also to the ability of Jews to adapt to American society; it enshrined the flavor of the old world but also housed stores and businesses serving the new American consumer; it celebrated the rapid acculturation of American Jews but also expressed the doubts and frustrations that accompanied the drive for Americanization."[42]

These interpretations encouraged an understanding of New York as a heritage site where American Judaism took root. A visit to a crumbling monument of Moorish architecture, the Eldridge Street Synagogue, inspired Roberta Brandes Gratz. A journalist and urban critic, Gratz helped to restore the building and turn it into a museum. She saw her project "less in terms of its relevance to the cultural life of the New York Jewish community than in terms of Jewish acceptance and presence in the wider context of American society and national heritage." Gratz affirmed that "Eldridge Street is an important vessel the same way that Trinity Church, North Church in Boston, or any of the other important churches that we think of as significant markers of American history" are. She wanted to "put a synagogue in that galaxy." Her activities meshed with her larger theories of urbanism and her commitment to local small-scale efforts to recycle buildings to preserve neighborhood complexity as opposed to massive renewal projects.[43]

These projects coincided with a burst of tourism to the Lower East Side by American Jews. The neighborhood became an icon of the American Jewish past, "a deliberate, willed act of creation." In fact, "tourism itself has helped to maintain the vitality of the Jewish neighborhood."

Eager to reclaim a piece of a dimly remembered—and often rejected—past, Jews signed up for tours to walk the streets, something impossible to do in suburban subdivisions. A Jewish graduate student, looking for a way to finance his studies, hit on historically informed walking tours. He established Big Onion, suggesting a takeoff on tourist-industry promotion of New York as the Big Apple. Significantly, one of the Big Onion's very first walking tours of the Jewish Lower East Side occurred on Christmas Day in 1991, explicitly targeting Jews seeking an alternative to Christian holiday celebrations.[44]

But nothing illustrated the impulse to transform New York Jewish history into American heritage better than the Lower East Side Tenement Museum. Its founder, Ruth Abram, grew up in the segregated South and chafed at the restrictions separating her as a white person from African Americans and the social exclusions separating her as a Jew from Christians. After she moved to New York, she discovered the power of an ordinary tenement building at 97 Orchard Street to promote her vision of interreligious and interracial toleration. The Tenement Museum possessed a redemptive mission. It preserved the experiences and cultural memories of people who had long been ignored, the "common ground of immigrants." Abram wanted visitors, young and old, to ponder the question, "How will we be one nation and at the same time enjoy, appreciate and certainly not be afraid of the profound differences we bring to the table based on background?" Yet Jews coming to visit either the Tenement Museum or the Eldridge Street Project tended to imagine that the whole neighborhood was somehow sacred. The streets themselves, not just the synagogues or the tenements, possessed mythic character.[45]

For many American Jews, the Lower East Side constitutes a "site of memory whose architectural, graphic, and olfactory sensuality stands so much at odds with the aesthetic, social and historical flatness of the suburban landscapes that have long been the locus of American Jewish life." Given the physical, social, and economic mobility of American Jews, they needed an enduring site of origin. The Lower East Side, long visited, photographed, described, and deplored, initially had escaped gentrification before succumbing in the 1990s. It retained Jewish stores and a small Jewish population, unlike other immigrant areas, ironically secured by affordable apartment houses sponsored by the ILGWU and the Amalgamated Clothing Workers Union. Accessible and located in

Rogarshevsky Parlor, by Keiko Niwa, c. 2010. The Lower East Side Tenement Museum, at 97 Orchard Street, carefully reconstructed rooms in the building to reflect the lives of past multiethnic immigrant residents. Originally the Rogarshevsky Parlor, representing eastern European Jews who lived in the building, displayed a funeral setting instead of the Sabbath setting pictured here. The brainchild of Ruth Abram, the Lower East Side Tenement Museum has flourished as an unusual, popular history museum, extending the attraction of the neighborhood itself as a touchstone of authentic Jewishness. Courtesy of the Lower East Side Tenement Museum.

New York City, which remained the source of Jewish American culture, a touchstone of authentic Jewishness even for those who lived thousands of miles west of the Hudson River, the Lower East Side became a site of memory, a metonym for New York as a Jewish city and a time when "language, politics, religion, culture and even kinship networks were intricately connected to an organic community"[46]—a time, in short, of promise.

Conclusion

In 2010, New York City's main charitable organization, UJA-Federation, decided to commission a survey of New York Jews within both the city and its New York State suburbs. The results surprised everyone. After years of a declining city population that was shifting to the suburbs, a new trend emerged: the number of New York Jews was growing, like the city itself. New estimates put the number of Jews in the city back up over a million, while suburbanization enjoyed more modest growth. Yet suburbanites moving to the city did not propel these changes, nor did immigration, the historical source of New York Jewish population increase. Rather, greater longevity among Jewish New Yorkers and a high birthrate among Hasidim and Orthodox Jews, especially in Brooklyn, fueled the numbers of Jews. In fact, almost half of all New York Jews were now under the age of twenty-five, another dramatic change. When combined with an expanding presence of Russian and other immigrant Jews in the city, the report highlighted significant differences from earlier eras. First, New York Jews were even more diverse than in the past, including around 10 percent biracial households. "The large number of bi-racial, Hispanic, and 'non-white' Jewish households," the report cautioned, "should serve as a reality check for those who are accustomed to thinking of all Jews as 'white.'" Second, this diversity extended to Orthodox Jews, which the report divided into three distinct groups: modern Orthodox, Hasidic, and Yeshivish. The latter two groups differed despite their common label as fervently pious Jews (*Haredim*). Third, poverty had also increased substantially, from 20 percent at the turn of the century to 27 percent of all Jews, especially among the elderly and Hasidim. Fourth, a significant minority of the city's wealthiest Jews gave no money to Jewish charities, a cause for alarm among stalwart supporters of UJA-Federation.[47]

The implications of these changes registered vividly in Brooklyn politics, where support for more conservative candidates and for Republicans emerged as a viable Jewish option. Orthodox Jews' concerns focused on public assistance that would specifically help them, such as money to support parochial education and succor the Jewish poor. Because most Hasidim voted as a bloc, following their rebbe's advice, New York politicians, fearful of antagonizing their leaders, tended to give them latitude to police their own. Many Hasidic groups had their own security patrols, emergency medical corps, and a rabbinic court system to handle criminal investigations. Yet issues of sexual abuse of young children, along with a growing disregard among a number of yeshivas for state laws on secular educational requisites, threatened the insularity of these communities. At the same time, the migration of young Jewish professionals to a revitalized brownstone belt in Brooklyn in such neighborhoods as Park Slope and Brooklyn Heights that had never previously attracted or welcomed Jews spurred a revival of left-leaning Jewish politics. In response to the Great Recession of 2008, Jewish political activism around economic justice concerns returned in grassroots movements as well as a new progressive third party, the Working Families Party (WFP). The WFP represented a coalition of African American, Hispanic, and Jewish activists who fought successfully for a fifteen-dollar-per-hour minimum wage.[48] Of course, most New York Jews, even most Brooklyn Jews, belonged to neither group but rather occupied a middle, largely liberal ground.

These contrary trends pointed to the vitality of New York Jewish life, its ongoing contradictions as well as competition between very different groups of Jews. On the one hand, ever larger numbers of Jewish children attended parochial schools, and the most popular names for boys in the city included such Orthodox Jewish favorites as Jacob, Moshe, Joshua, Jeremiah, Elijah, and Noah (not to mention David and Daniel). On the other hand, increased intermarriage among Jews made progressive politics and postmodern culture often of more significance Jewishly than religion was. Not only religion, class, and politics but also ethnicity, race, and sexual orientation divided New York Jews in the twenty-first century, not to mention attitudes toward Israeli policies on the West Bank. Yet despite these substantial differences, Jews continued to feel connected to each other enough to make their arguments reverberate throughout the city.[49]

In 2015, two very different Brooklyn Jews acquired national acclaim. Their fame spoke to the power of Jewish life in the postwar decades to produce politically engaged individuals dedicated to fulfilling the promise of America for all its citizens. Both of them grew up in working-class families; both graduated from James Madison High School; both excelled in their studies and went on to college. Then their paths diverged. Bernie Sanders (b. 1941), after spending a short time on a kibbutz in Israel, ended up settling in Vermont, where he built a career as an independent, socialist politician. Ruth Bader Ginsberg (b. 1933) married after graduating from Cornell, followed her husband first as he completed military service and then to Harvard Law School, before receiving her law degree from Columbia Law School. An articulate feminist and outstanding judge, she joined the United States Supreme Court in 1993, just two years after Sanders entered the United States Congress as a representative from Vermont. Both Ginsberg and Sanders have devoted their lives to changing America, making it a more just and equal society. Values that they learned in their Brooklyn Jewish homes and in the city's public schools combined to motivate them to lives of outstanding public service. Sanders's campaign to secure the Democratic Party's nomination for president galvanized hundreds of thousands of voters, who heard through his Brooklyn-accented speech the ideals of many New York Jews, such as a promise of a free college education. His vision and audacity as a Jew running for president amazed many observers. Similarly, Ginsberg's forthright support of gay marriage attracted admiration from supporters throughout America. These two figures exemplified a small fraction of the impact that New York Jews have exerted on the nation.[50]

Because Jews and New York developed a special relationship over many decades, they often became nearly synonymous. Sometimes, this translated into the coded language of anti-Semitism; something "too New York" was understood as a euphemism for "too Jewish." At other times, the closeness of Jews and New York has allowed creative figures to blur Jewish aspects of their work and substitute "New Yorkish" identities instead. But there is no question that American Jews in general have benefited from the cultural, political, and economic clout Jews acquired in New York that radiated to satellite communities of New Yorkers in other American cities. It has given American Jews not only a reference point for authenticity but also an opportunity to bask in recognition accorded Jews and Judaism in the United States.[51]

As New York gradually became a Jewish city, a process that began in the nineteenth century, it developed qualities that made it different from other American cities. Some of those attributes reflected Jewish passions for avant-garde culture and progressive politics; other urban characteristics stemmed from the rise of ethnic economic and residential niches. Jews helped to build New York, the physical city and the moral community embedded within it. In exchange, New York transformed Jewish life and religion, culture and society. In New York, Jews fashioned new ways to be American Jews and then enthusiastically exported their ideas and practices to others across the United States and around the world. American Jews made New York their capital city, a position of authority and influence that New York Jews have never ceded, just as the city has remained the nation's largest, its cultural, commercial, and financial capital. A city of promises and possibilities, it continually rewards its residents even as it struggles to fulfill its commitments to all who have placed their hopes in it.

Visual Essay

An Introduction to the Visual and Material Culture of New York City Jews, 1654–2015

DIANA L. LINDEN

Jews have long been referred to as the "People of the Book," signifying the importance of the ongoing study and interpretation of the Torah. Scholars of both Jewish and American history also depend on the written word located in such documents as books, letters, and newspapers, as well as records from all kinds of organizations constituting their primary sources.

This visual essay offers a different approach. It explores the beliefs, values, attitudes, and assumptions of New York Jewish history through an examination of visual and material culture, illuminating what we can learn from objects, artwork, and artifacts of the time.[1] The positioning of figures within a photograph, adaptations by Jews of objects from the surrounding American culture for new uses, or even what is purposely excluded by an artist in a portrait all provide insights and clues into social dynamics, the crafting of identity, the portrayal of class status, and the nature of gender relationships in Jewish America.

The coming pages trace the creation of a new dual identity of "American Jew" over the course of more than 350 years, using visual means to explore how those Jews strove to represent themselves, showing off, in many cases, their new American identities. A number of political currents and social influences intersected to produce a syncretic, American Jewish, identity in New York. The institutions that Jews developed, the customs that they adopted from their non-Jewish neighbors, the social exclusions to which they were subjected, and the caricatures against which they battled all worked together to forge this American Jewish identity and helped to establish New York as the capital of the Jewish world.

Jeff Gutterman, *View of Congregation Shearith Israel Cemetery*, photograph, 2011.
Courtesy of the artist.

Let's start down in Chatham Square, in 2015 part of New York City's
Chinatown. The Spanish-Portuguese Cemetery, built by Congregation Shearith Israel in 1682, stands as New York's oldest existing Jewish cemetery, although it was the second Jewish cemetery to be built by
the congregation. Raised high above street level, protected from vandals
and tourists by its sturdy padlocked metal fence, this historic cemetery
is exposed to weather and pollution that has eroded its tombstones,
rendering many epitaphs illegible and roughly pitting their smooth
surfaces with dents. Though not free to enter, a viewer can observe
from the gates how the gravestones are oriented (whether vertical or
horizontal), their size, and their design or shape. In other words, these
inanimate objects are communicating to us from behind the fence and
across many centuries.

Toward the left of center stands a two-foot-tall obelisk raised high
on a four-foot-tall stone base that makes it the tallest monument in the
cemetery. The presence of an obelisk is unusual for a Jewish cemetery

because it is not a traditional Jewish funerary form. This is an early example of Jews new to the colony borrowing established forms and symbols from the existing community. Colonial American Jews appropriated the obelisk design from Protestant cemeteries; the form originated in ancient Egypt, where it was associated with eternal life and light. Here, the obelisk's singular shape and height broadcasts the deceased's importance to the greater community. Even from the vantage point standing outside the locked gates, it can be assumed that the obelisk honors a man, rather than a woman, since women were kept out of the upper spheres of society where power was brokered and obtained. Indeed, the gravestone's inscription heralds the Reverend Gershom Mendes Seixas, the esteemed religious official of Congregation Shearith Israel. Seixas's duties equaled those of a rabbi, although he did not possess that title. In addition to serving as the congregation's hazan (or cantor), Seixas supervised kashrut and officiated at all life-cycle events.

The many surrounding tombstones conform to either one of two orientations: vertical slab stones favored by the Ashkenazim or horizontal ledger stones placed flat on the ground in the manner of the Sephardim. The tombstones are inscribed with varied texts that include biblical quotes, loving epitaphs, names, and birth and death dates, written in Ladino, Hebrew, and Dutch, among other languages, acknowledging the differing heritages of New York Jews in the colonial era. This cemetery has in effect become a site of cultural mixtures and intersections.

Just as an obelisk in a cemetery proclaims a man's high social status, Moses Levy used a portrait to broadcast his own importance. This Dutch merchant-class tradition proliferated in New Amsterdam, with sitting for a portrait an accepted means to mark one's achievement of wealth and status—few could afford to be art patrons. Portraits became one popular form of pictorial expression in colonial America, and these paintings were imbued with social messages. Moses Levy and his son-in-law Jacob Franks were the most prominent Jewish Anglo-German merchants who settled in New York in the early eighteenth century.[2] The very fact that they were able to commission such an expensive luxury item as a portrait testifies to their wealth and exalted position in the colony. Significantly, Levy and, in the next painting, members of his extended family chose to avoid any identifiable Jewish elements in their portraits. Levy wanted the paintings to establish his class position, rather than to highlight

Portrait of Moses Levy, attributed to Gerardus Duyckinck, c. 1735, oil on canvas, 45⅛ × 35¾ in. Photography by Dwight Primiano. Courtesy of Crystal Bridges Museum of American Art, Bentonville, Arkansas.

ethnicity. Folk painters worked from pattern books containing prints of stock poses, settings, and props derived from portraits of European aristocrats and royalty. Levy would simply look at the choices of settings and accouterments and pick and choose to assemble the prominent look he so desired. The Franks-Levy Family Portrait Collection comprises six

Portrait of Franks Children with Lamb, attributed to Gerardus Duyckinck, c. 1735, oil on canvas, 44½ × 35⅝ in. Photography by Dwight Primiano. Courtesy of Crystal Bridges Museum of American Art, Bentonville, Arkansas.

individual canvases, the most extensive surviving program of colonial American portraiture.[3]

In the first painting, Levy gestures out through a window to ships sailing nearby to indicate his merchant status and important connections to trade and economic growth, all statements of his masculinity and position within the male social sphere. The children in the second portrait are represented to convey their adherence to social mores and appropriate gender roles. The young boy is shown standing, his arm akimbo so that his elbow overlaps with a window view, connecting with the world beyond a domestic interior. His sister sits demurely at his

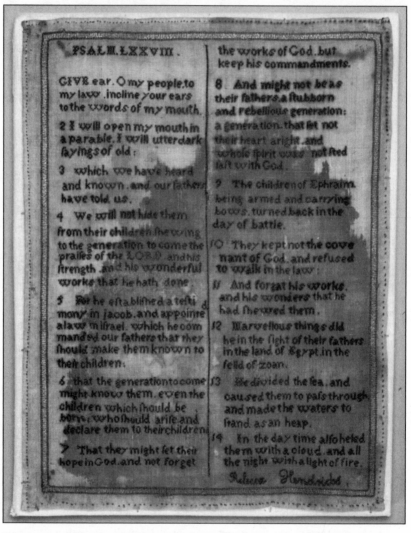

Rebecca Hendricks, sampler of the 78th Psalm, linen with cotton thread, late eighteenth century. Courtesy of American Jewish Historical Society, New York, NY, and Newton Centre, MA.

side, sheltered within the home, holding a rose in her uplifted hand and a lamb close to her side. Both the cultivated flower and tamed young animal are symbols frequently included in Protestant and Catholic European paintings to broadcast a young girl's virtues, chastity, and impeccable upbringing. In a sense, both children are props, just like the ships in Moses Levy's own portrait.

Good Jewish girls were to be kept busy with feminine chores and arts that would help to groom them into proper, marriageable young women. In the painted portrait of the young Franks daughter, she delicately held blossoms in her hand to indicate her youthful purity. It was widely believed that young girls' hands were best kept busy with such appropriate activities as making quilts and stitching samplers. The sampler pictured here was made by the hand of young Rebecca Hendricks. Using silk thread on linen, Hendricks stitched Jewish designs and text into a Christian-European form, uniting Judaica with Americana on her linen swatch. Young girls and adult women began to embroider fine needlework beginning in the Middle Ages and, by the sixteenth century, dutifully learned their stitches, alphabet, and lessons from set pattern books. Each measured stitch was also a lesson in patience and accuracy. Jewish women adopted embroidery in approximately 1650.[4] Samplers, the most common embroidered works of art and craft, are a literal sampling of different stitches through which women could display their virtuosity with a needle. They were also instructive of social mores, texts, and Bible verses.[5] Texts for colonial-era samplers were usually culled from biblical phrases and aphorisms. Hendricks embroidered a passage that reflects her dual identity as a colonial girl of breeding and a young Jewess. She stitched into cloth verses 1–14 of the 78th Psalm with the phrase "He commanded our fathers that they should make them known to their children; That they might [not] forget the words of God but keep his commandments" (Ps. 78:5, 7).[6]

When the first Jews arrived in New Amsterdam, the Dutch West India Company ordered Peter Stuyvesant, the last Dutch director of the colony of New Netherland, to permit them freedom of religious practice.[7] Just over one hundred years later, Jews were openly practicing their religion in New York without restraint. This prayer book demonstrates the growth and flourishing of the Jewish community. It was published in 1765/66 (5526). Isaac Pinto recognized that the majority of Jews did not know Hebrew and so translated the traditional texts into English. The

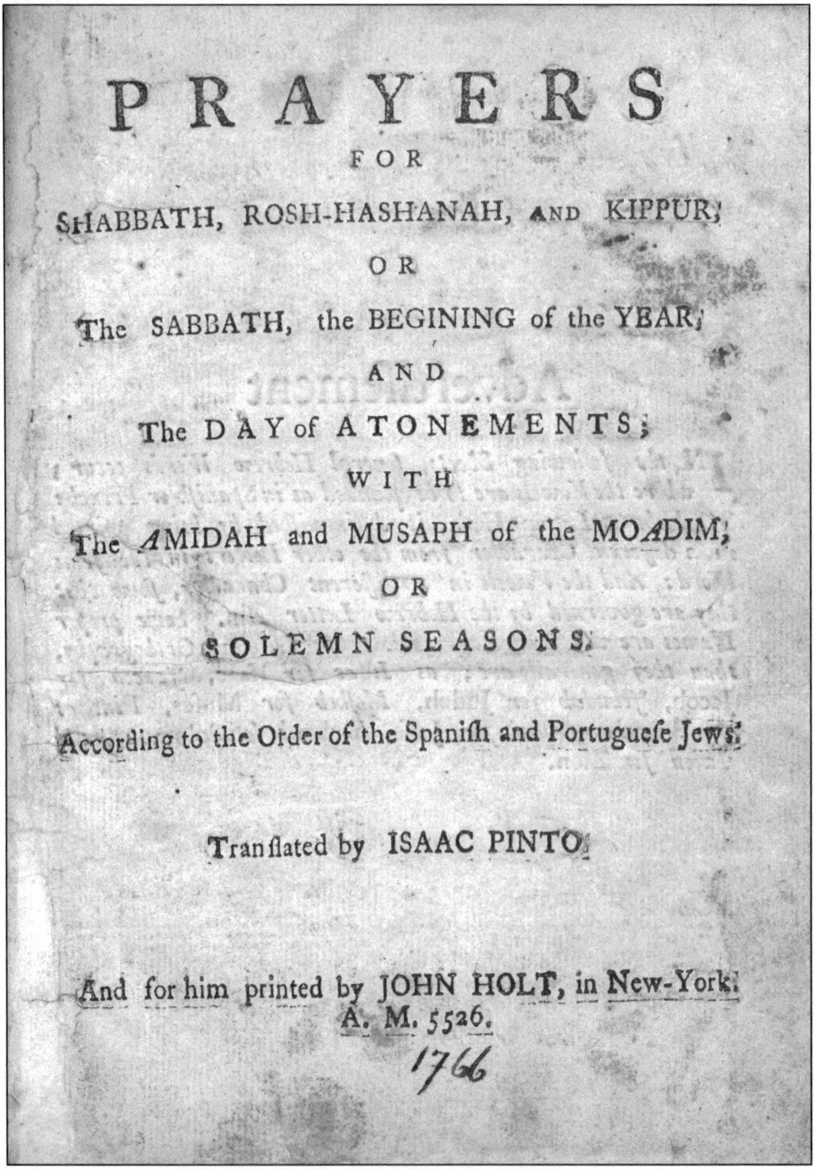

PRAYERS

FOR

SHABBATH, ROSH-HASHANAH, AND KIPPUR;

OR

The SABBATH, the BEGINING of the YEAR;

AND

The DAY of ATONEMENTS;

WITH

The *A*MIDAH and MUSAPH of the MO*A*DIM;

OR

SOLEMN SEASONS.

According to the Order of the Spanifh and Portuguefe Jews:

Tranflated by ISAAC PINTO.

And for him printed by JOHN HOLT, in New-York;
A. M. 5526.
1766

Prayers for Shabbat, Rosh-Hashanah, and Kippur, 1765/66, translated from the Hebrew by Isaac Pinto. Courtesy of the American Jewish Historical Society, New York, NY, and Newton Centre, MA, A. S. W. Rosenback Rare Book Collection.

liturgy and order of the prayers follow Sephardic custom. This prayer book (or siddur) is believed to have first been published anonymously, probably to avoid raising the ire of traditionalists, who often looked askance at liturgical translations. Such translations of traditional texts were often designed with women in mind; given their limited role in communal Jewish ritual and worship, they were not fluent in Hebrew, if they knew the language at all.

Unknown maker, *etrog* holder of the Louis (?) Gomez family of New York, late eighteenth century. Silver and cobalt blue glass. Engraved on the front is "E/BG/R/ MG" and on the back is "C/BG." 4 × 3¾ × 2¾ in. Courtesy of the American Jewish Historical Society, New York, NY, and Newton Centre, MA.

This beautiful, ornate *etrog* holder tells a story about the consumption of luxury goods in New York and also about the malleability of objects. Just as immigrants and refugees refashioned themselves upon arrival in New York, so too did the Gomez family's ornate mustard pot find a new identity and function. It was transformed from a fancy condiment holder from England to a prized Jewish ritual object—an *etrog* holder. The result, a syncretic object both Jewish and American, demonstrates the adaptability of the Gomez family and their devotion to both Judaism and status symbols.[8] The high-style pot, most definitely a luxury item, is made of silver, its body resting on three cabriole feet and topped off with a hinged lid. The front displays the family's monogram. Silver was a rare commodity in New York, and Jewish ritual objects available in Europe were not easily obtainable in the New World. For these reasons, the

Anonymous, *The Mill Street Synagogue*. Print on paper, undated. Courtesy of the American Jewish Historical Society, New York, NY, and Newton Centre, MA.

Gomez family transformed their fancy mustard pot into an *etrog* holder for the fall harvest festival of Sukkoth. The holder stayed within the family for six generations and symbolizes the early American Jewish experience, a blending of Jewish and European—here British—traditions, styles, and functions, refashioned on American soil.

During the Dutch period, Jews were required to build their homes close to each other on one side of New Amsterdam. A de facto Jewish neighborhood emerged. With the British conquest of the city, Jews were free to move but decided to remain centralized around Mill Street, which is where Congregation Shearith Israel began.[9] This undated print depicts the congregation's first synagogue, which was built by a non-Jewish mason, Stanley Holmes. At thirty-five square feet, this unassuming structure, consecrated in 1730, stood on a lot approximately 40 by 40 by 102 feet on a narrow street often called "Jews' Alley." Shearith Israel was New York's only Jewish congregation until 1825. Despite its modest size, the synagogue contained all the necessary accouterments of a Jewish house of worship, including a balcony with seating for

Torah scroll desecrated by two British soldiers during the Revolution. Photograph by Joanne Savio, in *Remnant of Israel: A Portrait of America's First Jewish Congregation, Shearith Israel*, by Marc D. Angel. Courtesy of Congregation Shearith Israel, New York.

women. In addition, the rear garden allowed for the construction of a booth for the festival of Sukkoth. This small, cottage-like structure vastly differs from the more elaborate synagogues built back in Amsterdam. Nothing about the exterior distinguishes it as a house of worship. New York's Jewish community in the 1730s lacked the population, wealth, and social prestige to build a synagogue approaching the grandeur of the Esnoga, the Spanish-Portuguese Synagogue in Amsterdam (built in 1671–1675). Instead, in terms of architectural style and scale, the members of Shearith Israel had to start anew. Modernization and relocation required a continuous shifting of artistic styles, so that this Dutch-style house became Jewish purely by its use as a synagogue. The serene setting of the print, complete with white picket fence and abundant greenery, evinces a familiarity with English landscape art.[10]

The very fact that this Torah exists at all is extraordinary. The historian Jonathan Sarna writes that "in colonial America, the presence of a Torah scroll served as a defining symbol of Jewish communal life and culture, of Jewish law and love."[11] This particular scroll, damaged by British soldiers during the American Revolution, comes down to us as a witness to and survivor of that war. That the Torah was not buried once it returned to the congregation, as is the custom when a scroll is desecrated, suggests that it was considered to be of value as a historical object. Someone made a choice to give preference to historical interests over religious obligation, and we are the beneficiaries. The very existence of a Torah from the colonial era indicates that there was a substantial-enough Jewish community to need and purchase one.

Mourning jewelry in the neoclassical style achieved popularity among American women, a fanciful token and a totem that brought the face and memories of a deceased loved one to mind while also signifying the owner's own mortality.[12] Only the wealthy could afford to commission jewelry, proof of their status and attention to the latest style. New York City was, and remains, a center of the jewelry industry. This exquisitely rendered, detailed mourning pendent typifies bereavement jewelry common to wealthy Christian families, but it is atypical because this piece was commissioned by Jews.

Jacob Hays had this double memorial locket crafted for his wife to mark the deaths of their two sons, Solomon and Joseph, in 1798 and 1801, respectively.[13] The unknown artisan's signature skill, displayed

Unidentified artist, memorial pendant for Solomon and Joseph Hays, 1801. Hair, gold, pearls, and pigment. Unknown/Memorial for Solomon and Joseph Hays/Yale University Art Gallery/Promised Bequest of Davida Tenenbaum Deutsch and Alvin Deutsch, L.L.B. 1958, in honor of Kathleen Luhrs.

here, was his intricate handling of human hair (from the two sons), beads, pearls, and wire. A lock of Solomon's blond hair forms the weeping willow at left, mirrored by Joseph's brown hair on the right. The craftsman dissolved the boys' hair to paint the left and right portions of the scene, which lends "a golden earthen tone to the background."

Know all Men by these presents, That *Jacob Levy Junr.*

do, by these presents, for good and valuable considerations, fully and absolutely Manumit, make Free, and set at Liberty *a female* slave, named *Mary Murray* hereby willing and declaring that the said *Mary* shall and may, at all times hereafter, exercise, hold, and enjoy, all and singular the liberties, rights, privileges, and immunities of *a* free *Woman* fully to all intents and purposes, as if *she* had been born free.—And *I* do hereby, for *myself, my* Executors, Administrators, and Assigns, absolutely relinquish and release all *my* right, title, and property whatsoever, in and to the said *female Slave Mary* as *my* slave. IN TESTIMONY WHEREOF, *I* have hereunto set *my* hand and seal, the *fifth* day of *March* one thousand eight hundred and *Seventeen*

SEALED AND DELIVERED IN
THE PRESENCE OF

S. Morton

Jacob Levy Jr. {LS}

City of New York, ss.

On the *sixth* day of *March* — 181*7* *Jacob Levy Junior* appeared before me, and acknowledged that *he* executed the above instrument, as *his* voluntary act and deed, for the uses and purposes therein mentioned. I allow it to be recorded.

Jacob Radcliff

By *Jacob Radcliff* Mayor, and *Richard Riker* Recorder, of the city of New-York,

It is hereby Certified, That pursuant to the statute in such case made and provided, we have this day examined *a* certain Negro Slave named *John Jackson* the property of *Jacob Levy Jr.*, aged *four & four months* ~~The Parents of said Slave~~ which slave *is* about to be manumitted, and *appearing to us ~~to be under forty five years of age, and of sufficient ability to provide for~~* we have granted this Certificate, this *Sixth* day of *March* ~~in the year of our~~ Lord, one thousand eight hundred and *Seventeen*

Jacob Radcliff

R. Riker

Certificate of manumission, New York Society for Manumission, New York, 1817. Collection of the New-York Historical Society, New York.

Chopped and cut blond hair fills the landscape below the memorials, and on the reverse, the two brothers' locks were plaited together, uniting the pair for eternity.[14] Jacob Hays and his wife, along with other wealthy Jews, influenced by their Christian neighbors but without renouncing their Jewishness or abandoning Jewish mourning practices, commissioned bereavement jewelry as a public statement of their private grief.

The arrival of African slaves in New Amsterdam in 1626 predated the arrival of the Jews from Recife, Brazil, and provided forced labor for the new colony. During parts of the seventeenth and eighteenth centuries, New York City was home to the largest urban slave population in North America.[15] While the story of slavery is usually cast as a southern experience, New York remained a slave state until 1827.

New York Jews did not differ from their Christian neighbors in that they also were slave owners. Jacob Levy Jr. was a prominent figure among New York Jews, connected by marriage to the Seixas family, and a member of Congregation Shearith Israel. He also was a slave owner. In 1814, George Roper, a slave, appealed to Levy, his owner, for his freedom, which Levy promised to him in three years' time. It appears that Levy was influenced by the New York Society for Promoting the Manumission of Slaves. Perhaps he was inspired by the pending legislation of 1827 to hasten the freeing of his other slaves: Mary Mundy, Samuel Spures, Edwin Jackson, Elizabeth Jackson, and James Jackson.[16] His manumission records, housed within the Manumission Society's holdings, suggests his involvement with abolition. Jews who acquired slaves, manumitted them, or chose not to own slaves on moral grounds demonstrated that living in New York involved them in one of the fundamental issues of our nation's founding—that of slavery.

Even without reading the contents of this Haggadah, the "quintessential Jewish prayer book for the home," or being able to hold it in your hand, consider the many facts that it helps to establish. That this Haggadah was published tells us that by 1837, there was a sizable observant Jewish population in New York sufficient to require the text used in the Passover seder.[17] The printer wrote out his name, Solomon Jackson, and profession on the cover page, an indication that Jews had expanded into traditionally Gentile businesses and occupations such as printing. Most likely, by necessity, their clientele was not limited to Jews; they

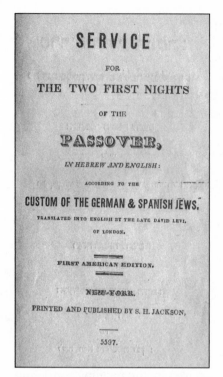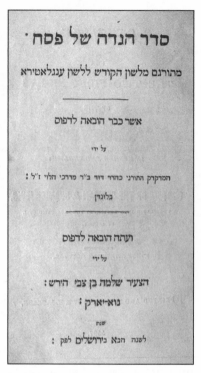

Solomon Jackson, *The First American Haggadah*, 1837. Gift of Leiner Temerlin, augmented by a grant from Madison Council, Hebraic Section, Library of Congress, Washington, DC.

produced works other than Jewish ritual volumes. Notice that Jackson described the Haggadah as the "First American Edition." By labeling it as the "first," Jackson announces with confidence his anticipation (and hope) that subsequent editions will be needed in coming years, on the basis of the assumption that there is, and will be, a market for Jewish ritual texts in New York. Finally, the cover provides insight into the makeup of New York's Jewish population at the time. The forty-three-leaf book was published in both the original Hebrew and English, which suggests that New York's Jews were by and large English speakers. The Haggadah conforms to both the "customs of the German and Spanish Jews," as is written on the cover. These words acknowledge the different linguistic and cultural strains of American Jews in the federal era.

"The Jewish Passover of 1858," *Frank Leslie's Illustrated News-paper*, April 10, 1858. Collection of the Library of Congress, Washington, DC.

Although the origins of American Jewry began with Sephardic, or Spanish, culture, even before the 1820s, Ashkenazi, or German, Jews outnumbered the Sephardim in New York.

What exotic creatures the Jews of New York must have seemed to their Christian neighbors. Their curiosity was satiated by illustrated newspapers such as *Frank Leslie's*, which enabled readers to be armchair voyeurs and anthropologists examining different cultures, such as Jews, from the sanctity of their plush parlors without ever needing to interact with them. Founded in 1855, *Frank Leslie's* targeted a rather broad and inclusive "middle" readership, mostly Christians of various denominations who were intrigued by Jews and their culture, which seemed mysterious in contrast to their own.[18] These images of matzo production on New York's Chatham Street illustrated a two-page spread titled "The Jewish Passover of 1858." The figures depicted conform to standard racial stereotypes. The article describes Jews as having "low stature, shining black eyes, crisp inky hair, hooked noses, stooping shoulders and eager movements." The author also asserts that despite their "loose morals" and dishonesty, all Jews are meticulous in their observance of the Passover rituals. The article concludes with a back-handed compliment that the city's Jews are "quiet, law-abiding good citizens, . . . among the very best of the adopted citizens of America." It is notable that a mainstream national newspaper would choose to run a relatively long (the paper ran sixteen pages in all), heavily illustrated feature about a minority population. One might also wonder how the journalist went about getting his information, as there are numerous errors, such as the suggestion that beef and fish are forbidden foods on Passover. The length of the 1858 illustrated article simultaneously demonstrates a growing awareness and interest in Jewish neighbors by Christian New Yorkers, while also maintaining an attitude of exoticism that portrayed Jews as people in need of interpretation.

Where Jews were allowed entry and with whom they socialized were important concerns as central European Jews climbed the social ladder. Some who had arrived at Castle Garden in the early nineteenth century went on to become prestigious, wealthy New Yorkers. Still, the doors of the city's posh Metropolitan Club and other men's clubs remained tightly closed to Jews despite their deep pockets. In 1852, six well-to-do German Jews established their own club, which they named the Harmonie Club.[19] Inside, members reveled in their German heritage, hosting boisterous communal singing and declamatory contests in German, the club's official language. By the century's end, such noteworthy members as the financer Joseph Seligman and the Lehman brothers felt it

DINING ROOM, HARMONIE CLUB, 10 EAST 60TH ST., NEW YORK.   McKim, Mead & White, Architects.   Wurts Bros. Photo.

Harmonie Club, established 1852. Postcard of the renovated Dining Room, 4 East Sixtieth Street, designed by the architect Stanford White, 1906. Courtesy of the Picture Collection, The New York Public Library, Astor, Lenox and Tilden Foundations.

time to bring the building up-to-date with the architectural style patronized by high society.

Club members awarded the commission to *the* premier architectural firm of the Gilded Age, Charles McKim, William Mead & Stanford White, whose patrons included Vanderbilts and Whitneys. In a 1906 article about the newly reopened Harmonie Club, the architectural critic Herbert D. Croly crowed, "No firm of architects in this country has had anything like the experience which McKim, Mead & White have had in designing club houses."[20] White's interpretation of an Italian palazzo fit for a Medici was lavishly decorated throughout with neoclassical details, such as here in the dining hall. Located at 4 East Sixtieth Street, the Harmonie Club represented the great distance that uptown German Jews placed between themselves and recent immigrants on the Lower East

Purim Association Fancy Dress Ball, March 15, 1881. Courtesy of the American Jewish Historical Society, New York, NY, and Newton Centre, MA.

Side. While Jews may not have been permitted entry to many of McKim, Mead & White's magnificent men's clubs, they were able to circumvent this prohibition by becoming architectural patrons in their own right.

In 1861, at the start of the Civil War, ten "jovial Hebrew young men," all young bachelor sons of Harmonie Club members, formed the Purim Association. Over the decades, its annual ball, such as this one held in 1881, became *the* highlight of the Jewish social calendar and an opportunity for much merriment.[21] Rather than simply a youthful bacchanal of dance and drink, the men hosted Purim Masquerades and Fancy Dress Balls as fund-raisers for Jewish charities. Seated prominently at center of this image, Queen Esther proudly directs the proceedings with masked revelers at her side. She raises her richly decorated arm with golden bracelets in the classic "Orator's Pose," as if to announce the evening's start. Just below the queen, in the shadows, are modestly dressed children in need of charity. The Punchinello and Esther drop coins their way, and at the composition's left, a girl lifts her skirt to form a basket to catch them. Uptown Jews envisioned the Purim Association's charitable dances as a retort to those who criticized Jewish "extravagance and propriety in public amusement."[22] Young Myer S. Isaacs, whose father edited the *Jewish Messenger*, cautioned revelers

Frederic Auguste Bartholdi, *Arm of the Statue of Liberty*, Philadelphia, Centennial Exhibition, 1876, photograph. Courtesy of the Granger Collection, New York.

that the Purim Ball must proceed in a "refined way that should fittingly represent the social side of Judaism."[23] Despite America's freedoms, New York Jews remained conscious of their minority position in society as they negotiated the tricky terrain of proper American Jewish forms of socializing.

The monumental uplifted hand of the Statue of Liberty is that of a woman, but neither her ethnic heritage nor cultural roots are made apparent. In nineteenth-century America, the artistic vocabulary of the neoclassical was understood as white and Anglo-Saxon. Yet the poetry of Emma Lazarus, a New York Sephardic Jew descended from one of the oldest Jewish families in America, bonded the monument to American Jewish history. Frederic Auguste Bartholdi intended his sculpture as a gift from the people of France to the United States on the occasion of its centennial to commemorate the enduring friendship of the two countries, as well as France's participation in America's war for independence.[24] Bartholdi never intended his statue either to celebrate American immigration or to serve as a grand welcoming figure to America.

Lazarus, with her poetry, recast the Statue of Liberty's meaning in a way that endures today. In order to raise funds to build a pedestal and place the monument in New York Harbor facing out to seaward, a planning committee approached her to write a sonnet. Lazarus wrote her fourteen-line "The New Colossus" in November 1883. Her words, subsequently affixed to the statue's base, transformed the Statue of Liberty into a welcome of "the wretched refuse" to America's "golden door." Despite the sculptor's original intentions, it was Lazarus's words that articulated the statue's message in the twentieth century; it became a beacon for people seeking self-determination and a new life in America, as well as a New York City icon. Ironically, Lazarus's poem did not become popular until after the United States restricted eastern and southern European immigration in 1924. Then, in the 1930s, it harked back to an ideal vision of American society as one welcoming immigrants to a new world. This interpretation of the meaning of immigration—as the movement of families across the ocean to seek a new life and not the passage of men temporarily seeking employment before returning home—expressed a widespread attitude among American Jewish immigrants. Although Lazarus was several generations removed from immigration, her encounters with Jewish immigrants at Castle Garden touched her deeply and awakened a passionate identification with these new Americans.

One of the most frequently reproduced photographs by the social reformer Jacob Riis is of this Jewish cobbler preparing for the Sabbath in his Ludlow Street coal cellar. The picture has carried different titles over the years, and with each change of name, the photograph is framed

Jacob Riis, "Where the Sound of Church Bells Never Goes," *Journal: Christmas Edition*, December 22, 1895, 6 ("Ludlow Street Hebrew Making Ready for Sabbath Eve," c. 1890). Courtesy of the Museum of the City of New York, New York, Jacob A. Riis Collection.

with a different moralizing tale. Some titles focus on the man's abject poverty, while others highlight his religious observance in a most inhospitable setting; occasionally his trade as a cobbler is mentioned. The photograph often has been cropped or edited, proving how malleable "realistic" photographs can be.[25] In uncropped versions, a second person stands next to the seated man, neutralizing the overwhelming sense of social isolation that Riis wanted to convey. The stunned look in the man's lonely eyes is not an accident. Aided by an assistant, Riis would suddenly burst into tenement apartments, camera in hand, shocking his subjects by shooting off a bright and loud magnesium-flash explosion. In a manner, Riis held people's public presentation hostage, denying them the right to control their own representation or even the publication of their photograph. Perhaps this man would have liked to tidy up, to present himself at his best, given the choice.

Riis reproduced this photo for the first time on page six of an eight-page photo essay titled "Where Santa Claus Will Not Go" in a special Christmas edition of William Randolph Hearst's *Journal,* on December 22, 1895.[26] In the original photograph, which bears the legend "Especially for *the Journal,*" the title is "Where the Sound of Church Bells Never Goes." The Christmas edition totaled forty pages in all, so almost one-fourth of the newspaper presented Riis's views on those who were excluded from the joys of the Christian holiday. All of the people Riis photographed for this piece, with the exception of the Jewish cobbler, lost out on a visit from Santa due to poverty or immoral behavior. Focusing on the cobbler's image with this original title highlights the man's exclusion from joyous church bells due to his Jewishness. Perhaps Riis sought not only to show "how the other half lives" in poverty and loneliness but also to convey a sense of social isolation.

Contemporary American Jews who see this photo today with the title *Ludlow Street Hebrew Making Ready for the Sabbath Eve in His Coal Cellar,* often unconsciously compare it to 1930s photographs of poor Polish Jews taken by Roman Vishniac. In this context, Riis's image suggests Jewish spiritual endurance and ability to transcend abject poverty through Sabbath observance, a far cry from any sense of isolation, loneliness, or spiritual deprivation that might have been conveyed to nineteenth-century viewers.[27]

Here sits a man to be reckoned with. In contrast to those who lived in the slums of Five Points or to Riis's abject subjects, the Jewish Freemason Levi Isaacs has the means to orchestrate his own visual representation. As we saw with the paintings of Moses Levy and his family, a portrait serves both to depict an individual and also to inscribe social identity. A commissioned portrait was a commodity, a luxury good whose ownership itself announced status.[28] Isaacs, who had recently been appointed as lodge master and was also a sexton of Congregation Shearith Israel, placed his body at a slight angle in relation to the camera lens, making his shiny pinky ring, his ornate lapel badge, and the apron festooned with symbols spread across his lap all easier for us to see. Calm and composed, Isaacs insists that we look at him, that we stand in admiration of his accomplishments, and that we recognize him as a very important man, just as Moses Levy had done decades before him.

Levi Isaacs in Freemason regalia, c. 1895, photograph. Courtesy of the American Jewish Historical Society, New York, NY, and Newton Centre, MA.

Over the course of the nineteenth century, New York Jews circulated and participated in secular organizations, many of which were not specific to Jews, to a greater degree than they had previously.[29] American Jewish men saw Freemasonry as "a means for social integration and an ideological system sympathetic to and derived from traditional Judaism."[30] A family man, a business man, a New Yorker, a sexton at his synagogue, which was the oldest in the United States, and a leader in his Masonic lodge, Isaacs took control of his multifaceted identity in America, ensuring that viewers saw him exactly in the esteemed manner in which he wanted to be seen.

What can a mass-produced postcard tell us about New York City Jewish life? In the late nineteenth century, concurrent with the great exodus of eastern European Jews to the United States, postcard designers and printers created a niche market targeting Jewish consumers, in particular women, offering a range of illustrated cards for Jewish holidays and life-cycle events. Many of the cards also pictured women, except for scenes set in synagogues, and brought Jewish women into "the visual universe of Jewish experience."[31] Women purchased the cards and exchanged them with friends and family, both in America and back in Europe. The cards pictured Jews—both women and men—of all ages engaged in observing holy days and using modern inventions (including ocean liners and telephones) that bridge distances and create a transnational Jewish world. Communication by postcard with "A Happy New Year" written in Hebrew and English across the front image enabled Jews on either side of the ocean to send inspirational pictures and words of good cheer in observance of their common holidays.

Here, at left, we see confident New York Jews who had previously made the voyage to America. They look swell and utterly modern. The men and women wear fine, brightly colored outfits and lack any obvious religious garments or objects, and though the men wear hats, some of them are clean shaven, a sign of their modern Orthodox Jewish practice. The American Jews extend their arms to the eastern European Jews in welcome. Perhaps, also, they intend to grasp their hands to pull these greenhorns, whose arms hang limply at their sides, into the modern world. Holding bundled parcels of their few belongings, wearing weathered hats or scarves, with rounded shoulders and faces cast slightly toward the ground, the newcomers express stasis rather than motion.

"A Happy New Year," New Year's postcard, c. 1900. Alfred & Elizabeth Bendiner Collection, Prints and Photographs Division, Library of Congress, Washington, DC.

These picturesque holiday cards provide clues to the lives of New York City Jews and how they chose to represent themselves to other Jews. The images on the front of the cards, pleasing, fanciful, and picturesque, are equal in value, despite their mass production, to the handwritten notes on their backs. If we were to read the cards and images literally, all was well for Jews in New York. Postcards, greeting cards, and the like allowed Jewish purchasers to choose how they would be represented. Such mass-produced cards satisfied their desire to be seen at their best: without grotesque stereotypes, looking healthy and fashionable, aware of holidays and traditions, and making good in the United States. The picture postcard was most often sunnier than the lives Jewish consumers actually lived and in a manner served as a note of self-congratulation on their new lives.

A busy day of work and shopping is about to begin in Brooklyn. A large clock, situated just below the store's name, Abraham & Straus, is forever frozen at 8:30 a.m. in this postcard as a crowd of customers—mainly women dressed with long skirts and coats with large hats on

"Customers at the Main Entrance Waiting for Opening," Abraham & Straus, Brooklyn, undated. Personal collection of Ronald Schweiger, Brooklyn Borough Historian, Brooklyn, New York. Courtesy of Ronald Schweiger.

their heads—wait eagerly for the shopping day to begin.[32] For immigrants, their newfound ethic of consumerism enabled women to buy and announce their status as Americans through purchasing just the right hat, right shoes, and right bag to match.[33] Young Jewish women, together with other New Yorkers, flocked to these Jewish-owned department stores. Like most young urban women, they wanted to purchase the most popular women's garments of the time: shirtwaists. These blouses, tucked in at the waist, created the much-desired slenderized "wasp waist," with a neat row of buttons down the front and a crisp snap to the shoulders. While the term "department store" was not in use prior to 1887, by the late 1860s, the concept of a grand shopping emporium had caught on with Americans.[34]

Brooklyn's Abraham & Straus and other impressive department stores employed young Jewish women as sales help, jobs they were proud to hold and a step above factory work in status, if not always in pay. This particular postcard was sent from one woman to another to share news about Bessie, a friend they had in common. The first woman wrote along the right side of the card, "This is where Bessie works." Immigrant women, especially those with a good command of English, could hold respectable jobs in stores like A&S, as it came to be known, enabling them to contribute to their family's finances and, perhaps, to save a bit of money for their own clothes and fun (and even a dowry).

New York City without bagels! Bakers on strike! From uptown on the East Side to the Lower East Side and from Brownsville, Brooklyn, to Williamsburg, Brooklyn, workers, including American Jews, marched the wide boulevards of the city and then gathered at Union Square each May 1 to celebrate May Day. This workers' holiday was founded in 1886 in the United States as part of the labor movement's fight for an eight-hour workday.[35] Approximately thirty thousand to fifty thousand laborers filled the streets of the city each May Day in the early 1900s. Here, three bakers stand as a united entity, on strike to demand a maximum ten-hour day, a minimum wage, recognition of their union, and the right to use the union's label.[36] The men balance on their shoulders a large wooden platform on which rests a gigantic loaf of bread measuring fifteen feet long and five feet wide; you can sense a bit of strain on the face of the man at the left. Rather than industrial workers, these men

Bakers and the Big Loaf, New York City, May 1, 1909, photograph. George Gratham Bain Collection, Library of Congress, Washington, DC.

were artisan bakers fighting to maintain their craft; that craft included making bagels, which vanished from the city during the strike. In the early twentieth century, New York City acquired prominence as a national center of bread baking. But for the workers, the bread that they held aloft communicated two meanings: it was, first, an example of their extraordinary talents and, second, the bread that they wanted to provide to their families with a decent wage.

On March 25, 1911, a deadly fire broke out in the Triangle Shirtwaist Factory on the cusp of Washington Square Park, which culminated in the worst labor tragedy to that date. The garment factory was littered with inflammable scraps of fabric and rags, so the fierce flames spread like quicksilver. The building's locked exits, buckling fire escapes, and inadequate safety measures led to the deaths of 133 young Italian and Jewish women, including teenagers, and 13 young men—a total of 146 workers. Many jumped from the windows located eight and nine stories above the street in an attempt to save their lives, only to die upon impact

"Awaiting Their Turn to Seek Lost Relatives," *New York American*, March 27, 1911, 2. Courtesy of the New York Public Library, New York.

with the sidewalk. The broken and burned corpses were lined up in rows along the sidewalks so that relatives could identify their daughters. Immigrant Jews from Russia and Galicia had previously witnessed mass deaths, as in the Kishinev pogrom of 1903, which in comparison had killed approximately 46 Jews. Far from the tsar's army in the United

"Grief Stricken Relatives Leaving the Morgue," *New York American*, March 27, 1911, 3. Courtesy of the New York Public Library, New York.

States, immigrant Jews suffered under the owners of garment factories, who frequently were German Jews who had arrived in the mid-nineteenth century and advanced to middle-class and managerial status. Max Blanck and Isaac Harris, joint owners of the Triangle Shirtwaist Factory, were exonerated at their trial from responsibility for the deaths of their workers.

Responses to the tragedy in New York City divided sharply along class, religious, and geographic lines, with newspapers catering to each group. White Anglo-Saxon Protestants, the city's wealthy and powerful, believed that, as with many emotions, grief should be kept private and under control. While they empathized with the mourning families' losses, they also sat in judgment of how they should behave in public and were aghast at the open weeping and pronounced agony that the mourners expressed without regard for judgmental eyes. Although William Randolph Hearst's *New York American* expressed support for the workers, his writers and photographers sensationalized an already sensational event, deploying features of period melodrama.[37] Hearst's staff "preyed on families," staging pictures at the morgue before and after the victims were identified, such as the two photographs shown here. The papers read by the survivors, such as the socialist Yiddish *Jewish Daily Forward*, saw no need to sensationalize or comment on the mourners' behavior. As the mouthpiece of Jewish immigrants, the *Forward* denounced the heartless capitalist Jews whose failure to recognize the Jewish union led to the tragedy. The *Forward* and its readers mourned openly and sorrowfully the promising, innocent lives lost.

Approximately twenty-five-thousand Levantine Sephardic Jews entered the United States between 1899 and 1925; most of them settled in New York. A minority within the Jewish minority, they were less educated and less prepared to succeed in the United States than were Jewish immigrants from eastern Europe. Many spoke Ladino (Judeo-Spanish); others spoke Greek or Arabic. Even under the umbrella term of "Sephardic Jews," these immigrants came from numerous countries, with different cultural and religious traditions.[38] But the needs of these differing groups were the same: to secure work, find housing, freely practice their religion, maintain ties with their homelands, and succeed as Americans. Sephardim used the Ladino press to secure recognition as Jews by the dominant Ashkenazim; the latter often failed to accept their fellow Jews, who manifested different ethnic appearances and customs. This particular issue of *La America* was written in both Ladino and Yiddish; prominent on the first page is an article, "To the Ashkenazic People," demonstrating Sephardic desire to connect with their coreligionists.

La America was just one of nineteen Judeo-Spanish periodicals published between 1910 and 1948; its editor was Moise Gadol, a Sephardic Jew from Bulgaria. All but two of the nineteen newspapers were

La America — אמיריקה — La America

L.A. AMERICA ORIENTAL SPANISH-JEWISH JOURNAL

THE ORIENTAL PRINTING & PUB. CO.

פיריאודיקו נאסיונאל ליטיראריו, פוליטיקו אי קומירסיאל.

Subscription Rates:
United States / Foreign
One Year .... $1.50 / 10 Francs
Six Months ... 0.75 / 5
Payable in Advance

Published Weekly By THE ORIENTAL PRINTING & PUB. CO.
180 Chrystie Street, New York, Telephone 4886 Orchard

PRICE TWO CENTS   NEW YORK, FRIDAY, MAY 12, 1911—5671 11 אייר ביום

צו דעם אידישע פאלק

די נעהיימניסע פון אילדיא מער־
קישען חוף

לה באלאור ריל זורנאל.

published in New York City. As German Jews and eastern European Jews had also done, Jews from lands such as Turkey and Syria established self-help charitable organizations, Etz Ha-hayim (Tree of life) and Rodfei Tsedek (Seekers of justice), to help their own. In 1911, the Hebrew Immigrant Aid Society (HIAS) opened its "Oriental Bureau" to serve the needs of the Sephardic Jewish Community.[39]

"This is a wonderful age we are living in," proclaimed the New York Jewish artist Max Weber in 1915. "Surely there will be new numbers, new weights, new colors, and new forms." Weber painted his passion for the urban and modern in *Chinese Restaurant* (1915), one of the artist's most heralded and reproduced works. With this composition, Weber displays his command of Picasso's synthetic cubism in its carefully arranged but seemingly haphazard placement of forms and the manner in which he shatters the face of the Chinese waiter, placing facial elements apart from each other. The distinct red and gold lacquer that decorated many

Max Weber (1881–1961), *Chinese Restaurant*, 1915, oil on canvas. Overall (sight): 39½ × 47½ in. (100.3 × 120.7 cm). Purchase 31.382, Whitney Museum of Art, New York.

Chinese restaurants, along with the black-and-white checkered floor linoleum, typifies the many "chop suey" houses that had sprung up in lower Manhattan. An early champion of modernism, Weber influenced other Jewish New York artists to experiment stylistically. Their works in painting and photography signaled the rise of Jewish involvement in modernism in the city.

For Weber, the exotic and the modern are represented in the restaurant's cuisine and staff. Both Weber and the waiter he has depicted were immigrants to America. But the two men were not equals. The Chinese Exclusion Act of 1882 prohibited Chinese immigration, while Jews were shifting to the "white" side of the color line.[40]

On a sunny day in Harlem, a congregation of Jews stands in front of their shul for a portrait as a community. In early twentieth-century

James VanDerZee, *The Congregation of the Moorish Zionist Temple of the Moorish Jews, Harlem*, 1929. Photograph by James VanDerZee. LC-DIG-ppmsca-05645, Prints and Photographs Division, Library of Congress, Washington, DC.

Harlem, Marcus Garvey's Universal Negro Improvement Association (UNIA) and the movement's interest in the history of the African diaspora inspired black Judaism.[41] In this group portrait in front of the brownstone that served as the Moorish Jews' synagogue, Rabbi Arnold Ford provides the sharp visual focus. His upper torso, wrapped in his white tallit (prayer shawl), sets him apart from his congregants. All of them, with the exception of a young boy, wear a hat or *kippah*, their heads covered in religious fidelity. The women, too, cover their heads. All appear to be dressed in their finest outfits for this posed group portrait.

While the content of contemporary Jewish and African American newspapers attests that other Jews questioned the authenticity of these Moorish Jews, they proudly displayed their faith in this formal photograph.[42]

"Yoo-Hoo, Mrs. Goldberg!" This signature greeting of *The Goldbergs* warmly welcomed audiences into Molly Goldberg's family apartment in the Bronx. Goldberg, played by the actress Gertrude Berg, cheerily

The Goldbergs Jigsaw Puzzle, Pepsodent, color lithograph. Published by Pepsodent Co., Chicago, Illinois, 1932. Collection of Yeshiva University Museum, New York.

shouted from her kitchen-window perch, dispensing home-spun wisdom in winning malapropisms. *The Goldbergs*, a popular radio and then television show sponsored by Pepsodent, was written and produced by Berg and also starred Berg as the matriarch of a Jewish family striving to do well.[43] The Tuesday-night fifteen-minute radio version debuted in November 1929, right after the disastrous stock-market crash. Berg, through her character, created the most modern, positive, and assertive popular image of a Jewish woman to that date. As Molly, she fearlessly took on such pressing issues as anti-Semitism and Hitler's war against the Jews. For most Americans, Berg's bubbly Mrs. Goldberg was their first, if only fictional, image of a Jewish New Yorker. Berg and Goldberg were so closely aligned in the public's mind as to be one and same.

During the 1930s, Gertrude/Molly stood second only to Eleanor Roosevelt in the quantity of letters received from the public. This fictional Jewish woman of the Bronx presented such a powerful image of motherly strength, tinged with Yiddish-inflected speech and her family's striving for a better life, that despite ethnic and geographic differences, many non-Jewish women nationally felt a kinship with Molly Goldberg.

The Jewish Palestine Exhibit at the New York world's fair. Miller Art Co., Inc., New York, 1939. Collection of Yeshiva University Museum, New York.

Although unknown today, before Lucille Ball's *I Love Lucy*, Berg created the first popular series about a New York family.

In 1939, New York City invited the world to visit the world's fair held in the borough of Queens. The Jewish Palestine Exhibit was an enticing advertisement for what did not yet exist: a Jewish national home. Since Palestine was under British mandate at the time, the organizers of the Jewish Palestine building were denied permission to situate their building among those of other nations. Allowed to construct a cultural exhibition in a different location on the fairgrounds, with accompanying public programs such as indigenous folk dance, the Zionist sponsors nonetheless aimed to cast the impression that Jewish Palestine was almost a nation-state. The pavilion featured on its façade a monumental hammered-copper relief sculpture titled *The Scholar, the Laborer, and the Toiler of the Soil,* by the acclaimed art deco sculptor Maurice Ascalon. Many New York Jews visited the Palestine pavilion, absorbing its presentation of a new type of Jewishness rooted in the soil, so different from their urban identity. This aspiring Jewish state in miniature reinforced through contrast Jewish New Yorkers' understanding of their own distinctiveness.[44]

In the hands of the American artist Ben Shahn, a trip to the post office could provide a lesson in civics. Shahn's mural for the New Deal art

Ben Shahn, *First Amendment*, 1941, egg tempera on canvas, Queens, New York. Photograph by Peter Morgan. Art © Estate of Ben Shahn / Licensed by VAGA, New York, NY.

programs, *First Amendment*, celebrates the Constitution's guarantee of freedom of religion and expression, values held dear by many New York Jews.[45] While Jews benefited from the separation of church and state, the First Amendment also guaranteed their right to speak out, protest, and unite as groups. Sharp diagonals lead us through the canvas's eight separate vignettes, each of which depicts citizens activating their constitutional rights. Painted in matte tones, men marching with fists upraised in protest and solidarity form unified groups to speak, work to keep the flow of news information going, and take their political grievances all the way to the Supreme Court. Shahn placed the Statue of Liberty's oxidized green hand and uplifted torch at the center to proclaim the centrality of freedom within his conception of America, articulating a slightly different vision from that of Emma Lazarus. The torch echoes the Socialist Party's symbol, also an uplifted torch, printed on the voter's ballot. In the late 1930s, the Statue of Liberty rose to symbolic prominence in response to the threat of war and existing limits on immigration. In black and white, Shahn re-created a conventional New York State voter's ballot, asserting, "the ballot being to my mind the guarantee of all our freedoms." Acutely aware of the rise of Hitler and the decision of President Franklin D. Roosevelt's administration not to increase immigration quotas to accommodate refugees, Shahn reinforced his pictorial vigor by writing to government officials when he was asked to alter his work. "The thing that I have tried to put into this mural, I feel very strongly," he explained. "I feel that it has profound significance for every American, more significance every day because of increasing threats to our rights and liberties." Shahn was successful in his argument. Shahn's mural was installed in a Queens post office in 1941, as World War II raged across the globe.[46]

By fixing the camera's lens on the front window of a Judaica shop on New York's Lower East Side, the photographer Marjory Collins supports the shop owner's desire to advertise his dual identities: a Jewish religious identity and a secular identity as an American patriot. "God Bless America," reads one banner, hanging next to a tallit. On one level, the shopkeeper announces, "It's great to be an American," demonstrating through his wares—religious books, a Torah scroll, books on Jewish humor and jokes, menorahs and candlesticks—just how free he felt as

Marjory Collins, *Window of a Jewish Religious Shop on Broome Street, New York*, 1942, photograph. FSA/OWI, Library of Congress, Washington, DC.

a Jew in New York City at a time when Nazi Germany was murdering Jews. Yet simultaneously, he also asserts his patriotism, perhaps partially to answer those who questioned Jews' commitment to the United States. The plate-glass window reflects iconic elements of the New York City urban landscape, such as the curved street lamp and fire escapes. Collins employed an urban aesthetic, deftly portraying the multiethnic and multicultural character of the United States. This window display on the Lower East Side also demonstrates the ongoing importance of the neighborhood for religious as well as Yiddish-reading New York Jews.

Collins joined Roy Stryker's Office of War Information (OWI), the renowned group of documentary photographers who worked under Stryker's direction. He provided his cadre of photographers with detailed shooting scripts. In the first incarnation, many of these photographers worked for the Resettlement Administration / Farm Security Administration (RA/FSA) to create and distribute images of the Dust Bowl and the Great Depression from throughout the South and the West. Assigned to document "hyphenated Americans," Collins's photos, such as this one, were duplicated and dropped behind enemy lines in Europe and in Asia in order to let ordinary citizens know that the United States supported peoples suppressed by fascist governments. OWI members were among the first Americans to view European atrocities through photos that made their way out of Nazi control.

These last photographs taken of Julius and Ethel Rosenberg, the infamous husband and wife accused of, convicted of, and ultimately executed for conspiring to pass nuclear secrets to the Soviet Union,

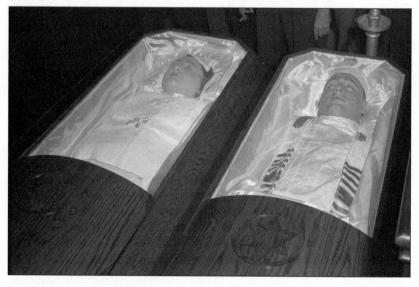

Anonymous, *Rosenbergs Lie in State*, Brooklyn, NY, news photograph, United Press International, 1953. © Bettmann/CORBIS.

illustrate the couple's desire to acknowledge posthumously their identities as Jews. Here, in a Brooklyn Jewish funeral home, with thousands of people waiting to pay their respects, the Rosenbergs lie in matching wood caskets with the Magen David (Jewish star) on the lids, which are lifted up for public viewing, in violation of traditional Jewish funerary practices. Revealed are husband and wife, always presented as a couple in the courts as in their deaths, dressed in white burial shrouds, following Jewish burial customs. Characteristic elements such as Julius's round, wire-rimmed glasses and mustache no longer appear. A neatly arranged tallit lies on Julius's shoulders and chest. The Rosenbergs were charged with conspiracy to commit espionage, and their case attracted international interest, eliciting strong passions and devoted support from many people, especially on the communist left. But their prosecution and execution were especially poignant for New York Jews. Both Julius and Ethel Rosenberg had grown up in the city and attended its public schools. On the Friday afternoon of their scheduled execution, many people gathered in Union Square hoping for a last-minute reprieve. However, some New York Jews vehemently opposed clemency for the Rosenbergs. The judge, attorney, and prosecutors were all Jews.

The comedian Lenny Bruce (1925–1966) graphically explained what made New York City and its residents Jewish, even when they weren't. As Bruce saw it, "If you live in New York or any other big city, you are Jewish. If doesn't matter if you are Catholic, you're Jewish. If you live in Butte, Montana you're going to be goyish even if you're Jewish. . . . Jewish means pumpernickel bread, black cherry soda and macaroons. Goyish means Kool-Aid, Drake's cakes and lime jello."[47] By contrasting "Jewish" with "goyish," Bruce transformed all New Yorkers into Jews, strengthening the Jewish identification of the city in the eyes of other Americans. New York and Jewish merged in Bruce's routine, making his listeners laugh with recognition at his boldness for saying what so many knew.

As stereotypes of Jewish men multiplied, Bruce mutated and reshaped each one. A Jewish intellectual? Well, while not an exact description of Bruce, he was sharp, verbal, and smart, although some people reduced him to just a smart aleck. Muscular Jew does not apply either, not to a man whose appetite for heroin and cigarettes abused his body; yet he

Anonymous photographer, *Lenny Bruce Being Frisked and Arrested*. NYWT&S
Collection, Prints and Photographs Division, Library of Congress, Washington, DC.

possessed the strength and courage to stand up and speak out during
the McCarthy era, when words were suppressed and free thought was
deemed dangerous. Bruce, like other New York Jews, such as the painter
Ben Shahn (see the earlier figure), revered the First Amendment and
Bill of Rights. Bruce was arrested numerous times on charges of obscenity; once the police arrested him for using the Yiddish word schmuck
(penis). Civil rights and free speech advocates, artists, writers, and comics spoke on his behalf at his trial in 1964 but to no avail. Bruce received
a posthumous gubernatorial pardon from New York State, the first ever
decreed in the state's history.

A woman effortlessly glides on a tightrope over the New York night
skyline, naked above the waist except for her bra. The story behind
this advertisement reveals the many supportive roles New York Jewish
women have played in America, especially in the garment and advertising industries. The Maidenform Company's "I Dreamed" campaign ran
for twenty years between 1949 and 1969, making it one of the longest
running advertising campaigns in history. The campaign took shape
around the kitchen table of a Jewish advertising executive and his wife.

"I Dreamed I Walked a Tightrope in My Maidenform Bra," 1961, advertisement. Courtesy of the Maidenform Collection, Archives Center, National Museum of American History, Smithsonian Institution, Washington, DC, and reprinted by permission of the Maidenform Company.

Similarly, the Maidenform bra company developed in reaction to the flat-chested flapper silhouette when Ida Cohen Rosenthal, a Jewish dressmaker working in a New York dress shop, fashioned a brassiere to enhance the natural female form in her dress designs. On the basis of positive reactions from her customers, she launched the Maidenform Brassiere Company in 1923 with her husband and another dressmaker.

Jewish women were not only a significant part of New York's female labor force, but they also played a major role in fashion design, beauty culture, and the advertising industry in the twentieth century. Like many others who did not conform precisely to Euro-American beauty ideals, Jewish women felt the need to align their bodies more closely with that standard. Their desires found expression in various innovations, some of which suggested a boldness, brashness, and sense of humor associated with New York Jews.

Howard Zieff's widely successfully campaign for Levy's Rye Bread first appeared in the city's subways, appealing to the inclusiveness of enjoying ethnic food. The series of posters, each presenting a different ethnic or racial type, offers a visual pun that assumes the people pictured would not be identified as Jewish. To be both Native American or African American or Chinese American and Jewish was inaccurately perceived as being a living oxymoron. Zieff recalled that he first encountered the Native American man near Grand Central Terminal, where he worked as an engineer. In order to amplify the man's non-Jewishness, Zieff outfitted him in a pastiche of Native costumes, more fictional Hollywood than accurate.[48] This "trickster" visual play brings to mind similarities between Native and Jewish humor, each with a dark tone of survival despite all odds. The ad campaign soon spread beyond New York and heralded an expanding consumption of both kosher food and "New York style" culture. Jewish New Yorkers were now exporting to the rest of the United States their particular fusion of Jewish and American urban identity, whether in the field of intellectualism (the New York Intellectuals) or painting (the New York school of art) or photography (the New York school of photography), inviting others to savor the combination. In the years following the campaign, rates of Jewish intermarriage climbed steadily, registering widespread acceptance of Jews as intimates of non-Jews.

Howard Zieff, "You Don't Have to Be Jewish to Love Levy's Real Jewish Rye," Doyle Dane Bernbach Ad Agency, New York, 1967. Courtesy of the Prints and Photographs Division, Library of Congress, Washington, DC.

"Let Our People Go," poster, Coalition to Free Soviet Jewry, New York City Center for Jewish History, mid-1970s. Courtesy of the American Jewish Historical Society, New York, NY.

Red and black, colors rich with symbolic meaning, are powerfully applied and contrasted in this poster demanding the release of Jews forced to remain in the Soviet Union. While red denotes strength, as well as bloodshed and fire, black stands for death, as well as evoking charred, coal-black burnt remains.[49] Each brings to mind violence and death during pogroms, the Shoah, and Stalin's murderous reign. The slogan "Let My People Go," here written with the more inclusive "our," instead of "my," motivated the movement. Originating from the nineteenth-century African American spiritual "Go Down Moses," the song references the Torah's account of the Exodus from Egypt. For many Americans, the definitive interpretation belongs to Paul Robeson, whose deep, rich bass-baritone voice conjured up images of Moses. New York City was home to the Coalition to Free Soviet Jews, as well as the Student Struggle for Soviet Jewry, not to mention the militant Jewish Defense League, whose slogan "Never Again" also became associated with the movement. With New York the site for numerous protests and marches, including the annual Solidarity Day rally held outside the United Nations, New York Jews played significant leadership roles in the Soviet Jewry movement. The capital city of American Jews, New York provided the numbers needed for massive rallies that kept the issue of rescue at the forefront of American politicians' minds and on the agenda of American Jews for several decades.

After Nan Goldin suffered a savage beating from her lover Brian, she made herself pretty for the photograph she would take of her mirror image, reapplying her red lipstick, which makes the red of her bruised, bloody eyes all the more evident. Fanciful earrings hang from her ears, and a pearl necklace runs around her neck. Within one face, the beauty of seduction and the rage of romantic, sexual obsession come together. Goldin drags us with her work into her world on the Lower East Side of New York in the 1980s, where heroin was king, apartments were dirt cheap, and the neighborhood was dangerous. This downtown world of

Nan Goldin, "Nan 1 Month after Being Battered," *The Ballad of Sexual Dependency*, 1984, Cibachrome photograph, 20 × 24 in. © Nan Goldin. Courtesy Matthew Marks Gallery, New York.

which she was a part refuted her upbringing as a "nice Jewish girl" in the suburbs outside Washington, DC. In reverse migration, she left home for the tenements. Her world and the people in it, who openly shoot drugs, have casual sex, sleep on filthy mattresses on filthy floors, and head out to punk nightclubs, no longer exist. The Lower East Side has been gentrified, excluding young artists, urban transplants, immigrants, and others from the rougher edges of life.

Gay men were dying in large numbers beginning in the early 1980s, and for many, remaining silent in the face of indifference was not an option. New York City, long a location of social and political organizing involving New York Jews, added to its reputation with the rise of

AIDS Coalition to Unleash Power, "Silence Equals Death," lapel button, c. 1987.

anti-AIDS activism. Angered by the government's gross mismanagement of the AIDS crisis, Gran Fury, a group of individuals committed to using the power of art to command social change, designed the "Silence = Death" poster campaign. In 1986, appropriating the pink triangle used by the Nazis to label gay men in the concentration camps, the group drew parallels between the Shoah and the pandemic. The following year, the Jewish playwright and gay activist Larry Kramer (b. 1935) called for a heated campaign of direct action; his combined energy and anger initiated the AIDS Coalition to Unleash Power (ACT-UP), based in New York. Famous actions of civil disobedience included the group's infiltration of the New York Stock Exchange to protest the high costs of medications; seizing New York's General Post Office on the eve of April 15, 1987, as bewildered bystanders filed tax returns; and "Stop the Church," an event in which close to five thousand protestors took over St. Patrick's Cathedral in response to the Catholic Church's

Amy Klein Reichert, *Miriam's Cup*, 1997, silver; Steven Smithers, silversmith, and Art Evans, photographer. Courtesy of the Jewish Museum, New York / Art Resource, NY, and Amy Klein Reichert.

opposition to AIDS education. Kramer's articulate activism, channeled into his play *The Normal Heart*, added the vision of gay Jews to New York City's reputation.

The feminist movement both transformed the visual arts and strongly influenced Judaism. Among New York's world-class museums is The Jewish Museum, established by the Jewish Theological Seminary. The museum's collections range from antiquities to contemporary religious and secular art. The museum has commissioned Jewish art as well as purchasing it, giving feminist Judaica greater visibility and prestige.

Formed from silver with small silver cymbals attached, artists Reichert's and Smithers's *Miriam's Cup* appeals to several of our senses. The shiny surface and the hanging cymbals glimmer when struck by light to entice our eyes; the gentle rattle of the small tambourines delights our ears; and the water within the cup quenches our thirst. Women have traditionally taken on a lesser role in the Passover seder than have men. In the 1970s, feminist Jews in New York City began to bring their voices to the feast of Passover in reclamation of their matriarchal ancestors.[50] For centuries, Passover celebrants have placed a cup of wine on the seder table for the prophet Elijah, who, it is said, will return to herald the coming of the Messiah. In recent years, some families have added a second cup—this one filled with water for Moses's sister, Miriam. The Torah relates that after the crossing of the Red Sea with timbrels—a percussion instrument similar to a tambourine—in hand, Miriam led the women of Israel in songs and dances of praise to God. "What are the sounds of freedom?" the artist Amy Klein Reichert has asked. "The wind rustling through grasses, the murmuring of exiles." What are the "desert sounds, a joyous song with a tambourine."[51]

The Jewish feminist movement provided Jewish women with a path that allowed them to combine critical features of their identities. Just as New York Jewish women had advocated for women's rights, including in the suffrage and labor-reform movements of the early twentieth century, they played key roles in what is now known as the second-wave feminist movement of the 1960s and 1970s. Women like Bella Abzug (1920–1988), a lawyer who represented a Manhattan district in the U.S. House of Representatives from 1971 to 1976, helped not only to secure civil rights, full protection under the law, and greater economic parity for women but also fundamentally rewrote women's social roles. A socialist Zionist, Abzug protested the "Zionism is racism" resolution at the United Nations in 1975.

Other second-wave Jewish feminists and co-founders with Abzug of the National Women's Political Caucus in 1971 included Betty Friedan, the author of *The Feminine Mystique* (1963) and first president of the National Organization for Women (NOW, 1966), and Letty Cottin Pogrebin, a founder of *Ms.* magazine (1972) and a prominent essayist on Jewish feminism. Together with younger New York women like Paula Hyman, who pioneered the Jewish feminist movement and demanded equality for Jewish women in Jewish religious life, they contributed to the identification of New York Jews with outspoken, politically active feminists, supporters of civil rights and peace movements.

In 2005, the German-born Jewish photographer Julian Voloj went searching for architectural elements, historical objects, and urban ruins that hinted at traces of New York City's rich Jewish heritage that had become obscured over time. He sought to create a visual catalogue of

Julian Voloj, *Untitled: Part of Forgotten Heritage Series: Uncovering New York's Hidden Jewish Past*, 2005, photograph. Courtesy of Julian Voloj.

what had been and what still exists today. Voloj assigns to us a task, if so inspired, to join his search for material remnants and to rediscover the vestiges of New York's Jewish past that remain potent in our time.[52]

Literally, Voloj's search sent him high and low, and he found himself up on the rooftop of Ahavas Israel Synagogue in Greenpoint, Brooklyn. His photograph emphasizes a Magen David located atop the synagogue's roof.[53] The metal bars were forged into the now familiar six-pointed star, creating a frame within a frame that directs the viewer's gaze to the blended Brooklyn and Manhattan skyline.

The Star of David's role as a framing device asks us to consider the role of Jewish history within the larger framework of the city. What is a New York Jew, and how are Jews pictured in the city's visual economy? Voloj's willingness to seek and to locate the once forgotten shows that Jewishness has not vacated New York, but rather, its nineteenth-century origins no longer command our view. Like an archeologist, Voloj unearths a hidden culture, people, and time and then brings it back to view in our contemporary era. His use of black and white for his images offers the sense of a document, of a survey, and of believability we used to see in newspapers. Voloj embeds the history of New York Jews within the broader fabric of the city at an unconscious level.

Spanning over three centuries, the objects and images offered for consideration in this visual essay have served as passports to the journey of becoming New York Jews. This journey has not been just temporal. Rather, this material culture calls our attention to a cultural journey in which Jews and Jewish objects have interacted with other cultures, with new ingredients with which to make art and ritual objects, and with an unfamiliar urban environment in which to establish their new home. Unlike Jewish participation in public political debates, such as those concerning slavery or World War II, through embroidery, portraits, and other crafts, we have gained entry into the domestic and private world of Jews in America. In his searing memoir, *The Fire Next Time*, the writer James Baldwin states what might seem obvious: that "African American" was a new identity brought about by slavery and that there is no equal to the African American identity in the world and African diaspora. His observations are pertinent to American Jews. The formation of New York Jewish identity was not established with the arrival of Recife refugees in New Amsterdam. Rather, the process of identity formation continues to evolve. Portraits, postcards, Purim Ball flyers, and political posters all serve to shape and announce what it meant historically to be a Jew in New York, as well as what it means today.

"Many American Jews," writes the author Douglas Rushkoff, "consider Israel the heart of Judaism. They write checks to Israel." Yet he notes that it is different for New York Jews and those of the greater New York Jewish Diaspora throughout the United States.[54] For these Jews, New York *is* the motherland. This new "ancestral" home replaces images of an often difficult and dangerous life in Europe or the Middle East with pictures of a challenging, but ultimately more welcoming, origin of Jewish American roots. Unlike in most American cities, New York's public schools close on the High Holidays, and food store clerks don't offer quizzical looks when asked for matzo meal in the springtime. Jewish life, rituals, and experiences have become incorporated into the fabric of New York and then have been communicated and shaped in the nation's imagination through popular culture, news media, and advertising. Politics, style, humor, music, painting, advertising, and photography all produced versions of a New York Jew so that, by the second decade of the twenty-first-century, most Americans recognize Jews as an important part of American culture. Many meanings and images of New York Jews have proliferated over the past three and a half centuries, representing their tremendous variation and vitality. As we have seen, these images permeate Jewish and American consciousness, traveling far and wide beyond the city itself.

ACKNOWLEDGMENTS

As any author knows, a particular pleasure accompanies writing acknowledgments, alongside trepidation lest one forget someone who matters. To begin with the pleasure, I can recall when this book, and the three that preceded it, were only a glimmer in the eye of Jennifer Hammer. She envisioned a history of New York Jews as early as 2004 and worked assiduously, overcoming many obstacles, to see it come to fruition. She recruited me to serve as general editor, and together we found a top-flight team of historians—Jeffrey S. Gurock, Annie Polland, Daniel Soyer, and Howard B. Rock—who wrote *City of Promises*, an award-winning three-volume history of Jews in New York City. Along with the art historian Diana L. Linden, who produced an innovative visual essay for each of the three volumes, they crafted a definitive history of New York Jews. This volume represents the final piece of Jennifer's project: a synthesis of *City of Promises*. I owe her an enormous debt of gratitude for her vision and fortitude and an enthusiasm that never flagged.

This book could not exist without the superb scholarship of Jeff Gurock, Annie Polland, Danny Soyer, and Howard Rock, as well as the insights of Diana Linden. It integrates their interpretations of New York's Jewish history and blends their language with my own. Synthesizing three excellent books proved much more difficult than I imagined. So much very fine writing needed to be condensed or cut that it took multiple drafts to reach a final manuscript. Both Jeff and Danny recognized my quandary and volunteered not only to read but also to reread and comment on earlier versions of this book. I am enormously grateful for their sharp editorial eyes and generous suggestions. They also kept me from several errors, though, of course, I remain responsible for any that may remain.

At NYU Press, Amy Klopfenstein proved an exceptionally able assistant when Jennifer was on maternity leave. Shannagh Rowland efficiently gathered permissions for the images in the book. I am grateful for their help, along with the rest of the team at the press.

A year's leave, or duty off campus in University of Michigan lingo, allowed me to make the transition with grace from director of the Frankel Center for Judaic Studies to faculty member and historian. My colleagues in Judaic Studies and in History have provided a congenial place to work and think. The staff at the Frankel Center has always been supportive. I particularly want to thank my colleagues at the Eisenberg Institute for Historical Studies for a fellowship in 2014–2015 that reduced my teaching duties for a semester and encouraged me to shift my focus from administration to scholarship.

Because this book draws on the three volumes of *City of Promises*, I benefited from fruitful discussions of those volumes with colleagues and students. Specifically, I want to mention the valuable responses of my students in the Sunday Night Study Group, a lively and sharp group of mostly suburban Detroit Jews who met monthly, ten months of the year, eager to learn about Jewish history, religion, and culture. They agreed to read each volume, which served as the basis for a significant segment of several class sessions, and they shared with me their impressions of what they read. Those remarks guided me as I rewrote this book. A different and complementary set of critiques from University of Michigan colleagues and graduate students (participants in the American Jewish Studies reading group) sent me to look for additional cultural material. I am particularly indebted to Mikhail Krutikov's helpful suggestions regarding New York's Yiddish literary culture, however inadequate my additions.

This book required more time to write than I expected. It took shape partly during a year of mourning. The death of my father, Martin Dash, in January 2015, reminded me forcefully of how my own story was deeply connected to the history I was telling. Although the printing industry warrants only a sentence in the book, I knew that I could not ignore my father's field of business, given its many Jewish dimensions. The following January, my grandson Elijah celebrated his bar mitzvah. That key rite of passage also deserved a sentence. My best and most critical editor and partner in life, MacDonald, put up with my absence during my year on sabbatical in New York City. He made me set a deadline on the rewriting and reminded me of my goals. I could never have finished this without his steadfast support.

In dedicating this book to my mother, Irene Golden Dash, and to my four grandchildren, Elijah Mateo Axt, Zoe Bella Moore, Rose Alexa

Moore, and Oren Jacob Moore, I wish to express my gratitude for my enormous good fortune to be embedded within four lively generations of New York Jews. My mother has lived a significant chunk of the history recounted in this book; her choices have contributed to New York Jewish culture. My grandchildren are just starting out to write new chapters of this history. I am fortunate to stand among them, glimpsing simultaneously past and future.

Deborah Dash Moore
Ann Arbor, August 2016

NOTES

ABBREVIATIONS

AJH   *American Jewish History*
AJHQ   *American Jewish Historical Quarterly*
AJAJ   *American Jewish Archives Journal*
PAJHS *Publications of the American Jewish Historical Society*

INTRODUCTION

1. Milton Lehman, "Veterans Pour into New York to Find That Its Hospitality Far Exceeds Their Dreams," *New York Times*, 8 July 1945, 51.
2. Rosenwaike, *Population History of New York City*, 98, 101.
3. Stern, Mellins, and Fishman, *New York 1960*, 10, 13–19, 27–28.
4. Kenneth T. Jackson, "Robert Moses and the Rise of New York: The Power Broker in Perspective," in Ballon and Jackson, *Robert Moses and the Modern City*, 67.
5. Milton Klonsky, "The Trojans of Brighton Beach," *Commentary*, May 1947, 466.
6. Richard I. Cohen, "Urban Visibility and Biblical Visions: Jewish Culture in Western and Central Europe in the Modern Age," in *Cultures of the Jews: A New History*, ed. David Biale (New York: Schocken Books, 2002), 741.
7. Moore, *At Home in America*, 3.
8. Bialystok, with a majority Jewish population in the late nineteenth century, produced similar identification by Jews with the city. See Rebecca Kobrin, *Jewish Bialystok and Its Diaspora* (Bloomington: Indiana University Press, 2010).
9. Rischin, *Promised City*, 294.
10. "Levi Strauss," Wikipedia, accessed 13 July 2011, http://en.wikipedia.org.
11. In this and the following pages, the text draws on the three volumes of *City of Promises: A History of the Jews of New York* (New York: NYU Press, 2012).
12. See, for example, Martin Shefter, ed., *Capital of the American Century: The National and International Influence of New York City* (New York: Russell Sage Foundation, 1993).

CHAPTER 1. FOUNDATIONS

1. Burrows and Wallace, *Gotham*, 1.
2. On the expulsion of Jews from Spain, see Salo W. Baron, *A Social and Religious History of the Jews*, 2nd ed., 18 vols. (New York: Columbia University Press, 1952–1985), 10:167–219.

3. Miriam Bodian, *Hebrews of the Portuguese Nation: Conversos and Community in Early Modern Amsterdam* (Bloomington: Indiana University Press, 1997), 6–17; Daniel M. Swetschinski, *Reluctant Cosmopolitans: The Portuguese Jews of Seventeenth-Century Amsterdam* (London: Littman Library of Jewish Civilization, 2000), 57–64; Jonathan Israel, *European Jewry in the Age of Mercantilism, 1550–1750* (Oxford, UK: Clarendon, 1989), chap. 1; Baron, *Social and Religious History*, vol. 10, chaps. 44–45; Faber, *Time for Planting*, 7.

4. Jonathan Israel, *The Dutch Republic: Its Rise, Greatness, and Fall, 1477–1806* (Oxford, UK: Clarendon, 1995), chaps. 11–15; Israel, *European Jewry*, 2–3, chap. 2; Swetschinski, *Reluctant Cosmopolitans*, 102–130; Simon Schama, *An Embarrassment of Riches: An Interpretation of Dutch Culture in the Golden Age* (New York: Knopf, 1987); Burrows and Wallace, *Gotham*, 14–17. Leo Hershkowitz, in "By Chance or Choice," notes that Jews constituted 4 percent of major investors in 1656 (5, 8).

5. Burrows and Wallace, *Gotham*, 29–40; Russell Shorto, *The Island at the Center of the World* (New York: Vintage, 2004), chap. 6.

6. Burrows and Wallace, *Gotham*, chap. 4; Henry Kessler and Eugene Rachlis, *Peter Stuyvesant and His New York* (New York: Random House, 1959), chap. 3.

7. David Franco Mendes, as quoted in Samuel Oppenheim, "The Early History of the Jews in New York, 1654–1664: Some New Matter on the Subject," *PAJHS* 18 (1909): 80; Oppenheim's version of the story is on 37–51.

8. On messianism, see Leibman, *Messianism, Secrecy, and Mysticism*; Samuel Oppenheim, "More about Jacob Barsimon, the First Jewish Settler in New York," *PAJHS* 29 (1925): 39–49.

9. Bernard Fernow, *Records of New Amsterdam*, as quoted in Oppenheim, "Early History of the Jews," 9, 67; Hershkowitz, "New Amsterdam's Twenty-Three Jews," 172; Hershkowitz, "By Chance or Choice," 1–2.

10. Fernow, *Records of New Amsterdam*, as quoted in Oppenheim, "Early History of the Jews," 68–69, 71–72; Marcus, *Colonial American Jew*, 1:217; Pool and Pool, *Old Faith in a New World*, 9–12. It is unclear how much property emigrants were permitted to take from Brazil and to what extent the twenty-three were victims of sharp practices by the captain. It is likely that they did not have the means to pay off their debt. The newly arrived Jewish merchants did not feel responsible to assume the debts of fellow Jews. Hershkowitz, "By Chance or Choice," 2.

11. Marcus, *Colonial American Jew*, 1:217; Peter Stuyvesant to Amsterdam Chamber of the West India Company, 22 September 1654, and approval of the burgomasters on 1 March 1655, in Oppenheim, "Early History of the Jews," 4–5; Hershkowitz, "By Chance or Choice," 2–3; Jaher, *Scapegoat in the Wilderness*, 89–91.

12. Hershkowitz, "New Amsterdam's Twenty-Three Jews," 172.

13. "Request of the Parnassim of Amsterdam to the Mayors of Amsterdam in Behalf of the Jews of New Netherland," in I. S. Emmanuel, "New Light on Early American Jewry," *AJAJ* 7 (January 1955): 17, 53–54.

14. "Reply of the Amsterdam Chamber of the West India Company to Peter Stuyvesant, 26 April 1655," in Schappes, *Documentary History*, 4–5; Oppenheim, "Early History of the Jews," 8; Hershkowitz, "New Amsterdam's Twenty-Three Jews," 172–179; James Homer Williams, "An Atlantic Perspective on the Jewish Struggle for Rights and Opportunities in Brazil, New Netherland and New York," in *The Jews and the Expansion of Europe to the West, 1450–1800*, ed. Paolo Bernardini and Norman Fiering (New York: Berghahn Books, 2001), 378.

15. Hershkowitz, "New Amsterdam's Twenty-Three Jews," 176; Marcus, *Colonial American Jew*, 1:236, 239–240; Oppenheim, "More about Jacob Barsimon," 47. On the changing status of Jews in Livorno, see Francesca Bregoli, *Mediterranean Enlightenment: Livornese Jews, Tuscan Culture and Eighteenth-Century Reform* (Stanford, CA: Stanford University Press, 2014).

16. Letter of Peter Stuyvesant to Board of Directors of the West India Company, 26 May 1655, 6 June 1656, in Oppenheim, "Early History of the Jews," 20, 21, 72–73.

17. William Pencak, *Jews and Gentiles in Early America, 1654–1800* (Ann Arbor: University of Michigan Press, 2005), 29–32; Oppenheim, "Early History of the Jews," 7, 19, 24, 32, 61; Marcus, *Colonial American Jew*, 1:233, 3:1226, 1418n3, 1419; Jonathan D. Sarna, "Colonial Judaism," in *Myer Myers: Jewish Silversmith in Colonial New York*, by David Barquist (New Haven, CT: Yale University Press Art Gallery, 2001), 12; "Naphtali Phillips," *PAJHS* 21 (1913): 183–184; Pool, *Portraits Etched in Stone*, 7–8.

18. For details of the petitions and responses to them, see "Oppenheim, "Early History of the Jews," 24–25, 27, 29, 31–37. See also "Naphtali Phillips," 179, 177, 182; Marcus, *Colonial American Jew*, 1: 226. Marcus sees the assessments not as discrimination but as signs that the wealthy Jews had brought considerable capital to New Netherland (*Colonial American Jew*, 1:238). In 1655, New Amsterdam's burghers implemented a second form of discrimination. Imposing a special assessment on city residents "to guard inhabitants against attack by the Indians," the city fathers assessed the seaport's prominent Jewish merchants, who made up only 5 out of the 210 citizens with ratable assets, the sum of one hundred guilders each. These merchants, composing one-thirtieth of the taxable population, had to pay one-twelfth the required amount.

19. For details of the petitions and responses to them, see Oppenheim, "Early History of the Jews," 37, 62–67; petition for citizenship, 1657, in Kohler, "Civil Status of the Jews," 88–89; Hershkowitz, "Amsterdam's Twenty-Three Jews," 178–179.

20. Kohler, "Civil Status of the Jews," 99; Pencak, *Jews and Gentiles*, 41–44, 55; Samuel Oppenheim, "The Jews and Masonry in the United States before 1810," *PAJHS* 19 (1910): 1–16; Marcus, *Colonial American Jew*, 3:1214. On religious and ethnic diversity in New York under the British, see Binder and Reimers, *All the Nations under Heaven*, chap. 1.

21. David Sorkin, "Is American Jewry Exceptional? Comparing Jewish Emancipation in Europe and America," *AJH* 96 (2010): 178–186.

22. Lois C. Dubin, *Port Jews of Hapsburg Trieste: Absolutist Politics and Enlightenment Culture* (Stanford, CA: Stanford University Press, 1999); Bregoli, *Mediterranean Enlightenment*, chap. 3–4.

23. Assessment rolls term the dwelling the "Jew synagogue" and list the house next door as rented to "the Jew Rabby [teacher]." Rent was eight British pounds.

24. Leo Hershkowitz, "The Mill Street Synagogue Reconsidered," *AJHQ* 53 (1963–1964): 404–414; N. Taylor Phillips, "Unwritten History: Reminiscences of N. Taylor Phillips," *AJAJ* 6 (1954): 78; Albion Morris Dyer, "Site of the First Synagogue of the Congregation Shearith Israel, of New York," *PAJHS* 8 (1900): 25; Jacob R. Marcus, "The Oldest Known Synagogue Record Book in North America," in *Studies in American Jewish History* (Cincinnati: Hebrew Union College Press, 1969), 44–53.

25. Pool and Pool, *Old Faith in a New World*, 40–45; Doris Groshen Daniels, "Colonial Jewry: Religion, Domestic and Social Relations," *AJHQ* 66 (1976–1977): 381–382. There was, of course, no rabbi. Nor would there be one for a hundred years. The sand that covered the floor, similar to the synagogue in Barbados, may have symbolized the sand that the Israelites crossed on their journey from Egypt to Palestine or may have been a remnant from the medieval era, when sand covered unheated public buildings for hygiene. Marcus, *Colonial American Jew*, 2:890–892. Miscellaneous letters on fund-raising can be found in "Manuscripts: Items Relating to Congregation Shearith Israel," *PAJHS* 27 (1920): 1–5. This includes a request from the hazan in Curaçao that "the asquenazum or Germans" who were "more in number" than the Sephardim in New York not be permitted "any More Votes nor Authority than they have had hitherto." The congregation ignored this request.

26. Faber, *Time for Planting*, 28.

27. Hershkowitz, "Some Aspects of the Merchant Community," 10–11, 19–20, 25–27; Marcus, *Colonial American Jew*, 2:636; Pool, *Portraits Etched in Stone*, 197–201, 218–223; Max J. Kohler, "Jewish Activity in American Colonial Commerce," *PAJHS* 10 (1902): 58–66; Kohler, "Phases of Jewish Life before 1800," *PAJHS* 3 (1895): 79–80.

28. Leo Hershkowitz, "Original Inventories of Early New York Jews (1682–1763)," *AJH* 88 (2002): 297–315, 316–322.

29. Michael Ben-Jacob, "Nathan Simson: A Biographical Sketch of a Colonial Jewish Merchant," *AJAJ* 51 (1999): 16–17. The importance of these early Jewish merchants is captured in Governor Bellomont's complaint to the Board of Trade that he was ill treated by most of the city's merchants: "were it not for one Dutch merchant and two or three Jews that have let me have money, I should have been undone." Quoted in Pool, *Portraits Etched in Stone*, 461.

30. Hershkowitz, "Some Aspects of the Merchant Community," 22–24; Marcus, *Colonial American Jew*, 2:542–545, 779–783.

31. Burrows and Wallace, *Gotham*, 126–129, 375; Graham Russell Hodges, *Root and Branch: African Americans in New York and East Jersey, 1613–1863* (Chapel Hill: University of North Carolina Press, 1999), 272–275.

32. Faber, *Jews, Slaves, and the Slave Trade*, 132–135; Leo Hershkowitz, *Wills of Early New York Jews, 1704–1799* (New York: American Jewish Historical Society, 1967), 15, 21–23, 60, 79n1, 129, 135–136, 158n1; Pool, *Portraits Etched in Stone*, 477, 468–469; Leo Hershkowitz, "Anatomy of a Slave Voyage, New York, 1721," *de Halve Maen* 76 (Fall 2003): 45–51; Ben-Jacob, "Nathan Simson," 26–30; Hodges, *Root and Branch*, 98; James G. Lydon, "New York and the Slave Trade, 1700 to 1774," *William and Mary Quarterly*, 3rd ser., 35, no. 2 (1978): 375–394. New York represented a minor part of the Atlantic slave trade, which was centered in the Caribbean. David Brian Davis, "The Slave Trade and the Jews," *New York Review of Books*, 22 December 1994.

33. Leo Hershkowitz, "Original Inventories," 293–296; Hershkowitz, *Wills of Early New York Jews*, 11–14, 79; Marcus, *Colonial American Jew*, 2:538; Snyder, "Queens of the Household," 18.

34. Marcus, *Colonial American Jew*, 3:1188–1190; Marc D. Angel, *Remnant of Israel: A Portrait of America's First Jewish Congregation* (New York: Riverside, 2004), 33; Pool, *Portraits Etched in Stone*, 7; Hershkowitz, "Original Inventories," 297, 299; Hershkowitz, "Some Aspects of the Jewish and Merchant Community," 13, 20. Pencak, in *Jews and Gentiles*, 45, sees election to the lower offices as a sign of discrimination. However, constables were exempt from militia service and jury duty, and the willingness of a number to run and serve may indicate that they did not see the office as dishonorable. In the *New York Journal* of 8 May 1749, the Coentjes Club declined to congratulate a Jewish neighbor who had lately moved to "Fudge Corner" because he had the habit of paying too much rent and raising the rent for the neighborhood.

35. Kohler, "Civil Status of American Jews," 94; Pencak, *Jews and Gentiles*, 41–44, 55 (quotes on the Assembly are from Pencak).

36. "The Earliest Extant Minutes of the Spanish and Portuguese Congregation Shearith Israel in New York, 1728–1786," *PAJHS* 21 (1913): 74 (10 October 1755); Sheldon Godfrey and Judith Godfrey, "The King vs. Gomez et al.: Opening the Prosecutor's File over 200 Years Later," *AJH* 77 (1991): 40.

37. Godfrey and Godfrey, "King vs. Gomez," 41–42; Snyder, "Queens of the Household," 17.

38. "Earliest Extant Minutes," 83–84 (30 January 1760); "From the 2nd Volume of Minute Books of the Congn: Shearith Israel in New York," *PAJHS* 21 (1913): 83, 84, 87 (17 July 1760, 6 August 1760, 11 September 1763); Pencak, *Jews and Gentiles*, 54–55; Snyder, "Queens of the Household," 16–17. Trouble in the women's gallery was not over. In 1760, what seemed more like a comic opera roiled the synagogue again. This time Judah Hays's wife, Josse, was "turned" out of her seat by Judah Mears, who wanted it for his daughter. The congregation tried to make peace by widening the seat so both could be accommodated, but to no avail. Judah, refusing to settle, was fined and threatened with excommunication. He refused to pay. Three years later, after Josse's death, Jacob Franks paid the fine, and Judah was readmitted to the "Rights and Ceremonies of the Synagogue," though his name no longer appeared in

congregational minutes. In 1796, the synagogue removed the offending *banca*, "the cause of much dissatisfaction." "Earliest Extant Minutes," 83–84 (24 June 1760).

39. Faber, *Time for Planting*, 55–56; Pool and Pool, *Old Faith in a New World*, 264–267, 502; Marcus, *Colonial American Jew*, 2:906–911.

40. "Earliest Extant Minutes," 4 (15 September 1728); Pool and Pool, *Old Faith in a New World*, 259, 286–287; Jacob Rader Marcus, *The Handsome Young Priest in a Black Gown: The Personal World of Gershom Seixas* (Cincinnati: American Jewish Archives, 1970), 4.

41. Faber, *Time for Planting*, 58–66; "Earliest Extant Minutes," 3 (15 September 1728), 53 (9 September 1746), 62–63 (22 October 1748).

42. Phillips, "Unwritten History," 96–97; Doris Groshen Daniels, "Colonial Jewry: Religion, Domestic and Social Relations," *AJHQ* 66 (1976–1977): 399–400; Frank Zimmerman, "A Letter and Memorandum on Ritual Circumcision, 1772," *PAJHS* 42 (1952–1953): 71–80.

43. Leo Hershkowitz and Isidore S. Meyer, eds., *The Letters of the Franks Family, 1733–1748* (Waltham, MA: American Jewish Historical Society, 1966), 87 (21 June 1741); Peter Kalm, *Travels in North America: The English Version of 1770*, 2 vols. (New York: Dover, 1964) 1:631; Pencak, *Jews and Gentiles*, 52. For a discussion of limitations of what can be known of Jewish religious practice in colonial America, see Gurock, *Orthodox Jews in America*.

44. "Earliest Extant Minutes," 79–80 (28 March 1758), 70–72 (13 September 1752), see also 68–70 (9 October 1747, 10 April 1752); "From the 2nd Volume of Minute Books," 111–112 (23–24 December 1771). Throughout the minutes, there is discussion of the appointment and pay of the *shochet* and *bodeck*. Letter from Hazan of Curaçao to Shearith Israel, 1753, in "Manuscripts: Items Relating to Congregation Shearith Israel," 6–7. See also letter from Kingston, Jamaica, 1758, expressing concern over kashrut because Shearith Israel was temporarily without a hazan. "Manuscripts: Items Relating to Congregation Shearith Israel," 10–11; "From the 2nd Volume of Minute Books," 111–112 (23–24 December 1771); Daniels, "Colonial Jewry," 400; Hershkowitz and Meyer, *Letters of the Franks Family*, 7–8 (9 July 1733); Edith Gelles, introduction to *The Letters of Abigaill Levy Franks, 1733–1748*, ed. Edith Gelles (New Haven, CT: Yale University Press, 2004), xxi–xxii.

45. "Earliest Extant Minutes," 75 (7 December 1755); Faber, *Time for Planting*, 71; Pool and Pool, *Old Faith in a New World*, 211–214; Jacob Kabakoff, "The Use of Hebrew by American Jews during the Colonial Period," in *Hebrew and the Bible in America: The First Two Centuries*, ed. Shalom Goldman (Hanover, NH: Brandeis University Press and Dartmouth College, 1993), 19; Marcus, *Colonial American Jew*, vol. 3, chap. 68.

46. "Earliest Extant Minutes," 3 (27 May 1729), 29 (11 September 1730), 76 (7 July 1756), 84 (30 January 1760); "From the 2nd Volume of Minute Books," 92 (17 November 1765); Faber, *Time for Planting*, 71–72; Pool and Pool, *Old Faith in a New World*, 341–347.

47. "Earliest Extant Minutes," 3 (15 September 1728), 16 (27 September 1731), 54–55 (1 December 1746), 61–62 (22 October 1748); Pencak, *Jews and Gentiles*, 48, 53 Hershkowitz, *Wills of Early New York Jews*, 118.

48. Hershkowitz, *Wills of Early New York Jews*, 1, 15, 33, 65, 75; Pool and Pool, *Old Faith in a New World*, 161; Marcus, *Colonial American Jew*, 2:949–950; Marcus, *American Jewry*, 14–17.

49. Joseph Jeshurun Pinto, *The Form of Prayer Which Was Performed at the Jews Synagogue in the City of New York on Thursday October 23, 1760* (New York, 1760), 1, 4; *Prayers for the Shabbath, Rosh-Hashanah, and Kippur . . .* , trans. Isaac Pinto (New York, 1766), iii–iv, 20; "Miscellaneous Items Relating to New York," *PAJHS* 28 (1920): 392–393; Pool and Pool, *Old Faith in a New World*, 88.

50. Kalm, *Travels in North America*, 1:130; Lee M. Friedman, "Dr. Hamilton Visits Shearith Israel," *PAJHS* 57 (1949): 183–184.

51. Hershkowitz and Meyer, *Letters of the Franks Family*, 66 (17 October 1739), 76 (6 July 1740), 78 (31 August 1740), 9 (9 July 1733), 87 (21 June 1741); Leo Hershkowitz, "Another Abigail Franks Letter and a Genealogical Note," *AJHQ* 59 (1969–1970): 224.

52. Phillips, "Unwritten History," 82.

53. Pencak, *Jews and Gentiles*, 48; Robert Cohen, "Jewish Demography in the Eighteenth Century: A Study of London, the West Indies and Early America" (PhD diss., Brandeis University, 1976), chaps. 5–6 (on intermarriage, see 112); Daniels, "Colonial Jewry," 389–392; Snyder, "Queens of the Household," 26–27.

54. Phillips, "Unwritten History," 87–88, 92; Snyder, "Queens of the Household," 24–25.

55. Daniels, "Colonial Jewry," 403; Hershkowitz, *Wills of Early New York Jews*, 12, 51, 81; Pool and Pool, *Old Faith in a New World*, 44. The sixty-five seats were adequate for weekly services but not for High Holiday services. Goldman, *Beyond the Synagogue Gallery*, 37–45, 59.

56. Snyder, "Queens of the Household," 23–24.

57. Leibman, *Messianism, Secrecy, and Mysticism*, 28–37, 50–51.

58. Barquist, *Myer Myers*, 35–40, 47–62.

59. Leibman, *Messianism, Secrecy, and Mysticism*, 182, 204.

60. Paul Needham, *The Celebrated Franks Family Portraits* (New York: Sotheby's, 2008), 20; Erica E. Hirshler, "The Levy-Franks Family Portraits," *Antiques*, November 1990, 1021.

61. For different interpretations of the parade, see Diner, *Jews of the United States*, 57; Moore, *Urban Origins of American Judaism*, 82; Sarna, *American Judaism*, 38; Beth S. Wenger, *Jewish Americans: Three Centuries of Voices in America* (New York: Doubleday, 2007), 11. The Christian observer was Dr. Benjamin Rush.

62. N. Taylor Phillips, "The Levy and Seixas Families of Newport and New York," *PAJHS* 4 (1896): 206; Pool, *Portraits Etched in Stone*, 350–351. Jacob Marcus argues that while Seixas was "a whole-hearted Whig," there is "no evidence whatsoever to substantiate the legend of patriotic leadership." He was one of the many who joined the American cause. Marcus, *Handsome Young Priest*, 15.

63. Phillips, "Unwritten History," 84–85. Patriots had to abandon the city. During the hasty retreat, amid the noise of cannon and musket fire, the merchant Isaac Moses

began to walk northward, refusing to ride on the Sabbath. Reaching the present Twenty-Third Street, he found a farm to shelter him. Saturday night, he and his family boarded a wagon and followed the army into Westchester. Like so many other New York Jews, he later made his way to Philadelphia.

64. Marcus, *Colonial American Jew*, 3:1257–1261, 1280–1282; Jay, quoted in Pencak, *Jews and Gentiles*, 68–69; Jaher, *Scapegoat in the Wilderness*, 121.

65. Burrows and Wallace, *Gotham*, 242–256; Stephen Birmingham, *The Grandees: America's Sephardic Elite* (New York: Harper and Row, 1971), 175.

66. Pool and Pool, *Old Faith in a New World*, 46, 169–170; Samuel Rezneck, *Unrecognized Patriots: The Jews in the American Revolution* (Westport, CT: Greenwood, 1975), 143; Abram Vossen Goodman, "A German Mercenary Observes American Jews during the Revolution," *AJHQ* 59 (1969–1970): 227; Cecil Roth, "A Jewish Voice of Peace in the War of American Independence: The Life and Writings of Abraham Wagg, 1719–1803," *PAJHS* 31 (1928): 33–74; Pencak, *Jews and Gentiles*, 63–64.

67. Edwin Wolf and Maxwell Whiteman, *History of the Jews of Philadelphia from Colonial Times to the Age of Jackson* (Philadelphia: Jewish Publication Society, 1957), chap. 7; Jacob Rader Marcus, ed., "Jews and the American Revolution: A Bicentennial Documentary," *AJAJ* 27 (November 1975): 141–144, 194–198.

68. Wolf and Whiteman, *History of the Jews of Philadelphia*, 146–152; Pencak, *Jews and Gentiles*, 202–230; Memorial of Rabbi Gershom Seixas and others to Council of Censors, December 1783, in Marcus, "Jews and the American Revolution," 214–216. Pennsylvania had a long strain of anti-Semitism (which may have caused many of New York's Jews to leave Philadelphia after the war). The Test Act was in part the work of the Lutheran senior minister Henry Muhlenberg, who accused the Jews of both atheism and declaring that the Christian messiah was an "imposter."

69. Herbert Friedenwald, "A Letter of Jonas Phillips to the Federal Convention," *PAJHS* 2 (1894): 107–109.

70. Gershom Seixas to Shearith Israel, 21 December 1783, in Marcus, "Jews and the American Revolution," 217–219; Pool, *Portraits Etched in Stone*, 353–354; Marcus, *Handsome Young Priest*, 12; "Items Relating to Gershom Seixas," *PAJHS* 27 (1920): 130–131.

71. A discussion of law may be found in Grinstein, *Rise of the Jewish Community*, 45–46; Isaac Jerushalmi, "Cultures, Practices, and Ideals of a New York Sephardic Congregation as Reflected in the Minutes of Shearith Israel, 1784–1789" (unpublished paper), 1–4, American Jewish Archives, Cincinnati; Pool and Pool, *Old Faith in a New World*, 260–262; Gershom Seixas to Board of Trustees of Shearith Israel, 22 September 1785, Seixas Papers, American Jewish Historical Society, New York.

CHAPTER 2. SHAKING OFF CONSTRAINTS

1. Burrows and Wallace, *Gotham*, chap. 21. For a useful overview of the Hamiltonian-Jeffersonian debate, see Stanley Elkins and Eric McKitrick, *The Age*

of Federalism: The Early American Republic 1788–1800 (New York: Oxford University Press, 1995); and Sean Wilentz, *The Rise of American Democracy: The Crisis of the New Order, 1787–1815* (New York: Norton, 2006).

2. Morris U. Schappes, "Anti-Semitism and Reaction, 1795–1800," *PAJHS* 38 (1948–1949): 145; Pencak, *Jews and Gentiles,* 74.

3. Marcus, *American Jewry,* 150–154, 157–158, 161–166. See also Sarna, *American Judaism,* 43; Faber, *Time for Planting,* 118–119, 123.

4. Jacob Rader Marcus, *United States Jewry, 1776–1985,* 3 vols. (Detroit: Wayne State University Press, 1989) 1:240; Hannah Adams quotes Hazan Seixas that there were seventy to eighty subscribers out of fifty families plus some unmarried, in Joseph L. Blau and Salo W. Baron, eds., *The Jews of the United States 1790–1840: A Documentary History,* 2 vols. (New York: Columbia University Press, 1963), 1:91; Minutes of the Board of Trustees of Congregation Shearith Israel, 28 May 1815, 27 July 1817, American Jewish Archives, Cincinnati.

5. *Bye Laws of the Congregation of Shearith Israel as Ratified on the 24 June 1805,* Lyons Collection, American Jewish Historical Society, New York; Minutes of the Board of Trustees, 21 July 1805, 12 October 1806, 11 January 1807, 6 October 1807, 16 April 1809, 22 October 1809, 8 May 1814, 8 March 1818, 5 April 1818, 16 January 1824. The board had its own rules of procedure, including a requirement of personal notification of every trustee at least six hours before a meeting, a $2.50 fine for speaking out of turn, and a $10 fine for leaving the meeting without permission. With regard to finances, only in the 1820s did the synagogue regain fiscal health. Hendrik Hartog, *Public Property and Private Power: The Corporation of the City of New York in American Law, 1730–1870* (Ithaca, NY: Cornell University Press, 1983); Burrows and Wallace, *Gotham,* 419–422; Sarna, *American Judaism,* 47.

6. "Manuscripts: Items Relating to Congregation Shearith Israel, New York," *PAJHS* 27 (1920): 19 (27 and 26 April 1796); Minutes of the Board of Trustees, 14 July 1814, 12 April 1815, 13 April 1815, 23 April 1815. None of the 1811 trustees was a member of the 1812 board. The new body included Hayam Solomon, son the of the famed revolutionary, representing Ashkenazim critical of laxity in religious observance, and Benjamin Judah, a synagogue gadfly who resigned in 1824 after being expelled on Yom Kippur eve for defying the *parnas* regarding an open door.

7. Burrows and Wallace, *Gotham,* 456–459; Grinstein, *Rise of the Jewish Community,* 48.

8. "Division in the New York Community, 1825," in Blau and Baron, *Jews of the United States,* 2:542–545.

9. Minutes of the Board of Trustees, 19 and 26 October 1825; Grinstein, *Rise of the Jewish Community,* 48–49. The city's Jewish population did not significantly increase until after 1825.

10. Israel Goldstein, *A Century of Judaism in New York: B'nai Jeshurun, 1825–1925* (New York: Congregation B'nai Jeshurun, 1930), 54–62.

11. Grinstein, *Rise of the Jewish Community,* 44–45, 49; Pool, *Portraits Etched in Stone,* 305.

12. Burrows and Wallace, *Gotham*, 748; Grinstein, *Rise of the Jewish Community*, 469.

13. Diner, *Time for Gathering*, 42–49. Population figures for 1860 are tentative. Some estimates are as low as eighteen thousand. Sarna, *American Judaism*, 63.

14. Moore, *B'nai B'rith*, 1–13.

15. Grusd, *B'nai B'rith*, chap. 1; Diner, *Time for Gathering*, 109–113; Grinstein, *Rise of the Jewish Community*, 109–114; Moore, *B'nai B'rith*, 39–42.

16. Moore, *B'nai B'rith*, 13–23; Grusd, *B'nai B'rith*, 33–48; Julius Bien, "History of the Independent Order of B'nai B'rith," *Menorah* (1886–1889): 123–125.

17. Tina Levitan, *Islands of Compassion: A History of the Jewish Hospitals of New York* (New York: Twayne, 1964), 27; Burrill B. Crohn, "The Centennial Anniversary of the Mount Sinai Hospital (1852–1952)," *PAJHS* 42 (September 1952–September 1953): 113–130.

18. Grinstein, *Rise of the Jewish Community*, 49–53, 472–478.

19. N. Cohen, *Encounter with Emancipation*, 42; Sefton D. Temkin, *Isaac Mayer Wise: Shaping American Judaism* (New York: Littman Library of Jewish Civilization, 1992), 36.

20. Blau and Baron, *Jews of the United States*, 2:484–493; *Asmonean*, 22 February 1850, 3 March 1850, 6 December 1850, 6 February 1851, 16 April 1851, 29 August 1851, 12 September 1851, 10 October 1851, 7 November 1851, 12 December 1851, 4 February 1853, 8 September 1854, 12 December 1854, 14 September 1855, 22 February 1856, 16 October 1857; *New York Times*, 27 December 1858; *Jewish Messenger*, 30 January 1857, 11 November 1859, 11 May 1860.

21. *New York Times*, 27 December 1858; *Asmonean*, 16 April 1851, 8 September 1854, 12 December 1854, 14 September 1855, 22 February 1856.

22. *New York Times*, 28 October 1855; *Asmonean*, 23 February 1855, 16 May 1856; *Jewish Messenger*, 11 March 1859, 20 May 1859, 10 September 1859, 21 June 1861, 3 September 1864.

23. *Jewish Messenger*, 3 March 1860, 20 March 1863, 20 October 1863; Philip Goodman, "The Purim Association of the City of New York, 1862–1902," *PAJHS* 40 (1950–1951): 134–144.

24. "The Sabbath," *Jewish Messenger*, 12 February 1848, 28; "To Correspondents," *Jewish Messenger*, 25 November 1859, 158; Bernard Drachman, *The Unfailing Light* (New York: Rabbinical Council of America, 1948), 227.

25. Alexis McCrossen, *Holy Day, Holiday: The American Sunday* (Ithaca, NY: Cornell University Press, 2000), 41–46.

26. "The Jew Wot Goes Ahead," *Asmonean*, 19 May 1854, 78; Emanuel Brandeis, "Desecration of Sabbath," *Asmonean*, 22 May 1854, 46; Nadel, *Little Germany*, 101; Dorothee Schneider, *Trade Unions and Community: The German Working Class in New York City, 1870–1900* (Urbana: University of Illinois Press, 1994), 32.

27. Burrows and Wallace, *Gotham*, chap. 22; Howard B. Rock, *Artisans of the New Republic: The Tradesmen of New York City in the Age of Jefferson* (New York: NYU Press, 1979), chap. 6.

28. Edmund Clarence Stedman, ed., *The New York Stock Exchange* (New York: Stock Exchange Historical Company, 1905), 1:23; Grinstein, *Rise of the Jewish Community*, 416–419; Marcus, *United States Jewry*, 1:181–182, 199, 358–359, 560, 642.

29. Burrows and Wallace, *Gotham*, chap. 38.

30. Ibid., chap. 27.

31. Shane White, *Somewhat More Independent: The End of Slavery in New York City, 1770–1810* (Athens: University of Georgia Press, 1991); Malcolm M. Stern, "Some Additions and Corrections to Rosenwaike's 'An Estimate and Analysis of the Jewish Population of the United States in 1790,'" *AJHQ* 53 (1963–1964): 385; "Manumitting Slaves, 1806–1809," excerpts from the minutes of the Society for Promoting the Manumission of Slaves and Protecting Such of Them as Have Been or May Be Liberated, New York 1806–1809, in Schappes, *Documentary History*, 118–121; "A Slave Promised His Freedom," legal paper promising freedom to George Roper from Jacob Levy, Jr., April 8, 1814, in Schappes, *Documentary History*, 134; Pool and Pool, *Old Faith in a New World*, 483; Jerome C. Rosenthal, "A Study of Jewish Businessmen in New York City as Reflected in the City Directories, 1776–1830" (unpublished paper, 1977), American Jewish Archives, Cincinnati; Ira Rosenwaike, "The Jewish Population of the United States as Estimated from the Census of 1820," *AJHQ* 53 (1963–1964): 131–135; Rosenwaike, *On the Edge of Greatness*, 95–96; Birmingham, *Grandees*, 191–199; Theodore Cohen, "Walter Jonas Judah and New York's 1798 Yellow Fever Epidemic," *AJAJ* 48 (1996): 23–34.

32. Burrow and Wallace, *Gotham*, 735–737; Diner, *Time for Gathering*, 8–13, 24–36.

33. Nadel, *Little Germany*, chap. 2; *New York Times*, 14 March 1856.

34. *Asmonean*, 30 October 1857; Glanz, *Studies in Judaica Americana*, 128–131; Feldman, "Jews in the Early Growth," 7–14; Vincent Carosso, "A Financial Elite: New York's German-Jewish Investment Bankers," *AJHQ* 66 (1976): 67–74; Birmingham, *"Our Crowd,"* chaps. 2–9; *The New York City Directory, 1856–57* (New York, 1857), available at ancestry.com. There were no Jews listed in the 1845 *New York Sun's* list of property owners with more than $100,000 in real estate. Stedman, *New York Stock Exchange*, 1:106–108. By 1855, a fourth of the city's top ten thousand taxpayers were immigrants. Burrows and Wallace, *Gotham*, 739.

35. Ernst, *Immigrant Life in New York City*, 63–64.

36. *Asmonean*, 2 November 1849, 7 December 1849, 8 February 1850, 22 February 1850, 7 March 1851, 19 March 1852; *Jewish Messenger*, 3 March 1865.

37. Burrows and Wallace, *Gotham*, 476, 745; Ernst, *Immigrant Life in New York City*, 46; Nadel, *Little Germany*, 99–103; Diner, *Time for Gathering*, 91; Beverly Hyman, "New York Businessmen, 1831–1835" (unpublished manuscript, 1977), American Jewish Archives, Cincinnati; *New York Times*, 14 March 1856; shearithisrael.org (accessed 16 February 2016).

38. Anbinder, *Five Points*, 17, 45.

39. Ibid., 17–19.

40. Ibid., 47, 98; 1860 Census, 2nd District, 6th Ward, Dwelling #608.

41. Ernst, *Immigrant Life in New York City*, 63–64.

42. See, for example, Philip Cowen, *Memories of an American Jew* (New York: International, 1932), 24–26, 36–37.

43. Burrows and Wallace, *Gotham*, chaps. 31–47; Robert Greenhalgh Albion, *The Rise of New York Port, 1815–1860* (New York: Scribner, 1939), 736–777 (figures on population growth and immigration).

44. Ernst, *Immigrant Life in New York City*, 69, 72.

45. Phyllis Dillon and Andrew Godley, "The Evolution of the Jewish Garment Industry, 1840–1940," in *Chosen Capital: The Jewish Encounter with American Capitalism*, ed. Rebecca Kobrin (New Brunswick, NJ: Rutgers University Press, 2012), 38, 42; Glanz, *Studies in Judaica Americana*, 126; Barkai, *Branching Out*, 86; Grinstein, *Rise of the Jewish Community*, 128; Nadel, *Little Germany*, 44–46, 63; Schneider, *Trade Unions and Community*, 9, 14–16.

46. N. Cohen, *Encounter with Emancipation*, 29; Feldman, "Jews in the Early Growth," 9; Dillon and Godley, "Evolution of the Jewish Garment Industry," 38–39. For overviews, see Hasia R. Diner, *Roads Taken: The Great Jewish Migrations to the New World and the Peddlers Who Forged the Way* (New Haven, CT: Yale University Press, 2015).

47. Feldman, "Jews in the Early Growth," 5; Barkai, *Branching Out*, 45–46; Nadel, *Little Germany*, 81; Jesse Pope, *The Clothing Industry in New York* (Columbia, MO: University of Missouri Press, 1905), 7–8. See also Mendelsohn, *Rag Race*.

48. Mathew Hale, *Wonders of a Great City* (Chicago: People's, 1877), 845; Glanz, *Studies in Judaica Americana*, 126; N. Cohen, *Encounter with Emancipation*, 29; Pope, *Clothing Industry*, 5–7; Mendelsohn, *Rag Race*, chap. 1.

49. Asa Green, *Travels in America* (New York: William Pearson, 1833), quoted in Glanz, *Studies in Judaica Americana*, 127; George C. Foster, *New York in Slices: By an Experienced Carver* (New York: W. F. Burgess, 1849), 14–15, quoted in Feldman, "Jews in the Early Growth," 3–7; N. Cohen, *Encounter with Emancipation*, 31; Isaac Mayer Wise, *Reminiscences*, ed. David Phillipson (Cincinnati: L. Wise, 1901), 17, 24.

50. Pope, *Clothing Industry*, 8.

51. Isaac Markens, *Hebrews in America* (New York: I Markens, 1888), 151.

52. America's first reform synagogue, founded in Charleston in 1825, was modeled more from American Unitarianism than from the German Reform movement. Sarna, *American Judaism*, 57–58, 84–87. The most important history of Reform Judaism is M. Meyer, *Response to Modernity*, chaps. 1–4. See also Michael A. Meyer, *The Origins of the Modern Jew: Jewish Identity and European Culture in Germany, 1749–1824* (Detroit: Wayne State University Press, 1967).

53. Sarna, *American Judaism*, 85; Steven Lowenstein, "The 1840s and the Creation of the German-Jewish Religious Reform Movement," in *Revolution and Evolution: 1848 in German-Jewish History*, ed. Werner Mosse (Tübingen: Mohr Siebeck, 1981); M. Meyer, *Response to Modernity*, 225–226.

54. M. Meyer, *Response to Modernity*, 225; Grinstein, *Rise of the Jewish Community*, 333–352; Diner, *Time for Gathering*, 114–116; Sarna, *American Judaism*, 73; Jick, "Reform Synagogue," 87.

55. Grinstein, *Rise of the Jewish Community*, 354, 368.

56. Ibid., 355–358.

57. Ibid., 353–371; Myer Stern, *The Rise and Progress of Reform Judaism: Temple Emanu-El of New York* (New York: M. Stern, 1895), 13–24, 30–31, 38–40; Benny Kraut, *From Reform Judaism to Ethical Culture: The Religious Evolution of Felix Adler* (New York: Ktav, 1979), 5.

58. Sarna, "Debate over Mixed Seating," 363–372, 374–379; Goldman, *Beyond the Synagogue Gallery*, 8–17; Grinstein, *Rise of the Jewish Community*, 364, 501–507; Minutes of Temple Emanu-El, 4 June 1854, 3 September 1854, 1 October 1854, 7 January 1855, 1 July 1855, 12 August 1855, Temple Emanu-El Archives, New York.

59. Goldman, *Beyond the Synagogue Gallery*, 86–87, 93–99; *Asmonean*, 8 February 1850, 22 February 1850, 24 March 1854, 4 January 1856, 22 May 1857; see also "Women and the Ceremony of Confirmation," in Marcus, *American Jewish Woman*, 1:186–189; Grinstein, *Rise of the Jewish Community*, 356; Sarna, "Debate over Mixed Seating," 363–371; Ann Douglas, *The Feminization of American Culture* (New York: Knopf, 1977); Gershom Greenberg, "A German-Jewish Immigrant's Perception of America, 1853–54," *AJHQ* 67 (June 1978): 326, 328; Pool and Pool, *Old Faith in a New World*, 361–367; *Jewish Messenger*, 11 May 1860, 18 May 1860, 25 May 1860, 6 March 1863. When Shearith Israel opened its Crosby Street synagogue in 1832, there were more seats in the ladies' gallery than in the men's section below. No other synagogue, however, had more seats for women than men.

60. Minutes of Temple Emanu-El, 4 June 1854, 3 September 1854, 1 October 1854, 7 January 1855, 1 July 1855, 12 August 1855.

61. *Asmonean*, 13 August 1852, 20 May 1853.

62. Wise, *Reminiscences*, 200–202; Temkin, *Isaac Mayer Wise*, 86; Hyman Grinstein, "The '*Asmonean*': The First Jewish Weekly in New York," *Journal of Jewish Bibliography* 1 (1939): 67–70; Guido Kirsch, "*Israels Herold*: The First Jewish Weekly in New York," *Historia Judaica* 2 (October 1940): 77–79; *Asmonean*, 19 April 1850, 10 May 1850, 8 October 1852, 26 November 1852, 22 July 1853, 13 January 1854, 3 February 1854, 19 May 1854, 23 June 1854, 30 June 1854, 4 August 1854, 8 September 1854, 5 November 1854, 30 May 1856, 21 August 1857.

63. Men such as Isaacs and Raphall, though not technically ordained as rabbis, were rabbis in everything but name, and this study uses that term as well as "Reverend" and "Dr." Goldstein, *Century of Judaism*, 110–114, 119–124; Grinstein, *Rise of the Jewish Community*, 91–92; Robert T. Swierenga, "Samuel Myers Isaacs: The Dutch Rabbi of New York," *AJAJ* 54 (1992): 607–615; David Philipson, *Max Lilienthal, American Rabbi: Life and Writings* (New York: Bloch, 1915), 46–59; Bruce L. Ruben, "Max Lilienthal and Isaac M. Wise: Architects of American Reform Judaism" *AJAJ* 60 (2003): 1–29; Pool and Pool, *Old Faith in a New World*, 190–191; Bernhard N. Cohn, "Leo Merzbacher," *AJAJ* 6 (1954): 21–24; Gershom Greenberg, "The Dimensions of Samuel Adler's Religious View of the World," *Hebrew Union College Annual* 46 (1975): 377–412.

64. Kraut, *From Reform Judaism to Ethical Culture*, chap. 1; Temkin, *Isaac Mayer Wise*, 1–30; Naomi W. Cohen, *What the Rabbis Said: The Public Discourse of Nineteenth-Century Rabbis* (New York: NYU Press, 2008), chap. 1.

65. J. D. Eisenstein, "History of the First Russian-American Jewish Congregation," *PAJHS* 9 (1901): 63–74; Alfred A. Greenbaum, "The Early 'Russian' Congregation in America in Its Ethnic and Religious Setting," *PAJHS* 62 (1972–1973): 162–169; Grinstein, *Rise of the Jewish Community*, 49–53, 172, 472–478; "The First New York Russian-Jewish Congregation, 1857," in Schappes, *Documentary History*, 373–375; Goldstein, *Century of Judaism*, 81–90, 93–94; Swierenga, "Samuel Myers Isaacs," 607–621; Minutes of B'nai Jeshurun, 25 November 1827, 12 May 1828, 28 December 1828, 6 June 1830, 7 August 1836, 21 August 1836, Jewish Theological Seminary, New York; Leo Hershkowitz, "Those 'Ignorant Immigrants' and the B'nai Jeshurun Schism," *AJH* 70 (1980): 168–179; Jick, *Americanization of the Synagogue*, 26; Myer Stern, *Rise and Progress*, 13–38.

66. "American Jews and the Damascus Affair: The Jews of New York to the President of the United States, August 24, 1840," in Schappes, *Documentary History*, 210–212; "Minister's Report on the Damascus Affair," ibid., 212–215, "State's Rights vs. Equality Abroad," ibid., 315–324; Rev. Isaac Leeser, "The Mortara Case," *Philadelphia Public Ledger*, November 25, 1858, ibid., 385–392; *Asmonean*, 7 February 1851; *Jewish Messenger*, 8 October 1858, 15 October 1858, 3 December 1858, 10 December 1858, 17 December 1858; Bertram W. Korn, *The American Reaction to the Mortara Case, 1858–1859* (Cincinnati: American Jewish Archives, 1957), 39. See also Kertzer, *Kidnapping of Edgardo Mortara*.

67. *Asmonean*, 8 November 1850, 23 March 1855, 24 April 1857, 1 May 1857, 19 June 1857; *Jewish Messenger* 1 January 1857, 9 September 1858, 21 October 1859, 4 November 1859, 11 December 1859, 18 December 1859, 10 February 1860, 1 June 1860, 21 September 1860, 22 February 1861, 21 August 1863, 24 June 1865; Grinstein, *Rise of the Jewish Community*, 432–439; Allan Tarshish, "The Board of Delegates of American Israelites, 1859–1878," *PAJHS* 49 (1959–1960): 16–36. In 1849, the newly arrived Isaac Mayer Wise, together with Isaac Leeser, attempted to assemble a national conference of congregations to discuss the state of the American congregations. Only eight congregations approved the project, and the meeting was never held. Indifference and apathy prevailed. Bertram W. Korn, "American Jewish Life in 1849," in *Eventful Years and Experiences: Studies in Nineteenth Century American Jewish History* (Cincinnati: American Jewish Archives, 1954), 35–38.

68. Goldstein, *Century of Judaism*, 110–114, 119–124; Grinstein, *Rise of the Jewish Community*, 91–92. The law forbidding Hebrews from returning an escaped slave to his or her master applied only to slaves escaping from foreign lands.

69. "Bible View of Slavery, Discourse of Rabbi Morris Jacob Raphall at B'nai Jeshurun, January 4, 1861," in *Documentary History*, ed. Schappes, 405–418; Kohler, "Jews and the American Anti-Slavery Movement," 154–155.

70. "Bible View of Slavery," 405–406, 686; Jayme Sokolow, "Revolution and Reform: The Antebellum Jewish Abolitionists," in *Jews and the Civil War*, ed. Jonathan D.

Sarna and Adam D. Mendelsohn (New York: NYU Press, 2010), 187–189; Korn, *American Jewry and the Civil War*, 16–19; Kohler, "Jews and the American Anti-Slavery Movement," 154–155.

71. *New York Times*, 2 October 1856.

72. Sarna, *Jacksonian Jew*, 109–113, 119; *Evening Star*, 18 February 1834, 15 September 1835, 9 November 1849, quoted in Leonard I. Gappelberg, "M. M. Noah and the *Evening Star*: Whig Journalism, 1833–1840" (PhD diss., Yeshiva University, 1970), 157–158, 167, 184–185; *Asmonean*, 30 October 1857.

73. *Asmonean*, 13 December 1850, 4 April 1851, 4 July 1851, 25 July 1856, 8 August 1856, 15 August 1856, 5 September 1856, 30 October 1857, 19 March 1858.

74. *Asmonean*, 26 October 1850, 10 January 1851, 5 June 1851. In the *Asmonean*'s 10 January 1851 issue, Lyon quoted from both the Old and New Testament to explain how the Bible can be misused and that the Bible supported the law.

75. N. Cohen, *Encounter with Emancipation*, 129–135; Sokolow, "Revolution and Reform," 125; "Government and Politics," in *The Almanac of New York City*, ed. Kenneth T. Jackson and Fred Kameny (New York: Columbia University Press, 2008), 367–368; *Jewish Messenger*, 25 March 1861, 2 January 1863; Nadel, *Little Germany*, 136.

76. Abram J. Dittenhoefer, *How We Elected Lincoln: Personal Recollections* (New York: Harper, 1916), 2–6, 16, quoted in Jonathan D. Sarna and Benjamin Shappell, *Lincoln and the Jews: A History* (New York: Thomas Dunne Books, 2015), 50.

77. Dittenhoefer, *How We Elected Lincoln*, 4–5, quoted in Sarna and Shappell, *Lincoln and the Jews*, 51.

78. Philip S. Foner, *Business and Slavery: The New York Merchants and the Irrepressible Conflict* (Chapel Hill: University of North Carolina Press, 1941), 251; Stedman, *New York Stock Exchange*, 1:128. A more recent book that covers the same ground generally confirms Foner's findings while noting that manufacturers at times had different interests from merchants, notably in seeking tariff protection. Sven Beckert finds that Republicans, while a small minority of New York's middle class, were most likely to be found in merchants involved in the western trade and manufacturers. Manufacturers were four times more likely to be Republicans than merchants were. However, the bulk of Jewish manufacturers were in the garment trade, which was deeply attached to the southern trade. Beckert, *Monied Metropolis*, chap. 3. See also Basil Leo Lee, *Discontent in New York City, 1861–1865* (Washington, DC: Catholic University of America Press, 1943), 8–13.

79. Jaher, *Scapegoat in the Wilderness*, 170, 186, 220–231, 237–238; *Asmonean*, 12 April 1850, 19 April 1850, 26 April 1850, 23 May 1851, 20 February 1852, 27 February 1852, 6 March 1852, 10 June 1853, 6 August 1853, 30 March 1855, 10 August 1855, 17 August 1855, 12 June 1857, 20 November 1857; *Jewish Messenger*, 27 July 1858, 30 March 1860, 23 April 1860, 18 June 1860, 13 November 1863, 5 December 1863. Jewish papers did their best to respond to aggressive Protestant missionaries who attempted to convert Jews.

80. Korn, *American Jewry*, chap. 6; "Revoking General Grant's Order No. 11," in Schappes, *Documentary History*, 472–476, 702–704; Marcus, *American Jewry*,

3:48–50; *Jewish Messenger*, 9 January 1863, 16 January 1863, 23 January 1863; *New York Times*, 8 January 1863. See also *New York Times*, 19 December 1862, 5 January 1863, 7 January 1863, 8 February 1863. For an excellent overview, see Jonathan D. Sarna, *When General Grant Expelled the Jews* (New York: Schocken, 2012).

81. Korn, *American Jewry*, 158–164, 173; *Frank Leslie's Illustrated Newspaper*, 21 March 1863, quoted in Gary L. Bunker and John J. Appel, "Shoddy Antisemitism and the Civil War," in Sarna and Mendelsohn, *Jews and the Civil War*, 320. Stedman does not list any Jews in his lengthy discussion of the gold trade and its fluctuations. Gold was extremely important for government finances during the war. Stedman, *New York Stock Exchange*, 150–152, 162. Many of Korn's references are to the *Jewish Messenger*. *Jewish Messenger*, 21 November 1862, 19 December 1862, 20 June 1863. Other instances of anti-Semitism are recorded in the *New York Times*, 11 January 1861, 28 September 1862, 8 February 1863, 2 April 1863, 27 July 1863, 2 November 1864.

82. Burrows and Wallace, *Gotham*, 887–901; Korn, *American Jewry*, 162–163; Simon Wolf, *The American Jew as Patriot, Soldier and Citizen* (Philadelphia: Jewish Publication Society of America, 1895), 284; Iver Bernstein, *The New York City Draft Riots: Their Significance for American Society and Politics in the Age of the Civil War* (New York: Oxford University Press, 1990), 34; Sarna and Shappell, *Lincoln and the Jews*, 159–161; *Jewish Messenger*, 26 July 1863, 28 August 1863, 4 September 1863. After the first day, most Germans abandoned violence, and some joined the authorities. Burrows and Wallace, *Gotham*, 894. The *Jewish Messenger* declined to report details of the riot. Instead, it asked "how many Jews were among the thousands [who] rose determined to commit every act repugnant to humanity?" The answer: "not one." *Jewish Messenger*, 26 July 1863.

83. Burrows and Wallace, *Gotham*, 903; *Jewish Messenger*, 26 October 1864, 4 November 1864; Bertram W. Korn, "The Jews of the Union," *AJAJ* 13 (1961): 221–224; Earnest A. McKay, *The Civil War and New York City* (Syracuse, NY: Syracuse University Press, 1990), 148; Beckert, *Monied Metropolis*, 135, 137; Ross L. Muir and Carl L. White, *Over the Long Term: The Story of J. & W. Seligman & Co.* (New York: J. & W. Seligman, 1964), 46; Lee, *Discontent in New York*, 175–177, 180–181, 204–205. Tailors' wages dropped from sixty-seven and a half cents per day to thirty-seven and a half cents per day in 1861. A number of trades staged wartime strikes. On the plight of women workers, working sixteen hour days, ravaged by inflation, see *New York Times*, 2 April 1864; N. Cohen, *Encounter with Emancipation*, 58; Edward K. Spann, *Gotham at War: New York City 1860–1865* (Wilmington, DE: SR Books, 2002), 109–112, 172.

84. Korn, "Jews of the Union," 239–243; *Jewish Messenger*, 28 April 1865; Emmanuel Hertz, ed., *Abraham Lincoln: The Tribute of the Synagogue* (New York: Bloch, 1927); Sarna and Shappell, *Lincoln and the Jews*, 217–219.

CHAPTER 3. ONE CITY, TWO JEWISH WORLDS

1. Martha Kransdorf, "Julia Richman's Years in the New York City Public Schools, 1872–1912" (PhD diss., University of Michigan, 1979), 58–127 (quote on 58); Selma

Berrol, "Julia Richman," in Hyman and Moore, *Jewish Women in America*, 2:1148–1149.

2. Kransdorf, "Julia Richman's Years," 66–72, 128–189 (quotes on 66–67, 72, 132–133); Howe, *World of Our Fathers*, 278; *New York Times*, 26 June 1912.

3. Berrol, "Julia Richman," 2:1148–1149.

4. Katznelson, "Between Separation and Disappearance," 186.

5. Rischin, *Promised City*, chap. 5; Nadel, *Little Germany*, 30–31; David de Sola Pool, "The Levantine Jews in the United States," *American Jewish Year Book* 15 (1914): 214–217.

6. Rischin, *Promised City*, 79–80; Miriam Weinstein, *Yiddish: A Nation of Words* (New York: Steerforth, 2001); Sarah Abrevaya Stein, *Making Jews Modern: The Yiddish and Ladino Press in the Russian and Ottoman Empires* (Bloomington: Indiana University Press, 2003).

7. Katznelson, "Between Separation and Disappearance," 184; Foner, *From Ellis Island to JFK*, 43, 45–47.

8. Andrew Dolkart, *Biography of a Tenement House in New York City: An Architectural History of 97 Orchard Street* (Santa Fe, NM: Center for American Places, 2006).

9. Ibid., 61.

10. Rose Radin, American Jewish Committee Oral Histories, New York Public Library; Rischin, *Promised City*, 76–95; Jacob Riis, *How the Other Half Lives* (1889; repr., New York: Norton, 2010), 75–94.

11. Dolkart, *Biography of a Tenement House*, 81–84.

12. Joselit, "Set Table," 27–33; Kirshenblatt-Gimblett, "Kitchen Judaism," 77–105; Joselit, *Wonders of America*, 137–140, 148; Aaron Domnitz, "Why I Left My Old Home and What I Have Accomplished in America," in Cohen and Soyer, *My Future Is in America*, 143; Heinze, *Adapting to Abundance*, 105–115.

13. Heinze, *Adapting to Abundance*, 133–134, 138–140; Joselit, "Set Table," 35.

14. Heinze, *Adapting to Abundance*, 89–104; Domnitz, "Why I Left," 144.

15. Enstad, *Ladies of Labor*, 22–31; Heinze, *Adapting to Abundance*, 89–104.

16. *One Hundred Years—1852–1952—The Harmonie Club* (New York: Harmonie Club, 1952); Glanz, *Studies in Judaica Americana*, 169–186; Jenna Weissman Joselit, "Fun and Games: The American Jewish Social Club," in *The Columbia History of Jews and Judaism in America*, ed. Marc Lee Raphael (New York: Columbia University Press, 2008), 246–262; Dinnerstein, *Anti-Semitism in America*, 36–42; Birmingham, *"Our Crowd,"* 141–150.

17. *One Hundred Years*; Glanz, *Studies in Judaica Americana*, 176, 179, 181.

18. Reuben Iceland, "At Goodman and Levine's," in Howe and Greenberg, *Voices from the Yiddish*, 300–303.

19. Herman Yablokoff, "Sitting in the Café Royale," in Howe and Libo, *How We Lived*, 288–289; "Café Intellectuals," *Commercial Advertiser*, ibid., 289–290; Howe, *World of Our Fathers*, 235–238; Edmund J. James, Oscar R. Flynn, J. R. Paulding, Charlotte Kimball, and Walter Scott Andrews, *The Immigrant Jew in America* (New York: B. F. Buck, 1906), 222–226.

20. Riis, *How the Other Half Lives*; Rebecca Zurier, *Picturing the City: Urban Vision and the Ashcan School* (Berkeley: University of California Press, 2006), 2–6; Blair, "Visions of the Tenement."

21. Alan Trachtenberg, *Reading American Photographs: Images as History, Mathew Brady to Walker Evans* (New York: Hill and Wang, 1989), 167.

22. Joel Smith, "How Stieglitz Came to Photograph Cityscapes," *History of Photography*, 20, no. 4 (1996): 322; Hans-Michael Koetzle, *Photo Icons: The Story behind the Pictures*, vol. 1 (Köln: Taschen, 2002), 136, 137. See also Elizabeth Anne McCauley, "The Making of a Modernist Myth," in *"The Steerage" and Alfred Stieglitz* (Berkeley: University of California Press, 2012).

23. Diner, *Time for Gathering*, 133–134; Ravitch, *Great School Wars*, 33–76; N. Cohen, *Encounter with Emancipation*, 92–96; Grinstein, *Rise of the Jewish Community*, 236, 244; Brumberg, *Going to America*, 3, 67–69, 74–75, 130–131, 138; James et al., *Immigrant Jew*, 185–186.

24. Howe, *World of Our Fathers*, 256–264, 273, 280–286; James et al., *Immigrant Jew*, 188–192, 194–196; Burrows and Wallace, *Gotham*, 781; Morris Raphael Cohen, *A Dreamer's Journey* (Boston: Beacon, 1949), 89.

25. George R. Adams, National Register of Historic Places Inventory, Nomination Form, United States Department of the Interior, National Park Service.

26. Leigh Schmidt, *Consumer Rites: The Buying and Selling of American Holidays* (Princeton: Princeton University Press, 1995), 169–174.

27. Christopher Gray, "Streetscapes: The A. T. Stewart Department Store: A City Plan to Revitalize the 1846 Marble Palace," *New York Times*, 20 March 1994.

28. "Banking on the Densely Populated East Side Is a Serious Business, but Has Amusing Features," *New York Tribune*, 15 May 1903, B4; *Jewish Daily Forward*, 4 October 1912.

29. "Latest Dealings in Realty Field," *New York Times*, 28 May 1911, XXI; Michael D. Caratzas, Research Report, Landmarks Preservation Commission, 13 October 2009, Designation List 419, LP 2363.

30. This ad ran in the *Yidishe gazeten* throughout 1887.

31. David Warfield, *Ghetto Silhouettes* (New York: James Pott, 1902), 81–82; Rischin, *Promised City*, appendix.

32. Day, *Urban Castles*, 37–41.

33. *Jewish Daily Forward*, 4 October 1912.

34. Kobrin, "Currents and Currency," 88–89; Domnitz, "Why I Left," 143.

35. Day, *Urban Castles*, 37.

36. "Banking on the Densely Populated East Side," *New York Tribune*, 15 May 1903; Domnitz, "Why I Left," 145; Day, *Urban Castles*, 37–41.

37. Kobrin, "Destructive Creators," 105–108; Kobrin, "Currents and Currency," 97–99.

38. Bernheimer, "Jewish Immigrant," 177; Lederhendler, *Jewish Immigrants and American Capitalism*, 41.

39. Daniel Soyer, "Introduction: The Rise and Fall of the New York Garment Industry," in Soyer, *Coat of Many Colors*, 4.

40. Dillon and Godley, "Development of the Jewish Clothing Industry," 21; Soyer, "Introduction," 8; Mary Wasserzug Natelson, "The Rabbi's House (Story of a

Family)," trans. Rachel Natelson (manuscript in possession of Annie Polland and Daniel Soyer), 64.

41. Isaac Rubinow, "Economic and Industrial Condition, New York," in *The Russian Jew in the United States*, ed. Charles S. Bernheimer (Philadelphia: JC Winston, 1905), 112–113.

42. Daniel Soyer, "Cockroach Capitalists: Jewish Contractors at the Turn of the Twentieth Century," in Soyer, *Coat of Many Colors*, 92–93.

43. Ibid., 98–108 (quote on 108); Weinstein, *Di idishe yunyons in Amerike*, 48.

44. Green, "Sweatshop Migrations"; Glenn, *Daughters of the Shtetl*, chap. 4.

45. Burton J. Hendricks, "The Jewish Invasion of America," *McClure's Magazine*, 12 March 1912, 126; Jesse Pope, *The Clothing Industry in New York* (1905), quoted in A. Karp, *Golden Door to America*, 111; Benjamin Stolberg, *Tailor's Progress: The Story of a Famous Union and the Men Who Made It* (Garden City, NY: Doubleday-American Mercury, 1944), 9.

46. Kraut, "The Butcher, the Baker, the Pushcart Peddler," 76; Heinze, "Jewish Street Merchants," 204, 206–207; Rischin, *Promised City*, 56.

47. Minnie Goldstein, "Success or Failure?," in Cohen and Soyer, *My Future Is in America*, 24–25, 28.

48. Kuznets, "Immigration of Russian Jews," 94–100; Samuel Joseph, *Jewish Immigration to the United States from 1881 to 1910* (New York: Columbia University Press, 1914), 140, 145.

49. John Bodnar, *The Transplanted: A History of Immigrants in Urban America* (Bloomington: Indiana University Press, 1986), 57–84; Glenn, *Daughters of the Shtetl*, 66–69; Judith E. Smith, *Family Connections: A History of Italian and Jewish Immigrant Lives in Providence, Rhode Island, 1900–1940* (Albany: State University of New York Press, 1985), 23–82; Domnitz, "Why I Left," 142–143.

50. Harry Golden, "East Side Memoir, 1910s," in Ribalow, *Autobiographies of American Jews*; Lower East Side Oral History Project, NS33–64, Tamiment Institute, New York.

51. Joseph, *Jewish Immigration*, 156–157; Bernheimer, "Jewish Immigrant," 403–404; Foner, *From Ellis Island to JFK*, 189–191; Samuel Chotzinoff, "Life on Stanton Street," in Ribalow, *Autobiographies of American Jews*, 264. The sociologist and settlement-house worker Charles Bernheimer's investigation of 225 families on one block in 1907 found that families relied on teenage children for between 44 and 69 percent of their total income. In one apartment, Bernheimer found a woman working as a pants finisher, earning $150 a year. Since rent typically was $10 a month and the woman had an eleven-year-old daughter to support, she took in a seventeen-year-old cousin, who earned $325 as a dressmaker. Bernheimer, "Jewish Immigrant," 179–180.

52. Michels, *Fire in Their Hearts*, 61, 100; Howe, *World of Our Fathers*, 108–109, 162.

53. Michels, *Fire in Their Hearts*, 15.

CHAPTER 4. FORGING COMMUNITY

1. "Temple Ahawath Chesed," *New York Herald*, 15 December 1870; "Architectural Improvements," *New York Times*, 3 December 1870, 6.

2. *New York Times*, 15 December 1870.

3. The Moorish style had rarely appeared in America until that time, except for P. T. Barnum's home in Bridgeport, Connecticut (1848), and the Crystal Palace built for the 1853 New York world's fair. Thus, architects for New York's Moorish synagogues turned to synagogue designs in central Europe, as well as in Cincinnati and San Francisco. Olga Bush, "The Architecture of Jewish Identity: The Neo-Islamic Central Synagogue of New York," *Journal of the Society of Architectural Historians* 61, no. 2 (2004): 180–201.

4. Kalmar, "Moorish Style," 84.

5. Rachel Wischnitzer, *Synagogue Architecture in the United States: History and Interpretation* (Philadelphia: Jewish Publication Society, 1955), 52–55; Jick, "Reform Synagogue," 89; Engelman, "Jewish Statistics in the U.S. Census of Religious Bodies," 130–133; Greenberg, "German-Jewish Immigrant's Perception," 321–322; *Asmonean*, 3 May 1850, 3 October 1851.

6. Grinstein, *Rise of the Jewish Community*, 370; Jick, "Reform Synagogue," 91.

7. "Layden, layden di kleyne stors [The small stores suffer]," *Forward*, 7 April 1902; see also the editorial in that issue on the subject: "Unser 'goody-goody' shtot regirung [Our 'goody-goody' city government]"; Anne Goldman, Lower East Side Oral History Project, NS33–58, Tamiment Institute, New York; Glenn, *Daughters of the Shtetl*, 133–135, 139; Rischin, *Promised City*, 85–86, 146–147; *Forward*, 4 February 1906; Domnitz, "Why I Left," 145.

8. Livia Garfinkel, "Reflections on Other Times, New York, 1881–1931," Brooklyn, 1981, Small Collections 5873, American Jewish Archives, Cincinnati; Glogower, "Impact of the American Experience," 263; Samuel Chotzinoff, "Life on Stanton Street," in Ribalow, *Autobiographies of American Jews*, 264; Golden, "East Side Memoir," 307; H. S. Goldstein, *Forty Years of Struggle for a Principle* (New York: Bloch, 1928), 32–33.

9. Polland, "May a Free Thinker Help a Pious Man?"; "Police Commissioner Bingham and Jewish Sabbath Observers," *Shabes zhurnal*, February 1909; "The Jewish Sabbath Association," *American Hebrew*, 8 January 1909, 265, 272, see also 15 January 1909, 286; Kehillah, *Jewish Communal Register*, 646; Bernard Drachman, "Jewish Sabbath Association," in Kehillah, *Jewish Communal Register*, 330.

10. Helen Harris, Lower East Side Oral History Project, NS33–60, Tamiment Institute, New York; Abraham Kokofsky, Lower East Side Oral History Project, NS33–64, Tamiment Institute, New York; Helen Rosenfeld, Lower East Side Oral History Project, NS33–75, Tamiment Institute, New York; Joseph Benjamin, "The Comforts and Discomforts of East Side Tenements," in *Report of the Year's Work* (New York: University Settlement Society, 1897), 27; "The Ghetto Market, Hester Street," *New York Times*, 14 November 1897, in Schoener, *Portal to America*, 55; Bertram Reinitz, "The East Side Looks into Its Future," *New York Times*, 13 March 1932; Richard Wheatley, "The Jews of New York," *Century Magazine*, January 1892, 327.

11. *Constitution of Kahal Adath Jeshurun with Anshe Lubz*, 1913, Collection of the Museum at Eldridge Street, New York.

12. Ibid.; Kehillah, *Jewish Communal Register*, 125 (insert); Solomon Foster, *The Workingman and the Synagogue* (Newark, 1910), 6; *New York Daily Tribune*, 20 September 1903; Edward Steiner, "The Russian and Polish Jew in New York," *Outlook*, 1 November 1902.

13. Sarna, *American Judaism*, 132 (quote); M. Meyer, *Response to Modernity*, 266.

14. Sarna, "Debate over Mixed Seating," 363–372, 374–379; Grinstein, *Rise of the Jewish Community*, 364, 410–412, 535.

15. Sarna, *American Judaism*, 147–148.

16. "Orthodoxy and Reform: The Controversy between Rabbis Kohut and Kohler," *New York Times*, 28 June 1885; Barnett Elzas, "Memoir of Alexander Kohut," in *The Ethics of the Fathers*, ed. Alexander Kohut and Max Cohen Elzas (New York: American Hebrew, 1920), xxxi; Sarna, *American Judaism*, 147–148.

17. Rebekah Kohut, *My Portion* (New York: T. Seltzer, 1925), 100–114; M. Meyer, *Response to Modernity*, 267.

18. Jick, "Reform Synagogue," 90–92.

19. Kohut, *My Portion*, 115; Diner, *Jews of the United States*, 124–127; Sarna, *American Judaism*, 150; "More Rabbis Needed," *American Hebrew*, 23 September 1887.

20. "Tiny Places of Worship: The Humble Synagogues of the Poorer East Side," *New York Daily Tribune*, 16 February 1896; Steiner, "Russian and Polish Jew in New York," 533; Schoener, *Portal to America*, 156.

21. Seat contract, 1887, signed by L. Matlawsky, secretary, collection of the Museum at Eldridge Street, New York.

22. Polland, *Landmark of the Spirit*, 32–48; "Mi Yodea," *American Israelite*, 16 September 1887, 4.

23. Jeffrey S. Gurock, "The Orthodox Synagogue," in *The American Synagogue: A Sanctuary Transformed*, ed. Jack Wertheimer (Hanover, NH: Brandeis University Press / University Press of New England, 1987), 47–53.

24. "Mi Yodea," 4.

25. Polland, *Landmark of the Spirit*, 99–103.

26. Ibid.,11. English did not become Eldridge Street's official language until 1899.

27. A. Karp, "New York Chooses a Chief Rabbi"; Polland, *Landmark of the Spirit*, 41–42.

28. Dinnerstein, "Funeral of Rabbi Jacob Joseph"; O'Donnell, "Hibernians versus Hebrews?"; Goren, *Politics and Public Culture*, 51–56.

29. Gurock, *American Jewish Orthodoxy*, 82–83; Polland, *Landmark of the Spirit*, 11.

30. Gurock, *Orthodox Jews in America*, 109–147 (quote on 133).

31. Hyman, "Immigrant Women and Consumer Protest," 93 (quote).

32. Ibid., 99 (quote), 100.

33. Ibid., 92–93, 99, 100, 102, 98 (quotes on 92, 102).

34. Diner, *Jews of the United States*, 100; Anbinder, *Five Points*, 254.

35. Rischin, *Promised City*, 10; Elizabeth Blackmar, "The Congregation and the City," in Goren and Blackmar, *Congregating and Consecrating*, 16.

36. John S. Billings, *Vital Statistics of the Jews in the United States*, 11th Census, Bulletin No. 19 (Washington, DC: U.S. Census Bureau, 1890); Diner, *Time for Gathering*, 65. These findings include all American Jews. Of the men surveyed, 5,977 were retail dealers; 3,041 were accountants, bookkeepers, and clerks; 2,147 were wholesale merchants and dealers; and 1,797 were commercial travelers.

37. Birmingham, *"Our Crowd,"* 154–178.

38. Howe, *World of Our Fathers*, 129.

39. *Jewish Messenger*, 31 March 1865, 23 March 1866.

40. Nadel, *Little Germany*, 66, 71.

41. "Shall We Foster Pauperism?," *Jewish Messenger*, 14 March 1873.

42. "Hebrew Benevolent and Orphan Asylum Society," *Jewish Messenger*, 7 March 1873.

43. "Co-operate!," *Jewish Messenger*, 28 February 1873.

44. "True Brotherhood," *Jewish Messenger*, 21 March 1873.

45. Anbinder, *Five Points*, 244. Inspiration from Christian missionaries in New York that used a district division probably inspired Isaacs.

46. They were the Hebrew Benevolent and Orphan Asylum, the Hebrew Benevolent Fuel Association, the Hebrew Relief Society, the Ladies Benevolent Society (Gates of Prayer), and the Yorkville Ladies Benevolent Society. Isaacs described the severity of New York conditions that winter of 1873 and turned to Jewish tradition as he invoked the Shema, the core Jewish prayer that proclaims the oneness of God: "As we have one God, one law, and are one people, so should we have one institution, where every case of distress might appeal with the certainty of immediate relief." "Remember the Poor!," *Jewish Messenger*, 19 December 1873.

47. Jewish Social Service Association, *Fifty Years of Social Service: The History of the United Hebrew Charities of the City of New York, Now the Jewish Social Service Association, Inc. New York City* (New York: C. S. Nathan, 1926), 22, 25; United Hebrew Charities, *First Annual Report of the Board of Relief of the United Hebrew Charities, 1874–1875*, 4–7, YIVO, New York.

48. Herman, "From Priestess to Hostess."

49. Beth S. Wenger, "Jewish Women and Voluntarism: Beyond the Myth of Enablers," *American Jewish History* 79, no. 1 (1989): 16–36.

50. Kohut, *My Portion*, 175.

51. Quoted in Joselit, "Special Sphere," 209.

52. "Souvenir," membership and summary of activities, 1895, 106, in Women's Organizations, RG4, Central Synagogue Archives, New York; Blackmar, "Congregation and the City," 16.

53. Hannah B. Einstein, "Sisterhoods of Personal Service," in *The Jewish Encyclopedia* (New York: Funk and Wagnalls, 1901–1906), quoted in Herman, "From Priestess to Hostess," 154; Hannah Leerburger, "President's Report, 1913," in *Annual Report of the A.C.S.H. Sisterhood of Personal Service, 1913*, 5–8, in Women's Organizations, RG4, Central Synagogue Archives, New York; Hannah B. Einstein, "The Federation of Sisterhoods," in *Twenty-Firth Annual Report of the United Hebrew Charities of the City of New York* (New York: United Hebrew Charities, 1899), 58.

54. United Hebrew Charities, *First Annual Report*, 4–7; Jewish Social Service Association, *Fifty Years of Social Service*, 50.

55. Kehillah, *Jewish Communal Register*, 994–997; Goren, *New York Jews and the Quest for Community*, 58–59; Rischin, *Promised City*, 98–99. The UHC assumed the major responsibility of helping recent immigrants by providing lodging, meals, medical assistance, and burial services and administering employment bureaus.

56. Soyer, *Jewish Immigrant Associations*, 61; Kehillah, *Jewish Communal Register*, 888–934.

57. Kehillah, *Jewish Communal Register*, 167–168, 816–817, 881; Rontch, *Di idishe landsmanshaften fun Nyu York*, 350–351.

58. Soyer, *Jewish Immigrant Associations*, 4–6.

59. Jacob Sholtz, Autobiography #5, American Jewish Autobiographies, RG102, YIVO, New York.

60. Soyer, *Jewish Immigrant Associations*, 117–120 (quote on 118).

61. Ibid., 144.

62. Tina Levitan, *Islands of Compassion: A History of the Jewish Hospitals of New York* (New York: Twayne, 1964), 89–92, 107–149; Kehillah, *Jewish Communal Register*, 119–124, 1014–1015; Soyer, *Jewish Immigrant Associations*, 142–160.

63. Levitan, *Islands of Compassion*, 107–149; Soyer, *Jewish Immigrant Associations*, 144–147.

64. Howe, *World of Our Fathers*, 47–50.

65. Soyer, *Jewish Immigrant Associations*, 138–141; Kehillah, *Jewish Communal Register*, 1241, 1243.

66. Eli Lederhendler, *Jewish Responses to Modernity: New Voices in America and Eastern Europe* (New York: NYU Press, 1997), chap. 1.

67. Diner, *Time for Gathering*, 8–35, 49–56, 219–226.

68. Steinmetz, *Yiddish and English*, 30–40; Sholem Aleichem, "Motl Peysi dem khazn's: In Amerike," in Green, *Jewish Workers in the Modern Diaspora*, 193.

69. Whitfield, *In Search of American Jewish Culture*, 36; Steinmetz, *Yiddish and English*, 41–65; H. L. Mencken, *The American Language: An Inquiry into the Development of English in the United States*, 4th ed. (1936; repr., New York, 1962), 368–369, 578, 633–636, and supplements 1 (1945/1962), 433–435, and 2 (1948/1962), 188–193, 259–262, 754.

70. Schor, *Emma Lazarus*, 17–20, 23–32, 46–49, 51–62, 67–79, 249–250; John Higham, "Transformation of the Statue of Liberty," in *Send These to Me*, 78–87; Francine Klagsbrun, foreword to *Emma Lazarus in Her World: Life and Letters*, by Bette Roth Young (Philadelphia: Jewish Publication Society, 1995), xii–xiii.

71. Stansell, *American Moderns*, 120–144 (quote on 134); Tony Michels, "Cultural Crossings: Immigrant Jews, Yiddish, and the New York Intellectual Scene" (unpublished paper, 2012).

72. Sanford Marovitz, *Abraham Cahan* (New York: Twayne, 1996), 153–156; Cahan, *Bleter fun may lebn*, 4:21–31; Alisa Braun, "Jews, Writing and the Dynamics of Literary Affiliation, 1880–1940" (PhD diss., University of Michigan, 2007), 20–67.

73. Moses Rischin, introduction to Hapgood, *Spirit of the Ghetto*, vii–x.

74. Stansell, *American Moderns*, 132, 134.

75. Antler, *Journey Home*, 74; Stansell, *American Moderns*, 121, 134.

76. Antler, *Journey Home*, 73–78, 82–85 (quote on 85); Stansell, *American Moderns*, 120–144 (quote on 134); Candace Falk, "Goldman, Emma," in Hyman and Moore, *Jewish Women in America*, 1:529.

77. Sandrow, *Vagabond Stars*, 72–78, 92, 104–109.

78. Nadel, "Jewish Race and German Soul," 15–16; Warnke, "Immigrant Popular Culture as Contested Space," 326–331 (quote on 326); Thissen, "Jewish Immigrant Audiences," 18.

79. Sandrow, *Vagabond Stars*, 132; Arthur A. Goren, "The Rites of Community," in *Politics and Public Culture*, 58–62 (quote on 61).

80. Sandrow, *Vagabond Stars*, 132–163, 170–189, 261–271; Warnke, "Theater as Educational Institution."

81. Daniel Soyer, "Kalisch, Bertha," in Hyman and Moore, *Jewish Women in America*, 1:715–717.

82. Burrows and Wallace, *Gotham*, 1151–1154, 1189, 1213; Daniel Pfaff, "Pulitzer, Joseph," in *American National Biography Online*, accessed 14 February 2016, www.anb.org.

83. Pfaff, "Pulitzer, Joseph."

84. Marcus, *United States Jewry*, 3:313–314; Susan Barnes, "Ochs, Adolph Simon," in *American National Biography Online*, accessed 14 February 2016, www.anb.org.

85. N. Cohen, *Not Free to Desist*, 74; "Adolph S. Ochs Dead at 77," *New York Times*, 9 April 1935; Harrison Salisbury, "New York Times," in *Encyclopedia of New York City*, ed. Kenneth T. Jackson (New Haven, CT: Yale University Press, 1995), 846–847; Tifft and Jones, *Trust*, 92–96; "The Frank Case," *New York Times*, 8 May 1914; Moore, *B'nai B'rith*, 107–108; Dinnerstein, *Anti-Semitism in America*, 181–184.

86. Michels, "Speaking to Moyshe," 53; Goren, "Jewish Press," 212; Rischin, *The Promised City*, 118; Moyshe Shtarkman, "Vikhtikste momentn in der geshikhte fun der yidisher prese in Amerike," in *Finf un zibetsik yor yidishe prese in Amerike, 1870–1945*, ed. J. Gladstone, S. Niger, and H. Rogoff (New York: Yiddish Writers Union, 1945), 17–19, 25–26; *Leksikon fun der nayer yidisher literatur*, vol. 7 (New York: Congress for Jewish Culture, 1968), 88–89.

87. Michels, *Fire in Their Hearts*, 53–56, 95–104; Rischin, introduction to *Grandma Never Lived in America*.

88. Heinze, *Adapting to Abundance*, 150, 153; Goren, "Jewish Press," 215, 217; Michels, "Speaking to Moyshe," 69.

89. S. Margoshes, "The Jewish Press in New York City," in Kehillah, *Jewish Communal Register*, 600–608, 612–632.

90. Irving Howe, Ruth Wisse, and Khone Shmeruk, introduction to *The Penguin Book of Modern Yiddish Verse*, ed. Irving Howe, Ruth Wisse, and Khone Shmeruk (New York: Viking, 1987), 22–25; *Leksikon fun der nayer yidisher literatur*, vol. 1 (1956), 207–210; vol. 3 (1960), 432–443; vol. 6 (1965), 554–563; vol. 8 (1981), 350–356; Morris Rosenfeld, "The Teardrop Millionaire," in *Morris Rosenfeld: Selections*

from His Poetry and Prose, ed. Itche Goldberg and Max Rosenfeld (New York: Yidisher kultur farband, 1964), 29; Braun, "Jews, Writing, and the Dynamics of Literary Affiliation," 72–121.

91. Howe, Wisse, and Shmeruk, introduction to *Penguin Book*, 28; Mani Leyb, "Ot azoy, azoy, azoy," in *Zishe Landoy: Zamlbukh aroysgegebn fun khaveyrim*, ed. Dovid Kazanski (New York: Farlag Inzl, 1938), 11.

92. Howe, Wisse, and Shmeruk, introduction to *Penguin Book*, 26–32; Wisse, *Little Love in Big Manhattan*, 21–44; Mani Leyb, "I Am . . . / Ich bitt . . ." in Howe, Wisse, and Shmeruk, *Penguin Book*, 128–132; *Leksikon fun der nayer yidisher literature*, vol. 5 (1963), 450–456.

93. Domnitz, "Why I Left," 151–152.

94. Krutikov, "Cityscapes of Yidishkayt."

95. Howe, *World of Our Fathers*, 445–451; *Leksikon fun der nayer yidisher literatur*, vol. 8 (1981), 678–720; vol. 1 (1956), 83–92; Goren, "Rites of Community," 67–71.

96. Josh Lambert, "Opatoshu's Eroticism, American Obscenity," in *Joseph Opatoshu: A Yiddish Writer between Europe and America*, ed. Sabine Koller, Gennady Estraikh, and Mikhail Krutikov (London: Routledge, 2013), 172–183; Norich, *Discovering Exile*, chap. 3.

97. Domnitz, "Why I Left," 148 (quote); Alan Mintz, "A Sanctuary in the Wilderness: The Beginnings of the Hebrew Movement in America in *Hatoren*," in *Hebrew in America: Perspectives and Prospects*, ed. Alan Mintz (Detroit: Wayne State University Press, 1993), 29–67.

98. Margoshes, "Jewish Press," 599; Z'vi Scharfstein, "Hebrew Speaking Clubs in America," in Kehillah, *Jewish Communal Register*, 566–567; A. Mintz, "Hebrew Literature in America"; Jonathan D. Sarna, "American Jewish Education in History," *Journal of Jewish Education* 64, nos. 1–2 (1998): 14–18.

99. Aviva Ben-Ur, "The Ladino (Judeo-Spanish) Press in the United States, 1910–1948," in *Multilingual America: Transnationalism, Ethnicity, and the Languages of American Literature*, ed. Werner Sollors (New York: NYU Press, 1998), 64–79.

100. Rischin, *Promised City*, 128–130; Michels, "Speaking to Moyshe," 67; Nadel, "Jewish Race and German Soul," 16; Nadel, *Little Germany*, 83.

101. Emma Goldman, *Living My Life* (New York: Knopf, 1931), 56, quoted in "Emma Goldman," in *Women of Valor*, Jewish Women's Archive, accessed 14 February 2016, http://jwa.org.

102. N. Cohen, *Encounter with Emancipation*, 233.

103. Howe, *World of Our Fathers*, 129.

104. Marcus, *United States Jewry*, 2:478; Friedman, "Send Me My Husband"; Abraham Oseroff, "The United Hebrew Charities of the City of New York and Subsidiary Relief Agencies," in Kehillah, *Jewish Communal Register*, 994–996, 1318–1327; Igra, *Wives without Husbands*; Peter Romanofsky, "'. . . To Rid Ourselves of the Burden . . .': New York Jewish Charities and the Origins of the Industrial Removal Office, 1890–1901," *AJHQ* 64, no. 4 (1975): 331; *New York Times*, 41 October 1905, 8 June 1914.

105. Judith Ann Trolander, *Professionalism and Social Change: From the Settlement House Movement to Neighborhood Centers, 1886 to the Present* (New York: Columbia University Press, 1887).

106. Marjorie N. Feld, "Lillian Wald," in *Encyclopedia*, Jewish Women's Archive, accessed January 18, 2017, https://jwa.org.

107. Marjorie N. Feld, *Lillian Wald: A Biography* (Chapel Hill: University of North Carolina Press, 2008); N. Feld, "Lillian Wald," in Hyman and Moore, *Jewish Women in America*, 2:1446–1449.

108. Adam Bellow, *The Educational Alliance: A Centennial Celebration* (New York: Educational Alliance, 1990), 41; D. Kaufman, *Shul with a Pool*, 92; Minutes of a Meeting of the Committee on Religious and Moral Work of the Educational Alliance, 4 May 1916, Records of the Educational Alliance, YIVO, New York.

109. "In a Wide Labor Field," *New York Times*, 19 May 1895.

110. Minutes of a Meeting of the Committee of Religious and Moral Work of the Educational Alliance, 4 May 1916; "In a Wide Labor Field." See also Cary Goodman, *Choosing Sides: Playground and Street Life on the Lower East Side* (New York: Schocken, 1979).

111. Soyer, "Brownstones and Brownsville."

112. Goren, *New York Jews*, 25.

113. Joselit, *Our Gang*, 2, 5–8; Gilfoyle, *City of Eros*, 264–265, 408n35.

114. Goren, *New York Jews*, 36.

115. Ibid., 36–38; Arthur A. Goren, introduction to *Dissenter in Zion: From the Writings of Judah L. Magnes*, ed. Arthur A. Goren (Cambridge, MA: Harvard University Press, 1982), 1–58; Moore, "New American Judaism," 41–42.

116. Goren, *New York Jews*, 52–55, 58–59, 82–84, 86–109, 159–213.

117. Samson Benderly, "The Present Status of Jewish Religious Education in New York City," and Bernard Dushkin, "Cheder Instruction," in Kehillah, *Jewish Communal Register*, 349–357, 397.

118. Goren, *New York Jews*, 240; Soyer, *Jewish Immigrant Associations*, 124–127.

119. Moore, "From Kehillah to Federation."

120. The New York and Brooklyn federations merged in 1943.

121. Walkowitz, *Working with Class*, 71–73; Jonathan Woocher, *Sacred Survival: The Civil Religion of American Jews* (Bloomington: Indiana University Press, 1986), 25; Kehillah, *Jewish Communal Register*, 1281–1313; *New York Times*, 24 June 1916; Moore, "From Kehillah to Federation," 134; Berkman, "Transforming Philanthropy," 150–153, 155–158.

CHAPTER 5. THE POWER OF POLITICS

1. Steven J. Zipperstein, *Elusive Prophet: Ahad Ha'am and the Origins of Zionism* (Berkeley: University of California Press, 1993), 204–205; Frankel, *Prophecy and Politics*, 473–484 (quote on 483).

2. Moore, *B'nai B'rith*, 74; Penkower, "Kishinev Pogrom," 191.

3. Frankel, *Prophecy and Politics*, 487–492; Penkower, "Kishinev Pogrom," 204.

4. Moore, "New American Judaism," 41–47.

5. N. Cohen, *Not Free to Desist*, 8–28.

6. Ibid., 27; Naomi W. Cohen, *Jacob Schiff: A Study in American Jewish Leadership* (Hanover, NH: Brandeis University Press, 1999); Ann E. Healy, "Tsarist Anti-Semitism and Russian-American Relations," *Slavic Review* 42, no. 3 (1983): 408–425.

7. Silver, "Louis Marshall"; N. Cohen, *Not Free to Desist*, 28.

8. N. Cohen, *Not Free to Desist*, 40–48, 57–58; Jeffrey S. Gurock, "The 1913 New York State Civil Rights Act," *AJS Review* 1 (1976): 93–120; Kehillah, *Jewish Communal Register*, 1415–1422.

9. N. Cohen, *Not Free to Desist*, 8–28, 40–48, 57–58; Kehillah, *Jewish Communal Register*, 1415–1422, 1426–1427; Panitz, "In Defense of the Jewish Immigrant," 63–64.

10. Rogow, *Gone to Another Meeting*, esp. 1–35, 225; Hasia R. Diner and Beryl Lieff Benderly, *Her Works Praise Her: A History of Jewish Women in America from Colonial Times to the Present* (New York: Basic Books, 2002), 252–253, 255; Martha Katz-Hyman, "American, Sadie," in Hyman and Moore, *Jewish Women in America*, 1:38–39.

11. Rogow, *Gone to Another Meeting*, 130–142; Diner and Benderly, *Her Works Praise Her*, 256–257. See also Edward J. Bristow, *Prostitution and Prejudice: The Jewish Fight against White Slavery, 1870–1939* (New York: Schocken, 1983).

12. Rogow, *Gone to Another Meeting*, 118; Katz-Hyman, "American, Sadie," 1:38–39.

13. Rogow, *Gone to Another Meeting*, 118–123; Katz-Hyman, "American, Sadie," 1:38–39.

14. Rogow, *Gone to Another Meeting*, 226; Peggy Pearlstein, "Brenner, Rose," in Hyman and Moore, *Jewish Women in America*, 1:175; Kehillah, *Jewish Communal Register*, 1137, 1232.

15. Diner, *Jews of the United States*, 181; Raider, *Emergence of American Zionism*, 10–13; Evyatar Friesel, "Brandeis' Role in American Zionism Historically Reconsidered," in *American Zionism: Mission and Politics*, ed. Jeffrey S. Gurock (New York: Routledge, 1998), 92–96; Naomi W. Cohen, "The Reaction of Reform Judaism in America to Political Zionism (1897–1922)," in Gurock, *American Zionism*, 31–32; Kehillah, *Jewish Communal Register*, 1340–1342.

16. Raider, *Emergence of American Zionism*, 18–19.

17. Kehillah, *Jewish Communal Register*, 1360–1361, 1370–1371; Deborah Dash Moore, "Hadassah," in Hyman and Moore, *Jewish Women in America*, 1:571 (quotes).

18. Simmons, *Hadassah and the Zionist Project*, 11; Raider, *Emergence of American Zionism*, 15–16; Michael Brown, "Szold, Henrietta," in Hyman and Moore, *Jewish Women in America*, 2:1368–1370; McCune, *"Whole Wide World without Limits,"* 23–26.

19. Michael Brown, *The Israeli-American Connection: Its Roots in the Yishuv, 1914–1945* (Detroit: Wayne State University Press, 1996), 145; Moore, "Hadassah," 1:572; Kehillah, *Jewish Communal Register*, 1360–1365; Simmons, *Hadassah and the Zionist Project*, 18.

20. Kehillah, *Jewish Communal Register*, 1340–1409.

21. Michels, *Fire in Their Hearts*, 125–216 (quotes on 136, 145); Epstein, *Profiles of Eleven*, 297–317.

22. Michels, *Fire in Their Hearts*, 125–178, 179 (quote); Frankel, *Prophecy and Politics*, 453–509.

23. Hillel Rogoff, *Meyer London: A biografye* (New York: Meyer London Memorial Fund, 1930), 78–79; Epstein, *Jewish Labor in the USA*, vol. 1, *1882–1914*, 358–360.

24. Cahan, *Bleter fun mayn lebn*, 4:606–607, 5:25–27, 240–241.

25. Society of Tammany or Columbian Order, *150th Anniversary Celebration: 1786–July 4–1936* (New York: Tammany Society, 1936), 65; Gustavus Myers, *The History of Tammany Hall* (New York: G. Myers, 1901), 257–258; Burrows and Wallace, *Gotham*, 995, 1145.

26. Rischin, *Promised City*, chap. 11.

27. Forman, "Politics of Minority Consciousness," 144; Fuchs, *Political Behavior of American Jews*, 25–27.

28. "Biographical Profiles," in Maisel, *Jews in American Politics*, 328, 334, 351; Myers, *History of Tammany Hall*, 166–167; Fuchs, *Political Behavior of American Jews*, 29, 32–46; Arthur Silver, "Jews in the Political Life of New York City, 1865–1897" (DHL diss., Yeshiva University, 1954), 7–8, 80, 107–108, 113–120. In 1892, Republicans nominated former congressman Edwin Einstein for mayor, making him the first Jew to head a major-party local ticket. Republicans hoped to attract Jewish votes to the state ticket with his candidacy. Tammany responded in part by increasing its nominations of Jews. Two years later, Tammany offered the mayoral nomination to the wealthy philanthropist Nathan Straus, but Straus withdrew when convinced by editors of the *American Hebrew* that he was simply being used to draw votes for Tammany's other candidates. Michels, *Fire in Their Hearts*, 46.

29. Burrows and Wallace, *Gotham*, 1092.

30. Burrows and Wallace, *Gotham*, 1092–1110; Epstein, *Jewish Labor in USA*, 115–116, 144–149; Tcherikower, *Geshikhte fun der yidisher arbeter bavegung in di fareynikte shtatn*, 290–294.

31. Ben Reisman, "Why I Came to America," in Cohen and Soyer, *My Future Is in America*, 67–68; Howe, *World of Our Fathers*, 287–295.

32. J. S. Hertz, *50 yor arbeter-ring in yidishn lebn* (New York: National Executive Committee of the Workmen's Circle, 1950), 15; Sachs, *Di geshikhte fun arbayter ring*, 3–6; Soyer, *Jewish Immigrant Associations*, 66–70.

33. Howe, *World of Our Fathers*, 522–543; Epstein, *Profiles of Eleven*, 49–110.

34. For an overview, see Nick Salvatore, *Eugene V. Debs: Citizen and Socialist* (Urbana: University of Illinois Press, 1982).

35. Kosak, *Cultures of Opposition*, 161–163.

36. Howe, *World of Our Fathers*, 298.

37. Ibid., 297–299; Orleck, *Common Sense*, 39–41, 48–49, 60; Greenwald, *Triangle Fire*, 32–46.

38. Greenwald, *Triangle Fire*, 50–75; Howe, *World of Our Fathers*, 301.

39. James et al., *Immigrant Jew*, 261.

40. See Morris Hillquit's autobiography, *Loose Leaves from a Busy Life* (New York: Macmillan, 1934).

41. Morris Hillquit, "Why I Am a Socialist," in Howe and Libo, *How We Lived*, 190; Epstein, *Profiles of Eleven*, 189–232; *Leksikon fun der nayer yiddisher literature*, vol. 3 (1960), 138–139; Howe, *World of Our Fathers*, 315.

42. Howe, *World of Our Fathers*, 315; Epstein, *Profiles of Eleven*, 159–188 (quote on 174); Rogoff, *Meyer London*.

43. Von Drehle, *Triangle*; Stein, *Triangle Fire*; Greenwald, *Triangle Fire*, 129–153.

44. *Jewish Daily Forward*, 26 March 1911; *Morgen zhurnal*, quoted in Goren, "Rites of Community," 62.

45. Goren, "Rites of Community," 63–67.

46. Rose Schneiderman, "An Appeal to Working People," in Howe and Libo, *How We Lived*, 187.

47. Stein, *Triangle Fire*, 124, 138; Orleck, *Common Sense*, 36–37, 44–45, 48, 103; Greenwald, *Triangle Fire*, 139–145.

48. Greenwald, *Triangle Fire*, 156–159; Von Drehle, *Triangle*, 209–214; Orleck, *Common Sense*, 131–132.

49. Thomas Henderson, *Tammany Hall and the New Immigrants: The Progressive Years* (New York: Arno, 1976), 177; Howe, *World of Our Fathers*, 313, 315; Dubofsky, "Success and Failure of Socialism," 367–368; Arthur A. Goren, "Socialist Politics on the Lower East Side," in *Politics and Public Culture*, 84–89, 95–97 (quote on 97).

50. Landesman, *Brownsville*, 113–119, 299–302.

51. Frederick C. Giffin, "Morris Hillquit and the War Issue in the New York Mayoralty Campaign of 1917," *International Social Science Review* 74, nos. 3–4 (1999): 115–128. See also Ross J. Wilson, *New York and the First World War: Shaping an American City* (Burlington, VT: Ashgate, 2014).

52. "Judge Hylan Opens Fight for Ballots," *New York Times*, 5 October 1917.

53. Henderson, *Tammany Hall and the New Immigrants*, 193–219; Dubofsky, "Success and Failure of Socialism," 371; Howe, *World of Our Fathers*, 278–280, 319–321 (quote 319); "Hylan Victory Is a Tammany Record," *New York Times*, 8 November 1917; Epstein, *Profiles of Eleven*, 213; Giffin, "Hillquit and the War Issue," 122–125.

54. Rosalyn Baxandall, "A Socialist in Congress: My Great-Uncle, Meyer London," *Jewish Currents*, September 2013, http://jewishcurrents.org. See also Gordon J. Goldberg, *Meyer London: A Biography of the Socialist Congressman, 1871–1926* (Jefferson, NC: McFarland, 2013).

55. Henderson, *Tammany Hall and the New Immigrants*, 222–234; Landesman, *Brownsville*, 304.

56. Lerner, "Jewish Involvement," reprinted in *American Jewish History*, ed. Jeffrey S. Gurock (New York: Routledge, 1998), 3: 963–982.

57. Orleck, *Common Sense*, 87–113 (quote on 91).

58. "Di pflicht fun amerikaner iden," *Tageblat*, 20 August 1914.

59. Soyer, *Jewish Immigrant Associations*, 161–171.

60. "American Jewish Joint Distribution Committee and Refugee Aid," *Holocaust Encyclopedia*, accessed 20 February 2016, www.ushmm.org.

61. Jonathan Frankel, "Jewish Socialists and the American Jewish Congress Movement," *YIVO Annual* 16 (1976): 202–341.

62. McCune, *"Whole Wide World without Limits,"* 49.

63. "An Inventory to the Stephen S. Wise Collection," American Jewish Archives, accessed 2 August 2010, www.americanjewisharchives.org; Kehillah, *Jewish Communal Register*, 1460–1461. See also Melvin I. Urofsky, *A Voice That Spoke for Justice: The Life and Times of Rabbi Stephen S. Wise* (Albany: State University of New York Press, 1982).

64. Frankel, *Prophecy and Politics*, 509–536; Kehillah, *Jewish Communal Register*, 1429–1440; "Jews Pick Members for Congress Today," *New York Times*, 10 June 1917.

65. N. Cohen, *Not Free to Desist*, 119. See also Carole Fink, *Defending the Rights of Others: The Great Powers, the Jews, and International Minority Protection, 1878–1938* (New York: Cambridge University Press, 2004).

66. "Likens Alien Bill to Pharaoh's Plan," *New York Times*, 20 April 1924.

67. Higham, *Strangers in the Land*, 194–299.

68. Ibid., 270–286; Madison Grant, *The Passing of the Great Race* (New York: Scribner, 1916), 81; N. Cohen, *Not Free to Desist*, 127.

69. N. Cohen, *Not Free to Desist*, 124–139; Woeste, "Insecure Equality."

70. Daniels, *Guarding the Golden Door*, 7–49 (quote on 47–48).

71. "Says 'Foreign Bloc' Fights Johnson Bill," *New York Times*, 2 March 1924; Chin Jou, "Contesting Nativism: The New York Congressional Delegation's Case against the Immigration Act of 1924," *Federal History* 3 (2011): 66–79, accessed 23 May 2011, http://shfg.org; *Biographical Dictionary of the United States Congress*, accessed 23 May 2011, http://bioguide.congress.gov; House Vote #90, 15 May 1924, *To Agree to the Report of Conference Committee on H.R. 7995, to Limit the Immigration of Aliens into the United States (P. 8651–1)*, accessed 23 May 2011, www.govtrack.us.

72. Higham, *Send These to Me*, 203–208. On name changing, see Kirsten Fermaglich, "'Too Long, Too Foreign . . . Too Jewish': Jews, Name Changing, and Family Mobility in New York City, 1917–1942," *Journal of American Ethnic History* 34, no. 3 (2015): 34–87.

73. Garland, "Not-Quite-Closed Gates," 199; "Population and Migration: Migration since World War I," in *The Yivo Encyclopedia of Jews in Eastern Europe*, accessed 4 February 2016, www.yivoencyclopedia.org; "Immigration Act of 1924," *Wikipedia*, accessed 4 February 2016, http://en.wikipedia.org.

74. Garland, "Not-Quite-Closed Gates," 199; Minnie Kuznetz, "I Haven't Lost Anything by Coming to America," in Cohen and Soyer, *My Future Is in America*, 302, 307–309.

CHAPTER 6. JEWISH GEOGRAPHY

1. Deborah Dash Moore, "Who Built New York? Jewish Builders in the Interwar Decades," *American Jewish History* 101 (2017).

2. Cahan, *Bleter fun mayn lebn*, 3:428.

3. Day, *Urban Castles*, 42–46; Gurock, *When Harlem Was Jewish*, 45–49.

4. Gurock, *When Harlem Was Jewish*, 28, 33; Cahan, *Bleter fun mayn lebn*, 3:430.

5. Rischin, "Toward the Onomastics of the Great New York Ghetto," 13–24; Moore, *At Home in America*, 8.

6. Moore, *At Home in America*, 19; Diner, *Lower East Side Memories*, 96–117.

7. Pritchett, *Brownsville, Brooklyn*, 11–18; Moore, "On the Fringes of the City," 256–257; quote from "Brownsville an Example of Rise of Values in Brooklyn Realty," *New York Herald*, undated clipping, A. J. Virginia Scrapbook, Jewish Division, New York Public Library.

8. Landesman, *Brownsville*, 58–60.

9. Ibid., 56, 78–79, 86, 88–89, 150; Moore, "On the Fringes of the City."

10. Kehillah, *Jewish Communal Register*, map following 80; Domnitz, "Why I Left," 149.

11. Hasia R. Diner, "Buying and Selling 'Jewish': The Historical Impact of Commerce on Jewish Communal Life," in *Imagining the American Jewish Community*, ed. Jack Wertheimer (Hanover, NH: Brandeis University Press, 2007), 28–41; Moore, *At Home in America*, 20; Gurock, *When Harlem Was Jewish*, 39; Rischin, *Promised City*, 56.

12. Rischin, *Promised City*, 57–58; James et al., *Immigrant Jew*, 289; Samuel Chotzinoff, *A Lost Paradise: Early Reminiscences* (1955; repr., New York: Arno, 1975), 182–188; Joselit, *Wonders of America*, 202–203. See also Merwin, *Pastrami on Rye*.

13. Joselit, *Wonders of America*, 208–215; James et al., *Immigrant Jew*, 223; Rischin, *Promised City*, 141.

14. Pritchett, *Brownsville, Brooklyn*, 25; Domnitz, "Why I Left," 149–150; Seward Park Branch Records, Manuscripts and Archives Division, Astor, Lenox, and Tilden Foundations, New York Public Library.

15. New York State Reconstruction Commission, *Housing Conditions: Report of the Housing Committee of the Reconstruction Commission of the State of New York* (Albany, NY: J. B. Lyon, 1920), 9.

16. Gurock, *When Harlem Was Jewish*, 140–141. On post–World War I racial tensions in American cities, see Arthur I. Waskow, *From Race Riot to Sit-In: 1919 and the 1960s* (Garden City, NY: Doubleday, 1966), 2, 21–22, 304–308.

17. On the tax-exemption law, see *Real Estate Record and Builders Guide* (hereafter *RERBG*), 5 March 1921, cited in Gurock, *When Harlem Was Jewish*, 42.

18. *RERBG*, 3 September 1921, 18 March 1922. On the citywide patterns over the decade of the 1920s, see New York City Tenement House Department, *Tenth Report, 1918–1929* (New York: Martin Brown, 1929), 36–49.

19. Regional Plan of New York and Its Environs, *Regional Survey of New York and Its Environs*, vol. 2, *Population, Land Values and Government: Studies of the Growth and Distribution of Population and Land Values and of Problems of Government, Regional Survey of New York and Its Environs* (New York: Regional Plan of New York and Its Environs, 1929), 62; *RERBG*, 21 September 1921, 26 February 1927.

20. Edwin Harold Spengler, *Land Values in New York in Relation to Transit Facilities* (New York: Columbia University Press, 1930), 19–24; Hood, *722 Miles*,

158–161, 174. See also Michael V. Gershowitz, "Neighborhood Power Structure: Decision Making in Forest Hills" (PhD diss., New York University, 1974), 28; Daniel A. Wishnoff, "The Tolerance Point: Race, Public Housing and the Forest Hills Controversy, 1945–1975" (PhD diss., City University of New York, 2005), 153–154.

21. Abraham Cahan wrote in his famous novel *The Rise of David Levinsky* about how a "boom" was "intoxicating a certain element of the population" of "Jewish carpenters, house-painters, bricklayers, or installment peddlers," emerging, in true rags-to-riches style, as "builders of tenements or frame dwellings." Abraham Cahan, *The Rise of David Levinsky: A Novel* (New York: Harper, 1917), 464, 480; Gurock, "Synagogue Imperialism."

22. Moore, *At Home in America*, 39 (quote).

23. Gurock, *When Harlem Was Jewish*, 27, 33–34.

24. Moore, *At Home in America*, 44–53.

25. Hood, *722 Miles*, 173–177; Plunz, *History of Housing*, 131.

26. Jackson Heights Investing Company v. James Conforti Construction Company, 222 A.D. 687 (1927), 73, 76, 100–101. See also Broun and Britt, *Christians Only*, 256.

27. For the evolution of the Russell Sage Foundation's approach toward Forest Hills Gardens, see Plunz, *History of Housing*, 117–120. See also, on the foundation, "Russell Sage Foundation," in Jackson, *Encyclopedia of New York City*, 1029. See also, on the rapid-transit issue, Gershowitz, "Neighborhood Power Structure," 26; Wishnoff, "Tolerance Point," 152; Jeff Gottlieb, "Benjamin Braunstein: Quiet, Genius at Work" (unpublished paper), formerly appearing at www.qjhs.org. On the Jewish population of Forest Hills as of 1930, see Horowitz and Kaplan, *Estimated Jewish Population*, 94. On the early settlers in the neighborhood, including the Forest Hills Gardens portion, see Jeff Gottlieb, "The Early Years: A Clearer View of Early Jewish Life in Forest Hills" (unpublished paper), formerly appearing at www.qjhs.org.

28. Kuznetz, "I Haven't Lost Anything," 302.

29. Moore, *At Home in America*, 62–80.

30. Moore, *At Home in America*, 19–24, 65–68; Wenger, *New York Jews*, 81, 83–84, 94.

31. For statistics on Jewish out-migration from older neighborhoods and resettlement elsewhere in the city, see Kehillah, *Jewish Communal Register*, 82, 85; Horowitz and Kaplan, *Estimated Jewish Population*, 22, 133, 157, 209, 239. See also, on relocation destinations, Grebler, *Housing Market Behavior*, 124–125. On the differing fates of Jews and African Americans in Harlem, circa 1920–1930, see Osofsky, *Harlem*, 130, 248; Gurock, *When Harlem Was Jewish*, 144–145, 156. On Washington Heights, see Robert W. Snyder, *Crossing Broadway: Washington Heights and the Promise of New York City* (Ithaca, NY: Cornell University Press, 2014).

32. Dolkart, "Homes for People"; Plunz, *History of Housing*, 151–157; Katherine Eva Rosenblatt, "Cooperative Battlegrounds: Farmers, Workers, and the Search for Economic Alternatives" (PhD diss., University of Michigan, 2016), 85–92, 102–103.

33. Plunz, *History of Housing*, 151–157; Dolkart, "Homes for People," 33–35; Rosenblatt, "Cooperative Battlegrounds," 105–113.

34. Trillin, "U.S. Journal."

35. Angel, *La America*, 20, 35–36, 146, 169; Ben-Ur, *Sephardic Jews in America*, 35–37.

36. Moore, *At Home in America*, 30.

37. Ibid., 23, 66, 71–73, 78–82; Rischin, *Promised City*, 93; Wenger, *New York Jews*, 85–89.

38. Moore, *At Home in America*, 23, 66, 73–74, 76; Wenger, *New York Jews*, 90–93 (quote on 93).

39. Moore, *At Home in America*, 21, 23; Wenger, *New York Jews*, 81.

40. Kazin, *Walker in the City*, 88, 107; Gay, *Unfinished People*, 298.

41. Adolph Schayes, interview with Jeffrey S. Gurock, 5 December 2008.

42. Stephen G. Thompson, "Co-op Housing: N.Y.C. vs. U.S.A.," *Architectural Forum*, July 1959, 132–133, 178. For a full discussion of Title 1 housing, see Joel Schwartz, *The New York Approach: Robert Moses, Urban Liberals, and the Redevelopment of the Inner City* (Columbus: Ohio State University Press, 1993).

43. "New Apartments Offer Terraces," *New York Times*, 26 April 1942; Marshall Sklare, "Jews, Ethnics, and the American City," *Commentary* 53, no. 4 (1972): 72 (quote).

44. All of these sources are derived from a clipping file, a compilation of newspaper articles titled "Forest Hills Housing, 1921–1971" at the Queens Public Library, Long Island Division; Sklare, "Jews, Ethnics," 72; Alison Gregor, "Away from the Limelight a Builder Makes His Mark," *New York Times*, 21 December 2006. See also the company's history of its endeavors, *Muss Development LLC: Building New York since 1906* (document provided to Gurock by Joshua Muss); Joshua Muss, interview with Gurock, 24 November 2008.

45. On the history of the LeFraks, see "LeFrak, Samuel J.," in *American National Biography Online*, accessed 19 January 2017, www.anb.org. On the LeFraks' early efforts in Queens, see "Forest Hills Gets New Apartments of Unusual Design," *New York Times*, 1 April 1951; James Trager, *The New York Chronology: The Ultimate Compendium of Events, People, and Anecdotes from the Dutch to the Present* (New York: Collins Reference, 2004), 455–456. On the family's approach to housing for less affluent residents, see Charles V. Bagli, "Blue-Collar Builders Expand Empire to Glitzier Shores," *New York Times*, 9 October 2007.

46. Ruth Glazer, "West Bronx: Food, Shelter, Clothing," *Commentary*, June 1949, 578–585.

47. Vivian Gornick, "There Is No More Community," *Interchange*, April 1977, 4; Vivian Gornick, "Commencement Address," in *City at the Center: A Collection of Writings by CCNY Alumni and Faculty*, ed. Betty Rizzo and Barry Wallenstein (New York: City College of New York, 1983), 84–87.

48. Zeitz, *White Ethnic New York*, 16; Snyder, *Crossing Broadway*, 24, 27–29, 150–152; Solomon Poll, *The Hasidic Community of Williamsburg: A Study in the Sociology of Religion* (New York: Schocken, 1969).

49. Bureau of Community Statistical Services Research Department, Community Council of Greater New York, *Bronx Communities: Population Characteristics*

and Neighborhood Social Resources, typescript (New York, 1962), 45–46, 69, 70; Horowitz and Kaplan, *Estimated Jewish Population*, 175, 217, 229, 233, 235; Naison, "Crown Heights in the 1950s," 143–152 (quote on 144–145).

50. Edgar M. Hoover and Raymond Vernon, *Anatomy of a Metropolis: The Changing Distribution of People and Jobs within the New York Metropolitan Region* (1962; repr., Cambridge, MA: Harvard University Press, 2014), 16.

51. Caro, *Power Broker*, 851–852; Freeman, *Working-Class New York*, 35, 37; Naison, "Crown Heights in the 1950s," 144; Emerson, *Always Magic in the Air*, 84–85.

CHAPTER 7. RAISING TWO GENERATIONS

1. Lederhendler, "New York City," 55; on the Yom Kippur method, see Moore, *At Home in America*, 243–245.

2. Lederhendler, "New York City," 55.

3. On gender differences, see Paula E. Hyman, *Gender and Assimilation in Modern Jewish History: The Roles and Representation of Women* (Seattle: University of Washington Press, 1995).

4. Marilyn Halter, *Shopping for Identity: The Marketing of Ethnicity* (New York: Schocken, 2000), 33–35. See also Roger Horowitz, *Kosher USA: How Coke Became Kosher and Other Tales of Modern Food* (New York: Columbia University Press, 2016).

5. Joselit, *Wonders of America*, 176, 187–188, 193–195; Heinze, *Adapting to Abundance*, 176–177.

6. Joselit, *Wonders of America*, 96–101.

7. McGill, "Some Characteristics of Jewish Youth," 266–267.

8. Pamela S. Nadell, "A Bright New Constellation: Feminism and American Judaism" in Raphael, *Columbia History of Jews and Judaism*, 387–388; Scult, *Judaism Faces the Twentieth Century*, 301–302.

9. Goren, "Traditional Institutions Transplanted," 62–78 (quote on 70–71).

10. Ibid., 71–72 (quote on 71).

11. Ibid., 75. Socialist Jews, rejecting Orthodox Jewish ritual requirements, established their own "Cemetery Departments" in such organizations as the Workmen's Circle, a socialist Jewish fraternal society.

12. On the rise of synagogue centers in New York during the 1920s, see Moore, *At Home in America*, 140–143. On Kaplan's break with Orthodoxy, see Gurock and Schacter, *Modern Heretic*, 106–134.

13. Gurock, *Judaism's Encounter with American Sports*, 66–67; Israel Herbert Levinthal, "The Value of the Center to the Synagogue," *United Synagogue Review*, June 1926, 19.

14. Gurock, *Judaism's Encounter*, 70–71; Merwin, *In Their Own Image*, 59; Wenger, *New York Jews*, 186.

15. Morris Freedman, "New Jewish Community in Formation: A Conservative Center Catering to Present-Day Needs," *Commentary*, January 1955, 36–37, 39, 43, 45, 46.

16. On the founding and early mission of the Forest Hills Jewish Center, see Wishnoff, "Tolerance Point," 159–164.

17. Jeffrey S. Gurock, "Devotees and Deviants: A Primer on the Religious Values of Orthodox Day School Families," in *Rav Chesed: Essays in Honor of Rabbi Dr. Haskel Lookstein*, ed. Rafael Medoff (Hoboken, NJ: Ktav, 2009), 271–294.

18. On the founding of the Yeshiva of Central Queens, see its brief institution history composed as part of its *Yeshiva of Central Queens Golden Jubilee Dinner Journal*, 3 March 1991, provided courtesy of the Yeshiva of Central Queens. See also Jeff Gottlieb, "Jamaica: Stronghold of the Jews" (unpublished paper), 7, formerly appearing at www.qjhs.org.

19. Undated report, c. 1957, on Solomon Schechter Schools in the Ben Zion Bokser Papers, Box 20, Ratner Center, Jewish Theological Seminary, New York; Ben Zion Bokser, "The Solomon Schechter Day Schools," *United Synagogue Review*, March 1957, 11; Harold U. Ribalow, "My Child Goes to Jewish Parochial School," *Commentary*, January–June 1954, 64–67.

20. United States Displaced Persons Commission, *Memo to America: The DP Story: The Final Report of the United States Displaced Persons Commission* (Washington, DC: Government Printing Office, 1952), 27, 38–39. I am grateful to William B. Helmreich for directing me to this source. See also Rosenwaike, *Population History*, 159. Ironically, immediately after the war, survivors from Germany and Austria found their own paths to America hindered by legal and bureaucratic definitions that included them as among unwelcomed refugees from a former enemy state, even though these so-called German expellees had had their citizenship stripped from them by Nazi edicts. Only in 1950 did the United States ameliorate this mischaracterization by amending displaced-persons legislation to allow approximately fifty-five thousand Jews to enter on a nonquota basis. V. Sanua, "Study of the Adjustment of Sephardi Jews." See also Sutton, *Magic Carpet*, 4.

21. On adjustment patterns of Jews from Germany in New York after World War II, see Joseph Berger, *Displaced Persons: Growing Up American after the Holocaust* (New York: Scribner, 2001); and Beth Cohen, *Case Closed: Holocaust Survivors in Postwar America* (New Brunswick, NJ: Rutgers University Press, 2007).

22. Kranzler, *Williamsburg*, 40–43; J. Mintz, *Hasidic People*, 30.

23. Mayer, *From Suburb to Shtetl*, 31; Kranzler, *Williamsburg*, 40–43.

24. On the Lubavitcher *farbrengen*, see J. Mintz, *Hasidic People*, 48–50, 97.

25. Heilman and Friedman, *Rebbe*, 158–160. See also Sue Fishkoff, *The Rebbe's Army: Inside the World of Chabad-Lubavitch* (New York: Schocken, 2003).

26. Stephen Steinberg, *The Academic Melting Pot: Catholics and Jews in American Higher Education* (New York: McGraw-Hill, 1974), 20–21; Marcia Graham Synott, *The Half-Opened Door: Discrimination and Admissions at Harvard, Yale and Princeton, 1900–1970* (Westport, CT: Greenwood, 1979), 158, 195. Communal pressures kept 20 percent of Harvard's study body Jewish, far above the 10 percent at Yale.

27. M. Sanua, "We Hate New York," 237; Lee J. Levinger, *The Jewish Student in America: A Study Made by the Research Bureau of the B'nai B'rith Hillel Foundation* (Cincinnati: B'nai B'rith, 1937), 94.

28. Broun and Britt, *Christians Only*, 107; Felix Morrow, "Higher Learning on Washington Square," *Menorah Journal*, Autumn 1930, 353; Hollinger, "Two NYUs," 255. On NYU's Depression-era reversal of policies, see Bender, *New York Intellect*, 291.

29. Hollinger, "Two NYUs," 256; Morrow, "Higher Learning," 348–349. There is a difference of opinion within the sources on the Jewish proportions at NYU, both uptown and downtown. Morrow has offered the figure of 93 percent in 1930, which, if correct, would make NYU more "Jewish" than CCNY was ("Higher Learning," 348). Broun and Britt, on the other hand, reported based on information from the school's registrar for 1931 that 45.3 percent of the uptown campus was Jewish, as opposed to 63 percent for downtown (*Christians Only*, 106–107). Hollinger has argued that in the 1920s, Jewish percentages in University Heights were less than 30 percent ("Two NYUs," 255). Bender has complicated matters by suggesting that by the end of the 1920s and into the Depression, economics moved NYU uptown to be more hospitable to Jews, and thus the numbers there rebounded to 54 percent from 30 percent in 1922 (*New York Intellect*, 291). On the easy commute from the Lower East Side, see Wechsler, *Qualified Student*, 133.

30. Sauna, "We Hate New York," 237; A. M. Rosenthal, "Of Course, It Is All Quite Obvious as to Why I Am So Moved," in Rizzo and Wallenstein, *City at the Center*, 67. On the cost of lunch at CCNY, see Sorin, *Irving Howe*, 15–17. On the cost of tuition at Columbia, see Nathan Glazer's memoir comments in Dorman, *Arguing the World*, 43–44. One luncheon staple, a "generous and highly seasoned chopped liver sandwich," cost fifteen cents, leaving enough for a soda or coffee.

31. R. Cohen, *When the Old Left Was Young*, 68–70. See also "City College Men Fight Rise in Fees," *New York Times*, 24 May 1932, 1; and "Protest Fee Plan for City Colleges," *New York Times*, 26 May 1932, 11.

32. On the academic achievements of CCNY's most outstanding alumni of that era, see CCNY Alumni Association, "City's Noble Laureates," accessed 19 January 2017, www.ccnyalumni.org.

33. Oshinsky, *Polio*, 96–97; Debbie Bookchin and Jim Schumacher, *The Virus and the Vaccine: The True Story of a Cancer-Causing Monkey Virus, Contaminated Polio Vaccine and the Millions of Americans Exposed* (New York: St. Martin's, 2004), 46. Salk had skipped several grades in elementary school, a common leap forward among New York's gifted public school youngsters, before gaining admission to Townsend Harris High School, essentially a publicly funded prep school. Every year, thousands applied for the two hundred coveted spots. If students survived pressures to succeed where four years of secondary training were crammed into three, they were virtually assured a seat at CCNY. Salk did just that.

34. Oshinsky, *Polio*, 98–104, 107.

35. L. Shands, "The Cheder on the Hill," *Menorah Journal*, March 1929, 269.

36. Steinberg, *Academic Melting Pot*, 9; Thomas Evans Coulton, *A City College in Action: Struggles and Achievements at Brooklyn College, 1930–1955* (New York: Harper, 1955), 8, 14; "Subway a 'Campus' for Many at Hunter," *New York Times* 2 October 1938, 54; R. Markowitz, *My Daughter, the Teacher*, 27. On Jewish male-to-female

proportions in colleges and universities, see McGill, "Some Characteristics of Jewish Youth," 256. See also, on young women sacrificing for their brothers' education, Wenger, *New York Jews*, 44.

37. Meyer Liben, "CCNY: A Memoir," in Rizzo and Wallenstein, *City at the Center*, 48; Sorin, *Irving Howe*, 17.

38. Dorman, *Arguing the World*, 44–46, 51–52; Liben, "CCNY," 48.

39. R. Markowitz, *My Daughter, the Teacher*, 52–54, 60–61.

40. Hal Draper, "The Student Movement in the Thirties," in *As We Saw the Thirties: Essays on Social and Political Movements of a Decade*, ed. Rita J. Simon (Urbana: University of Illinois Press, 1967), 182–188. See also, on the tuition crisis, R. Cohen, *When the Old Left Was Young*, 68–71, 211.

41. James Traub, *City on a Hill: Testing the American Dream at City College* (Reading, MA: Addison-Wesley, 1993), 39.

42. Although the application forms for admission into the program did not inquire about the student's religion, the majority possessed Jewish-sounding names and hailed from neighborhoods, when indicated, that were Jewish ones in the city. See, for these examples, a certificate, dated 17 September 1931, that lists twenty-eight senior ROTC cadets; nineteen possessed Jewish sounding names. These documents are on file at the Archives of the City College of New York (hereafter CCNY Archives).

43. Rudy, *College of the City of New York*, 404–419. See also "Expanded Historical Note on Department of Military Science (ROTC)," undated document, CCNY Archives. For an example of the group's publication, see the *Lavender Cadet*, November 1934, CCNY Archives; "Conclusions to Be Drawn," *Campus*, 25 February 1931, 2; "S.C. Charter Day Boycott Cuts Attendance to 1,000," *Campus*, 10 May 1935, 1; "Boycott Charter Day," *Campus*, 7 May 1935, 2; "Looking Backward," *Campus*, 31 May 1935, 2. See also untitled press release, dated 4 October 1939, describing the growth of ROTC at CCNY in the 1930s (CCNY Archives). On the athletes' support of ROTC and the administration, see Rudy, *College of the City of New York*, 419. See also, on CCNY's ROTC as the largest campus military group in the U.S., Irving Rosenthal, "Rumblings of Unrest and Empty Stomachs," in Rizzo and Wallenstein, *City at the Center*, 56. On athletes' support for a stance comparable to that of ROTC, see "5 More Suspended in City College Row," *New York Times*, 3 June 1933, 15; "186 Awards Made at City College," *New York Times*, 3 June 1933, 9; "Nation's Students 'Strike for Peace': Disorders Are Few," *New York Times*, 13 April 1935, 1–2.

44. Alfred Jospe, *Jewish Students and Student Services at American Universities* (Washington, DC: B'nai B'rith Hillel Foundation, 1963), 6, 7, 14.

45. Katznelson, "Between Separation and Disappearance," 193–195; Louis Weiser, "Memoir," American Jewish Committee Oral History Collection, New York Public Library. See also Leon Fink and Brian Greenberg, *Upheaval in the Quiet Zone: A History of Hospital Workers Union Local 1199* (Urbana: University of Illinois Press, 1989).

46. On the employment problems that Jews faced even with advanced degrees, see Wenger, *New York Jews*, 22–23.

47. Moore, *At Home in America*, 95–97; R. Markowitz, *My Daughter, the Teacher*, 75–92. See also David Hollinger, "Jewish Intellectuals and the De-Christianization of American Culture in the Twentieth Century," in *Science, Jews, and Secular Culture: Studies in Mid-Twentieth-Century American Intellectual History* (Princeton, NJ: Princeton University Press, 1998), 17–41.

48. Jonathan Freedman, *The Temple of Culture: Assimilation and Anti-Semitism in Literary Anglo-America* (New York: Oxford University Press, 1999), 158–175 (quotes on 167–168).

49. Ibid., 175.

50. Bell, "Three Faces of New York," 225.

51. Ibid., 224–227.

52. Vivian Gornick, "Commencement Address," in Rizzo and Wallenstein, *City at the Center*, 84–85; Trachtenberg, *Ralph Lauren*, 25–35.

53. Gaines and Churcher, *Obsession*, 13, 21, 35, 49, 65, 73–74, 178.

54. Kim Moody, *From Welfare State to Real Estate: Regime Change in New York City, 1974 to the Present* (New York: New Press, 2007), 2–8.

CHAPTER 8. MAKING NEW YORK JEWS

1. Moore, *Yankee Blues*, 137. The list included John Philip Sousa, Walter Damrosch, Leopold Godowsky Sr., Jascha Heifetz, Fritz Kreisler, John McCormack, Sergei Rachmaninoff, Leopold Stokowski, Moritz Rosenthal, Misha Elman, Igor Stravinsky, Victor Herbert, Ernest Bloch, and Willem Mengelberg.

2. Ibid., 71, quote on 137; en.wikipedia.org; accessed 8 February 2016.

3. Moore, *Yankee Blues*, 136–139 (quote on 137).

4. Ibid., 71.

5. Eli Lederhendler argues that New York Jewish culture and ethnicity depended "so strongly on the ethos of metropolitan 'New Yorkishness'" that it ultimately remained "hobbled" by that condition. He asks, why did "New York 'make' the Jews what they became, more than the reverse?" Lederhendler, *New York Jews*, 203.

6. Benjamin Pollak, "Plotting Gotham" (PhD diss., University of Michigan, 2014), 5, 16.

7. Alisa Braun, "Jews, Writing and the Dynamics of Literary Affiliation, 1880–1940" (PhD diss., University of Michigan, 2007), 20–67; Cahan, *Bleter fun mayn lebn*, 4:21–31; Sanford E. Marovitz, *Abraham Cahan* (New York: Twayne, 1996), 153–156. Many critics have asserted that the character of Levinsky is a thinly veiled stand-in for Cahan himself. But the character was actually the opposite of the author as he saw himself; while Levinsky was morally compromised and deficient in culture, Cahan devoted himself to the cause of social justice and cultural pursuits.

8. Sara B. Horowitz, "Yezierska, Anzia," in Hyman and Moore, *Jewish Women in America*, 2:1521–1522.

9. Carol Schoen, *Anzia Yezierska* (Boston: Twayne, 1982), 1–38 (quotes on 11).

10. Antler, *Journey Home*, 27–30; Alice Kessler-Harris, introduction to *Bread Givers*, by Anzia Yezierska (New York: Persea Books, 1975), v–xviii. See also Alan Robert Ginsberg, *The Salome Ensemble: Rose Pastor Stokes, Anzia Yezierska, Sonya Levien, and Jetta Goudal* (Syracuse, NY: Syracuse University Press, 2016).

11. For a good sense of scholarship on Roth, see Hana Wirth-Nesher, ed., *New Essays on "Call It Sleep"* (Cambridge: Cambridge University Press, 1996).

12. Anita Norich, "Paley, Grace," in Hyman and Moore, *Jewish Women in America*, 2:1028; Grace Paley, "The Loudest Voice," in *Collected Stories* (1959; repr., New York: Farrar, Straus and Giroux, 1994), 34–40 (quote on 34).

13. Paley, "Loudest Voice," 36; Elliot Cohen, "Jewish Culture in America: Some Speculations by an Editor," *Commentary* 3 (May 1947): 413, 415, quoted in Daniel Greene, "'Israel! What a Wonderful People!': Elliot Cohen's Critique of Modern American Jewry, 1924–1927," *AJAJ* 55, no. 1 (2003): 26–27 (see also 11–31).

14. Andrea Pappas, "The Picture at the *Menorah Journal*: Making 'Jewish Art,'" *American Jewish History* 90, no. 3 (2002): 205–238 (quotes on 217–218).

15. Norman L. Kleeblatt and Susan Chevlowe, eds., *Painting a Place in America: Jewish Artists in New York, 1900–1945*, exhibition catalogue (New York: Jewish Museum, 1991), 100.

16. Baigell, "From Hester Street to Fifty-Seventh Street," 32; Kleeblatt and Chevlowe, *Painting a Place*, 92–93; Milton Brown, *American Painting from the Armory Show to the Depression* (Princeton, NJ: Princeton University Press, 1955), 39–44, 137–138 (quote on 42).

17. Susan Laxton, "Stettheimer, Florine," in Hyman and Moore, *Jewish Women in America*, 2:1340–1341.

18. Kleeblatt and Chevlowe, *Painting a Place*, 94–95, 98.

19. Ibid., 105–114; Paul Avrich, *The Modern School Movement: Anarchism and Education in the United States* (Princeton, NJ: Princeton University Press, 1980), 145–153.

20. Baigell, "From Hester Street," 32; Kleeblatt and Chevlowe, *Painting a Place*, 99–100; Bellow, *Educational Alliance*, 123.

21. Quotes from "Concord," Metropolitan Museum of Art, accessed 21 February 2016, www.metmuseum.org.

22. "Mark Rothko," *Wikipedia*, accessed 21 February 2016, http://en.wikipedia.org.

23. Anne Wilkes Tucker has worked for many years to rehabilitate the New York Photo League. See Anne Wilkes Tucker, "The Photo League: A Center for Documentary Photography," in *This Was the Photo League: Compassion and the Camera from the Depression to the Cold War* (Chicago: Stephen Daiter Gallery and John Cleary Gallery, 2001), 9–20; quote from Anne Tucker, "The Photo League," *Creative Camera* 223–224 (July–August 1983): 1013; quote from Lili Corbus Bezner, *Photography and Politics in America: From the New Deal into the Cold War* (Baltimore: Johns Hopkins University Press, 1999), 24.

24. Morris Engel, quoted in Anne Tucker, "A History of the Photo League," *History of Photography* 18, no. 2 (1994): 175; W. Eugene Smith, interviewed by Beverly Bethune, 1975, quoted in Tucker, "Photo League," 1017.

25. Jane Livingston, *The New York School Photographs, 1936–1963* (New York: Stewart, Tabori, and Chang, 1992). Walter Rosenblum taught at Brooklyn College, Jerome Liebling at the University of Minnesota and then Hampshire College, Aaron Siskin at the Illinois Institute of Design and then the Rhode Island School of Design.

26. Singer, "Manhattan Nickelodeons," 5; Thissen, "Film and Vaudeville," 45; Heinze, *Adapting to Abundance*, 119, 204; Thissen, "Jewish Immigrant Audiences," 18–19; Peiss, *Cheap Amusements*, 149.

27. May, *Screening Out the Past*, 148 (quote), 174–175.

28. Heinze, *Adapting to Abundance*, 208–218; Neal Gabler, *An Empire of Their Own: How the Jews Invented Hollywood* (New York: Crown, 1988), 65–66; Matthew Bernstein, "Zukor, Adolph," in *American National Biography Online*, accessed 8 January 2016, www.anb.org.

29. Charles Musser (with David James), "Filmmaking," in Jackson, *Encyclopedia of New York City*, 404–405; Ann Douglas, *Terrible Honesty: Mongrel Manhattan in the 1920s* (New York: Farrar, Straus, and Giroux, 1995), 61; James Sanders, *Celluloid Skyline: New York and the Movies* (New York: Knopf, 2001).

30. Anita Norich, "From Lublin to New York: The Journal of Rivke Zilberg," *Frankel Institute Annual*, 2014, 18–20.

31. Anita Norich, "Singer, Israel Joshua," in *YIVO Encyclopedia of Jews in Eastern Europe Online*, accessed 16 February 2016, www.yivoencyclopedia.org. See also Anita Norich, *Discovering Exile: Yiddish and Jewish American Culture during the Holocaust* (Stanford, CA: Stanford University Press, 2007).

32. Howe, *World of Our Fathers*, 485–492; Doroshkin, *Yiddish in America*, 218; Whitfield, *In Search of American Jewish Culture*, 30.

33. Moore, *Yankee Blues*, 150; Joseph Horowitz, *Classical Music in America: A History of Its Rise and Fall* (New York: Norton, 2005), 423; Whitfield, *In Search of American Jewish Culture*, 61. On obscenity, see Josh Lambert, *Unclean Lips: Obscenity, Jews, and American Culture* (New York: NYU Press, 2013).

34. Most, *Making Americans*, 28; Jasen, *Tin Pan Alley*, xxii.

35. Jasen, *Tin Pan Alley*, 78–79; Kenneth Aaron Kanter, *The Jews on Tin Pan Alley: The Jewish Contribution to American Popular Music, 1830–1940* (New York: Ktav, 1982), 54–55, 58, 60, 113, 117, 142–143.

36. M. Alexander, *Jazz Age Jews*, 158–163; Whitfield, *In Search of American Jewish Culture*, 95–99; Douglas, *Terrible Honesty*, 355–359.

37. Stempel, *Showtime*, 192–194, 250–255; Douglas, *Terrible Honesty*, 102–103; Whitfield, *In Search of American Jewish Culture*, 69–71, 74–77, 155–157.

38. Moore, *Yankee Blues*, 139–141.

39. Bernstein and Haws, *Leonard Bernstein*, 1–11(quote on 5). One local newspaper wag reporting on Bernstein's surprise first appearance depicted it in competitive-

sports terms as "a shoestring catch in center field, . . . make it and you're a hero, muff it you're a dope. . . . He made it" (4).

40. Tim Page, "Leonard Bernstein and Television: Envisioning a Higher Purpose," in Bernstein and Haws, *Leonard Bernstein*, 88–91; Burton Bernstein, "A Brother's Recollection: The Maestro's New Medium," ibid., 92–97; Myers, *Leonard Bernstein*, 39–40.

41. Myers, *Leonard Bernstein*, 44. See also Lewis Nichols, "The Play," *New York Times*, 29 December 1944, 11.

42. Weegee, *Naked City* (1945; repr., New York: DaCapo, 2002); *Naked City*, Criterion Collection, DVD with commentary; Luc Sante, "The *Naked City*: New York Plays Itself," essay posted 19 March 2007, www.criterion.com. See also Anthony W. Lee and Richard Meyer, *Weegee and "Naked City"* (Berkeley: University of California Press, 2008).

43. Arthur Laurents, *Original Story By: A Memoir of Broadway and Hollywood* (New York: Applause Theatre and Cinema Books, 2001), 329–340; Irene G. Dash, *Shakespeare and the American Musical* (Bloomington: Indiana University Press, 2010), 80–82, 85–87 (quote on 86); Bernstein and Haws, *Leonard Bernstein*, 6–7.

44. Bernard Postal, "New York's Jewish Fare," *Congress Bi-Weekly*, 12 October 1964, 9.

45. Myron Kandel, "Tale of a Modern Dybbuk," *New York Times*, 1 November 1959, X3; Dan Sullivan, "Theater: 'The Tenth Man' Is Revived," *New York Times*, 9 November 1967, 54; John S. Radosta, "After 39 Years—a Hit," *New York Times*, 18 September 1960, X5; "London Critics Split on 'The Tenth Man,'" *New York Times*, 14 April 1961, 23.

46. Jeffrey Shandler, "Berg, Gertrude," in Hyman and Moore, *Jewish Women in America*, 1:139–141.

47. Zurawik, *Jews of Prime Time*, 17–28; Myrna Hant, "Molly Goldberg: A 1950s Icon," *Women in Judaism* 5, no. 2 (2008), http://wjudaism.library.utoronto.ca. See also Pearl and Pearl, *Chosen Image*.

48. Jeffrey Shandler, "Gertrude Berg," Jewish Women's Archive, accessed 25 August 2015, http://jwa.org.

CHAPTER 9. WARS ON THE HOME FRONT

1. On revamping of Jewish organizations, see Stuart Svonkin, *Jews against Prejudice: American Jews and the Fight for Civil Liberties* (New York: Columbia University Press, 1997).

2. "Anti-Nazis Hold Demonstration," *New York World Telegram and Sun*, quoted in *From Haven to Home*, www.loc.gov; for estimates of the size of rallies, see *American Jewish Year Book* 39 (1937–1938): 216–217. On public protest, see also Lookstein, *Were We Our Brothers' Keepers?*, 55, 83, 98. On the anti-Nazi boycott movement, see Moshe Gottlieb, "The Anti-Nazi Boycott Movement in the United States: An Ideological and Sociological Appreciation," *Jewish Social Studies* 35, nos. 3–4 (1973): 196–227.

3. "20,000 Jam Garden in Reich Protest," *New York Times*, 22 November 1938, 6.

4. For a history of the American Jewish Committee, see N. Cohen, *Not Free to Desist*; for the American Jewish Congress, see Urofsky, *Voice That Spoke for Justice*.

5. The geographical location of these New York–based national Jewish organizations and other institutions noted in this chapter was derived from the annual directory "Jewish National Organizations in the United States," published in the *American Jewish Year Book*. See, for example, the listing for 1941–1942 that appeared in volume 43, 521–602, and volume 47 (1945–1946), 560–610. For a history of the Joint Distribution Committee, see Yehuda Bauer, *My Brother's Keeper: A History of the American Jewish Joint Distribution Committee, 1929–1939* (Philadelphia: Jewish Publication Society of America, 1974). For a history of the United Jewish Appeal, see Marc Lee Raphael, *A History of the United Jewish Appeal, 1939–1982* (Providence, RI: Scholars, 1982).

6. On the mission and ideology of the Histadrut—especially its American context—see Raider, *Emergence of American Zionism*, xvi, 1, 25. On the mission and approaches of the Revisionist Zionists in America, see Medoff, *Militant Zionism in America*, 73–148. On the battles between Wise's Congress and the Revisionists, see David S. Wyman, *The Abandonment of the Jews: America and the Holocaust* (New York: Pantheon, 1984), 87, 90–92.

7. On the location of Lugee's, see its ad in *Jewish Life*, October 1946, 97.

8. On the proximity of these two groups and the mission of the Mizrachi, see *American Jewish Year Book* 43 (1941–1942): 558, 569.

9. For a flavor of communism among New York Jews, see Vivian Gornick, *The Romance of American Communism* (New York: Basic Books, 1978); on the Jewish Labor Committee, see the online exhibit, accessed January 21, 2017, http://www.nyu.edu.

10. On David Sarnoff and William Paley, see *American National Biography Online*, accessed 16 February 2016, www.anb.orgv.

11. For basic information on the names and number of media outlets in the city, see Mary Ellen Zuckerman, "Magazines," in Jackson, *Encyclopedia of New York City*, 714; Erica Judge, "Newspapers," ibid., 815–820. See also Aviva Ben-Ur, "In Search of the Ladino Press: A Bibliographic Survey," *Studies in Bibliography and Booklore* (Winter 2001): 10–52.

12. Lookstein, *Were We Our Brothers' Keepers?*, 55, 83, 98.

13. Penkower, "In Dramatic Dissent." See also Robert Skloot, "'We Will Never Die': The Success and Failure of a Holocaust Pageant," *Theatre Journal* 37, no. 2 (1985): 167–180.

14. "22,000 Nazis Hold Rally in Garden: Police Check Foes," *New York Times*, 21 February 1939, 1.

15. Melvin I. Urofsky, *American Zionism from Herzl to the Holocaust* (Garden City, NY: Doubleday, 1975), 399–400. See also Aaron Berman, *Nazism, Jews and American Zionism, 1933–1948* (Detroit: Wayne State University Press, 1990).

16. N. Cohen, *American Jews and the Zionist Idea*, 60–62, 87; Samuel Halperin, *The Political World of American Zionism* (Detroit: Wayne State University Press, 1961), 222–233, 236–237.

17. Zuroff, *Response of Orthodox Jewry*, 134.

18. Rafael Medoff, "'Retribution Is Not Enough': The 1943 Campaign by Jewish Students to Raise American Public Awareness of the Nazi Genocide," *Holocaust and Genocide Studies* 11, no. 2 (1997): 172, 174, 178–181.

19. Krasner, *Benderly Boys*, 360–367.

20. Haskell Lookstein, "May 1943: The Prayer Service That Almost Wasn't," email version of 1943 sermon delivered 18 April 2009 to Jeffrey Gurock.

21. "Adolf Hitler Was Once Teacher Here," *Commentator*, 26 February 1942, 1; "Concrete Action to Be Done by Every Type of Reader" and "Yeshiva Students Are Not Blameless," *Commentator*, 4 March 1943, 6.

22. Marsha L. Rozenblit, "The Seminary during the Holocaust Years," in *Tradition Renewed: A History of the Jewish Theological Seminary of America*, vol. 2, ed. Jack Wertheimer (New York: Jewish Theological Seminary of America, 1997), 289, 304.

23. Leff, "When the Facts Didn't Speak for Themselves"; Leff, "Tragic 'Fight in the Family,'" 3–4. See also Laurel Leff, *Buried by the Times: The Holocaust and America's Most Important Newspaper* (New York: Cambridge University Press, 2005).

24. Grobman, "What Did They Know?" See also Deborah Lipstadt, *Beyond Belief: The American Press and the Coming of the Holocaust, 1933–1945* (New York: Free Press, 1985).

25. Lookstein, "May 1943"; Krasner, *Benderly Boys*, 360–367.

26. Moore, *GI Jews*, 30–31, 39–40.

27. Ibid., 42–43; Alexander, "Irving Howe and the Holocaust," 101–102.

28. On the debate over the origins of the ditty, see Bee Wilson, "Bee Wilson Suggests Sending Salami Missiles to Iraq," *New Statesman*, 10 January 2003, www.newstatesman.com; and "Send a Salami to Your Boy in the Army," *The Big Apple* (blog), 14 October 2004, www.barrypopik.com; see also Merwin, *Pastrami on Rye*, 91–93. On soldiers coping with ham, see Moore, *GI Jews*, 49–85.

29. Landesman, *Brownsville*, 321; *Home News* (Bronx), 13 April 1943, 3; 18 April 1943, 11; M. Sanua, "From the Pages," 295–297, 327; *Commentator*, 4 February 1943, 1; 18 November 1943, 1; 16 December 1943, 1; 8 March 1945, 1.

30. *Home News* (Bronx), 4 April 1943, 8; 19 April 1943, 3; 26 April 1943, 1.

31. Stella Sardell, introduction to *Community Memories: The Syrian Jews of Brooklyn during World War II* (Brooklyn: Sephardic Community Center, 1984), 2, cited in M. Sanua, "From the Pages," 287. For an example of the "Roll of Honor," see *Victory Bulletin*, July 1942, 3; November 1942, 3, 5. All references to the newsletter are derived from Sephardic Archives, *The Victory Bulletin, July 1942–September 1945: Wartime Newspaper of the Syrian Jewish Community in Brooklyn* (Brooklyn, NY: Sephardic Archives, c. 1984).

32. *Victory Bulletin*, September 1942, 2; March 1943, 2; April 1944, 2; December 1944, 2; September 1945, 2, 10.

33. Stephen S. Wise, "The Victorious Leader: A Tribute to Franklin Delano Roosevelt," *Congress Weekly*, 20 April 1945, 7–8.

34. Moore, *At Home in America*, 202–227.

35. Fuchs, *Political Behavior of American Jews*, 129–130, 152–153; Feingold, *Time for Searching*, 212–217; Howe, *World of Our Fathers*, 391.
36. *Kehilath Jeshurun Bulletin*, 16 March 1945, 1; 16 April 1945, 1, Kehilath Jeshurun Archives, New York.
37. *Kehilath Jeshurun Bulletin*, 7 January 1944, 1; 14 January 1944, 3; 25 February 1944, 1; 12 January 1945, 1; 16 February 1945, 1; Max J. Etra, "Seven and Seventy," *Congregation Kehilath Jeshurun Dance Journal*, 1941, Kehilath Jeshurun Archives, New York; "Rabbinate Proclaims Fast Days for Jews," *Hamigdal*, February 1945, 9. Thanks to Rafael Medoff for sharing this latter source.
38. Sylvia and Jack Goldberg, interview with Jeffrey S. Gurock, 13 February 2009. (Tape of the interview in the possession of Gurock.)
39. Ibid.
40. Samuel Lubell, *The Future of American Politics*, 3rd ed. (New York: Doubleday Anchor, 1965), 206–208.
41. Moore, "Reconsidering the Rosenbergs," 21–37 (quote on 33).
42. Ibid., 33.
43. Ronald Radosh, quoted in ibid., 28. See also Ronald Radosh and Joyce Milton, *The Rosenberg File: A Search for the Truth* (New York: Holt, 1983).
44. There is extensive scholarship on the "New York Intellectuals." See, for example, Cooney, *Rise of the New York Intellectuals*; Wald, *New York Intellectuals*; Bloom, *Prodigal Sons*; Neil Jumonville, *Critical Crossings: The New York Intellectuals in Postwar America* (Berkeley: University of California Press, 1990).
45. Howe, *Margin of Hope*, 137; Cooney, *Rise of the New York Intellectuals*, 43, 50, discussed in Abrams, "Profoundly Hegemonic Moment"; Pierre Birnbaum, *Geography of Hope: Exile, the Enlightenment, Disassimilation*, trans. Charlotte Mandell (Stanford, CA: Stanford University Press, 2008), 3–4.
46. Joel Carmichael in *Midstream*, quoted in Deborah Dash Moore, *To the Golden Cities: Pursuing the American Jewish Dream in Miami and L.A.* (New York: Free Press, 1994), 249. See also Arthur A. Goren, "Spiritual Zionists and Jewish Sovereignty," in *Politics and Public Culture*, 155–164.
47. Raphael, *History of the United Jewish Appeal*; N. Jackson, *Converging Movements*, 171–206; Emily Alice Katz, *Bringing Zion Home: Israel in American Jewish Culture, 1948–1967* (Albany: State University of New York Press, 2015); Berkman, "Transforming Philanthropy," 170–171.
48. Recent scholarship on the Soviet Jewry movement includes Feingold, *"Silent No More"*; Lazin, *Struggle for Soviet Jewry*; Gal Beckerman, *When They Come for Us, We'll Be Gone: The Epic Struggle to Save Soviet Jewry* (New York: Houghton Mifflin Harcourt, 2010).
49. Feingold, *"Silent No More,"* 51–54, 57, 291.
50. Paul S. Appelbaum, "The Soviet Jewry Movement in the United States," in *Jewish American Voluntary Associations*, ed. Michael Dobkowski (Westport, CT: Greenwood, 1986), 617, 619; Orbach, *American Movement*, 27–28.
51. Lederhendler, *New York Jews*, 116–120, 188.

52. Orbach, *American Movement*, 8–9; Feingold, *"Silent No More,"* 80–86; Appelbaum, "Soviet Jewry Movement," 624. On the Jewish Defense League's critique of the Student Struggle, see Walter Ruby, "The Role of Non-violent Groups," in *A Second Exodus: The American Movement to Free Soviet Jews,* ed. Murray Friedman and Albert D. Chernin (Hanover, NH: Brandeis University Press, 1999), 207.

53. Appelbaum, "Soviet Jewry Movement," 625; Feingold, *"Silent No More,"* 93; Orbach, *American Movement*, 65–67.

54. Ruby, "Role of Non-violent Groups," 209.

55. Appelbaum, "Soviet Jewry Movement," 620. On the JDL, see also Janet Dolgin, *Jewish Identity and the JDL* (Princeton, NJ: Princeton University Press, 1977).

56. Feingold, *"Silent No More,"* 117, 122, 133, 143, 148, 188.

CHAPTER 10. OLD TURF, NEW TURF

1. "Emmanuel Celler," Jewish Virtual Library, accessed 21 October 2015, www.jewish virtuallibrary.org.

2. Maurice Carroll, "Emmanuel Celler, Former Brooklyn Congressman, Dies at 92," *New York Times*, 16 January 1981.

3. Jerry Kammer, "The Hart-Celler Immigration Act of 1965," Center for Immigration Studies, accessed September 2015, http://cis.org; New York City Department of City Planning, *The Newest New Yorkers: Characteristics of the City's Foreign-Born Population* (New York: City of New York, 2013), 4 (quote).

4. "Demographics of New York City," *Wikipedia*, accessed 9 February 2016, http://en.wikipedia.org; Derek Kravitz, "New York City Area's Jewish Population Rises," *Wall Street Journal*, 1 October 2013, www.wsj.com; United Jewish Appeal–Federation of Jewish Philanthropies of New York (UJA-Federation), *Jewish Community Study of New York: 2011* (New York: UJA-Federation, 2013), 47.

5. Glazer, "National Influence," 172–174.

6. Freeman, *Working-Class New York*, 271, 273; Thomas Bailey and Roger Waldinger, "The Changing Ethnic/Racial Division of Labor," in *Dual City: Restructuring New York*, ed. John Hull Mollenkopf and Manuel Castells (New York: Russell Sage Foundation, 1991), 47, 55; Samuel Kaplan, "The Bronx Arrangement," *New York Magazine*, 14 December 1970, 10; Joel Schwartz, *The New York Approach: Robert Moses, Urban Liberals, and the Redevelopment of the Inner City* (Columbus: Ohio State University Press, 1993), xv (quote); Philip Siekman, "The Rent Control Trap," *Fortune*, February 1960, 123.

7. Hillary Ballon, "Robert Moses and Urban Renewal: The Title I Program," in Ballon and Jackson, *Robert Moses and the Modern City*, 94–116, esp. 106–107.

8. Horowitz and Kaplan, *Estimated Jewish Population*, 197.

9. Caro, *Power Broker*, 850–894; Kenneth T. Jackson, *Crabgrass Frontier: The Suburbanization of the United States* (New York: Oxford University Press, 1985), 231–241; Horowitz and Kaplan, *Estimated Jewish Population*, 17; Robert E. Meyer, "How Government Helped Ruin the South Bronx," *Fortune*, November 1975, 143 (quote); Matthew P. Drennan, "The Decline and Rise of the New York Economy," in *Dual*

City: Restructuring New York, ed. John Hull Mollenkopf and Manuel Castells (New York: Russell Sage Foundation, 1991), 29–43.

10. Pritchett, *Brownsville, Brooklyn*, 5–6, 47–48, 97–100, 114–121, 162.

11. Freeman, *Working-Class New York*, 107, 117–118; Zeitz, *White Ethnic New York*, 150–151.

12. Freeman, *Working-Class New York*, 183–184; Pritchett, *Brownsville, Brooklyn*, 139–145; Sorin, *Nurturing Neighborhood*, 165; Ford, *Girls*, 4, 90–91, 94–96, 104. See also Ford, "Nice Jewish Girls," 133; Wendell Pritchett, "From One Ghetto to Another: Blacks, Jews and Public Housing in Brownsville, Brooklyn, 1945–1970" (PhD diss., University of Pennsylvania, 1997), 194 (quote).

13. Naison, "Crown Heights in the 1950s," 145.

14. Pritchett, *Brownsville, Brooklyn*, 149; J. Mintz, *Hasidic People*, 141, 143; Wishnoff, "Tolerance Point," 177; Lederhendler, *New York Jews*, 165.

15. Shapiro, *Crown Heights*, 72–77.

16. Lederhendler, *New York Jews*, 127–128; Joseph P. Fried, "City Charges Bias at Three Projects," *New York Times*, 28 May 1968, 27; "Changes in Parkchester Bring a Fear Oasis May Go," *New York Times*, 29 December 1968, 56.

17. Jeffrey S. Gurock, *Jews in Gotham: New York Jews in a Changing City, 1920–2010* (New York: NYU Press, 2012), 134–135.

18. Paul L. Montgomery and Francis X. Clines, "Thousands Riot in Harlem Area; Scores Hurt," *New York Times*, 19 July 1964, 1; Junius Griffin, "Harlem Businessmen Put Riot Losses at $50,000," *New York Times*, 21 July 1964, 22; "Store Ransacked in Riot Sues City," *New York Times*, 25 July 1964, 8; "The Root of the Trouble," *New York Times*, 23 July 1964, 26; Layhmond Robinson, "Negroes View of Plight Examined in Survey Here," *New York Times*, 27 July 1964, 1; Fred Powerledge, "Negro Riots Reflect Deep-Seated Grievances," *New York Times*, 2 August 1964, 133; Berson, *Negroes and the Jews*, 338–340. Interestingly, historical works that document the evolution of tensions between blacks and Jews also have not found explicit anti-Semitism in the 1964 riots. See, as an example, Murray Friedman, *What Went Wrong? The Creation and Collapse of the Black-Jewish Alliance* (New York: Free Press, 1995), which notes that "the degree of anti-Semitism involved was not at all clear" (214). Many other works do not mention the 1964 outbreak at all. Jewish Telegraphic Agency, *Daily News Bulletin*, 23 July 1964, 1; *Jewish Press*, 3 July 1964, 1; 10 July 1964, 1; 31 July 1964, 1.

19. Sam Welles, "The Jewish Elan," *Fortune*, February 1960, 160.

20. Podair, *Strike That Changed New York*, 38, 72, 77–78.

21. Ibid., 72–78; Cheryl Lynn Greenberg, *Troubling the Waters: Black-Jewish Relations in the American Century* (Princeton, NJ: Princeton University Press, 2006), 230.

22. J. Kaufman, *Broken Alliance*, 142–43 (quote), 148–149; Greenberg, *Troubling the Waters*, 230; Friedman, *What Went Wrong?*, 260; Podair, *Strike That Changed New York*, 2; Zeitz, *White Ethnic New York*, 161–163.

23. On the chronology of the three-stage strike and the text of the unsigned letter, see Podair, *Strike That Changed New York*, 115–124. On the text of the WBAI poem, see Weisbord and Stein, *Bittersweet Encounter*, 175–178. Ironically, the radio show

on WBAI was hosted by Julius Lester, an African American who later converted to Judaism and became a professor of Jewish studies. See also Richard Kahlenberg, *Tough Liberal: Albert Shanker and the Battle over Schools, Unions, Race, and Democracy* (New York: Columbia University Press, 2007).

24. On the connection between local black problems with Jews and the international scene, see Zeitz, *White Ethnic New York*, 64–66. On the relationship between the 1967 Israeli victory and New York Jewish assertiveness, see Freeman, *Working-Class New York*, 223–234 (quote on 224); on public opinion polls of black attitudes, see Freeman, *Working-Class New York*, 165–166.

25. On the history of the Teachers Union and its relationship with the United Federation of Teachers, see Zitron, *New York City Teachers Union*, 45–52; and Podair, *Strike That Changed New York*, 142. See also Ralph Blumenthal, "When Suspicion of Teachers Ran Unchecked in New York," *New York Times*, 16 June 2009, 15–16; Clarence Taylor, *Reds at the Blackboard: Communism, Civil Rights, and the New York City Teachers Union* (New York: Columbia University Press, 2011).

26. Freeman, *Working-Class New York*, 221.

27. For the opinions of a replacement teacher and his comparisons of his colleagues with the older teachers, see a personal account of life in a Brooklyn school: Charles S. Isaacs, "A J.H.S. 271 Teacher Tells It Like He Sees It," *New York Times Magazine*, November 24, 1968. On the return of Jewish teachers to their old neighborhood to teach minority youngsters, see Zeitz, *White Ethnic New York*, 167. For a sense among some older women teachers of not being appreciated for their efforts, see R. Markowitz, *My Daughter, the Teacher*, 171.

28. Greenberg, *Troubling the Waters*, 231 (quote); Friedman, *What Went Wrong?*, 261; Weisbord and Stein, *Bittersweet Encounter*, 165, 177–178.

29. On the founding of Kahane's Jewish Defense League, its connection to the teachers' strike, and its early activities during the time of these difficulties, see J. Kaufman, *Broken Alliance*, 157–158; Weisbord and Stein, *Bittersweet Encounter*, 201–204; Lederhendler, *New York Jews*, 192–194.

30. Tom Wolfe, "Radical Chic: That Party at Lenny's," *New York*, 8 June 1970, 53.

31. Greenberg, *Troubling the Waters*, 231; Rieder, *Canarsie*, 73 (quote), discussed in Podair, *Strike That Changed New York*, 144. The Anti-Defamation League, which before the strike had proclaimed that there was no "organized anti-Semitism in New York" and that blacks generally were less anti-Jewish than whites were, now noted that "raw undisguised anti-Semitism . . . is at a crisis level in New York City schools where, unchecked by public authorities, it has been building for more than two years." *New York Times*, 23 January 1969, 1.

32. Harris and Swanson, *Black-Jewish Relations*, 18–22, 30, 77, 105–106, 129.

33. Ibid., 19–20, 36–37, 60–61, 105–106.

34. Ibid., 18, 61, 93, 105, 129.

35. Ibid., 93.

36. Zeitz, *White Ethnic New York*, 174–176; McNickle, *To Be Mayor*, 205–208; Brecher and Horton, *Power Failure*, 83–86; Peter Khiss, "How Voter Swings Elected Lindsay," *New York Times*, 4 November 1965, 1, 50.

37. Brecher and Horton, *Power Failure*, 86–91; Glazer and Moynihan, *Beyond the Melting Pot*, xxvii.

38. Zeitz, *White Ethnic New York*, 176–187; Peter Khiss, "Poor and Rich, Not Middle-Class the Key to Lindsay Re-election," *New York Times*, 6 November 1969, 37.

39. Zeitz, *White Ethnic New York*, 190–192; Wishnoff, "Tolerance Point," 137–143, 181, 184, 188, 225.

40. Text of Bokser's remarks, from his papers at the Jewish Theological Seminary, are quoted in Wishnoff, "Tolerance Point," 190.

41. Murray Schumach, "Angry Crowd in Forest Hills Protests Housing," *New York Times*, 19 November 1971, 1; "A Silent Minority Supports Forest Hills Housing," *New York Times*, 23 November 1971, 36; Murray Schumach, "The Anguish of Forest Hills," *New York Times*, 28 November 1971, 1; "Forest Hills Project Protest Continues," *New York Times*, 29 November 1971, 52. Quotes from Wishnoff, "Tolerance Point," 231–232, quoting articles in *New York Times*, 25 November 1971; and *New York Times*, 21 November 1971.

42. Zeitz, *White Ethnic New York*, 191–193 (quotes on 193); Rieder, *Canarsie*, 16, 20, 22, 65, 69–71, 80, 110–111, 128, 129, 172, 184, 193–198, 207–214.

43. For a full discussion, see Shapiro, *Crown Heights*.

44. Goldschmidt, *Race and Religion*, 75.

45. Caro, *Power Broker*, 854.

46. UJA-Federation, *Jewish Community Study of New York: 2011*, 19–20, 39–40.

47. Freeman, *Working-Class New York*, 257–270. See also Peter Blake, "How to Solve the Housing Crisis (and Everything Else)," *New York*, 1 January 1970, 56; Wechsler, *Qualified Student*, chap. 11.

48. On the 1971 law and its implications, see Rosenblum, *Boulevard of Dreams*, 181; On "red-lining," see Freeman, *Working-Class New York*, 275.

49. Freeman, *Working-Class New York*, 274–275.

50. Kaplan, "Bronx Arrangement," 10; R. Meyer, "How Government Helped," 145; Rosenblum, *Boulevard of Dreams*, 181–183, 189, 203–05, Freeman, *Working-Class New York*, 281.

51. Massarik, "Basic Characteristics," 239, 242; Cohen and Ritterband, "Social Characteristics," 129, 140; Binder and Reimers, *All the Nations under Heaven*, 240–242. See also Eleanor Blau, "Population Shift Beset Jewish Community Here," *New York Times*, 21 August 1975, 73; and James Feron, "Tremont Temple Quits the Bronx," *New York Times*, 18 December 1976, 27; New School for Social Research, Center for New York City Affairs, *New York's Jewish Poor and Jewish Working Class: Economic Status and Social Needs*, typescript (New York, 1972), 10; Berl Steinberg, phone interview with Jeffrey Gurock, 11 November 2008 (notes in Gurock's possession); Edward C. Burks, "Middle Class Still Leaving City," *New York Times*, 29 May 1973, 22.

52. Allan M. Siegal, "Rent Is Primary Issue for Co-op City," *New York Times*, 6 September 1974, 73; James F. Clarity, "Co-op City, Home to 40,000, Is Given Tempered Praise," *New York Times*, 27 May 1971, 41; Rita Reif, "Some Subsidized Co-ops Far from Pioneers' Ideal," *New York Times*, 25 January 1976, 2, 6; Allegra

and Gary Gordon, interview with Jeffrey Gurock, 27 August 2009 (tape recording in Gurock's possession).

53. Murray Schumach, "Co-op City: A Symptom of Mitchell-Lama Ills," *New York Times*, 18 June 1975, 86; Samuel G. Freedman, "Co-op City: A Refuge in Transition," *New York Times*, 25 June 1986, B1; Don Terry, "Co-op City: A Haven Marred as Drugs Slip In," *New York Times*, 10 August 1989, B1; Sydney Schwartz, "Maintaining the Minyan: The Struggle of a Storefront Synagogue" (MA essay, Columbia University School of Journalism, 2005), 8, 9, 23; Robert E. Thompson, "As Change Intrudes, the Concourse Sells," *New York Times*, 13 August 1972, R1; Kaplan, "Bronx Arrangement," 10; Jack Luria, "A Pox on You, Riverdale," *New York Times*, 21 June 1972, 43.

54. Schumach, "Co-op City," 43, 53; Reif, "Some Subsidized Co-ops," 2; Joseph P. Fried, "Compromise Ends Co-op Strike," *New York Times*, 30 June 1976, B1; Francis X. Clines, "Grass Roots in Concrete," *New York Times*, 2 October 1976, S23; Leslie Maitland, "Co-op City: Paradise or Paradise Lost?," *New York Times*, 8 January 1979, B4. See also Freeman, *Working-Class New York*, 122.

55. UJA-Federation, *Greater New York Population Study*, 29.

56. Gurock, "Late Friday Night," 149.

57. UJA-Federation, *New York Jewish Population Study*, 69, 77, 87. See also Ansche Chesed, "History," accessed 22 February 2016, www.anschechesed.org; UJA-Federation, *1991 New York Jewish Population Study*, xviii.

58. Shokeid, *Gay Synagogue*, 81 (quote); Congregation Beit Simcha Torah, "Our History," accessed 22 February 2016, https://cbst.org.

59. Shokeid, *Gay Synagogue*, 16, 48, 63–64, 79, 81; Jewish Women's Archive, "The Feminist Revolution," accessed 21 October 2015, https://jwa.org.

60. On the numbers and status of the Jewish poor elderly from 1981 to 1991, see UJA-Federation, *Greater New York Population Study*, 10, 36, 37, 40; and UJA-Federation, *New York Jewish Population Study*, 1, 9, 10. On the numbers of elderly assisted and the greater concern with the problems of those who are poor, see UJA-Federation, *1991 New York Jewish Population Study*, xvi, 116–117.

61. Kugelmass, *Miracle of Intervale Avenue*, 221–224, 234–235, 262 (quote on 234).

62. Sue Fishkoff, *The Rebbe's Army: Inside the World of Chabad-Lubavitch* (New York: Schocken, 2010), 11–12; Heilman and Friedman, *Rebbe*, 170.

63. Rafael Medoff, "Esther Jungreis," Jewish Women's Archive, accessed 21 October 2015, http://jwa.org.

64. Carey Winfrey, "In Search of Bella Abzug," *New York Times*, 21 August 1977, 55, 60–61. See also Alan H. Levy, *The Political Life of Bella Abzug, 1920–1976: Political Passions, Women's Rights, and Congressional Battles* (Lanham, MD: Lexington Books, 2013).

65. Swerdlow, *Women Strike for Peace*, 4, 54, 146; Antler, *Journey Home*, 271–274.

66. Winfrey, "In Search of Bella Abzug," 60–61; Orleck, *Common Sense*, 87–91.

67. On the differing visions of Friedan's road to feminism and her life after the publication of her book, see Horowitz, *Betty Friedan*, 2–5, 224–227. See also Friedan's memoir, *Life So Far* (New York: Simon and Schuster, 2000), 131–141, 143–147.

68. See Gloria Steinem, *My Life on the Road* (New York: Random House, 2015), for her account of her political and intellectual feminism.

69. Letty Cottin Pogrebin, "Steinem, Gloria," in Hyman and Moore, *Jewish Women in America*, 2:1319 (quote). Biographers of Steinem differ over the extent of her Jewishness beyond her identification because of anti-Semitism. Letty Cottin Pogrebin has accorded Steinem the designation of Jew on the basis less of her father's background and more of her sense of self, "as an outsider," who "sees Jews as the quintessential out-group and because she feels drawn to the spiritual and social justice agenda of Jewish feminism." However, Caroline Heilbrun has quoted Steinem as saying, "I don't believe in either religion," Judaism or Christianity. "When I'm around Jews who feel there's something good about being exclusively Jewish, I emphasize the non-Jewish side of the family. When I'm around Protestants who think there is something good about being Protestant, then I emphasize the Jewish side." See Letty Cottin Pogrebin, "Gloria Steinem," in Hyman and Moore, *Jewish Women in America*, 2:1319–1323, which contains Pogrebin's characterization and a discussion of Steinem's larger career; and Carolyn G. Heilbrun, *The Education of a Woman: The Life of Gloria Steinem* (New York: Dial, 1995), 49. See also Horowitz, *Betty Friedan*, 229; and Marcia Cohen, *The Sisterhood: The Inside Story of the Women's Movement and the Leaders Who Made It Happen* (New York: Ballantine Books, 1989), 41–42. On disagreements among these leaders, see Antler, *Journey Home*, 276.

70. Letty Cottin Pogrebin, *Deborah, Golda and Me* (New York: Crown, 1991), 154–164; Friedan, *Life So Far*, 291–294.

71. Hyman, "Jewish Feminism," 300; Alan Silverstein, "The Evolution of Ezrat Nashim," *Conservative Judaism* 30, no. 1 (1975): 43.

72. Hyman, "Ezrat Nashim," 284–295.

73. Silverstein, "Evolution of Ezrat Nashim," 43–44. See also Stephen C. Lerner, "The Havurot," *Conservative Judaism* 24, no. 3 (1970): 2–15; Riv-Ellen Prell, *Prayer and Community: The Havurah in American Judaism* (Detroit: Wayne State University Press, 1989).

74. Quoted in Reena Sigman Friedman, "The Jewish Feminist Movement," in *Jewish American Voluntary Organizations*, ed. Michael N. Dobkowski (New York: Greenwood, 1986), 576.

75. Ibid., 575–581.

76. Susan Dworkin, "Henrietta Szold," *Response* 18 (Summer 1973): 39–45.

77. Nadell, "Bright New Constellation," 387–388. For a comprehensive history of the long road toward women's ordination among Reform Jews, see Pamela S. Nadell, *Women Who Would Be Rabbis: A History of Women's Ordination, 1889–1985* (Boston: Beacon, 1998), esp. 61–117.

78. Nadell, "Bright New Constellation," 393–394. On Ezrat Nashim's advocacy at JTS and reaction to the affirmative vote, see Wenger, "Politics of Women's Ordination," 514–515.

79. Nadell, "Bright New Constellation," 391; Antler, *Journey Home*, 268–269.

80. Fishman, *Breath of Life*, 2; Antler, *Journey Home*, 266–267; Hyman, "Jewish Feminism," 308. See also Pogrebin, *Deborah, Golda and Me*, esp. 42, 48–52, 235.

81. Blu Greenberg, *On Women in Judaism: A View from Tradition* (Philadelphia: Jewish Publication Society of America, 1994), 21–25, 27, 30–33, 47, 92–97, 135.

82. Stuart Ain, "A Pioneer at Age 12," *Jewish Week*, 14 May 2010, 11; Meira Beinstock, "Kagan Showed Great Wisdom in Her Youth," *Jerusalem Post*, 29 June 2010, 6. A number of dates have been offered for the beginnings of the Simchat Torah women's activity at Lincoln Square. The 1972 date relies on a study that interviewed women who assert that they were there at that moment. An alternative date is 1974, basically concomitant with Greenberg's emergence. See Cohen-Nusbacher, "Efforts at Change," 112n7.

83. For a full consideration of women's activities within modern Orthodoxy, see Gurock, *Orthodox Jews in America*, 274–280. See also, for a listing of contemporary women's *tefillahs*, Edah, "Women's Tefilla Groups," c. 2005, www.edah.org.

CHAPTER 11. A CHANGING CITY

1. For an extensive examination of Cosell's statement in the context of the city in decline, using many sports metaphors, see Mahler, *Ladies and Gentlemen*. This saga has also been the foreground to a movie of the same name on 1977 New York City's struggles. See also Rosenblum, *Boulevard of Dreams*, which recounts Cosell's remark and the television visual as a "terrifying image of devastation" (183).

2. Lee Dembart, "Carter Takes a 'Sobering' Trip to South Bronx," *New York Times*, 6 October 1977, A1, B16; James M. Naughton, "Ford Holds Rockefeller Blameless for Troubles," *New York Times*, 31 October 1975, 12.

3. Glazer, "National Influence," 167–168.

4. Brecher and Horton, *Power Failure*, 91–94.

5. Meyer, "How Government Helped," 143–145; Drennan, "Decline and Rise," 29–33; Thomas Bailey and Roger Waldinger, "The Changing Ethnic/Racial Division of Labor," in *Dual City: Restructuring New York*, ed. John Hull Mollenkopf and Manuel Castells (New York: Russell Sage Foundation, 1991), 43; Freeman, *Working-Class New York*, 273.

6. McNickle, *To Be Mayor*, 272–275.

7. Maureen Dowd, "Poll Finds New Yorkers' Pessimism Subsides," *New York Times*, 19 January 1985, 1; McNickle, *To Be Mayor*, 281–287; Brecher and Horton, *Power Failure*, 101–103.

8. McNickle, *To Be Mayor*, 287–292; Brecher and Horton, *Power Failure*, 105; Frank Lynn, "2 Nominees Clash in Race for Mayor with Harsh Words," *New York Times*, 14 September 1989, A1. See also, for an analysis of the 1989 mayoral campaigns, Mollenkopf, *Phoenix*, 165–185.

9. McNickle, *To Be Mayor*, 292–295; Celestine Bohlen, "Dinkins and Koch Vie for Jews' Votes," *New York Times*, 10 September 1989, 44; John Kifner, "The Mayor-Elect Inspires Pride, but It's Hardly Universal," *New York Times*, 9 November

1989, B1; Sam Roberts, "Almost Lost at the Wire," *New York Times*, 9 November 1989, A1.

10. Richard Levine, "Koch Confers with Dinkins on Transition," *New York Times*, 9 November 1989, A1. See also Mollenkopf, *Phoenix*, 184; and McNickle, *To Be Mayor*, 313.

11. Saskia Sassen, *The Global City: New York, London, Tokyo* (Princeton, NJ: Princeton University Press, 1991), 289n8.

12. Todd S. Purdam, "Crown Heights Drives Contest for Mayor," *New York Times*, 7 December 1992, B1; Todd S. Purdam, "White Hispanic Ticket Grabs at a Black Mayor's Coalition," *New York Times*, 15 June 1993, 128. See also Lankevich, *American Metropolis*, 242–243.

13. "Mayoral Meddling?," *Jewish Week*, 15 March 1996, 4; David Firestone, "In Mayor's Snub, a Hint of Strategy," *New York Times*, 26 October 1995, B1.

14. Gary Rosenblatt, "Between the Lines: How to React to Arafat," *Jewish Week*, 27 October 1995, 5.

15. Lankevich, *American Metropolis*, 252–253; Siegel, *Prince of the City*, 149.

16. Adam Dickter, "Getting in Their Two Cents? Mayoral Candidates Scramble for Equal Time at Brooklyn COJO Breakfast Honoring Giuliani," *Jewish Week*, 11 April 1997, 8; "Rudy, Ruth: In Their Own Words; Messinger 'Tough Not Mean,'" *Jewish Week*, 24 October 1997, 1; Adam Nagourney, "Poll Finds Most Voters Have No Opinion about Messinger," *New York Times*, 21 October 1997, A1, B2; Elizabeth Israels Perry and Rona Holub, "Messinger, Ruth," in Hyman and Moore, *Jewish Women in America*, 2:917–918.

17. Lawrence Kohler-Esses, "Still Fighting the 'War': As Combative Messinger Calls on Mayor to Heed Her Warnings, Supporters Rue Death of 'New Deal,'" *Jewish Week*, 7 November 1997, 12; Siegel, *Prince of the City*, 210, 215–216; Rudolf W. Giuliani, "A Blackout That Tested, and Proved, New York City's Character," WINS radio address, 11 July 1999, http://nyc.gov; Jim Yardley, "Jews and Blacks Try to Avoid Reprise of '91 in Crown Heights," *New York Times*, 4 April 1998, A1, B6. On AJWS, see its website, http://ajws.org (accessed 23 February 2016).

18. Adam Dickter, "A Friend 'Til the End: For Jewish Community, Giuliani Was America's Top Mayor," *Jewish Week*, 28 December 2001, 10.

19. Adam Dickter, "Jewish Vote Vital for Bloomberg," *Jewish Week*, 9 November 2001, 1.

20. Joyce Purnick, *Mike Bloomberg: Money, Power, Politics* (New York: Public Affairs, 2009), 4, 74, 87–88 (quote on 88).

21. Ibid., 168, 204, 223. See also "The New York Issue: High Life, New York above 800 Feet," *New York Times Magazine*, 29 May 2016.

22. Michael M. Grynbaum and Marjorie Connolly, "Good Grade for Mayor: Regret for His Third Term," *New York Times*, 20 August 2012.

23. Molly Ball, "The Pugnacious, Relentless Progressive Party That Wants to Remake America," *Atlantic*, 7 January 2016.

24. Steven M. Cohen, Jacob B. Ukeles, and Ron Miller, *Jewish Community Study of New York: 2011 Comprehensive Report* (New York: United Jewish Appeal–Federation of New York, 2011), 16, 18, 23, 27, 30.

25. Julia Moskin, "Everything New Is Old Again: The New Golden Age of Jewish-American Deli Food," *New York Times*, 27 May 2014; "Japanese Kosherfication," *What's Cookin' in NYC* (blog), Macaulay Honors College, accessed 23 February 2016, http://macaulay.cuny.edu; Merwin, *Pastrami on Rye*, 169–184. See also Danny Meyer, *Setting the Table: The Transforming Power of Hospitality in Business* (San Francisco: Harper, 2006); Sharon Zukin, *The Cultures of Cities* (Malden, MA: Blackwell, 1995), chap. 5.

26. Adam Pincus, "The Syrian Retail Touch," *Real Deal*, 1 January 2014, http://therealdeal.com; Barry Meir, "Crazy Eddie's Insane Odyssey," *New York Times*, 19 July 1992, F1; Paul Ritterband and Steven M. Cohen, *Report on Jewish Population of New York* (New York: Federation of Jewish Philanthropies of New York, 1984), 20 (table 2.7), 54–63 (maps). See also Sutton, *Magic Carpet*, 62, 66–67, 96–102; Zenner, *Global Community*, 138–141, 156, 162–166; Glazer, "National Influence," 173.

27. Michael Millken and Ivan Boesky both admitted guilt and went to jail for their illegal trading practices. Glazer, "National Influence," 169, 181–184; James B. Stewart and Peter Eavis, "Revisiting the Lehman Brothers Bailout That Never Was," *New York Times*, 29 September 2014.

28. Leslie Bennetts, "If You're Thinking of Living in Chelsea," *New York Times*, 2 May 1982, R9; Jan Morris, "The Future Looks Familiar," *New York Times*, 26 April 1987, SMA16; Samuel G. Freedman, "Real-Estate Boom Cited as Peril to Arts in City," *New York Times*, 15 April 1986, C13. See also Sharon Zukin, *Naked City: The Death and Life of Authentic Urban Places* (New York: Oxford University Press, 2009).

29. UJA-Federation, *Jewish Community Study of New York: 2002 Geographic Profile*, 110–111. On the transformation of Harlem, see "Migration of Affluent Whites to Harlem Forecast," *New York Times*, 28 May 1984, 23; Sam Roberts, "In Harlem, Blacks Are No Longer a Majority," *New York Times*, 6 January 2010, A16.

30. UJA-Federation, *Jewish Community Study of New York: 2002 Geographic Profile*, 35, 143, 169, 187.

31. Leslie Bennetts, "Woody Allen's Selective Vision of New York," *New York Times*, 7 May 1986, C1; Vincent Canby, "Hannah and Her Sisters," *New York Times*, 7 February 1986.

32. William J. Palmer, *The Films of the Eighties: A Social History* (Carbondale: Southern Illinois University Press, 1993), 284–285; McCann, *Woody Allen*, 14, 27, 35–36.

33. These included Westchester, Nassau, and Suffolk Counties but not New Jersey. UJA-Federation, *Jewish Community Study of New York: 2002 Geographic Profile*, 35, 36, 143, 169, 187. See also UJA-Federation, *Jewish Community Study of New York: 2002*, 25, 30.

34. Cohen, Ukeles, and Miller, *Jewish Community Study of New York: 2011 Comprehensive Report*, 16; Gil Stern Shefler, "Bukharan Jewish Community Thrives in NYC," *Jerusalem Post*, 12 July 2011; F. Markowitz, *Community in Spite of Itself*.

35. Michael Schapira, "André Aciman," *Full Stop*, 18 December 2012, www.full-stop.
net; "An Interview with Andre Aciman," *Bookslut*, March 2007, www.bookslut
.com; for an academic bio of Aciman, see the website of the Graduate Center of
CUNY, www.gc.cuny.edu (accessed 22 February 2016); on Lucette Lagnado, see
her website: www.lucettelagnado.com (accessed 22 February 2016); Gary Shteyn-
gart, *Little Failure: A Memoir* (New York: Random House, 2014).

36. Solomon, *Wonder of Wonders*, part 3; Jan Balakian, "Wasserstein, Wendy," in
Hyman and Moore, *Jewish Women in America*, 2:1456–1459 (quote on 1458).

37. Ben Brantley, "Theater Talkback: Tony Kushner and the Art of Empathy," *New
York Times*, 5 May 2011; for Kushner's bio, see the website of the Steven Barclay
Agency, http://barclayagency.com (accessed 22 February 2016). Kushner has been
critical of Israel, coediting a volume with Alisa Solomon, *Wrestling with Zion: Pro-
gressive Jewish-American Response to the Israeli-Palestinian Conflict* (New York:
Grove, 2003). In 2011, he was offered, then denied, an honorary degree from the
City University of New York. See Winnie Hu, "Reconsidering, CUNY Is Likely to
Honor Kushner," *New York Times*, 6 May 2011.

38. "Unprecedented $30 Million Capital Campaign Secures Future for Center for Jew-
ish History: Single Largest Fund-Raising Effort since Building Was Completed in
2000," PR Newswire, 24 January 2011, www.prnewswire.com.

39. Saidel, *Never Too Late to Remember*.

40. On the history of these institutions, see their websites: www.eldridgestreet.org,
www.tenement.org, and www.nycjewishtours.org.

41. Ingrid Abramovitch, "Hipification Reaches the Street Where Peddlers Once
Pushed Carts," *New York Times*, 16 November 1997, ST1, 6; Mark Russ Federman,
Russ & Daughters: Reflections and Recipes from the House that Herring Built (New
York: Schocken, 2013); Joseph Berger, "Streit's Matzo Factory, a Piece of Lower
East Side History, Is Moving On," *New York Times*, 6 January 2015.

42. Wenger, "Memory as Identity," 4–5.

43. Quoted in Kugelmass, "Turfing the Slum," 188.

44. Jenna Weissman Joselit, "Telling Tales: Or, How a Slum Became a Shrine," *Jewish
Social Studies* 2 (Winter 1995): 54; Seth Kamil, "Tripping down Memory Lane:
Walking Tours on the Jewish Lower East Side," in *Remembering the Lower East
Side*, ed. Hasia R. Diner, Jeffrey Shandler, and Beth S. Wenger (Bloomington:
Indiana University Press, 2000), 226–240 (quote on 227).

45. Quoted in Kugelmass, "Turfing the Slum," 184, 189.

46. Ibid., 199–200.

47. UJA-Federation, *Jewish Community Study of New York: 2011*, 19–30 (quote on 22).

48. Ibid.; Ball, "Pugnacious, Relentless Progressive Party."

49. Ellen Freudenheim, "Popular Baby Names in Brooklyn and New York City,"
About Travel: Brooklyn, NY, accessed 22 February 2016, http://brooklyn.about.
com; UJA-Federation, "Diverse Jewish Communities," chap. 7 in *Jewish Community Study of New York: 2011*, 211–252.

50. For a biography of Ruth Bader Ginsberg, see Malvina Halberstam, "Ginsberg,
Ruth Bader," in Hyman and Moore, *Jewish Women in America*, 1: 515–520; for

a biography of Bernie Sanders, see "Bernie Sanders Biography," Bio, accessed 24 June 2016, www.biography.com.

51. For a thoughtful discussion of these themes, see Rachel Gordan, "New York as the Capital of American Jews: What Has It Done to American Jewish History?," paper presented at the Biennial Scholars' Conference of the American Jewish Historical Society's Academic Council, Center for Jewish History, New York, 19–21 June 2016.

VISUAL ESSAY

1. Jules D. Prown, "Mind in Matter: An Introduction to Material Culture Theory and Method," in *Material Life in America, 1600–1860,* ed. Robert Blair St. George (Boston: Northeastern University Press, 1988), 18.

2. Needham, *Celebrated Franks Family Portraits,* 20.

3. Erica E. Hirshler, "The Levy-Franks Family Portraits," *Magazine Antiques,* November 1990, 1021.

4. Jonathan D. Krasner and Jonathan D. Sarna, *The History of the Jewish People: Ancient Israel to 1880s America* (New York: Berman House, 2006), 162.

5. For a brief and persuasive discussion of the art of embroidery in relation to the creation of separate male (public) and female (domestic) spheres and, therefore, the differences between their arts, see Amy Elizabeth Grey, "A Journey Embroidered: Gender Redefined," in *Invisible America: Unearthing Our Hidden Heritage,* ed. Mark P. Leone and Neil Asher Silberman (New York: Henry Holt, 1995), 140–141.

6. Ellen Smith, "Portraits of a Community: The Image and Experience of Early American Jews," in *American Jewish Women's History: A Reader,* ed. Pamela S. Nadell (New York: NYU Press, 2003), 19.

7. Joanne Reitano, *The Restless City* (New York: Routledge, 2006), 11.

8. Ellen Smith, "Portraits of a Community in America at the Time of the Revolutionary War," in *Facing a New World: Jewish Portraits in Colonial and Federal America,* ed. Richard Brilliant (New York: Prestel Munich, 1997), 13–14.

9. This is now the busy thoroughfare of South William Street in New York City's financial district.

10. David de Sola Pool's writings on Sephardic culture in New York City are essential readings. See, for example, David de Sola Pool, *The Mill Street Synagogue: 1730–1817* (New York: Shearith Israel, 1930).

11. Sarna, "Colonial Judaism," 13.

12. Erin E. Eisenbarth, *Baubles, Bangles, and Beads: American Jewelry from Yale University, 1700 to 2005* (New Haven, CT: Yale University Art Gallery, 2005), 17.

13. Robin Jaffee Frank, *Love and Loss: American Portrait and Mourning Miniatures* (New Haven, CT: Yale University Press, 2000), 130–132.

14. Ibid., 132.

15. Ira Berlin and Leslie M. Harris, introduction to *Slavery in New York,* ed. Ira Berlin and Leslie M. Harris (New York: New Press, 2005), 4–5.

16. Register of the Manumission of Slaves, New York City, 1816–1818, 2:51–52, now housed at the New-York Historical Society. Morris U. Schappes, ed., "Four

Documents Concerning Jews and Slavery," in *Strangers and Neighbors: Relations between Blacks and Jews in the United States*, ed. Maurianne Adams and John Bracey (Amherst: University of Massachusetts Press, 1999), 137–146.

17. Michael W. Grunberger, introduction to *From Haven to Home: 350 Years of Jewish Life in America*, ed. Michael W. Grunberger (New York: George Braziller, in association with the Library of Congress, 2004), 16–17.

18. Joshua Brown, "Reconstructing Representation: Social Types, Readers and the Pictorial Press, 1865–1877," *Radical History Review* 38 (Fall 1996): 5–38.

19. Birmingham, *"Our Crowd,"* 132, 148–149.

20. Herbert D. Croly, "The Harmonie Club House," *Architectural Record* 19, no. 4 (1906): 237–243.

21. Jonathan D. Sarna, "American Judaism," in Grunberger, *From Haven to Home*, 142; "Dancing for Charity: The Ball of the Purim Association Was a Grand Success," *New York Times*, 5 March 1890.

22. I. S. Isaacs, "Meyer S. Isaacs," *PAJHS* 13 (1905): 146.

23. Ibid.

24. Higham, *Send These to Me*, rev. ed., 71–80. Marvin Trachtenberg, *The Statue of Liberty* (New York: Viking Penguin, 1986).

25. My interpretation of Riis's photograph draws from the scholarship and input of the Riis expert Bonnie Yochelson. I appreciate her enormous generosity in sharing her knowledge of Riis and her research materials.

26. Bonnie Yochelson, *Jacob Riis 55* (New York: Phaidon, 2001), 118–119.

27. For a discussion of the changing history of this photograph, see Deborah Dash Moore, *Urban Origins of American Judaism* (Athens: University of Georgia Press, 2014), 117–119.

28. I want to thank the decorative arts scholar Karen Zukowski for providing insights into the furniture displayed in the photographer's studio. John Tagg, *The Burden of Representation: Essays on Photographies and Histories* (Minneapolis: University of Minnesota Press, 1988), 37.

29. It is not clear which lodge in New York Isaacs belonged to, according to Thomas M. Savini, director of the Masonic Library, Grand Lodge, New York (email correspondence with Diana L. Linden, 21 September 2010).

30. Alice M. Greenwald, "The Masonic Mizrahi and Lamp: Jewish Ritual Art as a Reflection of Cultural Assimilation," *Journal of Jewish Art* 10 (1984): 101.

31. Ellen Smith, "Greetings from Faith: Early-Twentieth-Century American Jewish New Year Postcards," in *The Visual Culture of American Religions*, ed. David Morgan and Sally M. Promey (Berkeley: University of California Press, 2001), 243–247.

32. "Big Change in a Big Store Which All Brooklyn Knows," *New York Times*, 2 April 1893. See also Heinze, *Adapting to Abundance*.

33. See Jenna Weissman Joselit, *A Perfect Fit: Clothes, Character, and the Promise of America* (New York: Henry Holt, 2001).

34. Robert Hendrickson, *The Grand Emporiums: The Illustrated History of America's Great Department Stores* (New York: Stein and Day, 1979), 33.

35. Donna T. Haverty-Stacke, *America's Forgotten Holiday: May Day and Nationalism, 1867–1960* (New York: NYU Press, 2009), 85–88.

36. Maria Balinska, *The Bagel: The Surprising History of a Modest Bread* (New Haven, CT: Yale University Press, 2008), 115–119. The Jewish bakers' union became famous for adding to their demands something for "which the Jewish labour movement was to become famous: that the bosses allow their workers to give one night's work to unemployed bakers" (ibid., 115).

37. Ellen Wiley Todd, "Remembering the Unknowns: The Longman Memorial and the 1911 Triangle Shirtwaist Fire," *American Art*, 23 no. 3 (2009): 65.

38. Ben-Ur, *Sephardic Jews in America*, 111. See also Angel, *La America*. The periodical *La America* began publication in 1910 as a national weekly. It continued to be published intermittently until 1925.

39. Helene Schwartz Kenvin, *This Land of Liberty: A History of America's Jews* (West Orange, NJ: Behrman House, 1986), 118–121.

40. Erika Lee, "The Chinese Exclusion Example: Race, Immigration, and American Gatekeeping, 1882–1924," *Journal of American Ethnic History* 21, no. 3 (2002): 36–62.

41. For a history of black Judaism, see Roberta S. Gold, "The Black Jews of Harlem: Representation, Identity, and Race, 1920–1939," *American Quarterly* 55, no. 2 (2003): 179–225.

42. The rediscovery of the history of Jews of African descent connected with pan-Africanist reappraisal of Egypt's relationship to the African continent. Solomon's lineage down to Emperor Menelik II of Ethiopia, coupled with the flight of Moorish Jews to Timbuktu in West Africa during the fourteenth century, reinforced plausible links between Judaism and African Americans, fueling a belief that they were true descendants of ancient Israelites. A small minority was inspired to adopt the faith.

43. Henry Bial, *Acting Jewish: Negotiating Ethnicity on the American Stage and Screen* (Ann Arbor: University of Michigan Press, 2005), 1–29, 40–48; Donald Weber, "The Jewish American World of Gertrude Berg: The Goldbergs on Radio and Television, 1930–1950," in *Talking Back: Images of Jewish Women in Popular Culture*, ed. Joyce Antler (Hanover, NH: Brandeis University Press / University of New England Press, 1998).

44. Barbara Kirshenblatt-Gimblett, *Destination Culture: Tourism, Museums, and Heritage* (Berkeley: University of California Press, 1998), 79–128.

45. For an in-depth examination of Shahn's mural, see Diana L. Linden, *Ben Shahn's New Deal Murals: Jewish Identity in the American Scene* (Detroit: Wayne State University Press, 2015).

46. Ben Shahn to Edward B. Rowan, 11 June 1940, Archives of American Art, Washington, DC.

47. Alfred J. Kolatch, *Great Jewish Quotations* (New York: Jonathan David, 1996), 74–75.

48. Duane Blue Spruce, ed., *Mother Earth, Father Skyline* (Washington, DC: Gustave Heye Center, National Museum of the American Indian, and Smithsonian

Institution, 2006), 38. Rachel Rubinstein, *Members of the Tribe: Native America in the Jewish Imagination* (Detroit: Wayne State University Press, 2010).

49. The Archives of the American Soviet Jewry Movement is housed at the American Jewish Historical Society in Manhattan (www.ajhs.org/aasjm).

50. Daniel Belasco helped me with my object selection. Many thanks.

51. Quote by Amy Klein Reichert from Jewish Museum, "Miriam Cup," accessed 28 January 2017, http://thejewishmuseum.org/collection/5027-miriam-cup.

52. Voloj's work is included in Alana Newhouse, ed., *A Living Lens: Photographs of Jewish Life from the Pages of the "Forward"* (New York: Norton, 2007). Voloj explains his photographic mission as being to rediscover forgotten Jewish history in New York City, as well as the "ways the culture is reborn and reinvented in a city in a permanent transition." Julian Voloj to Diana Linden, 5 February 2011.

53. Congregation Ahavas Israel is located at 108 Noble Street, Brooklyn, NY 11222. The congregation dates to the late nineteenth century; the building dates to 1903.

54. Lenore Skenazy, "Are New York Jews More Jewish?," *Forward*, 17 February 2010, 2.

SELECT BIBLIOGRAPHY

PERIODICALS
American Hebrew
American Israelite
Asmonean
Atlantic
Century Magazine
Evening Star
Forward
Jewish Messenger
Jewish Week
Morgen zhurnal
New York Daily Tribune
New York Herald
New York Times
Outlook
Shabes zhurnal
Tageblat
Victory Bulletin, July 1942–September 1945 (wartime newspaper of the Syrian Jewish community in Brooklyn, compiled by the Sephardic Archives)
Yidishe gazeten

PUBLISHED SOURCES
Abrams, Nathan. "'A Profoundly Hegemonic Moment': De-mythologizing the Cold War New York Jewish Intellectuals." *Shofar* 21, no. 3 (2003): 64–82.
Alexander, Edward. "Irving Howe and the Holocaust: Dilemmas of a Radical Jewish Intellectual." *AJH* 88, no. 1 (2000): 95–113.
Alexander, Michael. *Jazz Age Jews.* Princeton, NJ: Princeton University Press, 2001.
Anbinder, Tyler. *Five Points: The 19th-Century New York City Neighborhood That Invented Tap Dance, Stole Elections, and Became the World's Most Notorious Slum.* New York: Free Press, 2001.
Angel, Marc D. *La America: The Sephardic Experience in the United States.* Philadelphia: Jewish Publication Society of America, 1982.
Antler, Joyce. *The Journey Home: Jewish Women and the American Century.* New York: Free Press, 1997.

Baigell, Matthew. "From Hester Street to Fifty-Seventh Street: Jewish-American Artists in New York." In *Painting a Place in America: Jewish Artists in New York, 1900–1945*, edited by Norman L. Kleeblatt and Susan Chevlowe, 28–88. New York: Jewish Museum, 1991.

Ballon, Hilary, and Kenneth T. Jackson, eds. *Robert Moses and the Modern City: The Transformation of New York*. New York: Norton, 2007.

Barkai, Avraham. *Branching Out: German Jewish Immigration to the United States, 1820–1924*. New York: Holmes and Meier, 1994.

Bayor, Ronald H. *Neighbors in Conflict: The Irish, Germans, Jews, and Italians of New York City, 1929–1941*. Baltimore: Johns Hopkins University Press, 1978.

Beckert, Sven. *The Monied Metropolis: New York City and the Consolidation of the American Bourgeoisie, 1850–1896*. Cambridge: Cambridge University Press, 2001.

Bell, Daniel. "The Three Faces of New York." *Dissent* 8, no. 3 (1961): 222–232.

Bender, Thomas. *New York Intellect: A History of Intellectual Life in New York from 1750 to the Beginnings of Our Own Time*. New York: Knopf, 1987.

Ben-Ur, Aviva. *Sephardic Jews in America: A Diasporic History*. New York: NYU Press, 2009.

Berkman, Matthew. "Transforming Philanthropy: Finance and Institutional Evolution at the Jewish Federation of New York, 1917–1986." *Jewish Social Studies* 22, no. 2 (2017): 146–195.

Bernheimer, Charles S. "The Jewish Immigrant as an Industrial Worker." *Annals of the American Academy of Political and Social Science* 33, no. 2 (1909): 175–182.

Bernstein, Burton, and Barbara B. Haws. *Leonard Bernstein: American Original*. New York: HarperCollins, 2008.

Berson, Lenora E. *The Negroes and the Jews*. New York: Random House, 1971.

Binder, Frederick M., and David M. Reimers. *All the Nations under Heaven: An Ethnic and Racial History of New York City*. New York: Columbia University Press, 1995.

Birmingham, Stephen. *"Our Crowd": The Great Jewish Families of New York*. New York: Harper and Row, 1967.

Blair, Sara. "Visions of the Tenement: Jews, Photography, and Modernity on the Lower East Side." *Images* 4 (2010): 57–81.

Bloom, Alexander. *Prodigal Sons: The New York Intellectuals and Their World*. New York: Oxford University Press, 1986.

Brecher, Charles, and Raymond D. Horton, with Robert A. Cropf and Dean Michael Mead. *Power Failure: New York City Politics and Policy since 1960*. New York: Oxford University Press, 1993.

Broun, Heywood, and George Britt. *Christians Only: A Study in Prejudice*. New York: Vanguard, 1931.

Brumberg, Stephen F. *Going to America, Going to School: The Jewish Immigrant Public School Encounter in Turn-of-the-Century New York City*. New York: Praeger, 1986.

Burrows, Edwin G., and Michael Wallace. *Gotham: A History of New York City to 1898*. New York: Oxford University Press, 1999.

Cahan, Abraham. *Bleter fun mayn lebn*. 5 vols. New York: Forward Association, 1926–1931.

Caro, Robert A. *The Power Broker: Robert Moses and the Fall of New York*. New York: Knopf, 1974.

Cohen, Jocelyn, and Daniel Soyer, eds. *My Future Is in America: Autobiographies of Eastern European Jewish Immigrants*. New York: NYU Press, 2006.

Cohen, Naomi W. *American Jews and the Zionist Idea*. New York: KTAV, 1975.

———. *Encounter with Emancipation: The German Jews in the United States*. Philadelphia: Jewish Publication Society of America, 1984.

———. *Not Free to Desist: The American Jewish Committee, 1906–1966*. Philadelphia: Jewish Publication Society of America, 1972.

Cohen, Robert. *When the Old Left Was Young: Student Radicals and America's First Mass Student Movement, 1929–1941*. New York: Oxford University Press, 1993.

Cohen, Steven M., and Paul Ritterband. "The Social Characteristics of the New York Jewish Community, 1981." *American Jewish Yearbook*, 1984, 128–161.

Cohen-Nusbacher, Ailene. "Efforts at Change in a Traditional Denomination: The Case of Orthodox Women's Prayer Groups." *Nashim* 2 (Spring 1999): 95–113.

Cooney, Terry A. *The Rise of the New York Intellectuals: "Partisan Review" and Its Circle*. Madison: University of Wisconsin Press, 1986.

Daniels, Roger. *Guarding the Golden Door: American Immigration Policy and Immigrants since 1882*. New York: Hill and Wang, 2004.

Day, Jared N. *Urban Castles: Tenement Housing and Landlord Activism in New York City, 1890–1943*. New York: Columbia University Press, 1999.

Diner, Hasia R. *The Jews of the United States, 1654–2000*. Berkeley: University of California Press, 2004.

———. *Lower East Side Memories: A Jewish Place in America*. Princeton, NJ: Princeton University Press, 2000.

———. *A Time for Gathering: The Second Migration*. Baltimore: Johns Hopkins University Press, 1992.

Dinnerstein, Leonard. *Anti-Semitism in America*. New York: Oxford University Press, 1994.

———. "The Funeral of Rabbi Jacob Joseph." In *Anti-Semitism in American History*, edited by David Gerber, 275–301. Urbana: University of Illinois Press, 1986.

Dolkart, Andrew S. *Biography of a Tenement House in New York City: An Architectural History of 97 Orchard Street*. Santa Fe, NM: Center for American Places, 2006.

———. *Central Synagogue in Its Changing Neighborhood*. New York: Central Synagogue, 2001.

———. "Homes for People: Non-Profit Cooperatives in New York City, 1916–1929." *Sites* 30 (1989): 30–42.

Dorman, Joseph. *Arguing the World: The New York Intellectuals in Their Own Words*. New York: Free Press, 2000.

Doroshkin, Milton. *Yiddish in America: Social and Cultural Foundations*. Rutherford, NJ: Fairleigh Dickinson University Press, 1969.

Drennan, Matthew P. "The Decline and Rise of the New York Economy." In *Dual City: Restructuring New York*, edited by John Hull Mollenkopf and Manuel Castells, 25–42. New York: Russell Sage Foundation, 1991.

Dubofsky, Melvyn. "Success and Failure of Socialism in New York City, 1900–1918: A Case Study." *Labor History* 9, no. 3 (1968): 361–375.

Eisenstein, Judah. "The History of the First Russian-American Jewish Congregation: The Beth Hamedrash Hagadol." *PAJHS* 9 (1901): 63–74.

Emerson, Ken. *Always Magic in the Air: The Bomp and Brilliance of the Brill Building Era*. New York: Viking, 2005.

Engelman, Uriah Zvi. "Jewish Statistics in the U.S. Census of Religious Bodies (1850–1936)." *Jewish Social Studies* 9, no. 2 (1947): 127–174.

Enstad, Nan. *Ladies of Labor, Girls of Adventure: Working Women, Popular Culture, and Labor Politics at the Turn of the Twentieth Century*. New York: Columbia University Press, 1999.

Epstein, Melech. *Jewish Labor in the USA*. Vol. 1, *1882–1914*. 1950. Reprint, New York: Ktav, 1969.

———. *Profiles of Eleven: Profiles of Eleven Men Who Guided the Destiny of an Immigrant Society and Stimulated Social Consciousness among the American People*. Detroit: Wayne State University Press, 1965.

Ernst, Robert. *Immigrant Life in New York City, 1825–1863*. 1949. Reprint, Syracuse, NY: Syracuse University Press, 1994.

Faber, Eli. *Jews, Slaves, and the Slave Trade: Setting the Record Straight*. New York: NYU Press, 1998.

———. *A Time for Planting: The First Migration*. Baltimore: Johns Hopkins University Press, 1992.

Feingold, Henry L. *The Politics of Rescue: The Roosevelt Administration and the Holocaust, 1938–1945*. New Brunswick, NJ: Rutgers University Press, 1970.

———. *"Silent No More": Saving the Jews of Russia, the American Jewish Effort, 1967–1989*. Syracuse, NY: Syracuse University Press, 2007.

———. *A Time for Searching: Entering the Mainstream, 1920–1945*. Baltimore: Johns Hopkins University Press, 1992.

Feldman, Egal. "Jews in the Early Growth of the New York City Men's Clothing Trade." *AJAJ* 13 (1960): 3–14.

Foner, Nancy. *From Ellis Island to JFK: New York's Two Great Waves of Immigration*. New Haven, CT: Yale University Press, 2000.

Ford, Carole Bell. *The Girls: Jewish Women of Brownsville, Brooklyn, 1940–1995*. Albany: State University of New York Press, 2000.

———. "Nice Jewish Girls: Growing Up in Brownsville, 1930–1950." In *Jews of Brooklyn*, edited by Ilana Abramovitch and Sean Galvin, 129–136. Hanover, NH: University Press of New England / Brandeis University Press, 2002.

Forman, Ira. "The Politics of Minority Consciousness: The Historical Voting Behavior of American Jews." In *Jews in American Politics*, edited by L. Sandy Maisel, 141–160. Lanham, MD: Rowman and Littlefield, 2001.

Frankel, Jonathan. *Prophecy and Politics: Socialism, Nationalism, and the Russian Jews, 1862–1917*. New York: Cambridge University Press, 1981.

Freeman, Joshua B. *Working-Class New York: Life and Labor since World War II*. New York: New Press, 2000.

Friedman, Reena Sigman. "'Send Me My Husband Who Is In New York City': Husband Desertion in the American Jewish Immigrant Community, 1900–1926." *Jewish Social Studies* 44, no. 1 (1982): 1–18.

Fuchs, Lawrence H. *The Political Behavior of American Jews*. Glencoe, IL: Free Press, 1956.

Gaines, Steven, and Sharon Churcher. *Obsession: The Lives and Times of Calvin Klein*. New York: Birch Lane, 1994.

Garland, Libby. "Not-Quite-Closed Gates: Jewish Alien Smuggling in the Post-Quota Years." *AJH* 94, no. 3 (2008): 197–224.

Gay, Ruth. *Unfinished People: Eastern European Jews Encounter America*. New York: Norton, 1996.

Gilfoyle, Timothy. *City of Eros: New York City, Prostitution, and the Commercialization of Sex, 1790–1920*. New York: Norton, 1992.

Glanz, Rudolf. *Studies in Judaica Americana*. New York: KTAV, 1970.

Glazer, Nathan. "The National Influence of Jewish New York." In *Capital of the American Century: The National and International Influence of New York City*, edited by Martin Shefter, 167–174. New York: Russell Sage, 1993.

Glazer, Nathan, and Daniel P. Moynihan. *Beyond the Melting Pot: The Negroes, Puerto Ricans, Jews, Italians, and Irish of New York City*. 2nd ed. Cambridge, MA: MIT Press, 1970.

Glenn, Susan. *Daughters of the Shtetl: Life and Labor in the Immigrant Generation*. Ithaca, NY: Cornell University Press, 1990.

Glogower, Rod. "The Impact of the American Experience on Responsa Literature." *AJH* 69, no. 2 (1979): 257–269.

Goldman, Karla. *Beyond the Synagogue Gallery: Finding a Place for Women in American Judaism*. Cambridge, MA: Harvard University Press, 2000.

Goldschmidt, Henry. *Race and Religion among the Chosen People of Crown Heights*. New Brunswick, NJ: Rutgers University Press, 2006.

Goldstein, Eric L. "'A Childless Language': Yiddish and the Problem of 'Youth' in the 1920s and 1930s." In *1929: Mapping the Jewish World*, edited by Gennady Estraikh and Hasia Diner, 139–154. New York: NYU Press, 2013.

Gorelick, Sherry. *City College and the Jewish Poor: Education in New York, 1880–1924*. New Brunswick, NJ: Rutgers University Press, 1981.

Goren, Arthur A. "The Jewish Press." In *The Ethnic Press in the United States: A Historical Analysis and Handbook*, edited by Sally Miller, 203–228. New York: Greenwood, 1987.

———. *New York Jews and the Quest for Community: The Kehillah Experiment, 1908–1922*. New York: Columbia University Press, 1970.

———. *The Politics and Public Culture of American Jews*. Bloomington: Indiana University Press, 1999.

———. "Traditional Institutions Transplanted: The Hevra Kadisha in Europe and in America." In *The Jews of North America*, edited by Moses Rischin, 62–78. Detroit: Wayne State University Press, 1987.

Goren, Arthur A., and Elizabeth Blackmar. *Congregating and Consecrating at Central Synagogue*. New York: Central Synagogue, 2003.

Grebler, Leo. *Housing Market Behavior in a Declining Area: Long-Term Changes in Inventory and Utilization of Housing on New York's Lower East Side*. New York: Columbia University Press, 1952.

Green, Nancy, ed. *Jewish Workers in the Modern Diaspora*. Berkeley: University of California Press, 1998.

———. "Sweatshop Migrations: The Garment Industry between Home and Shop." In *The Landscape of Modernity: New York City 1900–1940*, edited by David Ward and Olivier Zunz, 213–233. Baltimore: Johns Hopkins University Press, 1992.

Greenwald, Richard. *The Triangle Fire, the Protocol of Peace, and Industrial Democracy in Progressive Era New York*. Philadelphia: Temple University Press, 2005.

Grinstein, Hyman. *The Rise of the Jewish Community of New York, 1654–1860*. Philadelphia: Jewish Publication Society of America, 1945.

Grobman, Alex. "What Did They Know? The American Jewish Press and the Holocaust, 1 September 1939–17 December 1942." *AJH* 68, no. 1 (1979): 327–352.

Grusd, Edward. *B'nai B'rith: The Story of a Covenant*. New York: Appleton-Century, 1966.

Gurock, Jeffrey S. *American Jewish Orthodoxy in Historical Perspective*. Hoboken, NJ: Ktav, 1996.

———. "Jewish Commitment and Continuity in Interwar Brooklyn." In *Jews of Brooklyn*, edited by Ilana Abramovitch and Sean Galvin, 231–241. Hanover, NH: University Press of New England, 2001.

———. *Judaism's Encounter with American Sports*. Bloomington: Indiana University Press, 2005.

———. "The Late Friday Night Orthodox Service: An Exercise in Religious Accommodation." *Jewish Social Studies* 12 (Spring–Summer 2006): 137–156.

———. *Orthodox Jews in America*. Bloomington: Indiana University Press, 2009.

———. "Synagogue Imperialism in New York City: The Case of Congregation Kehal Adath Jeshurun, 1909–1911." *Michael* 15 (2000): 95–108.

———. *When Harlem Was Jewish, 1870–1930*. New York: Columbia University Press, 1979.

Gurock, Jeffrey S., and Jacob J. Schacter. *A Modern Heretic and a Traditional Community: Mordecai M. Kaplan, Orthodoxy, and American Judaism*. New York: Columbia University Press, 1997.

Hapgood, Hutchins. *The Spirit of the Ghetto*. 1902. Reprint, Cambridge, MA: Harvard University Press, 1967.

Harris, Louis, and Bert E. Swanson. *Black-Jewish Relations in New York City*. New York: Praeger, 1970.

Heilman Samuel C., and Menachem M. Friedman. *The Rebbe: The Life and Afterlife of Menachem Mendel Schneerson*. Princeton, NJ: Princeton University Press, 2010.

Heinze, Andrew. *Adapting to Abundance: Jewish Immigrants, Mass Consumption, and the Search for American Identity*. New York: Columbia University Press, 1990.

———. "Jewish Street Merchants and Mass Consumption in New York City, 1880–1914." *AJAJ* 41, no. 2 (1989): 199–214.

Herman, Felicia. "From Priestess to Hostess: Sisterhoods of Personal Service in New York City, 1887–1936." In *Women and American Judaism: Historical Perspectives*, edited by Pamela Nadell and Jonathan D. Sarna, 148–181. Hanover, NH: Brandeis University Press / University Press of New England, 2001.

Hershkowitz, Leo. "By Chance or Choice: Jews in New Amsterdam, 1654." *AJAJ* 57 (2005): 1–13.

———. "New Amsterdam's Twenty-Three Jews—Myth or Reality?" In *Hebrew and the Bible in America: The First Two Centuries*, edited by Shalom Goldman, 171–183. Hanover, NH: Brandeis University Press and Dartmouth College, 1993.

Higham, John. *Send These to Me: Jews and other Immigrants in Urban America*. New York: Atheneum, 1975; rev ed., Baltimore: Johns Hopkins University Press, 1984.

———. *Strangers in the Land: Patterns of American Nativism, 1860–1925*. 1955. Reprint, New York: Atheneum, 1981.

Hollinger, David. "Two NYUs and the 'Obligation of Universities to the Social Order' in the Great Depression." In *The University and the City*, edited by Thomas Bender, 249–266. New York: Oxford University Press, 1988.

Hood, Clifton. *722 Miles: The Building of the Subways and How They Transformed New York*. New York: Simon and Schuster, 1993.

Horowitz, C. Morris, and Lawrence J. Kaplan. *The Estimated Jewish Population of the New York Area, 1900–1975*. New York: Federation of Jewish Philanthropies of New York, 1959.

Horowitz, Daniel. *Betty Friedan and the Making of "The Feminine Mystique": The American Left, the Cold War, and Modern Feminism*. Amherst: University of Massachusetts Press, 1998.

Howe, Irving. *A Margin of Hope: An Intellectual Autobiography*. San Diego: Harcourt Brace Jovanovich, 1982.

———. *World of Our Fathers: The Journey of the East European Jews to America and the Life They Found and Made*. New York: Harcourt Brace Jovanovich, 1976.

Howe, Irving, and Eliezer Greenberg, eds. *Voices from the Yiddish: Essays, Memoirs, Diaries*. 1972. New York: Schocken, 1975.

Howe, Irving, and Kenneth Libo, eds. *How We Lived: A Documentary History of Immigrant Jews in America, 1880–1930*. New York: Richard Marek, 1979.

Hyman, Paula E. "Ezrat Nashim and the Emergence of a New Jewish Feminism." In *The Americanization of the Jews*, edited by Robert M. Seltzer and Norman J. Cohen, 284–295. New York: NYU Press, 1995.

———. "Immigrant Women and Consumer Protest: The New York City Kosher Meat Boycott of 1902." *AJH* 70, no. 1 (1980): 91–105.

———. "Jewish Feminism Faces the American Women's Movement: Convergence and Divergence." In *American Jewish Women's History: A Reader*, edited by Pamela S. Nadell, 297–312. New York: NYU Press, 2003.

Hyman, Paula E., and Deborah Dash Moore, eds. *Jewish Women in America: An Historical Encyclopedia*. 2 vols. New York: Routledge, 1997.

Igra, Anna R. *Wives without Husbands: Marriage, Desertion, and Welfare in New York, 1900–1935*. Chapel Hill: University of North Carolina Press, 2007.

Jackson, Naomi. *Converging Movements: Modern Dance and Jewish Culture at the 92nd Street Y*. Middletown, CT: Wesleyan University Press, 2000.

Jaher, Frederic Cople. *A Scapegoat in the Wilderness: The Origin and Rise of Anti-Semitism in America*. Cambridge, MA: Harvard University Press, 1994.

Jasen, David A. *Tin Pan Alley: The Composers, the Songs, the Performers and Their Times*. New York: D. I. Fine, 1988.

Jick, Leon A. *The Americanization of the Synagogue, 1820–1870*. Hanover, NH: Brandeis University Press, 1976.

———. "The Reform Synagogue." In *The American Synagogue: A Sanctuary Transformed*, edited by Jack Wertheimer, 85–109. Hanover, NH: Brandeis University Press / University Press of New England, 1987.

Joselit, Jenna Weissman. *Our Gang: Jewish Crime and the New York Jewish Community*. Bloomington: Indiana University Press, 1983.

———. "A Set Table: Jewish Domestic Culture in the New World, 1880–1950." In *Getting Comfortable in New York: The American Jewish Home, 1880–1950*, edited by Susan Braunstein and Jenna Weissman Joselit, 19–73. New York: Jewish Museum, 1990.

———. "The Special Sphere of the Middle-Class American Jewish Woman: The Synagogue Sisterhood, 1890–1940." In *The American Synagogue: A Sanctuary Transformed*, edited by Jack Wertheimer, 206–230. Hanover, NH: Brandeis University Press / University Press of New England, 1987.

———. *The Wonders of America: Reinventing Jewish Culture, 1880–1950*. New York: Hill and Wang, 1994.

Kalmar, Ivan Davidson. "Moorish Style: Orientalism, the Jews and Synagogue Architecture." *Jewish Social Studies* 7, no. 3 (2001): 68–100.

Kaplan, Mordecai M. *Judaism as a Civilization: Toward a Reconstruction of American Jewish Life*. 1934. Reprint, New York: Schocken Books, 1967.

Karp, Abraham J. *Golden Door to America: The Jewish Immigrant Experience*. New York: Viking, 1973.

———. "New York Chooses a Chief Rabbi." *PAJHS* 44 (1955): 129–198.

Katznelson, Ira. "Between Separation and Disappearance: Jews on the Margins of American Liberalism." In *Paths of Emancipation: Jews, States, and Citizenship*, edited by Pierre Birnbaum and Ira Katznelson, 157–205. Princeton, NJ: Princeton University Press, 1995.

Kaufman, David. *A Shul with a Pool: The "Synagogue Center" in American Jewish History*. Hanover, NH: Brandeis University Press / University Press of New England, 1999.

Kaufman, Jonathan. *Broken Alliance: The Turbulent Times between Blacks and Jews in America*. New York: Scribner, 1988.

Kazin, Alfred. *A Walker in the City*. 1946. Reprint, San Diego: Harcourt Brace, 1979.

Kehillah (Jewish Community) of New York City, ed. *Jewish Communal Register of New York City, 1917–1918*. New York: Kehillah (Jewish Community) of New York City, 1918.

Kertzer, David I. *The Kidnapping of Edgardo Mortara*. New York: Vintage Books, 1998.

Kessler-Harris, Alice. Introduction to *Bread Givers*, by Anzia Yezierska, v–xxxvi. New York: Persea Books, 1975.

Kirshenblatt-Gimblett, Barbara. "Kitchen Judaism." In *Getting Comfortable in New York: The American Jewish Home, 1880–1950*, edited by Susan Braunstein and Jenna Weissman Joselit, 77–105. New York: Jewish Museum, 1990.

Kobrin, Rebecca. "Currents and Currency: Jewish Immigrant 'Bankers' and the Transnational Business of Mass Migration, 1873–1914." In *Transnational Traditions: New Perspectives on American Jewish History*, edited Ava F. Kahn and Adam Mendelsohn, 88–99. Detroit: Wayne State University Press, 2014.

———. "Destructive Creators: Sender Jarmolovsky and Financial Failure in the Annals of American Jewish History." *American Jewish History* 97, no. 2 (2013): 105–137.

———. *Jewish Bialystock and Its Diaspora*. Bloomington: Indiana University Press, 2010.

Kohler, Max J. "The Civil Status of the Jew in Colonial New York." *PAJHS* 6 (1898): 81–106.

———. "The Jews and the American Anti-Slavery Movement." *PAJHS* 5 (1897): 137–155.

Korn, Bertram W. *American Jewry and the Civil War*. Philadelphia: Jewish Publication Society of America, 1951.

Kosak, Hadassa. *Cultures of Opposition: Jewish Immigrant Workers, New York City, 1881–1905*. Albany: SUNY Press, 2000.

Kranzler, George. *Williamsburg: A Jewish Community in Transition*. New York: Feldheim, 1961.

Krasner, Jonathan B. *The Benderly Boys and the Making of American Jewish Education*. Hanover, NH: Brandeis University Press, 2011.

Kraut, Alan. "The Butcher, the Baker, the Pushcart Peddler." *Journal of American Culture* 6, no. 4 (1983): 71–83.

Krutikov, Mikhail. "Cityscapes of Yidishkayt: Opatoshu's New York Trilogy." In *Joseph Opatoshu: A Yiddish Writer between Europe and America*, edited by Sabine Koller, Gennady Estraikh, and Mikhail Krutikov, 160–171. London: Legenda, 2013.

Kugelmass, Jack. *The Miracle of Intervale Avenue: The Story of a Jewish Congregation in the South Bronx*. New York: Columbia University Press, 1996.

———. "Turfing the Slum: New York City's Tenement Museum and the Politics of Heritage." In *Remembering the Lower East Side*, edited by Hasia R. Diner, Jeffrey Shandler, and Beth S. Wenger, 179–211. Bloomington: Indiana University Press, 2000.

Kuznets, Simon. "Immigration of Russian Jews to the United States: Background and Structure." *Perspectives in American History* 9 (1975): 35–124.

Landesman, Alter. *Brownsville: The Birth, Development and Passing of a Jewish Community in New York*. New York: Bloch, 1971.

Lankevich, George J. *American Metropolis: A History of New York City*. New York: NYU Press, 1998.

Lazin, Fred A. *The Struggle for Soviet Jewry in American Politics: Israel versus the American Jewish Establishment*. Lanham, MD: Lexington Books, 2005.

Lederhendler, Eli. *Jewish Immigrants and American Capitalism, 1880–1920: From Caste to Class*. Cambridge: Cambridge University Press, 2009.

———. "New York City, the Jews, and 'The Urban Experience.'" *Studies in Contemporary Jewry* 15 (2000): 55.

———. *New York Jews and the Decline of Urban Ethnicity, 1950–1970.* Syracuse, NY: Syracuse University Press, 2001.

Leff, Laurel. "A Tragic 'Fight in the Family': The *New York Times*, Reform Judaism and the Holocaust." *AJH* 88, no. 1 (2000): 3–52.

———. "When the Facts Didn't Speak for Themselves: The Holocaust in the *New York Times*, 1939–1945." *Harvard International Journal of Press/Politics* 5, no. 2 (2000): 52–57.

Leibman, Laura Arnold. *Messianism, Secrecy, and Mysticism: A New Interpretation of Early American Jewish Life.* Portland, OR: Vallentine Mitchel, 2012.

Lerner, Elinor. "Jewish Involvement in the New York City Woman Suffrage Movement." *AJH* 70, no. 4 (1981): 442–461.

Linden, Diana L. *Ben Shahn's New Deal Murals: Jewish Identity in the American Scene.* Detroit: Wayne State University Press, 2015.

Lookstein, Haskel. *Were We Our Brothers' Keepers? The Public Response of American Jews to the Holocaust, 1938–1944.* New York: Hartmore House, 1985.

Mahler, Jonathan. *Ladies and Gentlemen, the Bronx Is Burning: 1977, Baseball, Politics, and the Battle for the Soul of a City.* New York: Farrar, Straus and Giroux, 2005.

Marcus, Jacob R., ed. *The American Jewish Woman: A Documentary History.* 2 vols. Cincinnati: American Jewish Archives, 1981.

———. *American Jewry: Documents; Eighteenth Century.* Cincinnati: American Jewish Archives, 1959.

———. *The Colonial American Jew, 1492–1776.* 3 vols. Detroit: Wayne State University Press, 1970.

Markowitz, Fran. *A Community in Spite of Itself: Soviet Jewish Émigrés in New York.* Washington, DC: Smithsonian Institution Press, 1993.

Markowitz, Ruth Jacknow. *My Daughter, the Teacher: Jewish Teachers in the New York City Schools.* New Brunswick, NJ: Rutgers University Press, 1993.

Massarik, Fred. "Basic Characteristics of the Greater New York Jewish Population." *American Jewish Year Book*, 1976, 238–248.

May, Lary. *Screening Out the Past: The Birth of Mass Culture and the Motion Picture Industry.* New York: Oxford University Press, 1980.

Mayer, Egon. *From Suburb to Shtetl: The Jews of Boro Park.* Philadelphia: Temple University Press, 1979.

McCann, Graham. *Woody Allen: New Yorker.* New York: Polity, 1990.

McCune, Mary. *"The Whole Wide World without Limits": International Relief, Gender Politics, and American Jewish Women, 1893–1930.* Detroit: Wayne State University Press, 2005.

McGill, Nettie Pauline. "Some Characteristics of Jewish Youth in New York City." *Jewish Social Service Quarterly* 14 (1938): 251–272.

McNickle, Chris. *To Be Mayor of New York: Ethnic Politics in the City.* New York: Columbia University Press, 1993.

Medoff, Rafael. *Militant Zionism in America: The Rise and Impact of the Jabotinsky Movement in the United States, 1926–1948*. Tuscaloosa: University of Alabama Press, 2002.

Mendelsohn, Adam D. *The Rag Race: How Jews Sewed Their Way to Success in America and the British Empire*. New York: NYU Press, 2014.

Merwin, Ted. *In Their Own Image: New York Jews in Jazz Age Popular Culture*. New Brunswick, NJ: Rutgers University Press, 2006.

———. *Pastrami on Rye: An Overstuffed History of the Jewish Deli*. New York: NYU Press, 2015.

Meyer, Michael A. *Response to Modernity: A History of the Reform Movement in Judaism*. Detroit: Wayne State University Press, 1988.

Michels, Tony. *A Fire in Their Hearts: Yiddish Socialists in New York*. Cambridge, MA: Harvard University Press, 2005.

———. "'Speaking to Moyshe': The Early Socialist Yiddish Press and its Readers." *Jewish History* 14, no. 1 (2000): 51–82.

Mintz, Alan. "Hebrew Literature in America." In *The Cambridge Companion to Jewish American Literature*, edited by Michael Kramer and Hanna Wirth-Nesher, 92–109. New York: Cambridge University Press, 2003.

Mintz, Jerome R. *Hasidic People: A Place in the New World*. Cambridge, MA: Harvard University Press, 1992.

Mollenkopf, John Hull. *A Phoenix in the Ashes: The Rise and Fall of the Koch Coalition in New York City Politics*. Princeton, NJ: Princeton University Press, 1992.

Moore, Deborah Dash. *At Home in America: Second Generation New York Jews*. New York: Columbia University Press, 1981.

———. *B'nai B'rith and the Challenge of Ethnic Leadership*. Albany: State University of New York Press, 1981.

———. "From Kehillah to Federation: The Communal Functions of Federated Philanthropy in New York City, 1917–1933." *AJH* 68, no. 2 (1978): 131–146.

———. *GI Jews: How World War II Changed a Generation*. Cambridge, MA: Harvard University Press, 2004.

———. "A New American Judaism." In *Like All the Nations? The Life and Legacy of Judah L. Magnes*, edited by William M. Brinner and Moses Rischin, 41–56. Albany: State University of New York Press, 1987.

———. "On the Fringes of the City: Jewish Neighborhoods in Three Boroughs." In *Landscapes of Modernity: Essays on New York City, 1900–1940*, edited by David Ward and Olivier Zunz, 252–272. New York: Russell Sage Foundation, 1992.

———. "Reconsidering the Rosenbergs: Symbol and Substance in Second Generation American Jewish Consciousness." *Journal of American Ethnic History* 8, no. 1 (1988): 21–37.

———. *Urban Origins of American Judaism*. Athens: University of Georgia Press, 2014.

Moore, MacDonald Smith. *Yankee Blues: Musical Culture and American Identity*. Bloomington: Indiana University Press, 1986.

Most, Andrea. *Making Americans: Jews and the Broadway Musical*. Cambridge, MA: Harvard University Press, 2004.

Myers, Paul. *Leonard Bernstein*. London: Phaidon, 1998.

Nadel, Stanley. "Jewish Race and German Soul in Nineteenth Century America." *AJH* 77, no. 1 (1987): 6–26.

———. *Little Germany: Ethnicity, Religion, and Class in New York City, 1845–1860*. Urbana: University of Illinois Press, 1990.

Naison, Mark. "Crown Heights in the 1950s." In *Jews of Brooklyn*, edited by Ilana Abramovitch and Sean Galvin, 143–152. Hanover, NH: University Press of New England, 2002.

———. "From Eviction Resistance to Rent Control: Tenant Activism in the Great Depression." In *The Tenant Movement in New York City, 1904–1984*, edited by Ronald Lawson, 102–112. New Brunswick, NJ: Rutgers University Press, 1986.

Norich, Anita. *Discovering Exile: Yiddish and Jewish American Culture during the Holocaust*. Stanford, CA: Stanford University Press, 2007.

O'Donnell, Edward. "Hibernians versus Hebrews? A New Look at the 1902 Jacob Joseph Funeral Riot." *Journal of the Gilded Age and Progressive Era* 6, no. 2 (2007): 209–225.

Orbach, William M. *The American Movement to Aid Soviet Jews*. Amherst: University of Massachusetts Press, 1979.

Orleck, Annelise. *Common Sense and a Little Fire: Women and Working-Class Politics in the United States, 1900–1965*. Chapel Hill: University of North Carolina Press, 1995.

Oshinsky, David M. *Polio: An American Story*. New York: Oxford University Press, 2005.

Osofsky, Gilbert. *Harlem: The Making of a Ghetto: Negro New York, 1890–1930*. New York: Harper and Row, 1964.

Panitz, Esther. "In Defense of the Jewish Immigrant (1891–1924)." *AJHQ* 55 (1965): 57–98.

Pearl, Jonathan, and Judith Pearl. *The Chosen Image: Television's Portrayal of Jewish Themes and Characters*. Jefferson, NC: McFarland, 1999.

Peiss, Kathy. *Cheap Amusements: Working Women and Leisure in Turn-of-the-Century New York*. Philadelphia: Temple University Press, 1986.

Penkower, Monte Noam. "In Dramatic Dissent: The Bergson Boys." *AJH* 70, no. 3 (1981): 281–309.

———. "The Kishinev Pogrom: A Turning Point in Jewish History." *Modern Judaism* 24, no. 3 (2004): 187–225.

Plunz, Richard. *A History of Housing in New York City: Dwelling Type and Social Change in the American Metropolis*. New York: Columbia University Press, 1990.

Podair, Jerald E. *The Strike That Changed New York: Blacks, Whites, and the Ocean Hill–Brownsville Crisis*. New Haven, CT: Yale University Press, 2002.

Polland, Annie. *Landmark of the Spirit: The Eldridge Street Synagogue*. New Haven, CT: Yale University Press, 2009.

———. "May a Free Thinker Help a Pious Man? The Shared World of the 'Religious' and the 'Secular' among Eastern European Jewish Immigrants to America." *AJH* 93, no. 4 (2007): 375–407.

Pool, David de Sola. *Portraits Etched in Stone: Early Jewish Settlers, 1681–1831*. New York: Columbia University Press, 1952.

Pool, David de Sola, and Tamar de Sola Pool. *An Old Faith in a New World: Portrait of Shearith Israel, 1654–1954*. New York: Columbia University Press, 1955.

Pritchett, Wendell. *Brownsville, Brooklyn: Blacks, Jews, and the Changing Face of the Ghetto*. Chicago: University of Chicago Press, 2002.

Raider, Mark A. *The Emergence of American Zionism*. New York: NYU Press, 1998.

Ravitch, Diane. *The Great School Wars: A History of the New York City Public Schools*. 1974. Reprint, New York: Basic Books, 1988.

Ribalow, Harold U., ed. *Autobiographies of American Jews*. Philadelphia: Jewish Publication Society of America, 1968.

Rieder, Jonathan. *Canarsie: The Jews and Italians of Brooklyn against Liberalism*. Cambridge, MA: Harvard University Press, 1985.

Rischin, Moses. Introduction to *Grandma Never Lived in America: The New Journalism of Abraham Cahan*, edited by Moses Rischin, xvii–xliv. Bloomington: Indiana University Press, 1985.

———. *The Promised City: New York's Jews, 1870–1914*. 1962. Reprint, Cambridge, MA: Harvard University Press, 1977.

———. "Toward the Onomastics of the Great New York Ghetto: How the Lower East Side Got Its Name." In *Remembering the Lower East Side: American Jewish Reflections*, edited by Hasia R. Diner, Jeffrey Shandler, Beth S. Wenger, 13–27. Bloomington: Indiana University Press, 2000.

Rock, Howard B. *Artisans of the New Republic: The Tradesmen of New York City in the Age of Jefferson*. New York: NYU Press, 1979.

Rogoff, Hillel. *Meyer London: A Biografye*. New York: Meyer London Memorial Fund, 1930.

Rogow, Faith. *Gone to Another Meeting: The National Council of Jewish Women, 1893–1993*. Tuscaloosa: University of Alabama Press, 1993.

Rontch, Isaac. *Di idishe landsmanshaften fun Nyu York*. New York: IL Peretz Yiddish Writers Union, 1938.

Rosenblum, Constance. *Boulevard of Dreams: Heady Times, Heartbreak, and Hope along the Grand Concourse in the Bronx*. New York: NYU Press, 2009.

Rosenwaike, Ira. *On the Edge of Greatness: A Portrait of the American Jew in the Early National Period*. Cincinnati: American Jewish Archives, 1985.

———. *Population History of New York City*. Syracuse, NY: Syracuse University Press, 1972.

Roth, Henry. *Mercy of a Rude Stream*. New York: St. Martin's, 1994.

———. *Shifting Landscape: A Composite, 1925–1987*. Ed. Mario Materassi. Philadelphia: Jewish Publication Society of America, 1987.

Rudy, Solomon Willis. *The College of the City of New York: A Centennial History, 1847–1947*. New York: City College Press, 1949.

Sachs, A. S. *Di geshikhte fun arbayter ring, 1892–1925*. New York: National Executive Committee of the Workmen's Circle, 1925.

Saidel, Rochelle G. *Never Too Late to Remember: The Politics behind New York City's Holocaust Museum.* New York: Holmes and Meier, 1996.

Sandrow, Nahma. *Vagabond Stars: A World History of the Yiddish Theater.* New York: Harper and Row, 1977.

Sanua, Marianne. "From the Pages of the *Victory Bulletin.*" *YIVO Annual* 19 (1992): 283–330.

———. " 'We Hate New York': Negative Images of the Promised City as a Source for Jewish Fraternity and Sorority Members, 1920–1940." In *An Inventory of Promises: Essays on American Jewish History in Honor of Moses Rischin,* edited by Jeffrey S. Gurock and Marc Lee Raphael, 235–263. Brooklyn, NY: Carlson, 1995.

Sanua, Victor D. "A Study of the Adjustment of Sephardi Jews in the New York Metropolitan Area." *Jewish Journal of Sociology* 9, no. 1 (1967): 25–33.

Sarna, Jonathan D. *American Judaism: A History.* New Haven, CT: Yale University Press, 2004.

———. "The Debate over Mixed Seating in America." In *The American Synagogue: A Sanctuary Transformed,* edited by Jack Wertheimer, 363–371. New York: Cambridge University Press, 1987.

———. *Jacksonian Jew: The Two Worlds of Mordecai Noah.* New York: Holmes and Meier, 1981.

Schappes, Morris, ed. *A Documentary History of the Jews of the United States, 1654–1875.* 1950. Reprint, New York: Schocken, 1971.

Schoener, Allon. *Portal to America: The Lower East Side, 1870–1925.* New York: Holt, Rinehart, and Winston, 1967.

Schor, Esther. *Emma Lazarus.* New York: Nextbook/Schocken, 2006.

Schwartz, Joel. *The New York Approach: Robert Moses, Urban Liberals, and the Redevelopment of the Inner City.* Columbus: Ohio State University Press, 1993.

Scult, Mel. *Judaism Faces the Twentieth Century: A Biography of Mordecai M. Kaplan.* Detroit: Wayne State University Press, 1993.

Shapiro, Edward S. *Crown Heights: Blacks, Jews, and the 1991 Brooklyn Riot.* Hanover, NH: Brandeis University Press, 2006.

Shokeid, Moshe. *A Gay Synagogue in New York.* New York: Columbia University Press, 1995.

Siegel, Fred. *The Prince of the City: Giuliani, New York, and the Genius of American Life.* San Francisco: Encounter Books, 2005.

Silver, Matthew. "Louis Marshall and the Democratization of Jewish Identity." *AJH* 94, nos. 1–2 (2008): 41–69.

Simmons, Erica B. *Hadassah and the Zionist Project.* Lanham, MD: Rowman and Littlefield, 2006.

Singer, Ben. "Manhattan Nickelodeons: New Data on Audiences and Exhibitors." *Cinema Journal* 34, no. 3 (1995): 5–35.

Slobin, Mark. *Tenement Songs: The Popular Music of the Jewish Immigrants.* Urbana: University of Illinois Press, 1982.

Snyder, Holly. "Queens of the Household: The Jewish Women of British America, 1700–1800." In *Women and American Judaism: Historical Perspectives,* edited by

Pamela S. Nadell and Jonathan D. Sarna, 15–45. Hanover, NH: Brandeis University Press, 2001.

Solomon, Alisa. *Wonder of Wonders: A Cultural History of "Fiddler on the Roof."* New York: Metropolitan Books, 2013.

Sorin, Gerald. *Irving Howe: A Life of Passionate Dissent.* New York: NYU Press, 2002.

———. *The Nurturing Neighborhood: The Brownsville Boys Club and Jewish Community in Urban America, 1940–1990.* New York: NYU Press, 1990.

Soyer, Daniel. "Brownstones and Brownsville: Elite Philanthropists and Immigrant Constituents at the Hebrew Educational Society of Brooklyn, 1899–1929." *AJH* 88, no. 2 (2000): 181–207.

———, ed. *A Coat of Many Colors: Immigration, Globalization, and Reform in the New York City Garment Industry.* New York: Fordham University Press, 2005.

———. *Jewish Immigrant Associations and American Identity in New York, 1880–1939.* Cambridge, MA: Harvard University Press, 1997.

Stansell, Christine. *American Moderns: Bohemian New York and the Creation of a New Century.* 2000. Reprint, Princeton, NJ: Princeton University Press, 2010.

Stein, Leon. *The Triangle Fire.* Philadelphia: J. B. Lippincott, 1962.

Steinmetz, Sol. *Yiddish and English: A Century of Yiddish in America.* Tuscaloosa: University of Alabama Press, 1986.

Stempel, Larry. *Showtime: A History of the Broadway Musical Theater.* New York: Norton, 2010.

Stern, Robert A. M., Thomas Mellins, David Fishman. *New York 1960: Architecture and Urbanism between the Second World War and the Bicentennial.* New York: Monacelli, 1995.

Sutton, Joseph A. D. *Magic Carpet: Aleppo-in-Flatbush: The Story of a Unique Ethnic Jewish Community.* New York: Thayer-Jacoby, 1979.

Swerdlow, Amy. *Women Strike for Peace: Traditional Motherhood and Radical Politics in the 1960s.* Chicago: University of Chicago Press, 1993.

Tcherikower, E. *Geshikhte fun der yidisher arbeter bavegung in di fareynikte shtatn.* New York: YIVO, 1945.

Thissen, Judith. "Film and Vaudeville on New York's Lower East Side." In *The Art of Being Jewish in Modern Times*, edited by Barbara Kirshenblatt-Gimblett and Jonathan Karp, 42–56. Philadelphia: University of Pennsylvania Press, 2008.

———. "Jewish Immigrant Audiences in New York City, 1905–1914." In *American Movie Audiences: From the Turn of the Century to the Early Sound Era*, edited by Melvyn Stokes and Richard Maltby, 15–28. London: BFI, 1999.

Tifft, Susan, and Alex S. Jones. *The Trust: The Private and Powerful Family behind the New York Times.* New York: Little, Brown, 1999.

Trachtenberg, Jeffrey A. *Ralph Lauren: The Man behind the Mystique.* New York: Little, Brown, 1988.

Trillin, Calvin. "U.S. Journal: The Bronx, The Coops." *New Yorker*, 1 August 1977, 49–54.

United Jewish Appeal–Federation of Jewish Philanthropies of New York (UJA-Federation). *Greater New York Population Study.* New York: UJA-Federation, 1981.

Typescript report maintained online at the Mandell L. Berman Institute North American Jewish Data Bank.

———. *The Jewish Community Study of New York: Geographic Profile: 2002*. New York: UJA-Federation, 2004. Typescript report maintained online at the Mandell L. Berman Institute North American Jewish Data Bank.

———. *The Jewish Community Study of New York: 2002*. New York: UJA-Federation, 2004. Typescript report maintained online at the Mandell L. Berman Institute North American Jewish Data Bank.

———. *The New York Jewish Population Study: Profiles of Counties, Boroughs and Neighborhoods 1991*. New York: UJA-Federation, 1995. Typescript report maintained online at the Mandell L. Berman Institute North American Jewish Data Bank.

———. *The 1991 New York Jewish Population Study*. New York: UJA-Federation, 1993. Typescript report maintained online at the Mandell L. Berman Institute North American Jewish Data Bank.

Von Drehle, David. *Triangle: The Fire That Changed America*. New York: Atlantic Monthly Press, 2003.

Wald, Alan M. *The New York Intellectuals: The Rise and Decline of the Anti-Stalinist Left from the 1930s to the 1980s*. Chapel Hill: University of North Carolina Press, 1987.

Walkowitz, Daniel. *Working with Class: Social Workers and the Politics of Middle-Class Identity*. Chapel Hill: University of North Carolina Press, 1999.

Warnke, Nina. "Immigrant Popular Culture as Contested Space: Yiddish Music Halls, the Yiddish Press, and the Processes of Americanization, 1900–1919." *Theater Journal* 48, no. 3 (1996): 321–335.

———. "Theater as Educational Institution: Jewish Immigrant Intellectuals and Yiddish Theater Reform." In *The Art of Being Jewish in Modern Times*, edited by Barbara Kirshenblatt-Gimblett and Jonathan Karp, 23–41. Philadelphia: University of Pennsylvania Press, 2008.

Wechsler, Harold S. *The Qualified Student: A History of Selective College Admission in America*. New York: Wiley, 1977.

Weinstein, Bernard. *Di idishe yunyons in Amerike*. New York: United Hebrew Trades, 1929.

Weisbord, Robert G., and Arthur Stein. *Bittersweet Encounter: The Afro-American and the American Jew*. Westport, CT: Negro Universities Press, 1970.

Wenger, Beth S. "Memory as Identity: The Invention of the Lower East Side." *AJH* 85, no. 1 (1997): 3–27.

———. *New York Jews and the Great Depression: Uncertain Promise*. New Haven, CT: Yale University Press, 1996.

———. "The Politics of Women's Ordination: Jewish Law, Institutional Power, and the Debate Over Women in the Rabbinate." In *Tradition Renewed: A History of the Jewish Theological Seminary of America*, vol. 2, edited by Jack Wertheimer, 483–523. New York: Jewish Theological Seminary, 1997.

Whitfield, Stephen. *In Search of American Jewish Culture*. Hanover, NH: Brandeis University Press / University Press of New England, 1999.

Wilentz, Sean. *Chants Democratic: New York City and the Rise of the American Working Class, 1789–1850*. New York: Oxford University Press, 1984.

Wilhelm, Cornelia. "Independent Order of True Sisters: Friendship, Fraternity, and a Model of Modernity for Nineteenth Century American Jewish Womanhood." *AJAJ* 54, no. 1 (2002): 37–63.

Wisse, Ruth. *A Little Love in Big Manhattan: Two Yiddish Poets*. Cambridge, MA: Harvard University Press, 1988.

Woeste, Victoria Saker. "Insecure Equality: Louis Marshall, Henry Ford, and the Problem of Defamatory Antisemitism, 1920–1929." *Journal of American History* 91, no. 3 (2004): 877–905.

Zeitz, Joshua M. *White Ethnic New York: Jews, Catholics, and the Shaping of Postwar Politics*. Chapel Hill: University of North Carolina Press, 2007.

Zenner, Walter P. *A Global Community: The Jews from Aleppo, Syria*. Detroit: Wayne State University Press, 2000.

Zitron, Celia Lewis. *The New York City Teachers Union, 1916–1964: A Story of Educational and Social Commitment*. New York: Humanities Press, 1968.

Zurawik, David. *The Jews of Prime Time*. Hanover, NH: Brandeis University Press, 2003.

Zuroff, Efraim. *The Response of Orthodox Jewry in the United States to the Holocaust: The Activities of the Vaad Ha-Hatzala Rescue Committee, 1939–1945*. New York: Michael Scharf Publication Trust of Yeshiva University Press, 2000.

INDEX

A native New Yorker, Jeffrey S. Gurock is Libby M. Klaperman Professor of Jewish History at Yeshiva University. His most recent book is *The Jews of Harlem: The Rise, Decline, and Revival of a Jewish Community* (NYU Press, 2016).

Diana L. Linden, a historian of American Art, is the author of *Ben Shahn's New Deal Murals: Jewish Identity in the American Scene*, which was selected as a finalist by the National Jewish Book Awards, Visual Arts category (2015), and co-editor, along with Alejandro Anreus and Jonathan Weinberg, of *The Social and the Real: Political Art of the 1930s in the Western Hemisphere* (2006).

Deborah Dash Moore is Frederick G. L. Huetwell Professor of History and Judaic Studies at the University of Michigan. A historian of American Jews, she has published an acclaimed trilogy examining the years from 1920 to 1960, including the experience of Jewish soldiers in World War II. Her work regularly garners awards.

Annie Polland is Senior Vice President for Programs and Education at the Lower East Side Tenement Museum, where she oversees the development of exhibits and programs. She is the author of *Landmark of the Spirit: The Eldridge Street Synagogue* (2009) and teaches at the Eugene Lang College at the New School.

Howard B. Rock is Professor of History, Emeritus, at Florida International University, where he has taught since 1973. His books include *Artisans of the New Republic: The Tradesmen of New York City in the Age of Jefferson*; *The New York City Artisan, 1790–1825: A Documentary History*; *Keepers of the Revolution: New Yorkers at Work in the Early Republic* (with Paul A. Gilje); *American Artisans: Crafting Social Identity,*

1750–1850 (with Paul A. Gilje); and *Cityscapes: A History of New York in Images* (with Deborah Dash Moore).

Daniel Soyer is Professor of History at Fordham University. He is the author, with Annie Polland, of *Emerging Metropolis: New York Jews in the Age of Immigration, 1840–1920* (2012), and co-editor of the journal *American Jewish History.*